John Christopher Hamm

The Unworthy Scholar from Pingjiang

Republican-Era Martial Arts Fiction

Columbia University Press

New York

Columbia University Press
Publishers Since 1893
New York   Chichester, West Sussex
cup.columbia.edu

Library of Congress Cataloging-in-Publication Data
Names: Hamm, John Christopher, 1957– author.
Title: The Unworthy Scholar from Pingjiang : Republican-era martial arts fiction /
    John Christopher Hamm.
Description: New York : Columbia University Press, [2019] | Includes
    bibliographical references and index.
Identifiers: LCCN 2018061395 (print) | LCCN 2019006201 (ebook) |
    ISBN 9780231549004 (e-book) | ISBN 9780231190565 | ISBN 9780231190565
    (cloth : alk. paper) | ISBN 9780231549004 (e-book)
Subjects: LCSH: Buxiaosheng, 1889–1957—Criticism and interpretation. |
    Buxiaosheng, 1889–1957—Influence. | Martial arts fiction, Chinese—20th
    century—History and criticism.
Classification: LCC PL2795.U28 (ebook) | LCC PL2795.U28 Z68 2019 (print) |
    DDC 895.13/51—dc 3
LC record available at https://lccn.loc.gov/2018061395

Columbia University Press books are printed
on permanent and durable acid-free paper.

Printed in the United States of America

Cover design: Lisa Hamm
Cover image: Photograph of Xiang Kairan, seated with monkeys. Used with
permission by Xiang Xiaoguang.

Contents

Acknowledgments

T he research and writing of this book have been supported by a research grant from the Chiang Ching-kuo Foundation, research and travel grants from the China Studies Program at the University of Washington, and research leave granted by the University of Washington's Department of Asian Languages and Literature and the College of Arts and Sciences. I offer my heartfelt thanks to all of the above for their assistance and encouragement.

My academic debts to the late Professor Fan Boqun and other scholars in the People's Republic of China will be evident from the text and notes. Here I would like to express my particular gratitude to Professor Xu Sinian, without whose pioneering research into Xiang Kairan's life and writings my own work would not have been possible and who has generously offered encouragement and comments on my project at several stages in its development.

I am grateful to the many colleagues in the field who have offered feedback on various portions of this work presented at conferences and workshops over the last decade. Earlier treatments of some of the material in this study have appeared in *The Oxford Handbook of Modern Chinese Literatures*, edited by Carlos Rojas and Andrea Bachner (New York: Oxford University Press, 2016), and *A New Literary History of Modern China*, edited by David Der-wei Wang (Cambridge, MA: Harvard University

Press, 2017). My particular thanks to the editors of these two volumes for their insightful comments and generous support.

More generally, I would like to express my gratitude to my colleagues in (and beyond) the Department of Asian Languages and Literature at the University of Washington. Over the years, at lunch, in the hallways of Gowen, and in living-room reading groups, you have shown by example the pleasure and value to be found in the study of the humanities and have reminded me that what sometimes seems the most solitary of callings thrives best in the nurturing soil of community.

My thanks also to the students in my University of Washington seminars on Republican-era periodicals, especially those who joined me in its first iteration to study *The Sunday* (*Xingqi* 星期): Laura Eshleman, Danny Huei Lin, Shih Chia-ying, and David Stone.

My thanks to the staff at the East Asia Library at the University of Washington, including Dr. Shen Zhijia and the endlessly helpful Richard Carkeek at Circulation, and my thanks to our department's Anna Schnell for her help with the illustrations.

I am indebted to the three anonymous reviewers for the Columbia University Press, who read my manuscript and offered invaluable comments and suggestions for revision. The errors and shortcomings that remain, needless to say, are my own responsibility. I am also deeply grateful to the editors at Columbia University Press, in particular Christine Dunbar, who has been instrumental in bringing this work to print.

I am grateful to Mr. Xiang Xiaoguang and his family for their generous permission to use the splendid photograph of Xiang Kairan seen on the cover of this volume.

A shout-out to my writing buddy, David Lewman, a good friend and true professional who kept my spirits up and my nose to the grindstone.

And my gratitude and love to my family, who make my work possible and worthwhile. Helen, Xiao Xue, Lyle, and Audrey. Toto too.

Notes on Conventions

I have tried to provide English-language translations of the titles of all Chinese-language literary works, articles, and Republican-era periodicals (but not contemporary Chinese journals) referred to in this study. In the main text and in discursive notes, the English version appears first, followed at the first occurrence by *pinyin* Romanization and Chinese characters. Unless otherwise noted, the use of traditional or simplified characters reflects the usage of the Chinese publication referenced. In notes whose function is purely documentary, as in the bibliography at the end of this volume, the English title appears in brackets after the Chinese *pinyin* and characters. A bracketed title that is capitalized sentence-style is one that I have provided myself; a bracketed translation capitalized headline-style is one that appears in the original publication.

When an author's name is followed by a name in brackets, the latter is the name under which a given item was originally published.

In many Republican-era periodicals, pagination begins anew with each item or article rather than running consecutively throughout the issue. I have omitted page numbers when referencing periodicals paginated in this fashion.

The Unworthy Scholar from Pingjiang

Introduction

T his book has become something different from what I originally imagined. When I first (too many years ago) began this project, I envisioned it as a prequel to my *Paper Swordsmen: Jin Yong and the Modern Chinese Martial Arts Novel.*[1] *Paper Swordsmen* is a study of the work of the late-twentieth-century writer commonly credited with bringing the distinctive Chinese genre of martial arts fiction (*wuxia xiaoshuo* 武俠小說) to its greatest heights and breaking down the wall that historically separated this popular genre from the canonical mainstream of modern Chinese literature. Interest in the genre's origins inevitably drew my attention to Xiang Kairan 向愷然 (1895–1957), "the generally acknowledged founding father of Republican-era martial arts fiction, that is to say, the leading figure of the first generation of the modern martial arts novel."[2] Xiang Kairan is remembered above all for his *Marvelous Gallants of the Rivers and Lakes* (*Jianghu qixia zhuan* 江湖奇俠傳; hereafter *Rivers and Lakes*) and *Chivalric Heroes of Modern Times* (*Jindai xiayi yingxiong zhuan* 近代俠義英雄傳; hereafter *Modern Times*), two novels that began serialization in 1923 under the pen name Buxiaosheng 不肖生, "The Unworthy Scholar." *Rivers and Lakes* and *Modern Times* are credited with igniting a craze for martial arts fiction and establishing some of the modern genre's characteristic features. But had this writer earned recognition as the "founding father" merely by being the first to catch the public's attention? What had he contributed to the developing traditions of martial arts fiction? Given China's long history of narratives on martial themes, what made Xiang Kairan's and his generation's fiction "modern"—was it different in nature from what preceded it, or did the adjective simply indicate these works' presence in an era identified as modern on extrinsic grounds? What was martial arts fiction's place in the wider panorama of Republican-era literature and culture? My initial investigations were shaped by these fairly obvious questions—questions about the characteristics, history, and significance of martial arts fiction as a genre.

As I proceeded, however, other questions increasingly occupied my attention, both because my provisional agenda seemed to require that they be answered before I could proceed and because of the intrinsic interest they held. Immersion in texts written by Xiang Kairan and his contemporaries quickly led me to question my assumptions about genre—not just about the genre of martial arts fiction but about the notion of genre, the historically contingent ways in which those involved in the production and consumption of texts perceive affinities and distinctions among texts and put these perceptions to various kinds of use. I had the good fortune to undergo this immersion in part by means of the outstanding collection of Republican-era periodicals held at the University of Washington's East Asia Library. Hands-on work with original periodicals here and at other institutions, and the rapidly expanding availability of periodical archives online, deepened my recognition of the importance of the material and visual contexts of the texts and led me to seek guidance from the perspectives of periodical studies, print culture, and publishing history. At the same time, my reading brought to the foreground and changed the tenor of the last of my original set of questions—that concerning the place of martial arts fiction in its contemporary literary context. Even as I developed a clearer picture of the ways in which Xiang Kairan's writings drew on and contributed to a tradition that identified itself with increasing assurance as martial arts fiction, I also became aware that, martial-arts-related material aside, the production and reception of his work was framed in fundamental ways by its identity as "fiction" in an era when the definition of this seemingly self-evident category was subject to intense debate.

Xiang Kairan published his first works of fiction in 1916 and his best-known works in the five-year period from 1923 to 1927. In January 1917 Hu

Shi 胡適 published his essay "Some Modest Proposals for the Reform of Literature" ("Wenxue gailiang chuyi" 文學改良芻議) in the journal *New Youth* (*Xin qingnian* 新青年); in May of the following year Lu Xun 魯迅 published his short story "A Madman's Diary" ("Kuangren riji" 狂人日記) in the same magazine; in January 1921 Mao Dun 茅盾 assumed editorial control over the leading fiction journal *The Short Story Magazine* (*Xiaoshuo yuebao* 小說月報). These three events were and are seen as milestones in the progress of a New Literature (*Xin wenxue* 新文學) movement led by progressive intellectuals associated with the broader New Culture (*Xin wenhua* 新文化) and May Fourth movements. The proponents of the New Literature called for a literature dedicated to the task of enlightening the people of the Chinese nation and fostering their participation in a rational and democratic modern society. They believed that China lacked such a literature and that it should therefore be built on the model of the modern literatures of Western nations, via coordinated efforts in translation, theory and criticism, and creative work. They understood the pinnacle of modern literature to be occupied by the genre known as fiction. The notions of literature and fiction that constituted their project were inspired by their understanding of the Western ideas to which these two terms referred; following usages established over the previous two decades, they translated these key terms by repurposing two words that had long been current in the Chinese language, using *wenxue* 文學 for "literature" and *xiaoshuo* 小說 for "fiction." But the enterprise of *wenxue*/literature, shouldering both universalist aspirations and national responsibilities, bore only contingent resemblance to *wenxue* in its previous sense of belles-lettres. And the *xiaoshuo*/fiction whose creation the progressives demanded answered to formal, thematic, aesthetic, and ideological standards modeled by the novels and short stories of the contemporary West—standards to which the heterogeneous writings traditionally gathered under the umbrella term *xiaoshuo* had never dreamed of owing allegiance.

In early usage the term *xiaoshuo* (literally "minor discourse" or "small talk") designated a bibliographic category rather than anything like a literary genre. Originally serving to classify minor and miscellaneous philosophical writings, by late-imperial times the category served as a catch-all for a wide range of texts with no obvious home elsewhere within the canonical organization of writings into classics, history, philosophy, and belles-lettres. The texts loosely gathered under the *xiaoshuo* umbrella employed a variety of linguistic registers, from the literary to the vernacular; took prose, verse, and prosimetric forms; and might be narrative, dramatic, descriptive, expository, argumentative, biographic, or anecdotal. Prose narrative texts for the most part clustered around the two poles of the short classical-language tale and the extended vernacular-language novel. The classical tale and the vernacular novel sprang from different literary ancestries but influenced each other over the course of their later development. Critics and commentators noted their kinship by the seventeenth century, though the two forms still shared membership in the *xiaoshuo* category with other types of texts. It was not until the late nineteenth and early twentieth centuries that the term *xiaoshuo* began to acquire, via Japanese usage, a meaning akin to that of the English "fiction," associated primarily with the modern Western short story and novel. This new (though not yet exclusive) meaning of the term granted the Chinese classical tale and the Chinese vernacular novel a viable claim to the label *xiaoshuo*—even as it raised the question, for literary progressives at least, of their fitness as representatives of what fiction was now conceived to be.[3]

When *xiaoshuo* became fiction, in other words, *xiaoshuo* was no longer *xiaoshuo*. *Xiaoshuo* in the older sense did not qualify as *xiaoshuo* in the new; it could only be bad fiction, old fiction, the primitive and limited predecessor to the modern literary genre. Its relics might merit academic study as part of the national heritage, but the new literature of the new nation could not afford to be burdened or contaminated by the corpse of the old *xiaoshuo*. The proponents of the new fiction, projecting onto the literary environment the same notion of modernity as a radical rupture from the past that informed the modernist cultural project more generally, aggressively laid claim to the critical high ground. And over the course of the 1920s a growing cadre of writers answered the call. Editors and publishers followed suit, and the readership for the new fiction expanded from a small core of the progressive intellectual elite to a broader segment of the educated reading public.

Xiaoshuo in the old sense, however, continued to be written and read throughout and beyond the Republican era. To say that something is *xiaoshuo* in the old sense requires qualification, for it would be a mistake to impute to premodern *xiaoshuo* a unified or unchanging identity. The scope of the category designated by the term had changed over time and varied according to the discursive purposes of those who invoked it. Once an affinity between *xiaoshuo* and "fiction" had been posited, moreover, even writers with the least allegiance to the New Literature could not help but feel the influence of the currents running through the literary field and affecting the choices of publishers and readers. The "old fiction" (*jiu xiaoshuo* 舊小說) of the early twentieth century was not the rotting corpse its critics claimed it to be. Nor was it the homogeneous entity their essentializing attacks implied. *Xiaoshuo*'s categorical scope subtly contracted, distancing some of the discursive, argumentative, dramatic, and notational material previously incorporated under the term in favor of imaginative prose narrative more akin to fiction in the modern sense. Within these loose parameters, however, thrived a variety of linguistic registers, fictional forms, aesthetic styles, ideological orientations, and artistic aims. These varieties of fiction in many cases absorbed narratological and structural innovations, included among their subjects many contemporary and topical matters, and interacted dynamically with the requirements and opportunities of the modern commercial publishing industry. At the same time, though, they declined to kowtow to the New Literature movement's restrictive aesthetic and ideological requirements. They drew freely on the language, material, narrative conventions, forms, hermeneutic codes, and epistemological assumptions of China's premodern varieties of *xiaoshuo* and offered these to audiences from whom they expected recognition and appreciation. This is the Republican-era *xiaoshuo* that this study intends to address: fiction that is of the modern age but that falls largely outside the scope of the modernist projects defined by the New Literature movement and its successors.

It is difficult to choose a term by which to refer to this fiction. Objections to the use of "traditional," "old," "old-style," or "old-school fiction" (舊派小說) are self-evident: such labels deny this fiction's contemporaneity and carry the scent of its critics' assumptions that it is a priori artistically fossilized and ideologically regressive. Republican-era detractors were also responsible for the two terms for this material most often encountered in subsequent literary historiography: Mandarin Ducks and Butterflies School (*Yuanyang hudie pai* 鴛鴦蝴蝶派) fiction and Saturday School (*Libai liu pai* 禮拜六派) fiction. The former denotes the romantic imagery prominent in love stories of the 1910s, and the latter, the periodical *Saturday* (*Libailiu* 禮拜六), known for featuring such stories. To the general critique implied by the term "old fiction," these labels add intimations of sentimentality, frivolity, and conscienceless commercialization. They also misrepresent the range and variety of fiction lying beyond the New Literature pale by implicitly equating it with a single thematic subgenre.[4] Over the last few decades a number of scholars have undertaken to reassess this body of fiction. One of the most comprehensive and sympathetic studies to date, by Fan Boqun 范伯群 and his colleagues, addresses its subject as *tongsu wenxue* 通俗文学, "popular literature."[5] The value of Fan's monumental work cannot be overstated; the use of the term *tongsu*, however, is susceptible to some of the same critiques that Milena Doleželová-Velingerová made of Perry Link's use of "popular" in his pioneering English-language *Mandarin Ducks and Butterflies: Popular Fiction in Early Twentieth-Century Chinese Cities*: on the one hand, "popular" as a critical term subsumes a slippery multiplicity of connotations; on the other, the varieties of fiction meant to be encompassed under this category include some that are not "popular" in any ordinarily accepted sense of the word.[6] Recent efforts to link the fiction formerly known as Butterfly with concepts of vernacular modernity—that is, with local attempts to negotiate transnational modernity by means of the media that both transmit that modernity and exist as constituent elements of it—might suggest the use of the term "vernacular fiction" or "vernacular literature."[7] Whatever the critical validity of such an approach, though, these particular terms are unavailable, having long been co-opted, within the twentieth-century context, as references to the vernacular-language movement (*baihua yundong* 白話運動) that was a central element of the New Literature's modernist project.[8]

The difficulty of finding a satisfactory way to refer to this fiction is compounded by the fact that I intend no single unified tradition, concept, or corpus such as is implied by a division of modern Chinese literature into the New Literature and its Other. I mean rather to admit into discussion notions, elements, and varieties of fiction informed by premodern understandings and practices of *xiaoshuo*. In an attempt to circumvent at least partially the multiple ambiguities inherent in the word *xiaoshuo* and its further translation as "fiction," I will therefore use "*xiaoshuo*," the Romanization of the Chinese term, to refer to the vast body of fictional narratives whose forms, ideas, and practices are significantly shaped by (though by no means slavishly reproductive of) premodern traditions. I will refer to fiction in the sense championed by Hu Shi, Lu Xun, and Mao Dun as "New Literature fiction" or "May Fourth fiction"; the term "New Fiction" must be reserved for an earlier, related, yet distinct project, the "Revolution in Fiction" (*xiaoshuo jie de geming* 小說界的革命) spearheaded by Liang Qichao's 梁啓超 1902 journal of the same name, *New Fiction* (*Xin xiaoshuo* 新小說). I will attempt to use "fiction" alone only in places where the context makes the referent clear or where the distinctions just mentioned are not immediately relevant. When I use the terms "Butterfly literature" or "Butterfly fiction," they should be understood to carry scare quotes and to refer to the concept of a literary Other constructed by New Literature critics and their inheritors.

This study, then, has become as much an exploration of the life of *xiaoshuo* in a period remembered for the birth of the New Literature as an investigation into the origins of the modern martial arts novel. Had I originally identified Republican-era *xiaoshuo* per se as the subject of my study, I might have chosen a different body of material. Fan Boqun puts at the head of his study what he terms "social and romantic" (*shehui yanqing* 社會言情) fiction—late-Qing and Republican-era *xiaoshuo* on human relationships in contemporary society, urban society in particular.[9] The category comprehends what are arguably the most common and popular varieties of *xiaoshuo* from the period, offering the prospective researcher a voluminous corpus in a wide variety of literary forms from the entire span of decades in question. The subject matters dealt with are also often close to or identical with those favored by the authors of New Fiction, offering rich opportunities for comparative study or for approaches seeking to transcend or deconstruct the assumption of a New Literature / old literature divide.[10] The body of Xiang Kairan's work presents a corpus far less vast (a circumstance that in some ways works to an individual researcher's advantage) but one that still engages the most prominent textual forms of Republican-era *xiaoshuo* and its salient discursive features. Therefore, using Xiang Kairan's writings as a window on *xiaoshuo* is, I believe, defensible. And understanding the habits, constraints, possibilities, and status of *xiaoshuo* is essential to an understanding of Xiang Kairan's work.

Even for the relatively circumscribed purposes of an investigation into the history of martial arts fiction, a focus on the oeuvre of one particular author might legitimately be questioned. Xiang Kairan's established reputation as the modern genre's founding father arguably merits either challenge or clarification. But to the extent that my efforts have been colored by the insights of literary sociology, the study of print culture, and periodical studies, this volume's choice of what seems to be an antique author-and-works approach may be even more subject to critique.[11] I have attempted here to be conscious of the limitations of an authorial approach to literary history even while availing myself of the opportunities it offers. For these opportunities are indeed rich. Just as martial arts fiction provides a productive point of approach to the larger question of Republican-era *xiaoshuo*, so the work of Xiang Kairan provides an abundantly rewarding point of entry to the Republican-era martial arts novel. And while reading texts in relation to a historical author may be an inveterate habit of modern literary criticism and historiography, producing and consuming texts with reference to an authorial persona is no less a habit of many literary cultures—Republican-era China's most definitely among them— and as such constitutes a necessary (though not sufficient) focus of historical inquiry. I attempt to contextualize Xiang Kairan's career and his works in relation to genre, literary form, thematic subgenre, contemporary literary debates, and social and cultural history and to use his works to illuminate some larger questions that present themselves within these contexts. At the same time, finally, I have to confess to a fascination with and an affection for the distinctive preoccupations and devices evident in the work of this particular author, and I have endeavored here to acknowledge the pleasures of reading Xiang Kairan even while exploring the broader issues to which his work grants us access.

GENRE AND LITERARY CATEGORIES

To move from talking about martial arts fiction to talking about *xiaoshuo* is to talk about genre in two different senses of the word. A genre is a class or type. A type is an abstraction derived from concrete instances; in the study of literature, a genre is an act of categorization that establishes connections between certain texts and distinguishes the texts so connected from other texts and groupings of texts. The possible criteria by which any given text might be judged similar or dissimilar to another are multitudinous, in theory perhaps infinite. Does any given set of shared characteristics qualify as constituting a genre, or do we reserve the term for some particular level or mode of categorization? In Western traditions of literary criticism and historiography, the term has been employed to refer to categories defined by criteria ranging from fundamental expressive strategy (e.g., the lyrical or the dramatic), to historically contingent literary form (e.g., the romance or the novel), to interlinked conventions of setting, character, plot, and theme (e.g., detective fiction or the western). Genette's influential intervention into twentieth-century genre theory designates categories of the first type as "modes" and dismisses those matters of content and theme that define categories of the third type as irrelevant to the question of genre per se, which properly concerns such larger expressive formations as the novel.[12]

It is with the third type of categorization that we are concerned when we talk about martial arts fiction. Genette readily acknowledges that "a generic category like the novel can be subdivided into specifications that are less extensive but more detailed, such as picaresque novel, sentimental novel, detective novel, etc." and allows that "nothing prevents these latter from being christened . . . 'subgenres.'"[13] But the identification of subgenres in this sense seems to afford little scope for dealing with the ways in which narrative and thematic material retains recognizable identity while crossing boundaries of form and medium. A premodern Chinese narrative of crime and judicial retribution, for instance, might manifest itself as a classical-language tale, a vernacular short story, a stage drama, or the performance of an oral storyteller, just as a twentieth-century western might take the form of a novel, a film, a television series, or a radio broadcast. Although in the present study I do concern myself primarily with the written word and with subdivisions within the field of fictional prose narrative, the transmedial circulation of martial arts material is essential to the understanding of my topic. One approach that allows for such transmedial circulation is Cawelti's model of "formula stories."[14] While considering questions of setting, characters, and theme, however, his model privileges narrative archetype—it is no accident that he takes the classical detective story as the primary example for his analysis. Cawelti's "formula" approach is therefore less ideal for understanding a body of material such as Chinese martial arts fiction and film, which embraces a range of common story lines (e.g., revenge, transmission, competition, romance). For the purposes of this study, I will depart from Genettean orthodoxy and use the awkward term "thematic genre" to refer to a body of narrative material interlinked by fluid conventions of setting, characters, and narrative tropes. Martial arts fiction is thus the literary subset (literary not in an evaluative sense but in the sense of employing the medium of the written or printed word) of a thematic genre of martial arts adventure that also includes martial arts films, opera, comic books, and other forms and media.

If martial arts fiction is a thematic genre, then *xiaoshuo* in the sense I address it in this study is a literary genre, a distinctive subtype of literary discourse. If we define literary discourse in general as those uses of language marked through manner or convention as figurative rather than instrumental or transparently referential, then literary genres are the subtypes whose mutually defining relationships and distinctions structure the ecology of literary discourse as a whole. These relationships and distinctions are historically contingent; while a pure formalism might posit the literariness of a discourse as inherent in a text, I understand it as contingent upon recognition by its users and therefore the product of constant negotiations. Generic subtypes of literary discourse shift over time and differ across cultural formations. In the case of Republican-era *xiaoshuo*, accordingly, we are looking neither at a category native to Western traditions of literary practice and criticism nor at an element of a stable Chinese ecology of literary genres. What we have instead is a subtype of literary discourse that seems to echo in certain ways models of both Western fiction and premodern Chinese *xiaoshuo* yet that emerges in a distinctive form during an unusually unstable and hence productive juncture in cultural and literary history. To sketch the overall contours of the protean and contested ecology of literary discourse within which Republican-era *xiaoshuo* exists is beyond the ambition of the present study, and I will content myself with attempting to identify some of *xiaoshuo*'s defining characteristics. To the extent that I am referencing Xiang Kairan's fictional works in order to identify the properties of a type of literary discourse, I am engaged in outlining a poetics of *xiaoshuo*.[15] Considered as resources available to the author plying his craft, features of this poetics may be thought of as elements of *xiaoshuo* rhetoric; considered as points of reference in an audience's reception of the texts, they may be thought of as aspects of *xiaoshuo* aesthetics. To the extent that I am referencing the properties I have identified in order to offer readings of some of Xiang Kairan's works, the project I am engaged in is one of criticism and interpretation. I hope that the relationship between the project of poetics and the project of criticism proves to be synergistic rather than reductively circular.

In addition to thematic genre and literary genre, genre in a third sense plays a role in this study. This is genre in the sense in which we encounter it when we walk (or used to walk) into a bookstore and look for the Fiction section, or perhaps Literary Fiction or Science Fiction or Romance—likewise when we would go to a Blockbuster Video store and head for Family or Foreign. The categories operant in such cases may seem at first glance to be of the same order as, maybe even identical with, thematic genres as I have just defined them. At issue here, though, are not simply intertextual affinities of setting, character, narrative trope, and so forth but also, and more fundamentally, the devices by which the producers and marketers of cultural commodities address their audiences. With the emergence of mass-media marketplaces, and in the days before Amazon and Netflix developed algorithms to put to surgically effective use the vast and detailed troves of consumer information to which they have access, what we might call market genres served as broad categories of negotiation between the various agents (producers, consumers, distributors, gatekeepers) in the cultural-commodity economy. The meaningful units in the marketplace for fiction, for example—fiction here in the broad sense of prose narrative literature—were not simply individual texts or editions of texts or the works of certain authors but also recognizable and distinctive categories of texts. It was in part through reference to these categories that audiences expressed their preferences, that publishers sought to incite and answer audience demands, and that authors and editors shaped their production of fictional texts.[16]

THE PLAN OF THIS STUDY

The first chapter of this study presents a biography of Xiang Kairan, intended to situate his writings in the context of his life and career and his life and career in the context of his times. The second chapter approaches his writings in terms of the dominant generic form they assume: *xiaoshuo*. I take Xiang Kairan's textual representations of himself as author and narrator and the recurrent fictional motif of monkeys and apes as points of entry into the characteristics of his *xiaoshuo*. The textual presence and functions of the author-narrator are inseparable from *xiaoshuo*'s fascination with the strange or marvelous (*qi* 奇), its declared intention of serving as a record of events, and its interest in the communicative process of transmission. These elements, their ramifications, and their interactions—including both their synergy and the tensions among them—are essential to the poetics of *xiaoshuo* as a genre in the Republican era. Embedded in this poetics are an uncertainty about the value of *xiaoshuo* and presumptions about its limitations that echo critiques by contemporary progressive critics yet derive from premodern discourse on the genre.

Xiang Kairan's contemporary and colleague Bao Tianxiao relates that the Republican vogue for martial arts fiction began, and the modern genre of martial arts fiction was created, through the marriage of Xiang Kairan's unique literary talents with the entrepreneurial vision of the publisher Shen Zhifang 沈知方—a marriage for which Bao played matchmaker. Modern scholarship has by and large accepted Bao's account. Chapter 3 undertakes to unpack this version of the genre's origins, examining in more detail the question of in just what sense Xiang and Shen's collaboration may be said to mark the creation of *wuxia xiaoshuo* as a thematic genre. It begins by reviewing the history of notions of fictional subtypes in China and the late-Qing interest in the question of genre, then proceeds to examine the status before the 1920s of two particular thematic genres: detective fiction and fiction of martial arts and chivalry. Key to my investigation is the fact that *Modern Times*, one of the founding works of modern martial arts fiction, was featured in Shen Zhifang's magazine *Detective World* (*Zhentan shijie* 偵探世界). I argue that while this placement may seem at first glance no more than an editorial convenience, it was in fact a concrete factor in the process by which *wuxia xiaoshuo* achieved its modern identity and exemplifies the logic by which the process took place. Shen Zhifang contributed to the birth of modern martial arts fiction by defining and promoting a marketable thematic genre, and it was the established success of detective fiction that provided him with the model for genre in this sense. The invention of martial arts fiction is not so much the invention of a genre as the deployment of a new notion of genre as a marketable category, in which a distinctive thematic genre, epitomized by the work of a high-profile author, is linked to particular considerations of medium and form.

Chapter 4 begins by moving from the question of thematic genre to these more concrete issues of literary form and the material presentation of texts. I first introduce the traditional Chinese linked-chapter novel (*zhanghui xiaoshuo* 章回小說): the history of the term, the genealogy and characteristics imputed to the category, and the form's status amid the early twentieth century's changing perspectives on fiction. I then examine the redeployment of the linked-chapter novel in fiction periodicals from Shen Zhifang's World Book Co., Ltd., which exploit the synergy between chapter fiction and periodical publishing as part of their appeal to the market and their response to the challenges of the New Literature. The presentation of Xiang Kairan's two major novels establishes an affinity between martial arts adventure as a thematic genre and the literary form of the linked-chapter novel that becomes a prominent element of modern martial arts fiction's identity. The two novels' histories also demonstrate two different responses to the vicissitudes of serialization. While *Modern Times* achieves a certain structural and thematic closure despite the challenges of serialization, *Rivers and Lakes* exploits—or is exploited by—serialization's logic to the point of continuing to reproduce itself beyond the original author's immediate control, both as unauthorized text and as cinematic adaptation. A text whose original success was attributable in part to the wedding of its material to a specific literary form thus becomes a prominent example of the transmedial propagation of thematic genre.

Marvelous Gallants of the Rivers and Lakes, Xiang Kairan's most famous novel, serves as the center of gravity for chapter 5. Beginning in 1928, *Rivers and Lakes* served as the inspiration for a series of films made under the title *The Burning of Red Lotus Temple* (*Huoshao honglian si* 火燒紅蓮寺). The box-office success of these films launched the Republican-era craze for martial arts fantasy films and magnified Xiang Kairan's reputation as an author. But this same success attracted the attention of critics who condemned such films and the fiction behind them for injuring the nation's citizenry by fostering superstition. The twentieth-century promotion of scientific rationalism as an essential element of a modernizing nationalist ideology problematized the status of the supernatural material that had long figured prominently in *xiaoshuo*'s fascination with the strange. Xiang Kairan's fiction addresses this problem directly in several works, most notably in the novella *Strange Phenomena of the Rivers and*

Lakes (*Jianghu guaiyi zhuan* 江湖怪異傳), which articulates *xiaoshuo* as a discursive realm exoticized and energized by the tension between the strange, on the one hand, and modern notions of facticity and rationality, on the other. It is the strange in this sense, and not the martial arts per se, that is the central concern of *Rivers and Lakes*. The novel situates the strange topographically in the Rivers and Lakes of its title and embeds it socially in master-disciple lineages devoted to the transmission of the mysterious Way. The process of transmission serves as one of the principal engines of the novel's plotting; so too does the threat of sexual desire that shadows the asexual reproduction of the marvelous made possible through the relationship of master and disciple. The authority of transmitted narrative, meanwhile, binds together the seemingly disparate facets of the strange gathered under the mantle of *xiaoshuo*, ranging from the milieu of the supernatural to instances of alternative historiography.

The final chapter focuses on the second of the Xiang Kairan's seminal pair of martial arts novels, *Chivalric Heroes of Modern Times*. It begins by examining the roots of *Modern Times* in the work that marked Xiang Kairan's debut as a novelist and made his reputation as a writer: *The Unofficial History of Sojourners in Japan* (*Liudong waishi* 留東外史). *Sojourners* echoes the linked-chapter novels of its day in its thematic focus on the excesses and hypocrisies of life in the modern city. It is distinctive, though, in taking Tokyo and not Shanghai as the setting for its exploration of the urban dystopia, thereby foregrounding the issue of Chinese national identity. And it prefigures the subgenre with which Xiang Kairan was soon to become associated by assigning the martial arts a minor yet powerful role in the narrative. The modern city, the negotiation of Chinese identity in the face of foreign presences, and, of course, the Chinese martial arts are all central concerns of *Modern Times*. The novel presents the earliest extended elaboration of the legend of the historical martial artist Huo Yuanjia. Later retellings of the tale, including Bruce Lee's cinematic role as Huo's fictional student Chen Zhen, exploit the material for anti-Japanese nationalism and triumphalist rejections of China's reputation as the "sick man of Asia." Xiang Kairan's novel presents a more hesitant and nuanced account of the Chinese martial artist's encounters with the foreign and the modern. His Huo Yuanjia stands up against challenges to Chinese dignity and falls to the perfidy of foreign villains. The more fundamental challenge Huo confronts, however, is that of adapting the Chinese martial arts to the needs and opportunities of modern, urban, mediatized, and transnational society. The problem is again that of transmission: of the balance between continuity and change, identity and difference, in the passing of an inheritance from one set of hands to another. And just as the novel's diegesis shifts the world of the martial arts from the otherworldly Rivers and Lakes to the cosmopolis under the sign of history, so too does its thematic agenda suggest possibilities for martial arts fiction and *xiaoshuo* in general beyond the traditional parameters of entertainment and moralizing didacticism. Yet the text declines to engage these possibilities fully. This disinclination situates the text and its author in an ambivalent position analogous to that of its ultimately tragic protagonist and bespeaks limitations inherent in the self-concept of *xiaoshuo*.

CHAPTER ONE

The Writer's Life

X iang Kairan 向愷然 (childhood name Taijie 泰階, given name Kui 逵, courtesy name Kaiyuan 愷元) was born on the sixteenth day of the second lunar month in the sixteenth year of the Guangxu reign period—March 6, 1890, by the Gregorian calendar.[1] His family's ancestral home was in Pingjiang 平江 county in Hunan, northeast of the provincial capital Changsha, perhaps eighty-some kilometers as the crow flies but much farther by the mountain roads; he was born, however, fifty kilometers south of Changsha, in the Xiangtan 湘潭 county seat on the Xiang 湘 River, where his father owned a shop that manufactured and sold umbrellas. As the son of a moderately comfortable family, he began his education at the age of four (five *sui* 歲) in a traditional schoolroom. The family closed the umbrella shop when he was ten and relocated to the countryside east of Changsha; he recalls the schoolroom where he then boarded in his 1923 "Three Monkey Tales" ("Sange hou'er de gushi" 三個猴兒的故事). In 1903, at the age of thirteen, he enrolled in the recently established Provincial Industrial College (Shengyuan shiye xuetang 省垣實業學堂) in Changsha, a government-run school offering Western-style curricula including mining and civil engineering. And it was here that he engaged with the public events of his day in a way that was to shape his life decisively.

Also in 1903 another Hunanese, Chen Tianhua 陳天華 (1875–1905), arrived in Japan to pursue his own education. Chen quickly became involved in the revolutionary activities for which the community of overseas students provided fertile ground: he organized in Japan and back in China, published incendiary pamphlets, and was a founding member of Sun Yat-sen's Revolutionary Alliance (Tongmenghui 同盟會), established in Tokyo in August 1905.[2] In November of the same year, the Japanese Ministry of Education issued new regulations governing Chinese students in Japan. Intended to dampen a growing political activism, the regulations instead prompted protests, strikes, and mass returns of students to China. On December 7 an editorial in the *Asahi Shimbun* 朝日新聞 credited the Chinese students' actions to a misunderstanding of the regulations and to "that self-indulgent and mean self-will that seems peculiar to Chinese nationals."[3] Chen Tianhua responded by composing a testament calling upon his comrades to give the lie to this calumny, and the following day he drowned himself in Tokyo Bay. A fellow Hunanese revolutionary, Huang Xing 黃興 (1874–1916), arranged to have Chen's remains returned to Changsha and on May 29, 1906, held a public funeral service for him at Yuelu Mountain 岳麓山 south of the city. The local government was powerless to stop the demonstration but took note of those in attendance. Xiang Kairan was among them. He was soon expelled from the Provincial College. With this road to education and career closed off, his family elected the alternative favored by so many aspiring Chinese students of the time and, selling a plot of land to finance the venture, placed him on a steamer from Shanghai to Japan.

Xiang Kairan's first stint in Japan lasted from the latter part of 1906 to early 1911. He enrolled at the Kobun Institute (Kōbun Gakuin 宏文学院), a school established to prepare Chinese students for study at Japanese universities; the revolutionaries Chen Tianhua and Huang Xing and the future literary giant Lu Xun were only a few among the luminaries who passed through its gates.[4] What specific course of academic study Xiang Kairan pursued is not clear. His extracurricular activities are somewhat better documented. He joined the Revolutionary Alliance, continuing the political proclivities that had brought his previous studies to an abrupt end. Under the guidance of a fellow Hunanese, Wang Zhiqun 王志群 (Runsheng 潤生, 1880–1941)—also a student at Kobun, and also a member of the Alliance—he deepened his study of the martial arts, a pursuit in which he had had at least a casual interest since childhood. And by all accounts, including his own, he was an enthusiastic participant in the life of drinking, gambling, and whoring indulged in by some segments of the overseas Chinese community.

By March 1911 Xiang Kairan had returned to Changsha and was involved in the establishment of a martial arts study group. In September of the following year he made what was apparently his first sale of a piece of his writing, publishing a treatise on "The Art of Pugilism" ("Quanshu" 拳術) in *Changsha ribao* 長沙日報 (*Changsha Daily News*). He used the proceeds to fund his return to Japan. The intervening eighteen months, of course, had seen the Wuchang Uprising of October 1911, the ensuing Xinhai Revolution, the establishment of the Republic of China in January 1912, and the subsequent abdication of the last Qing emperor. The extent of Xiang Kairan's involvement in these momentous affairs is unclear. Family members recall tales of his participation in the Wuchang Uprising's failed predecessor, Huang Xing's bloody Huanghuagang Uprising at Guangzhou in April, but there is no mention of such involvement in the author's published writings or any independent documentation thereof.[5] In several later fictional pieces, the author-narrator takes pains to distance himself self-deprecatingly from the events surrounding the Xinhai Revolution. The 1925 *Repent and Be Saved* (*Huitou shi an* 回頭是岸) describes the period before his return to Japan as follows:

> In the Renzi year of the Republic (1912), I held an extremely minor position in Yuezhou [north of Changsha]. At that time the Republic of China had just been established, and the Nationalist Party, reorganized from the Revolutionary Party, lorded it high and mighty in Hunan. Although not a genuine old-school revolutionary myself, while studying in Japan before Xinhai I'd happened to become quite close with a number of revolutionaries; and much to my surprise, once the Revolution had succeeded, I found myself alongside these genuine old-school revolutionaries in reaping a few rewards.[6]

A 1922 recollection of the pregnant period between the Wuchang Uprising and the declaration of the establishment of the Republic likewise makes no overt reference to the political situation:

In the 11th month of the Xinhai year (1911), I lived at the offices of the *Dahan bao* 大漢報 in Changsha. I held no position at this office; the manager simply let me live there because of our personal connections. Living there at the time the same as me was also one Liu Tuigong from Xinning. Although this Liu Tuigong was quite young, his education and character were quite good. He possessed a most inimitable talent, namely an aptitude for conversation. Odd anecdotes and curious occurrences of all sorts—I really don't know how he was able to keep so many of them in his head! The weather at that season was bitterly cold, and neither of us had any professional responsibilities. Every night, as the people in the office busied themselves with their various tasks, he and I would sit close to the stove and talk over every conceivable kind of nonsense. Stories of spirits, ghosts, and weird events made up the greater part of the tales he told.[7]

The fact that the newspaper *Dahan bao* was established in support of the Revolutionary Alliance suggests Xiang's association with the movement. But this passage, like the previous, portrays Xiang Kairan as no more than a fellow traveler and mines this moment from the past for what we will come to recognize as key themes in Xiang's fictional practice: the sociability of tale telling, the fascination with the strange, and the pleasure of entertainment as a sphere distinct from either political or professional concerns, fostered within the environment of the press.

These recollections were penned a decade or more after the fact, at the height of Xiang Kairan's career as a professional writer and in the context of the production of fictional texts. At the time, however, Xiang Kairan's involvement with the political upheavals of the day seems to have run deeper than these vignettes suggest. His second stay in Japan was brief. At some point in 1913 he returned to Hunan, where he held an administrative position at a leather factory in Yueyang and, in concert with Wang Zhiqun and with financial support from the provincial government, resumed organizing a society for the study and teaching of the martial arts. His return most likely occurred after the escalation of political tensions following the assassination of the Nationalist Party's Song Jiaoren 宋教仁 (1882–1913) in March. In July, when Hunan's military governor Tan Yankai 譚延闓 (1880–1930) declared his support for the Second Revolution against President Yuan Shikai's growing abuse of power, Xiang Kairan served as an officer in the anti-Yuan First Army under Cheng Zikai 程子楷 (1872–1945). The Second Revolution sputtered; Tan Yankai reversed his allegiance in August; Cheng Zikai, under threat of arrest, went into exile in Japan; so too, for a third sojourn across the East China Sea, did Xiang Kairan.

During this third sojourn, Xiang Kairan studied at Central University (Chūō Daigaku 中央大學) in Tokyo. His course of study is unclear, and it is not certain whether he completed a degree. By the latter part of 1915 he was back in China and affiliated with the Jiangxi branch of Sun Yat-sen's Chinese Revolutionary Party (Zhonghua gemingdang 中華革命黨). It was in December 1915 that Yuan Shikai declared his intent to restore the monarchy, which the Xinhai Revolution had overthrown, and install himself as the first emperor of a new dynasty—sparking revolt in the south, the formation of a National Protection Army, and warfare between Yuan and his opponents. Yuan's renouncement of his imperial ambitions in March 1916 did not resolve the crisis, and in the Haizhu Incident of April 12, representatives of the National Protection Army were gunned down when negotiations with agents of Guangzhou's governor Long Jiguang 龍濟光 (1867–1925) erupted into violence. Xiang Kairan, posted to Guangzhou at the time on behalf of the anti-Yuan Jiangxi Revolutionary Army, found himself in some peril. By the end of June, though—after Yuan's death on June 6—he had made his way to Shanghai, where he set aside direct involvement in the tumultuous politics of the day and assumed the role of a professional writer.

His turn toward the world of print had begun earlier, apparently around the time of his most recent return to China. The latter half of 1915 saw the serialization of "The Art of Pugilism"—presumably the same text as that published in *Changsha ribao* four years earlier—in the periodical *Chung Hwa Novel Magazine* (*Zhonghua xiaoshuo jie* 中華小說界).[8] Beginning in March 1916 the same magazine then published Xiang Kairan's "Matters Pugilistic, Seen and Heard" ("Quanshu jianwen lu" 拳術見聞錄), a sequel of sorts to "The Art of Pugilism," devoted not to the exposition of principles and techniques but to meditations on the art and brief classical-language biographies and anecdotes of martial artists.[9] March 1916 also saw the publication of a collection of anecdotes on tiger hunting, "Turning Pale" ("Bianse tan" 變色談), in *Elements of People's Rights* (*Minquan su* 民權素), a literary magazine with close ties to anti-Yuan journalists and intellectuals.[10] And between August and December a series of long classical-language tales appeared in *Ocean of Fiction* (*Xiaoshuo hai* 小說 海).[11] The work that established Xiang Kairan's reputation as a writer, however, was the ninety-chapter vernacular-language novel *The Unofficial History of Sojourners in Japan* (*Liudong waishi* 留東外史), published by People's Rights Publishing (Minquan chubanbu 民權出版部) in May 1916 under the name Pingjiang Buxiaosheng 平江不肖生. The novel exhaustively relates the debauched misadventures of Chinese students and expatriates; the opening states that the author began penning it toward the close of 1914, that is, during his third stay in Japan.

I will discuss certain of the formal, rhetorical, and thematic aspects of this first spate of Xiang Kairan's writings at later points in this study. For the purposes of this preliminary overview of his authorial career, though, it is worth noting that "Matters Pugilistic, Seen and Heard" represents a bridge between his previous publication on the martial arts and his nascent career as a writer of *xiaoshuo* 小說 (fiction). The collection presents itself as a record of actual persons and events and is by no means fiction in the sense of deliberately invented content, yet it marks a turn toward narrative and includes material that will reappear in more elaborated form in Xiang Kairan's later works, including (as the longest and final item in the text) a biography of the martial artist Huo Yuanjia 霍元甲. These early explorations of narrative did not entail an abandonment of expository or discursive writing; Xiang Kairan continued to produce non-narrative writings on the martial arts until the end of his life. Nor did they entail an immediate embrace of what we might call martial arts fiction as such. Although these early writings include martial arts characters, incidents, and themes, and it is possible to trace resonances and links between them and Xiang Kairan's later martial arts novels, the early fictional works are also closely allied to such then-popular subtypes as social satire, romance, tales of the strange, and historical fiction. Finally, Xiang Kairan's early narrative writings demonstrate facility with a range of linguistic and formal options for *xiaoshuo*: classical-language tales, both of the anecdotal "jottings" (*biji* 筆記) variety and of the linguistically more florid and narratively more elaborate type in vogue in the years surrounding the founding of the Republic, and vernacular-language fiction in the expansive linked-chapter (*zhanghui* 章回) form.

Shanghai was Xiang Kairan's primary residence for the next five years, although he made several trips back to Hunan—to serve a stint as an officer in a local militia in 1917 and to work once again with Wang Zhiqun in a martial arts organization in 1919. He continued to write, though he produced nothing that approached the success and popularity of *Sojourners*. One more classical-language tale, a "tale of strange passion" (*qiqing xiaoshuo* 奇情小說), appeared in 1917.[12] Shanghai's Taidong shuju 泰東圖書局 published another short collection of martial anecdotes in the classical language, under the same title as the appendix to the earlier "Art of Pugilism."[13] Two little-known short novels, *Annals of the Dragon and Tiger* (*Longhu chunqiu* 龍虎春秋, 1919) and *The Flying Head at Midnight* (*Banye feitou ji* 半夜飛頭記, 1920?), constitute early attempts at presenting martial arts and fantastic material within the vernacular chapter-novel form.[14] Little else is known about his activities during these years. There is no record of any immediate engagement with the cultural and political ferment surrounding the 1919 May Fourth Movement, and it was primarily on the strength of *Sojourners* that he was remembered as a writer at the beginning of the century's third decade, five years after that novel's first publication.

It was *Sojourners* that recommended Xiang Kairan to Bao Tianxiao 包天笑 (1876–1973), a veteran of Shanghai's literary and publishing circles, when Bao began seeking contributors for a new fiction periodical. Bao tells the story in colorful detail in his memoirs. He doesn't specify the date but implies that it was sometime around the February 1922 launch of *The Sunday* (*Xingqi* 星期), a small-format weekly fiction and entertainment magazine published by Great Eastern Books (Dadong shuju 大東書局). For some time Bao had wanted to locate the man who had written *Sojourners*, but despite the novel's fame, the author's current whereabouts were unknown. "Some said he'd already gone home to Hunan, some that he'd returned to Japan, but there was no consensus on the matter," writes Bao. A break comes when another Hunanese litterateur, Zhang Mingfei 張冥飛 (1894–?), reveals Xiang's current residence in Shanghai. He warns, though, that the gentleman in question is not much given to receiving visitors, and if you *do* look him up, he continues, you'd best do so late in the day, or better yet at night. Aha! says the savvy Bao: an opium smoker. Just so, laughs Zhang. The very next day Bao makes his way to a narrow alley off Xinzha Road 新閘路. He finds the author in the upstairs room he shares with a dog, a monkey, and a mistress. At four in the afternoon Xiang Kairan has just risen and is scarcely ready for company. "He needed to satisfy his craving before he had any energy, and so without standing on ceremony I settled down across from him on the opium couch." Bao left Xiang's lodgings that night with the promise of two contributions for *The Sunday.*[15]

One of Xiang's contributions was the *Supplement to the Unofficial History of Sojourners in Japan* (*Liudong waishi bu* 留東外史補)—one of several sequels he produced to the novel that had first made his reputation.[16] The second was "A Hunter's Miscellany" ("Lieren ouji" 獵人偶記), a series of classical-language anecdotes about hunters and tigers in the wilds of his native Hunan.[17] As with Xiang Kairan's earlier writings, it is possible to trace thematic and formal links between these two works and the genre of martial arts fiction. What Bao's account highlights, however, is not the literary genealogy of the genre but the personal networks and commercial decisions that led to its emergence. Pleased with the success of his mission, Bao shows the Hunan tales to Shen Zhifang 沈知方 (1882–1939), a friend and colleague from his days with an earlier periodical, *The Grand Magazine* (*Xiaoshuo daguan* 小說大觀).[18] "Where did you unearth this treasure?" exclaims Shen. Shen, the most aggressively entrepreneurial of Shanghai publishers, had recently founded the World Book Co., Ltd. (Shijie shuju 世界書局; hereafter World Books). In a bid to challenge Great Eastern in the entertainment-periodical market, he launches his flagship *The Scarlet Magazine* (*Hong zazhi* 紅雜誌; hereafter *Scarlet*) in August 1922; among *Scarlet*'s sisters will be something new, the first Chinese periodical devoted to a specific popular-fiction genre—*Detective World* (*Zhentan shijie* 偵探世界). What Bao has shown him motivates Shen to contract Xiang Kairan to write for his magazines. And with his characteristic instinct for creating new market niches, Shen commissions Xiang to pen something novel and quite specific: "first-class romantic fiction in the sword-immortal and knight-errant vein" (劍仙俠士之類的一流傳奇小說).[19] Pingjiang Buxiaosheng's *Rivers and Lakes* began serialization in *Scarlet* in January 1923 and *Modern Times* in the first issue of *Detective World* in the summer of the same year. Bao's visit to Xiang Kairan's garret thus resulted not only in contributions for *The Sunday* but also—as he tells it—in the revival of Xiang Kairan's career as an author and in "the launching of the first wave of Shanghai's *wuxia xiaoshuo*" (開上海武俠小說的先河).[20]

The next chapter of this study examines the question of to what extent and in what sense the encounter between Bao Tianxiao and Xiang Kairan might be said to be responsible for the creation of the modern genre of *wuxia xiaoshuo*. As far as Xiang Kairan's career, it is undeniable that the writings he published in Bao Tianxiao's *The Sunday* marked the beginning of his most productive period as a writer. The year 1922 saw not only the commencement of *The Sunday*'s serialization of the *Supplement* to *Sojourners* but also the publication by Minquan chubanbu 民權出版部 of the seventy-chapter continuation (*xuji* 續集) of the original novel, together with a few short pieces in *The Sunday* and in World Books' new *The Merry Magazine* (*Kuaihuo* 快活). Both *Rivers and Lakes* and *Modern Times* began serialization in 1923; so did yet another sequel to *Sojourners*, *A New History of Sojourners in Japan* (*Liudong xinshi* 留東新史), in the *Xinwen bao* 新聞報. Ten-chapter volumes of *Rivers and Lakes* and *Modern Times*, collected from the serializations, began to appear before the end of the year; they were joined by a novella published in book form and by at least nine short stories placed in *The Sunday*, *Scarlet*, *Detective World*, and *The Story World* (*Xiaoshuo shijie* 小說世界).

His membership in a short-lived literary group organized by Yuan Hanyun 袁寒雲 (Kewen 克文, 1889–1931) in 1923 signals the recognition, both by the author and by his associates, of his place in the community of Shanghai's littérateurs.[21] Yet neither his work as a writer nor his socializing was limited to the world of entertainment literature. He was associated as editor and contributor with the *Panorama of National Skills* (*Guoji daguan* 國技大觀), an encyclopedic volume on the Chinese martial arts published in September 1923. In the same year he became a lay disciple of a Buddhist teacher. And in 1925 he would expand his study of the martial arts to include the increasingly popular *taijiquan* 太極拳. A reminiscence by his son Xiang Yixue 向一學 (born 1918) paints a perhaps romanticized picture of Xiang Kairan's Shanghai lodgings as a hub of the socialization and storytelling that fed his work as a writer:

Shanghai celebrities, heads of secret societies, masters of the martial arts, stalwarts from every walk of life—he was on the closest of terms with all of them. The house was filled with visitors, coming and going as they pleased. Formal introductions were rarely made; people would simply introduce themselves with a salute amid the flow of conversation and later leave without bothering to say goodbye. Sometimes there would be two or three groups of various people present, and my father would chat and joke in high spirits, talking about everything under the sun, past and present, domestic and foreign. His powers of memory were excellent, and when he heard people's stories, anecdotes, and gossip, he would selectively record them in his mind; when the time came to write he could then pour them out in an unbroken flood.[22]

In 1924, *Modern Times* was cut short by the closing of *Detective World*, but *Rivers and Lakes* flowed on, and the novel *Jade Pendant, Golden Bracelet* (*Yujue jinhuan lu* 玉玦金環錄) succeeded *New History* on the pages of *Xinwen bao*. World Books added a three-volume book edition of *New History* to the accretive volumes of *Modern Times* and *Rivers and Lakes*; a full twenty short stories appeared, the majority in *Scarlet* and its successor *Scarlet Rose*. Only eight or so short stories were published in 1925, but they were joined by another new serialized novel, *Repent and Be Saved* (*Huitou shi an* 回頭是岸), in *New Shanghai* (*Xin Shanghai* 新上海) and by an independent sequel of sorts to the still-serializing *Rivers and Lakes*, *Young Gallants of the Rivers and Lakes* (*Jianghu xiaoxia zhuan* 江湖小俠傳), published in book form by World Books.

In 1926, then, the flood came to a halt. Xiang Kairan published only four or five short stories in this year. *Repent and Be Saved* broke off in the middle of its eighth chapter, after fifteen installments, in December 1926. An editor's note in the January 1927 issue of *New Shanghai* explained that "Buxiaosheng has returned to Hunan, and *Repent and Be Saved* will pause for one or two issues,"[23] but no further installments appeared, nor any mention of the novel, through the remainder of the magazine's life. Xiang Kairan's signature work, *Rivers and Lakes*, came to an even more puzzling juncture in its publication. In July 1926 the novel, now in its eighty-sixth chapter, rather hastily wraps up two major plot lines that have been spun out for some tens of chapters, and then, through the voice of the narrator, announces its conclusion—leaving open, nevertheless, the possibility of a continuation or sequel at some later date.[24] The "Editor's Remarks" ("Bianyu suohua" 編餘瑣話) in the same issue announce that Buxiaosheng's work will reappear in the periodical's third volume with the continuation of *Modern Times*, which had been interrupted by *Detective World*'s cessation. Yet the first issue of the new volume in January 1927 brings not *Modern Times* but a resumption of *Rivers and Lakes*, prefaced with a lengthy explanation by the author-narrator (discussed in chapter 4) of his decision to continue the novel. This unexpected continuation then proceeds at a halting pace. It runs for just four issues, through the end of chapter 88, before disappearing. Only after three issues have passed without an episode of *Rivers and Lakes*—a gap of a month and a half's time, on account of a Lunar New Year break in publication—does the editor offer his apologies and explain that the novel must "pause for a few issues" because the author has gone to Hunan to take up an office and "does not at present have time to write." "But I can promise our readers," he goes on, "that as soon as his affairs have settled down a bit, he will be sending us the continuation."[25] Sure enough, before the month is out, the editor returns with the "happy tidings" that Buxiaosheng has resumed his submissions. "It is truly moving that amid the welter of military correspondence he is willing to make the time to write for our *Scarlet Rose*. [The manuscript] is already in the hands of our typesetters."[26] And in the following issue the serialization resumes with the commencement of chapter 89. It continues in this fashion until the 106th chapter in December 1928 (*Scarlet Rose* 4, no. 34), when it ends in midcourse without further explanation.

The logic and mechanics of *Rivers and Lakes*'s serialization will be examined in more detail in chapter 3. Most relevant here is the fact that the latter portion of the novel was written not by Xiang Kairan but by someone else, evidently *Scarlet Rose*'s editor, Zhao Tiaokuang 趙苕狂 (1893–1953). Xiang Kairan had indeed left Shanghai and abandoned his authorial career in order to take an administrative post in the military. Some scholars credit him with the first two chapters of the continuation, 87 and 88, suggesting that he at first entertained some hope of keeping up with his writing, or perhaps made an attempt to respond to his editor's importunities, before finding the project impractical.

Xiang Kairan's departure took place in the context of the tumultuous political and military events of the day—events that, while of concern to all citizens of China, could well have seemed particularly pressing to a Hunan native with revolutionary affiliations resident in Shanghai. The first step of Chiang Kaishek's Northern Expedition, which aimed to eliminate warlordism and foreign influence and reunify the nation under Nationalist rule, was to establish control of Hunan in preparation for the drive north from Guangdong to the Wuhan cities on the Yangtze. The Hunan general Tang Shengzhi (唐生智, 1889–1970), whose armies had been integrated into the National Revolutionary Army in the spring of 1926, occupied Changsha in July. Xiang Kairan's ancestral hometown, Pingjiang, was one of the Nationalists' first objectives when they pushed forward in mid-August. By December the Nationalists could claim authority over seven provinces. In the early months of 1927, however, as operational and ideological rifts widened between Chiang Kaishek and the Nationalist headquarters in Wuhan, the latter groomed Tang Shengzhi as the center of a military counterweight to Chiang and his forces. Meanwhile, the Nationalists' Communist allies and other radical elements organized labor unions and farmers' associations in preparation for the social revolution, which they saw as the next stage of the struggle. Hunan was a center of such activities, and Changsha was perhaps the most radical city in China. The counties around Changsha were the subject of Mao Zedong's famous "Report on the Investigation of the Peasant Movement in Hunan" ("Hunan nongmin yundong kaocha baogao" 湖南農民運動考察報告), written in March 1927, in which he sketched his vision of the peasantry as the source of violent social revolution.

It was at this juncture, evidently in February or March 1927, that Xiang Kairan left Shanghai to take a position as secretary at the headquarters of the First Division of the Thirty-Sixth Corps of Tang Shengzhi's Fourth Army Group (previously the Eighth Army). His divisional commander was Liao Lei 廖磊 (1890–1939); Liu Xing 劉興 (1887–1963) commanded the Thirty-Sixth Corps. We know very little of Xiang Kairan's motives and aims. Was he tiring of the pressures of making a living with his pen? Was residence in Shanghai—an obvious objective in the war and already a site of leftist agitation—beginning to seem problematic, even dangerous? Was he stirred by loyalty to his native province or by the revolutionary aspirations that had shaped his life in the past? Did he have personal connections in Tang Shengzhi's camp, or did the exigencies of the time simply open promising opportunities for a man of his talents and background? Clues in his writings and in the contours of his career suggest all of these factors as possibilities, but as to their relative weight, it is difficult to hazard a surmise.

Xiang Kairan was garrisoned with the Thirty-Sixth Corps at Xiaogan 孝感, northwest of Wuhan. Chiang Kaishek's armies took Nanjing in

March and Shanghai in April—at which point Chiang initiated his bloody purge of Communists and their supporters. In May, as the Nanjing forces moved into northern Anhui and northern Jiangsu, the Wuhan army under Tang Shengzhi advanced into Henan. Back in Changsha garrison forces commanded by an officer under Tang's Thirty-Fifth Corps launched their own violent suppression of local labor unions and farmers' associations. The beleaguered Communists led the doomed Nanchang Uprising in August and the equally ill-fated Autumn Harvest Uprisings in Guangdong, Hubei, and Hunan in September; the Hunan uprising, led by Mao Zedong, included a unit from Pingjiang and attempted in vain to capture the Pingjiang county seat. In late August, when the warlord Sun Chuanfang 孫傳芳 (1885–1935) mounted a counteroffensive against the Nationalist's Nanjing forces, Tang Shengzhi sent units to Anhui under Liu Xing and He Jian 何鍵 (1887–1956) intended to coordinate with Sun. After Sun's defeat, Tang declined to attend a September meeting aimed at reunifying the Nationalist leadership, which then launched a punitive expedition against him in October. His forces retreated to Hunan; in November Tang escaped to Japan. The remnants of his armies capitulated with the Nationalist authorities, and many were assigned to the Fourth Army Group commanded by Bai Chongxi 白崇禧 (1893–1966) for the final push to Beijing in May 1928. Over the byzantine course of these campaigns, Xiang Kairan evidently followed the Thirty-Sixth Corps from Hubei to Anhui and back to Hunan. By the autumn of 1928 he was garrisoned with the Thirty-Sixth, now under Liao Lei's command, in the Kaiping 開平 district of Tangshan 唐山 northwest of Tianjin, and may have been involved in the Nationalist civic administration of Tianjin.[27] He followed Liao Lei in his reassignment to Beiping (as Beijing was now renamed) but then, sometime in early 1929, resigned his military commission. Xiang Kairan was evidently already on the sidelines when warfare between Chiang and his warlord allies broke out again in March.

It was in late March that rumors began to circulate in the Shanghai press that Xiang Kairan had died. The earliest such report that Xu Sinian's researches have identified appears in the *Shanghai Pictorial* (*Shanghai huabao* 上海畫報) of March 24. In early April Bao Tianxiao noted that the details of Xiang's alleged demise were unclear but nonetheless took the occasion to publish a reminiscence. Similar reports and memorials followed. Zhang Mingfei countered in July with the news that Xiang Kairan was alive and in Tianjin, and the facts were seemingly settled with the *Beiyang Pictorial*'s (*Beiyang huabao* 北洋畫報) publication of a letter and recent photograph from Xiang Kairan in August.[28] In the meantime, however, the rumor had kindled further controversy. The author's purported demise raised questions about the authenticity of writings bearing his name, both the continuation of *Rivers and Lakes*, which had been serialized in *Scarlet Rose* through the last month of 1928, and a *New Tale of the Swordsmen* (*Xin jianxia zhuan* 新劍俠傳) announced for publication in the *New Liaoning News* (*Liaoning xinbao* 遼寧新報). By the end of August Xiang Kairan was evidently negotiating with Shanghai publishers about the unauthorized portions of *Rivers and Lakes* and about future writing projects. World Books' Shen Fangzhi sent a representative north to arrange both settlement and contract. Xiang Kairan returned to Hunan in November for his father's final illness. By April or May 1930 he was once again residing in Shanghai and had resumed his career as a writer.

The resumption of his pre-1927 life was brief, however, and far less productive than before. An authorized continuation and conclusion to *Rivers and Lakes* that is said to have been under discussion never appeared. He did complete *Modern Times*, the final chapters of which were published by World Books in March 1932. The only writing to appear in the Shanghai periodical press was a series of reflections on the practice of *taijiquan* serialized in the *Xinwen bao* 新聞報 in 1930.[29] This piece seems to have signaled the direction in which Xiang Kairan's interests were increasingly tending. At some point in 1932 he returned to Changsha to serve as secretary of the Hunan Institute for the Practice of the National Arts (Hunan guoshu xunlian suo 湖南國術訓練所), a martial arts organization established by He Jian, now governor of the province. For the next five years, until the outbreak of war with Japan, his activities centered on the promotion of the martial arts, as administrator and instructor, and his occasional publications likewise focused on the same concerns.

After the outbreak of hostilities in July 1937, Xiang Kairan and the martial arts organizations he helped direct contributed to patriotic and support activities. By some accounts he led a unit of the local self-defense forces organized after the Japanese began attacks into Hunan in 1938. Later in that year he joined the staff of his old superior Liao Lei, now in command of the forces defending the Anhui wartime government at Lihuang 立煌 (today Jinzhai 金寨). There he married for the third time, with a former student from the Hunan Martial Arts Association, twenty years his junior. Liao Lei died of a stroke in October 1939 and was entombed at Xiangshan Temple 響山寺. Xiang Kairan remained at Lihuang, serving in the provincial government and for a time teaching classical Chinese literature at Anhui College 安徽学院. In 1944 he was appointed supervisor of the reconstruction of Xiangshan Temple, which had been destroyed in a Japanese attack the previous year. When Japan's surrender in 1945 was followed by civil war between the Nationalists and the Communists, Xiang Kairan held a post under the Nationalist commander Xia Wei 夏威 (1893– 1975) at Bengbu 蚌埠, but he was at Lihuang when it was temporarily seized by Communist forces in September 1947 and was detained by the PLA for several days. The officer who interviewed him urged Xiang Kairan to take a teaching position at the recently established Jiamusi College 佳木斯高校 in Heilongjiang, but when Xiang declined, he was released, and he and his family were granted travel documents for safe passage.[30]

Xiang Kairan took his family to Bengbu, then later, via Nanjing and Hankou, back to Hunan. He was in Changsha when its government welcomed the advancing Communist forces in 1949. Though he resumed writing, his works did not find an audience: the first part of an *Unofficial History of the Revolution* (*Geming yeshi* 革命野史), which he seems to have been working on as early as 1946, was published in 1950 but disappeared unnoticed.[31] From 1954 on he drew a salary from the provincial Institute of Literature and History 文史馆. The mid-1950s saw the beginnings of the new regime's incorporation of the martial arts into state-sponsored physical-education programs. At a martial arts exhibition, Xiang Kairan was received by the head of the national Sports and Physical Culture Commission, He Long 賀龍 (1896–1969), an erstwhile PLA field commander whose early career as a butcher-knife-wielding bandit in Hunan would not have been out of place on the pages of Xiang Kairan's fiction. He encouraged Xiang to begin work on a history of the Chinese martial arts. The last work Xiang Kairan was to publish during his lifetime, however, was "The Phoenix Greets the Sun" ("Danfeng chao yang" 丹凤朝阳), which appeared in the provincial literary magazine *New Sprouts* (*Xin miao* 新苗) in 1957.[32] This tale recounts how the phoenix, paying a congratulatory birthday visit to the sun, brings an entourage of magpies (*xique* 喜鹊) who chirp glad tidings in repetitive unison. The sun insists that he wants to hear "the hundred birds sing together" (百鸟齐鸣), but the magpies shout down the crows as pessimists, the partridges as recidivists, and so forth; the mimic blackbirds (百舌鸟) find favor for a time by imitating the magpies but when commanded to sing their own song can only fall silent. The mode of satirical allegory is unusual, even unprecedented, for Xiang Kairan. While the content is obviously motivated by the Hundred Flowers Campaign of 1956–1957, it is hard not to read it as also expressive of the personal perspective of an author whose writings—to say nothing of his lifestyle and values—were ill suited to the expectations of the new social and ideological regime. The tale's publication surely did not serve him well when the Hundred Flowers Campaign was succeeded by the Anti-Rightist Movement. Xiang Kairan, branded a "rightist element," died of a stroke on December 27, 1957.

CHAPTER TWO

Xiang Kairan's Monkeys

Xiaoshuo *as a Literary Genre*

WRITING AS PROFESSION AND THE BRAND
OF THE BUTTERFLY

How did Xiang Kairan view his role as a writer of fiction, and how did he understand the craft in which he was engaged? How did his conception of the nature of *xiaoshuo* shape the fiction he wrote? A point of entry into these questions is suggested by Bao Tianxiao's visit to Xiang Kairan's lodgings in 1921 or early 1922—the meeting that Bao's 1974 memoir credits with producing Xiang Kairan's contributions to *The Sunday*, revitalizing Xiang's writing career, and indeed igniting the Republican-era craze for martial arts fiction. Among the residents Bao finds at Xiang Kairan's lodgings is a monkey. "The Monkey in Xiang Kairan's Home" is the title of an anecdote Bao subsequently publishes in *The Sunday*:

> Mr. Xiang Kairan raised a monkey at his home. It was a male. One day a monkey trainer came to the door. He had with him a monkey of about the same size, but female. When the two monkeys saw one another, they stroked one another's bodies and made a marvelous show of affection. Mr. Xiang had it in mind to buy the monkey as a mate for his own, but when the monkey trainer saw the situation he

demanded an exorbitant price. The monkey was in fact already withered and thin. You could have bought one like it for no more than four or five dollars. Mr. Xiang was willing to pay ten, but the man still refused the offer. Then, as the monkey trainer made ready to leave, the two monkeys linked their hands together and would not let go. They had to force them apart. Mr. Xiang's monkey wailed in grief the whole night through.[1]

Monkeys appear in a photograph of Xiang Kairan dated 1926. The author is seated at a table upon which a pair of monkeys, chained at the neck, play with a piece of fruit as the writer busies himself with paper and pen. Though obviously taken in a studio rather than at Xiang Kairan's lodgings, the photograph corroborates Bao's portrait of the author's fondness for (among others) simian companions. Beyond that, though, it visually suggests an affinity between the monkeys and the very endeavor of writing. But in just what way are the two connected? Do the monkeys inspire the author? Do they divert him from his task? Does his writing

FIGURE 2.1 Xiang Kairan at a writing desk with monkeys, Shanghai, 1926.

Source: Scan provided by Mr. Xiang Xiaoguang.

mimic their play? Does his pen somehow evoke them from the paper with which they share the tabletop? And do we discern, in this droll tableau, any echoes of the grief and thwarted desire of the monkey whose tale Bao Tianxiao recorded?

The photograph dates from the end of the ten-year period in which Xiang Kairan was most active as a writer of fiction. In a broad sense, of course, his writing career can be said to span almost the entirety of his adult life. His earliest known publication, "The Art of Pugilism," appeared in 1912, when he was twenty-two years of age (or twenty-three *sui*), and his last, "The Phoenix Greets the Sun," shortly before his death at age sixty-seven. He was without question a *wenren* 文人, a literatus; he devoted his early life to acquiring an education founded on literacy in the narrow sense and entailing the broader social literacies that accompany it, and he subsequently relied on these competencies as the foundation of his livelihood and status. For much of his life, however, this livelihood and status centered not on writing fiction but on the deployment of his literacies in a series of secretarial, administrative, and educational capacities. There is nothing unusual in this; the majority of his peers in the world of commercial writing likewise either found occasional employment or made ongoing careers as editors, teachers, administrators, or entrepreneurs. If Xiang Kairan's case stands out, it is only for the brevity and intensity of his career as a fiction writer. The period of his life in which he relied primarily if not exclusively on the sale of fiction to support himself and his family began in 1916 with the publication of *Sojourners* and ended toward the end of 1926 with the sudden interruption of the previous years' voluminous output.[2] His attempt to return to a writer's life in the early 1930s was short-lived and relatively unproductive, and thenceforth any writing he did for commercial publication seems to have been either a sideline or a fairly fruitless endeavor to resume his earlier role. The popularity of his fiction from that single decade nonetheless granted him lifelong recognition. We can see both the enduring strength of the reputation these works engendered and something of the relationship between authorial renown and the more persistent realities of life as a *wenren* in Xiang Kairan's account of his 1947 detention by Communist troops, who, knowing him from his martial arts novels, offer him a teaching job and ask him to help with "a few literary tasks, such as writing handbooks, propaganda material and so forth."[3]

The encounter between the erstwhile martial arts novelist and the troops of the People's Liberation Army can serve to draw our attention to another feature of Xiang Kairan's authorial career: the dissociation of his fiction writing from his involvement with the political and social events of his day. The author's life spanned the momentous events of modern Chinese history, from the late-Qing tides of reform and overseas study through the Revolution and the establishment of Republic, the failed Second Revolution against Yuan Shikai and the years of warlord rule, Chiang Kaishek's Northern Expedition and the Nanjing Decade, the War of Resistance against Japan, civil war between Nationalist and Communists, the founding of the People's Republic of China, and the early years of the new regime, up to the Hundred Flowers and Anti-Rightist Movements. Far from merely being contemporary with these events, Xiang Kairan was actively engaged with many of them. Yet he did not embrace those currents of thought that envisioned the writing of fiction as an instrument of social and political engagement. In 1902, four years before Xiang Kairan's first journey to Japan, Liang Qichao, also in Japan, argued in the first issue of his journal *New Fiction* (*Xin xiaoshuo* 新小說) that "if one intends to renovate the people of a nation, one must first renovate its fiction."[4] In 1922, just as Xiang Kairan's authorial career was poised to flourish, Lu Xun explained how he had abandoned youthful dreams of saving his countrymen through the practice of medicine in favor of literary endeavor: "The most important thing to be done was to transform their *spirits*, and of course the best way to effect a spiritual transformation—or so I thought at the time—would be through literature and art."[5] Twenty years further on, Mao Zedong insisted that "literature and art fit well into the revolutionary machine as a component part, that they operate as powerful weapons for uniting and educating the people and for attacking and destroying the enemy."[6] But in 1931 Xiang Kairan, returning to the writing life he had set aside in order to play a role in the nation's military and political struggles, resumed the text of *Modern Times* with the following passage:

In the 15th year of the Republic (1926), I, Buxiaosheng, had written this *Tale of Chivalric Heroes* only as far as the 65th chapter, when because of my affairs I departed Shanghai and was unable to continue writing. That was now five whole years ago; and I had long ago decided simply to end [the book] midcourse. As far as I was concerned, writing fiction was entirely for the sake of making a living. I am not a military man, capable of drilling troops or fighting battles, and so I am unable to obtain even the most insignificant position in the military world. Nor am I a politician, capable of flapping my lips and drumming my tongue, and so I am unable to operate in the world of politics. Much less do I have any particular scientific knowledge or specialized technical skills that would allow me to scrape together a bowl of rice in the worlds of education or business. So utterly unskilled, I truly had no means to make a living, and could only rely upon this feeble brush of mine, scratching out a bit of irrelevant fiction and thereby swindling of bowl of rice for my sustenance. But five years ago, Providence unexpectedly stretched out its hand, and I was able to obtain an itinerant position in the interior. Once I could give up writing fiction without being reduced to starvation, I was quite happy to set this feeble brush of mine aside. I had always presumed that those who bought and read this irrelevant fiction did so in any event only to pass the time and that it made no real difference whether this book was completed or not. Little had I imagined that a good number of readers would write letters to inquire, directly or indirectly, and add their encouragements that I bring the novel to completion.

In the course of my travels through the provinces of Henan and Zhili over the last few years, I have seen and heard various matters similar in character to those found in the previous eight volumes of this book. What's more, as it so happens, I have lost that itinerant position and needs must resume my old profession. It seems to me that rather than starting a new project from scratch and leaving the book's readers in a state of disappointment, it would be better first to complete the present work; and thus, once more, I take my feeble brush in hand, and write as follows.[7]

This astonishing intervention into the text addresses two interrelated questions: that of the author's motives and that of the nature, status, and value of fiction. In a tone of wry self-deprecation, the author-narrator represents himself quite frankly as a commercial writer and disavows any aim or motivation beyond financial expediency. It is significant, in this regard, that in listing the professions for which he is unfit he specifies those arenas most often associated in his day with service to the nation: the military, politics, science, and education. He portrays these fields of worthy and public endeavor as polar opposites to the profession of fiction writing. Writing fiction is the last recourse of one unable to earn a livelihood in one of these more constructive roles, and the author is ready to abandon the pursuit when offered a better way to fill his rice bowl. The product, fiction, is empty of intrinsic worth, serving only the "irrelevant" function of amusing readers in times of idleness.

With very little effort one can project this view of the fiction writer's condition onto our photographic portrait, where the author is shadowed by his monkeys—playful, humanoid but not fully human, fruit in hand, chains about their necks. Yet in contemplating the textual self-portrait it is difficult to distinguish between convention, pose, and cri de coeur. It will be productive to consider Xiang Kairan's self-portrait as a writer from three perspectives: the discernible facts of the author's career, modern-era critiques of popular fiction, and premodern understandings of the nature and functions of *xiaoshuo*.

We should not assume that the textually incarnate narrator speaks as the unmediated voice of the historical author. We can, however, note that the facts and stance this passage sets forth tally with the circumstances of Xiang Kairan's career. He produced fiction for publication almost exclusively in those periods when he held no other employment. While it is possible that the demands of the various secretarial and administrative posts he held left little time for creative writing, there is no evidence that he regretted the tradeoff, actively sought to continue writing fiction, or welcomed the resumption of an authorial career. External sources reinforce the impression that for all his delight in swapping stories Xiang Kairan found the pressures of writing for publication onerous. Yu Shuwen (1907–1996) recollects a conversation with Xiang Kairan in Anhui during the War of Resistance in which the author reportedly claimed that he had devoted his most earnest efforts to his maiden work, *Sojourners*. At the time when he was writing *Rivers and Lakes*, however, "I had been living in Shanghai for some time, leading a debauched existence, sunk in brothels, dance halls, bars, and opium dens the whole day through; producing long-form fiction was the only way I could earn the writers' fees that would support my extravagances and pay off my mountain of debts." *Rivers and Lakes* deliberately exploited readers' appetites "so that I could satisfy my own wish for uninterrupted remuneration; there's no possible comparison between [writing of this kind] and writing to advance one's views or to educate and benefit society."[8] Through the elaborate show of modesty in the passage from *Modern Times* we can discern, to be sure, pride in the author's reputation, and in the playful manipulation of his material we see an unmistakable pleasure in his craft. But the author-narrator makes no claim to be moved to write by any need for self-expression; nor does he present writing fiction as a vital tool for the advancement of any of the political or societal agendas with which the historical Xiang Kairan was involved, much less of the enlightenment agenda claimed by the New Literature.

Xiang Kairan's characterization of his writing reads almost like a confession of the sins with which so-called Butterfly fiction was charged by its detractors. Criticism of literature not aligned with the New Literature project began with the birth of that project in the latter 1910s. Critiques multiplied and intensified around the time of Shen Yanbing's 沈雁冰 (Mao Dun 茅盾) assumption of editorial responsibilities at *The Short Story Magazine* (*Xiaoshuo yuebao* 小說月報) in 1921, an event that adherents perceived as a defining moment in the New Literature's triumph over the old. Attacks were again renewed in the early 1930s, prompted by an escalating sense of national crisis, the Left's calls for proletarian and revolutionary literature, and anxiety over the film industry's reinvigoration of commercial mass culture. Although the emphasis varies over time and from author to author, clear themes persist throughout this tradition of criticism. Butterfly literature is artistically primitive, inflexible, and repetitive. Its antiquated forms are matched by its promotion, either overt or unconscious, of outmoded values and regressive ideologies. When not inculcating reactionary ideas, it dedicates itself to mere entertainment, indulging in a frivolity that abnegates the responsibilities of true literature and contributes through distraction to moral and social inertia. Those who produce it are motivated by a combination of vested interest in the status quo, dilettantish self-indulgence and desire for fame, and crass commercial motives; some of the more virulent attacks label them "literary beggars" and even "literary prostitutes." The commercial imperative ensures that this literature panders to the basest impulses of its intended audience rather than guiding them toward understanding and meaningful action.

In such critiques, the term "old literature" may lump premodern literary forms together with literature produced for the contemporary marketplace, while the term "Butterfly literature" focuses primarily on the latter. And although "Butterfly literature" may include the essay, drama, and verse, its most common expressions are fictional, so that "Butterfly fiction" is often taken to epitomize, and serves as a metonymic reference to, "Butterfly literature" and even "old literature" as a whole.[9]

The attacks on "old literature" and "Butterfly fiction" were informed by the New Literature movement's concepts of literature's nature and purpose, and they were an integral part of its strategies for claiming territory and status within the literary field. At the same time, however, these attacks also echoed tropes and concepts that had circulated in premodern literary discourse and that shaped particular understandings of *xiaoshuo* for both its aficionados and its detractors. Orthodoxy ideology accorded the greatest value to those texts and types of texts that were understood to convey the Way, the moral patterning of the cosmos, society, and the individual. *Xiaoshuo*, "small talk" or "minor discourse," referred, by definition, to texts that were marginal to this central enterprise. The defining quality of inconsequentiality persisted even as the identity of the texts so designated shifted from the minor philosophical discourses and inferior historiography intended by early bibliographers to the popular narratives in various forms and linguistic registers comprehended by late-imperial uses of the term.[10] For critics, the triviality of *xiaoshuo* and its consequent undesirability as a distraction from more fruitful objects of study were exacerbated by the more active moral dangers posed by its shaky grounding in facticity and its fondness for unorthodox subject matter, including violence, sexual passion, and the supernatural. Supporters championed *xiaoshuo* in terms that left unchallenged many of the fundamental presumptions of such critiques. They averred *xiaoshuo*'s historicity and its value as a record of matters outside the purview of formal historiography. They argued—sometimes with tongue firmly in cheek—for the didactic benefits of portrayals of aberrant behavior. While admitting *xiaoshuo*'s nugatory character, they maintained that diversion and play (*youxi* 遊戲) served a role as indispensable complements to weightier undertakings. And they circumvented critiques of the unreliability and moral unorthodoxy of the contents of *xiaoshuo* by elaborating an aesthetics that focused on the structural and narratological artistry of the texts.[11] Significantly absent from the discussion, however, was explicit acknowledgment of the degree to which the literate elite employed *xiaoshuo* as a literary medium of increasing range and depth. From the late Ming on, the elaboration of the aesthetics of *xiaoshuo* in commentaries and prefaces went hand in hand with the reworking of transmitted texts and the creation of new fictional texts ab nihilo in the service of personal expression, moral inquiry, and social and political critique—practiced, with rare exceptions, under the cover of a discourse that insisted on the marginality and triviality of the genre.

While it is legitimate, therefore, to understand the apologia at the commencement of chapter 66 of *Modern Times* both as an expression of views that guided the historical author's career decisions and as an acknowledgment of attitudes that exposed his work and that of his peers to attacks from the New Literature camp, it is necessary to recognize it also as an iteration, indeed a performance, of perspectives that were integral to the self-identity of *xiaoshuo* as understood before the encroachment of Western regimes of fiction. Recognizing the author-narrator's assertions that he was motivated by purely commercial concerns, aimed only to entertain his readers, and considered his writings nugatory does not require that we evaluate these claims according to the standards of the New Literature's "universal humanist discourse centering on *wenxue* (literature) rather than *xiaoshuo* (small talk)."[12] We can take these claims as points of entry into an understanding of Xiang Kairan's fiction, not as a rationale for dismissing it or the final word on the subject. We can allow for the possibilities of irony and self-deprecation in Xiang Kairan's self-characterization, of course, but more fundamentally, we can ask about the characteristics and logic of *xiaoshuo* as a literary genre—the terms by which it conducts itself and seeks to engage with its readers. A reading of Xiang Kairan's writings in terms of their negotiation of elements of the literary traditions of *xiaoshuo* realigns and quickens our understanding of these writings and of the networks of texts and literary practices of which they are a part.

Literary historiography in the first decades of the People's Republic of China canonized May Fourth critiques that cast Butterfly literature as a regressive countercurrent to the New Literature.[13] Challenges to this historiography began to emerge in the post-Mao 1980s.[14] In their broadest aspect, these challenges were tied to a reconsideration of the logic and legacies of the May Fourth cultural project.[15] Within the specific field of literary studies, scholars began to analyze the degree to which the May Fourth's New Literature had laid claim to cultural capital through a logic of differentiation, defining itself and staking its place in the literary field through the construction of literary Others. Questioning of the May Fourth literary paradigm encouraged new attention to previously marginalized aspects of the Republican-era literary scene, Butterfly literature among them. Some scholars have striven to refute the specific charges leveled against Butterfly literature;[16] others to examine this literature in a new light, clarifying Butterfly literature's place in a literary tradition or illuminating its unique perspectives on Chinese modernity;[17] and others to read Republican-era literature without reliance on the assumptions established by such categories as Butterfly and May Fourth.[18] In my present attempt to read Xiang Kairan's fiction on something like its own terms, I am obviously indebted to these efforts. I endeavor to avoid treating either Butterfly fiction or May Fourth literature as reified categories, while at the same time I remain sensitive to the fact that the author, like his peers, editors, and readers, was influenced by contemporary discourses that often proposed facile distinctions between "new" and "old" literature. My aim in shifting my focus away from such categories is not so much to recuperate an alternative modernity in the sense of an overarching ideology or cultural discourse as it is to explore the more specific literary question of the poetics and aesthetics of Republican-era *xiaoshuo*. What were the features of *xiaoshuo* as Xiang Kairan understood the genre? In what way and to what ends did he deploy received elements of the genre, and how did he negotiate between allegiance to a tradition of *xiaoshuo*, on the one hand, and the shifting discursive and institutional tides of Republican China's literary scene, on the other?

THE NATURE AND CHARACTERISTICS OF *XIAOSHUO*

In order to explore Xiang Kairan's understanding and practice of *xiaoshuo*, let us turn from the passage in *Modern Times*, penned in 1931, to a brief self-portrait sketched during the early heyday of his career as an author of fiction. Like the photographic portrait, this sketch features not only the author but monkeys as well. "Three Monkey Tales" ("Sange houer de gushi" 三個猴兒的故事), published in 1924 in the final issue of the first volume of *Scarlet Magazine*, begins with the narrator's introduction to the stories he is about to relate:

> When I find myself idle or bored, I always enjoy taking the strange and bizarre things I've heard about or seen in the past and playing them over again in my head, just like a movie. The more bizarre the matter is, the greater the number of times I play it over. It often happens that while playing over some comical matter I unwittingly break out into loud laughter, all by myself. The members of my family don't know what's going on, and always imagine that a visitor has arrived. At times they even come over and ask me who it is I'm talking and laughing with.
>
> What I've replayed in my mind the greatest number of times, and what I think are the most bizarre and interesting, are three tales about monkeys.[19] One of them is something I saw with my own eyes, and two of them I heard from someone else, but even though I heard them from someone else, they are not the products of empty invention. As I take the opportunity to write them out, I myself feel that they are quite a bit richer in interest than ordinary *xiaoshuo* conjured up out of nothing.[20]

This introduction can serve, first of all, as a gloss of sorts on the author's photographic portrait. If we assume that the narrator here speaks for the author, then the monkeys in the photograph are not simply the writer's companions but his inspiration, his subject matter, and at the same time his goal; what he claims to be aiming for in his fiction is the recreation of the monkeys in his mind. And if we examine the narrator's remarks more analytically, we find that they can serve not exactly as a definition of fiction (*xiaoshuo* 小說) but at least as an index to several salient characteristics of the genre: the role of the author-narrator, the functions of recording and transmission, the aim of entertainment, and the fascination of the strange.[21]

Narrator and Author

The first of these characteristics is the prominence of the author-narrator within the text. The text of "Three Monkey Tales" begins in a voice that identifies itself as that of the narrator of the tales that constitute the bulk of the text and discusses the sources of the stories he is about to relate and his motives for relating them.[22] This narratorial persona invites his readers to identify him with the "I" who appears as a minor character in the first of the tales, the one involving events the narrator claims to have seen and experienced firsthand. And his reference to the process of materializing the tales as text—taking the opportunity to write them out—further encourages readers to impute the narratorial voice to the historical author, Xiang Kairan, under whose name the text appears in print. The majority of Xiang Kairan's published texts employ and manipulate this same identification between author, narrator, and (at times) diegetic character. In some of the texts the narrator is covert—the story seemingly tells itself. More often the narrator makes his presence evident by commenting on the characters and events of the narrative or by calling attention to the fact and circumstances of the narration. While the narrator who thus brings himself to the readers' attention sometimes remains anonymous, he frequently identifies himself with the author, either by directly naming himself or by referencing dates, places, and circumstances associable with the historical author. The information provided is often so concrete that Xiang Kairan's biographers have mined it for details of his life and career.

Structurally, the autobiographical vignettes appearing in Xiang Kairan's fiction most often supply a frame that introduces the principal narrative. They are in some cases quite brief but in others take on a length and complexity that gives them the character of an independent narrative level. Over a third of the text of the 1924 short story "The Death of Boxing Master Li Cunyi" ("Quanshujia Li Cunyi zhi si" 拳術家李存義之死), for instance, is devoted to the narrator's account of the circumstances in which he heard the tale from a friend and to his reflections on the affair;[23] the entire first chapter of the 1925 *Repent and Be Saved* elaborates the experiences of the author-narrator leading up to an acquaintance's account of the events to which the remainder of the novel is devoted. In these instances the author-narrator, for all his prominence, serves to frame stories about other characters. But in other cases he is a participant or protagonist in the events of the tale, and the text as a whole takes on the character of an autobiographical anecdote. Examples of tales of this sort include the personal encounters with tigers related in the 1924 "Turning

Pale" ("Bianse tan" 變色談)[24] and the account of a brawl in a Hunan marketplace in the 1923 "My Hands-On Experience in the Study of the Martial Arts" ("Wo yanjiu quanjiao zhi shidi lianxi" 我研究拳腳之實地練習).[25] All of the narrative variations surveyed so far involve an author-narrator who speaks in the first-person voice. But the 1924 *Young Gallants of the Rivers and Lakes* (*Jianghu xiaoxia zhuan* 江湖小俠傳) takes a different approach. The opening chapters strike a familiar note, relating the experiences of Buxiaosheng in the Hunan countryside, leading up to his meeting with a character who relates to him the events that make up the primary narrative, but Buxiaosheng here appears as a character in a third-person narration: "The story goes that in the Spring of the second year of the Republic, Buxiaosheng was in Changde prefecture in Hunan, engaged in a business that ordinary merchants generally ignore."[26]

The variation in narratological technique we find here bespeaks Xiang Kairan's interest in experimenting with the formal features of fictional discourse. At the same time, the formulaic opening of this last passage ("The story goes . . ."), drawn from the rhetorical toolbox of traditional vernacular fiction, reminds us of the resources he makes use of and the conventions within which his experimentation takes place. The author-narrator in Xiang Kairan's fiction combines narratological conventions from the two dominant forms of pre-twentieth-century *xiaoshuo*: short classical-language and extended vernacular-language prose narrative. The shorter classical-language *xiaoshuo* (including the forms that modern scholarship has categorized as *biji xiaoshuo* 筆記小說, "note-form *xiaoshuo*"; *zhiguai* 志怪, "records of anomalies"; and *chuanqi* 傳奇, "transmissions of the marvelous") favors covert narration. However, it often includes a passage at the beginning or end in which the recorder of the text acknowledges the source of the tale, and it may also carry appended commentary. Xiang Kairan's early collection of classical-language anecdotes about martial artists, the 1919 *Matters Pugilistic, Seen and Heard* (*Quanshu jianwen lu* 拳術見聞錄), faithfully replicates these formal characteristics. The loquacious and recurrently present narrator of his chapter-form novels, on the other hand, is that traditionally associated with vernacular fiction, and the explicit identification of the narrator with the persona of the author is typical of developments in the vernacular novel seen since the late nineteenth century.[27]

It would be misleading to think of either the classical- and vernacular-language varieties of *xiaoshuo* or of the narratorial practices typically associated with each as entirely distinct. Xiang Kairan demonstrated his facility in both forms at the commencement of his authorial career, with the 1916 publication of the initial ninety chapters of *Sojourners* on the vernacular side of the field and the anecdotes of "Turning Pale" and "Matters Pugilistic, Seen and Heard" and the more elaborate *chuanqi*-like tales published in *Ocean of Fiction* on the classical side. His subsequent production shows not only an increasing focus on vernacular narrative—a shift typical of the age—but also several adaptations of his own classical-language texts into vernacular versions. These adaptations make it clear that narrative material could pass easily from one formal and linguistic mode to another and also demonstrate how narratorial roles and strategies made the transition and adapted to the new environment. Xiang Kairan's work typifies in this respect the mingling of registers, forms, and genres facilitated by late-Qing and early-Republican periodicals, which offered shared ground for publication.[28] "The Reverend Wulai," one of the classical tales in *Ocean of Fiction*, begins with a typical account of the origins of the tale:

> When the Reverend Wulai presided over Yingjiang Temple, the precincts were pure and tranquil, unsullied by any speck of worldly dust. People spoke of the rigorous perfection of his monastic discipline, little knowing that he had never in his entire life had any contact with the fairer sex. After he passed away, the Reverend Huihai related his entire history to me. In the eighth month of last year, Huihai too attained Buddhahood. Grieving for Wulai and in remembrance of Huihai, I made this record of their affairs. [29]

Probably in 1920, Xiang Kairan published the thirteen-chapter vernacular novel *The Flying Head at Midnight*, which also begins with an account of the text's origins:

> As I take up my brush to write this book, my breast is filled with unfathomable emotion, for the events in this book have lingered in my mind for the space of five or six full years. During these five or

six years there has not been a single moment in which I have not wanted to write out in detail the events of this book and so provide readers with something to chat about over their tea or wine—and to show, what's more, that the knights-errant and sword-immortals who so amaze the people of our age are not in fact entirely a matter of empty fabulation. But during these five or six years, idle though I have been, my mind has not been unoccupied, and I have simply found no opportunity to pick up my brush and write about the affair. The impressions that have lingered in my mind for five or six years have become ever more distant, ever more dim, and gradually begun to disappear. As luck would have it a friend came by to see me today. As we were chatting, this friend happened to mention that four years ago he had read among some fiction the tale of one Reverend Wulai. The plot, he felt, was quite extraordinary, but the account was unfortunately too simple. He had forgotten the author's name and didn't know who it was who had written it. When I, Buxiaosheng, heard this, I said with a smile: You, sir, think it's too simple; I too feel the same way. You don't know the truth of these affairs, however, and so merely think it too simple, but I for my part feel even more strongly that that account leaves out far too many events. My friend asked in surprise: So you've also read that account and even know the truth of these affairs as well? I replied: I haven't merely read it, and I don't merely know; I've personally met with the Reverend Huihai spoken of in the account, and it was he himself who told me every detail of the affair. What that account relates is only a general outline of the matter; it hasn't even written out one part in ten of the whole. My friend asked: Since you know it in such detail, why don't you make it into a book? Besides giving people something with which to occupy their leisure, it might even serve as a corrective influence and convince a few of them not to take so many of those concubines that bring a family to ruin. Said I: I first had this thought in mind before you even read that account. It's just that over the years I'd nearly forgotten about it, and if you hadn't brought it up just now it never would have occurred to me. But now, by good fortune, I find myself at leisure and my mind unoccupied as well, and you, sir, have come along to give me a reminder. So why don't I take advantage of this opportunity and spend a few days' time writing this business out, fulfilling the wish I've harbored these last few years? My friend, delighted, said: Excellent! You go ahead and write. I won't disturb you further; I'll come back in a few days and give it a read. So after my friend had left I took out paper and brush and wrote as follows. [30]

The expansiveness of the vernacular relative to the classical—not only in lexicon and sentence structure but even more prominently in content and in volubility, even repetitiveness, of expression—is self-evident. The passage makes several points about the nature and purposes of fiction that I will take up in this chapter. Most immediately relevant, though, is its demonstration of the transformation of the laconic narrator of the classical tale into the garrulous and individualized author of the vernacular novel. The reported circumstances of the story's transmission remain the same. But the simple statement of the recorder's motives ("grieving for Wulai and in remembrance of Huihai") has become a ruminative narrative of the author's changing states of mind. The original transmission of the tale from Huihai to the writer has been joined by a second scene, dramatized in dialogue, of give and take between the writer and a tale-loving friend. And beyond being fleshed out in psychological and social dimensions, the writer both names himself within the text as Buxiaosheng and identifies himself as a professional author—at least to those readers who get the joke and recognize him as the writer of that earlier tale whose name the friend is unable to recall. The transformation of "The Reverend Wulai" into *The Flying Head at Midnight* thus illustrates both the permeability of the borders between the two formal antipodes of *xiaoshuo* and the distinctive characteristics they still retain.

Functionally, then, the narrators in Xiang Kairan's vernacular fiction combine the authenticating role of the narrators of classical-language tales with the various roles played by the storytelling narrator of the traditional novel: describing and explaining, passing judgment on events and characters, managing and calling attention to the progress of the narrative, simulating interaction with the audience or readership, and revealing personal characteristics and opinions.[31] At the same time, the narrator frequently claims identity with the historical author and contributes to the construction of a distinctive authorial persona. In "identifying the author with the narrator and dramatizing the writing situation," Xiang Kairan's works are even more emphatic than the fin de siècle novels identified by Hanan as demonstrating the emergence of "the involved author."[32] The prominence of the author-narrator results not simply from the wealth and specificity of personal details provided in certain individual texts but also and more significantly from the accretion and intertextual referencing of such details across a number of texts published over the years. Xiang Kairan's shorter novels and short fiction, which frequently dramatize the circumstances of the author's reception or recording of the tale, play at least as important a role in this process as the long serialized novels, in which personalized authorial interventions are more sporadic. The author-narrator of the tales amalgamates with the protagonist of the autobiographical pieces.

When representing himself as a protagonist, Xiang Kairan is consistently self-deprecating—watching from the sidelines as the older boys in the schoolhouse play chess in "Three Monkey Tales," stricken with terror when encountering tigers in "Turning Pale," scrambling to find his footing in his slick foreign-style shoes when caught in a brawl in "My Hands-On Experience in the Study of the Martial Arts."[33] Paratextual material, however, in the form of editorial notes, commentaries appended to the novels, and advertisements published alongside the texts in books and magazines, encourages readers to understand such self-representations as nothing more than seemly modesty on the part of an author who has studied overseas, served with the military, and practiced martial arts with the masters of the day. The authorial persona that emerges is that of a man both worldly and eccentric; a native of Hunan, familiar with its jungles, beasts, hunters, and shamans; a denizen of cosmopolitan Shanghai, seasoned by his rakish student days in Tokyo; an adept in the martial arts, intimate with Buddhist holy men and the tricksters and toughs of the real-life Rivers and Lakes; a scholar versed in the classics and prepared to answer the call to service in the government or military; a convivial raconteur; and a successful author.

The commercial publishing world of the day actively promoted the reputations and personas of the authors it marketed to the reading public. The tales Xiang Kairan told contributed to the construction of his distinctive persona, while that persona at the same time conditioned the reception of his work. The interdependence of oeuvre and authorial persona is implicit in Bao Tianxiao's witticism on the conditions for the success of Xiang Kairan's martial arts fiction: "By that time Shanghai's so-called love stories and romance novels were beginning to cloy, and it was high time for a change of flavor; it's like when Jiangnan dishes become too sweet, and some Hunan spice makes a welcome change."[34]

Recording Events, Transmitting the Strange

Just as the opening of "Three Monkey Tales" indicates Xiang Kairan's deployment of narrators adapted from those of traditional Chinese *xiaoshuo* to the purposes of commercial periodical fiction, so too does it illustrate his texts' endorsement of several features of *xiaoshuo*'s understanding of its own nature and status that are closely tied to the narrator's presence. Chief among these are the notion of fiction as a record of actual events, a consequent interest in the process of transmission, and, above all, a fascination with the strange.

Historiography was the earliest and most revered form of narrative writing in the literary system of premodern China. Both the writings that were subsumed under the shifting premodern category of *xiaoshuo* and those that modern scholars recognize as fiction were heavily indebted to historical writing for their form, rhetoric, and motivating assumptions.[35] *Xiaoshuo* in its earliest senses served in part as a bibliographic rubric and conceptual home for material that did not belong in the orthodox histories. As Andrew Plaks has pointed out, the distinguishing criterion was a distinction between matters of public and private life, not one between historicity (facticity) and fictionality (inventedness); both historiography and *xiaoshuo* were understood to be records of actual events.[36] Modern scholars seeking the roots of fiction (in our contemporary sense) in premodern *xiaoshuo* have echoed late-Ming critics in viewing the classical tales of the Tang dynasty as exhibiting a decisive turn toward aesthetic elaboration and conscious fabrication.[37] But the presumption or at least the pose of recording actual events remained a central feature of traditional forms of fiction into the twentieth century. Henry Y. H. Zhao even sees the emulation of historiography by the traditional novel as reaching a climax in the early twentieth century, as new models of fiction and new expectations of its role brought the contradictions between historicity and fictionality to the fore.[38]

The author-narrator in many of Xiang Kairan's narratives explicitly addresses the question of the authenticity of his material—and consciously or unconsciously expresses the tension Zhao perceives as well. In the opening to "Three Monkey Tales" the narrator expresses full awareness of the fact that writers of fiction may simply make things up, but he is confident that the tales he has to tell, witnessed with his own eyes or heard from reliable sources, "are quite a bit richer in interest than ordinary *xiaoshuo* conjured up out of nothing." "The Death of Boxing Master Li Cunyi" (1924) is another of the many narratives that explicitly present themselves as a record of facts. I have already noted the large proportion of this text devoted to recounting the circumstances in which the author-narrator recalls having heard the tale; even more striking is the fact that the piece is followed by a corrective sequel, "The Unfounded Rumor of Li Cunyi's Taking His Art to the Grave" ("Li Cunyi xunji echuan" 李存義殉技訛傳), in which the author addresses readers' concerns about the veracity of the original account.[39] Fidelity to events, to a historical personage, and in this case to the enterprise of the martial arts is required even in narratives offered for the entertainment of the readers of a fiction periodical. This is not to say that Xiang Kairan was indifferent to the demands of varying literary forms and publication contexts. "Luo Seven" ("Luo Qi" 羅七), an item in the 1919 *Matters Pugilistic, Seen and Heard*, includes the following appended note:

> Last year I enlarged upon this account and made a *xiaoshuo* of over two thousand words. I named the piece "Luo from Anhui" and sold it to the *xiaoshuo* bureau of the Commercial Press. This piece however is a documentary account. Storytelling involves variations, and it has been several decades [since the events of the tale]; so how can one ensure that it is not an invention? Thus the writer has heard it; thus the reader may take it as having been read.[40]

The comment addresses the question of the reliability of transmitted information, an issue I will take up shortly. In terms of the present topic of discussion, it is revealing in that it demonstrates the perception of a distinction between a "documentary account" (*jishi* 紀實) included in a "record of matters seen and heard" (*jianwen lu* 見聞錄) and an elaboration of that account produced for sale as *xiaoshuo* to a magazine. The elaboration mentioned here was "Luo of Anhui" ("Wan Luo" 皖羅), a classical-language tale published in *Ocean of Fiction* in 1916.[41] Recalling that the author took "The Reverend Wulai," another tale published in the same venue in the same year, as the germ for elaboration into the novel *The Flying Head at Midnight*, we find a neat paradigm for the expansion of narrative from documentary account to classical tale to vernacular chapter novel. Yet while the progressive elaboration of material clearly involves formal and linguistic differences, it does not necessarily entail abandoning the assertion of authenticity; *The Flying Head at Midnight*, as we have seen, begins with a lengthy dramatization of the author-narrator's claims to privileged knowledge of the facts. Claims of authenticity, whether couched in terms of the historicity of events or of the reliability of sources, function as a generic marker of *xiaoshuo* and a constitutive element of its discourse.[42]

As we have already seen, in some cases Xiang Kairan's texts claim fidelity not to events as such but to an *account* of events received from another source. To some extent this move serves to hedge the author-narrator's bets, distancing him from responsibility for the facticity of the content of the narrative. But the gesture serves also to foreground the importance of transmission—the transferral of the narrative, whatever it may be, from one person to another. As Plaks points out, "in both the historical and the fictional branches of the Chinese tradition, the final justification for the enterprise of narrative may be said to lie in the *transmission* of known facts, a point perhaps not unrelated to the use of the character *chuan* 傳 (with its alternate reading) to refer to a broad range of narrative forms."[43] Plaks goes on to argue that transmission assumes and validates the truth value of what is transmitted, but his remark also underlines the relational dimension of the practice of *xiaoshuo*. Allen's *Shifting Stories: History, Gossip, and Lore in Narratives from Tang-Dynasty China* addresses the social dimensions of the literati fad for telling, collecting, and recording the stories that came to play so prominent a role in the historiography of *xiaoshuo*. Her discussion of the framing statements found in the texts—the remarks on sources and the circumstances in which a writer or recorder received the narrative he inscribes—focuses on the value of such statements as evidence of the context and functions of the tales' production.[44] As we contemplate the descendants of these framing statements we find in narratives produced for periodical publication in the early twentieth century, we can bear in mind that the issue of transmission is relevant both to the origins of a circulating tale and to its destination and objectives. Every text presumes a reader, of course. But Xiang Kairan's *xiaoshuo*, wedding the classical tale's acknowledgment of sources with expansive dramatizations of the storytelling context drawn in part from the vernacular-fiction tradition, not only put the interpersonal interactions through which a tale is given life at the heart of the practice of *xiaoshuo* but further invite the reader to understand him- or herself as a part of the process. While the author of the text may be a unique individual and a talented professional, he is also, like the reader, a lover of tales and a link in the chain of their transmission rather than their unitary source. The text the author produces continues the tale's previous circulation. The reader's enjoyment of the tale—and perhaps then even his or her account of it to a friend, or the act of passing along the latest copy of a periodical—reiterates the author's role as someone who both receives and forwards the narrative. In replicating the author's role, the reader also joins the author and other readers in the community of those sharing the tale. To note that this conjuration of imagined community serves in part a commercial purpose—that it dovetails with publishers' efforts to build an engaged readership as a market strategy—need not diminish, and may in fact increase, our recognition of the adaptability of the discourse of traditional *xiaoshuo* to changing social and media contexts.

Yet what makes a tale worth passing along? Plaks notes that transmission implies an endorsement of value and thus (at least at some level) truth. The narrator of "Three Monkey Tales," as we have seen, sees fidelity to fact as adding to the interest and worth of the stories he has to tell. But if facticity increases the savor of his tales, what makes them worth telling in the first place is that the events they recount are "strange and bizarre" (*xiqi guguai* 稀奇古怪) enough to provide diversion in idle moments. And while bizarre or unusual happenings arguably have universal appeal as topics for storytelling, Xiang Kairan's characterization of his subject matter here echoes that particular fascination with the strange that characterized premodern Chinese *xiaoshuo*. I follow Zeitlin in using the English term "the strange" as shorthand for a cluster of Chinese words with overlapping albeit distinct connotations and semantic ranges: *yi* 異, divergent, differing from the norm; *guai* 怪, anomalous, freakish, abnormal; and *qi* 奇, marvelous, rare, exceptional, amazing.[45] The role of the strange as a distinctive, even defining feature in Chinese traditions of extrahistoriographic narrative is evident in the terminology modern scholars have adopted to designate some of that tradition's seminal forms, from the "records of anomalies" (*zhiguai* 志怪) that took shape in the Six Dynasties period to the "transmissions of the marvelous" (*chuanqi* 傳奇) of the Tang. Pu Songling's (1640–1715) Qing-dynasty revival of the classical-language tale took the title *Records of the Strange from the Idle Studio* (*Liaozhai zhiyi* 聊齋誌異); Pu Songling's successor Yuan Mei (1716–1797) famously confirmed the terrain of fiction as that lying outside the bounds of orthodox Confucian discourse by naming a *xiaoshuo* collection *What the Master Did Not Speak Of* (*Zi bu yu* 子不語).[46] By the end of the Qing dynasty the classical-language tale of the strange had populated the new medium of commercial mass publishing and engaged the myriad new manifestations of strangeness engendered by China's encounters with modern nations, cultures, and technologies.[47] And the same fundamental concern for the unusual and the astounding informed the parallel tradition of vernacular-language fiction; thus, by way once again of titular example, Ling Mengchu's 凌濛初 (1580–1644) collections of vernacular tales published under the title *Striking the Table in Amazement at the Marvels* (拍案驚奇). Liang Shi maintains that "*qi* is nothing less than a central generic feature of traditional Chinese *xiaoshuo*."[48] All of which is simply to say that there is nothing strange about the prominence of the strange in Xiang Kairan's fiction, as heralded in the titles of his works: *Marvelous Gallants of the Heroes and Lakes* (*Jianhu qixia zhuan* 江湖奇俠傳, 1923), *Strange Phenomena of the Rivers and Lakes* (*Jianghu guaiyi zhuan* 江湖怪異傳, 1923), *Strange Characters of the Rivers and Lakes* (*Jianghu yiren zhuan* 江湖異人傳, 1924), *Marvelous Characters of Modern Times* (*Xiandai qiren zhuan* 現代奇人傳, 1929). In prizing the strange, in seeing the sharing of unusual, bizarre, and/or wondrous incidents with an audience as his primary imperative, Xiang Kairan expresses the essence of *xiaoshuo* as he understands it and signals his affiliation with familiar *xiaoshuo* traditions to his potential readership.

Recognizing the centrality of the strange in Xiang Kairan's fiction and its role in affirming a particular conception of *xiaoshuo* raises additional questions. One is that of the definition of the strange. What constitutes *yi*, *guai*, and/or *qi*, and what qualifies a person, occurrence, or tale for membership in the categories these terms designate? Another is that of the function and value of accounts of the strange. Campany has demonstrated that early "records of anomalies" served a cosmological function: by describing phenomena at or beyond the boundaries of the normative order, they clarified that order's contours and dimensions.[49] The narrator of "Three Monkey Tales" claims no other aim than that of diverting himself and others in moments of boredom. Does he truly intend nothing further than entertainment? And whether he does or not, what are the functions of entertainment, and what value is assigned to it? Further, what is the relationship between the strange and facticity? We have seen that the author-narrator deems his tales more entertaining precisely because they are both extraordinary and grounded in fact, but this very claim admits the possibility that the strange might sometimes depart not just from the commonplace but also from the verifiably true or the actually possible. What is the status of such departures, of fiction in the sense of fabrication? And what forms might such departures take: do differences obtain between events that although fabricated accord with the known functioning of the world and those that violate the boundaries of possibility? What territory does the strange share with the supernatural? Chapter 5 of this study, which examines Xiang Kairan's *Marvelous Gallants of the Rivers and Lakes*, will return to the exploration of these questions, whose presence shapes the author's work and embeds it in those negotiations between the fascinations of the strange, the imperatives of recording, the dynamics of transmission, the aim of entertainment, and the role of the narrator that together define the flexible poetics of *xiaoshuo*.

XIANG KAIRAN'S MONKEYS

So far, I have identified certain basic characteristics of the poetics of *xiaoshuo*—properties that define *xiaoshuo* as a generic discourse—while at the same time beginning to explore some of the distinctive expressions of these characteristics in Xiang Kairan's fictional writings. Subsequent chapters of this study will refer to elements of this poetics and elaborate them further in the course of examining the historical emergence of *wuxia xiaoshuo* as a thematic subgenre, the form of the traditional linked-chapter novel, and the diegetic and discursive worlds of Xiang Kairan's most famous works. In the remainder of the present chapter I would like to explore the figuration of *xiaoshuo* in certain of Xiang Kairan's texts. The narrator of "Three Monkey Tales" suggests that the qualities he prizes in fiction are somehow epitomized in the stories he is about to share; they are the ones he has "replayed in [his] mind the greatest number of times." And as noted earlier, the monkeys at the center of these three stories echo the monkeys and apes that recur in others of Xiang Kairan's texts. What is it about monkeys that lends itself in such exemplary manner to tale telling, and what do Xiang Kairan's monkeys reveal about the tale telling that is at the heart of *xiaoshuo*? Let me begin with brief summaries of the "Three Monkey Tales."

The first tale, the one allegedly based on personal experience, relates how the author/narrator boards at a primary school in the Hunan countryside, where he and his classmates are in the habit of stealing food and playing games at night after their teacher has retired. One night they find a monkey trying to steal poultry from the school courtyard by stuffing ducks and chickens into bags. When they drive it off, it leaves its bags behind. Beginning the next night the students find their brushes and school supplies mysteriously vandalized, and they soon discover that the culprit is the monkey. At the locals' urging, they hang the monkey's lost bags under the schoolroom eaves; the bags disappear during the night, and the vandalism ceases. The second tale, heard though not witnessed, concerns a martial artist hired as a watchman by a landlord living near the school in the first story. The fastidious watchman is infuriated to find his room and bedding repeatedly sullied. By lying in wait he discovers that the culprit is once again a thieving monkey. He lays a trap by night, captures what he thinks is the monkey in a sheet, thrashes it thoroughly, and then, in front of his master, the household, and the assembled farmhands, triumphantly opens the sheet to reveal . . . a stolen ham. The third and final story tells of a trained monkey whose wealthy master sends it out every day to purchase his daily dose of opium. A marketplace vendor tricks the monkey into spending the money given it on fruit; the monkey takes to stealing the daily opium to make up the difference. The boss of the opium hall surprises the thief, by accident strikes it dead, and then tries to conceal the prized creature's death from its wealthy and powerful owner. But when the truth comes out the owner takes him to court, and the boss is forced to recognize the monkey as his adoptive son and give it full funeral rites; the opium hall subsequently goes bankrupt and closes. "This business was told to me by Wu Yingpei from Fujian; there's nothing at all made up about it. You have to admit that it's quite an interesting affair."

As promised, then, the tales are distinguished by the "interest" or "flavor" (*quwei* 趣味) of the incidents (*shi* 事) at their core. The flavor lies in the quality of the strange or unusual, made more piquant by their alleged facticity. And in these particular tales, the strange manifests itself above all in the monkey's capacity for blurring the boundaries between the human and the nonhuman. At the heart of each tale are the monkey's unexpectedly humanlike actions. At first it is simply the actions, the behaviors, that mimic human activity: the attempt to stuff squawking poultry into a bag, described in such vivid detail in the first tale, or the capacity to make purchases in the marketplace related in the third. But the resemblance becomes more uncanny as it becomes clear that the monkeys, far from simply aping human actions, are motivated by emotions, desires, and complex intentions. When it despoils the schoolboys' writing materials, the first tale's monkey may be moved by spite, a desire for vengeance, the intent to force the return of its bags, or some combination of all of these; in any event, the cessation of its ravages once his own property is returned clearly demonstrates an understanding of quid pro quo, even of justice. The third tale's monkey seems at first merely to be performing a task by rote. But subsequent events show that is not only subject to temptation but clever enough to plan and carry out a scheme to conceal its misdeeds. And while the second tale plays out as slapstick comedy, it also derives interest precisely from foregrounding the question of intentionality—of leaving us wondering whether the monkey dropped the stolen ham in fright or deliberately used it to fool the headstrong watchman.

Monkeys reveal themselves to be wondrously human. Humans show themselves to be monkeys as well.[50] The first tale's monkey enters the story as a poultry thief. But its actions are anticipated, on some level even evoked, by the mischief, thievery, and gluttony of the gang of schoolchildren who discover it—a band of little monkeys if ever there was one. If anything, the monkey's arrangement for the return of its bags displays an understanding of principle higher than theirs. In the second tale, the monkey succeeds in "making a monkey" of the watchman, tricking him into performing an antic spectacle in front of an uproarious crowd. The opium hall boss in the final tale is likewise forced to make a public spectacle of himself—in this case, what's more, in a fashion that requires him to recognize himself literally as the monkey's next of kin, "a monkey's uncle" as the English idiom goes. The tales' blurring of the lines thus involves both the anthropomorphizing of monkeys and the simianization of humans and lends itself in part to humorous aspects of the strange.[51]

Monkeys are the central subject of each of the "Three Monkey Tales," the embodiment of the strangeness that justifies the narrative. In others of Xiang Kairan's writings monkeys play a more peripheral role, and in certain cases their peripherality takes the particular form of liminality, of marking and motivating the narrative passage from the familiar to the marvelous. The most striking example of this gatekeeping function appears in the unfinished novel *Repent and Be Saved*. The Buddhist-inspired title (literally "Turn your head and there is the shore") derives from the novel's alleged didactic value and, more proximately, from the episode that motivates the narration of events: a glimpse of an attractive young woman at a nunnery. The entire first chapter of the text serves as an elaborate preface to the story proper (*zhengwen* 正文).[52] It tells how the author-narrator, serving in a government office in Yuezhou 岳州 after the establishment of the Republic, makes the acquaintance of a member of the *yamen* staff, one Mr. Yuan 袁. Invited to Mr. Yuan's home over New Year's, he is delighted to find two pairs of monkey (*housun* 猴猻) servants who serve the guests tea and patrol the residence with gongs at night as watchmen. Mr. Yuan tells that he originally had three pairs of monkeys but was forced to make a present of one female to a superior and then had to kill its mate when it became unmanageable with grief. He relates a wealth of lore on the capture and training of monkeys and promises that they will perform for his guests after dinner. The onset of bad weather forces the narrator and his companions to depart early without having seen the show. The narrator and a single companion seek to return the following day, founder in the new-fallen snow, and are forced to seek refuge at the only building in sight, Lord Qu's Cloister 瞿公庵. Here they see the mummified remains of Lord Qu and catch a sight of a mysterious young girl. When they finally make their way to Mr. Yuan's home, he tells them the story of the cloister's founder; this is the tale that will constitute the main body of the (incomplete) text.[53]

The monkeys' role as gatekeepers for the primary narrative goes beyond their simple presence in the introductory chapter. It is Mr. Yuan who relates the tale that the narrator in turn transmits to his readers. At Mr. Yuan's residence the monkeys serve as gatekeepers in a literal sense, welcoming invited guests with tea and guarding against intruders. Mr. Yuan plans to stage a performance by the monkeys for his guests' entertainment but ends up telling his tale instead; the narrative in effect is the monkey show, standing in for the promised performance. The monkey lore and anecdotes Mr. Yuan shares before the commencement of the primary narrative highlight the entertainment value of monkeys and the identification of monkeys with entertainment. And Mr. Yuan's very name, homophonous with "ape" (*yuan* 猿), bespeaks his kinship with his simian attendants and their roles.

A second instance of monkeys serving as gatekeepers makes clearer the stakes in this liminality: not merely a passage from the mundane to that which is marvelous enough to warrant narration but also a distinction between the morally normative and the heterodox. This instance is the tale of Hu Zhizai 胡直哉, introduced late in the text of *Modern Times*. In a manner typical of the interlocking biographies (*zhuan* 傳) that make up the fabric of the novel, Hu Zhizai enters the narrative in chapter 69 as a comrade of another character, Liu Ti'an 柳惕安, whose own background and career are introduced (beginning in chapter 67) when an associate of the central character Huo Yuanjia 霍元甲 encounters Liu in Shanghai. With Liu Ti'an's story, the narrative of *Modern Times* makes a noticeable and temporary tonal shift, from the exploits of martial artists in a more or less verisimilitudinous turn-of-the-century China toward the more fantastic incarnations of the strange typical of *Rivers and Lakes*, characterized by esoteric arts, otherworldly immortals, sorcery, demons, and bizarre creatures. The author/narrator explicitly marks this shift at the beginning of chapter 68, making overt reference to *Rivers and Lakes* before providing his readers with a systematic account of the nature and organization of the school into which Liu Ti'an is initiated and a description of the early stages of his training in the art of mystical energy swords (*jianshu* 劍術).[54]

Hu Zhizai, the son of a magistrate, is as a youth disinclined to the study that would allow him to follow in his father's Confucian footsteps and is drawn instead to the monkey trainers, magicians, and martial artists who pass by their home. One day he is entranced by the performance of a beguiling female tightrope walker and then watches as the troupe of acrobats to which she belongs gets into a duel of sorcery with a group of passing hunters. The supposed acrobats turn out to be outlaws seeking vengeance against Hu Zhizai's father, Magistrate Hu, who some years ago executed their master for banditry and sorcery; the hunters for their part have been summoned by the local Cao family to aid them against a demon bedeviling their daughter. Hu Zhizai goes to seek the hunters' assistance in protecting his father from the outlaws but instead encounters an aged traveler accompanied by a trained monkey (*mahouzi* 馬猴子). The demon harassing the Cao girl turns out to be the monkey's escaped companion. The traveling monkey master recaptures the truant beast, resolving the Cao family's troubles, and assures Hu that his father has nothing more to fear from the outlaws. Hu Zhizai takes the monkey master as his teacher and disappears. Reappearing five years later, he tells how he has been in Mongolia with his master, descending upon caravans in dust storms with the two monkeys to engage in Robin Hood–style plundering of ill-gotten wealth. Thus his career up to the time when he encounters Liu Ti'an and is drawn into the net of the novel's story.

The gatekeeping or liminal function of the monkeys here functions differently from that in *Repent and Be Saved*. There they signal the appearance of the strange and serve as a figure for the tale the narrator will pass on to the reader; here they lure the protagonist into the realm of the strange. At first, in fact, the monkeys are merely notional, one potential feature of the fascinating world of the Rivers and Lakes; Hu Zhizai, hearing the sound of gongs from his study, knows that "it must either be a magician or a monkey-show" (69:5, 516). In the world into which he is then drawn, the strange manifests itself in various interconnected forms—the martial arts, magic, nonhuman creatures, eccentric characters, marginal members of society. But monkeys dwell at their heart of this world, not merely as gateways to the strange but as a dramatic expression of its essence. They are both the demons that torment the Cao family daughter and the instruments of the monkey master's chivalric exploits.

Within the text, Hu Zhizai's father reminds us of the relationship between the world of the strange and the Confucian orthodoxy that he as a scholar and government official represents. When Hu Zhizai urges that they turn for aid against their enemies to the hunters summoned by the Cao family, Magistrate Hu replies:

"When one's own righteousness is insufficient to conquer evil, then one can only seek aid from those versed in the black arts; this is called fighting poison with poison. But such behavior is a sin against the Teachings, and deserves only scorn from the learned. I have comported myself according to Principle my whole life. Such behavior is not for our family to engage in."

(69:5, 20)

Despite his remonstrations, of course, his son chooses to engage with the world beyond the pale of Confucian Principle and eventually to become a disciple of the monkey master. And the text's own implicit allegiance appears to be clear. While it grants a voice to the arguments for orthodoxy, it owes it very existence to that which Magistrate Hu rejects. It is Hu Zhizai's fascination and engagement with the unorthodox, his entry into the world of the Rivers and Lakes, that merits narration; had he never left his study, there would be no tale to tell. The episode, like the novel in which it appears, is another instance of that embrace of "what the Master did not speak of" (子不語) that persistently informs and even defines the traditional discourse of *xiaoshuo*.

The Hu Zhizai episode makes clear a further key feature of the world of the strange: the connection between the strange and unorthodox and the impulse of sexual desire. Monkeys and apes serve to figure this connection as well. When Hu Zhizai is lured to the fairground by the sound of the gongs, his conscious thoughts are of magicians and monkey shows, but what he finds when he arrives is the female acrobat:

> Hu Zhizai saw that while the girl was not what you would call beautiful, her features were pleasingly regular; a short jacket with tight sleeves showed her every movement to advantage, lively and nimble, and he found her quite attractive. At this time Hu Zhizai was already thirteen years of age and had felt the first stirrings of passion. Finding the girl so attractive, he wished to get closer.

(69:5, 6)

The girl is monkeylike, prancing nimbly in her short jacket, but so too is Hu Zhizai, albeit in another sense: his inability to govern his mind and desires.[55] The conventional figure of the ungovernable monkey mind is explicitly referenced in one of our other texts, *Repent and Be Saved*. Here, in a similar situation, it is the narrator who is distracted and bewitched by the glimpse of the young girl in the cloister:

> With my thoughts and feelings in turmoil [more literally, "my heart a monkey and my mind a horse"], I took my leave and departed. As we walked to the Yuan Family Village, my mind was not at peace for a single moment. It wasn't until we saw old Mr. Yuan, and he related to me in detail the history of Master Qu, that I felt as if a basin of cold water had been poured on my back, completely extinguishing the wicked fires that consumed me.[56]

In *Repent and Be Saved*, the male narrator's sexual desire is allegedly quelled by the story that Mr. Yuan tells; Mr. Yuan is of course the owner and master of this text's trained monkeys, and we have already learned that he was forced to kill one monkey driven mad by desire and grief. *Rivers and Lakes* deals with Hu Zhizai's sexual desire in another fashion. First of all, it displaces it. Nothing comes of Hu Zhizai's attraction for the female acrobat; the narrative instead shifts the question of sexuality onto the situation at the Cao household. The rape of the Cao daughter by a demonic monkey displaces male desire onto the nonhuman. Even in this nonhuman form, however, male desire is exculpated. As the affair is resolved, the monkey master promises to punish the offending creature, but, echoing Magistrate Hu's earlier condemnation of the Cao household, explains that it is primarily the daughter who bears the blame:

> "I have no intention of making excuses, but there is too much about that Miss Cao that incites lust, and Cao Hanlin is far too lax in supervising her. Otherwise, just think: I live in Shandong, and on the road from Shandong to here there is no shortage of young and beautiful daughters of good families; why should [the monkey] have bestowed his attentions upon the Cao family household alone?"
>
> (70:5, 40)

The monkeys and Hu Zhizai, meanwhile, are allowed to redeem themselves by sublimating their energies into deeds of chivalry and derring-do beyond the frontier.

Tales of monkeys and ape spirits abducting human females are easy to find in Chinese folklore and in the fiction traditions that draw on that lore. Glen Dudbridge, for instance, reviews a set of legends of this sort in his investigation into the background of the Sun Wukong material;[57] Xiang Kairan presents a variation on the tale in his 1924 story "The White Ape in the Gaolan Gate-tower."[58] And rejection of male heterosexual desire and a corresponding misogyny are persistent themes in literary representations of martial heroism—most notoriously in *The Water Margin*—and indeed through the broader range of Chinese vernacular fiction and of the culture in which it was embedded. In these regards, Xiang Kairan's monkey stories once again merely give us instances of already familiar tropes. They are distinctive, however, in the extent to which they employ the image of the monkey to figure a homology, and even a confusion, between sexual desire and that love of the strange that is understood to be the essential motive of fiction.

The homology is most perfectly expressed in the title of another of Xiang Kairan's short stories, the 1923 "Curiosity or Lust?" (*Haoqi yu haose yu* 好奇歟好色歟).[59] My English rendition of the title, intended to be idiomatic, is less than ideal. The affective connotations of the English "lust" are perhaps more brutal than those of the Chinese *haose*, and I have rendered as simple nouns the two phrases that are in the original verb-object combinations. A clumsy overtranslation might be "being fond of the strange, or being fond of that which is sensually attractive?" I should hasten to make clear that no monkeys or apes appear in this story. The author-narrator relays, with much circumstantial and verisimilitudinous detail, two yarns told to him by a friend visiting his Shanghai lodgings. In both stories, the friend's curiosity and penchant for reckless chivalry lead to brawls with hoodlums from the Shanghai underworld. The fact that in both cases the initial object of his curiosity is an attractive young woman prompts the interdiegetic audience (the narrator and another friend) to needle the teller as to whether he was moved by "curiosity or lust." In the course of the second narrative, the tale teller unabashedly relates the moment at which, realizing the mysterious woman he has met at a theater is in fact an ordinary prostitute, "I figured I might as well set aside my curiosity, and start putting my lust into practice." The homology between the two impulses allows one to substitute seamlessly for the other.

The two are at some level interchangeable: differing in their objects but identical as motions of desire.

When monkeys appear in Xiang Kairan's fiction, they are typically linked with the strange, with sexual desire, or with both. The capacity to signify the strange on the one hand, lust on the other, grants the figure of the monkey a productive polysemy. And the signifying monkey (if I may) gains further complexity from the fact that these two associations allow it to occupy both sides of the circuit of desire. As the epitome of the strange, the uncannily human nonhuman, both eerie and comical, it is an object of desire—an ideal target for that desire for the strange that gives rise to the production and transmission of stories, to the practice of *xiaoshuo*. As the epitome of lust (and notoriously curious as well), it is the desiring subject. The duality of positions makes the monkey an invaluable tool in games of displacement. The men swapping tales in the author-narrator's rooms in (the monkeyless) "Curiosity or Lust?" are ready to admit—if not without a bit of banter—their susceptibility to both the desire for a good story and the desire for a beautiful woman. This text's internal staging of the practice of *xiaoshuo*, that is, of narrative realized through transmission, subtly encourages the reader similarly to validate his or her own enjoyment of the text with little or no hesitation over the indulgence of desire. Other texts, however, employ the monkey to estrange the relationship between different circuits of desire. In *Repent and Be Saved*, as I have detailed, the gatekeeping monkeys at the scene of narration introduce a tale that is *about* the encounter with an object of desire, yet the tale allegedly serves the function of obliterating the very (monkeylike) desire that the encounter stirred. In this case, the moralizing discourse of the narrative cancels (or at least pretends to cancel) the narrative's desirous content with a finality that admits no congruence between the pleasures of tale telling and those of sex. The homology that the monkey figures thus becomes a tension, a contradiction; the claim that *xiaoshuo* can embrace curiosity while rejecting lust is destabilized by the shadow of a congruence between the two.

Antecedents for this tension are easily found in premodern discourse on the nature and value of *xiaoshuo*. The Ming scholar Hu Yinglin saw a congruence between readers' conflicted attitudes toward *xiaoshuo* and their conflicted feelings about women and sex: "Men's love and hatred for fiction are comparable to their love and hatred for sex and beauty in women."[60] Pronouncements by orthodox moralists and sporadic bans by government officials from the Yuan dynasty onward did not merely suspect connections between *xiaoshuo* and immoral or aberrant conduct but denounced them as self-evident fact.[61] Critics understood the extracanonicity of *xiaoshuo* as a literary form to be indistinguishable from the heterodoxy of its subject matter, and they saw its perniciousness not in the abstract terms of a structural congruence between the desire for the strange and sexual desire but as a concrete instrumentality: *xiaoshuo* taught immoral behavior. Contemporary attacks on Xiang Kairan's novels, though voiced most forcefully by figures associated with progressive literary currents, often echoed traditional moralistic criticism of *xiaoshuo* as an incitement to immorality. *Sojourners* was grouped with novels of the demimonde as a "textbook on whoring," and *Rivers and Lakes* was accused of fostering superstition and encouraging gullible youth to run off into the mountains in search of immortal masters.[62] Although Butterfly fiction's critics were informed by a new consciousness of *xiaoshuo*'s inadequacy relative to the new standards for fiction and motivated in their attacks by the desire to establish a new position for themselves in a fluid literary field, elements inherited from traditional discourse on *xiaoshuo* found their way into the substance of their critiques.

Similarly, ambivalences and limitations inherent in premodern concepts of *xiaoshuo* were inherited by Xiang Kairan and other Republican-era practitioners of the genre. *Xiaoshuo* texts since at least the Ming dynasty typically justified their heterodox or even scandalous contents with apologies for the virtues of entertainment and claims for the instructional value of the exposure of vice—claims whose tenor ranges from the sincere through the perfunctory to the tongue in cheek.[63] Xiang Kairan's own texts, as we have seen, reproduce these defensive strategies, portraying *xiaoshuo* as an amusement to share over tea or wine and leavening this celebration of diversion with occasional gestures toward moral didacticism. The foregrounding of the amusement function is arguably energized by the broader flourishing of a culture of entertainment in Shanghai and other urban centers and the crucial role that commercial publishing played in this culture.[64] Claims for the stories' didactic value need be read neither as a confession of the true motivation for tale telling nor as a facile display of disingenuousness; they simply confirm the extent to which the texts' representation of their own character and functions remains grounded in an inherited understanding of *xiaoshuo*. It is this same understanding that limits the possibility that a love of sharing stories might be understood as a vocation rather than an amusement and that writing stories for profit might be seen as a profession rather than a merely expedient means of filling one's rice bowl; it shapes the author-narrator's presentation of himself in his texts and informs the texts' highly charged ambivalence about the project of *xiaoshuo*—the mix of passion, amusement, delight, anxiety, and dismissiveness that we find figured in Xiang Kairan's monkeys.

CHAPTER THREE

Thematic Subgenre

Martial Arts Fiction

A s we saw in chapter 1, Bao Tianxiao in his 1974 memoir assigns himself credit for introducing Xiang Kairan to World Book Co. Ltd.'s Shen Zhifang and thus for "the launching of the first wave of Shanghai's *wuxia xiaoshuo*" that eventuated from this fateful encounter. In a reminiscence penned some years earlier, however, he seems to attribute a much less decisive role to Xiang Kairan's contributions to the genre:

> Upon encountering Mr. Xiang's chivalrous and forthright manner I regretted that we had not met earlier, and I commissioned him to write for each issue of *The Sunday*. The robust style of his *New Unofficial History of Sojourners in Japan* [sic] concealed a delicacy within its vigor, and it far surpassed his previous work. Unfortunately *The Sunday* ceased publication after a year, and Mr. Xiang then poured his energies into the so-called chivalric fiction that was fashionable for a time. He would simply take a well-known item of anecdotal fiction and stretch it out into tens of thousands of words. He was rebuked for this by his contemporaries, but this was actually not his greatest strength.[1]

The memoir's more triumphant account benefits from the perspective of the postwar era, when the success of Jin Yong and other "new school" writers had confirmed the longevity and popularity of martial arts fiction and established a place for Xiang Kairan as a founding father. The version just quoted is excerpted from a reminiscence that Bao published in 1929 in response to the rumors of Xiang Kairan's death, at a time when the precipitate success of the *Red Lotus Temple* films was affording fantasy martial arts material a spectacular but not universally appreciated place in urban popular culture. Several points of the 1929 account are worth highlighting. It characterizes Xiang Kairan's martial arts fiction as not on a literary par with others of his writings. It refers to the fiction in question as *xiayi xiaoshuo* ("chivalric fiction"); has *wuxia xiaoshuo* not yet become the default term, or does Bao have some reason to avoid using it? It describes Xiang's compositional process and the resultant texts as the deliberate attenuation of preexisting anecdotal material and alleges that readers found this tiresome (though it is not clear in the Chinese whether what earns rebuke is the attenuation, the novels more generally, or even Xiang Kairan the man). Most interesting of all, though, is the claim that when *The Sunday*'s demise threatened the livelihood it had provided, Xiang Kairan found he could survive as an author by capitalizing on an already existing vogue for fiction on martial themes. There is no mention of the guiding hand of Shen Zhifang and no suggestion that, however successful Xiang Kairan may have been in producing such material, he had any role in instigating the vogue. So, did Xiang Kairan and Shen Zhifang create the modern martial arts novel? Did martial arts fiction exist before *Rivers and Lakes* burst upon the scene? How common was martial arts material in narrative literature of the late Qing and early Republic? What status did it enjoy? What forms did it take, and with what themes did it engage? To what extent, and in what particular ways, did the publication of *Rivers and Lakes* mark a milestone in this material's history? How was Shen Zhifang involved, and how decisive was his influence?

This chapter's topic is *wuxia xiaoshuo* as a thematic genre. I am using the term "thematic genre" to refer to a body of narrative material interlinked by fluid conventions of setting, characters, and narrative tropes. Thematic genres are often transmedial, finding expression in cinematic, oral, dramatic, and visual arts as well as in written literature. Within the literary sphere, the categories defined by thematic genres are by no means the only sorts of categories operant, and a thematic genre may or may not stand in fixed relationship with categorizations defined by form, linguistic register, ideology, expressive mode, or other criteria. The question of the criteria by which literary categories are identified is in fact crucial to an understanding of the history of Republican-era martial arts fiction. I will argue that Shen Zhifang and Xiang Kairan's intervention does indeed mark a turning point in the history of martial arts fiction. What made their intervention decisive, however, was not the invention of a new thematic genre per se; a variety of fiction on martial and chivalric themes was already under production during the first two decades of the twentieth century. Shen Zhifang's real contribution lay in giving this popular but heterogeneous material a defined and marketable genre identity by associating it with a particular author and a particular form. The tools he used for his project were the resources and strategies of the commercial publishing industry, and his model was the established success of detective fiction as a marketable thematic genre. An illuminating perspective on this process is afforded by *Rivers and Lakes*'s sister work, *Modern Times*, which was serialized on the pages of Shen Zhifang's *Detective World*. Xiang Kairan's seminal novels represent not so much the creation of a genre as the conscious deployment of genre in a new sense: the deliberate and explicitly marked wedding of elements of thematic genre to particular considerations of form, medium, and market.

FICTION AS A GENRE AND GENRES OF FICTION

Notions of *xiaoshuo* as a literary genre, a distinctive form of literary discourse, first glimmered in the late seventeenth century but did not begin to coalesce until the late nineteenth, in part through dialogue (and confusion) with Western ideas of fiction. But notions of what I am calling thematic genres, namely groupings of narrative material by subject, setting, and theme, have a longer and sturdier pedigree in China, traceable at least to the Song dynasty. The *Extensive Records from the Taiping Reign* (*Taiping guangji* 太平廣記, comp. 977–978 CE), the most comprehensive compilation to its time of miscellaneous narrative material, organizes its more than seven thousand items under ninety-two topics, from "Immortals" (*Shenxian* 神仙) to "Barbarian Peoples" (*Man Yi* 蠻夷).[2] Early records of storytelling in the Song capitals also indicate that professionals specialized in particular types of material; the *Record of the Splendors of the Capital* (*Ducheng jisheng* 都城紀勝, 1235) explains that "the storytellers can be divided into four groups: those who specialize in social tales, mysteries, and miracle tales; those who deal in military adventures; those who explicate sutras by telling religious tales; and those who relate historical events."[3] In the Ming dynasty, when the full-length linked-chapter novel emerged as a prominent narrative form, its most distinguished exemplars, the "four masterworks" (*sida qishu* 四大奇書), became de facto benchmarks for thematic subtypes: *The Romance of the Three Kingdoms* (*Sanguo zhi yanyi* 三國志演義) for historical romances, *The Water Margin* (*Shuihu zhuan* 水滸傳) for heroic legends, *The Journey to the West* (*Xiyou ji* 西遊記) for supernatural fantasy, and *The Plum in the Golden Vase* (*Jinpingmei* 金瓶梅) for novels of romance and manners.[4] This categorization or some variation of it runs as an undercurrent to many of the prefaces and commentaries appended to the novels of the Ming and Qing dynasties. One late example, a preface to the nineteenth-century *A Tale of Romance and Heroism* (*Ernü yingxiong zhuan* 兒女英雄傳), cleverly associates *The Journey to the West*, *The Water Margin*, *The Plum in the Golden Vase*, and *The Dream of the Red Chamber* with "anomalies, feats of strength, disorder, and the spirits" (怪力亂神) respectively—four topics reportedly shunned by Confucius (*Lunyu* 論語 7:21) and that later came to be associated with the miscellaneous narratives lumped under the rubric *xiaoshuo*.[5] Indeed, this work's introductory chapter makes clear that the novel's very title heralds a synthesis of two thematic metagenres, the romantic (*ernü* 兒女) and the heroic (*yingxiong* 英雄).[6]

The New Fiction movement of the late Qing, in introducing Western models and ideas of fiction, both solidified notions of fiction as a distinctive form of literary discourse and brought renewed attention to the question of the subcategories of fiction. "In the West, each and every object or affair has its own proper name, and categories are differentiated without careless cross-borrowing. As far as fiction is concerned, each form has its own distinct name."[7] Exactly what criteria differentiate fiction's subcategories? The author of the 1907 passage just quoted goes on to cite (in English) the Western forms "Romance, Novelette, Story, Tale, Fable," without however providing further explanation. A seminal approach to the issue written five years earlier, Liang Qichao's 梁啓超 "China's Only Literary Journal: *New Fiction*" ("Zhongguo weiyi zhi wenxue bao *Xin Xiaoshuo*" 中國唯一之文學報新小說), touches upon several different parameters for categorizing fiction, including linguistic register and length, but gives primary attention to characterizing a series of fictional types: historical fiction (歷史小說), political fiction (政治小說), military fiction (軍事小說), adventure fiction (冒險小說), detective fiction (探偵小說), romantic fiction (寫情小說), supernatural fiction (語怪小說), anecdotal fiction (劄記小說), and dramatic fiction (傳奇小說).[8] While the last two categories testify to the continuing currency of traditional perceptions of *xiaoshuo* as a miscellany of narrative and dramatic forms, the other categories represent distinctions not of language or form but of subject matter and theme, and it is the thematic categories that first dominate late-Qing typologies of fiction in both theory and practice.

Discussions of the types and subtypes of fiction were structured by and constituted an essential element of the New Fiction movement's fundamental agenda of promoting a new, foreign-inspired practice of fiction over the derelict native tradition. Liang Qichao's first rallying cry for the New Fiction, his 1898 "Preface to the Translation and Publication of Political Novels" ("Yi yin zhengzhi xiaoshuo xu" 譯印政治小說序), took the form of an introduction to a specific subgenre imported from the West and Japan.[9] The vogue for the political novel at the turn of the century testified to a widespread receptiveness to Liang's vision of this particular genre's ideological aims.[10] At the same time, it reinforced the perception that fiction properly assumed the form of a particular thematic subtype. Other thematic types soon followed. An essay published in *New Fiction* in 1905 states clearly the need for the importation of new fictional genres: "The strategy for remedying [the moribund state of Chinese fiction] must begin with the importation of political fiction, detective fiction, and scientific fiction. In all of Chinese fiction, the qualities of these three cannot be found, yet it is these three above all that are the crux of fiction as a whole."[11] Traditional Chinese fiction, lacking these most vital components, was viewed as a sparse and narrow field. As Liang elsewhere puts it:

> I believe that beyond revering heroism and cherishing romance, humankind also possesses a subsidiary characteristic, namely fearing ghosts and spirits. With these three, one can encompass the entirety of Chinese fiction. But with the evolution of narrative literature in the West, nearly all [realms of] ideation are brought together and dealt with; it cannot be delimited by these three.[12]

Liang clearly views the thematic categories of the indigenous narrative tra-dition as limited in number and restricted in scope. It is important to note, however, that these categories' perceived shortcomings lay not merely, or even chiefly, in their typological sparseness. The reformers' goal was not a "revolution in fiction" for its own sake but rather the deployment of fiction as a tool for national enlightenment. And just as the fictional subgenres promoted for import were those most closely associated with crucial bodies of modern knowledge, so the native genres were seen as those most heavily burdened with regressive moral and social tendencies:

> Although Chinese fiction is included in the nine schools of litera-ture and philosophy, very few good works have been written since the time of Yu Chu. Stories about heroes are all patterned after *The Water Margin*, whereas those about love imitate *The Dream of the Red Chamber*. Taken as a whole, Chinese novels invariably teach us either robbery or lust. Lost in a vicious circle, the novelists are unable to rise above the quagmire. For this reason, knowledgeable men often scorn the mere mention of fiction.[13]

The late Qing's newly elaborated typologies for the expanding domains of fiction manifest themselves not only in theory—in analytical and polemical essays—but also in publication practice—the organization and tables of contents of literary periodicals. Here too it was Liang Qichao who took the lead. The table of contents of the first issue of his *New Fiction* (1902) places the titles and authors of individual contributions under rubrics similar to though not identical with those presented in the essay/advertisement just noted. Illustrations (*tuhua* 圖畫) and essays (*lunshuo* 論說) are followed by a series of thematic categories for chaptered vernac-ular novels (historical fiction, political fiction, scientific fiction, etc.), then by miscellaneous literary forms: dramas (傳奇), Cantonese plays (廣東戲本), jottings (雜記), miscellaneous lyrics (雜歌謠). The same categorizers appear as rubrics in a smaller typeface preceding the title of each work on the first page of its presentation. Later issues of the journal varied the catego-ries somewhat. Other periodicals followed suit. With the exception of *Illustrated Fiction* (*Xiuxiang xiaoshuo* 繡像小說, 1903), which added classifiers only after a year of publication and only as title-page headings, the other chief fiction periodicals of the late Qing—*New New Fiction* (*Xinxin xiaoshuo* 新新小說, 1904), *The All-Story Monthly* (*Yueyue xiaoshuo* 月月小說, 1906), and *Forest of Fiction* (*Xiaoshuo lin* 小說林, 1907)—imitated *New Fiction* in foregrounding thematic categories in their tables of contents and/or as headers for individual titles. These thematic categories applied almost exclusively to long, serialized fiction; when the new category of "short-form fiction" or the "short story" (*duanpian xiaoshuo* 短篇小說) first appeared in *The All-Story Monthly*, it was placed alongside the other miscellaneous forms (anecdotal fiction, miscellaneous notes, etc.), and instances of the form were not designated with thematic headings.[14]

In the last years of the Qing and the first of the Republican era, the thematic types that dominated the approach of Liang Qichao and his immediate imitators begin to cede importance to the other, more formalistic categories whose discongruent company they had shared all along. In 1912, for example, writing on "The categorization of fiction" ("Xiaoshuo zhi fenlei" 小說之分類), Guan Daru 管達如 discusses three parallel sets of parameters. Under the heading of "Categorization by characteristic qualities" (性質上之分類) he surveys such familiar thematic subtypes as the martial (武力的), the romantic (寫情的), the supernatural (神怪的), and so forth. But given equal weight and even precedence in his discussion are "Categorization by literary type" (文學上的分類), which distinguishes texts by their use of classical, vernacular, and rhymed literary forms (文言體、白話體、韻文體), and "Categorization by form" (體制上之分類), which notes differences between the structure and narrative approaches of "note-style" (筆記體) and "linked-chapter" (章回體) fiction.[15] Even more striking than Guan's theoretical revalorization of linguistic and formal approaches to the categorizing of fiction is the fact that the periodical that published his essay, *The Short Story Magazine* (*Xiaoshuo yuebao* 小說月報), almost entirely dispensed with thematic categories in the presentation of its material. The first issue's table of contents simply allocates material to the categories of long-form fiction (長篇小說), short-form fiction (短篇小說), translations (譯叢), notes (筆記), belles-lettres (文苑), new knowledge (新智識), and reformed drama (改良新劇). Thematic designators continued to be absent from subsequent issues' tables of contents, although they occasionally appeared above the title on the first page of a text. Their main presence, in fact, was not in association with the periodical's own fictional material but in its advertisements. The many full-page advertisements for novels from *The Short Story Magazine*'s publisher, the Commercial Press, invariably employed the familiar thematic designators to characterize their products.

Many variations of approach can be found in the proliferating fiction periodicals of the teens. Thematic categories remained prominent, for example, in the quarterly *The Grand Magazine* (*Xiaoshuo daguan* 小說大觀, 1915). Its table of contents, like that of *The Short Story Magazine*, designated the two broad categories of long form and short form. Under these categories, though, each title was then preceded by a thematic designator. And these designators were repeated not only on the first page of each text but also on the separate calligraphic title page, printed on colored paper, that prefaced each individual item. The prominence of the thematic categorizers here was matched by the proliferation of their number. In this and other contemporary publications, the six to ten categories employed by Liang Qichao's *New Fiction* were replaced by a dazzling range of subtypes: detective, social, and military fiction were joined by "fiction of the European war" (歐戰小說), "tragic romantic fiction" (哀情小說), "youth fiction" (輕年小說), "fiction of extraordinary sentiment" (奇情小說), and a host of others. One scholar of Republican-era fiction offers a list of some 150 such categorizors.[16] The extraordinary excrescence of thematic categories became in effect the breakdown of this branch of genre theory, entirely congruent with its diminishing importance in theoretical discussions. Invented seemingly at will and with reference to no overarching system, the thematic designators became useless as tools of classification and analysis and served instead as blazons of a given work's affiliation with familiar models and, simultaneously, its novelty.[17] By the end of the teens, their migration from title pages and tables of contents to advertisements was virtually complete. Rather than expanding the realm of fictional practice and thereby invigorating the spirit of the nation, fictional "genres," in the sense of thematic categories, were now employed primarily to market fiction to its readers.[18]

DETECTIVE FICTION

This survey of the perception of thematic genres in the late Qing and early Republic affords a context for appreciating the very different identities and status of the two thematic genres showcased side by side in the 1923 *Detective World*: detective fiction and martial arts fiction.

Detective fiction was among the types foregrounded for promotion in Liang Qichao's manifestos for New Fiction. Indeed, the 1896 publication of translations of Sherlock Holmes in his newspaper *The Chinese Progress* (*Shiwu bao* 時務報) predated his earliest theoretical pronouncements and can be seen as "the vanguard of the whole fiction-for-mass-education movement."[19] Promoting *New Fiction* in 1902, Liang describes the genre: "[As to] detective fiction, its marvelous plots and extraordinary imaginings frequently surprise one's expectations. *The Chinese Progress* has in the past translated a few samples, but these amounted to no more than the smallest taste. This journal will select widely from among the most new and extraordinary texts of the Western nations for translation."[20] From its inception, thus, the genre was unmistakably marked as an imported and progressive form of fiction. The very name (*tanzhen* 探偵 in Liang Qichao's early usage, soon regularized as *zhentan* 偵探) was adopted from Japanese; the texts were translated from Japan and the West, with original works by Chinese authors only gradually gaining a foothold. Commentators sometimes noted the genre's affinities with certain elements of the native narrative tradition but generally proceeded to dismiss the connection. The tales of Lord Bao and other righteous judges were perceived as lacking in the deduction and evidence gathering essential to true detective fiction and to move perilously close to the orbit of the discredited native genre of *shenguai* (the supernatural). Guan Daru could go so far as to claim that "This kind of fiction also [like scientific (*kexue*) fiction] did not exist in China. . . . Detective fiction is the most intricate in its design and must moreover adhere closely to reality in every respect; that it could not appear in China is not to be wondered at in the least."[21]

Guan's comments suggest several different aspects of detective fiction's "newness" and its perceived suitability for the goals of the New Fiction's reform-oriented promoters. Enthusiasm for the genre was directed in part toward its literary qualities. Liang Qichao's remark about "marvelous plots and extraordinary imaginings" refers not only to the thrilling events that make up the core of a detective story but also to the manner of their narration. Commentators admired the careful plotting required by the genre, and though some of the devices employed in the narration of the classical detective story—the first-person narrator, the manipulation of the reader's knowledge through flashbacks and the withholding of information, etc.—found a difficult reception at first, it was in large measure through the translation of detective fiction that such narrative techniques became familiar to Chinese readers and authors.[22] As already noted, however, the reformers' goals were social and political rather than literary as such. From this perspective, detective fiction's virtues lay in its protagonists' combination of moral rectitude, intellectual acumen, and not infrequently physical courage and in the genre's vision of a society in which scientific logic and modern technology lent their support to justice and the rule of law.[23] To some today, the imputation of such progressive ideals to what is at heart an entertainment genre may seem a misprision.[24] But it is important to recognize that the perceived "modernity" that accounts at least in part for the enthusiastic reception detective fiction received in China resides as much in the genre's settings and textural details as in its ideological superstructure. The opening lines of a typical story—this from the first issue of *The Short Story Magazine*—promptly establish the tale's typological affiliations: "I had just sat down at my desk to read the paper one day when the telephone rang. I picked it up, and an urgent voice called out, 'Is that the detective Mr. Gelai?' I said that it was. 'Then come to the Heishi Jewelry Store right away!'"[25] At the same time, the casual immediacy of the first-person narration and the diegetic apparatus of telephone, newspaper, and jewelry store join to provide a bracing, almost naturalistic snapshot of modern urban life.

This passage's easy recognizability as an example of detective fiction brings our attention to a further aspect of the form's history: the distinctiveness and stability of its generic markers. Many of this thematic genre's characteristic features of setting, incident, characterization, plot structure, and narrative approach were established at the moment of its birth in the West with Edgar Allan Poe's 1841 "The Murders in the Rue Morgue." Arthur Conan Doyle's Sherlock Holmes tales elaborated on these features without altering their essential character,[26] and when Holmes and his amanuensis Watson entered China in the last years of the nineteenth century, the implicit authority of the foreign model only reinforced the firmness of the generic conventions. The form's recognizability and integrity are reflected in the fact that the term *zhentan xiaoshuo* was not only among the first thematic categorizers to be introduced in late-Qing

Chinese fiction but also, into the Republican period, remained one of the most persistent and unchanging in its deployment. And as thematic categorizers generally faded from the tables of contents and title headings of periodicals in the 1920s, *zhentan xiaoshuo* remained one of the most likely to reappear in discussions of fiction, in the titles of columns or special issues, and in advertisements.

By one reckoning, translated works made up some two-thirds of the fiction published in China in the last years of the Qing and the early years of the Republic, and detective stories represented two-thirds of all translated fiction.[27] Although native authors in the genre found it impossible to escape the shadow of their translated models and inspirations, their own production was far from inconsiderable. Cheng Xiaoqing 程小青 (1893–1976; creator of Huo Sang 霍桑, "China's Sherlock Holmes") and other specialists emerged, and there was hardly an author working in the popular periodical press of the 1910s and 1920s who did not try his hand at the form, through translation, original creation, or both. Translated and native works remained popular into the war years of the 1930s and 1940s. Detective fiction must thus be accounted one of the New Fiction movement's great successes—a genre that far outlived the political fiction in whose company it was first introduced and that reached audiences far wider than the elite circles to whom Liang Qichao first proposed his "revolution in the world of fiction." From another perspective, of course, this success was a loss—the degeneration of a potentially progressive form into a commodified vehicle for escapist entertainment.[28] But even in the post–May Fourth world, when the political and aesthetic agendas of the New Culture relegated detective fiction to the outcast status of the "old" and benighted, authors and enthusiasts of this thematic genre continued to lay claim to some of its previous cachet as a force for the improvement of society and the thinking man's entertainment literature.[29]

MARTIAL ARTS FICTION

The late Qing and early Republican periods saw a reinvigoration of China's rich tradition of literature on martial, chivalric, and military topics.[30] Just as late-Qing and early-Republican-era interest in Western technology, paradigms of knowledge and rationality, and law and civic society provided a broad extraliterary context for the reception of detective fiction, so too did the same period's interest in various aspects of martiality prepare the soil for new production of fiction on martial themes. One response to the widespread sense of a national crisis brought on by both internal weakness and external threat was a call for the promotion of a martial spirit in the people of the Chinese nation. Liang Qichao's 1904 *The Chinese Way of the Warrior* (*Zhongguo zhi wushi dao* 中國之武士道) interprets the traditional *xia*'s 俠 ("gallant" or "knight-errant") altruism and disdain for the law as a willingness to sacrifice the self for the sake of the people and the nation. The work collects its material from the historical records of pre-Qin statesmen and cultural heroes but draws upon Liang's perceptions of Meiji Japan for the "way of the warrior" (Japanese *bushido*) of its title and its vision of a martial ideology infused with a nationally specific spirit. The writings of Liang Qichao and his contemporaries portrayed the martial spirit as an essential element of historical Chinese civilization obscured or repressed by centuries of neo-Confucian orthodoxy and the rule of the "foreign" Manchu dynasty. Mapping contemporary political tides onto their readings of Chinese history, they associated the revival of the martial-chivalric spirit with the ideology of revolution and, by extension, with secret societies and the tactics of assassination.[31]

Distinct from but often allied with the promotion of a Chinese martial spirit were late-Qing and Republican-era movements to reshape the traditional Chinese martial arts into a form of modern physical culture. Western ideas of race, hygiene, and eugenics facilitated a literal interpretation of the metaphoric characterization of China as the "sick man of East Asia" (*dongya bingfu* 東亞病夫): the nation's geopolitical weakness was seen as instantiated in and at least in part attributable to the physical debility of its people. The remedy for this condition was the strengthening of the citizenry by means of a modern, scientific program of physical culture. The sports and physical-education curricula of Western nations provided the essential models for emulation; Japan's reinvention of judo and other martial arts traditions in conformity with these models suggested a template for creating a physical culture that looked to the new international standards while both drawing on and promoting the indigenous cultural heritage. During the last decade of the Qing, individual martial artists and private organizations began championing modernized versions of the Chinese martial arts. The most prominent and successful of such organizations was the Pure Martial Athletic Association 精武體育會

(originally the Pure Martial Calisthenics Association 精武體操會), founded in Shanghai in 1910 before establishing branches throughout China and Chinese communities overseas. The association's first martial arts instructor was the Tianjin-born Huo Yuanjia 霍元甲 (1868–1910), whose reputation mushroomed after rumors attributed his death to poisoning by a Japanese rival. The programs championed by the association and similar organizations were vehemently rejected by New Culture critics, who viewed the traditional martial arts as an irredeemable manifestation of the violence and superstition endemic to "feudal" culture. But modernized versions of the martial arts—systematized, purged of "unscientific" elements, assimilated to models of sports and hygiene, taught by open-access and even co-ed organizations rather than passed on via secretive master-disciple lineages—gained popularity among urban populations and proved so conformable to the Nationalist Party's cultural agenda that the Nanjing government consecrated them as the "national arts" (*guoshu* 國術) and established a Central Academy for the National Arts 中央國術館 in 1928.[32]

Xiang Kairan seems to provide a direct link between Republican-era martial arts activity and the production of martial arts fiction. The recognized father of the fictional subgenre also practiced the martial arts, was engaged in their teaching and promotion through private and government-sponsored organizations from as early as his student days in Japan, and authored nonfictional treatises and essays on the martial arts as well as martial arts fiction. His material passed through the borders between fictional and nonfictional treatments; Huo Yuanjia, whose life is the subject of the final portion of the 1916 appendix to his "Art of Pugilism," is the chief protagonist of one of his most famous novels, the 1923 *Chivalric Heroes of Modern Times*, one of whose central themes is the modernization of the martial arts. And fictional and nonfictional treatments of the martial arts occupied closely related niches in the environment of the print culture of his times. Thus the "Art of Pugilism" and its appendix were published, as were other martial arts treatises, in a special section of *Chung Hwa Novel Magazine*; some years later, the latest volume of *Marvelous Gallants of the Rivers and Lakes* shared an advertisement with the ostensibly nonfictional *Secret Teachings of the Chinese Martial Arts* (*Zhonghua wushu michuan* 中華武術秘傳) from the same publisher.[33] As significant as these connections are, however, they do not constitute a sufficient account of Xiang Kairan's alleged creation of modern martial arts fiction. We saw in the previous chapter that he perceived his occupation as a writer of fiction as quite distinct from his vocation as a practitioner and promoter of the martial arts. And if we widen our focus from the individual author to the thematic genre, we find that the development of the category of *wuxia xiaoshuo* in late-Qing and Republican-era China is much more complex and decentered than that of *zhentan xiaoshuo*.

To appreciate the differences between the history and status of *zhentan xiaoshuo* and those of *wuxia xiaoshuo*, we could do worse than to begin by noting that unlike the former, the latter term was not employed by the New Fiction advocates to designate a fictional subtype. The New Fiction movement did play a role in introducing the term *wuxia* into modern Chinese usage. Although an association between *wu* and *xia* in Chinese culture can be traced at least as far back as the Warring States period, the bisyllabic compound *wuxia* gained currency only in the early years of the twentieth century. It was borrowed from Japanese usage, and the proximate source may have been the patriotic adventure fiction of the novelist Oshikawa Shunrô 押川春浪 (1876–1914).[34] Remarks on this author's works in the journal *Forest of Fiction* (*Xiaoshuo lin* 小說林) in 1908 claim that the "citizens [of Japan] all take martial chivalry (*wuxia*) as their responsibility" (其國民咸以武俠自命) and refer to several of Oshikawa's novels containing the phrase *wuxia* 武俠 (*bukyô*) in their titles.[35] The compound had begun to circulate several years earlier, however. Its first use seems to have been in a 1905 entry in *New Fiction*'s "Miscellaneous Remarks on Fiction" series that credits *The Water Margin* with "bequeathing the model for martial chivalry (*wuxia*) and allowing society to reap its benefits."[36] The term *wuxia* thus enters the language in the context of a discussion of fiction but not yet as the designation of a fictional subtype per se. That step was taken in 1915 when *The Grand Magazine* (*Xiaoshuo daguan* 小說大觀), edited by Bao Tianxiao, published Lin Shu's classical-language short story *Fu Meishi* 傅眉史 under the rubric *wuxia xiaoshuo* 武俠小說.[37] Rather than staking out a unique claim to territory, however, *wuxia xiaoshuo*, "fiction of martial chivalry," joined a small crowd of other descriptors employed to label fiction with martial and/or chivalric content: "fiction of combat arts" (*jiji xiaoshuo* 技擊小說), "fiction of chivalric righteousness" (*xiayi xiaoshuo* 俠義小說), "fiction of righteous chivalry" (*yixia xiaoshuo*

義俠小說), "fiction of courageous righteousness" (*yongyi xiaoshuo* 勇義小說), "fiction of chivalric passion" (*xiaqing xiaoshuo* 俠情小說), and so forth.

Given Liang Qichao's interest in the martial spirit and his faith in the power of fiction as an agent of national enlightenment, it was inevitable that his New Fiction project should endorse fiction promoting martiality. But the gulf between his advocacy of a native martial spirit and his distrust of native fiction and its subtypes produced confusion about what models a new martial fiction might follow and the name under which it might pursue its mission. As we have just seen, the very term *wuxia* entered the modern Chinese language via the pages of Liang Qichao's journal *New Fiction* and in the context of praise for *The Water Margin*'s spirit. In the journal's inaugural issue, however, Liang Qichao unsparingly relegated *The Water Margin* to the camp of benighted indigenous fictional genres:

> Now everywhere among our people there are heroes of the green forests. The ceremony of "swearing an oath of brotherhood in the Peach Garden" in *The Romance of the Three Kingdoms* and of "oath-taking in the Liang Mountain" as in *The Water Margin* is rampant. Dreams of having "big bowls of wine, big slices of meat, sharing gold and silver and weighing them on a scale, and putting on complete suits of clothes," as these heroes did, fill the minds of the lower classes. This has gradually led to the formation of secret societies such as the Old Brothers and the Big Swords, culminating in the Boxer Movement, which was responsible for the loss of the capital and for bringing foreign troops into China. This was all because of fiction.[38]

The categories in his 1902 "China's Only Literary Journal: *New Fiction*" include "adventure fiction" (*maoxian xiaoshuo* 冒險小說), "devoted to encouraging the people's spirit of exploration and adventure," and "military fiction" (*junshi xiaoshuo* 軍事小說), "dedicated to nourishing the martial spirit of the nation's citizens."[39] These categories look to foreign models for definition and validation; "adventure fiction" cites *Robinson Crusoe* as an archetype, and the description of "military fiction" specifies that "its material will all be taken from translations." The native texts *The Romance of the Three Kingdoms* and *The Water Margin* are consigned to the category of historical fiction, pointedly snubbed as sources of inspiration for the martial virtues.[40]

One of the most striking fictional elaborations of martial and chivalric themes inspired by the New Fiction movement is "Tales of Knights-Errant: The Biography of Spared-the-Blade" ("Xiake tan: Daoyusheng zhuan" 俠客談: 刀餘生傳), published in the first two issues of *New New Fiction* (*Xin xin xiaoshuo* 新新小說) in 1904. *New New Fiction* was edited by Chen Jinghan 陳景韓 (Lengxue 冷血, 1877–1965), who also contributed to its content, "Spared-the-Blade" included. While Chen Jinghan seems to have shared Liang Qichao's belief in the power of fiction to enlighten society, his politics leaned toward revolution rather than Liang Qichao's reform agenda. A radical ideology finds exaggerated expression in "Spared-the-Blade," which relates how a traveler abducted by bandits is introduced to the alternate society his captors have established. Their organization has departments for industry, commerce, research and education, and so forth; most spectacular, though, are the execution chambers, where victims are systematically bathed, killed, dismembered, and rendered into useful substances, with the useless remains finally consigned to the furnace. The targets of this harrowing operation are those whose debilities burden society: "To opium addicts—death! To women with bound feet—death! To those over fifty—death! To cripples—death! To those carrying infectious diseases—death!"[41] The *xia* here becomes the agent for the radical implementation of a eugenics inspired by social Darwinism; "knights-errant" hasten the process of natural selection for the benefit of the nation.

New New Fiction's significance for our understanding of late-Qing and early-Republican developments in martial arts fiction lies not only in the way that "Spared-the-Blade" and other works employ martial and chivalric material in the expression of radical and revolutionary ideologies but also in the journal's experiments with the categorization of fictional subtypes. In the first issue, the organization of material closely resembles that of Liang Qichao's *New Fiction*. The table of contents lists various thematic genres of fiction—political fiction, social fiction, historical fiction, etc.—and places under each category a featured fictional work identified by title and author. The various categories of fiction are followed by a "Miscellany" (*zalu* 雜錄). "Tales of Knight-Errantry," credited to Lengxue 冷血, appears under the category of "Social Fiction" (*shehui xiaoshuo* 社會小說). With the third issue, however, the organization of the table of contents changes dramatically. "Tales of Knight-Errantry" has been elevated to the title of the first of three main sections, the others being "Additional Material" (*fulu* 附錄) and the "Miscellany." Four works of fiction, each with an apposite subtitle, appear under "Tales of Knight-Errantry." The continuation of *The Unofficial History of the Philippines* (*Feiliebin waishi* 非列賓外史), which commenced in the first issue under the categorizer "Historical Fiction" (*lishi xiaoshuo* 歷史小說), is now subtitled "Southeast Asian Tales of Knight-Errantry" (*Nanya kiake tan* 南亞俠客談); a sequel to the original "Spared-the-Blade" is subtitled "Tales of Knight-Errantry from a Century in the Future" (*Bainian hou zhi xiake tan* 百年後之俠客談). An announcement explains that the periodical will be published in sets of twelve issues, each set devoted to a particular topic; "in this issue, for example, the topic is knight-errantry" (如此期內。則以俠客為主義。).[42] The journal seems to have ceased publication after the tenth issue, leaving its plans unfulfilled. The project nonetheless illuminates several interrelated factors: the reenergized attention given to the idea of the martial-chivalric spirit, the catholicity and flexibility of the idea, the interest in the identification of fictional types and subtypes, and the role of periodical publishing in defining these types.[43]

The expression of revolutionary ideologies was but one of many manifestations of martial and chivalric material in the fiction of the last years of the Qing dynasty and the first decade of the Republic.[44] Those engaged in producing the era's flood of translations from foreign literature used the inherited vocabulary and imagery of *xia* to render into Chinese a wide range of fiction involving chivalry, principle, passion, and struggle. This practice accommodated foreign material to native preconceptions but at the same time expanded the range of themes with which *xia* was associated and renewed the contemporary relevance of the concept. The overlapping circles of writers associated with the Southern Society (Nanshe 南社) and the fiction periodical *Saturday* (*Libailiu* 禮拜六) penned tales exploring the links between chivalry and passion (*qing* 情). Lin Shu's 1908 *Anecdotes of the Combat Arts* (*Jiji yuwen* 技擊餘聞) spurred a fad for short classical-language martial tales spiced with local color that lasted for well over a decade. *The Short Story Magazine* was only one of many magazines that regularly published such tales; many of the pieces printed in its column "Supplemental Anecdotes of the Combat Arts" ("Jiji yuwen bu" 技擊

餘聞補) in 1914 and 1915 were included in a collection published in book form in 1916 under the title *Gathered Tales of Martial Arts and Chivalry* (*Wuxia congtan* 武俠叢談)—further evidence of the growing currency of the term *wuxia*.[45] Such collections of classical-language tales provided the model for Xiang Kairan's first martial fiction, his 1916 "Matters Pugilistic, Seen and Heard." By the beginning of the 1920s, publishers' advertisements listed such collections alongside editions of and sequels to nineteenth-century martial- and supernatural-themed vernacular novels such as *The Three Knights and Five Gallants* (*Sanxia wuyi* 三俠五義) and *The Story-teller's Jigong* (*Jigong an* 濟公案).[46] Other martial and chivalric material from China's earlier literary traditions continued to circulate as well: from Tang-dynasty tales of swordswomen, through Ming novels including *The Water Margin* and *The Romance of the Three Kingdoms*, to the wealth of martial anecdotes in Qing *biji* collections, this heritage lived on in new editions, in revised and rewritten versions, and in adaptations for the storyteller's teahouse and the opera stage. My aim is not to recuperate all of these phenomena as elements of a single tradition. My point is rather that, for all the cross-fertilization of their imagery, characters, plots, and themes, and despite their often evident consciousness of drawing from a storehouse of shared cultural material, these literary productions evince diversities of form and of ideology so great as to render the notion of a thematic genre inapplicable in any but the most superficial and contingent sense. The profusion of terminology noted earlier—the unsettled and redundant evocation of "fiction of chivalric righteousness," "fiction of chivalric passion," "fiction of combat arts," and so forth—is only symptomatic of a more fundamental absence: that of any single core set of characteristics that might define a *wuxia* genre. The contrast with detective fiction, whose introduction as a new and foreign fictional type vested it with a clearly prescribed set of formal conventions and a concomitantly focused range of signification, could not be greater.

The Sunday's *"Special Issue on Martial Arts and Chivalry"*

During the latter half of the 1910s and into the beginning of the 1920s, the currency of the term *wuxia xiaoshuo* gradually spread. But it by no means gained immediate ascendancy, much less exclusivity, as a label for fiction on chivalric or martial themes; nor did the writings designated as *wuxia xiaoshuo* demonstrate an obvious tendency toward uniformity of formal or thematic characteristics. Testimony both to the category's increasing visibility and to its continuing heterogeneity is offered by the "Special Issue on Martial Arts and Chivalry" ("Wuxia hao" 武俠號) published in March 1923 as the fiftieth and final issue of Bao Tianxiao's *The Sunday*.

The "Martial Arts" issue was one of four special issues *The Sunday* published during its year-long run. It was not only the last but also the most unusual: the previous special issues—on "Marriage" ("Hunyin hao" 婚姻號) in no. 13, "Childrearing" ("Shengyu hao" 生育號) in no. 26, and "Maids and Concubines" ("Bi qie hao" 婢妾號) in no. 41—had each featured a theme congruent with the periodical's characteristic focus on the domestic and romantic aspects of life in contemporary society. Does the concluding issue's departure from the magazine's established concerns represent a response to a perceived shift in readers' interests, a planned change of editorial direction too tardily implemented, a careless final cast of the dice? One can only speculate on the editor's precise motives. It is evident, however, that despite the ambivalence toward martial arts fiction he seems to display in his 1929 piece on Xiang Kairan, Bao Tianxiao played a non-negligible role in defining and promoting this thematic genre. He was editor of *The Grand Magazine* in 1915 when it made the first use of the rubric *wuxia xiaoshuo* to designate a piece of fiction, and here, several months after the commencement of *Scarlet Magazine*'s serialization of *Rivers and Lakes*, born of his matchmaking, he foregrounds *wuxia* as the theme of the final issue of his popular weekly.

Although the selection of *wuxia* as the focus of the issue provides prima facie evidence of this topic's growing appeal, it is difficult to argue from the evidence of the issue's contents that fiction on martial and chivalric subjects has found a genre identity in the sense of any consensus on formal or thematic conventions. Within the more than two dozen items, long and short, perhaps the most explicit expression of something like a genre consciousness is to be found in Hu Jichen's 胡寄塵 (Hu Huaichen 胡懷琛, 1886–1938) "A Chivalrous Youth" ("Xia shaonian" 俠少年). This brief (roughly four hundred characters) story tells of an impoverished young husband who braves his in-laws' scorn and his fellow townsmen's incomprehension to share his meager resources with a beggar found lying in the snow. In prefatory remarks, the author recasts the familiar distinction between romantic and heroic fiction as a matter of style:

"The brush and ink that compose romantic fiction should rightly be soft and lingering; the brush and ink that compose martial arts fiction should rightly be bold and forthright. As the matters they record are not the same, so their style should rightly be different as well."[47] He further references a specific textual model for his response to Bao Tianxiao's request for *wuxia* material: Chen Lengxue's 1904 "Tales of Knights-Errant," which he first read some years ago and a copy of which Bao recently gave him for his renewed perusal. Hu's tale is a creditable successor to his avowed model, both in its angular and forceful prose style and in its foregrounding of chivalric altruism over—or in this case without the slightest hint of—martial prowess as such. The norms it so deliberately articulates, however, are anything but universally recognized by the other contributions to the issue.

Bao Tianxiao, for the opening item that he customarily contributed to each issue of *The Sunday*, here presents "A Female Gallant for the World" ("Shijie nüxia" 世界女俠), a sketch of a thoroughly modern swordswoman. The protagonist takes her name, Zhang Feixia 張飛俠 ("Flying Gallant Zhang"), from the fact that she can indeed fly—not, as the narrator quickly clarifies, by means of any sort of magic but rather through the power of science; she has invented a set of wings that she stores in a case and can attach to her body when she finds it necessary to fly through the heavens. She has trained in the martial arts since childhood and has also studied abroad, in England, America, France, Germany, and Russia. Although she would be unstoppable as an assassin, easily surpassing such classical models as Hongxian or Yinniang, she disdains to kill or to concern herself with acts of private vengeance. She devotes herself instead to eradicating social inequality, and although she is Chinese, her allegiance is global and the scope of her activities worldwide. Her foes are militarists, capitalist tycoons, and the governments they support. She runs an international ring of spies and agents, lectures to socialist parties and secret organizations, organizes strikes, destroys armaments factories and military laboratories, establishes trade schools funded by money stolen from banks and big corporations, and manages disaster relief. Decades later, after the international revolution has achieved its final success, she dies, unmarried and childless but looking upon the youth of the world as her progeny. Zhang Feixia, too, is the progeny, on one level, of late-Qing fictional figures who joined elements of the avenging swordswoman from the Chinese literary tradition with themes of revolution, liberation, and anarchy.[48] She likewise echoes contemporary cinematic representations that employed the technology of the film medium and exploited the imaginative resonance of modern technological wonders to envision women in flight.[49] Bao's text shows little interest in delving too deeply into any ideological implications this sensational figure might harbor; it approaches more closely than many other contributions to the issue *The Sunday*'s hallmark mix of facile progressivism with a fixation on the modern female as the object of discourse. The author presents the whole in characteristically casual *baihua* prose and with fluid association standing in for structured plotting.[50]

Bi Yihong's 畢倚虹 (Bi Zhenda 振達, 1892–1926) "Minutes from the Society of Female Gallants" ("Xia she ji" 俠社記) also imagines the modern swordswoman; in this case the narrative is more tightly focused, portraying a single board meeting of a secret society, as is the avenging heroines' agenda, which concentrates on fighting the oppression of women. Other stories bring *xia* material to bear on contemporary or near-contemporary political and military struggles. The protagonist of Wu Lingyuan's 吳陵園 "Only a Chapter in the Tale" ("Zhe buguo yi hui shu" 這不過一回書), frustrated with the ineffectiveness of the Revolutionary Party, proposes to organize a band of martial artists to take more direct action against the corrupt warlords who are leading the nation to ruin. The stalwarts of Wang Houzhe's 王后哲 "Two Heroes of Molin" ("Molin shuangxia" 秣林雙俠), operating in the more optimistic days of the 1911 Revolution, make common cause with the troops of the Revolutionary Army in defending a town against the depredations of bandits. Yu Bai's 羽白 "The Unbending Thumb" ("Bu qu zhi muzhi" 不屈之拇指) celebrates military virtues and sacrifice for the nation. Still other tales put martial skills and/or chivalrous spirits in service to more private ends: punishing local tyrants and sexual predators (Zhang Biwu's 張碧梧, "Flying Blades in the Night" ["Heiye feidao" 黑夜飛刀]), rescuing an errant young man from ruin at the hands of an unscrupulous courtesan (Fan Yanqiao 范烟橋 [Fan Yong 鏞, 1894–1967], "An Unexpected Guest" ["Busu zhi ke" 不速之客]), or pursuing the feuds and glories of the marginal society of the Rivers and Lakes (Ranli 髯李, "A Thwarted Hero" ["Shiyi de yingxiong" 失意的英雄]). Perhaps the most intriguing tales on the thematic level are those whose unusual deployments of *xia* material bespeak cynicism or playfulness about the issue's project. Shen Jiaxiang's 沈家驤 "Old Wounds"

("Jiuchuang" 舊創) features an unreliable first-person narrator who uses the vocabulary of chivalry and heroism to justify what is clearly a life of sordid crime. Yao Gengkui's 姚賡夔 (1905–1974) "The Strange Gallant" ("Guaixia" 怪俠) details the baffling powers and anarchic deeds of a champion whose identity is withheld until the last lines of the story: "Readers, do you know who he is? Have you ever had any dealings with him? Ha ha! He's no 'strange gallant'; he is in fact none other than the universally beloved . . . *Money*."[51]

Self-conscious manipulation of readers' expectations such as we find in these last two examples is sometimes taken as evidence of a genre's maturation, even of its over-ripening. In the case of *The Sunday*'s "Special Issue on Martial Arts and Chivalry," however, what we find is a hodgepodge of elements that, for all their (over)familiarity, show little sign of having gelled into a set of dominant formulas. The heterogeneity of subject matter and thematic agenda is matched by that of form. There are *biji*-style anecdotes of no more than a few lines' length; classical-language *chuanqi* tales with more elaborate plotting and more richly descriptive prose; vernacular short stories in a variety of traditional and Europeanized prose styles; and, ranging across the parameters of length, structure, and language register, considerable experimentation with the possibilities of narrative voice. In addition, extraliterary ties to the contemporary revival of the Chinese martial arts are evident in Lu Weichang's 盧煒昌 (1883–1943) hyperbolic encomium of "national calisthenics" (*guocao* 國操) as a panacea for the ills of the human race and in advertisements for various instruction manuals.

THE CREATION OF A GENRE?

The questions posed at the beginning of this chapter remain so far unanswered. In what sense can Xiang Kairan be said to have created modern martial arts fiction, and what was Shen Zhifang's role in the process? Evidence of the abundance and variety of fiction on martial and chivalric themes in the years leading up to 1923 makes the first of these questions more salient, even as it provides the necessary context for suggesting an answer to the second. In a literary and cultural environment well saturated with martial and chivalric fiction of various kinds, Shen Zhifang laid claim to a defining position not by commissioning an author to write something unheard of or create a thematic genre ex nihilo but rather by enlisting Xiang Kairan in the service of his project of giving this popular yet amorphous material a more fixed, recognizable, and marketable identity. The serialization of *Modern Times* on the pages of *Detective World* brings Shen Zhifang's project into clearer perspective; the yoking of martial arts to detective fiction illuminates the extent to which Shen Zhifang's conception of *wuxia xiaoshuo* as a distinctive and marketable thematic genre was modeled on the genre identity that detective fiction already possessed.

This conception of genre, and Shen Zhifang's conscious deployment of it, grew out of the previous decades' uses of fictional subtypes and was shaped by the increasingly competitive world of periodical publishing in the 1920s. Fiction magazines proliferated in the early 1920s. The self-consciously progressive literary journals that sprung up in the aftermath of the 1919 May Fourth Movement dreamed of dealing an ideological and aesthetic deathblow to the established popularity of what they referred to as "Saturday School" or "Mandarin Duck and Butterfly School" fiction; from the perspective of the publishing industry, however, they simply added another sector to a burgeoning and variegated literary marketplace. Far from being cut off, the circulation of popular (by which I here mean only non–May Fourth) literature only increased. A provisional tally shows two popular-literature periodicals founded in 1917, three in 1918, five in 1919, one in 1920, eight in 1921, nine in 1922, eleven in 1923, and seven in 1924.[52] The numbers reflect a growing market for fiction and a corresponding intensification of the competition between Shanghai's publishing firms.[53]

One of the publishing world's most spirited rivalries, particularly in the arena of popular periodical publishing, was that between the World Book Company (Shijie shuju 世界書局) and Great Eastern Books (Dadong shuju 大東書局). Shen Zhifang founded World Books in 1921 and moved aggressively to establish the company as a presence in the trade book and popular periodical markets before later moving on to challenge the Commercial Press and Zhonghua Books (Zhonghua shuju 中華書局) in the textbook arena.[54] World Books's flagship fiction journals were *The Scarlet Magazine* (*Hong zazhi* 紅雜誌), launched in August 1922 with Shi Jiqun 施濟群 as editor, and its continuation as *The Scarlet Rose* (*Hong meigui* 紅玫瑰), beginning in July 1924 under the editorship of Zhao Tiaokuang 趙

苔狂. These two were among the most prominent and enduring fiction journals of the 1920s, with the latter title ending publication only in 1932. They were joined under the World Books imprint by the shorter-lived ten-day *The Merry Magazine* (*Kuaihuo* 快活, 1922–1923), the monthly *The Home Companion* (*Jiating zazhi* 家庭雜誌, 1922–1923), and the biweekly *Detective World* (*Zhentan shijie* 偵探世界, 1923–1924).[55] Shijie's rival, Great Eastern, had been founded in 1916 by Lü Ziquan 呂子泉 (b. ~1881) and Shen Junsheng 沈駿聲. Its lineup of fiction journals comprised the monthly *The Recreation World* (*Youxi shijie* 遊戲世界, 1921–1923), the semimonthly *The Half Moon Journal* (*Banyue* 半月, 1921–1925), *The Sunday* (*Xingqi* 星期, 1922–1923), the monthly *Violet Petals* (*Zilan huapian* 紫蘭花片, 1922–1924), and the semimonthly *Violet* (*Ziluolan* 紫羅蘭, 1925–1930). The eminent Zhou Shoujuan 周瘦鵑 (1895–1968) served as the editor of all of these Great Eastern journals except *The Sunday*, for which the publisher engaged the similarly popular and widely networked Bao Tianxiao.

The competition emblazoned in the two publishers' rival color schemes played itself out in the appointment of editors—in response to Great Eastern's employment of the renowned Zhou Shoujuan, Shen Zhi-fang enlisted Yan Duhe 嚴獨鶴 (1889–1968), a prominent author and the editor of *Xinwen bao*'s 新聞報 supplement "Kuaihuo lin" 快活林, to lend his name and prestige to Shijie's line of periodicals without being actively involved in their production—and in a back-and-forth of "special issues, featured authors, and contests for readers."[56] One specific arena for the rivalry was the publication of detective fiction. While detective fiction could be found in many, even most, fiction periodicals of the period, Great Eastern took the lead in highlighting the genre in its publications. *The Half Moon Journal*, for instance, featured in its inaugural issue (September 16, 1921) the first installment of Zhang Biwu's "A Battle of Wits Between Two Heroes" ("Shuangxiong douzhi ji" 雙雄鬥智記), the tale of a contest between the iconic Huo Sang and the master thief Luo Ping 羅蘋; the serialization ran through the periodical's entire first year of publication.[57] *The Half Moon Journal* no. 6 (November 11, 1921) was a "Special Issue on Detective Fiction" ("Zhentan xiaoshuo hao" 偵探小說號). The plates at the front of the magazine presented portraits of Arthur Conan Doyle and Edgar Allan Poe, plus illustrations of scenes from the former's stories. The issue's fiction included new translations of Holmes and Lupin stories and a new Huo Sang tale from Cheng Xiaoqing. And alongside the fiction were Zhang

Shewo's 張舍我 "Miscellaneous Chats on Detective Fiction" ("Zhentan xiaoshuo zatan" 偵探小說雜談), short filler pieces on the genre's history and characteristics. Detective stories continued to be a reliable part of the magazine's regular offerings, and issue 15 (April 11, 1922) saw the first appearance of a regular column, "The Detective's Friend" ("Zhentan zhi you" 偵探之友), devoted to detective fiction and related features.

The presentation of detective fiction in *The Half Moon Journal* and other Great Eastern periodicals is the logical extension of the migration of notions of fictional subtypes from the literary manifesto to the table of contents and thence to the advertisement. A thematic genre with a distinctive pedigree and perhaps the most stable constellation of formal characteristics and thematic concerns is further reified through the promotion of well-known authors and their equally well-known fictional creations and through the development of an associated discourse of commentary and appreciation. The agent of this reification is a commercial publisher seeking to consolidate readership by establishing a distinctive identity, and the means by which the publisher pursues his strategy are the devices—special issues, columns—proper to the periodical as a medium. Detective fiction as it appears in the Great Eastern periodicals of the early 1920s has become a genre in the particular sense with which early-twenty-first-century audiences and critics are most familiar: not merely a thematic genre in the purely literary sense but a set of formulae at play in the culture industry's negotiation of the exchanges between producers and consumers.

Between producers and consumers, and between one producer and another—for World Books's launch of *Detective World* clearly represents an attempt to answer and outdo Great Eastern's self-promotion as a leader in the publication of detective fiction.[58] Beginning with its first issue in June 1923, *Detective World* included all the elements of Great Eastern's presentation of the genre: translations of foreign works, original stories by Chinese authors, and associated nonfiction articles. It strove moreover to expand and improve upon these elements. Tang Zhesheng credits the periodical with promoting native writers in a genre still dominated by foreign models and with stimulating the critical discourse through the range and quality of its nonfiction material.[59] But *Detective World* did more than strengthen detective fiction's identity as a marketable thematic genre. It also extended this type of genre identity to a new category: that of *wuxia xiaoshuo*, martial arts fiction.

Publishers had paired detective fiction with fiction on martial themes before the appearance of *Detective World*. An advertisement for Jiaotong shuju from March 1922 lists available books of both types under the heading "If you want to read fiction, read detective fiction and chivalric fiction" (要看小說最好看偵探小說與俠義小說): "The spirit of our nation's people is listless and unenergetic; reading detective fiction and chivalric fiction has the benefit of energizing the spirit and invigorating the heart and mind. Our nation's society is treacherous and deceitful; reading detective fiction and chivalric fiction has the benefit of broadening one's experience and teaching the distinction between good and evil."[60] These sweeping justifications echo the New Fiction movement's claims for the ameliorating virtues of fiction without, however, specifying the connections between these virtues and the characteristics of the two varieties mentioned or making any distinctions between the two.

Detective World similarly justifies its joint presentation of detective and martial arts fiction by stressing their thematic affinities. To be sure, familiar arguments about detective fiction's unique promotion of rational thinking and a scientific worldview can be found on the pages of the magazine.[61] They are present only in attenuated form, however, in the publisher's remarks in the inaugural issue. Shen Zhifang takes note of fiction's traditional role as a medium for edification and its recent rise to the summit of the literary world in response to influence from the West. Chinese fiction, he claims, is dominated by social and romantic works; he attributes the relative lack of enthusiasm for detective fiction to "the placidity and lack of resourcefulness of our national character." But as he goes on to laud the virtues of detective fiction, he characterizes its benefits not so much in terms of the advancement of society through scientific thinking as in terms of guarding oneself against the snares of the world: "It seems to me that although the gentleman may disdain cunning and craft, those of us who find ourselves floundering in the ocean of human life cannot avoid knowing something about these matters." As for joining detective fiction with fiction of martial arts (*wuxia*) and adventure (*maoxian* 冒險), he explains that "the three spring from a single source, and when joined together can illuminate one another."[62] Lu Dan'an 陸澹盫, the magazine's editor, likewise explains that "the works in this magazine will chiefly be detective fiction, supplemented by martial arts fiction and adventure fiction. This is because the qualities of both martial arts and adventure are rather closely associated with the life of the detective."[63] As Cai Aiguo points out, this rationale foregrounds the sensational aspects of detective fiction over the edifying rationality its proponents were so fond of citing.[64] An ad in the second issue for works of detective fiction published by World Books explicitly characterizes the books in the language of martial adventure rather than that of ingenious crime solving: "Detective Fiction—Promoting the Martial Spirit—Stimulating the Air of Righteous Chivalry" (偵探小說·提倡尚武精神·標榜義俠風氣).[65]

Very few works appearing in the magazine are explicitly identified as belonging to the "adventure" type.[66] It is detective and martial arts fiction that fill the pages. Each issue of *Detective World* features installments of two serializations, one of martial arts fiction and one of detective fiction. Xiang Kairan's *Modern Times* makes up the martial arts serialization for the magazine's entire run, matched on the detective side by the serialization of a series of novellas by Cheng Xiaoqing.[67] Among the shorter works—the stories published in their entirety in a single issue and the novellas presented over two issues or occasionally more—one to perhaps three pieces in the martial arts vein typically stand against over half a dozen works of detective fiction.[68] And in the nonfiction fillers that round out the magazine, the detective genre holds unchallenged sway; the true crime anecdotes, notes on the art of detective fiction, and so forth are matched by no similar secondary texts on martial arts or martial arts fiction.[69] It is clear that, as Shen Zhifang puts it in his "Manifesto," martial arts fiction is "guest" to the detective story's "host" (以賓屬主).[70] The lack of parity between the two genres is not merely a matter of the page count. The magazine's detective fiction is self-reflective and theorized in a way its martial arts fiction is not, outfitted with an exegetical and appreciative apparatus and set within broader literary and extraliterary contexts.

In other respects, however, the magazine takes pains to foreground its martial arts fiction and Xiang Kairan's *Modern Times* in particular. These efforts begin on the cover, which features detective fiction in the magazine's title but martial arts fiction in the illustration: the cover of each issue illustrates the current installment of Xiang Kairan's *Chivalric Heroes of Modern Times* (figure 3.1). Two full chapters of *Modern Times* appear in each issue, printed as the final item before the editor's notes and colophon. The layout of *Detective World* is simpler than that of World Books' *Scarlet*, and *Modern Times* in its serialized form lacks the text

FIGURE 3.1 The cover of
Detective World no. 14
(December 1923), illustrating
a scene from *Modern Times.*

Source: Author's photograph, from a copy
in the collection of the University of
Alberta Libraries.

illustrations and typographic features that, as we shall see in the next chapter, make the serialization of *Rivers and Lakes* so visually distinctive. But the inclusion of extensive commentary by the editor Lu Dan'an, printed both within the lines of text (in smaller font) and at the end of each chapter (in indented blocks), gives the text of *Modern Times* a unique presence on the page. And the content of this commentary, which addresses both the events and characters of the tale and the artistry of its author, imparts prestige and importance to the text and contributes to the establishment of aesthetic and ideological criteria for its appreciation. In short, *Detective World* presents *Modern Times* in such a way as to highlight both the work and the presence of martial arts fiction in the magazine as a whole.

Shen Zhifang's promotion of martial arts fiction and of Xiang Kairan as the martial arts author par excellence had already begun with *The Scarlet Magazine*'s serialization of *Rivers and Lakes*. Shi Juan, focusing on the publication and reception of *Rivers and Lakes*, has convincingly argued that Shen Zhifang's contributions lay in envisioning a type of fiction that would exploit the contemporary popularity of martial and chivalric themes, in identifying Xiang Kairan as the suitable author to manifest his vision, and in using his mastery of the paratextual tools available to commercial publishing—including serialization, advertising, and commentary—to promote Xiang Kairan's fiction aggressively.[71] In terms of content, *Rivers and Lakes* was arguably the more influential of Xiang Kairan's two seminal novels. It enjoyed a longer serialization than *Modern Times*, in a magazine with a higher reputation and wider appeal than *Detective World*. It was the inspiration for a series of phenomenally popular films, the 1928 *The Burning of Red Lotus Temple* and its sequels. And its tale of rival schools employing superhuman martial arts in the pursuit of generation-spanning feuds played a key role in establishing templates for the plotlines, narrative structure, character types, and themes of a mainstream of martial arts fiction that can be traced through Buxiaosheng's imitators and contemporaries; Huanzhulouzhu 還珠樓主 and other authors of the later Republic; the postwar "new school" dominated by Jin Yong 金庸, Liang Yusheng 梁羽生 and Gu Long 古龍; and all the way to many authors active in print and online today. While *Modern Times*' more earthbound tales of martial artists active on the margins of modern history and society are not without literary successors, its legacy is perhaps more evident in the cinematic tradition. Whatever the relative weight of the two novels' influence, in any case, they both share the burden of manifesting—indeed, of helping construct—a newly heightened consciousness of *wuxia xiaoshuo* as a distinct thematic genre of fiction. And it is in *Detective World*, where martial arts fiction stands shoulder to shoulder with detective fiction, that we can discern this new consciousness most clearly.

Shen Zhifang presumably hoped that the inclusion of martial arts fiction in a detective magazine would broaden the magazine's appeal. He saw the two (or, counting adventure fiction, three) types as sharing kindred features and attracting a diverse but somehow integrated audience. But the matching of martial arts fiction with detective fiction is an act more ambitious and creative than a simple pairing of preexisting and equal entities. It is a move that implicitly confers upon a body of popular yet inchoate material some of the qualities enjoyed by a fictional subtype with clearly recognizable formal and thematic characteristics, a large and established readership, and a reservoir of prestige inherited from its foreign and reformist antecedents. An integral element of the strategy is the link-age of the emergent thematic genre's name with the name of a distinctive author—distinctive in persona, in literary style, and in unique association with the target genre. Whether we designate this move as an act of creation or of recognition is perhaps immaterial. The modern martial arts novel achieved definition as a thematic genre in part through Shen Zhi-fang's promotion of Buxiaosheng's work, and the identity that it achieved was made possible in part by detective fiction's prior achievement, and modeling, of a marketable thematic genre identity.

CHAPTER FOUR

Form and Medium

The Serialized Linked-Chapter Novel and Beyond

The previous chapter has argued that Shen Zhifang's promotion of Xiang Kairan and his works simultaneously contributed to and was aided by the conscious definition of *wuxia xiaoshuo* as a thematic genre. It is in part the conscious deployment of this thematic genre as a marketable entity on a par with detective fiction that distinguishes modern martial arts fiction from the rich and varied mass of fiction on martial and chivalric themes from which it emerged. The present chapter turns from the question of thematic genre to questions of form and medium. In the first two decades of the twentieth century, martial and chivalric themes found expression in a variety of literary forms as well as in nonliterary media. Xiang Kairan wrote martial arts fiction in both the literary and vernacular linguistic registers and as short stories and collections of anecdotes as well as long-form novels. The phenomenal success of his *Rivers and Lakes* and *Modern Times*, however, established a privileged connection between modern martial arts fiction and the novel. From Xiang Kairan's imitators and successors in the Republican era, through the postwar masters Jin Yong and Liang Yusheng in Hong Kong, all the way to contemporary producers of martial arts fiction for readers online—all have worked primarily in long-form fiction, to the point where *wuxia xiaoshuo* can reasonably be translated as "the martial arts novel" rather than "martial arts fiction," short-form works being ancillary to the central tradition. What's more, until the stylistic and formal experiments of Gu Long 古龍 and Wen Rui'an (Woon Swee Oan) 溫瑞安 in the late 1960s and 1970s, long-form martial arts fiction, even as it absorbed techniques and sensibilities associated with fiction in its modern and Western forms, still maintained conscious affiliations with the formal and narratological features of the traditional Chinese linked-chapter novel (*zhanghui xiaoshuo* 章回小說). And affiliation with the particular form of the linked-chapter novel served as both a token of and a medium for a deeper affiliation with the discursive parameters of the "different fiction" of *xiaoshuo*.

Like the definition of martial arts fiction as a thematic genre, so too was the association between martial arts fiction and the traditional linked-chapter novel strengthened by World Books' presentation of Xiang Kairan's two major works. World Books highlighted the synergy between characteristic features of the linked-chapter novel form (including linguistic register, narratorial voice, scope of content, and the internal structuring of the text) and certain specific contexts of literary production in Republican-era China (the role of the periodical press in the commercial publishing industry and the contentious discourse over "new" and "old" fiction) to the point that it is not inappropriate to recognize the serialized linked-chapter novel as a distinctive mediatized form. The Republican-era serialized linked-chapter novel was not the province of martial arts fiction alone: it found perhaps its most ideal expression in *Scarlet*'s serialization of the social novel *New Shanghai Tides*. But the presentation of *Rivers and Lakes* and *Modern Times* as serialized linked-chapter novels contributed to the identity and success of these works and of the thematic genre they were heralded as representing. At the same time, however, the appeal of these texts supported their continuation beyond the limits of periodical serialization, and the success of the thematic genre spilled beyond strictly literary expressions into adaptations in other media.

THE LINKED-CHAPTER NOVEL

The identification of the linked-chapter novel as a form with a central role in the premodern tradition of Chinese fiction is a product of modern literary historiography. We can see in the remarks of Qing-dynasty critics and commentators the perception that works that will later be described as *zhanghui xiaoshuo* share characteristics that distinguish them from other forms of writing. By the eighteenth century, likewise, the term *zhanghui* has entered circulation, as in *The Story of the Stone*'s mention of dividing material into chapters (*fen chu zhanghui* 分出章回) as part of a process of composition and revision.[1] It is not until the first decade of the twentieth century, however, that we find *zhanghui xiaoshuo* explicitly identified as a type of Chinese fiction—identified still, at this point, in terms of representative texts and a concomitant sense of historical tradition and not yet through a catalogue of defining characteristics.[2] This tentative establishment of the category took place in the context of the late-Qing "Revolution in Fiction." It was motivated in part by that movement's urgent interest in the nature and roles of *xiaoshuo* and found expression within the expansion of the print medium that both drove and facilitated the movement as a whole.

By the middle of the twentieth century, literary historiography had reached a consensus on the defining features of the form. The typical Chinese *zhanghui xiaoshuo* was and is understood to be a vernacular prose narrative of extended length, relating a tale of expansive scope, involving a multitude of characters and interwoven plot lines. The text is divided into numerous narrative units of roughly equal length—the eponymous *zhang* or *hui* chapters—which are furnished with individual titles, often in the form of parallel couplets. The narrative is presented through a voice that simulates a professional storyteller's address to his audience, commenting on characters and actions and drawing attention to the artful manipulation of narrative material, the latter most characteristically at the junctures between chapters: "If you want to know what happened next, read on!" The formal segmentation of the text into interconnected units often works hand in hand with a structural predilection for building the narrative out of discrete episodes involving various members of the large cast of characters. But the linking of formal and structural segments was not indefinitely extensible; the classic linked-chapter novels of the Ming and Qing dynasties were finite texts, bringing their narratives to clearly defined resolutions, often via architectural symmetries in which balanced groups of chapters played a role.[3] A number of these novels later inspired sequels, that is, new works that used characters and plot elements from the original novel to create a narrative that extended beyond the parent work's intended closure.[4] And the late Qing saw a vogue for chapter fiction taking the form of what we can call series as distinct from sequels: open-ended continuations of the episodic adventures of a particular figure or group of figures, published in successive volumes. In extending the traditional injunction to read the next chapter to a call to buy the next volume, these series join traditional narrative rhetoric with the dynamics of a burgeoning commercial publishing industry.[5] In the context of the present study it is also worth noting that these series typically centered on the exploits of martial heroes—the champions gathered around the righteous Judge Bao or the eccentric martial/magical monk Ji Gong.[6]

Concomitant with the delineation of the form's characteristics emerged an account of its history. Its distinctive voice and structure were understood to have roots in the segmented sequential storytelling sessions of professional performers in the Song and Yuan dynasties. The Ming saw the development and consolidation of *zhanghui xiaoshuo* as a written form, the mid-Qing the production of unique masterworks (*The Scholars*, *The Story of the Stone*), and the nineteenth century a long stretch of imitation, formulaicism, and sequels. The late-Qing Revolution in Fiction spurred the conscious definition of the form; reinvigorated it, introducing new subject matters and making it a vehicle for new intellectual and political projects; and challenged it, by bringing it into dialogue with new theories and models of fiction from abroad.

Both the renewed interest in fiction and a proliferation of periodical publications fed, and were in turn fed by, the late-Qing growth of the publishing industry. Like novels in series, commercial periodicals served publishers in their quest to provide a continuous flow of material to the buying public. Periodicals differed from series in that they appeared at regular (at least in theory) and frequent intervals and in that the unit of recurrence was the periodical, a kind of textual assemblage, rather than any specific individual text. Fictional texts appeared in general-interest periodicals and newspapers as well as in dedicated fiction journals, and they accommodated themselves to the periodical medium in a variety of ways. It is no surprise to find an awareness of congruencies between the developing conventions of periodical publication and the traditional form of the linked-chapter novel. We may take as an example the first issue of Liang Qichao's iconic *New Fiction* (*Xin xiaoshuo* 新小說, 1902). A call for contributions defines as the first category of desired material "chapter-form novels of over ten chapters and dramatic librettos of over ten scenes"

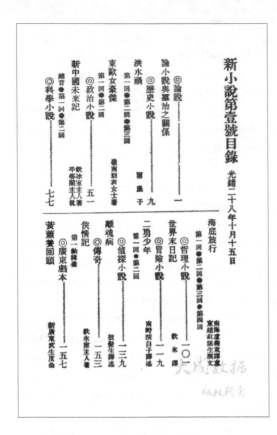

FIGURE 4.1 *New Fiction* 1, no. 1 (1902), first page of the table of contents. For serialized novels, the title is followed by an enumeration of the chapters printed in the current issue.

Source: Author's scan, from a copy in the collection of the University of Washington Libraries.

(章回體小說在十數回以上者及傳奇曲本在十數齣以上者).[7] The table of contents lists the issue's fiction under the thematic categories previously discussed; following the individual titles we then see, in most cases, an enumeration of chapters: "Chapter 1, Chapter 2" (figure 4.1). The works of fiction lacking such annotation are complete in this issue, and those furnished with it will be continued; in the latter case, the conventional closing "If you want to know the full story, wait and hear the next chapter's explanation!" (要知端的且聽下回分解) directs readers simultaneously to the next unit of the text and the next issue of the publication.[8] Des Forges notes that scholarship on serialized publication in China has typically seen "the conventions of linked chapter (*zhanghui*) vernacular fiction of the Ming and Qing as a direct and unproblematic precursor to the installment form."[9] It is often assumed, that is, that a set of textual conventions that allegedly had its basis in one mode of production and communication (oral storytelling sessions) comes home to a new mode of distribution (installment publication) that gives the conventions renewed function and validation. As Des Forges goes on to demonstrate, however, this account of a "natural fit" is complicated by the fact that the earliest fiction published in chapter-length installments eschewed the narratorial hooks between one chapter and the next, while the first installment novel to include them was published in a newspaper one page at a time, eliminating any congruence between unit of narrative and unit of publication and limiting such phrases' function to the rhetorical and ornamental.[10] When *New Fiction* and later periodicals link textual structure with installment form, they do so not as the result of some process of natural evolution but rather by editorial choice.

While long-form fiction in serialization dominates the literary periodicals of the first decade of the twentieth century, short fiction gains ground in the 1910s. The shift may have been in part a response to reader frustration with the discontinued journals and unfinished novels of the previous period, in part an editorial strategy for varying the content of literary periodicals and in part an exploration by authors of the possibilities for short fiction revealed by foreign models. Some writers and critics reveal a nascent awareness of the Western-style short story as a form defined not by word count but by a distinctive perspective and aesthetic.[11] But editors of the time seem to have used the terms *duanpian xiaoshuo* 短篇小說 (short fiction) and *changpian xiaoshuo* 長篇小說 (long fiction) primarily as simple indicators of a work's length. Inclusion in one category or the other implicitly indicated whether a piece of fiction was complete in a given issue or continued in other numbers, but the terms were otherwise value free and broadly inclusive. We see them used in this fashion, for instance, in the table of contents of the February 1915 issue of *Short Story Magazine* (*Xiaoshuo yuebao* 小說月報) (figure 4.2)—one of the leading literary periodicals of the 1910s and 1920s and one that despite its English title (provided by the publisher on the colophon page) published fiction in both long/serialized and short/nonserialized forms from its first issue on.

In the latter years of the 1910s, however, writers and critics associated with the New Culture and May Fourth movements took steps to appropriate and redefine the terminology as part of their advocacy of a radically new literature that would serve in the vanguard of a broader

FIGURE 4.2 *Short Story Magazine* 6, no. 2 (February 1915), first page of the table of contents. Fiction is categorized as "long form" (*changpian*) or "short form" (*duanpian*).

Source: Author's scan, from a copy in the collection of the University of Washington Libraries.

struggle between old and new cultural ideologies. Building on the discourse of the previous generation, they employed the term *xiaoshuo* not as the miscellaneous category of premodern bibliographers but as a surrogate for the English "fiction." This newly (and nebulously) identified literary category was in turn seen as constituted by two distinct genres, the "novel" and the "short story." To render these two concepts, the terms *changpian xiaoshuo* and *duanpian xiaoshuo* were pressed into service—a move that required disassociating them from their previous, more neutrally descriptive meanings. Thus Hu Shi's 1918 "On the Short Story" ("Lun duanpian xiaoshuo" 論短篇小說) takes pains to explain that "the 'short story' of the West . . . has a definite scope within literature and a particular character; something is not called a 'short story' simply on the basis of its length. . . . The short story is a piece of writing that is able to provide complete satisfaction by using the most economical literary methods to describe a most essential and interesting segment or aspect of reality."[12]

He goes on to make clear that of the two genres, the short story and the novel, it is the former that most perfectly embodies the radical modernity expressed by fiction in the new sense of the word. The short story joins lyric verse and the one-act play in manifesting a global literary trend toward brevity and concision—a trend motivated both by internal literary factors and by modern life's overarching drive toward "economy." It is in this regard, above all, that China's current literature falls (as it were) short:

> The Chinese literature of today is the least concerned with "economy." The masters of archaic prose and writers of hackneyed *Strange Tales* fiction can only record wooden accounts of how "at a certain time, at a certain place, a certain person did a certain thing"; they haven't the slightest notion that the representation of event and the evocation of emotion are entirely dependent upon discrete particulars. The writers of long-form fiction are capable only of creating interminable novels in the mode of *The Nine-Tailed Tortoise*; they don't know the slightest thing about form or composition, much less literary economy. It is impossible to remedy these two flaws without promoting the most economical of all forms—without promoting the true "short story."[13]

In this passage Hu Shi uses the term *duanpian xiaoshuo* in the new sense but *changpian xiaoshuo* in the old, underscoring (almost in contradiction of his earlier disavowal of brevity alone as the criterion for the "short story") a default association between length and outmoded fictional form. And while he does not identify the category of *zhanghui xiaoshuo* as such, much less mention the practice of serialization, the example he cites would have been instantly recognizable to his readers as a paradigm of *zhanghui* form, of sheer length, and of extended publication: Zhang Chunfan's 張春帆 popular *Nine-Tailed Tortoise* (*Jiuwei gui* 九尾龜) ran to a staggering total of 192 chapters, originally serialized in a variety of newspapers and published in twelve successive collections (*ji* 集) between 1906 and 1910.[14]

For May Fourth critics, *zhanghui xiaoshuo* thus epitomizes the ills of Chinese fiction or, more precisely, of those writings that fall into the new category of "fiction" in its most capacious sense yet utterly fail to realize the genre's modern essence.[15] The naming and description of *zhanghui xiaoshuo* goes hand in hand with its relegation to the dustbin of literary history; the form is recognized in order to serve as the past against which the "new fiction" defines its modernity. In the 1922 "Naturalism and Modern Chinese Fiction" ("Ziranzhuyi yu Zhongguo xiandai xiaoshuo" 自然主義與中國現代小說), Shen Yanbing 沈雁冰 (Mao Dun 茅盾) wastes no time in identifying *zhanghui xiaoshuo* as the first and most egregious of the three types of "old school" (*jiupai* 舊派) fiction he undertakes to dissect, and he seems to be irked not only by the form's tenaciousness and ubiquity but especially by its combination of features he values—the use of the vernacular language and the portrayal of contemporary society—with others he despises—a wooden form, a shopworn narratorial toolkit, a lifeless ideological perspective.[16] Shen Yanbing's discussion is significant not only for its substance but also for the forum in which it appears. Hu Shi's 1918 essay had been published in the journal *New Youth* for a core audience of engaged intellectuals (in the same issue as Lu Xun's "Diary of a Madman" ["Kuangren riji" 狂人日記], which was hailed as the first modern short story in Chinese); Shen Yanbing's 1922 article appears in *The Short Story Magazine*, the flagship literary periodical from China's leading publisher, Commercial Press, shortly after Shen had assumed the role of the magazine's general editor. In terms of publication venue, the advocacy of new fiction and the critique of the old have moved from an elite margin into the mainstream. And it is no surprise to find that advocacy is matched by practice: serialized fiction is absent from the first issues of *The Short Story Magazine* produced under Shen's watch.[17]

Literary historiography rightly portrays Shen Yanbing's establishment of a "New Tides in Fiction" column for *The Short Story Magazine* in 1920 and his assumption of general editorship of the magazine in 1921 as a victory for the Literary Research Association and the New Literature project more generally. But the victory was by no means a conquest either of the discursive realm of fiction or of the publishing market. To the contrary, the new fiction's enhanced profile invigorated the literary scene and helped spark the founding of numerous periodicals, some allied with the New Literature program but others not.[18]

New Literature critics had favorite targets for attack among the new journals. There was *The Story World* (*Xiaoshuo shijie* 小說世界), whose unveiling in 1923 by *The Short Story Magazine*'s own publisher, Commercial Press, allowed the May Fourth camp to howl betrayal and distance themselves from the base mercenary motives of their host. There was *Saturday* (*Libailiu* 禮拜六), whose 1921 revival after an earlier run had ended in 1916 made it ripe for characterization as the resurrected corpse of a dead literature and whose very name (together with a notorious advertisement) seemed to epitomize a reactionary notion of literature as mere diversion for the leisure hours; through the term "Saturday School" (*Libai liu pai* 禮拜六派), the magazine earned the dubious honor of serving as synecdoche for the New Literature's characterizations of its venal, immoral, and outmoded literary Other. *Scarlet*, the magazine that serialized Xiang Kairan's *Rivers and Lakes*, was singled out for critique as well. And if we turn to *Scarlet* (and its successor *Scarlet Rose*), we find that the linked-chapter novel plays a prominent role in the magazine's design and presentation. This prominence does not merely consist in the publication of texts that take linked-chapter-novel form. Rather, it involves coordinating the texts with the magazine's publication schedule, situating the texts within the magazine's overall organization, and employing the tools of graphic design, all in such a way as to harmonize the formal features of the text with the mechanics of periodical serialization and to suggest a privileged affinity between the linked-chapter novel form and the magazine's own identity. I argue that in continuing to serialize linked-chapter novels after New Literature critics had declared the form dead, *Scarlet* was not mindlessly manipulating a literary corpse but reanimating the linked-chapter novel with a spirit consciously, even defiantly informed by the practices of commercial periodical publication. Next I will examine the most distinctive of *Scarlet*'s presentations of the linked-chapter novel, its serialization of Zhou Shouju's *New Shanghai Tides*. I will then return to the serialization of Xiang Kairan's novels in *Scarlet* and elsewhere.

THE SERIALIZED LINKED-CHAPTER NOVEL: *NEW SHANGHAI TIDES*

Scarlet, published by Shen Zhifang's World Books, began weekly publication in August 1922 under the editorship of Yan Duhe 嚴獨鶴. It published fifty issues through July 27, 1923, then two weeks later began a second fifty-issue volume (*juan* 卷). After the conclusion of the second year's run, the magazine was relaunched as *The Scarlet Rose*, which began publication in August 1924.

The first issue's table of contents lists the titles and authors of the magazine's contents in three groups: a first untitled group, a second headed "short-form fiction" (*duanpian xiaoshuo* 短篇小說), and a third headed "long-form fiction" (*changpian xiaoshuo* 長篇小說) (figure 4.3). Beginning from the ninth issue, the previously untitled first group acquires the label "amusement columns" (*youxilan* 遊戲欄). The magazine's layout gives a distinctive form to this tripartite grouping of material. For the bulk of the magazine, individual pages are divided into upper and lower registers of text. The upper register carries the amusement pieces one after another; the lower runs the short fiction. Both the upper and lower registers contain twelve columns of text; each column of the upper register contains fourteen characters, each column of the lower twenty-six (figure 4.4). Exempt from this double-register layout are special materials that may appear at the beginning of the issue, advertising pages interspersed throughout, and, most notable in terms of the present inquiry, the long-form fiction section at the tail end of the magazine.

The first issue's table of contents lists a single piece of long-form fiction: *New Shanghai Tides* (*Xin Xiepu chao* 新歇浦潮), by Haishang Shuomengren. Haishang Shuomengren 海上說夢人 (The Shanghai Teller of Dreams) is the pen name of the author Zhu Shouju 朱瘦菊 (1892–1966), and *New Shanghai Tides* (hereafter *New Tides*) is a sequel to his best-known work, *The Shanghai Tide* (*Xiepu chao* 歇浦潮), which was serialized in the supplement of the Shanghai newspaper *Xin Shenbao* 新申報 from 1916 to 1921 under the editorship of Wang Dungen 王鈍根.[19] *New Tides*, like its predecessor, reflects the early Republican-era vogue for "Black Curtain" (*heimu* 黑幕) fiction—fiction that inherited from late-Qing "castigatory fiction" (*qianze xiaoshuo* 譴責小說) a mandate for social satire and critique and claimed to draw aside the curtains to reveal the grotesque and scandalous features of contemporary Chinese society.[20] Many of the same critics who objected to the linked-chapter novel on formal grounds also attacked Black Curtain fiction as ideologically bankrupt, and while Black Curtain fiction did not exclusively take the form of the linked-chapter novel (short classical-language anecdotes and collections of the same enjoyed wide circulation), Black Curtain themes dominated the linked-chapter novels of the early Republican years, and many readers and

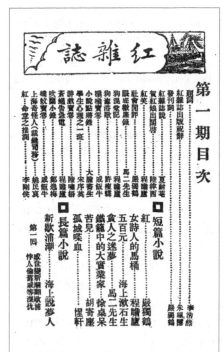

FIGURE 4.3 *The Scarlet Magazine* 1, no. 1 (August 1922), table of contents. Uncategorized items are followed by "short fiction" (*duanpian xiaoshuo*) and "long fiction" (*changpian xiaoshuo*); the latter provides the couplet-form chapter title of the first installment of *New Tides*.

Source: Author's scan, from a reprint in the collection of the University of Washington Libraries.

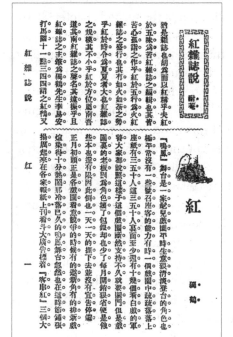

FIGURE 4.4 *The Scarlet Magazine* 1, no. 1 (August 1922). Double registers of text: miscellaneous items on the top, short fiction on the bottom.

Source: Author's scan, from a reprint in the collection of the University of Washington Libraries.

critics assumed a close association, even an identity, between Black Curtain themes and contemporary manifestations of the traditional vernacular novel.[21]

Scarlet's table of contents displays not only *New Tides'* title and author but also the full title of the first *hui* or chapter: "Chapter 1: Responding to Changes in the World, New Tides Roil the Huangpu; Resisting Larceny, an Old Relation Broods on Revenge" (*Diyi hui: Gan shibian xinchao fan Xiepu; bei ren tou jiuqi deng shenchou* 第一回 感世變新潮翻歇浦 悖人偷舊戚等深仇). The naming of the *hui* and the display of its couplet-form title immediately establish expectations that the text is not merely long-form fiction but that it will also bear the specific characteristics of the traditional linked-chapter novel. At the same time the listing serves as a marker of serialization practice. It implies that the issue will contain one complete segment, or *hui*, of the novel; this in fact proves to be the case. The installment runs to sixteen full pages of text, closing with the scene of a character's encounter with a pickpocket and the cliffhanger address to readers characteristic of the form: "So were the fifty dollars in bills actually missing from his pocket or not? You'll have to wait for the next chapter to explain!" The text proper is followed by a parenthetical clarification: "The next issue will continue with the publication of the second chapter."[22] The chapter, the structural property that defines the literary form, functions at the same time as the installment, the mechanism for the text's division between and continuance across the consecutive issues of the magazine.

The layout of the novel's text reinforces the table of contents' distinction between "long-form fiction" and "short-form fiction," further reifies the chapter as a unit of both internal form and serial presentation, and additionally indexes yet another aspect of the novel's identity: its potential publication as an independent book. Unlike the upper and lower registers in which the short fiction and miscellaneous pieces are housed, the novel's text occupies the entirety of each page, in eleven thirty-one-character columns of larger type. The formatting makes clear that one has entered a separate section within the magazine, and this awareness is buttressed by the illustrations and the pagination. Two pages of illustrations, the recto and verso of a single leaf, separate the densely printed short fiction from the more expansive novel text. Each of these two pages carries two illustrations, the only illustrations within the issue apart from occasional spot designs at the beginning or end of an item.[23] The chapter

FIGURE 4.5 *The Scarlet Magazine* 1, no. 1 (August 1922). The opening of *New Tides*: one of the two pages of illustrations fronting the chapter, faced by text in large type occupying the entire page.

Source: Author's scan, from a reprint in the collection of the University of Washington Libraries.

number and title couplet appear at the margin of each illustration page; beyond illustrating the chapter's contents, thus, the twin pages of paired illustrations echo the couplet's stylized and parallel framing of the material (figure 4.5). Finally, the pagination of the novel text is separate from that of the rest of the magazine. A single set of page numbers threads together the various items of the short fiction/miscellany section—in the first issue, they run to sixty pages altogether; following the illustrations, the novel's text begins again with page 1. And the novel's pagination is continuous across the issues of the magazine. Chapter 1 in the first issue ends on page 16, and Chapter 2 in issue 2 begins with page 17. By the end of the fiftieth chapter the novel has reached page 798. The fifty-first issue, the first of the magazine's second year, continues with chapter 51 but recommences the pagination at page 1, thereby superimposing another aspect of the magazine's publishing logic—a division into annual volumes—onto the presentation of the novel's text.

The practice of giving the pages of the novel a consecutive pagination separate from that of the individual issues of the periodical underscores both the novel's continuity and its independence. The plates prepared for the novel's magazine serialization are ready to be used without alteration for publication in book form.[24] Even were this book not to materialize, its potential existence is already evident to the magazine's reader, adumbrated for example by a notice printed at the end of the nineteenth installment (December 15, 1922), recommending the World Books printing of the novel's predecessor, *Shanghai Tides*, available at a discount for a limited time. Book publication of *New Tides* first becomes a reality in June 1924, when World Books issues the first forty chapters in four *ji* 集. This is nearly a year after the fortieth chapter's appearance in *Scarlet* 1, no. 40 (May 18, 1923), and slightly anticipates the novel's completion in vol. 2, no. 48 (July 4, 1924). The book publication is presumably timed to capitalize on interest generated by the serialization's conclusion. The term *ji* ("collection") here refers simultaneously to the four physical volumes of the publication and to the ten-chapter sets of text distributed among these volumes. The migration from serialization to book publication entails a certain restructuring of the material: the first *ji* contains two prefaces, by Yan Duhe and Zhao Tiaokuang 趙苕狂; the twenty pages of illustrations belonging to each decade are assembled at the front of the proper volume; and each volume contains the table of contents for all four *ji*. Yet the echoes of serialization are not entirely absent from this moment of book publication. The narrative rhetoric of suspense and continuation—"the next chapter will explain"—remains at the end of each chapter except the fortieth, from the end of which similar language from the serialized text has been excised. No next chapter is promised, although the narrative is in full career. Readers who purchased these four *ji* would need to wait for the publisher to continue or complete the novel with the publication of another set of *ji*; the publisher was presumably waiting for the serialized text's completion— and perhaps also for the market's response to the first forty chapters.[25]

New Tides' serialization proceeds with great regularity through the course of *Scarlet*'s publication. Each weekly issue carries a single complete chapter prefaced by its illustrations; each chapter reliably runs to sixteen pages (eight leaves) of text, with rare variations of fourteen or eighteen and occasional vacancies on the final verso filled in with an advertisement or a notice. The steady rhythm falters only after eighty-seven issues and eighty-seven chapters. Chapter 88 is split into two eight-page installments carried in vol. 2, nos. 38 and 39. The novel is absent from vol. 2, no. 40, in which the editor explains that "Haishang Shuomengren is on a trip to Hangzhou and has not sent the eighty-ninth chapter of *New Tides*. We therefore have no choice but to omit it from this issue. In any case this great work will come to its close in only two more chapters. We ask our esteemed readers to control their impatience and wait to see how it concludes."[26] Chapter 89 is likewise split between two issues, vol. 2, nos. 41 and 42; the novel is again absent from nos. 43 through 47 and then concludes with the ninetieth chapter in vol. 2, no. 48.[27] The magazine's one hundredth issue is its last, pending its restart under the title *The Scarlet Rose* in August 1924. And so the life span of the periodical and the life span of the novel in its original serialized form are very nearly coterminous.

Variations on this treatment of serialized linked-chapter novels can be found in other periodicals from World Books. *Merry Magazine* (*Kuaihuo* 快活; a weekly launched in January 1922 under the editorship of Li Hanqiu 李涵秋) divided its fiction into short-form (*duanpian*) and long-form (*changpian*) in the table of contents. The long-form serializations in the early issues included "new-style" fiction and a classical-language love story by Xu Zhenya 徐枕亞 as well as an item in linked-chapter novel form, Li Hanqiu's *Strange Things Witnessed Over the Last Ten Years* (*Jin shinian mudu zhi guai xianzhuang* 近十年目睹之怪現狀); the serializations alternate from issue to issue rather than being serialized continuously. *The Home Companion* (*Jiating zazhi* 家庭雜誌; January 1922, monthly, ed. Jiang Hongjiao 江紅蕉) more closely approximated *Scarlet*'s presentation of linked-chapter novels. *Companion* mixed domestic-themed short- and long-form fiction with articles on family and household management; short fiction was interspersed among the nonfiction articles, while serialized long-form fiction was grouped together at the rear of each issue. Although the table of contents furnished no categories, it made the serialized material readily identifiable through the specification, between title and author, of a particular issue's installment ("Chapter 1"). From its first issue the magazine began serializing one prosimetric ballad (*tanci* 彈詞) and two linked-chapter novels, Bi Yihong's 畢倚虹 *A Troubled Household* (*Kunao jiating* 苦惱家庭) and the editor's own *After the Wedding* (*Jiahou guangyin* 嫁後光陰). These linked-chapter novels were published in one full chapter per issue. Each chapter was individually paginated and prefaced by two pages of illustrations keyed to the events highlighted in the couplet chapter-title.

Just how distinctive such treatment of the linked-chapter novel was becomes evident when we compare others of *Scarlet*'s contemporaries. The 1921 relaunch of *Saturday* primarily featured short fiction. The first issue included the initial installments of two serialized items: Tianxuwosheng's 天虛我生 "Who Am I?" (*Wo wei shei* 我為誰), a piece of "new-style" fiction with a first-person narrator-protagonist, and "The Chopped-Finger Gang" (*Duanzhi dang* 斷指黨), a detective story by Cheng Xiaoqing. Tianxuwosheng's novel was labeled as long form in the table of contents, but neither serialization was in traditional linked-chapter novel form nor received presentation any different from that of the issue's short fiction. *The Half Moon Journal* (*Banyue* 半月; September 1921, fortnightly, ed. Zhou Shoujuan 周瘦鵑) likewise began with two serializations. These were in no way differentiated from the short fiction in the table of contents, and while one of them, Haishang Shuomengren's 海上說夢人 *Traces of Powder and Rouge* (Shengfen canzhi lu 賸粉殘脂錄), was in linked-chapter novel form and offered with a complete chapter in each issue, its layout was identical with that of the rest of the magazine's material. For a final example, *The Sunday* (*Xingqi* 星期, March 1922, weekly, ed. Bao Tianxiao 包天笑), which was later to serialize Buxiaosheng's *Supplement to the Unofficial History of Sojourners in Japan* (*Liudong waishi bu* 留東外史補), began by serializing Laozhugu's 老主顧 exposé *The True Nature of the Stock Exchange* (*Jiaoyisuo xianxing ji* 交易所現形記); although the text was in linked-chapter novel form, the table of contents gave no indication of that fact, the formatting of the text was the same as that of the short fiction, and the first issue's installment ended partway through the first chapter, with the simple notice "Continued" (*weiwan* 未完). Rarely, in short, do we find the elements we see in *Scarlet*'s presentation of the linked-chapter novel—the coordination of chapters with issues, the identification of the linked-chapter novel form in the table of contents, the foregrounding of the form's features through devices of layout and illustration—and never in such emphatic conjunction as in *Scarlet*.

Scarlet's serialization of *New Tides* achieves an almost ideal harmony between the internal formal features of the text and the mechanics of periodical serialization: in the deployment of *hui* as serial units, in the dependable regularity of these units' length and periodicity, and in the commensurability of the novel's text and the periodical's overall run. This harmony foregrounds key characteristics of the linked-chapter novel form and creates an association between that form and the periodical's own identity. The association is significant in that it constitutes a conscious investment in a literary form that prominent voices in the literary field have written off as moribund, if not already a living corpse. From the point of view of the New Culture and May Fourth movements, the "new" in the title *New Tides* is ironic or, better yet, a travesty. For what it promises is not "new," a radical break from the "old." It promises rather the very opposite: more of the same. *New Tides* is simply more of the old *Tides*. The logic of the sequel reproduces the logic of serialization: continuation, repetition, potentially endless extensibility. And the logic of the sequel is in turn reproduced in the seemingly inexhaustible reproduction of an "old" literary form, the linked-chapter novel. I argue, to the contrary, that *Scarlet*'s investment in the linked-chapter novel is a creative act. Rather than simply reproducing the traditional linked-chapter novel (if so essentialized an entity can be said to have ever existed), it reinvents it as the serialized linked-chapter novel, a form uniquely suited to the medium of periodical literary publication, and gives it a currency independent of those questions of content, technique, and ideology on the basis of which the modern validity of the linked-chapter novel was most commonly challenged.

What Chen Jianhua has called "the silence of the Butterflies"—the disinclination on the part of those writers whom May Fourth critics represented as the "Saturday School" or the "Mandarin Duck and Butterfly School" to take up the gauntlet and contest the grounds on which literary prestige and authority were to be claimed—has often been noted.[28] But what seemed to be a silence in the arena of theoretical debate was of course matched by a veritable uproar in the realm of literary production; the production of writings not identified with New Literature positions only increased in response to New Literature challenges and gains and at least through the 1920s found audiences larger and apparently more varied than those won by the self-professed vanguard of literary change. This response should not be measured in quantity of production alone nor imputed only to the writers who produced literary texts. *Scarlet*'s exploitation of the affinities between the linked-chapter novel form and the practice of serialization is a deliberate editorial choice. This choice invests serialization with significance as a contribution to contemporary debates about the nature of fiction and the roles of literature. The editor's linking periodical fiction to the essential identity of the magazine constitutes a definitive and, in the context of the times, almost defiant investment in the form. The form's significance is articulated in part through what might be considered extraliterary aspects of the text, that is, elements of publication practice, organization, and design that lie outside the parameters of the text considered as a linguistic artifact in the abstract. The materiality of the text and its imbedding in a frankly commercial context are not, as May Fourth polemicists would have it, shameful badges of "begging" or "prostitution" but rather elements of its identity and tools for its engagement with its audience and the production of meaning.

The ideal harmony between text and serialization seen in *Scarlet*'s serialization of *New Tides* was rarely—if ever—replicated. The fates of Zhu Shouju's two other serializations from more or less the same period demonstrate how difficult it might be for a serialized novel even to achieve simple completion: one was aborted after five chapters when the magazine carrying it ceased publication; the other was cut off midcourse at chapter 46, allegedly because of pressures brought to bear over the plot's mirroring of a contemporary scandal.[29] But these false starts and curtailments do not vitiate my point about the roles of the linked-chapter novel form and the practice of periodical serialization in the production of meaning; if anything, one might argue, they foreground the significance of the text's temporal situation and materiality. Let us now turn to the publication history of Xiang Kairan's most famous works.

SCARLET'S SERIALIZATION OF *RIVERS AND LAKES*

Xiang Kairan began publishing fiction in 1916 with works in a variety of forms: the "jottings" (*biji* 筆記)-style anecdotes of "Matters Pugilistic, Seen and Heard" and "Turning Pale," the longer classical tales published in *Sea of Fiction*, and his first novel, *The Unofficial History of Sojourners in Japan*. I will address aspects of the content and themes of *Sojourners* in chapter 6 of this study; for the present suffice it to say that in its seemingly inexhaustible narration of the scandalous behavior of Chinese students and exiles in Japan it clearly fits the thematic mold most closely associated with the late-Qing- and early-Republican-era linked-chapter novel, that of Black Curtain fiction. Ninety chapters, organized into five sets (*ji* 集) of from sixteen to twenty chapters each, were published in the fifth month of 1916.[30] Six years later in 1922, at the outset of the most productive five years of Xiang Kairan's authorial career, the original publisher, People's Rights Publishers (Minquan chubanbu 民權出版部), issued a sequel containing an additional seventy chapters in five "continuing sets" (*xuji* 續集). The previous ninety chapters were then considered to constitute the original volume (*zhengji* 正集, "sets proper"), and *Sojourners* as a whole consisted of 160 chapters. Even as he published the sequel or second half of the novel with his original publisher, the author produced additional continuations and extensions for other venues. The *Supplement to the Unofficial History of Sojourners in Japan* (*Liudong waishi bu* 留東外史補) began serialization in the same year in Bao Tianxiao's *The Sunday*; the *Supplement* was unfinished when the magazine folded but was published as a book by Great Eastern Books in 1926. And a *New History of Sojourners in Japan* (*Liudong xinshi* 留東新史) was serialized in the "Forest of Happiness" ("Kuaihuo lin" 快活林) supplement of the Shanghai *Xinwen bao* 新聞報 between 1923 and 1924, then published in book form by World Books in 1924.[31] The publishing history of *Sojourners* illustrates how the world of commercial publishing exploited the voluminous and extensible form of the linked-chapter novel in a manner that made porous the boundaries between book publication, sequels, and serialization.

The publication of *Modern Times* directly bridged the gap between serialization and book form. An editor's note in the first issue of *Detective World* in June 1923 announces it as a work in eighty chapters. The magazine published two full chapters in each of the first twenty-three issues, then four in its twenty-fourth and final number in May 1924, bringing the novel through chapter 50. Ten-chapter sets (*ji* 集) collecting the serialized material were published in book form beginning in Autumn 1923. These ceased after the magazine folded, but in 1926, three additional five-volume sets of new material appeared, bringing the text through chapter 65. There it remained poised until 1933, when the publication of nineteen chapters in four sets carried the eighty-four-chapter work to its conclusion.[32] It is the text of these final chapters that begins with the authorial apologia quoted in chapter 2 of this study.

When *Scarlet* began serializing *Rivers and Lakes* in January 1923, it adapted the devices employed for the concurrent serialization of *New Tides* in order to highlight the identity of Buxiaosheng's novel as another example of the linked-chapter novel form but at the same time to promote its uniqueness both as an individual work and as the harbinger of the newly defined genre of *wuxia xiaoshuo*. An advance notice in *Scarlet* 1, no. 21, alerts readers that "The long-form novel *Marvelous Gallants of the Rivers and Lakes* by Buxiaosheng will begin serialization in the next issue."[33] This notice names neither the category of linked-chapter novel nor that of martial arts fiction, although the novel's subject matter can be inferred from the title. With the commencement of the novel's publication in no. 22, the unique framing of the novel begins on the table of contents (figure 4.6). This table of contents replicates the previous issues' tripartite classification of material as entertainment items, short-form fiction, and long-form fiction, listed in upper and lower registers on the page, but it precedes these double registers by listing *Rivers and Lakes* in a single column running from the top to the bottom of the page. The novel's title is in type the same size as the magazine's; it is headed with a rubric in smaller type, "long-form martial arts fiction" (*changpian wuxia xiaoshuo*), which simultaneously places the item in the preestablished category of long-form fiction and distinguishes it as an example of a thematic subgenre. The text's allegiance to the linked-chapter novel form it shares with *New Tides* is made clear through the identification of the issue's installment as *Diyi hui* 第一回, the first chapter. Instead of providing the chapter title, however, as it does for *New Tides*, the listing then specifies the quantity of text presented: five folios (*wuzhang* 五張), that is, ten pages of text recto and verso. This choice may reflect anxiety over violating the congruence between text chapter and magazine installment that *Scarlet* has established in its printing of *New Tides*. The editor in fact takes pains to provide an explicit explanation of this practice: "*Marvelous Gallants of the Rivers and Lakes* has begun serialization in this issue. Because the original text is overly long, each chapter will be printed in its entirety across two issues. Readers please take note."[34]

Mirroring the listing in the table of contents, the actual text of the novel is given pride of place at the front of the magazine, opposite *New Tides* at the rear. Its format echoes that of its long-form peer, with page-length columns of text in large type; the text of *Rivers and Lakes*, however, is further distinguished by a graphic decoration picturing warriors on horseback, repeated across the top of each page, reducing the

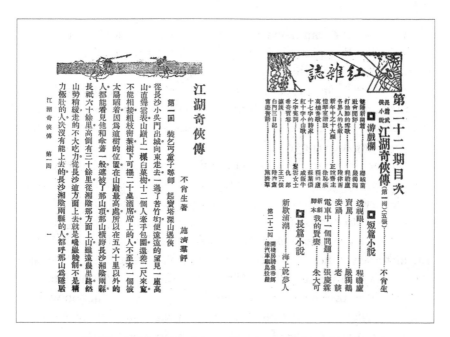

FIGURE 4.6 *The Scarlet Magazine* 1, no. 22 (January 1923): The table of contents foregrounds *Rivers and Lakes* and is immediately followed by the first page of the text.

Source: Author's scan, from a reprint in the collection of the University of Washington Libraries.

characters per column to twenty-seven from *New Tides'* thirty-one. Each chapter of the novel is indeed serialized across two consecutive issues of the magazine.[35] Illustrations in the same format as those for *New Tides*—two pages of two illustrations each, keyed to the first and second lines of the couplet chapter heading—appear at the head of each chapter's second installment. The illustrations are excluded from the pagination, which is independent of the magazine's other contents and runs continuously from one chapter to the next. Chapter length is generally greater, but also more variable, than *New Tides'* dependable fifteen to sixteen pages of text, typically running between eighteen and twenty-two pages total (that is, across two issues), though on occasion dipping to sixteen or rising to twenty-four. The text for each chapter's first installment runs to the end of the last column of type on the final page of the dedicated folios, cutting off in the middle of a sentence if the typesetting so requires and then resuming midsentence at the start of the next issue. At the tail end of each chapter, that is, in every other issue, appears commentary by Shi

Jiqun 施濟羣. The commentary text seems clearly tailored with an eye to filling out that page of the magazine, for it runs longer or shorter according to how far the chapter text falls short of the final verso of its allotted space.[36] One of the functions of the commentary text is thus to align the units of the novel with the material contingencies of periodical publication—even as the splitting of chapters in midsentence blithely abandons any such congruency.

We see the interplay between the novel's immanent identity as an independent text and the desire to integrate it with the periodical's rhythms and identity at other levels of presentation as well. The halfway mark in *Scarlet*'s hundred-issue lifespan sees additional changes. Throughout the magazine's first year, each issue is assigned a simple number, from 1 to 50. The first issue of the second year of publication is designated in the table of contents as "Issue 51" 第五十一期 but on the cover as "Volume 2 Issue 1" 二卷一期. The cover now characterizes the magazine as a "fiction weekly" (*xiaoshuo zhoukan* 小說週刊). The category *xiaoshuo* assumes greater dominance over the table of contents as well, for there the previous category of "entertainment columns" has disappeared, and all of the contents now fall under the two categories "short-form fiction" and "long-form fiction," the former including pieces of the sort that would have previously been subsumed under the "entertainment" rubric.[37] *Rivers and Lakes* takes its place beside *New Tides* under the long-form section of the table of contents, no longer given pride of place ahead of the other listings; the actual text likewise joins its serialized fellow at the end of each issue. The table of contents continues to specify the number of folios (*zhang*) printed but now matches the *New Tides* listing in printing the chapter title as well. With the start of its second year, the magazine also commences a new volume or set (*ji* 集) of the novel's text; vol. 2, no. 1's table of contents identifies the text as "Rivers and Lakes, Set II" (*Jianghu qixia zhuan er ji*) and numbers the issue's chapter as "Chapter 1" (*Diyi hui*). When we turn to the text, however, we find that while the opening page notes "Set II" after the title, the chapter is numbered in sequence with its predecessors as "Chapter 16" (*Dishiliu hui* 第十六回), and, unlike in the case of *New Tides*, the page numbers also continue in uninterrupted succession. Subsequent issues continue to note "Volume II" in the table of contents, but not at the head of the text proper, while the table of contents' numbering of the chapters reverts to the original sequence immediately in vol. 2, no. 2. Vol. 2, no. 31 designates "Chapter 31" as the beginning of "Set III" (*Disan ji* 第三集), making clear that the division of the novel into *ji* refers not to the annual volumes of the magazine's publication but to an internal division of the text into *ji* of fifteen chapters each.

This basic pattern of presentation is followed through vol. 2, no. 40. Beginning with vol. 2, no. 41, each issue publishes a full chapter of *Rivers and Lakes*, running between eighteen and twenty-nine pages (nine to fifteen folios) of text. The acceleration of the novel's publication serves *Scarlet*'s agenda for publishing linked-chapter novels in two ways. First, as *New Tides* reaches its completion and disappears from the magazine's pages, *Rivers and Lakes'* expanded presence fills out an expected quota for novel serialization.[38] Second, the accelerated publication schedule allows *Rivers and Lakes* to reach the end of its forty-fifth chapter—the third fifteen-chapter *ji*—just as the magazine completes its second year and reaches its one hundredth and final issue. An announcement on the final page of chapter 45, page 917 of the aggregate text, declares: "Since this book has not yet concluded, beginning from the forty-sixth chapter it will accordingly be published in this company's new fiction weekly *Scarlet Rose*. We respectfully hope that you esteemed gentlemen who enjoy reading it will take notice."[39]

River and Lakes *in* Scarlet Rose

Scarlet's serialization of *Rivers and Lakes* echoes its serialization of *New Tides* and similarly serves to integrate the form of the linked-chapter novel with the medium of periodical publication, to the benefit of both. The continuation of the serialization in *Scarlet Rose* affirms the continuity between the new magazine and the old. Over the course of its serialization in *Scarlet Rose*, however, *Rivers and Lakes* evolves into an entity that expands dramatically, and in several different fashions, beyond the partnership between Buxiaosheng's textual production and its periodical host. Most simply, the novel moves from periodical serialization to publication as a book—a common and planned-for transition and one we have already noted in the case of *New Tides*. At the same time, periodical serialization proves itself to be an engine whose logic and demands override individual authorial agency in the production of the text. The demands of the periodical medium join with the imperatives of an emerging thematic genre, as the success of *Rivers and Lakes* makes a major contribution to the establishment of the martial arts linked-chapter novel as a larger textual category with conjoined formal and thematic features. And lastly, the themes and imagery of the martial arts novel detach themselves from strictly textual expression as the translation of *Rivers and Lakes* to the silver screen launches the first wave of martial arts film.

Let us begin with the continuation of the novel's serialization. As the name makes clear, *Scarlet Rose* is not so much a new periodical as a relaunch of *Scarlet*. Its first issue is published on August 2, 1924, maintaining the rhythm established by the August 1922 and August 1923 inaugurations of *Scarlet's* first and second volumes; it begins, like *Scarlet*, as a weekly published in fifty-issue volumes;[40] it is nominally edited, like *Scarlet*, by Yan Duhe 嚴獨鶴;[41] and its contents and formatting mirror closely those of its predecessor. One change appears in the table of contents, which no longer provides categorizing labels under which the pieces are listed but merely distinguishes fiction from miscellaneous pieces through the use of larger and smaller type respectively. This practice establishes an equivalency between long-form fiction, that is, serialized novels, and short-form fiction; within the body of the magazine, however, familiar devices maintain the distinction between the two. Long-form fiction appears at the rear of the issue and is given formatting identical with *Scarlet's* layout for serializations, including the type size that distinguishes them from shorter, independent pieces. *Rivers and Lakes* even displays the same decorative border across the top of each page and begins in the first issue of *Scarlet Rose* with page 919 and the first half of chapter 46—a seamless continuance of the novel's previous run.[42] In *Scarlet Rose*, *Rivers and Lakes* is once again paired with a panoramic social novel revealing the tangle of lives in the modern city—in this case *New Yangzhou Tides* (*Xin Guangling chao* 新廣陵潮), a sequel to one of the most popular linked-chapter novels of the teens, Li Hanqiu's 李涵秋 (1873–1923) *Yangzhou Tides* (*Guangling chao* 新廣陵潮), composed by Cheng Zhanlu 程瞻廬 (1879–1943) on the basis of fragmentary material left by that novel's late author.[43] For the greater part of its lifespan the magazine will continue the practice, established with *Scarlet's* initial presentation of *Rivers and Lakes*, of running two serialized linked-chapter novels, one a "social novel" (*shehui xiaoshuo* 社會小說) variously inflected towards satire, Black Curtain, melodrama, and/or romance, and one a martial arts adventure. This pairing confirms the martial arts genre as content for the vessel the linked-chapter novel form provides, on a par with the familiar and ubiquitous social novel (and thus raises the possibility of thematic complementarity between the two).

Rivers and Lakes continues to run a half-chapter each issue through the fifty issues of Scarlet Rose's first year and into the second. But suddenly, at the conclusion of chapter 86,[44] the narrator rather hastily wraps up two major plot lines that have been spun out for some tens of chapters and then channels the voice of the author to announce:

> As for the enmity between the two lineages, even to this very day it has yet to be entirely resolved. I, however, having written up to this point, am not in the mood to extend the tale any farther, and shall take leave of my readers for the time being. Given the vastness of China, it's impossible to say how many inexhaustible stories remain to be written of marvelous men and marvelous events. One of these days, perhaps, if the spirit moves me, I shall write another volume or two for my readers' entertainment.[45]

The "Editor's Remarks" in the same issue offer further explanation:

> Buxiaosheng's Marvelous Gallants of the Rivers and Lakes, eighty-six chapters in all, has concluded its publication with the present issue. We have now asked him to continue with the composition of Chivalric Heroes of Modern Times, to be presented in the third volume of our magazine. Beginning with the next issue we will publish my Shattered Jade and Sunken Pearls. This is merely for the purpose of filling in the interval and allowing Buxiaosheng to rest for a bit. Our esteemed readers are all understanding individuals, and I beg your indulgence toward my unworthy scribblings.[46]

Zhao Tiaokuang's remarks confirm the expectation that a social novel will be paired with a martial arts novel by excusing the publication of his linked-chapter-novel romance as a temporary expedient pending the return of Buxiaosheng's work. Modern Times, as we have seen, had ended unfinished at chapter 50 when Detective World ceased publication, but the claim made here, that Scarlet Rose will fill its martial arts slot by resuming the serialization of Modern Times, is not fulfilled. Zhao's Shattered

Jade ends in the final issue of *Scarlet Rose*'s second year. When the third volume commences in January 1927 it carries not the promised continuation of *Modern Times* but rather the reappearance of *Rivers and Lakes*, prefaced with an elaborate narratorial disquisition:

> When *Marvelous Gallants of the Rivers and Lakes* had reached the eighty-sixth chapter, I originally intended to end it there and absolutely not continue it any further unless an appropriate opportunity should arise. There were still quite a few places where the book hadn't explained things that needed explaining or followed up on things that ought to be followed up on. So why bring it to such a muddled and casual conclusion, before I had explained matters clearly, one by one, and followed up on everything properly? No matter how able in conjecture and skilled in surmise my readers may be, they will never figure out the reason for this unless I confess it in my own words. So just what is the reason? It's actually quite funny to tell. Over the last few years I have been taking the fiction I write and selling it for cash, on the basis of the word count, in order to meet the expenses of life. It's not just that, for this reason, what I've written can't match such novelists as Shi Naian and Cao Xueqin—spending any number of years' worth of time, taking their drafts through any number of revisions before they took shape as perfected works of fiction. Because of this commercial character, I'm concerned only with rapid production, and don't even have the time to read my work a second time; I punctuate as I write, and as soon as I've finished a chapter or several pages' worth of draft, I rush right off to trade it in for money. Adding to my misfortune, I enjoy a certain meager and undeserved reputation in today's fiction circles, and the novels for which I've accepted commissions from various clients may number as many as five or six at a time. I write one or two chapters of this one and hand them over for use, then set it aside to work on that one, and once again—after no more than one or two chapters, or at most three-thousand-some characters—I have to send it off. I can't see it until it has been published, for I have no master draft at home. A given novel may have as many as several hundred names of people and places, and at the least several dozen. I rely entirely on my memory for these, and after several thousands or tens of thousands of

words, it's painfully easy to get them muddled! For these reasons I had made up my mind to bring one or two of the novels to a hasty close and ease a bit of the burden on my brain. It hadn't occurred to me that after eighty-six chapters letters of censure from my readers would come thick and fast. It was as if they were coercing me, giving me no choice but to continue writing it properly. Although the pressure leaves me feeling a bit anxious, I am at the same time quite honored that fiction of a commercial character such as mine should be able to win such favor from my readers. Once again, therefore, I marshal my spirits, and present to my readers *Rivers and Lakes* from the eighty-seventh chapter on. So let me now tell how after the burning of Red Lotus Temple . . .[47]

And so the serialization resumes. It disappears from the magazine once again, this time for good, in January 1929. I shall return shortly to the details of the serialization. First, though, let us take note of the passage's representation of the practice of writing fiction. In July the narrator presents himself as a chronicler succumbing before the inexhaustible fecundity of his material; in January, resuming his labors, he admits to the role of a jaded fabricator eager to make the chore of producing fodder for a hungry public as painless for himself as possible. The author-narrator readily confesses the sins often imputed to serialized fiction, in China and elsewhere: prolixity, carelessness, and, more fundamentally, the monetary imperative that motivates these formal and aesthetic flaws.[48] And he acknowledges the resultant gap between a commercial product and a "perfected work of fiction," lovingly crafted and reworked by its author over a period of years if not decades before being released to its public. In short, this apologia sounds many of the same notes as the similar passage, discussed in chapter 2 of this study, with which the author resumed *Modern Times* after a five-year hiatus. Yet it is not clear whether what we hear here is the voice of the author at all. As we shall see, the latter chapters of the novel were a forgery published under the name of Buxiaosheng, and exactly where the historical author's production of the text gave way to the work of his stand-in, the projected author that the success of the novel created, is a matter still under debate.

The novel's unexpected and elaborately explained resumption proceeds at an uncertain pace. The serialization runs for four issues, through the end of chapter 88, and then disappears. Only after three issues have passed without an episode of *Rivers and Lakes*—a gap of a month and a half's time, on account of a Lunar New Year break in publication—does the editor offer his apologies and explain that the novel must "pause for a few issues" because the author has gone to Hunan to take up office and "doesn't have time at present to write." "But I can promise our readers," he continues, "that as soon as his affairs have settled down a bit, he will be sending us the continuation."[49] Sure enough, before the month is out, the editor returns with the "happy tidings" that Buxiaosheng has resumed his submissions. "It is truly moving that amid the welter of military correspondence he is willing to make the time to write for our *Scarlet Rose*. [The manuscript] is already in the hands of our typesetters."[50] And in vol. 3, no. 11, the serialization resumes with the commencement of chapter 89. But publication is now intermittent, most typically with a chapter in two installments followed by an absence of two issues.

Scarlet Rose continues to serialize *Rivers and Lakes* in this fashion through December 1928. In vol. 4, no. 34, the text of the novel's 106th chapter concludes on page 2,612 of the continuous pagination, ending, as have its predecessors, with the linked-chapter novel's traditional invitation to read on: "If you wish to know what happened next, please listen to the next chapter's account." *Rivers and Lakes* is absent from the next issue, as is not unusual, but so too is its current counterpart, Yan Duhe's 嚴獨鶴 social linked-chapter novel *A Dream of the Human Sea* (*Renhai meng* 人海夢). In his notes at the head of the issue the editor apologizes for *Human Sea*'s absence. He promises that it will be made up next time with a full chapter of either *Rivers and Lakes* or of *Human Sea* and, further, that arrangements will be made for more reliable publication of serialized fiction in the future.[51] The first promise is not fulfilled; vol. 4, no. 36, the last issue of the fourth volume, provides installments of neither of the current serializations and must apologize yet again for the absence of *Human Sea*. The editor does include a lengthy preview of the upcoming fifth volume of the magazine, which explains that Yao Min'ai's 姚民哀 *Dragons of the Four Seas* (*Sihai qunlong ji* 四海群龍記) will publish a full chapter (*hui*) in every issue and will be paired not with one social novel but with two appearing in alternation—the continuation of Yan Duhe's *Ocean* and Cheng Danlu's 程瞻廬 fledgling *Hilarious New History* (*Huaji xinshi* 滑稽新史). One of these upcoming attractions, Yao Min'ai's *Dragons*, is given its own full-page ad in addition to mention in the editor's notes; what's more, as a special gift to the magazine's readers, the present issue presents the novel's first chapter in full.[52] Thus, with some fanfare and perhaps a bit of mystery, Yao Min'ai's *Dragons* comes to replace Xiang Kairan's *Rivers and Lakes* as *Scarlet Rose*'s serialized martial arts novel.

RIVERS AND LAKES AS GENERIC AND MATERIAL PARADIGM

Let us talk first about the fanfare, that is, the presentation and marketing of Yao Min'ai's fiction. There is more to *Dragons'* succession to *Rivers and Lakes'* place than a simple series of texts related to a common thematic category. *Scarlet Rose*'s presentation of Yao's fiction confirms and clarifies the extent to which the magazine has created a role for the serialized chapter novel in the construction of its own identity, its election of martial arts fiction as one candidate for filling this role, the subordination of individual texts to the role's requirements, and the deployment of elements of the periodical's materiality and visual design in the articulation of this role. Yao Min'ai's early fiction, much of it in the classical register, dealt primarily with social and romantic themes.[53] In July and August 1922, *The Half Moon Journal* (*Banyue* 半月) published one of his first forays into martial arts material, "A Record of the Sanyi Tavern in Qicun" ("Ji Qicun Sanyidian" 記齊村三義店. This medium-length story (approximately 9,600 characters on twenty-five pages) was serialized in three consecutive issues of the magazine, with none of the trappings of the linked-chapter novel. Yao solidified his reputation as an author of "secret society" (*danghui* 黨會 or *banghui* 幫會) novels—martial arts tales seasoned with purportedly authentic representations of the rituals, personalities, lore, and secret jargon of the underworld of the Rivers and Lakes—with the following year's *Highwaymen of Shandong* (*Shandong xiangma zhuan* 山東響馬傳), a tale inspired by and exploiting the notoriety of the Lincheng train robbery of May 1923.[54] *Highwaymen* appeared in World Books' *Detective World*, which was serializing Buxiaosheng's *Modern Times*, but while *Modern Times* was published in regular two-*hui* installments formatted so as to highlight the congruence of the linked-chapter novel form and periodical publication, *Highwaymen* appeared in six irregularly spaced segments, totaling some 44,000 characters on 101 pages, the text free of the apparatus of couplet chapter-titles and narrator-staged cliffhangers, printed in a format identical with that of the bulk of the issue's contents.[55] Similar treatment was afforded to the series of long-form tales Yao published in *Scarlet Rose* beginning in February 1926, concurrent with that magazine's ongoing serialization of Buxiaosheng's *Rivers and Lakes*. *Blood of the Stallion* (*Longju zouxue ji* 龍駒走血記) and its successors are each published in from four to a dozen continuous installments.[56] The installments are numbered, in most cases identified as "sections" (*jie* 節) or "chapters" (*zhang* 章), and also in most cases furnished with short (noncouplet) titles. Yet the absence of the explicit textual and narratorial markers of the traditional linked-chapter novel surprisingly compels the editor to explain to his readers the relationship between one installment and the next; thus, at the head of the third installment of *Stallion*: "This piece as a whole is divided into four sections. The first and second sections have already been published in the sixteenth and seventeenth issues of this periodical respectively."[57] The editor likewise steps in to explain the relationship between the four tales in the series; thus, at the beginning of the second, *The War of the Three Phoenixes*: "This piece has been written to follow *Blood of the Stallion*, but they deal with two different matters. You can therefore read them either separately or together. It will be published in a total of four installments."[58] Despite strong similarities of material, language, and narrative design, it is clear that Yao Min'ai's series of serialized tales is meant not to infringe upon *Rivers and Lakes*' status as one of the two linked-chapter novel serializations anchoring the periodical. A novel by Yao serialized in a rival publication has, in contrast, all the standard trappings of the linked-chapter novel form.[59]

Once *Rivers and Lakes* disappears, however, Yao Min'ai's fiction steps directly into its role. In content and language, *Dragons* is much of a piece with Yao's secret-society tales previously published in *Scarlet Rose*. Unlike them, though, its text is organized into chapters designated as *hui*, each with a couplet title and the elaborate closing—narratorial stage-managing, including a final couplet and a hook for the subsequent *hui*—characteristic of the linked-chapter novel form. It is printed in the larger type *Scarlet Rose* employs for its linked-chapter novels. Like the other linked-chapter novels, it also maintains old styles of punctuation and paragraph formatting, even though by this time the bulk of the periodical's contents have adopted the "modern" punctuation championed by the New

FIGURE 4.7 *Scarlet Rose* 5, no. 1 (February 1929): The first page of Yao Min'ai's *Dragons*, with a graphic header inherited from *Rivers and Lakes*. Note that the facing final page of a Cheng Xiaoqing detective story is printed in double registers and with modern-style punctuation.

Source: Author's scan, from a copy in the collection of the University of Washington Libraries.

Literature movement. *Dragons* is distinguished from the other linked-chapter novels and further branded as the successor to *Rivers and Lakes* through its inheritance of its predecessor's martial-themed graphic header (figure 4.7). Its supertitle designates it not, like its predecessors, as a "secret-society novel" (黨會小說) but as "secret tidings of the Rivers and Lakes" (江湖秘聞)—a label that reinforces its affinity with Xiang Kairan's iconic novel. And its signal role in the branding of the periodical's own identity is marked by the resumption of the practice of aligning the serialized linked-chapter novel's text with the magazine's yearly run.[60] Yet the adaptation of Yao Min'ai's martial arts fiction to the linked-chapter novel form extends beyond the agenda of the magazine alone. When *Highwaymen*, the work that established his reputation, was published in book form, it was edited and recast as a linked-chapter novel.[61] *Blood of the Stallion* and its three sequels from *Scarlet Rose*, likewise, were combined, divided into couplet-titled *zhanghui* chapters, and renamed *Bold Gallants of the Rivers and Lakes* (*Jianghu haoxia zhuan* 江湖豪俠傳) for book publication.[62]

Yao Min'ai reflects on the linked-chapter novel form at the beginning of the first of *Dragons'* sequels, the 1930 *Bandit King*. The first *hui* of the text proper is preceded by an eight-page "Important Announcement at the Opening of This Book" ("Benshu kaichang de zhongyao baogao" 本書開場的重要報告), which explains why the new annual volume of *Scarlet Rose* is presenting *Bandit King* instead of resuming the unfinished narrative business of *Dragons* in a second volume (*ji*) of that novel. The author/narrator declares that he has gathered material on the deeds of more than fifty heroes and heroines of the secret societies of the Rivers and Lakes and, rather than dispersing it among pieces of short fiction, had envisioned weaving it into a vast "martial-arts secret-society social novel in a linked-ring form, separable into parts but combinable into a whole." His talents, however, are not sufficient to do the material justice in the manner of the structural models for such a work, *The Water Margin* and *The Scholars*. The majority of today's readers, moreover, hold a "faster is better" attitude and would find a novel of the requisite hundreds of *hui* too tedious to read. The author has therefore divided his material into a series of discrete yet interconnected works. "The readers have a bit more freedom; they can read on continuously at any time, and can also leave off in the middle as they like."[63]

The author, presumably in concert with his editor, seeks the balance between the appeal of the linked-chapter novel form and the needs and habits of contemporary periodical readers. The serialization of *Rivers and Lakes* had foundered on the impulse to extend indefinitely the affinity between episodic structure and serial publication. Yao Min'ai's novels, even as they assume the mantle of Buxiaosheng's serialization, employ a different strategy. Like Hu Shi, the author addresses the connection between literary form and a need for speed that is integral to the modern experience. But he shuns Hu Shi's conclusion that the short story is the optimal form for modern fiction. Short fiction would not do justice to his material; instead of "using [the material] up by throwing together some short pieces, scattered like dogs and chickens," he opts to modify the form of the linked-chapter novel, exploiting the possibilities for segmentation and connection available through the medium of periodical publication. The attempt to honor and preserve a familiar form while adapting it to contemporary sensibilities is quite conscious, and it is made explicit to the readers; indeed, the "Announcement" that broaches the problem is itself performative of the issues involved. It begins by identifying some of the distinctive formal features of the linked-chapter novel: "According to the standard practice of old-style fiction, at the head of each entire work stands a statement of a few 'general principles,' and each individual chapter then begins with some sort of poem or lyric." But in an age when people are unwilling to take a train unless it's an express, much less proceed to their destination by cart or foot, the practice of furnishing the front of a novel with general principles, prefaces, and dedications has fallen into disuse, and most works launch right into the action of the first *hui*. It's only the need to explain the relation between *Bandit King* and its predecessor *Dragons* that compels the author to employ the old practice of introductory remarks. And the utilitarian title he gives these remarks bespeaks on yet another level the adaptation of inherited form to present needs.

Not all of the martial-arts-themed fiction of the early 1920s, whether published through World Books or elsewhere, was in linked-chapter novel form. By no means did all of the linked-chapter novels of the period belong to the genre of martial arts fiction. It is clear, however, that World Books publications actively promoted the linked-chapter novel form as one among several options for the production and circulation of fiction—not out of ignorance of or disinterest in contemporary literary developments but from a conscious desire, informed no doubt by an assessment of audience preferences, to make use of modes of expression marked as indigenous and familiar. World Books further elected the thematic genre of martial arts fiction as an appropriate match for the linked-chapter novel form. And in a strategy that increased the symbolic capital of the genre, the form, the author, and the publisher simultaneously, it presented the martial arts linked-chapter novel fiction of Xiang Kairan as the exemplar of this felicitous pairing, the formal and generic mold into which other texts might step.

BEYOND THE AUTHOR

The fanfare surrounding *Dragons*' replacement of *Rivers and Lakes* thus gives us further insight into the periodical's role in constructing genre and form and the relationship between the two. A related but different set of questions attends the mystery of this succession or, more precisely, of *Rivers and Lakes'* disappearance from the pages of the magazine. On the face of it, to be sure, this disappearance was scarcely a mystery at all. As we have already seen, the volatility of Republican-era commercial publishing, the particular mechanics of serialization, and the universal vicissitudes of human life ensured that the midcourse cessation of a serialized novel was by no means uncommon. *Scarlet Rose's* practice of providing its readers with frequent updates and previews of its contents makes the editor's silence on the fate of *Rivers and Lakes* after the fourth volume of the magazine seem somewhat unusual; on the other hand, though, the serialization's previous history of stops and starts, the report that the author had returned to his native Hunan to take up office, and the subsequent portrait of his author stealing time to write amid pressing military duties suggested a ready explanation for the interruption or even termination of the periodic supply of text.

Mystery and controversy surfaced nonetheless. Early in 1929, only a few months after *Scarlet Rose's* serialization of the novel had ceased, rumors that Xiang Kairan was dead began to circulate in the Shanghai press.[64] By the end of the summer these tales had been refuted by more accurate reports that he was alive and in the north. Before being laid to rest, however, the reports of his demise drew attention to another issue: the question of the authenticity of works published under his name. Papers in the north questioned the authorship of a novel announced for serialization under Xiang Kairan's name in the *Liaoning xinbao* 遼寧新報, while Shanghai tabloids such as *Qiongbao* 瓊報 and *Tanbao* 灘報 accused *Scarlet Rose's* editor Zhao Tiaokuang of forging the later chapters of *Rivers and Lakes*.[65] The news of Buxiaosheng's continued existence was followed by the tidings that he had resumed, or intended to resume, his writing career; these were followed in turn by reports that he had approached publishers in Shanghai in order to discuss prospects for the future but also to seek settlement for infringements on his name. *Rivers and Lakes*, although the most prominent instance of such infringement, was not the only one:

> Pingjiang Buxiaosheng Mr. Xiang Kairan, after receiving eight thousand *yuan* as a special gift of thanks from World Books [for] *Rivers and Lakes*, has now engaged a lawyer to sue Shihuan shuju 時還書局 in provisional court. Shihuan has made a steady profit on martial arts

novels, among them the book *The Tale of the Flying Head at Midnight*. The first two volumes were indeed by Mr. Xiang; afterward Shihuan engaged the Fisher-Hermit of Sijiang to continue it and bring it to completion. On the cover of the book, however, they omitted the Fisher-Hermit of Sijiang's name and wrote only Buxiaosheng. With this evidence in hand Mr. Xiang has initiated a formal suit. On Shihuan's part Haishang Shushisheng Sun Yusheng has engaged a lawyer for the defense. There's certain to be a spell of "tongues like swords and lips like spears"![66]

The author, far from dead, asserts the ownership of his intellectual property in a court of law. While the case illustrates the development of copyright in Republican-era China,[67] Xiang Kairan's efforts throw into relief the power of the forces against which he struggles—not a death of the author in the Barthesian sense of the bankruptcy of the hermeneutic valence of notions of authorial design but rather a death or even transcendence of the author in the sense of textual production that escapes individual control. The media attention to Xiang Kairan's activities testifies to the concretization of perceptions of the author as an individual in society, even a celebrity, an object of interest beyond the texts he has created. But the pen name under whose sign he has created those texts, and on the basis of whose creations his identity as an author is constructed, is susceptible to deployment by other agents—writers, publishers, distributors—with vested interests in expanding, through continuation, sequelization, and imitation, the body of texts enjoying that pen name's consecration. The extension of particular works and the extension of the authority of the authorial name, even if eventually checked, contribute to the formation of a larger body of texts marked as sharing particular characteristics—in other words, a thematic genre. Thus it is that we see the consolidation of martial arts fiction as a genre linked both with specialized publishing concerns and with the shadow of the "founding father's" name.

The unauthorized continuation of *Rivers and Lakes* involved not only the later chapters of the magazine serialization but also the book publication of the novel. Gu Zhen's 顾臻 study of the novel's publication history indicates that while *Rivers and Lakes* was in the course of being serialized in *Scarlet* and then *Scarlet Rose*, World Books was simultaneously printing it in book form, using the plates already prepared for the magazines.[68]

Volumes (*ji*) of ten *hui* appeared, presumably as the requisite chapters finished serialization, up through volume 7 and chapter 70; the eighth *ji* then included chapters 71–78, and the ninth chapters 79–86, at which point the original serialization declared itself at an end. Chapters 87–94 and 95–104 of the resumed serialization were subsequently included in a tenth and eleventh *ji* respectively. The magazine's final chapters, 105 and 106, printed in *Scarlet Rose* at the end of 1928, were likely destined to commence a twelfth *ji* that was aborted, as was the serialization, by the rumors of the author's death and the legal complications attendant upon his reappearance.[69] But the truncation of World Books' publication was not the end of the novel—neither of the text nor of its reproduction. Editions under other publishers' imprints included further chapters in additional *ji*, sometimes (though not always) attributing the new material to one Zouxiaosheng 走肖生.[70] As early as June 1930 an edition from Puyi shuju 普益書局 ran to fourteen *ji* and 134 *hui*. A slightly later edition (April 1931) from the same publisher reorganized the material from the fifty-fifth *hui* onward, subdividing and retitling chapters to make a total of 160 *hui*; this was evidently the source of the edition commonly republished today.

Gu Zhen makes two points about this history that are worth iterating here. One is that World Books, despite having made a settlement of some sort with Xiang Kairan, seems nonetheless to have remained involved in the novel's less legitimate afterlife. The colophon for the 1931 Puyi shuju edition credits World Books as the distributor; a 1935 edition from Wenyi chubanshe 文藝出版社 likewise credits World Books as both printer and distributor. Even after the official World Books editions, printed with the plates from the original serialization, came to an end, the publisher clearly found ways to maintain an interest in the publication of the novel's unauthorized extensions. The second is that the impetus for the extension of the text and for publishers' interest in it came not from the novel's own popularity alone but also from the adaptation of the material into a new medium. The 1931 Puyi shuju edition appeared under the variant title *Marvelous Gallants of the Rivers and Lakes: The Burning of Red Lotus Temple* (江湖奇俠傳火燒紅蓮寺). *The Burning of Red Lotus Temple*, referring to a central incident in the novel's plot, was also the title of the film version produced by Mingxing Film Company in 1928.

The Burning of Red Lotus Temple opened at the Palace Theater (Zhongyang daxiyuan 中央大戲院) in Shanghai on May 13, 1928, and was an immediate success, breaking box-office records for a domestic film, reversing Mingxing's previously foundering fortunes, and launching what came to be seen as the first wave of Chinese martial arts cinema.[71] It was by no means the first martial arts movie produced in China. The Shanghai film industry had already produced a number of films with martial arts subjects and themes, drawing on indigenous material while often borrowing from the filmmaking techniques and mise-en-scène of Hollywood swashbucklers. But none of these earlier films had anything near the success and impact of *Red Lotus Temple*. Neither did *The Gallant's Revenge* (*Daxia fuchou ji* 大俠復仇記), a two-part film based on another portion of *Rivers and Lakes* produced by Mingxing and released in the same year.[72] Between 1928 and 1931, Mingxing followed the initial *Red Lotus Temple* with seventeen sequels as well as other martial-arts-themed films; other studios followed suit with a wave of imitations, often in multipart series and frequently blazoned with *The Burning of . . .* as a title. These films used what at the time were groundbreaking special-effects techniques to represent the superhuman abilities, sorcerous arts, and strange creatures found in Buxiaosheng's novel and its imitators. Their novelty and technical success in bringing the fantastic world of the Rivers and Lakes to the screen were evidently major elements in their appeal to their audiences.[73] By one count, over 240 such "martial arts fantasy films" (*wuxia shenguai pian* 武俠神怪片) were produced in the four years following *Red Lotus Temple*'s success, representing approximately 60 percent of Chinese domestic film production for the period. The flood of martial arts films flowed from some fifty different studios, many of them small and newly established to capitalize on the craze, and the output was enthusiastically received by Chinese audiences throughout Southeast Asia as well as within the country.[74]

Rivers and Lakes can thus be credited not only with initiating the Republican-era craze for martial arts fiction but also with inspiring what is even today one of the most distinctive genres of Chinese cinema. For the purposes of the present investigation, the significance of *Red Lotus Temple* lies in part in the fact that it reproduces within a new medium the dynamics of serialization, series, and genre. Mingxing allegedly had no plans to produce more than a single film; it was the popular and financial success of the original *Red Lotus Temple* that drove it to produce seventeen sequels.[75] As the films have been lost, it is difficult to ascertain whether they constituted a serial—in the sense of a single overarching narrative suspended at critical moments in such a way as to stoke desire for the next installment—or simply a series of related but distinct episodes.[76] In either case, though, they present a paradigmatic process of extension from a single work to continuations and sequels and then to other works taking the original as their model. *Red Lotus Temple*'s role in establishing the genre of martial arts film parallels *Rivers and Lakes*'s role in establishing the genre of the martial arts novel; taken together, the two illustrate how genre in the thematic sense is not restricted to a single form or medium.

This is not to say that a single work can create a thematic genre *ab ovo*. Genres exist in the perception that bodies of texts share certain characteristics. The texts affiliated with the genre, like all texts, draw from multiple sources and are not constructed solely from those features understood to qualify them for genre membership. But a given text can play a significant role in defining the characteristics seen as constitutive of a given genre, and a given text's potency in reifying the significance of certain characteristics is amplified when that text propagates itself through continuation, sequelization, and imitation. *Rivers and Lakes* plays this seminal role in Republican-era martial arts fiction and *Red Lotus Temple* in Republican-era martial arts film, and, of course, the two do not simply represent two discrete and parallel cases but are rather linked in a larger process of transmedial propagation. A full account of *Rivers and Lakes'* migrations through various Republican-era media would take into account its adaptation into comic books (*lianhuanhua* 連環畫) and for the opera stage as well and the role these and other mediated forms played in constructing a martial arts imaginary as a persistent element in modern Chinese popular culture. This chapter began by investigating the historical relationship between the thematic genre of martial arts fiction and a particular literary form—the linked-chapter novel—and a particular medium—periodical publishing. It concludes with this glance toward the much broader phenomenon to which this contingent historical relationship contributed: a transmedial martial arts genre that was to persist and continually transform through and beyond the twentieth century and to spread from the Chinese base so important to its identity out into global circulation.

CHAPTER FIVE

Marvelous Gallants of the Rivers and Lakes

G iven that *Marvelous Gallants of the Rivers and Lakes* is the work
that cemented the reputation of the author known to this day as
the father of modern martial arts fiction, one might naturally
expect to find in this novel the template for the subgenre's subsequent
development. In some respects one can. On the formal level, as the previous chapter argued, *Rivers and Lakes* contributed to the establishment of
a special (though not exclusive) relationship between martial arts fiction
and the traditional linked-chapter novel. In terms of content, as the current chapter will in part demonstrate, *Rivers and Lakes* helped confirm
its titular milieu as the setting for tales of martial adventure and rivalries
between various master-disciple lineages (sects or schools) as essential
grist for the mill of the plot. Readers of later martial arts fiction, however,
as well as devotees of its cinematic cousin the martial arts film, are likely
to be surprised by the relative lack of attention given by *Rivers and Lakes*
to the martial arts as such. Its sister novel, *Modern Times*, to some degree
makes up for this lack, and it will be discussed in the final chapter of this
study. But the protagonists of *Rivers and Lakes* are not so much martial
artists as "swordsmen" (*jianke* 劍客) or "sword-immortals" (*jianxian* 劍仙),
practitioners of mystical arts and masters of magical combat associated
with their pursuit of a spiritual Way. The novel's supernatural content is
rooted in the tales of spirits and anomalies that were a central part of

premodern *xiaoshuo*'s mandate to address the strange and the marvelous (*qi* 奇). Twentieth-century modernizing ideologies removed these roots from the soil of the beliefs of which they were a part, exposing them to the withering light of scientism and requiring that supernatural fiction construct new rationales for its continued existence. The response we find in Xiang Kairan's fiction addresses the ontological status of the supernatural and in so doing proposes a role for *xiaoshuo* in the modern age. This chapter's discussion of this response will begin from the questions framed by critics of the cinematic adaptation of *Rivers and Lakes*.

THE SUPERNATURAL AND THE ROLE OF FICTION

The Banning of Red Lotus Temple

The flood of martial arts films precipitated by Mingxing Film Company's 1928 adaptation of *Rivers and Lakes* into *The Burning of Red Lotus Temple* slowed to a trickle by 1932. The decline can be attributed to multiple causes, including market glut, the inferior quality of some of the films, a changing public mood in the face of the threat from Japan, the growing influence of left-wing filmmakers, and changes in the industry attendant upon the introduction of sound-film technology. The most direct cause, however, was interdiction by the Nationalist government. A National Film Censorship Committee (NFCC) was established in 1931 and empowered to license films approved for exhibition. While it withheld or revoked licenses for a variety of films both foreign and domestic, some 70 percent of the films it banned were domestic productions belonging to the genre of martial arts fantasy (*wuxia shenguai* 武俠神怪).[1] The eighteen installments of *Red Lotus Temple*, the most prominent and influential of such films, were among those singled out. *Red Lotus Temple* was issued a license on June 27, only to see it revoked on July 21.[2] In response to an appeal from Mingxing's Zhang Shichuan 張石川, who argued that the losses resulting from the prohibition would cripple the domestic film industry's ability to compete with Hollywood imports, the NFCC approved the exhibition of versions of the *Red Lotus Temple* films carefully edited to remove objectionable content.[3] But the Ministry of the Interior subsequently issued a new prohibition, noting that *Red Lotus Temple* was adapted from *Rivers and Lakes*, a novel that had been denied a publication permit on the grounds that its contents were "absurd and unreasonable, and ran counter to the spirit of the Party."[4]

Although the Nationalist government's intervention contributed to a dramatic slowdown in the production of martial arts films after 1931, it did not sound a death knell either for *Red Lotus Temple*, which was to enjoy further sequels, rereleases, and remakes, or for the genre of martial arts cinema as a whole, whose subsequent vitality is too well known to require rehearsal here. Of present interest are the criteria by which *Red Lotus Temple* and its kin were banned. Instead of being included in the NFCC-promoted categories of films of "science, patriotism, and adventure," the martial arts fantasy films fell afoul of the new law forbidding the screening of films "injuring the dignity of the Chinese people" (有損中華民族之尊嚴者), "violating the Three Principles of the People" (違反三民主義者), "damaging social morality or the public order" (妨害善良風俗或公共秩序者), or "promoting superstition and heterodoxy" (提倡迷信邪說者).[5] And it was primarily the last of these offenses of which they were deemed culpable. They were perceived, that is, less as martial arts films than as films of fantasy; any adventurous or patriotic potential of the martial (*wuxia*) was outweighed and negated by fantasy's (*shenguai*) affinities with the heterodox and superstitious. The wave of fantasy martial arts films launched by *Red Lotus Temple* coincided with a renewed campaign against superstition mounted by the left wing of the Nationalist Party between 1927 and 1930. The campaign's concrete targets included religious communities of monks and nuns, religious properties (with their revenues), and festivals and worship rituals, but the attendant intensification of antisuperstition rhetoric also fueled the critique of *shenguai* plays and films and contributed to the government bans.[6]

The word I am translating here as "fantasy," *shenguai* 神怪, might be more literally rendered as "spirits and anomalies." The compound was used as early as the Han dynasty to refer to beings and phenomena beyond ordinary human experience. Early appearances of the term in Chinese film commentary are descriptive rather than pejorative. In 1927 the Shanghai Film Company released *The Cave of Silken Web* (*Pansi dong* 盤絲洞), an adaptation of the episode of Monkey King Sun Wukong's encounter with spider demons from the traditional novel *Journey to the West* (*Xiyou ji* 西遊記). A prerelease publication includes an article entitled "My Views on Fantasy Films" ("Wo zhi shenguai yingpian guan" 我之神怪影片觀) by

Cheng Xiaoqing, the dean of Chinese detective fiction. Cheng attributes the Chinese taste for *shenguai* films to a long tradition of fiction in the same mode and to the fledgling state of scientific thinking (*kexue guannian* 科學觀念) in China as compared to the West—where, he believes, *shenguai* films are accordingly rare, but he allows that *shenguai* films can "refresh people's perspectives by opening a realm outside the scope of actual life."[7] Within a few years, however, a far less forgiving view has come to the fore. Critics identify *shenguai* with superstition and charge *shenguai* films with abetting an infantile, antiscientific worldview that hinders China's emergence as a modern nation:

> Using "the spirits" to repress any and all real-life endeavors, using "the spirits" as the ultimate measure of all things and affairs—this lingering poison is still deeply rooted in the minds of the great majority of the populace of China. As we all know, in the tempestuous age of our scientific twentieth-century present, this "poison" is something that should be annihilated. And yet circumstances are in fact quite different; rather than finding a way to annihilate this sort of mentality, our great nation instead encourages it. The sins of old-style drama and fantasy films alone are immense.[8]

Antisuperstitious currents had been an element of Chinese reform movements since the late Qing.[9] Twentieth-century reformers' attacks on superstition in some respects echoed the ambivalence toward popular religion often expressed by the pre-twentieth-century Chinese elite. But where the latter defined itself in terms of moral concerns, the former was grounded in more radical ontological objections. The premodern gentry, especially those inclined toward Confucian fundamentalism, viewed dealings with ghosts and spirits as perilous and morally compromising but did not disallow the existence either of such powers or of arts for negotiating with them. The orthodox Confucian's disdain for the admittedly potent resources of heterodoxy is precisely the position articulated by Hu Zhizai's father in the episode from *Modern Times* discussed in chapter 1. Modern reformers, however, viewed the entire complex of popular religious beliefs, together with the practices and social institutions with which they were interwoven, as superstition, "deluded belief" (*mixin* 迷信), a false understanding of the world. It was not the gods and spirits who were dangerous; it was *belief* in them that was dangerous, because it was false. Belief in gods, spirits, and heavenly oversight of a moral order supported the repressive ideologies and social institutions of China's "feudal" past; such belief occluded—and betrayed by its very falsity—the rational, scientific understanding of the world on which the building of a modern secular society and a rich and powerful nation were seen to depend.

Reformist attacks saw an intimate connection between popular beliefs and the popular cultural forms that promulgated them. Liang Qichao's epochal 1902 treatment of the powers of fiction and its potential for renovating the nation lists superstition as one of the ills for which traditional *xiaoshuo* was culpable:

> Nowadays our people are deluded by such superstitious practices as geomancy, physiognomy, divination, and praying to spirits to bring good fortune and to exorcise calamities. The superstitious belief in geomancy has driven people to oppose the construction of railroads and the opening of mines. Disputes over the site for a grave can embroil an entire clan in armed fighting and merciless killing. Processions and festivals intended to welcome the spirits or offer thanksgiving to the gods annually cause people to squander millions of dollars, waste their time, stir up trouble, and drain the national economy. This is all because of fiction.[10]

Here, as throughout the essay, Liang Qichao intends "fiction" not in the now presumptive sense of imaginative literary narrative but in the sense of a continuum of popular culture that includes written texts, oral performance, theater, and ritual. The restriction of *xiaoshuo* to a literary sense was essential to the refashioning of the term as an equivalent for the English word "fiction" in its meaning as a modern literary category. The literarization of fiction by the polemicists and literary historians of the May Fourth generation established definitions that left premodern *xiaoshuo* beyond the pale and positioned it as embedded in the matrices of primitive belief and practice from which modern artistic forms and media were understood to be free.[11] The critics of the early 1930s could therefore characterize *shenguai* films as "running counter to the principles of cinema," while consigning their textual predecessors to the self-evidently irredeemable category of "old-style *xiaoshuo*" (舊小說); they cast superstition's presence in the cinema as a betrayal but in old-style fiction as a given.[12]

The critics and government censors of the Nationalist era targeted martial arts fantasy films more vigorously than they did the fiction that inspired them. Xiang Kairan's novels met with government disfavor—as we have seen, *Rivers and Lakes* was refused a publication license—and criticism of the films not infrequently took note of their printed parentage. Even when doing so, however, they pointed out that the films were "even more broadly distributed than the books, and more severe in the harm they cause."[13] The fact that the films were seen as a greater danger stemmed not only from the perception that they reached a wider and less educated public than their written counterparts but also from the new and unsettling characteristics of cinema as a medium. Films, like plays, were viewed by people in groups; their communal audience was a physical and social reality, not merely an "imaginary community" constructed rhetorically by a written text or implicit in its distribution.[14] And films as a visual medium went far beyond plays in their ability to give form to imagined places, creatures, and events, paradoxically using modern technology to impart the semblance of the real to the fantastic and unscientific. The film scholar Bao Weihong argues that the *Burning* films epitomize what both audiences and critics experienced as the incendiary potential of the affective medium of cinema.[15]

Deracinated Spirits: Supernatural Fiction in a Modern World

The claim that the literary, dramatic, or cinematic representation of spirits and magical powers promotes superstitious belief relies on the presumption that audiences understand such plays and films in a simplistically literal way. This is the mode of reception that Liang Qichao imputed to popular culture at the turn of the century and the mode that the critics of the 1930s imputed to the audiences for martial arts fantasy films. Mao Dun, describing the cheers and applause with which audiences greeted the onscreen entry of characters in *Red Lotus Temple*, insisted that "their comments on a film are never that such and such a star's portrayal of such and such a character is good in this way or bad in that way; they comment on what the Kunlun School is like, and what the Kongtong School is like! For them, a film is no longer a 'play'—it's reality!"[16] Critics regularly characterized the audiences for martial arts fantasy films as young and/or uneducated and so impressionable and incapable of distinguishing fantasy from reality, superstition from fact, that they parroted the speech and manners of their cinematic heroes, ran away from home to seek teachers in the mountains, and burned incense inside movie theaters in worship of the gods onscreen.[17]

As discussed in chapter 2, the strange (*yi* 異), the marvelous (*qi* 奇), and the weird (*guai* 怪) were defining concerns of premodern *xiaoshuo*. Many types of material populated these overlapping categories; unusual creatures, bizarre coincidences, eccentric personalities, extremes of emotion or virtue, expressions of talent, and distinctive words or deeds of famous individuals might all be considered strange enough to merit recording and transmitting as *xiaoshuo*. But "spirits and anomalies" (*shen guai*) occupy a dominant position within the corpus. How did such elements—entities, powers, and occurrences beyond the boundaries of ordinary human existence—mesh with another of *xiaoshuo*'s defining concerns: historicity? Before scientific rationalism's generation of the paired categories of "religion" and "superstition," did premodern *xiaoshuo* presume a literal belief in its gods and spirits, such as twentieth-century critics assumed was invoked by *shenguai* films? Did the extremities of the strange ever undermine *xiaoshuo*'s claims to facticity and its desire for validation as historiography's closest kin?

Judith Zeitlin's overview of the reception of Pu Songling's *Liaozhai's Records of the Strange*, the most widely read late-imperial collection of supernatural tales, surveys a range of approaches that readers might take to these stories. Zeitlin identifies three primary interpretive strategies that evolved successively between the seventeenth and nineteenth centuries: a first that accepted anomalies as fact and concerned itself with the way in which they define and support the normative moral order, a second that focused on the tales' function as a means of authorial self-expression, and a third that primarily addressed literary style and narrative technique, the discourse rather than the story.[18] While the first strategy accords with what Campany identifies as the impulse behind the emergence of anomaly accounts in the early medieval period, the second and third approaches distance themselves from the question of the stories' facticity. As such, they provided twentieth-century readers and scholars of anomaly tales with acceptable models for engagement at times when "the literature of the strange was ... tainted with politically undesirable associations of superstition."[19]

By the twentieth century, the widespread acceptance of an enlightenment discourse that relegated spirits and anomalies to the false consciousness of superstition posed even greater challenges for would-be writers than it did for scholars or ordinary readers of the premodern corpus of the strange. Spirits relegated to the category of "superstition" are spirits deracinated, "no longer the messengers of an overarching plausibility structure that ha[d] once been the ultimate source of meaning."[20] If the supernatural is a priori false, what justifies its being spoken of or deployed? New models of fiction rejected *xiaoshuo*'s traditional ties with historiography, allowing and even celebrating invention as central to the fictional project. At the same time, however, a heightened sense of fiction's responsibilities in an age of national crisis privileged models of "realism" that required fiction to reflect material and social realities and presumed that fiction and the arts shaped readers' consciousness and actions in quite direct ways. For the intellectual elite, paternalistic and condescending attitudes toward "the masses" made these expectations particularly compelling in the case of cultural forms circulating among or directed at the general public. When Lu Xun, whose 1925 *Brief History of Chinese Fiction* identified myths and legends as one of the roots of fiction and traced the circulation of supernatural material in fiction's premodern antecedents, reworked stories of gods and anomalies in his 1936 *Old Tales Retold* (*Gushi xinbian* 故事新編), he could reasonably anticipate that an educated readership would recognize his work as operating in allegorical and expressionistic modes. But a baldly literal understanding—a belief in the facticity of fictive events, scientifically impossible phenomena, and an immanent moral design to human existence—was the only mode of reception elite critics could imagine for the audiences of *Red Lotus Temple*.

Several of Xiang Kairan's fictional works directly address the questions of superstition and the facticity of supernatural manifestations of the strange. The most forthright and extended treatment appears in *Strange Phenomena of the Rivers and Lakes* (*Jianghu guaiyi zhuan* 江湖怪異傳). This novella (a text in twenty-one short chapters of varying lengths) was printed in a handsome illustrated single volume by World Books in October 1923, the year in which both *Rivers and Lakes* and *Modern Times* began publication.[21] Unlike the two voluminous serializations for which

Xiang Kairan is chiefly remembered, it neglects the martial arts entirely, mixing tales of the supernatural with structural and narrative features borrowed from the popular subgenre of detective fiction.

The text begins by raising the question of the persistence of shamanism (*wu* 巫), that is, of practices purporting to mediate with the gods and spirits. It attributes the existence of such practices to the ever-present threats of illness, the capriciousness of the law, and the unfathomability of the roads to success and failure in life; shamans thrive by supporting people's desperate search for aid and justice in the face of these vicissitudes. Thus far the argument supports the text's characterization of shamanism as *mixin*, "deluded beliefs" or superstition. But the chapter's close introduces a note of doubt. "What's more, the shamans do in fact possess quite a few ways of raising demons to wreak havoc, such that they have become a force to be reckoned with in and of themselves" (4). The phrase "raising demons to wreak havoc" (*xing yao zuo guai* 興妖作怪) metaphorically connotes stirring up trouble; is its use here ironic, or is there a hint that it may retain something of its literal sense?

After a survey of some of the shamanistic practices of Hunan, described as a hotbed of superstition, the narrative proper begins in chapter 3 with the disappearance of a member of the Changsha gentry, one Peng Lihe 彭禮和. His anxious family hires a spirit medium who discovers Peng's corpse hanging in the provincial examination hall. The magistrate judges the death a suicide and closes the case. But the scion of another gentry family, Fu Jizu 傅繼祖, has his suspicions aroused when a local *fengshui* practitioner, Luo Man 羅滿, hints that Peng was driven to his death by ghosts. Fu decides to investigate. His informant avers that Peng was not only a devotee of planchette writing (*fuji* 扶乩, a common spiritual practice among the late-Qing elite) but also a student of magical arts (*qimen dunjia* 奇門遁甲) and that he had been killed as a result of struggles between rival sects over a powerful talisman (*lingpai* 領牌) in Peng's possession. Continuing inquiries reveal a series of other, tangentially related cases involving witchcraft, possession, and supernatural retribution. Fu Jizu's investigation into the truth of Peng's demise is at the same time an investigation of the veracity of the proliferating tales of demons and magic that his probings uncover.

Thus described, *Strange Phenomena* seems to pit the scientific rationalism that detective fiction was averred to champion against the belief in falsehoods that tales of the supernatural were accused of promoting. And the outcome of the Peng case appears to signal a clear victory over superstition. Peng's evident suicide was indeed a murder motivated by his talisman. The talisman was not, however, a potent magical relic but rather the hiding place for a key document in a contested inheritance, and although his murderers were shamans and spirit mediums, they were driven not by a struggle for spiritual power but rather by squabbles over an item they were scheming to sell to the highest bidder. Peng's sorcerous battle against the Demon Mother of Black Mountain (Heishan guimu 黑山鬼母) turns out to be mere invention; Luo Man's narration of this episode in chapter 9, allegedly on the basis of Peng's own account, constitutes one of the most spectacular scenes in the novel, but it is grimly answered by Luo's confession in chapter 19 of the truth of how he lured Peng to his death—a tense scene worthy of a noir thriller. Even the spirit medium's discovery of Peng's body, the seemingly supernatural event that sets the plot into motion, is revealed in the end to have been staged by the culprits.

Yet the triumph of scientific rationality is neither complete nor clearcut. Although key supernatural events are exposed as fraudulent or fictive, others are left to stand unchallenged. A case in point is the figure of Li Bingrong 李炳榮, a shaman and sect leader who is deeply involved with Peng Lihe and with other strands of the narrative. He is instrumental in the final resolution of Peng's case, and in the aftermath, the text gives Li's own life story (chapter 20). This minibiography records his schemes and machinations but also his practice of magic and dealings with the spirits; it begins, for instance, with the anecdote of his learning from a woodpecker the charms and gestures that allow him to unlock magically the door of a room in which he has been imprisoned. The narrator presents this material without qualification or disclaimers. In the text's final chapter, then, the narrator identifies himself with the historical author and directly expounds his views on ghosts and magic. Scientific knowledge has its limits: "On the question of whether or not ghosts exist, neither side has been able to present reliable evidence. Everyone in the world today says that science reigns supreme, and yet there has never yet been a proper method for investigating the question of ghosts; no one dares to state conclusively that they exist, but no one dares to state conclusively that they don't" (189). Citing his own experience of phenomena inexplicable by science, the narrator goes on to opine that ghosts do exist, though they are not necessarily harmful to living humans, and that magic exists as well, though it operates through the cultivation of psychic energy (*qi* 氣) and not by the command of spirits.

What is most significant for Xiang Kairan's practice of *xiaoshuo*, however, is not this bald statement of personal opinions concerning the supernatural but rather the way in which the text figures the hermeneutics of *xiaoshuo* as the basis of knowledge of the world. Detective stories presume a homology between the reader and the fictional detective, with the former shadowing the latter in the discovery of truth.[22] But *Strange Phenomenon*'s Fu Jizu is no Holmesian master of ratiocination and forensic science. The text introduces him as a member of a club (*wanyi tuan* 玩意團) of Changsha playboys who begin to weary of their accustomed pursuits of drinking, whoring, and theatergoing. "It just so happened that the Sherlock Holmes detective stories were in tremendous vogue at this time; and this crowd, under the sway of this fictionalizing influence, undertook the study of the arts of detection" (15). But their efforts are marked by the muddle-headedness characteristic of contemporary Chinese society:

> In a society such as this—without system, without order, without reason, without standards—no matter what kind of science you use to analyze people's intentions and attitudes, it is still quite difficult to discern any authentic right and wrong or black and white. So it was with this business of detection; any thorough understanding was impossible, needless to say, and it was nothing more than chasing the wind and clutching at shadows, succeeding only by chance.
>
> (15–16)

The young men's "detection" is directed primarily toward snooping out information about family secrets and local beauties until the Peng case catches Fu's attention. And even then, their investigations rest not on the analysis of physical evidence but on the collection and exchange of accounts, often over a cup of wine or a pipe of opium. The process exactly mirrors Xiang Kairan's textual representations of the storytelling on which his own fiction is modeled. At one point one of Fu Jizu's associates mocks the tall tales Fu has collected as "a chapter straight out of *The Investiture of the Gods*" (54), referring to the Ming novel of magical warfare held to epitomize the tradition of *shenguai* fiction. Rather than being an exercise in scientific knowledge empowered to dispel the murk of superstition, *Strange Phenomenon*'s detection, itself of fictional parentage, proves to be an instance of that transmission of narratives among networks of acquaintances that constitutes *xiaoshuo* as traditionally understood.

Xiang Kairan's short story "A Black Cat and a Strange Case" ("Heimao yu qi'an" 黑貓與奇案) likewise frames its presentation of supernatural events with references to both inherited and imported models of fiction.[23] The story tells how the bizarre and seemingly impossible actions of a black cat lead an unwitting tradesman and a canny magistrate to uncover a case of adultery and murder. But the narrator prefaces the story proper with an excursus in which he criticizes the tales of Judge Bao and Judge Shi, righteous magistrates celebrated in popular nineteenth-century novels, for their accounts of crimes solved through the intervention of birds and beasts. At issue, at least at first, are both the implausibility of the events in such tales and the superstitious implication of the intervention of some higher power: "Among the readers of such hogwash (那類荒唐故事) would be uneducated women and children intellectually incapable of discerning truth from falsehood. There would also be traditionalists who cling to their belief in karmic retribution and who, their doubts notwithstanding, lack the courage to question the veracity of what they read" (147). As he continues, the narrator also takes these earlier texts to task for what is more of a professional flaw: their ignorance of the forensic science that informs modern crime stories. "[Discerning readers] might very well ridicule the authors as deficient in knowledge concerning crime detection. Unable to portray their heroes properly, these writers could only resort to accounts of the supernatural (神鬼無稽的情節) to hoodwink the gullible" (147). Yet the tale our narrator is about to tell has caused him to reconsider his own assumptions:

> Today, however, I unexpectedly encountered someone from Hofei in Anhui who had just come to Shanghai. Quite by chance, he told me about an extraordinary case that took place in his native town toward the end of last year. The case actually demonstrates that some accounts involving the supernatural are not at all wild fantasies, certainly not the unfounded fabrications of those who set them down

in writing (絕對不是著那類小說的人憑空捏造). My intention here is not to advocate superstition. But during these times of loss of personal trust and decline in social mores, if I can discover and present a few of these deeply touching stories, they can perhaps be regarded as helpful in areas where laws are ineffectual and where the detective's ability to reason falls short. The ancient sages and worthies had this very idea when they set up their teachings based on the existence of ghosts and spirits.

(147–48)

The narrator's relationship to his material is complex and in the final analysis perhaps not entirely coherent. He takes pains to distance himself from "superstition." In attributing the tale to an acquaintance and insisting that supernatural tales are not necessarily "the unfounded fabrications of those who set them down in writing," he takes refuge in the familiar ploy of faithfully recording what he has heard while declining to testify to the veracity of the events. In arguing for the social utility of such tales, likewise, he presents a case for their ameliorative influence that does not necessarily depend on the stories' facticity as such. And while this trust in the stories' didactic potential allies the narrator with the aims of "the ancient sages and worthies," he stops short of actually endorsing "the existence of ghosts and spirits," which the sages instrumentally averred. Yet all these careful qualifications seem to crumble as the narrative draws toward its resolution. The black cat's strange behavior leads to the exhumation of the corpse of a merchant and the discovery that he was killed by a steel rod driven into his skull. Confronted with the evidence, the man's widow confesses that she and her lover committed the crime and that the latter took his inspiration from a Judge Bao tale of a man murdered with a nail. Here the narrator again takes his predecessors to task for their ignorance of forensics:

The person who wrote the Judge Bao stories had never read anything about legal procedure, however, so he had no knowledge of autopsies. When corpses were examined for legal reasons, every bone and sinew was taken apart, cleaned off, and scrutinized. There was no possible way a metal nail of considerable length driven through the middle of the skull could escape notice. Had the sergeant not believed the fictional story of Judge Bao, he might not have committed this extraordinary crime.

(157)

But this critique of earlier fiction's failings in its representation of physical and procedural reality leads into a final endorsement of the proposition that events in this world are shaped by the operations of a higher moral power: "That he would place his trust in the idea of using a nail as a murder weapon, but not in that of an animal acting to write a wrong, ultimately became the reason for his inability to escape the karma of a just retribution. How can we deny the remarkable irony in all this (也不可謂 不巧了)?" (157).

To what should we credit the triumph of justice? Is it the power of modern science to arrive at the truth through "taking apart, cleaning, and scrutinizing," or is it the power of karma to operate through a brute beast? Did the criminal err by giving credence to the Judge Bao tales or by failing to recognize what they taught? Despite avowals of allegiance to the enlightenment perspective and modest disclaimers as to its own aims, the text declines to exorcize fully the ghost of a nonsecular framework of meaning. The narrator invites the reader to be both conscious of and skeptical of a range of possibilities as to the significance of the story's events. The final invitation is to appreciate "the remarkable irony in all this"; *qiao* 巧, the word that Wong translates as "irony," carries connotations of both serendipity and cleverness and could apply equally to the story and the discourse, to the events reported and to their rendering as a tale.

Here, as in *Strange Phenomena* and in Xiang Kairan's fiction more generally, the issue is not in the end whether the events recounted accord with a scientific worldview nor whether the author believes in their facticity. Fully aware of the status of the supernatural in a society that accords normative status to scientific rationalism, the text employs elements of *xiaoshuo*'s inherited poetics—the delight in the strange, the authority granted to transmitted narrative and the exculpability this authority confers—to create a discursive space where that which scientism disallows enjoys potential or provisional existence. Han Yunbo understands the recasting of the preposterous as the aestheticized fantastic to be one of Xiang Kairan's fundamental contributions to modern martial arts fiction.[24] Zhang Zhen, focusing on the martial arts films sired by *Rivers and Lakes*, argues that the anarchic overlapping of science and magic in popular culture was an essential characteristic of a vernacular modernity deemed monstrous by China's elites.[25] My argument here is that in Xiang Kairan's fictional texts, this overlapping and aestheticization is effected through the deployment of some of the constitutive elements of *xiaoshuo* discourse. The subtle repurposing of elements of *xiaoshuo* poetics created the conditions under which readers might approach the strange—both the surface strangeness of events and the now-estranged proposition of their shaping by a higher power—with simultaneous skepticism and acceptance, a Coleridgean willing suspension of disbelief that arguably enhanced the savor of the strange as forbidden fruit. At the same time, though, this repurposing weighted the character of *xiaoshuo* itself toward fictionality in a nugatory sense that left it vulnerable to attacks from its critics.

MARVELOUS GALLANTS OF THE RIVERS AND LAKES

Liu Chi: The Topography and Social Networks of the Strange

Xiang Kairan's single most famous work, *Marvelous Gallants of the Rivers and Lakes* (*Jianghu qixia zhuan* 江湖奇俠傳), is a novel of the strange, and it constructs the strange in good measure (though not exclusively) through the presentation of the supernatural.[26] The film versions, through their incendiary visibility, may have drawn the brunt of critics' ire, but they succeeded, and invited trouble, in large part because of their effectiveness in realizing material essential to the novel's own vision. The centrality of the strange is signaled by the presence in the novel's title of the key word *qi* 奇, rendered in my translation as the adjective "marvelous." The adjective serves grammatically as a modifier to the noun *xia* 俠, "gallants," but the relative weight of the two words is suggested by the author's defense of a lengthy excursus: "Though some of the characters I've written about in the last ten-odd chapters are not gallant, there's not a one who isn't marvelous (*qi*)."[27] The noun phrase *qixia* is modified by another noun phrase, *jianghu* 江湖, "rivers and lakes," and the resultant four-character phrase *jianghu qixia* modifies a final noun, *zhuan* 傳, which I have left implicit in my Englishing of the title. The word *zhuan* frequently serves in the titles of *xiaoshuo*, whether classical language or vernacular. In its broadest sense it means simply an "account," but its genealogical and associative links with the biographies (*zhuan* 傳) of formal historiography suggest the possibility that the account may be organized around the life stories of particular individuals.[28] At the same time, the character's alternate reading (*chuan* 傳, "to transmit") reminds us that an account exists for the purpose of being passed on to others. The title thus adumbrates several aspects of the novel worth further examination: its locating of the strange in individual characters and in a particular landscape and its interest in the dynamics of transmission on structural, thematic, and generic levels.

It will be useful to begin discussion of these issues with a glance at the novel's narrative contents and structure. The first four chapters relate the upbringing of one Liu Chi 柳遲, the only son of a minor gentry landowner dwelling near the Hunan provincial capital, Changsha. The boy's name—Chi, "tardy"—connotes the arrival of an heir late in the father's life; this late arrival, and an infancy plagued by sickness, lead Liu senior and his wife, Madam Chen 陳, to dote on the child and indulge his many eccentricities. Liu Chi is grotesque in appearance:

> His eyebrows, thick as a broom, met at the middle, like a single stroke across his forehead. His eyes were deeply set, and the upper and lower lashes tangled together. Every morning when he woke up they were glued together by the rheum his eyes had excreted, making it impossible for him to open his eyes; only after Madam Chen herself had taken water and washed them clean for him was he able to open them up to see the world around him. His forehead was quite a bit higher than that of ordinary people, and his cheekbones ran from the corners of his eyes to his temples. His lips were thin, his mouth huge, so that when he opened it up it looked like that of a perch. A sallow complexion was shot through with a greenish tinge. He was given to fits of crying, and when he bawled, that gaping perch-like mouth of his was enough to frighten anyone who saw it.
>
> (1:1, 2)

As he grows, his grotesque appearance is discovered to be matched by extraordinary intellectual gifts. These two singularities, and their startling coexistence, embody the strange in the innate qualities of an individual.

The circumstances of Liu Chi's birth, meanwhile, locate the meaning of the individual's existence in the continuity of the patriliny, the transmission of the ancestral line.

Despite his gifts, Liu Chi is uninterested in either the content of the orthodox Confucian education given him or the socialization it entails. He is given instead to odd preoccupations and spends his days consorting with beggars and itinerants. At around age twelve, he encounters a wandering Daoist priest and immediately begs to be taken as his student. The Daoist brings Liu Chi to his temple and instructs him in meditation. At a convocation some months later Liu Chi learns that his arrival has fulfilled a destined tally of thirty-six disciples in his master's school, but he is then directed to continue his studies at home while serving his aging parents. Two years later he encounters another master, the Golden Arhat Lü Xuanliang (Jin luohan Lü Xuanliang 金羅漢呂宣良), a senior member of the same school as his first teacher, whom he only now learns is known as the Laughing Daoist (Xiao daoren 笑道人). From his two teachers' conversation, Liu Chi gains his first inkling of a longstanding feud between this school, the Kunlun lineage (Kunlun pai 崑崙派), and the rival Kongtong lineage (Kongtong pai 崆峒派). And before taking leave of his new disciple, the Golden Arhat makes an appointment to meet with him again on Mount Yuelu 岳麓山 at Mid-Autumn of the following year.

Liu Chi now vanishes from the narrative, not to reappear for fifty-some chapters. This opening account of his education has nonetheless introduced several elements of the ensuing narrative. The gathering of the Laughing Daoist's students in the second and third chapters provides glimpses of many characters and hints of situations and events that will be developed as the story proceeds. The ongoing conflict between the Kunlun and Kongtong lineages will prove to be the warp into which many of the narrative strands—both those adumbrated here and those later introduced—are directly or indirectly threaded. Among these strands is a longstanding feud between the residents of Pingjiang 平江 and Liuyang 瀏陽 counties over the fertile riverlands at Zhaojiaping 趙家坪, a feud into which the rival lineages are drawn through the ill-considered intervention of another of the Laughing Daoist's disciples. Liu Chi's Mid-Autumn meeting with the Golden Arhat upon Mount Yuelu, which comes to pass in the seventy-first chapter, serves to gather the welter of intervening material together under at least a gestural continuity and closure. The aftermath of the meeting finds Liu Chi involved in the extirpation of the villainous monks who make their lair at Red Lotus Temple, and embedded in the tale of Red Lotus Temple is the famous story of the assassination of Ma Xinyi 馬心儀 by his erstwhile sworn brother.

Discussions of *Rivers and Lakes* typically treat the battle over Zhaojiaping, the Kunlun-Kongtong conflict, and the episodes of the Red Lotus Temple and the Ma assassination (*ci Ma* 刺馬) as the most prominent elements of its narrative content. The extent to which these elements can be said to constitute a plot, in the sense of a unified and overarching narrative structure, is debatable. The subsequent sections of this chapter will examine further the question of the novel's structure; given the dizzying complexity of the novel's plotting, however, the opening Liu Chi episode is perhaps less useful as a roadmap to potential narrative destinations than as an introduction to settings, narrative tropes, and associated thematic concerns.

In speaking of the novel's setting, it is worth noting first of all its frequent references to features of Hunan geography, both natural and manmade, and the history, customs, and lore associated with them. The text in fact opens with just such a reference, introducing Liu Chi via an account of a local landmark (a towering tree atop Hermit Mountain 隐居山) near his family home. Such details of local geography and regional traditions help construct the distinctive Hunan flavor for which Xiang Kairan's writings were admired. They overlap with other elements of setting that do not so much anchor the action to specific places on a map as locate it within certain iconic environments: the countryside, waterways, temples, and the forests, mountains, and caves of the unpeopled wilderness. These marginal and fluid environments construct the novel's setting in a more abstract sense, that is, the milieu of its titular Rivers and Lakes.

I have elsewhere sketched the role of the Rivers and Lakes, "the geographic and moral margins of settled society," in the history of martial arts fiction.[29] The discursive connotations of this milieu in Xiang Kairan's novel can be illustrated by examining the scene of Liu Chi's first encounter with the Golden Arhat. Charged with delivering birthday gifts to a relative, Liu Chi uses the powers he has gained from his study of esoteric arts to take a shortcut over a mountain, only to find that he has been preceded in this seemingly trackless wilderness by a white-haired ancient commanding two giant eagles:

No sooner had Liu Chi seen the ancient's majestic bearing than a sense of extreme reverence rose up unbidden from the depths of his heart; and right there beneath the rock face he set down the bundle of birthday gifts he was carrying and knelt down before the ancient, saying: "Your disciple Liu Chi is committed to the Way. I beg and implore my venerable master to show the Way to his disciple!" Having said which, he began kowtowing as briskly as if he were pounding garlic. At this sight the ancient let out a laugh that echoed through the clouds above and left Liu Chi's eardrums ringing. When his laughter had died away the ancient said, "What on earth are you doing kneeling here, child?" Liu Chi stretched forward and said, "I beg you, venerable master, to show the Way (*dao* 道) to your disciple." "There are no rice paddies (*dao* 稻) up here in the mountains!" said the ancient. "If you're looking for paddies you've got to go down into the fields." "The *dao* your disciple seeks," said Liu Chi, "is the *dao* of the Way and its Virtue (*daode* 道德), not the *dao* of paddies and fields. I beg my master to take pity on his disciple, who has struggled for years without finding a gate to the Way." The ancient nodded, smiling, and said, "So even a young child like yourself knows about studying the Way. But the Way is manifold; just which Way is it that you wish to study?" Liu Chi said, "Your disciple has not yet entered the gate. I know only that I wish to study the Way, not which Way it is that I should study. I will gladly study whatever my master sees fit to instruct." The ancient said, "Very well then. I shall teach you the Way. But you must recognize me as your master." "Of course I shall recognize you as my master!" said Liu Chi joyfully. "Your disciple prostrates himself before you!" And as he spoke he kowtowed once again.

(3:1, 39)

Although the scene here is a craggy mountaintop rather than a body of water, the setting equally represents the physical and social marginality that defines the Rivers and Lakes. Liu Chi's adventure occurs when he departs the well-trodden paths of common human activity. In abandoning the main road Liu Chi gives kinetic and spatial expression to that separation from the ordinary—that quality of the extraordinary, *qi* 奇—already marked by his grotesque form and behavioral eccentricities.

The marginal equates with the marvelous, and the Rivers and Lakes are the domain of the strange. The first signs of the marvelous that Liu Chi encounters are the actions of nonhuman creatures, the antics of the twin eagles. The eagles lead Liu Chi to their master, the Golden Arhat. And in recognizing each other as master and disciple, Liu Chi and the Golden Arhat perform the relationship that structures the community of the Rivers and Lakes as envisioned in the novel.

The relationship between master and disciple is predicated upon the transmission of a body of knowledge, practice, and understanding referred to as the Way. It is the practice of the Way that effectively defines the "marvelous gallants" (*qixia* 奇俠) of the novel's title, and the episode under discussion makes clear that the Way too is extraordinary, in the sense of being removed from the concerns of quotidian life and orthodox institutions. It is Liu Chi's prior training in the Way that emboldens him and allows him to leave the well-trodden paths and his leaving the well-trodden paths that in turn allows his encounter with a new representative of the Way. In punning "the Way" against the "rice paddies" that serve as society's economic foundation, the Golden Arhat teasingly suggests the Way's distinction from ordinary life—and, at the same time, its analogous character as a field of potentially fruitful labor. Liu Chi's setting aside his bundle in order to bow before the Arhat likewise dramatizes the extent to which pursuit of the Way represents an alternative to normative social obligations.

But what is this Way? What is it that its followers actually do? The novel's Way is a spiritual path, linked with elements of the Confucian, Buddhist, and Daoist traditions yet unique and distinct from all three; it is never clearly defined and implicitly indefinable. In proclaiming that the Way is manifold (*dao you qianduan* 道有千端) the Golden Arhat suggests both that it manifests itself in many forms and that those who pursue it may take many different paths. Central to the novel's interests are the "sword-immortals" (*jianxian* 劍仙) who study "the art of the sword" (*jianshu* 劍術), which is not a technique of physical combat but the mastery of spiritual weapons including beams of light, ghostly hands, and swords of flying energy. These techniques are presented as methods of self-cultivation and self-defense ancillary to the Way proper, and they are joined by other displays of spiritual development such as prognostication, astral projection, cloud travel, and teleportation. The lines between such esoteric arts and the more physical martial arts, on the one hand, and sorcery, illusion, and garden-variety trickery, on the other, are often blurry. From time to time the narrator or one of his characters makes technical or moral distinctions between various of these practices, but it is difficult to identify any single consistent system or set of definitions as underpinning the carnival of phenomena encompassed by the practice of the Way. On the diegetic level, Liu Chi's declaration that "I will gladly study whatever my master sees fit to instruct" is an appropriate expression of humility and openness to the master's teachings. From a hermeneutic perspective, though, we can understand it as an admission that for the purposes of the narrative the Way serves as a floating signifier. The Way is not merely extraordinary; it *is* The Extraordinary, an empty vessel replete with the marvelous and strange. But the concrete manifestations of the Way fall into the category of the supernatural—phenomena that are impossible in a world governed by the laws of modern science.

The importance for the novel of this empty vessel lies not only in its valence as a sign of the marvelous and its power as the source of phenomena strange enough to merit narration but also in the structures of interpersonal relationship involved in the study of the Way. Knowledge of the Way and of the practices that lead to its realization exists only through transmission, and transmission from master to disciple creates the lineages that constitute the social organization of the marvelous world of the Rivers and Lakes. Lineages are virtual kinship networks, entailing the full range of familial relationships—lineage brothers and sisters, lineage nephews and uncles, lineage grandmasters and grand-disciples and so forth. Sworn brotherhood, the mode of virtual familiality so prominent elsewhere in Chinese martial and heroic traditions, plays but a secondary role in Xiang Kairan's *Rivers and Lakes*, chiefly in the episode of the Ma assassination.[30] Throughout the majority of the novel the focus remains firmly on the master-disciple relationships that the transmission of the Way requires. Liu Chi's story makes clear the importance of such relationships for the would-be disciple, a seeker of the Way. But they are equally important for the master, whose art dies without a disciple to receive its transmission. Zhu Zhenyue 朱鎮岳, an elder of the Kunlun lineage, makes this point upon meeting the newly initiated Liu Chi:

"The most difficult thing for us swordsmen to obtain is a disciple who can inherit the 'robe and almsbowl.' For every ten swordsmen who attain the Way, no more than two or three are fated to have someone to whom they can transmit their art. The other seven or eight may accept disciples just the same, even as many as a hundred disciples or more, yet in the end they can't look for success from a single one of them. And so it is that this Way of ours wanes from one generation to the next."

(3:1, 32)

The novel represents traditional Chinese society as organized around the transmission of the patriliny and the communities of the Rivers and Lakes as organized around the transmission of the Way. Despite the Way's role as a sign of the marvelous, despite the heterodox practices associated with its pursuit, and despite the marginality geographically figured in the Rivers and Lakes, human endeavor is structured identically in the two social realms. The structural homology intensifies the possibility of a divergence or even conflict of allegiances: taking a master is in effect recognizing an alternate father. Liu Chi's entry into the Kunlun lineage thus spurs discussion of how he will fulfill his filial obligations to his natal parents. And the issues of allegiance and filiality are thematized even more complexly in the story of Yang Tianchi 楊天池, to whom the narrative turns after leaving Liu Chi in chapter 4. Yang Tianchi, born to a gentry family, is lost while still an infant by a careless nurse. He is adopted by the peasants who find him, and they raise him under the name Yishe'er 義捨兒 ("Foundling"); later he is initiated into the Kunlun lineage by the Laughing Daoist. His natal parents, meanwhile, desperate to hide the loss of the family's heir from the grandparents, buy a replacement infant from a starving tailor and raise him as Yang Jixin 楊繼新 (implying "Successor"). Yang Jixin's later adventures also involve him with the Golden Arhat and the Kunlun lineage. The narrative requires that each of the Yangs negotiate his relationships with and responsibilities toward his adoptive parents, natal parents, and lineage master—as well as with his doppelgänger. But once again, the complications that arise serve in the end to affirm the congruent structures and shared moral imperatives of mainstream society and the communities of the Rivers and Lakes. Both are devoted to the continuance of the line through patriarchal succession; both are equally concerned, in other words, with the problem of transmission.

Recognizing transmission as one of the novel's central thematic concerns may partly explain what may strike at least some readers today as a puzzling tentativeness to the Liu Chi episode. The narrative of his upbringing and encounters with the Laughing Daoist and Golden Arhat certainly contains enough eccentric characters, odd phenomena, and unexpected developments to qualify as a tale of the strange, but it arguably lacks an arc of tension, climax, and resolution and is moreover devoid of martial arts action, apart from the brief interpolated tale of the Golden Arhat's duel against the magical swords of Kongtong's Dong Lutang 董祿堂. One can justly dismiss such complaints as motivated by expectations irrelevant to the novel's own aesthetic and point (as the original chapter commentary does) to the episode's structural function as a "lead-in" (*yinzi* 引子) and to its role in establishing characters and relationships that will reappear later in the text.[31] But one can also note that in telling how master and disciple find each other, how the Way is passed on and the paternal line at the same time given its due, the episode is in a sense complete: it gives full and satisfying attention to matters at the novel's thematic heart.

The Reverend Lan and the Problem of Desire

One of the novel's most distinctive figures is the hunter and shaman Reverend Lan (Lan fashi 藍法師), a character adapted from Xiang Kairan's earlier short fiction. The history of the Reverend Lan material illustrates Xiang Kairan's frequent habit of recycling and reworking narrative matter. The successive versions also chart the early contours of his writing career, including the role of Bao Tianxiao's *The Sunday* in the evolution from tales of Hunan exotica to the martial arts novel. Lan first appears in one of the author's earliest publications, the set of classical-language hunting tales appearing in 1916 under the joint title "Turning Pale."[32] The third of these anecdotes tells of one Mr. Lan of Xinning 新寧 in southern Hunan, a man of "extraordinary abilities" (*yineng* 異能), who hunts tigers with a combination of martial prowess, bravado, and magic and who loses the use of an arm in an epic encounter with a three-legged tiger. Six years later, *The Sunday*'s publication of the classical-language "A Hunter's Miscellany"

("Lieren ou ji" 獵人偶記) was followed by that of the vernacular "Tales of the Reverend Lan" in two parts: "Reverend Lan Catches a Ghost" ("Lan fashi zhuo gui" 藍法師捉鬼) and "Reverend Lan Fights a Tiger" ("Lan fashi da hu" 藍法師打虎).[33] The second of these retells the story of Lan and his three-legged nemesis. Although Bao implies in his memoirs that it was "A Hunter's Miscellany" that excited Shen Zhifang's interest in Buxiaosheng, it seems not improbable that the Reverend Lan stories played a role as well. Shen's *Scarlet Magazine* published a third Reverend Lan story, "The Toad Demon" ("Hama yao" 蝦蟆妖), in March 1924, while the serialization of *Rivers and Lakes* was in its thirty-first chapter.[34] Lan then appears as a character in chapter 56 of *Rivers and Lakes*, published in *Scarlet Rose* in December 1924. He maintains a prominent role in the narrative through chapter 71: chapters 58–62 relate a version of the exorcism previously narrated in "Reverend Lan Catches a Ghost," chapters 62–64 tell once again of his encounter with the three-legged tiger, and chapters 69–71 rework his encounter with the toad demon.

The reuse of narrative material involves almost no recycling of concrete passages of text. For instance, not only in the transition from the classical-language "Turning Pale" to the vernacular "Reverend Lan" but equally in the transition from the short story to the novel, the tale of the three-legged tiger is expanded, reorganized, given variant details, and cast into new language, even as the core of the episode's plot and certain striking scenes and images remain the same. The most significant aspect of the transformation, of course, is the integration of anecdotes that were previously freestanding (though linked by a common protagonist) into the vast and sprawling fabric of the novel. A sketch of the novel's deployment of the Reverend Lan material will serve both to exemplify some of *Rivers and Lakes'* structure and characteristic narrative strategies and to lay the groundwork for further exploration of its thematic concerns.

In chapter 55, the narrator returns his attention to Liu Chi, unseen since chapter 4, when the Golden Arhat sent him home to continue his practice under his parents' roof and charged him with honoring an appointment at Mount Yuelu on Mid-Autumn of the following year. Liu Chi's parents have abandoned their hopes of his forging a successful career but are still determined that he marry and continue the ancestral line. They take him to Xinning to meet the family of a prospective bride. Liu Chi, uninterested in currying favor with his potential in-laws, wanders off into the mountains, where he tumbles into a tiger pit. While languishing there he overhears a conversation between two disciples of an as yet unnamed master. The elder disciple confesses that he has violated the master's rule against sexual misconduct and vows to end his own life in a show of remorse and repentance; the two also discuss a third disciple, who has recently suffered wounds to his arm (chapter 56). As the elder disciple departs, the younger frees Liu Chi, identifies himself as Zhou Jirong 周季容, his errant senior brother as Lu Rui 盧瑞, the third disciple as Lan Xinshi 藍辛石 or Reverend Lan, and their common master as one Fang Shaode 方紹德 (57). He brings Liu Chi to meet Fang, who then sends Lan and Liu to exorcise the spirits that have begun bedeviling Liu's marriage prospect; the story from "Reverend Lan Catches a Ghost" is thus integrated into the novel by making the possessed victim Liu Chi's intended (58–60). After settling the spirits and taking leave of Liu Chi, Reverend Lan encounters a mysterious figure at a bridge. The narration interrupts the incipient episode with a history of Lan's background and character, then returns to the figure at the bridge—a young woman who turns out to be the last of the spirits from the exorcism incident, seeking vengeance on Lan (60–62). Lan defeats the spirit and returns to his home and his practice until the local gentry beseech his aid in ending the scourge of the three-legged tiger (62–64). It is his battle with the tiger that leaves him with the wounds Liu Chi has heard about back in chapter 56, before Lan has even been named.

Recovering from his wounds and devoting himself to his practice, Lan receives a visit from his senior fellow-disciple Lu Rui. The narrator takes the opportunity to recount Lu Rui's background and upbringing—an account within which is also embedded the story of Lu's first master, the opera performer and martial artist Hu Dagezi 胡大個子 (chapters 64–66). The focus shifts yet again to tell of the young life and career of the general Sun Kaihua 孫開華 (66–67). A character in Sun's story turns out to be Fang Shaode; the obligatory intervention relates Fang's birth, upbringing, training, and adventures up through his encounter with General Sun, in the aftermath of which Fang travels to Miao-minority regions of Hunan (67–68). There he meets Reverend Lan and takes him as his disciple (69). Lan tells his master about his encounter with the toad demon (69–70), and Fang, seeking a more worthy inheritor of his arts, elects Lu Rui—reconnecting the narrative with the strands abandoned in chapter 66.

But Lu Rui also errs and calls on Reverend Lan (as first told in 64) to ask him to aid with his last rites. With Reverend Lan and Zhou Jirong as witnesses, Lu Rui immolates himself with magical fire atop Mount Yuelu. Also present is Liu Chi, who has come to the mountain to keep his Mid-Autumn appointment with the Golden Arhat—who in turn appears and declares that the purpose of the appointment was precisely to allow Liu Chi to learn from Lu Rui's fate, of which the Golden Arhat had long ago had mystical foreknowledge. The Golden Arhat's revelations in chapter 71 thus resolve not only the narrative strands initiated in chapter 56, when the character of Liu Chi first connects with that of Reverend Lan, but also elements from the novel's opening chapters. In yet one more act of narrative closure, the scene on the mountaintop also reveals the conclusion of Lan's adventure with the toad demon, which Lan had concealed from his teacher (and the readers) when he told the tale in the previous chapter.

The novel thus makes the preexisting Lan episodes integral parts of a larger narrative web that is almost bewildering in its complexity. The interval of diegetic time between Liu Chi's first encounter with Fang Shaode's disciples in chapter 56 and their reunion on Mount Yuelu in chapters 70–71 is evidently no more than a matter of weeks, months at best. But the intervening fifteen chapters of text encompass multiple storylines spanning many decades of time.[35] The expansion of the temporal scope comes largely from the narrative convention of the biography (*zhuan* 傳): the provision of a chronologically organized sketch of the background and upbringing of each new character introduced. The introduction of characters is often occasioned by master-disciple relationships, and these relationships likewise play a central role in the majority of the characters' biographies. In this way transmission serves simultaneously as a thematic motif and as a device for narrative juncture, motivating and structuring the interweaving of diegetic content.[36]

The weaving together of the narrative strands—through foreshadowing, flashbacks (analepsis) and flashforwards (prolepsis), interruption, digression, intersection, resumption, and repetition—is effected in part through the help of overt narratorial intervention.[37] The narrator's voice provides persistent reminders of the fact that the narrative exists by virtue of the storyteller's interaction with his audience and thus of the centrality of transmission in another sense to the generic self-identity of *xiaoshuo*. When Lu Rui appears at Reverend Lan's door in chapter 65, for instance:

> Lan Xinshi realized that the arrival was his senior fellow-disciple Lu Rui. Just who was this Lu Rui? He was the stalwart that Liu Chi heard talking with Zhou Jirong back when he was trapped in the wilderness. I daresay my readers still recall that the substance of their conversation was Lu Rui's violation of the precept against lust and his determination to admit his crime and end his own life. Lu Rui has already told in his own words the story of his offense, but since his background and career are also relevant to our story, it will be best to take this opportunity to provide an account of these matters.
>
> (64:3, 86)

Here the narratorial voice functions less as an expression of the personalized author-narrator than as an exercise of the storytelling rhetoric of traditional vernacular fiction. But while the interventions sometimes seem heavy-handed, necessitated by a narrative so digressive and convoluted as to threaten to spin out of control, they at the same time display a certain bravado, a performer's delight in displaying his art before his audience, and to this extent the storyteller's voice is part and parcel of the construction of Xiang Kairan's distinctive authorial persona.

The combination of originally or potentially independent narrative strands into a larger narrative fabric, the layering and interweaving of narrative elements that the voice of the author-narrator so ostentatiously manages, deepens and complicates the material's thematic implications. Even considered on its own, the Reverend Lan material epitomizes *Rivers and Lakes'* fascination with the strange. Lan amalgamates and intensifies the strange in its various manifestations, including some we have not yet considered. His habitat, the wilds of Hunan, represents in an extreme form the marginality of the Rivers and Lakes; to this geographic and topographic marginality it adds an ethnic dimension, for these jungles are the home of his people, the non-Han Miao minority. Reverend Lan's personal appearance dramatizes his ethnic and cultural alterity, presenting not only an electric charisma but a striking contrast between his dark skin and strapping physique and the bearing and garb of a Confucian scholar.[38] The realm of the non-Han Miao is also the realm of the nonhuman. Animal instances of the nonhuman are dominated by the tigers and monkeys so prominent elsewhere in Xiang Kairan's fiction. Liu Chi's entry into Miao lands and into the narrative territory of the Reverend Lan material is marked by his blundering into a tiger pit, and tiger hunting is one of Lan's signature occupations; rescued from the pit, Liu Chi is entertained with tiger and monkey lore, and we later learn that Lan's master Fang Shaode was raised by monkeys as a child (albeit in Sichuan, not here in Hunan). But the nonhuman includes spirits as well as animals, and the line between the two is in fact porous. Reverend Lan calls upon the spirits to aid him in his struggles against his foes, and his adversaries transform themselves variously into human, animal, and patently demonic forms.

In part by means of such transformations, the Reverend Lan stories link these various manifestations of the strange—geographic, ethnic, animal, supernatural—to problems of sexuality, gender, and desire. The first Reverend Lan episode the novel presents is his exorcism of the spirits bedeviling the Liu 劉 family's marriageable daughter. The daughter has experienced her possession as a sexually suggestive nightmare of being carried off by five men. Reverend Lan uses his magic to trap the five spirits in earthen jars, but one escapes because of the family's negligence. As he returns from his exertions, drunk from a celebratory feast, he encounters a young woman weeping by a bridge in the dark. She explains that she has been driven out by an abusive husband and mother-in-law and begs Lan to escort her home. The narrative takes pains to make the temptation she offers real to the reader by dwelling on her comeliness, detailing her flirtatious conversation with Lan, and stretching the account of their interaction out over several chapters. Lan, however, is wary and unmoved; he pretends weakness to her charms only to force her to reveal herself as the last of the spirits from the Liu household, then pins the spirit beneath a bridge in its true form as a rooster. The episode imagines sexuality as desire incited by the female, indulged and abetted by demonic forces but subdued by the heroic male. It expresses the same ambivalence toward desire—its estrangement, the displacement of its fascinations onto an animal other—that the first chapter of this study found figured in Xiang Kairan's monkeys.

The later episode of the toad demon echoes this model of sexual desire and further suggests its relevance to the problem of transmission. In this case the waterside temptress is an alluring young woman who demands that Lan show her his gratitude for the harvest he has reaped over several nights of toad hunting. A toadlike reek from her body that Lan smells as his spirit briefly wavers before her temptation burdens male desire for the female with a visceral revulsion. Most significant are the circumstances in which this tale is told. After Reverend Lan has taken Fang Shaode as his master, Fang explains that he can teach Lan lesser magical arts (*fashu* 法術) but not the Way (*daofa* 道法), for Lan's primal male energy (*yuanyang* 元陽) is no longer in its virginal state. Lan insists he has never had congress with a woman, but Fang prompts him to think of instances when he might have been tempted, and upon hearing the tale of the toad demon explains that Lan's essence was stolen the moment he felt temptation's pull. The danger of desire—male heterosexual desire, presumptively—lies in its threat to the circuit of transmission between master and disciple. In its ideal form, the marvelous transmission of the Way is not simply patrilineal: it excludes entirely the female and the attendant problem of sexual desire.

Rivers and Lakes' interlacing of narrative strands puts the Reverend Lan stories in dialogue with other material that similarly reflects on the role of sexual desire in the enterprise of transmission. As previously mentioned, the narrative context for the Reverend Lan stories is Liu Chi's wandering into Miao lands, and no sooner has Liu Chi entered Miao territory than he blunders into a tiger pit, where he overhears the tale of Lu Rui's misadventures, which provide a straightforward demonstration of the dangers of unchecked desire. The temptress to whom Lu Rui succumbs is Miao, uses sorcery to undermine Lu Rui's resolve, and reveals her hideous true aspect once the deed is done; like the toad-demon tale, the episode thus expresses revulsion for a desire that is projected onto the female, the supernatural, and in this case the ethnic other. Lu Rui ascribes responsibility for his fall to evil karma from a previous lifetime (*qiansheng de yuannie* 前生的冤孽), and we later learn how he hesitated at the vow of chastity when taking Fang Shaode as his master:

Lu Rui thought to himself: "This requirement is too difficult! I'm not worried about cutting off the Lu family's posterity, but at this point I have no idea whether or not maintaining my virginity for my entire life is going to be an easy thing to do. Since he has this rule, though, if I want to follow the master's teachings of the Way all I can do is promise to observe it." And having thought this through, he went ahead and promised, saying, "I am willing to obey."

(70:3, 165)

Lu Rui chooses the transmission of the Way over transmission of the family line, ignorant of the power of karma, sorcery, and desire to subvert his choice.

Fate's designs encompass not only Lu Rui but also Liu Chi, whom the Golden Arhat brings to Mount Yuelu to learn from Lu Rui's end. The Golden Arhat accompanies his pronouncements to Liu Chi in chapter 71 with admonishments to Reverend Lan, further underlining the shared themes of the three storylines. But Liu Chi's own story acknowledges the imperative of the family line, with its implicit acceptance of at least carefully controlled sexuality. Li Chi ends his initial sojourn at the Laughing Daoist's temple and returns to attend to his parents when his lineage elder Ouyang Jingming reminds him of his filial obligations: "'I've heard of students of the Way casting aside concubines and abandoning their children, but I've never heard of any casting aside their father and abandoning their mother. If you can even cast aside your father and mother, then what good is the Way even if you attain it? There's no art of the Way in the whole world, what's more, that teaches unfilial behavior!'" (3:1, 34).

True filiality, of course, requires not merely tending to one's parents but also continuing the ancestral line. Liu Chi's mother reminds him of his obligations in a vivid and humorous exchange in chapter 55. Her efforts to secure grandchildren bring Liu Chi to Xinning, where his tale intersects with those of Reverend Lan and Lu Rui; they also trigger the possession of the Liu family's daughter, which we learn serves the providential purpose of aborting a match not karmically ordained. The narrative thus finesses the potential for conflict between the familial and spiritual axes of transmission by granting that Liu Chi must and will father children while continually forestalling realization of this obligation. The same dynamic informs the later episode of Liu Chi's adventures with a bandit queen (chapters 155–158, within the continuation authored by Zhao Tiaokuang); the plentiful suggestions of their mutual interest and possible pairing are swept away by the Golden Arhat's sudden appearance and declaration that "You are destined to marry late, and now is not yet the time" (158:5, 434). The text concedes on an ideological level the carefully regimented sexual desire allowed for in the Confucian model of transmission yet distances even this possibility through continuous narrative deferral. It imagines instead an idealized asexual transmission, a model that estranges sexual desire, setting it to haunt and so energize the landscapes, creatures, powers, and social bodies of the strange.

Fantasy and History: The Ma Assassination

Blame for the perception that fantasy martial arts fiction and film promoted superstitious beliefs and false consciousness must be assigned in part to Xiang Kairan's publisher, World Books. Shi Juan's analysis of the aggressive advertising campaign supporting *Rivers and Lakes'* book publication demonstrates that while early ads highlighted the novel's presentation of the strange, later ads increasingly insisted on the facticity of the material.[39] Two forms of authentification were invoked: common knowledge, that is, the currency of legends and tales among the population, and the identity and authority of the author. An ad published in *Xinwen bao* in June 1929 illustrates the latter:

> What kind of a person is Buxiaosheng? Readers may imagine him as a frail scholar; little do they know that he is himself a gallant possessed of consummate skills. The hundred and more marvelous gallants and sword-immortals found in the book are all his kin and fellow disciples; the sword-immortal "Xiang Leshan" is none other than Buxiaosheng's grandfather! And so everything in the book is actual fact.
>
> Fiction born of empty invention quickly proves tedious to read! For the truth and falsity of the plot immediately become apparent.
>
> Not a single sentence of *Marvelous Gallants of the Rivers and Lakes* is fabricated, and so it is that everyone reads it with tremendous pleasure.[40]

Shi Juan believes that the insistence on facticity was intended to counter the very tediousness the ad imputes to other products of invention; the strategy echoes the author's own claims in his "Three Monkey Tales" for the superior entertainment value of fact-based stories. The ascription to the author of a role equivalent to that of his characters takes to a new extreme the promotion of authorial personae that was a common feature of the marketing of fiction, sounding a rather different note from the deprecatory self-portraits the author provides in his texts.

Rivers and Lakes' claims concerning its own facticity, likewise, are more nuanced than the enthusiastic credulity promoted by the advertising campaign. The Reverend Lan material, which presents the strange in its most exotic forms, spiced with ethnic otherness, sexual transgression, nonhuman creatures, and the supernatural, offers a case in point. The text avers the authenticity of the events it narrates even as it brands them as superstition. When Lan buries the spirits who have bedeviled the Liu household, he tells the neighbors not to disturb the spot and warns of disaster to anyone who disregards his instructions. The narrator informs us that "the Hunanese are terribly superstitious" (60:3, 41) and so have passed Lan's warning on to the present day; he also tells us that those ignorant or heedless enough to violate the warning invariably suffer misfortune. Is it then still superstition, a groundless belief? The sequel to the episode, when Reverend Lan exposes the true form of the final spirit and pins it beneath a bridge, occasions more expansive ruminations in this vein:

> It's all very strange. No one who hadn't seen with his own eyes the rooster beneath the bridge would ever believe that such a preposterous and nonsensical thing could happen. I, Buxiaosheng, have a friend from the Liu family in Xinning. Back when Reverend Lan erected an altar and subdued the spirits at his family home, he wasn't yet born; today this friend of mine is already thirty years old. It's said that to this very day that rooster is still pinned to the sand beneath the bridge by a knife through its breast. It's unable to move, unable to eat or drink, and while it doesn't seem to be dead neither does it seem to be alive. [Even] women and children all know that it's a demon that Reverend Lan subdued at this spot, and no one dares to approach or touch it. From time to time an unwitting child or a passerby who doesn't know the inside story tries to approach, but as soon as they come to within ten feet of the rooster they are struck with an unbearable headache, sometimes even falling unconscious to the ground. The Hunanese have always had a superstitious belief in spirits and anomalies. For some decades, therefore, no one

has dared to touch that rooster. . . . What's more, in the region of Xinning and Baoqing, the sites connected with Reverend Lan's strange and unfathomable deeds are not limited to this bridge alone.

(62:3, 64)

The citation of a source with a personal connection to the narrated events, the reference to associated physical locales, and the appeal to common knowledge are all devices used in classical-language *xiaoshuo* to assert the authenticity of an anecdote.[41] They run counter to the distancing suggested by "it's said" (*jushuo* 據說) and the more comprehensive charge of misguided counterfactuality generally conveyed by the term "superstition." It is almost as if the author-narrator uses "superstition" not so much to brand beliefs as mistaken as to signal awareness that they are outmoded, discordant with contemporary ideological standards, a survival or leftover (as the etymology of the English word may imply) of a prior understanding of the world.[42]

Other passages echo *Strange Phenomena* and "The Black Cat" in suggesting that the jury is still out on science's authority to give a comprehensive account of the world. Chapter 23 presents an account of a magical flying sword imbued with power from the blood of a male and female pair of virgins. "This account is of course groundless hearsay (*wuji zhi tan* 無稽之談)," allows the narrator. "But since there are many matters even more groundless than this in the whole *Tale of Marvelous Gallants*, I can't omit it here simply on the grounds that it is groundless" (23:1, 332). The word *wuji* 無稽 can be used to mean "absurd," "preposterous"; if it is understood in this sense here, the passage reads as a frank confession of the tale's irreality. More literally, however, *wuji* means "without proof," thus "groundless" or "unfounded." And the possibility that the narrator is casting his material not as specious but as still open to verification becomes more evident in his later comments on the tale of Sun Yaoting 孫耀庭:

If one were to tell his history to the ordinary sort of person full of scientific understanding, it goes without saying that they would deride it as utterly absurd (*huangmiu* 荒謬)! Even I, who earnestly believe that there is no marvel that does not exist somewhere within the vastness of creation, felt that it was groundless (*wuji* 無稽)

hearsay when I first heard someone tell the history of Sun Yaoting. It was only later when my experience had gradually broadened that I came to understand that the matter of Sun Yaoting was not absurd in the least. Assuming, on the basis of an extremely childish scientific understanding, the absurdity of what is beyond the reach of one's mind and senses—*that* would be truly absurd![43]

(92:4, 7)

Xiaoshuo lays claim to a discursive terrain in which transmitted narratives of the strange enjoy a fundamental authority. In the Republican-era context, supernatural manifestations of the strange gain notoriety and marketable appeal precisely because of the intensity of the challenge they present to normative modernizing ideologies. But the strange is not restricted to the supernatural, either in the premodern *xiaoshuo* tradition or in Xiang Kairan's fiction. One of *xiaoshuo*'s roles is to serve as unofficial history, *waishi* 外史 or *yeshi* 野史, recording and transmitting matters overlooked by official historiography. Within this portion of *xiaoshuo*'s domain, strangeness consists not so much in challenges to common assumptions about the laws of reality (though these are sometimes involved) as in the revelation of unknown, private, or alternative aspects of the persons and events of public history. *Rivers and Lakes* embraces this role most prominently in the episode of the Ma assassination. The story is based on the notorious incident of Governor-General Ma Xinyi's 馬新貽 (1821–1870) assassination in Nanjing by one Zhang Wenxiang 張汶祥. An official investigation attributed the deed to personal grievances between Zhang and Ma. Rumors elaborated on the alleged grievances, while conspiracy theories hinted at others' involvement and deeper political motives; the resulting tales circulated in various written and dramatic forms as well as in general gossip.[44] In Xiang Kairan's telling, Ma Xinyi 馬心儀, a prefectural magistrate, is captured by the Sichuan bandit chieftains Zheng Shi 鄭時 and Zhang Wenxiang. The bandits invite Ma to swear brotherhood with them, seeing in him an opportunity to abandon outlawry and forge legitimate careers. Ma, under the pressure of circumstances, can only agree. Ma's own career subsequently thrives, thanks in part to the outlaws' behind-the-scenes assistance. He is appointed governor of Shandong, and the brothers come to join him, but Ma seduces their wives, then betrays them to government troops when their outlaw past begins to come to light. Zheng is killed but Zhang escapes. After years of plotting and several foiled attempts, Zhang finally catches up with Ma in Nanjing and exacts vengeance for his fallen brother.

The novel incorporates the episode of the Ma assassination by means of its typical strategies of interruption and digression. The beginning of chapter 80 finds us at Red Lotus Temple; Liu Chi and his companions rescue Inspector-General Bu 卜巡撫, a Qing official who has been imprisoned by the villainous monks. The narrative then backtracks to tell the story of Bu's capture from his own perspective. At a climactic moment, when a monk whom the abbot Zhiyuan has ordered to execute Bu is suddenly struck dead, the narrator interrupts to begin Zhiyuan's *zhuan*, the chronological account of his life, which he began under the lay name Yang Conghua 楊從化. When Yang Conghua takes the monk Wugou 無垢 as his master, we meet Wugou's elder disciple Zhang Wenxiang. Noting that Zhang Wenxiang is best known for his role in the Ma assassination, the narrative now launches into that tale. The events leading up to Ma's assassination unfold over some nine chapters before being fissured by a ten-chapter digression into stories surrounding another character, Sun Yaoting 孫耀庭; the narrative then relates Zhang Wenxiang's assassination of Ma Xinyi and, in chapter 106, returns to Bu's rescue, last mentioned some twenty-six chapters ago.

In terms of plotting, the Ma episode is stitched into the novel's fabric not only by Zhang Wenxiang's connection with Red Lotus Temple but by several other characters and narrative threads as well. Thematically the episode presents the Rivers and Lakes in a variant aspect: as the Greenwoods (*lülin* 綠林), the exilic margins inhabited by men whose talent and ambition cannot find accommodation within the orthodox but restrictive channels of success through government service. The outlaws of the Greenwoods seek not the realization of an otherworldly Way but an alternate path to recognition and favor. The tragedies that befall them implicate the orthodox structures of power for narrowness and hypocrisy. Sexual desire still functions as both an engine of disaster and a symbol of moral failing, though its dangers here are imagined more in terms of a threat to brotherhood than as a challenge to the transmission of a lineage. Ma's lechery epitomizes his villainy, and the hidden pleasure chamber where he seduces his sworn brothers' wives mirrors the dungeons beneath Red Lotus Temple where the archvillain Abbot Zhiyuan practices his depravities. But the ground for Ma's betrayal is prepared by Zheng Shi's own weakness for the female sex and his success in convincing his brother Zhang to join him in taking as wives the two beguiling sisters they encounter on their journey toward Shandong. Zhang, brotherhood's avenging champion, never consummates his relationship with his nominal bride.

In its representation of outlawry and brotherhood the Ma episode operates within the diegetic and thematic territory immortalized by *The Water Margin*, one of the landmarks in the tradition of the vernacular-language linked-chapter novel. In its representation of its own intent and status, the episode claims the motivation that ranks alongside fascination with the strange as one of the defining imperatives of *xiaoshuo*: the transmission of an authentic account. The author-narrator claims that Zhang Wenxiang confessed the true story of his relationship with Ma Xinyi only to Minister of Justice Zheng Dunjin 鄭敦謹 (1803–1885; unrelated to the story's bandit chieftain Zheng), who carried the secret to his grave. All previous accounts of this notorious case are fabrications, deliberately concealing even what fragments of truth their authors may have known. But:

> In the course of my investigations into the background of the Red Lotus Temple, I tracked down Zheng Dunjin's son-in-law, who eavesdropped on Zhang Wenxiang's confession that day from behind a screen, and it was only thus that I got to the bottom of the matter. If I were not to make an accurate record of these events, [the true account] would vanish, which would be a great pity. What's more, if I didn't add this episode to my tale of chivalric gallants, the preposterous and bizarre [episode of] Red Lotus Temple would be quite without foundation! For these reasons, although even women and children all know the story of Ma's assassination by Zhang Wenxiang, I shall write it out from beginning to end according to what I have discovered, heedless of the expense of words, and speak out on behalf of a hero who suffered wrongful death at the hands of tyrannical authority!
>
> (82:3, 321)

There are two points to make about the author-narrator's account of the transmission of the tale. The first is that he portrays the transmission as honoring the same moral logic that defines the actions of the characters within the tale. The account to which readers have privileged access is that given by Zhang to Minister Zheng. When the captured Zhang is pressed on his motives for assassinating Ma, he insists that it is only to Minister Zheng that he will reveal his story. Minister Zheng, dispatched to Nanjing by imperial order, has no idea why he has been singled out by Zhang, a man he has never before heard of or met. Only when they come face to face does he realize that the two in fact encountered each other some years ago, when Zheng refused the advances of the lust-addled wife of a man in whose residence he was staying. His upright behavior was witnessed and lauded by a bandit who just happened to have broken in to burglarize the house. The intruder was of course none other than Zhang Wenxiang, who now, on the strength of this demonstration of moral integrity, identifies Minister Zheng as the only worthy recipient of his tale of brotherhood and betrayal.[45] The recognition of male virtue epitomized by resistance to sexual desire incited by lascivious women thus shapes both the events of the episode and the course of its transmission, and this homology invites readers to a greater investment in the material, suggesting that in receiving the tale they join simple spectatorship with some degree of participation in the story's moral imaginary.

The second point to note is the catholicity of the authority that transmission grants and the heterogeneity of the material over which this authority extends. In some cases, both in Xiang Kairan's fiction and in the *xiaoshuo* tradition more broadly, the citation of sources serves to locate authenticity more in the transmission of a story than in the facticity of its contents as such. Here however the detailed account of transmission serves not to defer responsibility but to assert absolute historicity. The writing of a record is driven by the moral imperative to keep the truth of events from vanishing from knowledge and by the even more compelling need to speak out for—"give vent to anger" (*chu qi* 出氣) for—a righteous man wronged. The assertion of a moral imperative hints at possible tensions between this averredly historical episode and the "preposterous and bizarre" (*huangtang guiguai* 荒唐詭怪) matter of Red Lotus Temple. The statement that the Ma assassination provides a "foundation" (*laiyou* 來由, a "cause" or a "reason") is ambiguous in scope; does the Ma episode simply provide a narrative pretext for the more fantastic material, or is it intended to share the mantle of its historicity?[46] From a certain standpoint the text's mixture of pseudohistory with tales of the supernatural is a forced wedding that breeds a monster, an aesthetic flaw on a par with its deliriously digressive structure. From another perspective, though, the result demonstrates the power of the web of narrative transmission to find and bind together material disparate in source, content, and even ontological status under the mandate of the strange and beneath the capacious discursive mantle of *xiaoshuo*.

The Final Chapters and the Flattening of the Strange

The resumption of *Rivers and Lakes'* serialization in *Scarlet Rose* in January 1927 required a relaunching of the novel's narrative arc, some major strands of which had been at least provisionally resolved when the serialization came to an apparent end in July of the previous year. Like the novel's early chapters, the restart recounts a bit of lore from northeastern Hunan, a local custom that ends up embroiling martial artists, adepts of the Way, and their rival lineages. The precipitating event in the opening chapters was the feud over the Zhaojiaping riverlands; in this case it is an annual lion-dancing competition between Changsha and nearby Xiangyin 湘陰 county. When Xiangyin hires a ringer, an itinerant martial artist from Shandong named Zhao Wu 趙五, the Changsha gentry turn for help to Liu Chi. He recommends to them a hidden talent, one Yu Bashu 余八叔. Zhao Wu and Yu Bashu—with their backstories, teachers, teachers' backstories, and so forth—serve as the points of entry into the narrative web of the novel's last fifty-odd chapters. Though not from Xiang Kairan's hand, these chapters are a part of the novel as it has been received and transmitted, and their departures from the earlier chapters throws some aspects of Xiang Kairan's own work into clearer relief.

These chapters interweave new material with characters and plotlines from the earlier portion. While the narrative still delights in digression, it is more focused (or, one might argue, more simplistic) than before in developing a central organizing story that centers on a new villain, the Weeping Daoist (Ku Daoren 哭道人), and on the alliance of the Kunlun and Kongtong lineages to foil the menace he presents. The conflict proceeds through a series of encounters, climaxing with the allies' triumph at a tournament (*leitai* 擂台) the Weeping Daoist has convened and their destruction of his lair. Xiang Kairan's Hunan lore and flashes of naturalistic dialogue and incident are shouldered aside by increasingly implausible and grandiose adventures, frequently envisioned as large-scale public spectacles. Highlights include an initiation ceremony on an island teeming with fabulous monsters, where fifty virgin female disciples impale themselves on stakes and are then restored to life (chapters 110–111), and a duel between the Weeping and Laughing Daoists conducted through the combatants' deployment of weaponized powers of weeping and laughter (chapter 139). Spectacular excesses of the strange and the supernatural are now the main substance of the novel, and as a result the strange, while more grandiose, feels strangely flattened.

The novel's final decade of chapters constitutes a sort of coda made up of several episodes that revisit earlier characters. And several of these episodes introduce another new element into the novel: a topical or allegorical mode, in which the events of the novel echo contemporary political concerns. In the aftermath of his defeat in chapter 151, the Weeping Daoist encounters Abbot Zhiyuan, chief villain of the Red Lotus Temple episode, unseen since chapter 106. Zhiyuan has returned to lay life and established a new base of operations—not a heterodox sect or a trap-filled lair but what is described as a colony, a formerly desert isle that he has populated with desperadoes and their families and developed into a thriving community. From this island base he schemes to seize control of provinces along the coast, and toward this end he allies himself with the King of the Eastern Barbarians, whose island realm has long harbored designs against the Chinese nation.

The episode shifts the focus of the novel's conflicts away from factional strife within the marginal terrain of the Rivers and Lakes and toward a direct challenge to established political authority. Challenge to political authority is of course a persistent theme in the literary and cultural traditions of the *xia* and the Rivers and Lakes, whether in the deeds of Sima Qian's assassins and wandering knights or in the Liangshan bandits' struggles against and on behalf of the Song government and court. Several passages in the earlier chapters of *Rivers and Lakes* link the struggle between the Kunlun and Kongtong lineages to Han Chinese resistance against the Manchu Qing dynasty.[47] While these passages suggestively adumbrate the engagement with ethnic and political themes by some later martial arts fiction, particularly the novels of Jin Yong, they remain peripheral and inert within the novel itself. Zhiyuan's new schemes foreground the question of political sovereignty, and his alliance with the

Eastern Barbarians baldly assign it a contemporary topicality, unmistakably referencing the threats to the Republic of China posed by internecine warfare and Japanese aggression. The Drunken Gallant of Jiangnan (Jiangnan jiuxia 江南酒俠), a hero introduced during the Weeping Daoist episodes, aids Zhiyuan and his accomplices in capturing the key coastal city of Xiamen. He then reveals that the apparent victory was only an illusion and that he has actually imprisoned Zhiyuan within a magical jade cup. The crime for which he calls Zhiyuan to account is not treason but rather sexual misconduct, the defilement of honest women at Red Lotus Temple. At the same time, however, the Drunken Gallant expresses regret at his inability to extirpate completely the threat from the Eastern Barbarians, thereby evoking a traditional mapping of sexual discipline onto political loyalty.

The Drunken Gallant also intervenes in the novel's final episode. The annual battle over Zhaojiaping is approaching, and the conflict between the Kunlun and Kongtong lineages threatens to erupt once more. Intercepting the adept Hongyun laozu 紅雲老祖 on his way to aid the Kongtong faction, the Drunken Gallant shows him a vision of a dispute between his disciples escalating into an inferno in which foreign soldiers cast souls into the devouring flames. Hongyun agrees that he must do whatever he can to save the innocent from imminent disaster. The Drunken Gallant next kidnaps the heads of the Kunlun and Kongtong lineages and again presents visions to urge them to work together, not against one another. When the proud elders balk, he reveals that he has entrapped them in a magical structure from which only a promise of cooperation will allow escape; only then do they agree to abandon their longstanding enmity.

While this episode resolves (in perfunctory fashion) one of the novel's primary narrative strands, it also, like the previous episode, asserts the priority of the national community over that of the Rivers and Lakes. And it does so in part by shifting the text's mode of signification toward the allegorical. It is not merely the case, that is, that the narrative presents agents and events of the Rivers and Lakes reaching out from their accustomed margins to impinge upon orthodox institutions or the community at large; this much could be said of several core episodes of the novel, such as the assassination of Viceroy Ma (an episode inspired by a historical incident) or the kidnapping of Prefect Bu by the monks of Red Lotus Temple (an entirely fictional event). The more fundamental shift lies in the fact that the significance of these later episodes is generated not so much by any intrinsic narrative energy or by the fascination of esoteric lore as by their figural reference to events and situations other than themselves—contemporary concerns over factional conflict and foreign aggression. The text signals the referentiality of these episodes by foregrounding acts of illusion and representation: Zhiyuan's conquest of Xiamen is a fantasy conjured by the Drunken Gallant, who likewise presents his case against factionalism through moving pictures displayed in a crystal ball. In operating as topical allegories, almost as the textual equivalent of political cartoons, these late episodes might seem to vindicate the claim that the rise and popularity of martial arts fiction directly reflect public concern with Republican-era warlordism.[48] This claim in turn could conceivably be deployed in an attempt to assimilate martial arts fiction to hoary narratives of a mainstream of modern Chinese literature defined (and burdened) by an "obsession with China." But these gestures toward allegory and topicality mark a turn away from the notion of historicity that informed the episode of the Ma assassination and thus from the earlier chapters' performative allegiance to a particular model of what *xiaoshuo* is and how it functions. Just as exaggeration flattens the strange, so allegorization denatures historicity. It is valid to see national and nationalistic concerns as informing Xiang Kairan's fiction and the genre of martial arts fiction as a whole, but these concerns manifest themselves less through allegory than through a form of cultural nationalism—a national identity constructed through reference to cultural traditions. This cultural nationalism finds its most evident expression in *Rivers and Lakes*' sister work, *Modern Times*, the subject of the final chapter of this study.

CHAPTER SIX

Chivalric Heroes of Modern Times

Part of *Rivers and Lakes'* legacy lies in the novel's influence, via the *Red Lotus Temple* films, on the emergence of Chinese martial arts cinema. This cinematic legacy has in turn affected the way later readers have experienced the novel and how scholars perceive its place in literary and cultural history. A similar dynamic obtains for *Modern Times*. The most iconic figure in the entire body of martial arts film is arguably Bruce Lee, who in the early 1970s brought the martial arts genre and indeed Chinese film as a whole to the attention of audiences worldwide. One of the roles that showcased Lee's wedding of the martial arts with sensual machismo and ardent Chinese nationalism was that of Chen Zhen, who in *Fist of Fury* (*Jingwu men* 精武門, 1972) avenges his teacher's death upon the treacherous Japanese before meeting apotheotic martyrdom before the guns of an international firing squad.[1] Although the character of Chen Zhen was invented for the film, Xiang Kairan's *Modern Times* can indirectly claim credit for his conception. The fictional Chen Zhen's teacher is the historical Huo Yuanjia 霍元甲, the first martial arts instructor at the Shanghai Pure Martial Athletic Association. Written accounts of Huo Yuanjia's life and death began to circulate soon after his demise in 1910. Xiang Kairan told the story several times, and an extended account of Huo Yuanjia's career serves as the structural and narrative framework for *Modern Times*.[2] The account in *Modern Times* has been the direct or indirect source for the recensions and reinventions of the Huo Yuanjia legend that continue to thrive in fiction, film, and television up through the present day—including numerous representations of the fictional student first played by Bruce Lee.[3] Although *Fist of Fury*'s Chen Zhen was conceived as an emendation of sorts to the Huo Yuanjia legend, answering the earlier stories' poignant tragedy with a more dynamic, even chauvinistic, triumphalism, the spirit (and at times even narrative elements) of the film are often imputed to Xiang Kairan's fictional treatment. One aim of this chapter is to free Xiang Kairan's Huo Yuanjia from the posthumous shadow of Chen Zhen and read him in the context of his textual home in *Modern Times*.

Commentary and scholarship on Xiang Kairan's writings find it impossible to resist the temptation of reading *Modern Times* alongside *Rivers and Lakes*. The two novels are the author's best-known works. They began publication in the same year, as serializations in sister periodicals from World Books. They exhibit so many similarities in language, form, narratorial rhetoric, narrative structure, representational mode, and subject matter as to seem cut from the very same cloth, yet they are somehow distinct in scope and themes. The similarity of their titles is far from unique, for it is echoed in the titles of others of Xiang Kairan's works as well as those of his inspirations and imitators. The two titles' presentation of semantic variation framed by and at the same time challenging a mirrored structure nonetheless reinforces the impulse to consider them as the complementary components of a couplet of parallel verse. The two-character modifiers at the beginning of both titles, *jianghu* 江湖 (Rivers and Lakes) and *jindai* 近代 (modern times), seem to epitomize both the congruity and the contrast. One phrase is locative, one temporal. One novel reveals the native home of the strange, of the martial arts, and of those who pursue them; the other explores this world's encounter with the tides of a teleological and universalizing history.[4]

"These two works both served as trailblazers for modern Chinese martial arts fiction," says Han Yunbo 韩云波 in a typical remark; "the former more fully inherits and continues tradition, while the later more fully expresses the modernity of '*wuxia.*'"[5] Scholars addressing the modernity of *Modern Times* most often characterize its literary modernity—its role in the transformation of late-Qing- and early-Republican-era chivalric fiction (*xiayi xiaoshuo* 俠義小說) into modern martial arts fiction (*wuxia xiaoshuo* 武侠小说)—in terms of a broader ideological modernity. While *Rivers and Lakes* is burdened by its blithe trafficking in what canonical figures of literary modernity branded as superstition and feudal value systems, *Modern Times* redeems itself by sounding patriotic and progressive notes. "The work is anti-imperialist without being xenophobic and recognizes Western learning without fawning over the foreign."[6] For some scholars, thus, *Modern Times* offers an avenue for assimilating Xiang Kairan as an author and, through him, martial arts fiction as a genre and even Butterfly fiction as a whole into a narrative of modern Chinese literature that is more inclusive than May Fourth literary orthodoxy yet still informed by a nationalist spirit and enlightenment values.[7]

My discussion of *Modern Times* will focus not so much on the question of the novel's own modernity as on its representation of its protagonist's encounters with modernity in the form of certain defining aspects of modern life: the global system of nation-states, the urban environment, scientific rationalism, modern technology, and the mass media. I will argue that these encounters serve to foreground the problem of transmission, which the previous chapter identified as an axis of structural congruity and substantive differentiation between the Rivers and Lakes and its societally orthodox other. Intrinsic to the process of transmission are both continuity and change, as some practice, knowledge, or identity travels from one generation of inheritors to the next. Clinging for a moment longer to the conceit of parallelism, we might say that *Rivers and Lakes* delights in and even fetishizes what is transmitted and thus implicitly emphasizes the integrity of the line, while *Modern Times* brings its attention to the challenges presented by changing times, the changes that tradition might make in response, and the extent to which a tradition responsive in such a way can be said to maintain its authority and even its identity. Even as it suggests the parameters of later deployments of the Chinese martial arts as a vehicle for cultural nationalism, it attempts to imagine the modernization of the martial arts through new forms of transmission. And in so doing, it does in fact undertake an at least tentative exploration of the boundaries and possibilities of that art of transmission we know as *xiaoshuo*.

The redactions of the Huo Yuanjia legend epitomized by Bruce Lee's Chen Zhen portray the Japanese as the chief villains and primary foils for Chinese masculine identity. Xiang Kairan's *Modern Times*, as we shall see, has the Japanese play a key narrative role, yet it introduces them only quite late in the text. In order to appreciate the role of the Japanese in *Modern Times* and the novel's overall thematic concerns, including those that distinguish it from later versions of the Huo Yuanjia legend, it will be helpful to glance at the representation of Japan and the Japanese in Xiang Kairan's first novel, *The Unofficial History of Sojourners in Japan*.

Chapter 1 has already described the importance of Japan to Xiang Kairan's own life and career. It was study in Japan that provided a route for continuing his education when his schooling ran afoul of his youthful political activism. It was his sojourns in Japan that provided the material and in certain senses the inspiration for the literary work that established him as an author of *xiaoshuo*. One would only expect that his experiences there between the ages of fifteen and twenty-five would have a significant effect (as similar experiences did for so many of his peers) on his understanding of his world and of himself, including his sense of identity as a Chinese.[8] The discussion below will address *Sojourners'* representation of interactions between Chinese and Japanese and its expression of the role of an imagined Japan in the construction of Chinese selves.

Depravity in the Modern City

For an example of the kinds of characters and incidents that comprise the novel's narrative, we may look to the case of Zhu Fuquan 朱甫全, whose story is related in chapter 6.[9] Zhu Fuquan comes to Japan not on a government stipend but backed by a substantial family fortune. Unfamiliar with local conditions, he looks for guidance to a fellow clansman, Zhu Zhong 朱鐘, who is only too happy to show him how to spend his money, above all in the pursuit of Japanese girls. After an extended apprenticeship in the brothels, Zhu Zhong introduces Zhu Futian to a tailor's daughter, Yoshida Nakako 吉田仲子; Zhu Zhong is involved with Nakako, but he is unable to satisfy her sexual appetite and so is eager to pass her on to some third party. Zhu Futian is so taken with the young and pretty Nakako that he decides to make her his concubine, intending eventually to bring her back to China. At Zhu Zhong's urging and for a handsome bride-price, Nakako agrees to a formal union. All seems well until Zhu Futian's wife back in China balks at the arrangement. She pressures her father-in-law to cut off the flow of funds to Japan; Zhu Futian's blizzard of letters home goes unanswered, and he finds himself quickly sinking into debt. Nakako, disenchanted with the sudden turn from a life of luxury to daily visits to the pawnshop and tirades from the landlord, to say nothing of her brow-beaten master's loss of ardor, demands a formal separation—including, of course, monetary compensation. In a flash of inspiration, Zhu Futian forges a letter from home announcing the imminent arrival of five hundred *yuan*, and on the strength of this document he convinces Zhu Zhong, who as a government-funded student commands good credit, to stand surety for a short-term, high-interest loan from a Japanese moneylender. After dismissing Nakako, Zhu Futian lingers in Japan just long enough to purchase the diploma he has neglected to earn during his previous years in the country, then flees home to China, leaving Zhu Zhong saddled with his debts.

The elements of this episode are replayed throughout the novel in inexhaustible repetition and variation. Characters are ruled by their desires, above all for sex and money. In the scramble for the most immediate possible gratification, no relationship, no institution, and no ideal is exempt from manipulation. Education and service to the nation, the ostensible reasons for Chinese sojourners' presence in a foreign land, are irrelevant, dispensable, or, if discovered to be tactically advantageous, conveniently subject to the same market rules that govern the exchange of the novel's central commodity, sex. Face is to be saved if possible, but there is almost nothing that cannot be brazened out if necessary. While Chinese males are the central agents of the narrated action and apparent focus of critique, men and women, Chinese and Japanese, are all equally committed to the game of self-gratification and mutual manipulation. Chinese are as apt to swindle Chinese, and Japanese Japanese, as each the other. The predictable disasters attendant upon the characters' breathtakingly short-sighted schemes bring no enlightenment, but only a stirring of the stew of desires and resentments that generates further gamesmanship and misadventure.

Although this summary of Zhu Fuquan's career serves as a useful example of the setting, scope, and tone of the novel's narrative materials, it is less representative of the work's general narrative texture. Zhu Fuquan's story is presented to the reader in a form only slightly more expanded than that given here, in a focused account occupying a page or two of text. Such brief, integral, and self-sufficient narratives do occur within the novel from time to time, as intradiegetic anecdotes, illustrative asides, or (as here) prolegomena to more extended series of events. But the wider narrative fabric within which they are imbedded is prolix rather than succinct, multistranded rather than unitary, retardatory and endlessly fissile rather than answerable to any teleological urgency or discipline. The novel begins with the character Zhou Zhuan 周撰, a lecherous and conniving "old Japan hand" from the same mold as Zhu Fuquan, and is structured around the leisurely narration of his adventures and those of his circle of acquaintances. A character, action, or relationship commences winding its way through conversations, meals, ruminations, trysts, and excursions, only to be shunted from the stage by an entirely different train of events, which might be raised in conversation, occasioned by a chance encounter, or introduced by the narrator out of the blue. The new narrative vector may or may not reach a determinate point before itself suffering a similar fate. Once faded from the stage, a given element of the plot may reappear almost immediately or only after numerous chapters; rediscovered, it may retain something like its original contours or reveal a latent fusion with some other sequence of events. Zhu Fuquan's compact story, thus, serves as a node for a tangle of events involving Zhu Zhong and his family and friends: the problem of Zhu Fuquan's debts; the efforts of Zhu Zhong's usurious father, Zhu Zhengzhang 朱正章, to forge a business alliance with the Japanese moneylender; the seduction of his sister, Zhu Hui 朱惠, by a classmate; the father's attempt to blackmail the classmate; the classmate's enlistment of other characters in a counterblackmail involving a Japanese newspaper reporter; and so on, seemingly ad infinitum, with each of these strands intersecting with other recurrent figures and ongoing storylines and leavened with material of purely incidental interest. The narrative texture of *Sojourners*, in short, is what will later serve for Xiang Kairan's novels on marvelous and martial themes.

The narrative techniques of multiplicity, indirectness, prolixity, and retardation are associated, of course, with traditional Chinese vernacular linked-chapter fiction in general. *Sojourners'* thematic concerns link it to several more specific categories of contemporary and near-contemporary fiction—exposé fiction, the courtesan novel, urban fiction, and overseas-student literature. In its focus on the revelation of contemporary society's hypocrisy and excess it echoes that body of late-Qing fiction that David Wang refers to as exposé fiction.[10] As Wang argues, the commonly encountered characterization of these novels as *qianze xiaoshuo* 譴責小說, "tales that chastise and excoriate," imputes to them an agenda of normative satire and so does less than full justice to that dizzying absence of ethical and intellectual moorings they not only parade before the reader but also in some sense perform.[11] *Sojourners'* particular focus on the libidinal carnival indicates a secondary linkage with another prominent late-Qing thematic subgenre, that of the "courtesan" or "depravity" novel. Its geographic imaginary, however, is not that of the (allegedly) typical courtesan novel, which reduces the social world to a microcosm contained within the walls of the brothel;[12] its landscape is the city of Tokyo, in which the interior spaces of hostels, restaurants, gambling dens, and bordellos are connected by avenues and meticulously specified tram lines and woven by the intersecting itineraries of recurrent characters into a vaster fabric of expatriate enclaves, police precincts, commercial and entertainment districts, residential neighborhoods, suburbs, scenic areas, and outlying spas. This fictional conjuration of urban space suggests *Sojourners'* affinity with the body of Shanghai fiction analyzed by Des Forges, a literary product with a distinctive aesthetic in which the narrative tropes of simultaneity, interruption, and excess serve both to represent the city of Shanghai and to circulate a vision of urban modernity among a geographically dispersed readership.[13] Des Forges's model is useful here in part because it specifies a novelistic subgenre more distinctive than is suggested by the general rubric of exposé fiction, in part because it shifts the chronological perspective. Viewing *Sojourners* merely as an offspring of the late-Qing exposé tradition places the novel at the twilight of a genre, when (according to Lu Xun's still influential account) the outraged if undisciplined fires of social criticism had sunk to the vulgarity and blackmail of Black Curtain fiction (*heimu xiaoshuo* 黑幕小說). Des Forges's schema of the Shanghai urban novel, in contrast, defines a fictional form and attendant consciousness that took shape in the 1890s and retained vigor well into the 1920s and beyond.[14]

Des Forges argues for Shanghai's unique status as the metropole that simultaneously acts as the material (publishing) and imaginary (narrative) center of a modern urban sensibility. *Sojourners* obviously diverges from his model by making Tokyo rather than Shanghai the locus of its action. One might account for this divergence by pointing out Shanghai's persisting centrality as both site of the novel's publication and crucial (if off-stage) geographic and economic nexus for many of its characters' activities or by positing the urban imaginary as fashioned in and for Shanghai but then transferable to other fictional locales. In any event, *Sojourners'* setting constitutes an important point of difference not only from the Shanghai-based urban novel but within the larger context of exposé fiction as well. While recent scholarship has emphasized that late-Qing exposé fiction's unmasking of the perceived hypocrisy and corruption of Chinese society, governmental institutions, and mores cannot be reduced to a simple "response" to Western pressures and influence, it is undeniable that the encounter with the non-Chinese other in many ways shaped this fiction and the intellectual milieu in which it took form. But whether laying bare the grotesqueries of "traditional" society or those of "modernizing" countercurrents, exposé fiction most often made contemporary China its setting. Exceptions include Zeng Pu's 曾樸 (1872–1935) 1903 *Niehai hua* 孽海花 [A flower in the sea of sins], which includes an account of the courtesan Fu Caiyun's 傅彩雲 adventures in Europe, and Li Boyuan's 李伯元 (1861–1906) 1905 *A Brief History of Enlightenment* (*Wenming xiaoshi* 文明小史), which anticipates *Sojourners* with several episodes concerning Chinese students in Japan; one might also bear in mind the parallel subgenre of science fantasy, which might send Chinese travelers on journeys to speculative utopias and dystopias.[15] But *Sojourners* breaks new ground by devoting itself exclusively to the escapades of Chinese outside their home country and is accordingly recognized as the progenitor of the still thriving genre of "overseas-student literature" (*liuxuesheng wenxue* 留學生文學).

The Japanese Other

As a portrait of early-Republican-era Chinese students in Japan, *Sojourners* invites comparison with a slightly later and apparently quite different body of literature: those foundational texts of May Fourth fiction that represent the same milieu. Lu Xun's 1922 "Preface to *A Call to Arms*" ("*Nahan* zixu" 《呐喊》自序) portrays the author's student experience in Japan as the original impetus for the literary career that almost single-handedly launched the project of May Fourth fiction. The early short stories of Yu Dafu 郁達夫 (1896–1945), a pioneer of May Fourth fictional Romanticism, are likewise set in Japan, and they are widely read as fictionalized accounts of the author's student days. "Chenlun" 沉淪 [Sinking] (1921), the best known of this set of stories, is typical in its subject, themes, and narrative approach. It relates the deepening despair of a Chinese student in Japan for whom sexual frustration is inextricably entangled with a sense of national and racial inferiority. His repression and shame drive him to masturbation and voyeurism, and these, in a vicious cycle, to deeper shame and repression; progressively alienated from both Japanese society and his own countrymen, he ends the narrative at the seashore, contemplating suicide after a humiliating encounter with a Japanese prostitute, gazing toward his distant homeland and crying out, "Oh China, my China, you are the cause of my death!. . . I wish you could become rich and strong soon!" The story is renowned for its introduction to Chinese literature of the techniques of internal focalization, that is, the refraction of the world through the consciousness of a single main character; for the alienation and psychosexual morbidity of that central fictional consciousness; and for its exploration of the links between sexuality and national identity.[16]

The similarity between "Sinking" and *Sojourners* lies not merely in the setting and subject matter but also in the thematic preoccupation with the libidinal and in the apparent desire to provide an exhaustive and unstinting record of a diseased condition. The enumeration of these points of comparison, of course, only facilitates an even more detailed articulation of the points at which the two texts so markedly diverge. "Sinking" examines the condition of a single character, *Sojourners* the misadventures of a sprawling cast. "Sinking" provides an internally focalized and subjective account, *Sojourners* an external and descriptive narration. In "Sinking" the subjective fragmentation of the narrative allows the emergence of only the most rudimentary plot; in *Sojourners* emplotment disintegrates under the sheer profusion of character and incident. Yu Dafu's protagonist is swept toward final self-destruction through his internalization of external prejudice and his inability to realize his desires. Buxiaosheng's characters bring indiscriminate and recurrent disaster upon themselves and others through their unchecked pursuit of self-gratification. The target of Yu Dafu's exposure is the individual and national psyche, and its flaw a weakness symbolized by and manifested as emasculation; the target of Buxiaosheng's is the behavior of a social group, the predatory sexual hyperactivity of whose members is the most primal expression of their self-centeredness and undisciplined appetite.

The enumeration of these differences still amounts to not much more than a recapitulation of oft-noted ideological distinctions between May Fourth fiction and its late-Qing and early-Republican predecessors and of the alternative formal and rhetorical strategies through which their divergent social and artistic agendas found articulation. For a deeper understanding of the implications of Yu Dafu and Buxiaosheng's shared narrative and thematic material, we may turn to Shih Shu-mei's analysis of Japan's role in Chinese modernity. Shih suggests that the protagonists of Yu Dafu's stories can best be understood in the context of Chinese intellectuals' conflicted response to a Japan that played two ostensibly distinct roles: that of a metropolitan culture, exemplifying the successful transition to (Western) modernity and mediating that modernity for a China eager to catch up, and that of an imperial culture, reproducing within the local arena the West's posture of domination and its colonizing strategies. The Japanese woman as object of libidinal desire embodies the impulse to "love the [modern Western] other through Japan." And the humiliating inability to realize that desire marks the cultural moment at which complete capitulation to the discursive authority of the West erases the traditional self, leaving Chinese male self-identity emasculated, afflicted with melancholy and self-loathing.[17] In these terms, Buxiaosheng's protagonists can be said to exist on the prelapsarian side of that watershed of consciousness, when the other of modernity, mediated through Japan and projected onto the female, is still perceived as available for appropriation and manipulation by the narcissistic and self-indulgent Chinese male. An underlying sense of entitlement informs the narrator's stance toward his material, allowing him to present with enthusiasm behavior he at the same time earnestly castigates as unconscionable. The internal challenges that destabilize this stance derive, as previously discussed, from a moral ambivalence woven into the poetics of *xiaoshuo* and not from Yu Dafu's radical questioning of psychological and national identity.

The Role of the Martial Arts

Within the world of *Sojourners*, a distinctive note is struck by the presence and practice of the martial arts. The martial arts are embodied principally in the figure of Huang Wenhan 黃文漢, one of the central cast of recurring characters. At his first appearance, in chapter 4, Huang Wenhan is introduced as a native of Hubei, a longtime resident of Japan and occasional student who knows a bit of martial arts. His primary claim to fame, however, is as an accomplished whoremonger, so fully the peer of the Zhou Zhuan who commences the narrative that admirers of the two speak of "the Southern School of Zhou and the Northern School of Huang" (南周北黃). Zhou Zhuan claims as his inspiration the five keys to amorous success imparted to *The Water Margin*'s Ximen Qing 西門慶 by the old bawd Granny Wang 王婆: Pan An's 潘安 looks, a donkey's tool, Deng Tong's 鄧通 wealth, an artist's attention to detail, and an idler's abundance of time (*Pan, lu, Deng, xiao, xian* 潘驢鄧小閑).[18] Huang Wenhan dismisses these criteria as variously improbable or trivial and has instead devised a formula that summarizes his own techniques for bending women to his will: "bullshit, the squeeze, the cops, pimping, and brute force" (*chui, yao, jing, la, qiang* 吹要警拉強). The last item refers not to rape but to the use of his martial skills to guard against blackmail or to gain the upper hand in a dispute.

The introductory characterization of Huang Wenhan as an unapologetic rake with no compunctions about using force when trickery or suasion fail is borne out by the ensuing episode, in which he takes Zheng Shaotian, an intimate of Zhou Zhuan's as well as a disciple of his own techniques, to visit a pair of prostitutes. Huang and Zheng arrive at the sisters' dwelling only to find two pairs of Japanese military boots at the door. Although Zheng is quite ready to abort the excursion at this point, Huang dismisses his qualms, demands that the flustered elder sister make them welcome in a waiting room, and soon, goaded by the conviction that he's being given the brush-off, barges in on the sisters and their stunned but reflexively courteous guests. When the Japanese officers, brazening the situation out, suggest that they and their new acquaintances share a meal, Huang calls their bluff. He eats voraciously and drinks with abandon, ringing up an enormous tab. The Japanese present him with the bill; he seizes one of their greatcoats, announces his intention to pawn it, and strides for the door. The officers follow, and he fells one with his fist.

When the military men implore him to be reasonable, he seeks out a policeman and is quickly vindicated in his expectation that, facing constituted civil authority and the prospect of public embarrassment and professional repercussions, his foes will meekly apologize and slink off to pay the bill.[19]

To a reader of Republican-era martial arts fiction or the various premodern narratives from which the genre draws, Huang Wenhan's pursuit of sexual gratification clearly marks him as a deviant from the chivalric code. His deviance lies not merely in that flagrant rejection of any selfless or charitable behavior which is trumpeted by his rules for whoring but more fundamentally in his violation of a taboo against sexual indulgence, a taboo integral to the martial tradition. The very terms by which he is first introduced provide a pointed reminder of this taboo and its most famous literary expression. Huang's five-character formula is a response to Zhou Zhuan's (it is also, in this context, a parody of the similar oral formulae for the transmission of martial techniques),[20] Zhou Zhuan's formula is borrowed from Ximen Qing, and Ximen Qing is traditional Chinese fiction's most notorious libertine. But *The Water Margin*, the Ming novel that first portrays Ximen Qing and his exploits, is also traditional fiction's quintessential representation of martial prowess and the codes of brotherhood that surround it. And a central element of its martial code is a sexual asceticism that repeatedly expresses itself in (or perhaps reveals its basis in) murderous misogyny. In *The Water Margin* the expression of male sexual desire is at best a dangerous and humiliating admission of weakness, at worst the very emblem of villainy.[21] Various Qing novels respond to *The Water Margin*'s vision by exploring the rapprochement of martial valor with the valorizing authenticity of *qing* 情 (passion) and with the proper neo-Confucian regulation of desire and the family.[22] Huang Wenhan's sexual adventurism, however, is as distant from these works' idealized harmonies of libido and martiality as it is from *The Water Margin*'s uncompromising rejection of desire.

Far from merely dividing his energies between the martial arts and sexual conquest, Huang Wenhan at times actually uses the former to facilitate the latter. The fifth element of his formula frankly declares as much. Prominent among the narrative instances of the connection is his courtship of a Westernized Chinese women's rights advocate, the "heroine" (*nü yingxiong* 女英雄) Miss Hu 胡女士. Huang uses his commanding physical presence to push his way through the admirers who throng Miss Hu at her first appearance at a public meeting. Miss Hu is favorably impressed by his bearing and vigor, and as he escorts her from the gathering, the martial artist's stable footing enables him to catch her, and cop a quick feel, when she is thrown off balance by a lurch of the streetcar they are riding. Although from the perspective of the martial tradition Huang's deployment of his abilities in such a way may amount to a betrayal of the art, in terms of the concerns he shares with his co-protagonists his skills are clearly an asset. In the case of Miss Hu, for instance, they enable him to carry off a prize bitterly contested by his compatriots. By clearly drawing a contrast between the élan with which he achieves this triumph and the risible efforts of his rivals, the narrative casts his efforts in an admiring if still cynically knowing light. And the elevation of Huang Wenhan's erotic adventures to a somewhat more exalted plane extends well beyond the single instance of Miss Hu. The narrative of his encounter with the leading geisha of a provincial town in chapter 13 is unstinting in its account of the tricks by which entertainers squeeze the most out of their customers, on the one hand, and in its admission of Huang's enjoyment of status and opportunities he would not command back in Tokyo, on the other, yet it still portrays their tryst as the reward of Huang's generosity of spirit and the communion of two passionate souls. The romantic rhetoric that attends the scene, even if read as ironically intended, still imparts an emotional and poetic richness absent from the burlesque renditions of other characters' sordid affairs.

Huang Wenhan's adventures involve not only the female objects of his desire but also male rivals to its realization. The early episode of his encounter with the military officers at the prostitutes' lodgings neatly illustrates this point; by the end of this scene, indeed, the excursion's original erotic goal evaporates before the intensity of the competition between the male players. Details of imagery and dialogue make clear that much of what is at stake is a virility defined by one-upmanship. "Are we inferior to them somehow?" Huang demands of one of the sisters, challenging the Japanese for her attention, and of his companion Zheng, "You're not scared just because they've got swords at their belts, are you?" (4:22). But biological and psychological parameters of competition soon expand to incorporate the national as well. One of the officers compliments Huang on his command of the Japanese language, verifies that he is a student, then inquires why he is visiting a brothel rather than attending class. Huang leaps to the offense:

> "Where do you get off saying something like that? This is the first time the two of us have met; how can you be such a boor as to try and teach me my manners? So you know I've come here to get an education, do you? Let me tell you something, and I won't bother being polite. When I was back in my own country, I heard it said that your honored nation's girls were the prettiest, and the easiest too. My forefathers left me an inheritance of hundreds of thousands, and when I got tired of whoring back in China, I decided to come to your honored nation for an advanced course of study. It's precisely to do my coursework that I came here today. Do you want to tell me there's something wrong with that?"
>
> (4:23)

In contrast to the self-doubt on display in May Fourth writings, the mapping of the national onto the libidinal here generates an aggressive assertion of resource, potency, and privilege.[23]

Huang Wenhan is by no means the one-dimensional Chinese chauvinist this episode taken in isolation might suggest. Of the central group of recurrent characters, he is to be sure the one most sensitive to questions of national image and most outspoken in asserting Chinese pride. At the same time, though, he is also the one most fluent in the Japanese language and most comfortable with the intricacies of Japanese social and cultural life. While more than a few of his compatriots blunder through their years in Tokyo unable to speak a word of the local language and ignorant of the most basic forms of courtesy, Huang sets off into the countryside on solo walking tours that bring him into vital contact with Japanese from varied strata of society. It is precisely the depth of his interaction with the Japanese that lands him in situations where the relationship between the two nations becomes an issue and that allows him to address the issue in terms both spirited and nuanced. His violations of local mores, as in the scene just discussed, are not dictated by ignorance but guided by deliberate manipulation of the interstices between insider knowledge and outsider status.

The multidimensionality of Huang Wenhan's perspective is expressed in, and indeed exemplified by, his practice of the martial arts. A key episode in this regard is his visit to a Japanese archery range in chapters 32–33. Accompanied by his friend Guo Zilan 郭子蘭, a Hunan native studying at a college of physical education, he first calls on a Japanese sword teacher of his acquaintance, a Mr. Yoshikawa 吉川, who will escort them to the range. Guo and Yoshikawa fall into a conversation about the relative merits of Chinese and Japanese swordsmanship, and when Yoshikawa slights the Chinese tradition—why is it that the whole world knows Japan's art of the sword, while no one has heard of China's?—Huang challenges him to a test of skill, faces his bamboo sword barehanded, and topples him with a single sudden blow. Yoshikawa is saved from further embarrassment by the arrival of friends, including a judo exponent who is also eager to match himself against Huang and Guo. Although producing no dramatic victory for either side, the ensuing contests are embarrassing and exhausting for the judo enthusiast, who excuses himself when the others set out for the archery range. Arriving at the range, Huang and his companions are immediately impressed with the bearing and skills of the resident master, a disciple of the Heki lineage 日置流 of *kyudo* 弓道. They share tea with him before participating in a team contest. The master, pleased with Huang's and Guo's diligent and respectful approach to the art, invites them to join his association, an invitation they for their part are happy to accept; as he signs the ledger, Huang notes that the other names in the book are of prominent members of society, including military officers, jurists, and professors.

Huang's acceptance into this august company is a recognition not only of his own skills but also, by extension, of Chinese entitlement to equal standing. The element of national pride is even more explicit in the earlier, more combative encounters at Yoshikawa's residence, where Huang uses Chinese arts to expunge what he sees as a slight to Chinese honor. At the same time, however, these episodes evince an admiration for aspects of Japanese culture embodied in its martial arts. This admiration is not only voiced by Huang Wenhan but also expressed by the narrator, through overt declaration of the virtues of the Japanese martial system and through careful exposition of the details of its practice. At this juncture, at least, character, narrator, and historical author seem to be in full harmony; it is easy to correlate the perspective represented here with Xiang Kairan's advocacy of the Japanese model for the systematization and dissemination of martial training in such works as the 1923 *Panorama of National*

Skills. What is of more immediate interest here, though, is the role this perspective plays within the particular fictional parameters of the *Unofficial History of Sojourners in Japan*. The practice of the martial arts serves simultaneously as a vehicle for a positive, even triumphant assertion of Chinese identity and for intelligent, respectful interaction with Japanese society. In both aspects it functions to differentiate the character of Huang Wenhan from his feckless compatriots, allowing him a more positive appraisal and establishing him on a mimetically more elevated plane. It rescues neither him nor the novel as a whole from the general moral chaos that exposé fiction represents and enacts. It does, however, present in distinctive shape a possibility for personal and national integrity—a possibility that rarely finds expression in any form within the exposé tradition. In this sense, and not merely in facile displays of triumph over Japanese opponents, *Sojourners* prefigures *Modern Times'* exploration of the role of the Chinese martial arts in the encounter with modernity.

CHIVALRIC HEROES OF MODERN TIMES

At the heart of the Huo Yuanjia legend is a tale of nationalistic martyrdom. Huo, a champion of China's martial arts, is struck down by foul play at the hands of the Japanese. In many tellings of the tale this fate is the tragic coda to a series of stirring triumphs over foreign challengers—Russian, American, European, and finally Japanese. In Xiang Kairan's *Modern Times*, however (and this seems to accord with what can be reconstructed of the historical record), Huo Yuanjia never actually engages in physical contest with a Western opponent. Instead of triumph, the novel offers frustration: Huo seeks in vain, over the course of eighty-four chapters, to measure the Chinese martial arts against the West. Rather than competing against foreign champions, he struggles with the conditions of a modern world that both creates the desire for so straightforward a vindication of potency and continually forestalls its realization.

Origins and Transmission

Xiang Kairan's narrative approaches Huo Yuanjia through the story of another martial artist, Broadsworder Wang Wu 大刀王五, and first introduces Wang Wu through his association with Tan Sitong 譚嗣同

(1865–1898), one of the martyrs of the 1898 reform movement. This opening establishes the question of the nation's fate and an air of heroic sacrifice as the backdrop for the martial tales that will follow. Wang Wu's own tale is prefaced by that of his teacher, Zhou Liang 周亮. From the outset, thus, the text both foregrounds the centrality of master-to-student transmission in the world of the martial arts and sets into motion a narrative process in which the handing off of the narrative thread from one character to the next echoes, and in some cases directly parallels, the transmission of the arts from one generation to the next. The content of Zhou Liang's and Wang Wu's tales further highlight the central importance of transmission. Both center on episodes in which a renowned martial artist is humbled in an encounter with a master whose talents lie hidden beneath an unprepossessing exterior, and both explore the roles of talent, reputation, and recognition in establishing the networks of relationships that constitute the Rivers and Lakes. The narrative then returns to the figure of Tan Sitong and to the question of the role of the martial arts in the nation's crisis—without, however, providing a satisfying answer to the question it has raised. It tells how Tan Sitong, inspired in his reformist ambitions by the historian Sima Qian's accounts of pre-Han generals and assassins, practices the martial arts and cultivates the acquaintance of men of renown, Wang Wu among them. Getting wind of the court's backlash against the reformers, Wang Wu offers to escort Tan to safety, but Tan refuses on the grounds that change will never come without the blood of martyrs. The national hero draws from the martial arts only the courage to face tragic martyrdom, and the martial artist is granted no practical avenue for putting his talents to use. Wang Wu can do no more than voice his admiration for Tan's vision, weep, and then remove himself to Tianjin—where he will first encounter Huo Yuanjia.

The narrative transition from Wang to Huo occurs at the juncture of the fourth and fifth chapters. Wang Wu lingers through the first half of the novel in an exiguous capacity, reappearing at spare intervals and primarily to motivate the introduction of subsidiary characters and events. The only major incident remaining in his own story is his death, which occurs in the forty-fourth chapter, roughly at the halfway point of the eighty-four-chapter novel. In the aftermath of the Boxer Uprising Wang Wu lingers in the capital, grieving for the disaster and the sufferings of Chinese citizens at the hands of the rampaging Allied troops. He is gunned down by a company of German soldiers eager to avenge their legate's death at Boxer hands and ignorant of any distinction between the Boxers and such pugilists as the renowned Wang Wu. Wang Wu's death vindicates his master's warnings about the perils of reputation and stages the tragedy of the traditional martial hero's fate in a world marked by foreign incursion and unconquerable new technologies. Wang Wu's life and career are cut short by the unsought intrusion of this new order; Huo Yuanjia's career, in the novel's telling, centers on his deliberate attempts to engage it.

The narrative sutures that link the story of Wang Wu to that of Huo Yuanjia are reinforced by broad structural symmetries. After Huo is introduced, via Wang, at the juncture of chapters 4 and 5, the first major arc of Huo's story extends (with interpolations) through the end of chapter 19, where Huo triumphs over a Boxer opponent. The beginning of chapter 20 reintroduces Wang, on a slender pretext and only long enough to launch another series of interpolated tales that extend into chapter 44. At this point the narrative rejoins Wang, telling of his death at Boxer hands, and after Wang's death we return to Huo, for a new sequence of events that will frame the last forty chapters of the novel. Both the introduction of the central character through a chain of preliminary figures and the organization of the material in rough decades of chapters employ and consciously refer to the devices of the premodern vernacular novel, most notably *The Water Margin*, and the function of both devices is to highlight the thematic connections between the two characters' biographies. The narrator spells out the connection for his readers:

> Because of the chaos of the Boxer bandits, Wang Wu lost his life in vain, yet because of the chaos of the Boxer bandits, Tianjin's Huo Yuanjia accomplished a tremendous deed and gained tremendous renown. The same talent, the same ambition, the very same situation, and yet the outcomes were so entirely different—of those present at the time, there was nary a one who did not sigh with regret for Wang Wu and nary a one who did not delight in Huo Yuanjia's good fortune.
>
> (44:3, 41)

However different the outcomes may be, at least for the present, the parallels establish a common frame of signification for the two heroes' experiences. And Wang Wu's tale could not be more clear in signaling the peril inherent in the "tremendous renown" identified as the fruit of Huo Yuanjia's deeds.

Wang, arriving in Tianjin, sees evidence of Huo's prowess and first hears his name. At this point the narrator inserts an account of Huo's background and early career. The story of Huo Yuanjia's early life foregrounds the question of patrimony—specifically, the problems attendant upon the patrilineal transmission of an inheritance. The inheritance in question is the "Trackless Art" (Mizongyi 迷蹤藝), a system of martial arts practiced by members of the Huo 霍 clan of Jinghai 靜海 county in Tianjin. It is unclear, notes the narrator, whether the art's name refers to its mysterious origins or to its foes' inability to grasp its subtleties; in either case, the name clearly indexes the art's inaccessibility and thus the weight of the Huo clan's proprietary claim. So jealously guarded is the art that even the clan's own female members, destined to marry out of the family, are forbidden to learn it. The young Huo Yuanjia is excluded from the transmission as well; he is so weak and sickly that his father fears that training in the martial arts will only embroil the boy in conflicts he has no hope of winning and so discredit the family name. But Huo Yuanjia spies on his brothers' training and practices in secret. When a challenger bests the family's champion, it is Huo Yuanjia who steps forward, astonishes his clansmen by prevailing, and is then embraced by his father as a rightful successor.

The tale of Huo Yuanjia's childhood develops the novel's already established interest in talent, semblance, and the question of recognition. Here these concerns play their parts in an almost Arthurian fable of birthright: a rightful heir languishes unrecognized until the revelation of hidden worth vindicates his place in the succession. The resolution of the tale is affirmative; on the face of things, both the protagonist and the patriliny to which he succeeds enjoy the fruits of his triumph. At the same time, though, the story adumbrates problems that will beleaguer the ensuing narrative. Is the body of the protagonist essentially sound; has the patrimony succeeded in correcting, overcoming, or compensating for what seemed to be an innate deficiency? And what, exactly, is the logic of the patrilineal transmission? Do certain standards of fitness attenuate the presumption of patrilineal inheritance; if they do, what validity can the system of patrimony still claim? Although the text does not frame the issues in precisely these terms, it pointedly follows the story of Huo Yuanjia's triumph with an excursus on the viciousness of the martial world—not only the spite and enmity engendered by restricted transmission and the obsession with reputation but also the cruelty of various conventions for dueling. The chapter commentary targets even more explicitly the damage inflicted upon China's cultural heritage by the practice of restricted transmission: "Under these circumstances, can we even hope to see the arts progress? The Huo family's Trackless Art—not transmitted to those of other surnames, kept private rather than public—shares the common defect of the realm of the arts, and it is for this reason that the author has taken pains to point it out" (5:1, 60). The debut that thrusts Huo Yuanjia into the limelight simultaneously places him under the shadow of the ills that haunt the tradition, in the form of the enmity and scheming of his family's hereditary rivals, the Zhao clan. Yet he has ambitions that extend beyond the familiar parameters of the Rivers and Lakes. These ambitions manifest themselves at first simply as a desire to see something of the world. With permission and funding from his father he goes into Tianjin to open an herb store. When aspirants attracted by his renown seek him out, he accepts the most sincere of them as his disciple. Although he respects clan rules by not teaching his disciple the restricted "Trackless Art," this acceptance of an outsider marks the first step toward a new model of transmission. And here in the treaty port of Tianjin he encounters a new order of challenge—not from a rival from the Rivers and Lakes, contesting standing and reputation within that recognized milieu, but from a foreigner, a Russian strongman, whose very presence assigns the arts Huo champions a new and broader dimension of significance.

The Challenge of the Modern

It is Huo who reads the Russian's presence as a challenge. When his disciple brings him news of the strongman's appearance at a Tianjin theater and complains that the visitor has not obtained Huo's permission to "sell his arts" (*maiyi* 賣藝), Huo at first dismisses the matter: he is not some territorial boss to whom outsiders must tender respect. But when he discovers that the ad for the performance declares the Russian, along with a German and an Englishman, the world's three strongest men, he takes the absence of a Chinese as a deliberate slight and proceeds to the theater to

FIGURE 6.1 Huo Yuanjia and the Russian strong-man. Illustrations from chapter 14 of *Modern Times*.

Source: From Pingjiang Buxiaosheng 平江不肖生, *Jindai xiayi yingxiong zhuan* (*di er ji*) 近代俠義英雄傳 (第二集) , 2nd printing (Shanghai: Shijie shuju, 1924). Author's scan, from a copy in the collection of the University of Oregon Libraries.

demand satisfaction (figure 6.1). There he hears an even more galling provocation, as the strongman declares that his visit has confirmed the widespread characterization of China as the "sick man of Asia" (*Zhongguo shi dongfang de bingfu guo* 中國是東方的病夫國; 14:1, 179), a nation of weaklings unaware of the importance of physical culture. The furious Huo Yuanjia sends the performer a challenge to no-holds-barred combat. The Russian, negotiating through his interpreter, professes himself unwilling to fight without understanding more about the Chinese martial arts and proposes friendship, collegial discussion, then perhaps an exhibition match. Huo refuses. The Russian, unwilling either to fight or to retract publicly his claim to be the strongest man in the world, promptly departs China and the novel.

The episode foregrounds a powerful set of issues yet fails to give them a dramatically satisfying or conceptually unambiguous resolution. It aborts the showdown between Chinese and foreign fighters that will become a staple of later versions of Huo Yuanjia's story and a cliché of martial arts cinema. Although the Russian's withdrawal can be counted a victory of sorts for Huo, it is hard to read the absence of an actual physical contest as anything other than a disappointment—a disappointment exacerbated by the narrator's conclusion of the episode in a few brief sentences.[24] The central issue raised by the encounter is that of the role of the Chinese martial arts in a multinational and modernizing world. The theater in which the strongman performs epitomizes this world and its particular manifestation in the treaty port city of Tianjin. The theater is cosmopolitan, a space in which Chinese and foreigners intermingle, though with clearly established distinctions and hierarchies. It is a commodified space, in which access to economic resources serves as a prerequisite for participation and as an index of status. And it is a space that employs modes and media of communication distinct from the networks of reputation and private affiliation that inform the Rivers and Lakes: handbills, newspapers, public speech, and performance. Within this space and employing these media, the Russian invokes a discursive framework that defines modern physical culture as linked with science and the nationalist project in both its racial and civic aspects:

> "The science of physical education concerns the strength of the race and the prosperity of the nation. How can it be that there is not a single organization in the entire country devoted to its study and improvement? Because of my wish to let the Chinese know the value of physical education, I will display my skills in Tianjin for a week, then proceed to Beijing, Shanghai, and other locales to perform. I earnestly welcome China's strongmen and experts in physical education to come forward and join me in this study."
>
> (15:1, 180)

Huo's very involvement with the Russian implies an admission of the validity of the discursive terms of engagement articulated here. And though the episode concludes with the Russian's departure from China— the Russian's capitulation to Huo's immediate demands—Huo's project of mastering this new discourse of the national body is left conflicted and incomplete. It remains unclear how Huo will coordinate his passion for the new ideals with his continuing allegiance to the social and discursive structures within which his inheritance is embedded; it remains unclear whether the Chinese martial arts as a practice are a valid candidate for integration into the modern system of physical education. Quite willing to overlook the Russian's performance when it is presented to him in terms of the prerogatives of the Rivers and Lakes, Huo is galvanized into action once he perceives it in terms of "winning face for the Chinese" (*ti Zhongguoren zhengzheng mianzi* 替中國人掙掙面子; 14:1, 175). He finds support not only from his disciple but more importantly from his cosmopolitan friend Nong Jingsun 農勁蓀, a scholar fluent in English and held in rare respect by the foreign community in China. The only response Huo will consider, nonetheless, is a duel, more proper to the vicious traditions of the Rivers and Lakes than to the scientific and purportedly fraternal world of physical culture.[25] And once he has succeeded in driving his opponent away, he is left to fret over the inaccessibility of this new world. "Although I drove him off in a rage, what he said on stage today actually spoke right to China's greatest defect. If I weren't tied up at present with these trivial matters of business, I would truly like to step up and devote all my efforts to promoting China's martial arts. What good does it do for me, one single man, to be strong?" (15:1, 190–91).

No sooner has Huo begun to contemplate the martial arts' place in a modern society than he is confronted with the problem in what is perhaps its most traumatic and grotesque manifestation: the Boxer Uprising. Huo's discussion with Nong Jingsun on promoting the martial arts is interrupted by a visit from Xie Liankui 解聯魁, the son of an old acquaintance. Xie, clownishly garbed in a yellow robe and red turban, enthusiastically describes the magical arts and "spirit boxing" (*shenquan* 神拳) by which the Boxers will drive the foreigners from China, and he invites Huo to join them. Huo declines. Soon after, hearing of Boxer massacres of Chinese Christian converts, he has Nong Jingsun write up posters inviting refugees to seek safety with him in Tianjin. Fifteen hundred converts flock to his compound. With the aid of Nong and local merchants, he defends them from Boxer attacks and finally, learning of preparations for a final assault with cannon, speeds to the Boxer camp and strikes their leader down in front of his assembled minions.

The Boxers played a central role in Republican-era discussions of the Chinese martial arts. For many, the iconoclasts of the May Fourth generation in particular, the Boxers confirmed the martial arts' identification with the superstition and violence of China's irredeemable "feudal" past; for certain groups of reformers, they were an aberration that distracted from the martial arts' potential to serve as a culturally appropriate vehicle for nation-building physical education.[26] Huo's conversation with Nong marks him as a potential spokesman for the latter position. In his response to Xie, he distinguishes superstitious and heterodox forms of the martial arts from a version that seems both rational and Confucian in its humanism:

> Huo Junqing [Yuanjia], having heard him out, understood that this was sorcery like that of the White Lotus Cult. How could a man as upright and farsighted as himself listen to such iniquitous nonsense? He merely gave a faint smile and said, "I'm deeply grateful to you for your kindness, Brother Xie, in coming so far to see me. I'm afraid, though, that I've always been of a rather dull-witted disposition, and have never been willing to believe in any kind of gods or spirits. The martial arts that I've studied are quite expressly taught by human beings, and I don't believe in any 'spirit boxing.' If some expert in this 'spirit boxing' dares to match himself against my 'human boxing,' I'll be happy to oblige him at the time and place of his choosing—I'm not afraid of how awesome his 'spirit boxing' might be."
>
> (15:1, 193)

His subsequent deeds not only vindicate the superiority of his "human boxing" but also neatly contrast the destructive fanaticism of the Boxers' supposed patriotism with his own altruistic and forward-thinking defense of his countrymen. To Xie, however, Huo disingenuously disclaims any interest in national affairs:

> "The realm of the Great Qing doesn't need the assistance of ordinary folk like ourselves; nor are the foreign devils something that we ordinary folk could ever manage to get rid of. I'll have to trouble you, Brother Xie, to return to Beijing and give this Han fellow [the Boxer leader] my thanks. I, Huo Yuanjia, am just a petty businessman, and

seeking a profit is all I understand; I know nothing about doing great deeds for the sake of the nation."

(15:1, 193)

One can easily imagine a disinclination to engage in debate with the foolish and dogmatic youth before him. The disavowal is nonetheless striking, particularly in that it so precisely inverts his immediately preceding complaint to Nong about the entanglements of business. It echoes Huo's stance toward the Russian in establishing narrow, even peremptory terms outside of which Huo is unwilling to negotiate the issues he feels compelled to confront.

The episode illustrates not only some of the problems facing Huo in defining a modern identity for the martial arts but also the tensions between Huo's project and the choices made by the author/narrator of his tale. As early as the contest between Wang Wu and Shanxi Dong 山西董 in chapters 3 and 4, the author has demonstrated his ability to relate the details of a physical encounter between martial artists. The account of Huo's strike against the Boxer leader adopts a different narrative strategy, one emphasizing not concrete techniques but the unfathomability of Huo Yuanjia's prowess. Huo dons an assassin's garb, downs in one gulp a bottle of Gaoliang wine, and speeds from his compound so swiftly that even his comrades fail to note his passing. He arrives at the Boxer camp as the leader, Han Qilong 韓起龍, is boasting to his followers of the ruin he will visit upon Huo Yuanjia and the Christian converts:

> Before the next words were even uttered, Huo Yuanjia had flown forward with the speed of the wind. A hand rose, a blade fell; with a "chop chop," Han Qilong's two arms, each still grasping a pistol in its hand, were separated from his body, and his body fell from the table where he'd been standing to the ground.
>
> In the instant before Han Qilong's arms were severed, the "heavenly troops" filling the field heard a cry: "Huo Yuanjia has arrived!" Yet not a one of them saw so much Huo Yuanjia's shadow. As Han Qilong's body toppled over, they again heard a cry: "Huo Yuanjia takes his leave!"; and half of those present were so terrified that the weapons fell from their hands of their own accord. Han Qilong did

not lose his life on this occasion, but without his arms he was henceforth a cripple.

(19:2, 33)

The brutal assault shows Huo's contempt for Han, who is clearly unworthy of the courtesies that might be due to a challenger from the traditional martial fraternity. The narrator's telling seems designed to mock the Boxers' claims to "spiritual" powers; it does so, however, by portraying Huo's abilities as seemingly supernatural, and in so doing it undermines the episode's efficacy as a demonstration of "human" martial arts, passed from man to man in a rational daylight world. There is a disconnect between, on the one hand, the author-narrator's and commentator's support of Huo's ambitions for a rational, modern system of the martial arts and, on the other, the narrator's responsibility in his capacity as storyteller to give his audience a thrilling tale, marvelous (*qi*) in both content and delivery. *Xiaoshuo*'s commitment to the strange must have its due, even at the expense of the real-world project to which the episode gestures.

Shanghai

The Boxers, as noted earlier, provide a structural and thematic bridge between the figures of Huo Yuanjia and Wang Wu. Wang Wu's death in the post-Boxer turmoil in chapter 44 allows the narrator to contrast the tragedy of his fate with the glory and renown won by Huo. As this narrative bridge returns us to Huo's story, the question of the fruits of renown hangs heavy in the air. The narrative arc of the novel's second half in essence replicates the incident of the Russian strongman. A foreign athlete, O'Brien, insults the Chinese people, prompting Huo Yuanjia to issue a challenge; negotiations ensue, leading in the end not to a match but only to the foreign champion's withdrawal. In this instance, though, the tale is writ much larger. The narrative, with its complications and digressions, extends over some forty chapters. The challenge to O'Brien takes Huo to Shanghai, which replaces Tianjin as the primary setting for the action. There Huo Yuanjia finds himself increasingly embroiled in the commercial, legal, social, and media practices of life in the modern metropolis—to the point where urban modernity, not some foreign athlete, becomes his principal antagonist. Within these chapters, Huo's dealings with O'Brien are replicated in miniature in yet another incident, a similarly aborted challenge to a pair of foreign wrestlers, black and white. And even when the long-anticipated match with O'Brien has come to naught, the irrevocable complications of his experiences in Shanghai propel Huo Yuanjia simultaneously toward a new model for the social role and context of the martial arts and toward a death no less premature and inglorious than Wang Wu's.

The opening of the O'Brien episode articulates several of the elements that will shape ensuing events: Huo Yuanjia's fervor to answer any challenge to Chinese honor, his unpreparedness to deal with the unfamiliar contexts and practices within which these challenges appear, and the crucial role of his associate Nong Jingsun in mediating between Huo and an alien world. When Nong, brandishing a newspaper, walks in on Huo as he discusses the martial arts with his disciple, Huo can't even be bothered to read O'Brien's advertisement because of the foreign words with which the text is sprinkled. But no sooner has Nong summarized the insulting challenge than Huo, jumping to his feet in righteous indignation, vows to travel to Shanghai to confront the foreigner. In Shanghai, Nong's assistance proves indispensable, for the proposed match with O'Brien must be arranged with reference not to the customs of the Rivers and Lakes but rather to the legal and economic protocols of a transnational capitalist system. Nong explains to Huo that O'Brien represents the interests of his sponsors and investors, not his own personal honor. Arranging the match requires negotiating with his agent, one Wolin 沃林, over details of licensing, wagers, date and venue, a contract, lawyers, and financial guarantors. Huo is contemptuous of the need for anything beyond a man's word: "I've never in my life understood this business they call 'the law'" (45:3, 58). It develops, nonetheless, that his own motivations are less unalloyed than he first represents; he accedes to Wolin's proposal of a substantial wager in part because the financial commitments he has made to friends in the name of brotherhood (*yiqi* 義氣) have imperiled his own family's finances.

The first round of negotiations in chapters 45–46 with Wolin marks only the beginning of a tortuous and ultimately fruitless process. When an agreement is finally signed in chapter 55, Huo returns to Tianjin to seek social and financial backing. He encounters disappointing resistance from his family but gathers supporters from among the martial community and adopts Nong's suggestion of a new-style *leitai* 擂台 (a "challenge platform," that is, a ring or arena)—one not just dedicated to personal reputation but aimed simultaneously at financial profit and promotion of the martial arts. Returning to Shanghai in chapter 64, he struggles to promote the *leitai*, and by the time O'Brien and Wolin, warned of Huo's prowess by a spy, forfeit the match by absconding from Shanghai, the processes that will lead to Huo's death are already in inexorable motion. Though foiled in his attempt to battle a foreigner, he must contend with the unsought enmity of Chinese rivals. Physical exertion and the stress of his responsibilities exacerbate his congenital infirmity. And the insistent solicitude of a Japanese physician proves to mask a jealous enmity that first pushes Huo Yuanjia into unwanted trials against Japanese challengers, then leads to his poisoning at the doctor's hands.

In effect, Huo finds himself confronting his Western antagonists in an arena far from the one he originally envisions. The contest of physical strength and martial skill never transpires; the manipulation of the legal, economic, and media practices of modern urban life replaces the exchange of blows. Who wins? Huo Yuanjia claims the moral high ground, to be sure. His integrity, perseverance, and valor stand in clear contrast to the Westerners' deviousness, self-interest, and pusillanimity, and the reader can be expected to share the disdain Huo expresses for his opponents' machinations. Under Nong Jingsun's tutelage, however, Huo does his best to master the skills required by life in the modern metropolis. He succeeds to the point that he can employ them to sidetrack an unwanted challenger; when one Zhang Wenda 張文達, a giant from Shandong, comes seeking vengeance for his disciple's humiliation at Huo's *leitai*, Huo and Nong send him off to arrange a *leitai* of his own, smugly (and, in the event, mistakenly) confident that he will be foiled by the bureaucratic complexities and financial burdens involved. Zhang serves as an intratextual comic foil, a gullible lout whose enthusiastic immersion in the temptations of city life highlights the Confucian composure with which Huo engages the new environment. Intertextually, Huo Yuanjia's dealings in and with the modern city stand in clear contrast with those of *Sojourners'* Huang Wenhan. Huo's interest in the ways of the city is purely instrumental, and he seeks to employ them only to the extent that they will further the aims defined by his practice of the martial arts. Huang Wenhan, as we have seen, adumbrates the martial arts' potential for serving as a vehicle of enlightened transnational exchange. But he is also, and foremost, an avid pursuer of the opportunities and pleasures the city offers, so adept in its ways that he can boast of a signature Art of Whoring in which his martial skills are assigned a merely auxiliary role.

In any event, Huo Yuanjia's moral superiority is unable to compensate fully for the Westerners' superior mastery of the devices of modern life. In his early encounter with the Russian in Tianjin, it was Huo who had insisted on terms of engagement; this ended in driving his antagonist away. Here in Shanghai, the roles are reversed. When, frustrated with the pace of deliberations with O'Brien, Huo seeks a match against a pair of American wrestlers, the conditions proposed by the other party are so restrictive—no punches, kicks, headbutts, elbow jabs, shoulder strikes, or finger techniques—that he stalks out of the negotiations in disgust. For the long-sought O'Brien match, Huo exercises extremes of patience, but to no avail; when the strongman and his agent Wolin divine that events may not play out in their favor, they simply decamp, and the painstakingly established pledges and guarantees prove powerless to constrain them. Although Nong Jingsun insists that the Westerner's forfeiture constitutes a victory, Huo finds it hard to summon a sense of triumph, in part because the debacle further worsens his financial plight. Readers, for their part, are likely to see corroboration of foreigners' diminutive moral stature as a disappointing substitute at best for the climactic physical confrontation the text has anticipated for so long.

Another substitute for the martial confrontation between Chinese and foreign bodies occurs in the form of incidents, anecdotes, and discussions that contrast the nature and merits of Chinese and Western medical knowledge. These tales and vignettes emerge from Huo's experiences and widening circle of acquaintances in cosmopolitan Shanghai. One burden they share is that of Chinese medicine's superiority; this theme is evident, for instance, in one of the earliest of such episodes, in which a practitioner of the Marrow-Changing Classic (*yijin jing* 易筋經) uses his mastery of the life force (*qi* 氣) to draw pottery shards from the skull of a man on whom the doctors at a modern hospital were afraid to operate (chapter 55). Another recurring theme, however, is the virtue of the Western passion for obtaining and sharing knowledge, particularly in comparison with the Chinese penchant for secrecy and restrictive transmission.

The two themes intertwine most spectacularly in the tale of a German doctor who opens a hospital in Hong Kong (chapter 75). He uses X-rays to diagnose a Chinese patient with lung disease, and he gives him only six months to live. Unwilling to concede to this fate, the patient consults a Chinese herbalist, recovers fully, and returns to the hospital to berate the Western physician. The doctor takes further X-rays; convinced of the miraculous recovery, he asks the patient to sacrifice himself for the benefit of mankind and donate his lungs for study at the Imperial Hospital in Berlin. The proposal sends the patient into a fury. The doctor shoots him dead, dissects him, and sends his lungs off to Europe with an explanatory note. His duty to science done, the doctor then shoots himself to satisfy the victim's family and the law. The tale vindicates both Chinese knowledge and the Western fervor for learning. The incident exacts a sacrificial victim equally from each of the two traditions, but, tellingly, it is the representative of the West who perceives a need for such sacrifice to feed his tradition's demands.

In any event, the digressions and discussions that testify to the value of China's traditional bodies of knowledge serve in the end only to underscore the tragedy of the main tale to which they play counterpoint—the tale of the Chinese champion's ruin. The proximate agent of this ruin is a Japanese character, the doctor Akino. Akino echoes the complex of roles assigned to the Japanese in *Sojourners*. He represents himself as conversant with the mysteries of Western medicine and Western knowledge more generally but at the same time claims a special pan-Asian kinship with the Chinese—a kinship that in Chinese eyes amounts to little more than theft. While Westerners harm the Chinese through their arrogance and unscrupulous self-interest, the need to vindicate Japanese self-worth drives Akino and his countrymen to acts of deliberate malice, masked by appeals to fellowship and mutual benefit—most centrally, to poisoning Huo Yuanjia under the guise of offering him medical assistance. Yet what drives Huo to seek medical attention in the first place is something whose roots predate either Japanese or Western involvement in his tale: the intrinsic problem of his physical integrity.

Is Huo Yuanjia fundamentally sound? Are his martial arts a heritage of strength, an antidote for illness, or a compensatory performance that bespeaks ongoing infirmity? These questions were first raised in the fraught tale of his inheritance and reframed in his response to the

Russian strongman's challenge to the "sick man of East Asia." They reappear in the second half of the novel as his illness resurfaces. One of Huo's backers in Shanghai, Peng Shubai 彭庶白, introduces him to the martial artist Qin Heqi 秦鶴岐. After the two have demonstrated their arts to each other, Qin privately volunteers to Peng an assessment of Huo's condition. He perceives that Huo suffers from an illness of the lungs. What's more, the external form of martial arts Huo practices (*waijia gongfu* 外家工夫) has developed his external power out of proportion to his internal strength, to the extent that the exertion of that power harms him as well as his opponent. "If he persists in this aggressive and competitive spirit, entering into fights on the slightest pretext—given his martial skills, winning the victory will hardly be a problem, but each time he wins, his lifespan will be shortened by five years at the least." (54:3, 234).

Some while later, when Huo has opened his *leitai* and awaits his match with O'Brien, he accepts an invitation to visit an English merchant and physical-culture enthusiast, Ban Nuowei 班諾威. Casually trying out the Englishman's exercise equipment, he accidently breaks a metered strength-testing machine, and Nong Jingsun explains to their astonished host how Chinese martial artists employ a dynamic whole-body power different from foreign weightlifters' brute strength. That night, though, Huo begins to suffer severe chest pains, and his companions recall Qin Heqi's warnings about overexertion. Qin, called to consult, refers Huo to an acupuncturist, Huang Shiping 黃石屏 or "Divine Needle Huang" 神針黃, whose ministrations bring relief. But the news that O'Brien and Wolin have fled, forfeiting the long-awaited match—the Englishman Ban was a spy, sent to test Huo's powers—sends Huo into a relapse: "Huo Yuanjia stamped his foot and said in a bitter voice, 'Blast it! How is it that right when my luck goes awry even this iron-sinewed body of mine lets me down? It just keeps on falling ill—it's absolutely infuriating!' He rubbed his chest with both hands as he spoke, and couldn't help but stifle a groan" (77:6, 36).

Unwilling to impose further on Divine Needle Huang, Huo finally agrees to consult a practitioner of Western medicine recommended by Peng, the Japanese Akino 秋野. Akino turns out to be a student of judo, eager to learn the secrets of a renowned Chinese martial artist. Huo easily bests him in an ostensibly friendly match that once again exacerbates Huo's condition. A later meeting with a delegation of Japanese martial artists, into which Huo is pressured against his will, turns rather more ugly; in the aftermath, Akino administers shots and pills, and Huo soon vomits blood and dies. The text leaves no doubt that he has been poisoned by the treacherous Japanese. From a broader perspective, though, his congenital infirmity, his ill-advised training regimen, his physical exertions, and the burdens he has so eagerly shouldered have all led him to this fatal point. His attempts to champion his inheritance as he understands it in the arena of the modern city have exposed the limitations of that inheritance's strength. As Qin Heqi diagnosed, "He comes to grief not at his enemy's hands, but at his own" (54:3, 232).

A New Mode of Transmission

Both Huo Yuanjia's aims and the means by which he seeks to realize them shift over the course of his sojourn in Shanghai. His original motive is a determination to answer personally O'Brien's challenge to Chinese strength; it gradually shifts toward the related but broader project of promoting the martial arts as a tool for building the strength of the people of the Chinese nation. This shift, in turn, posits a fundamental change in the way the martial arts are transmitted and in the kinds of communities the process of transmission creates. Or, to put it another way, the desire to repurpose the martial arts toward the creation of a different kind of community requires a new practice of transmission.

Earlier episodes have laid the groundwork for these changes. We have seen already how Huo's own education reveals some of the limits and tensions of the received modes of master-to-disciple transmission, how Huo tentatively tests the limits of the traditional model by accepting a disciple from outside his clan, and how the Russian strongman's challenge, revealing both foreign arrogance and the uncomfortable truth of Chinese weakness, first stirs Huo's ambition to promote the martial arts. O'Brien's new challenge and the ensuing negotiations in Shanghai with O'Brien's agent and with Chinese sponsors and supporters engage Huo and Nong in renewed discussion of these issues. But the first move toward attempting a new strategy occurs when Huo returns to Tianjin in search of further support and is rebuffed by his family. His father and elder brother see a public match against an unknown foreigner as an unwarranted risk and are anxious about the financial obligations Huo is incurring. It is at this point, as the tension between Huo's heritage and his ambitions becomes acute, that Nong proposes the *leitai*.

Nong's *leitai* is not merely an expansion of Huo's Shanghai venture beyond the original aim of a match against O'Brien but also a reimagining of the challenge platform as previously known in the Rivers and Lakes and (as several characters point out) on the pages of fiction. It departs from tradition first of all in being a commercial venture. When Huo demurs at the idea of selling tickets, Nong explains that this procedure, beyond relieving the Huo clan's financial difficulties, is also necessary to defray the expenses of the O'Brien match and, in any case, only accords with international norms for sporting competitions. The new *leitai*'s second and even more fundamental innovation is in its purpose. Martial artists customarily opened a *leitai* in order to establish a reputation or for other purely personal ends. Huo's *leitai* will be intended not to aggrandize Huo but rather to gather champions from all over China to present a unified response to foreign arrogance and aggression. To achieve this end, it will make use of the new media of communication and their hub in the metropolis of Shanghai. "The notion is both original and apt," opines Peng Shubai when he first hears the plan:

> "If you were to try it in any of the provinces of China's interior, you wouldn't necessarily be able to call many people together. But Shanghai is where China and the West mingle, with transport by land and sea to the four corners of the world. We just have to put together a few advertisements in various languages, and publish them in the newspapers, both Chinese and foreign. Within a few weeks, not just everyone in the nation, but everyone in the whole world will know about it!"
>
> (64:4, 158)

The press has been involved in Huo Yuanjia's career since he arrived in the northern treaty port city of Tianjin, where a printed handbill brought the Russian's performance to his attention and where the newspapers trumpeted his resistance against the Boxers to the nation at large.[27] Now Huo's supporter Nong Jingsun employs the press for his own purposes, promoting the *leitai* through networking, advertisements, and press conferences. It eventually opens with great ceremony. On the first day a single challenger appears, a hot-headed youngster who gives his name only as Donghai Zhao 東海趙, "Zhao from Donghai." Zhao brushes aside Huo's insistence that the *leitai* is meant to challenge foreigners, not fellow Chinese, and once the fight begins, he is blind to Huo's attempts to treat him gently, finally forcing Huo to trounce him with a spectacular throw. Enthusiastic press coverage of the bout brings crowds to the venue on the following days but discourages challengers. As the days drag on without further event, the crowds fade, further promotion proves fruitless, Huo's purse is drained, and the *leitai* finally closes with a whimper. Nong Jingsun's mastery of the tools of the modern media was not so complete as he imagined. More fatally, he had misread the readiness of the martial community, and of the public, to embrace his new vision. The *leitai*'s failure to break the mold of tradition is underscored by the sequel, when the defeated Zhao's master, Zhang Wenda, opens his own *leitai* to challenge Huo, driven by the old Rivers and Lakes imperatives of factional rivalry and revenge.

Even as the *leitai* fails, however, it opens another avenue for the realization of a new form for the martial arts. On the day when Huo, already anxious about the *leitai*'s faltering fortunes, receives the disheartening news that O'Brien has forfeited their match, Nong tries to cheer him up with two new propositions he has received. One is an offer to serve as bodyguard to a Shanghai millionaire and instructor to his sons and nephews. Huo rejects this offer out of hand, indignant that anyone could think that mere money might tempt him to play watchdog and, worse, forgo his responsibility to select students on the basis of their character. Problematic as the old forms of transmission might be, money alone cannot serve as the basis for a viable alternative. The second proposition seems to offer a different path. Eminent figures in education circles wish to fund and establish a school that will promote physical education through the Chinese martial arts. The project is still in the planning stages, Nong cautions, but it vindicates the *leitai* by opening an opportunity that will benefit the whole nation.

"Up until now, those in education circles have generally been obsessed with a superstitious faith in Western learning. Anything foreign was good, and anything native to China, no matter what it might be, was uniformly rejected. In this day and age, when foreign physical education holds sway throughout the nation, who would dare say anything about promoting the Chinese martial arts? The credit for bringing the education world to its senses, and making them take the initiative to promote [the martial arts], is due to our opening the *leitai*."

(77:6, 35).

Plans for the school are finalized at a banquet held by its sponsors in honor of Huo's victory over Zhang Wenda. Huo is in a less than celebratory mood; he insists that there is no glory to be claimed from fighting his own countrymen and laments that he was not born in the age before modern weaponry, when his martial skills might have served the nation on the field of battle. He announces, though, that he is prepared to serve as instructor at the school. While the clan elders will not change the rule forbidding teaching the Trackless Art to outsiders, they have announced that Huo Yuanjia will not be punished for any violations and so is free to proceed as he sees fit. A new body for the Chinese martial arts—the Jingwu Athletic Association (Jingwu tiyu hui 精武體育會), a civic organization that members of China's modern urban society may freely join—is born. Huo Yuanjia's encounters with the urban, transnational, commodified, and mediatized fabric of modern life bear fruit in the creation of a new vehicle for the transmission of the personal and national heritage of the Chinese martial arts, a vehicle that seems to hold the promise of freeing that heritage from the infirmities and limitations that have hitherto plagued its transmission from one generation to the next.

Mediality and Fiction

The establishment of the Jingwu Athletic Association marks the realization of a vision the novel's protagonist has pursued since his entry into the narrative. Yet the novel has little to say about this new embodiment of China's martial arts. The vision of the martial arts as a model for a new mode of transmission and a keystone of Chinese citizenship and national strength is defined primarily through the negative examples of its others: on the one hand, the traditional world of the Rivers and Lakes, with its feuding, secrecy, and ambivalent relationship with the law and established institutions of authority; on the other, the mirage of transnational modernity proffered by the Japanese, whose appeals to cultural kinship and Pan-Asian solidarity mask a malevolent self-interest. In the aftermath of the match with Zhang, Huo, weakened by his exertions and burdened with new responsibilities at the school in addition to his anxieties over family finances, is again afflicted with his old ailment. He seeks out Dr. Akino, with ultimately fatal consequences. Concerning the Jingwu Athletic Association, the realization of the dream for which the protagonist has given his life, the novel tells us nothing beyond the disheartening fact that students were scant, for, Huo's renown notwithstanding, few were moved to dedicate themselves to the hard work of training. Similarly, although several subsequent fictional and cinematic versions of the Huo Yuanjia story have taken up his democratization of the martial arts—it is a theme that lends itself to a variety of treatments, including the antitraditional, the popularist, and the nationalistic—the novel's primary legacy to subsequent popular culture has been not its portrait of reimagined institutions of transmission but rather its staging of a drama of betrayal and humiliation that cry out for retribution. In this respect, the novel and its successors can be read as instantiating Jing Tsu's argument that victimization constitutes a key modality for modern Chinese cultural identity.[28] In the more specific context of Xiang Kairan's writings and career, the novel's lack of narrative investment in the realization of Huo Yuanjia's vision also reflects the author's understanding of the discursive scope and limitations of *xiaoshuo*.

As noted toward the beginning of this chapter, *Modern Times* stands out among Xiang Kairan's fictional works in the degree to which it gestures toward concerns beyond those by which traditional *xiaoshuo* defined its aims, that is, entertainment and moralizing didacticism. Its narrative material engages the question of the Chinese nation's standing in the international order and, in its treatment of the martial arts, the question of the modern viability of traditional culture and the social institutions that transmit it. Its protagonist's views on the latter question seem to mirror those of the historical author, as expressed in his nonfictional writings on the martial arts and in his lifelong commitment to martial arts practice, study, and education. Huo Yuanjia's possibilities as a fictional spokesman for Xiang Kairan's extrafictional agenda make all the more striking the extent to which the text of the novel evokes the parameters of *xiaoshuo* to foreclose the possibility of instrumental engagement with matters beyond the genre's established discursive terrain.

This proclivity manifests itself as early as the novel's first chapter. By opening with the figure of the renowned martyr Tan Sitong, the novel situates itself against themes of the nation and its history, giving the nod to *xiaoshuo*'s traditionally acknowledged kinship with historiography and at the same time providing fuel for advocates who seek to recuperate the novel, its author, and martial arts fiction in general to certain narratives of national literature. Yet in employing Tan Sitong as a device for introducing Broadsworder Wang Wu, the text acknowledges that *xiaoshuo* may have concerns distinct from those of historiography:

> This book is in essence a portrait of the chivalric heroes of the last twenty years, and in writing of the chivalric heroes of the last twenty years, one must of course open the proceedings by requesting the presence of a hero "whose deeds echo through the ages, whose fame fills the universe." Now, of the chivalric heroes of the last twenty years, there are quite a few who stand shoulder to shoulder with Broadsworder Wang Wu in fame and in deeds. The only proper procedure has been to choose one whose time period and role are suitable to the text in terms of the characters and events that the book intends to relate and so to begin writing from there.
>
> (1:1, 2)

Implicit here is the distinction between the public figures and grand events with which historiography concerns itself and the lesser-known individuals and private deeds that *xiaoshuo* is at liberty to record. What is addressed directly, though, is the separate issue of artistry, of *xiaoshuo*'s requirements concerning the selection and arrangement of material. Suitability to the structural and aesthetic requirements of the text carries at least as much weight as the intrinsic import of the material. And the text foregrounds its own artistry—its purposes as text rather than as an index of extratextual reality—for the reader's attention and appreciation.

Similar priorities obtain not only in the case of the introductory gambit involving Tan Sitong and Wang Wu but equally with regard to the Huo Yuanjia material. If my discussion so far has given the impression that the bulk of the text is concerned with Huo Yuanjia's adventures, then I have gravely misrepresented the work. *Modern Times* is as exuberantly digressive as the others of Xiang Kairan's chapter novels. Huo Yuanjia's story indeed provides the framework, structural and thematic, of the novel as a whole, but it is a framework that is attenuated to an extreme degree by the inclusion of anecdotes, tales, and minibiographies of dozens of martial artists and other colorful figures. Such digressions far outweigh the Huo Yuanjia material proper in terms of quantity and through their complexity sometimes render the narrative design and thematic direction I have imputed to the narrative barely distinguishable.[29] At the point in the tale where Huo, in Shanghai, first encounters Peng Shubai, the narrator breaks off to introduce Peng's uncle, Peng Jizhou, an official in Shaanxi, and to tell the tale of his dealings with the bandit Hu Jiu. The excursus prompts the narrator to address the question of the novel's design directly:

> [The story of how] Peng Jizhou himself brought along his constable Zhu Youjie to call upon Hu Jiu by night and then returned to his *yamen* has already been completed. Now, as I continue writing this account, I need only explain what was behind this whole affair, and then get back to the main story of how Peng Shubai aided Huo Yuanjia in setting up his *leitai* in Shanghai. Most of my readers are undoubtedly thinking that since I'm telling the tale of Huo Yuanjia, I should just go right ahead and write it in a direct and straightforward manner, without deliberately complicating manners, setting the main story off to one side, time and again, heedless of the tedium, devoting my writing to these irrelevant digressions and driving my readers to exasperation.
>
> You must understand, dearest readers, that although in composing this *Tale of Chivalric Heroes* I have not made Huo Yuanjia the central character throughout the entire text, yet all the many and various matters that arise invariably derive from the thread of Huo Yuanjia. And if I were simply to write out the events of Huo Yuanjia's entire life in a book of some three or five chapters, then wouldn't I have to take each one of these related tales and write it up as a short story, starting from scratch over and over again? If I wrote in this manner, not only would I find it uninteresting as a writer, but I dare say you too, dearest readers, would feel that it was fairly dull.
>
> (51:3, 154)

The passage obviously speaks to the comparative aesthetics of short fiction and the chapter novel; more fundamentally, though, it champions the pleasures of narrative texture. It presumes and cultivates a readerly interest in the formal aspects of fiction, laying bare the narrative's machinations in an invitation to the reader to savor the author-narrator's skills. And it prioritizes the pleasures of this aesthetic negotiation over the exigencies of the matter ostensibly at hand—the matter of our chivalric hero Huo Yuanjia. One can argue that many of the interpolated stories reinforce certain themes of the primary narrative—the trials and limitations of master-disciple transmission, for instance, or the challenges of life in the modern metropolis. One could also argue that the frustration they create by delaying the flow of the primary narrative reproduces on the level of readerly experience the frustration that bedevils the protagonist in his desire to prove himself against a foreign challenger. But the text, in the voices of both narrator and commentator, makes clear that the digressions are meant to be entertaining in their own right and, further, that their obfuscation of the primary narrative constitutes a form of pleasure. The author-narrator, no less than his protagonist, is a master of the Trackless Art.

Of the text's concrete strategies for elaborating and delaying the narrative, two in particular stand out. One is the technique familiar from traditional fiction going back at least to *The Water Margin*, whereby one character's encounter with another within the diegesis provides the pretext for a change of narrative direction. In *Modern Times*, many of the links between one character and the next either begin from or lead to the relationship between master and disciple. The introduction of a certain figure occasions an account of his martial training and thus of his master's career, or a chance encounter between two martial artists leads to the establishment of a master-disciple relationship. In such cases, the handing off of the narrative thread from one character to the next directly replicates the networks of transmission that constitute the world of the traditional martial arts. This handoff is conducted by the text's extra-diegetic narrator, employing the traditional simulation of the interaction between a storyteller and his audience, often (as in the example above) explicitly drawing attention to his manipulation of the narrative and the readerly pleasure it supposedly affords.

A second mechanism for introducing digressive material is intradiegetic narration. The pleasures of digressive storytelling are modeled for the reader by characters within the novel who tell stories to other characters; the characters within the stories they tell take a similar delight in storytelling, creating multiple levels of nesting narration. The first and most prominent of the intradiegetic narrators is none other than Huo Yuanjia. When invited by Xie Liankui to join the Boxer cause, Huo makes his excuses to the misguided youth, then proceeds to regale Nong Jingsun with tales of the elder Xie's exploits: "In any case we've got time on our hands today, and since I've gotten this far in the tale, I might as well tell you the amusing story of what happened to him in Caozhou" (16:1, 207). Nong, for his part, as Huo's interlocutor, provides a diegetic echo and instantiation of that audience typically implied in the narrator's address to the reader:

> When Nong Jinsun heard this, he couldn't help but interrupt to ask, "So just who was it that they mistook him for? Why did they need to mobilize such a crowd of troops to come and capture him?"
>
> Would you like to know how Huo Yuanjia responded? Just wait for the seventeenth chapter to tell more!
>
> (16:1, 212)

The chapter commentary that follows invites the reader to admire the introduction of intradiegetic narration as another cleverly deployed device from the author's technical arsenal. The representation of Huo Yuanjia as a storyteller establishes a functional correspondence between the author-narrator and his protagonist. That Huo should choose to assume this role, however, right at the point in the narrative when he is sidestepping a call (however misguided) to devote the martial arts to the nation's service, underlines the gulf between the potential utility of the martial arts and the allegedly inconsequential pleasures of storytelling.

The author-narrator's perception of a gulf between the work of the nation and his career as a writer of fiction finds particularly acute expression in the portions of the novel written after Xiang Kairan's return to Shanghai in 1930. The completion of *Rivers and Lakes* was the single major accomplishment of his short-lived return to fiction writing after several years of direct involvement in the nation's military and political struggles. But the novel's text resumes at the beginning of chapter 66 with the extended narratorial interpolation discussed in chapter 1 of this study: a disclaimer of any motivation on the author's part beyond making a living and of any value to his fiction beyond satisfying his readers' craving for the entertainingly strange. Chapter 67 then makes a noticeable and indeed explicitly signaled departure from the this-worldly material characteristic of *Modern Times* by assigning no less a figure than Sun Yatsen a set of sword-immortal bodyguards in the mode of the by now notorious *Rivers and Lakes*. The author seems to be taking special pains to flag his fictional representations of martial adventure as divorced from direct engagement with real-world concerns, whether of national struggle or of the democratization of the martial arts.

The representational practice of *Modern Times* remains defined by Xiang Kairan's commitment to what he understood to be the nature, aims, and poetics of *xiaoshuo*. Whether one understands this commitment as an embrace or as an imprisonment is in the end a matter of critical inclination. In any event, the understanding of *xiaoshuo* as peripheral, both in its proper subject matter and in its claims to moral authority, forecloses the possibility that the novel might imagine itself as instrumental. The historical author Xiang Kairan may have shared with his fictionalized character Huo Yuanjia a belief in the potential of the Chinese martial arts to strengthen the nation, but he did not share the faith in fiction's own nation-building potential professed by some of his late-Qing predecessors, much less the dream of cultivating a radically new consciousness by means of reinvented fictional modalities pursued by some of his New Literature contemporaries. His fictional representation of Huo Yuanjia and his associates evinces little ambition of venturing beyond the parameters of entertainment.

Yet if an "old school" perception of the scope of *xiaoshuo* mandates a disjunction between the representation of the martial arts for entertainment purposes and the martial arts' potential role in the formation of society and the nation and between Xiang Kairan's fictional practice and his lifelong activism on behalf of the Chinese martial arts, a common ground emerges in *Modern Times'* awareness of its own mediality. The old sense of *xiaoshuo* connotes not only peripherality but sociality as well. Entertaining narrative functions as a currency of social exchange between teller and audience. The rhetoric of *xiaoshuo*, as we have seen, frequently evokes the dynamics and relationships of its putatively originary contexts, whether of the swapping of anecdotes between friends or of the public performance of a professional storyteller. *Modern Times*, like Xiang Kairan's other fictional works, weds a narratorial persona inherited from the storytelling rhetoric of traditional fiction to a perception of the author as the producer of a mass-mediated commodity. The resultant author-narrator is neither traditional fiction's teller of tales to an audience of intimates nor the New Literature's voice of conscience baring itself in the public arena. It is a persona that embraces the commodified mediation facilitated by new technologies and institutions for the dissemination of fiction, and it in fact positions itself as a valuable element of the commodity. On the other end of an exchange initiated by the narrativized author and mediated through the publishing industry stands the buying public. Without committing ourselves unreservedly to Anderson's model of "imagined communities," we can recognize that the author-narrator's address constitutes the audience, if not inevitably as a "nation," at the least as public community, democratized by commerce and unrestricted by temporal and geographic exigencies. The public evoked in this way by the narration finds extratextual reification in the commonality of the consumers, the buyers and readers, of the text.

The author-narrator's representation of his objectives establishes an additional mode of congruence between his activity and that of his protagonist. In making Huo a storyteller, he creates Huo in his own image, and in retailing his own stories to a mass audience, he replicates some aspects of Huo's quest to bring the martial arts to a general public. The difference between that exchange of stories among friends and intimates modeled in the diegesis, in other words, and the marketing of fiction as a form of commodified print culture echoes the difference between the traditionally restricted transmission of the martial arts and the standardized public instruction promoted by Huo Yuanjia. Does the transition from private transmission to public dissemination represent a gain or a loss? The answer lies, of course, in the scales on which gain and loss are measured. Some sense of the text's own ambivalence may be gathered from Huo's exchange with Cheng Youming 程友銘, the adept who uses his skills to draw pottery shards from a man's skull:

> "From what Mr. Qin has said, what you practice is the technique
> of the Marrow-Changing Classic. I'm curious as to whether or not
> there is any substantial difference between your Marrow-Changing

Classic and that currently printed and distributed by commercial publishers."

Cheng Youming said, "I received it through oral transmission. The movements are somewhat different from those recorded in the book. The book, however, makes no record of the essentials, and the movements are wrong in a number of places as well. But if someone were to practice on the basis of what's in the book, as long as he was able to persevere, he would still gain considerable benefit."

(55:3, 245–46)

This is a measured endorsement at best. The quality of what is publicly disseminated does not match that of what is privately transmitted. On the other side of the balance is the broader access facilitated by the democratization of the art. Absent from the equation in this formulation is the question of the economic and cultural capital that might accrue to the publishers and authors engaged in the democratizing process. Yet economic benefit is precisely what the author has identified as the essential motive for his own production of texts for mass distribution.

In recognizing and invoking in this manner the author-audience relationships made possible by mass-mediated print culture, *Modern Times* shares ground with other fiction of the late Qing and early Republic. What distinguishes it from other texts is the way in which it echoes these relationships diegetically by means of its representation of the changing mediatory structures of the martial arts. The community of consumers of the modern fictional text—its public—is structurally and functionally analogous to the community of practitioners of the martial arts as mediated through commercial publications and open-membership organizations. This is the kind of public the novel's Huo Yuanjia seeks to address through a new dissemination of the martial arts; this is the kind of public the historical Xiang Kairan addressed both as a martial arts educator and promoter and as an author of fiction. The text's suturing of nodes of tale telling with nodes of martial transmission and its representation of Huo Yuanjia as a devoted raconteur underscore this homology. The point is not that Huo Yuanjia serves as a projection of an authorial persona—a plausible but reductionist reading—but rather that the correspondence allows us to recognize how the text's reflections of modern mediality exceed its surface-level replication of traditional notions of the limited scope of *xiaoshuo*. In reaching beyond traditional models of communication and transmission, in exploiting new institutions' and new technologies' potential for constituting new social formations, Xiang Kairan's martial arts *xiaoshuo* joins the martial arts as a medium for negotiating the experience of modernity. And in its ambivalent assessment of the gains and losses brought by the apparently inevitable emergence of modern mediality, *Modern Times* reflects as much on the role of fiction and the limits of *xiaoshuo* as it does on the future of the martial arts.

Conclusion

The Unworthy Scholar from Pingjiang

The previous chapter of this study opened with a glance at Xiang Kairan's first novel, *Sojourners*. The opening of *Sojourners* presents the earliest instance within Xiang Kairan's body of fictional works of an elaborate performance by a narrator claiming identity with the historical author, who, in addressing his motives for writing, speaks to the question of the value and nature of *xiaoshuo*. In a recollected vignette, he casts Buxiaosheng (the author in his role as writer) as both narrator and object of narration: "The fifteenth day of the twelfth month of the third year of the Republic; dust and clouds obscure the sky, dim shadows fill the room. This time and this place—such is Buxiaosheng's memory of sitting down in a Tokyo hotel to begin writing *The Unofficial History of Sojourners in Japan*" (1:1).

Posing, on his readers' behalf, the questions of what the book is about and why he wrote it, the narrator then proceeds to divide his countrymen in Japan (apart from diplomatic and economic officials) into four categories: students, merchants, those on government funds who devote themselves not to study or commerce but to whoring and gluttony, and exiles from the Second Revolution. Buxiaosheng, however, claims membership in none of these categories. In Tokyo since Meiji 40 (1907),[1] supported by family funds, he has pursued his studies through graduation yet "spent twenty-five days of any given month in the realm of wine and women" (1:2).

Now facing the prospect of returning home with no substantive accomplishments to present to "the elders of my native home," he has conceived the notion of composing this record of the follies of the third group and the bad apples among the fourth "as a slapdash way of fulfilling my responsibilities." He expresses the pious hope that the book will first of all warn its readers to avoid its characters' examples and, second, warn those represented on its pages to reform their ways. "And third, if those who come later do in fact imitate those within the book, and those within the book repeat the deeds the book records, then I can only hope that a Buxiaosheng will once again appear, willing to sacrifice his personal virtue and continue writing *The Unofficial History of Sojourners in Japan* in a declaration of war against the forces of depravity" (1:2).

This apologia at the head of Xiang Kairan's career as a writer of fiction neither mentions the strange (*qi* 奇) as such nor argues for the entertainment value of fictional narrative. The extraordinariness of the material is framed in negative moral terms, as "despicable acts" (*choushi* 醜事) and "vile reports" (*esheng* 惡聲), and this moralization of the strange serves to support a claim for the novel's didactic value. Even this defense, however, concedes the novel's status as an inferior and heterodox mode of discourse, one that strays from the practices of the ancients even as it invests itself in their ideals: "The ancients set great store in not speaking of evil but praising the good; this book however overlooks the good while exalting the evil. There are those who will revile me. But Buxiaosheng is my name while I am alive and will serve as my posthumous title when I am dead; let them go ahead and revile me as they like!" (1:2).

The standing of the novel thus implicates, even determines, the standing of its author. The sense of the pen name "Buxiaosheng" is key here; indeed, the link between the novel's motives and its creator's identity as an author could not be asserted more strongly than in this passage defending the very name under which he chooses to write. *Buxiao*, most commonly understood as meaning "unworthy" or "feckless," is sometimes used as a first-person humilific. Traditional etymologies derive the sense of "unworthy" from that of "dissimilar, unlike" and further associate the phrase with its homophone "unfilial" (*buxiao* 不孝), equating unworthiness with the failure either to serve or to emulate one's forebears.[2] Buxiaosheng is thus the Unworthy Scholar, and on the surface the name expresses those very fears of disappointing familial expectations that allegedly spur the novel's production.[3] But what then accounts for the defiance with which the author-narrator wields the name in the face of his detractors? Xiang Kairan reportedly once glossed his pen name with reference to a passage from the Daoist philosopher Laozi: "'All the world says that, while my Dao is great, it yet appears to be inferior [*buxiao* 不肖] (to other systems of teaching). Now it is just its greatness that makes it seem to be inferior. If it were like any other (system), for long would its smallness have been known!'"[4]

While it is possible that this reading represents a later reinterpretation of the name on the author's part,[5] it also seems plausible to understand a Daoist celebration of eccentricity as informing the narrator's ostentatious disregard for the Confucian-inspired critics he imagines: the heterodoxy that appears to be a congenital flaw could from this perspective be a mark of greatness. The author-narrator's presentation of himself and his work is thus ambiguously positioned between humility and hubris. Whether we see rote pieties thinly masking a delight in the scandalous or playful self-assurance undercut by internalized doubts, the author's conflicted stance toward his chosen genre is plainly on display.

As I argued in chapter 2 of this study, this conflicted stance is facilitated by, even overdetermined by, constituent aspects of an inherited understanding of *xiaoshuo*. But its rehearsal here also achieves a particular historical resonance, for the 1916 birth of Buxiaosheng—the commencement of Xiang Kairan's career as an author—occurs during a critical juncture in the development of modern Chinese fiction. In employing the form of the vernacular linked-chapter novel to present a mordant satire of contemporary society, *Sojourners* continues a trend instigated in part by Liang Qichao's 1902 manifesto for a New Fiction. And the novel's publication by People's Rights Publishing, an offspring of the revolutionary newspaper *People's Rights* (*Minquan bao* 民權報), echoes the association between this type of fiction and the political tides of the late Qing and the first years of the Republic. Yet by 1916 this association had become attenuated and even challenged outright. People's Rights Publishing had been established in 1914 after the paper was shut down by Yuan Shikai's censors. The publishing house and its journal *Elements of People's Rights* (which published Xiang Kairan's "Turning Pale") downplayed political agitation in favor of literary expression and were a prominent venue for the classical-language romantic tales that were later to become labeled as "Mandarin Ducks and Butterflies" fiction. In 1915 Liang Qichao lamented the betrayal of his New Fiction vision by the mendacious and irresponsible productions of contemporary fiction writers.[6] The same year saw the founding of *Youth* magazine (soon *New Youth*), a forum for the New Culture movement's calls for radically new paradigms in the forms and functions of fiction. In the year of *Sojourners'* publication, scandalous exposés akin to those from which Xiang Kairan's novel was woven gained renewed prominence and marketability under the name of "Black Curtain" fiction. Two years later, Black Curtain fiction became an initial target of New Culture attempts to define a new fiction in part by savaging established forms and aesthetics as moribund, while Lu Xun's "Diary of a Madman" gave new paradigms a dramatic first instantiation. Xiang Kairan published *Sojourners*, in short, just as conditions ripened for a redefinition of *xiaoshuo*, one that took what had previously been the vanguard of fictional practice and recast it as a regressive holdover. Under the terms of this redefinition, the author-narrator's textual performance reads not as an informed deployment of *xiaoshuo* genre tropes in the service of self-examination and self-presentation but rather as a confession of allegiance to a discredited status quo.

That the New Culture movement's call for a new fictional paradigm emerged in part as a response to the devolution of Liang Qichao's politically engaged New Fiction into Black Curtain scandalmongering and Butterfly sentimentality and commercialism is a familiar claim, one integrated into the received historiography of modern Chinese literature. We must perceive this historiography as shaped by the new literature's own polemical representations of its inspirations, aims, and value, but we must also perforce recognize many of the narrative's constituent elements—the existence of certain literary forms and the discovery and exploration of seemingly new literary possibilities; the association of these various literary options with the cultures, literary practices, and ideologies of certain social groups; the interventions of political movements and of the expanding commercial publishing industry; and so forth—as validly descriptive of historical reality, consequently as historically contingent and so in one sense unique to the Chinese case. Yet while respecting the granularity of the phenomena, we must also understand both the phenomena and the narratives constructed around them as participating in a transnational literary modernity.

A common approach to the question of Chinese literary modernity is to examine the validity of the claims to modernity implicitly or explicitly made by those texts that were understood by their authors and audiences as undertaking a radical break from the literary past—namely, the new literature of the May Fourth and New Culture movements, with its predecessors and descendants. How does the break manifest itself: in linguistic register, rhetoric, voice, form, content, ideology, praxis? How clean is the break: has the modern truly dawned, or is the project haunted by the unexorcised ghosts of the past? Does the modern dawn as the first morning of a new world, or has it been foreshadowed (forelightened?) by previous dawns, false, tentative, or forgotten? How long does the light of the modern shine, and at what point in history do we find it darkened by trauma, despair, betrayal—or are these sorrows indeed constituent of the modern? Can the Chinese modern be Chinese; do explicitly Chinese affiliations, whether elected or inescapable, compromise participation in a universal modernity? To the extent that such questions revolve around the identification and evaluation of texts (and, most often, writers) that might constitute the corpus of modern Chinese literature, they disregard the systemic production of Chinese literary modernity and its place in the global reproduction of associated systems.

Andreas Huyssen has christened that "volatile relationship between high art and mass culture" that characterizes "the culture of modernity" with the name "the Great Divide." Locating the birth of modernism in the literary art of such mid-nineteenth-century figures as Gustave Flaubert (1821–1880) and Charles Baudelaire (1821–1867), he notes that its emergence "cannot be adequately understood on the basis of an assumed logic of 'high' literary evolution alone. Modernism constituted itself through a conscious strategy of exclusion, an anxiety of contamination by its other: an increasingly consuming and engulfing mass culture."[7] The opposition between high literature (art, culture) and low (non)literature (art, culture), in other words, is a constitutive element of literary modernism. Works that lay claim to literary modernity cannot do so through their engagement with modern social conditions, modern aesthetics, or a consciously modern subjectivity alone but must make implied or explicit reference to a mass cultural other against which their position is defined and characterized as "high." From a systemic perspective, thus, modernity inheres not within the modernist works but in the gestalt that generates high and low in symbiosis. It is this gestalt that Fan Boqun figures as the two wings of a bird, the pure (*chun* 纯) and the popular (*tongsu* 通俗), lacking either of which the body of modern Chinese literature would be unable to take flight.[8]

Huyssen's interest lies primarily in the discursive operations of this gestalt, in the Euro-American sphere he sees as its native habitat, and (as his title makes clear) in the era subsequent to its nineteenth-century emergence, up to the late-twentieth-century advent of the postmodern. Pierre Bourdieu's work on the establishment of the modern literary field shares a similar understanding of mid-nineteenth-century Europe as a point of origin.[9] In analyzing this originary moment, Bourdieu seeks to ground discursive formations in institutional structures and sociological positions. High and low face each other not across a Great Divide but within a dynamic field structured by the tensions between perpendicular axes of heteronomous and autonomous value, that is, of economic value esteemed by society as a whole and of aesthetic value proper to a newly autonomous literary field. The higher the position an individual or institutional agent claims in relation to one axis, the greater the resistance to a corresponding ascent along the other. High art and vulgar commerce define each other through claims of mutual exclusivity, while various agents' strategic negotiation of positions relative to these twin standards of value constitutes and situates the literary field as a whole.

It does not require a simplistic belief in material determinism or a Marxist theory of base and superstructure to note that Bourdieu's sociological model presumes the technological, institutional, and economic development of the publishing industry through which the literary field conducts its operations and thus that these material factors join institutional and discursive elements in constructing literary modernity. A focus on the material conditions of textual production, and in particular on the importance and specific dynamics of the periodical circulation of literature, constitutes one of several significant interventions made by Michel Hockx in his consideration of the relevance of Bourdieu's models to an understanding of modern Chinese literature.[10] Hockx points out that the New Literature's construction of a Butterfly other as an object of attack replicates a classic strategy for newcomers seeking literary authority: "It is always in the interest of the recognition-seeking avant-garde to argue that the literary establishment of its time has squandered the autonomous principle of literature and succumbed to the lures of more profitable, heteronomous forms of capital."[11] He sees a modern Chinese literary field allowing for such strategies as beginning to take shape after the suppression of the Taiping Rebellion in the latter nineteenth century, that is, slightly later than the developments analyzed by Bourdieu. But a literary field in the broad sense of an "interest community" of writers, publishers, booksellers, and critics can be found in China at least as early as the late sixteenth century, during the Ming dynasty. A primary dynamic structuring this earlier manifestation of a literary field was the interplay between the autonomous principle of literary value and the heteronomous principle of political usefulness. As the nineteenth-century growth of the commercial publishing industry magnified the potential for and influence of economic capital, profit joined but did not replace politics as an axis of heteronomous value. The modern Chinese literary field must therefore be understood as structured along not two axes but three: an autonomous principle of literary value, a heteronomous principle of economic value, and a partially heteronomous principle of political authority, claiming validation in the name of the nation and its people.[12]

These various models aid us in seeing more clearly the affinities between the modern Chinese literary system and global patterns of literary modernity as well as the historical specificities of the Chinese case. The fact that the New Culture movement's rhetoric, strategies, and literary choices were deeply imbedded in, even overdetermined by, the unique political and cultural crises Chinese intellectuals faced at the dawn of the twentieth century should not blind us to the fact that their choices also answered to rules defining modern literary fields around the globe and affirmed the Great Divide between high and low on which these fields depended. At the same time we must acknowledge the distinctive authority within the Chinese literary field (it is surely not an entirely unique presence) of a principle neither economic nor aesthetic, a principle constituted through the linking of literature to the fate of the nation—the impulse behind what C. T. Hsia dubbed modern Chinese literature's "obsession with China," conditioned by the literate class's historic role as shepherds of the masses, adapted to new notions of a nation and its citizenry, and feverishly energized by an awareness of national crisis and the trauma of the collapse of traditional institutions of intellectual authority.[13] The presence of this third, political principle created additional complexities and allowed for novel strategies for the negotiation of position and capital in the literary field. The fact that the ostensible stakes were not merely economic and aesthetic value but the fate of the nation as well contributed to the virulent, winner-take-all tone that came to characterize literary polemics and granted the resultant structures and positions a striking tenacity.

In addition to facilitating an understanding of modern Chinese literature that locates it within global patterns of literary modernity, a systemic perspective can act as a counterbalance to the assumption that it is only those texts, authors, and genres that find themselves on the more elevated side of the Great Divide that deserve the attention of literary historians and critics. In challenging this assumption, the aim should not be to rehabilitate literature relegated to the swamps of the Low by resettling it on higher terrain—a move that would only validate literary study's implication in terraforming the landscape it seeks to survey. Nor should it be to deny that the distinction between High and Low exists. The Great Divide's presence, to be sure, is constructed and contingent rather than immanent any given text, but its very contingency, and the agents and processes involved in its construction, are proper and necessary objects of literary inquiry. Essential to this inquiry is an understanding that all elements of a literary system are involved in its creation. This is not to say that power is equally shared, for the negotiation of authority, dependent upon capital of various sorts, animates the literary field both synchronically and diachronically. But to the extent that we, as readers and as scholars, can decline even provisionally to identify with one given position—in particular one among those that claim ascendance through the successful appropriation of autonomous symbolic capital—then we can open ourselves to a more holistic understanding of the system and to an appreciation of the choices made by the literatures that find places for themselves elsewhere within the field.

The focus of this study has been the choices made by one particular author: those that Xiang Kairan as a writer made concerning, among other things, genre, language, form, subject matter, representational mode, narrative structure, narrative voice, and self-presentation. These choices entailed other choices involving literary affiliations, professional networks, publication venues, and potential audiences. As such they were in some sense individual but certainly not autonomous; they were conditioned, rather, by the possibilities made available by the collective actions of imbricated groups including reading audiences, colleagues and peers, editors and publishers, critics and commentators. The significance of this study therefore lies in part in what the case of Xiang Kairan's activities as a writer of *xiaoshuo* reveal about the networks in which he was engaged and the system of which these networks were a constituent part. The difference between the author/narrator's self-presentation in the opening of *Sojourners* and what we find when *Modern Times* recommences in its sixty-sixth chapter (see chapter 2 of this study) can legitimately be read as the difference between the provocative playfulness of a fledgling author first stretching his wings and the resignation of a man fifteen years older turning his hand once again to an all-too-familiar craft. But it is also the difference between a perception of the linked-chapter novel as a vehicle for audacious satire suitable for book publication by a publisher with a lingering aura of literary distinction and revolutionary valor and a perception of the linked-chapter novel's value as grist for the mills of a publisher striving to outpace competitors in providing a staple diet of entertainment, familiar yet appealingly spiced, to its readership market. It would be a mistake to impute the latter perception only to New Literature critics and a further mistake to accept uncritically the valuation they attached to it. The continuing life of the linked-chapter novel as a literary genre into the 1940s and beyond, and the increasingly diversifying manifestations of martial arts fiction as a thematic subgenre up through the present day, have been driven by choices made by agents on various levels—choices vindicated as meaningful and productive by the very history of these forms.

In the years following the appearance of *Rivers and Lakes* and *Modern Times*, consensus on the conventions of martial arts fiction coalesced, in good measure on the basis of the possibilities articulated by these two works. While the elaboration and reinforcement of genre characteristics allowed for considerable variation, including the articulation of further subgenres and signature authorial styles, it also involved a closing off of possibilities and a habituation of martial-arts-related material to the confines—one might almost say the ghetto—of genre literature, presumed to belong by default to the subliterary terrain of the Low. Over the course of the twentieth century there are instances of authors working outside the thematic subgenre who draw on similar material (Lao She's 老舍 1934 "Soul-Slaying Spear" ["Duanhun qiang" 斷魂槍] is a well-known example) and of authors working within the subgenre but widely perceived as having transcended its confines and ascended to a more expansive literary terrain—most notably Jin Yong 金庸. The position occupied by Xiang Kairan's works is unique. While contributing foundational elements to modern martial arts fiction, they also carry a wealth of material and possibilities beyond those that will become reified as the thematic subgenre's defining characteristics. This is perhaps even more true of *Modern Times* than of *Rivers and Lakes*. The novel's catholicity and the author's consciousness of both the links and the disjunctures between his personal commitment to the martial arts and his role as a purveyor of martial arts entertainment fiction contribute to the novel's avoidance of the glassy-eyed lack of irony that marks much of the subsequent development of martial arts fiction and film in either the romantic *wuxia* 武俠 or chauvinistic *gongfu* 功夫 substrains. Considered not as martial arts fiction but as manifestations of "traditional fiction," or what I refer to in this study as *xiaoshuo*, Xiang Kairan's body of work similarly defies easy definition. It embraces the rhetorical conventions and ostensibly trivial ambitions that New Literature critics saw as defining the reactionary backwardness of premodern prose narrative and its contemporary descendants. Yet it engages with the project of literary modernity—on a systemic level, as I have argued, but also through the author's redeployment of these very conventions and ambitions. For Xiang Kairan, *xiaoshuo*'s defining features of recording and transmitting events, highlighting the strange, and providing entertainment become the constituent elements of a mode of literary production designed to engage, delight, and satisfy the widening readerships of contemporary Chinese society, and the inherited persona of the author-narrator becomes a vehicle for that negotiation of the roles of storyteller, professional writer, and citizen of a changing China that history demanded of the Unworthy Scholar from Pingjiang.

Notes

INTRODUCTION

1. John Christopher Hamm, *Paper Swordsmen: Jin Yong and the Modern Chinese Martial Arts Novel* (Honolulu: University of Hawai'i Press, 2005).

2. Fan Boqun 范伯群, "Lun Minguo wuxia xiaoshuo dianji zuo Jindai xiayi yingxiong zhuan" 论民国武侠小说奠基作《近代侠义英雄传》 [An Analysis of "The Legends of Modern Chivalric Heroes"—Foundation of Martial Arts Fiction in the Period of the Republic of China], *Xinan daxue xuebao (shehui kexue ban)* 西南大学学报 (社会科学版) 37, no. 1 (January 2011): 37.

3. See Judith T. Zeitlin, "*Xiaoshuo*," in *The Novel*, vol. 1: *History, Geography, and Culture*, ed. Franco Moretti (Princeton, NJ: Princeton University Press, 2006), 249–61; and Sarah M. Allen, "Narrative Genres," in *The Oxford Handbook of Classical Chinese Literature (1000 BCE–900CE)*, ed. Wiebke Denecke, Wai-yee Li, and Xiaofei Tian (New York: Oxford University Press, 2017), 273–87. For further references on the history of the term and the writings it designates, see the discussions in chapters 2 and 4.

4. On the origins of these terms see E. Perry Link Jr., *Mandarin Ducks and Butterflies: Popular Fiction in Early Twentieth-Century Chinese Cities* (Berkeley: University of California Press, 1981), 7–8, 166, 176–77. As Link points out, both terms were originally descriptive rather than pejorative and were limited in scope of reference; New Literature critics made them terms of scorn and broadened their application then bequeathed this usage to later historiographers. See also Fan Boqun 范伯群, ed., *Zhongguo jin- xiandai tongsu wenxue shi* 中国近现代通俗文学史 [A history of recent- and modern-era Chinese popular literature], 2 vols. (Nanjing: Jiangsu jiaoyu chubanshe, 1999), 1:13–18; and Xueqing Xu, "The Mandarin Duck and Butterfly School," in *Literary Societies of*

Republican China, ed. Kirk A. Denton and Michel Hockx (Lanham, MD: Lexington Books, 2008), 47–51.

5. Fan Boqun, ed., *Zhongguo jin- xiandai tongsu wenxue shi*. See also the more concise single-author treatment in Fan Boqun 范伯群, *Zhongguo xiandai tongsu wenxue shi* 中国现代通俗文学史 [A history of modern Chinese popular literature] (Beijing: Beijing daxue chubanshe, 2007).

6. Milena Doleželová-Velingerová, review of *Mandarin Ducks and Butterflies* by E. Perry Link Jr., *Harvard Journal of Asiatic Studies* 44, no. 2 (December 1984): 581–83.

7. Chen Jianhua 陈建华, *Cong geming dao gonghe: Qingmo zhi Minguo shiqi wenxue, dianying yu wenhua de zhuanxing* 从革命到共和: 清末至民国时期文学, 电影与文化的转型 [From revolution to republic: the transformation of literature, film, and culture from the late Qing to the Republican era] (Guilin: Guangxi shifan daxue chubanshe, 2009).

8. A recent issue of the journal *Renditions*, "in a frank attempt to revise conventional literary history," employs the term "Republican urban fiction" without, however, expansively clarifying the rationale behind this particular label. Theodore Huters, "Cultivating the 'Great Divide': Urban Literature in Early Twentieth-Century China," *Renditions* 87 and 88 (Spring and Autumn 2017): 7.

9. Fan Boqun, ed., *Zhongguo jin-xiandai tongsu wenxue shi*, 1:37–438.

10. For examples of such approaches, see, e.g., Huters's discussion of Zhao Tiaokuang's "The Pawnshop" and Lu Xun's "Kong Yiji" in "Popular Literature and the 'Great Divide'"; Chen Jianhua's analysis of Zhou Shoujuan's "A Gramophone Record" and Mao Dun's "Creation" in "An Archaeology of Repressed Popularity: Zhou Shoujuan, Mao Dun, and their 1920s Literary Polemics," in *Rethinking Chinese Popular Culture: Cannibalizations of the Canon*, ed. Carlos Rojas and Eileen Cheng-yin Chow (London: Routledge, 2009), 101–9; and Alexander Des Forges, "Street Talk and Alley Stories: Tangled Narratives of Shanghai from *Lives of Shanghai Flowers* (1892) to *Midnight* (1933)," PhD diss., Princeton University, 1998.

11. Michel Hockx, assessing the potential impact of the work of Bourdieu and other theorists of literary sociology upon the study of Chinese literature, predicts that "the literary text and its authors will remain the central focus of scholars' attention for decades to come." See Michel Hockx, ed., *The Literary Field of Twentieth-Century China* (Honolulu: University of Hawai'i Press, 1999), 19. The publication of the present study at least falls within his anticipated horizon.

12. Gérard Genette, *The Architext*, trans. Jane E. Lewin (Berkeley: University of California Press, 1992).

13. Genette, *The Architext*, 75.

14. John G. Cawelti, *Adventure, Mystery, and Romance: Formula Stories as Art and Popular Culture* (Chicago: University of Chicago Press, 1976).

15. Cf. Tzvetan Todorov, *The Poetics of Prose*, trans. Richard Howard (Ithaca, NY: Cornell University Press, 1977).

16. The field of cinema studies has given fuller attention to the function of genre as a marketing device than has the (generally undernourished) field of popular literature

studies. Cawelti's study of formula fiction gives some attention to marketing; the classic sociological study of a popular fiction subgenre, addressing both the institutions of production and the dynamics of readership, is Janice Radway, *Reading the Romance* (Chapel Hill: University of North Carolina Press, 1984).

1. THE WRITER'S LIFE

1. There are many lacunae in our knowledge of Xiang Kairan's life and career as a writer and frequent discrepancies among the published sources, which include statements by the author, reminiscences by family members, accounts by colleagues and contemporaries, and official biographies. I here rely on Xu Sinian 徐斯年 and his associates' "Pingjiang Buxiaosheng Xiang Kairan nianbiao: zengbu gao" 平江不肖生向愷然年表 (增补稿) [Chronological table for Pingjiang Buxiaosheng Xiang Kairan: expanded and revised version] *Pinbao* 品报 31 (July 2015): 2–28. The journal *Pinbao* is electronically distributed; several earlier and perhaps more accessible versions of Xu Sinian's article are listed in the bibliography to this volume. For an English-language biography see Roland Altenburger, "Xiang Kairan," in *Dictionary of Literary Biography*, vol. 328: *Chinese Fiction Writers, 1900–1949*, ed. Thomas Moran (Detroit: Thomson Gale, 2006), 235–40.

2. On Chen's life and ideas see Ernest P. Young, "Ch'en T'ien-hua (1875–1905): A Chinese Nationalist," *Papers on China* 13 (1959): 113–62.

3. Translation from John K. Fairbank and Kwang-ching Liu, eds., *The Cambridge History of China*, vol. 11: *Late Ch'ing, 1800–1911*, part 2 (Cambridge: Cambridge University Press, 1980), 358.

4. On the Kobun Institute, see Douglas Robertson Reynolds, *China, 1898–1912: The Xinzheng Revolution and Japan* (Cambridge, MA: Council on East Asian Studies, Harvard University, 1993), 49–52. On Chinese students in Japan in general, the classic study is Huang Fu-ch'ing, *Chinese Students in Japan in the Late Ch'ing Period* (Tokyo: Centre for East Asian Cultural Studies, 1982).

5. See Xu Sinian, "Nianbiao," 5.

6. Xiang Kairan [Buxiaosheng 不肖生], *Huitou shi an* 回頭是岸 [Repent and be saved], *Xin Shanghai* 新上海 [New Shanghai] 1, no. 1 (May 1925).

7. Xiang Kairan, "Lan fashi ji: Lan fashi zhuo gui" 藍法師記: 藍法師捉鬼 [Reverend Lan catches a ghost], *Xingqi* 星期 [The Sunday] no. 34 (1922). Xu Sinian, "Nianbiao," 5, cites the same passage.

8. Xiang Kairan, "Quanshu" 拳術 [The art of pugilism], *Zhonghua xiaoshuo jie* 中華小說界 [Chung Hwa Novel Magazine] 2, nos. 7–12 (July–December 1915).

9. Xiang Kairan [Xiang Kui Kairan 向逵愷然], "Quanshu jianwen lu" 拳術見聞錄 [Matters pugilistic, seen and heard], *Zhonghua xiaoshuo jie* 中華小說界 [Chung Hwa Novel Magazine] 3, nos. 3–5 (March–May 1916); included as an appendix in the monograph publication of "Quanshu" by Zhonghua shuju 中華書局 in December 1916.

10. Xiang Kairan [Kairan 愷然], "Bianse tan" 變色談 [Turning pale], *Minquan su* 民權素 [Elements of people's rights] no. 16 (March 1916). On *Minquan su* 民權素 see Link,

Mandarin Ducks, 166–67; and Yuan Jin 袁进, *Zhongguo wenxue de jindai biange* 中国文学的近代变革 [The early-modern transformation of Chinese literature] (Guilin: Guangxi shifan daxue chubanshe, 2006), 44–58.

11. "Wulai chanshi" 無賴禪師 [The reverend Wulai] in *Xiaoshuo hai* 小說海 [Ocean of fiction] 2, no. 8 (August 1916); "Zhu Sangongzi" 朱三公子 [Third master Zhu] in 2, no. 10 (October 1916); "Danchi xue" 丹墀血 [Blood on the palace steps] in 2, no. 11 (November 1916); and "Wan Luo" 皖羅 [Luo of Anhui] in 2, no. 12 (December 1916); all published under the name Kairan 慨然.

12. "Kou hun" 寇婚 [Stolen wedding], in the Beijing-based *Cunxin* 寸心 [Heart] no. 3 (July 1917), under the name Buxiaosheng 不肖生.

13. Xiang Kairan [Xiang Kui Kairan 向逵慨然], *Quanshu jianwen lu* 拳術見聞錄 [Matters pugilistic, seen and heard] (Shanghai: Taidong tushu ju, 1919).

14. *Longhu chunqiu* 龍虎春秋 [Annals of the dragon and tiger], in twenty chapters, was published by Shanghai's Jiaotong tushuguan 交通圖書館 in 1919, under the name Xiang Kui Kairan 向逵慨然. It is mentioned in Xu Sinian, "Nianbiao," 8; and Altenburger, "Xiang Kairan," 237; I have not seen a copy of the text. *Banye feitou ji* 半夜飛頭記 [The flying head at midnight], thirteen chapters, was evidently first published in 1920 by Shanghai's Shihuan shuju 時還書局. The copy I have seen was published in 1923 by Shanghai's Wuqiang shuju 武強書局 under the name Xiake shanren 俠客山人 (although the narrator identifies himself as Buxiaosheng in the opening chapter). Later in the 1920s—after the success of *Rivers and Lakes* and *Modern Times*—Shihuan shuju published a series of sequels to *Flying Head* authored by Sishui yuyin 泗水漁隱, i.e., Yu Yinmin 俞印民 (1895–1949); in some editions and some secondary literature, these sequels are attributed to Xiang Kairan. See Xu Sinian, "Nianbiao," 8–9.

15. Bao Tianxiao, *Chuanying lou huiyi lu* 釧影樓回憶錄 [Memoirs of bracelet shadow chamber] (Taipei: Longwen chubanshe, 1990), 457–58. See also the account of the visit in Bao Tianxiao [Manmiao 曼妙], "Zhuiyi Buxiaosheng" 追憶不肖生 [Remembering Buxiaosheng], *Jingbao* 晶報 [The Crystal], April 3, 1929. For overviews of *The Sunday*, see Wei Shaochang 魏绍昌 et al., ed. *Yuanyang hudie pai yanjiu ziliao* 鸳鸯蝴蝶派研究资料 [Research materials on the mandarin duck and butterfly school] (Hong Kong: Sanlian shudian, 1980), 334–36; and Fan Boqun, *jin-xiandai*, 2:647–51.

16. Xiang Kairan [Buxiaosheng 不肖生], *Liudong waishi bu* 留東外史補 [Supplement to the unofficial history of sojourners in Japan], *Xingqi* [The Sunday] nos. 32–48 (1922–1923); published in book form by Dadong shuju, 1926.

17. Like the *Supplement*, "A Hunter's Miscellany" harks back to his previous publications, in this case the 1916 "Turning Pale." Another set of tiger anecdotes entitled "Turning Pale," but this time in the vernacular, appeared in *Flowers of Society* (*Shehui zhi hua* 社會之花) in 1924.

18. Note that Bao gives Shen Zhifang's name as Shen Zifang 沈子方; in some sources 沈芝芳 also appears.

19. Bao Tianxiao, *Chuanying lou*, 458.

20. Bao Tianxiao, *Chuanying lou*, 458.

21. There is, however, no evidence that he joined either of the two better-known societies of popular writers, the Green Society (Qing she 青社) and the Star Society (Xing she 星社), both founded in 1922.

22. Xiang Yixue 向一学, "Huiyi fuqin de yisheng" 回忆父亲的一生 [Remembering my father's life], in Pingjiang Buxiaosheng 平江不肖生, *Jianghu qixia zhuan* 江湖奇侠传 (Changsha: Yuelu shushe, 1986), 567.

23. Xu Zhuodai 徐卓呆 [Zhuodai 卓呆], "Fagao hou" 發稿後 [Post-production], *Xin Shanghai* 新上海 [New Shanghai] 2, no. 4 (January 1927).

24. The conclusion of chapter 86 in the magazine serialization is the end of chapter 106 in the editions most commonly circulated today. On the reorganization of the chapters and the publication history of the novel generally, see Gu Zhen 顾臻, "*Jianghu qixia zhuan* banben kao ji xiangguan wenti yanjiu" 《江湖奇侠传》版本考及相关问题研究 [A study of the editions of *Marvelous Gallants of the Rivers and Lakes* and related issues], *Suzhou jiaoyu xueyuan xuebao* 苏州教育学院学报 30, no. 3 (June 2013): 21–32.

25. Zhao Tiaokuang 赵苕狂 [Tiaokuang 苕狂], "Huaqian xiaoyu" 花前小語 [Remarks before the flowers], *Hong meigui* 紅玫瑰 [Scarlet rose] 3, no. 7 (March 5, 1927).

26. Zhao Tiaokuang 赵苕狂 [Tiaokuang 苕狂], "Huaqian xiaoyu" 花前小語 [Remarks before the flowers], *Hong meigui* 紅玫瑰 [Scarlet rose] 3, no. 10 (March 26, 1927).

27. In addition to Xu Sinian's "Nianbiao," see the details in Gu Zhen 顾臻, "Guanyu Xiang Kairan suo zai sanshi liu jun jiben qingkuang" 关于向恺然所在第三十六军基本情况 [On the circumstances of the Thirty-Sixth Corps to which Xiang Kairan was attached], *Suzhou jiaoyu xueyuan xuebao* 苏州教育学院学报 27, no. 3 (September 2010): 13–14. For a general account of the Northern Expedition I have relied on John K. Fairbank, ed., *The Cambridge History of China*, vol. 12: *Republican China 1912–1949*, part 1 (Cambridge: Cambridge University Press, 1983).

28. See Xu Sinian, "Nianbiao," 15–17, for a detailed account of relevant articles.

29. Reprinted under the title "Xiang Kairan xiansheng lian taijiquan de jingyan" 向愷然先生練太極拳的經驗 [Mr. Xiang Kairan's experience practicing *taijiquan*], in Wu Zhiqing 吳志青, *Taiji zhengzong* 太极正宗 [The orthodox tradition of *taiji*] (Shanghai: Dadong shuju, 1936; repr. Hong Kong, Jinhua chubanshe 錦華出版社, n.d.). An English translation by Paul Brennan, as "My Experience of Practicing Taiji Boxing," can be found at https://brennantranslation.wordpress.com/2016/07/31/xiang-kairans-taiji -experience/.

30. In a 1953 account of the incident addressed to the head of the Hunan Propaganda Department, Xiang Kairan relates that "They [the Communist officers] had all read my novels. They said that the ideology of my fiction was similar to their own, consistently sympathetic to the proletariat, never praising the government or the bourgeoisie; and they wished that I might go to Jiamusi to be a professor at the university. Regrettably, my sense of family obligation was too strong; at the time I had five young children who wouldn't be able to live without me, and so I was unwilling to accede to [the officer's] wishes." Quoted in Xu Sinian, "Nianbiao," 24. *Yisiqi huabao* 一四七畫報 [One-four-seven pictorial] 17, no. 7 (December 4, 1947), contains an article entitled "Pingjiang

Buxiaosheng Xiang Kairan, feiju tuoxian jingguo xiangji" 平江不肖生向愷然, 匪窟脫險經過詳記 [A detailed account of Pingjiang Buxiaosheng Xiang Kairan's experiences in escaping the perils of the bandits' lair]; this account, purportedly based on the reporter's interview with Xiang Kairan, presents the author's exchanges with his interrogator in a different light. "The next day, so-called administrative chief Shi Zirong and the rest interrogated him as to his name. Mr. Xiang replied forthrightly and without hesitation, and Shi and the rest were filled with admiration. They asked if he had ever read the works of Mao Zedong, Guo Moruo, Lu Xun, and so forth? He replied: I have read nothing later than the Tang and Song dynasties. . . . They then asked, are you willing to go to Jiamusi to serve as an instructor? He replied: To be honest, I have never read works of the Marxist sort, and if I were to teach what I'm most familiar with—Laozi, Zhuangzi, the Four Books and the Five Classics—I'm afraid it might not be quite to your taste." This article appears to be identical with the one that Xu Sinian, "Nianbiao," 24, cites from the *Jishi bao* 記事報 [The record] of December 10, 1947, under the title "Ming xiaoshuojia Pingjiang Buxiaosheng feiku tuoxian jingguo" 名小說家平江不肖生匪窟脫險經過 [Famous novelist Pingjiang Buxiaosheng's experiences in escaping the perils of the bandits' lair]; I have not seen the original of the latter article.

31. Xiang Kairan's "Li Zongren Yang Du tong yi wenzi xianzhi yu Yuan Shikai" 李宗仁楊度同以文字現知于袁世凱 [Li Zongren and Yang Du display their learning to Yuan Shikai], published in the Anhui *Xin xuefeng* 新學風 [New scholarship] no. 1 (1946), bears the subtitle "Materials for the *Unofficial History of the Revolution*, Part One" (《革命野史》材料之一). Xu Sinian, "Nianbiao," 26, notes *Geming waishi*'s publication in 1950 by Yuenan zhizi yinshu chang 岳南鑄字印刷廠. I have not seen a copy of this text.

32. Xu Sinian, "Nianbiao," 26. A text available online at Wenshi shiyi 文史拾遺 (http://www.changsha0731.cn/wssy/index.php?m=content&c=index&a=show&catid=8&id=340) identifies itself as based on a manuscript copy rather than on the published version.

2. XIANG KAIRAN'S MONKEYS: *XIAOSHUO* AS A LITERARY GENRE

1. Bao Tianxiao 包天笑 [Chuanying 釧影], "Xiang Kairan jia zhi hou" 向愷然家之猴 [The monkey in Xiang Kairan's home], *Xingqi* 星期 [The Sunday] no. 46 (January 14, 1923).

2. Altenburger, "Xiang Kairan," 240, makes this same point.

3. Quoted from Xu Sinian, "Nianbiao," 25.

4. Liang Qichao, "On the Relationship Between Fiction and the Government of the People," trans. Gek Nai Cheng, in *Modern Chinese Literary Thought: Writings on Literature, 1893–1945*, ed. Kirk A. Denton (Stanford, CA: Stanford University Press, 1996), 74.

5. Lu Xun, "Preface" to *Cheering from the Sidelines*, trans. William A. Lyell, in *Diary of a Madman and Other Stories* (Honolulu: University of Hawai'i Press, 1990), 23–24.

6. Mao Zedong, "Talks at the Yan'an Forum on Literature and Art," in Denton, *Literary Thought*, 459.

7. Xiang Kairan [Pingjiang Buxiaosheng 平江不肖生], *Jindai xiayi yingxiong zhuan* 近代俠義英雄傳 [Chivalric heroes of modern times], 5 vols. (Taipei: Shijie shuju, 2004), 4:200–1.

Except in instances where I have reason to refer specifically to the serialized text, I will hereafter reference this edition when citing *Modern Times*, giving chapter:volume, page. (66:4, 200–1) is thus chapter 66, volume 4, pp. 200–1.

8. Yu Shuwen 余叔文, "*Jianghu qixia zhuan*" 江湖奇侠传, in *Wentan zayi quanbian* 文坛杂忆全编 [Reminiscences of the literary world], ed. Gu Guohua 顾国华, 6 vols. (Shanghai: Shanghai shudian chubanshe, 2015), 1:119. Another colorful account can be found in "Wenzhang zengming zhi Xiang Kairan" 文章憎命之向恺然 [Xiang Kairan, abhorring the writer's fate], *Laoshi hua* 老實話 [Straight talk] no. 35 (1935): 10–11: "Writing was always a matter of painstaking effort for Xiang. He was unwilling to dash things off in a half-hearted manner and would often pace his room the whole night through, pondering deeply and wracking his brains before producing some marvelous effect; completing a single piece of writing meant wringing out his very heart's blood. The greatest cross he had to bear was the fact that the mistress he doted on presumed upon their relationship, and other than this [i.e., writing] he had no means to satisfy her demands for paints and powders, perfumes and mahjong. Whenever he saw a close friend he would speak of his hardships, and he once talked angrily of smashing his inkstone and breaking his brushes in two." The article, published in a Beiping-based periodical several years after Xiang Kairan's return to the south, is anonymous, and the sources of its claims are unknown; it appears in a column entitled "Roadside Gossip" [Daoting tushuo 道聽途說].

9. See Link, *Mandarin Ducks*, 16–18, 62–63. Contemporary critiques of Butterfly literature are collected in Wei Shaochang 魏紹昌, *Yanjiu ziliao*, 1–83; and Rui Heshi 芮和师 et al., eds., *Yuanyang hudie pai wenxue ziliao* 鸳鸯蝴蝶派文学资料 [Materials on mandarin duck and butterfly school literature] (Beijing: Zhishi chanquan chubanshe, 2010), 637–832. Rui Heshi organizes the materials chronologically, Wei Shaochang according to the canonical precedence of the authors.

10. Sheldon Hsiao-peng Lu, *From Historicity to Fictionality: The Chinese Poetics of Narrative* (Stanford, CA: Stanford University Press, 1994), 39; Robert E. Hegel, *Reading Illustrated Fiction in Late Imperial China* (Stanford, CA: Stanford University Press, 1998), 12.

11. On traditional critique and defense of *xiaoshuo*, see, e.g., Henry Y. H. Zhao, "Historiography and Fiction in Chinese Culture," in *The Novel*, vol. 1: *History, Geography, and Culture*, ed. Franco Moretti (Princeton, NJ: Princeton University Press, 2006), 78–83; Martin W. Huang, *Desire and Fictional Narrative in Late Imperial China* (Cambridge, MA: Harvard University Asia Center, 2001), esp. chap. 3, "From *Yu* to *Qing*: Desire and Fictional Narrative," 57–85; and Liang Shi, *Reconstructing the Historical Discourse of Traditional Chinese Fiction* (Lewiston, NY: Edwin Mellen, 2002), 111–22, *passim*. On the poetics of *xiaoshuo* (particularly the linked-chapter novel) as developed in the Ming and Qing, see especially Andrew H. Plaks, *The Four Masterworks of the Ming Novel* (Princeton, NJ: Princeton University Press, 1987); and David L. Rolston, ed., *How to Read the Chinese Novel* (Princeton, NJ: Princeton University Press, 1990).

12. Chen Jianhua, "Canon Formation and Linguistic Turn: Literary Debates in Republican China, 1919–1949," in *Beyond the May Fourth Paradigm: In Search of Chinese Modernity*, ed. Kai-Wing Chow et al. (Lanham, MD: Lexington Books, 2008), 55.

13. See the selections from literary histories produced between 1955 and 1961 collected in Wei Shaochang, *Yanjiu ziliao*, 85–121.

14. For reflections on the history of Butterfly historiography, see Chen Jianhua, "Repressed Popularity."

15. See, e.g., the essays collected in Milena Doleželová-Velingerová and Oldrich Král, eds., *The Appropriation of Cultural Capital: China's May Fourth Project* (Cambridge, MA: Harvard University Asia Center, 2001); and Chow, *Beyond the May Fourth Paradigm*. Kirk Denton, "Lu Xun, Returning Home, and May Fourth Modernity," in *The Oxford Handbook of Modern Chinese Literatures*, ed. Carlos Rojas and Andrea Bachner (New York: Oxford University Press, 2016), 34n2, surveys reconsiderations of May Fourth modernity in recent studies from a variety of academic fields.

16. See Fan Boqun, *Jin- xiandai*, esp. 1:1–6; Denise Gimpel, *Lost Voices of Modernity: A Chinese Popular Fiction Magazine in Context* (Honolulu: University of Hawai'i Press, 2001).

17. On Butterfly literature and the "sentimental-erotic tradition," see C. T. Hsia, "Hsü Chen-ya's *Yü-li hun*: An Essay in Literary History and Criticism," in *Chinese Middlebrow Fiction from the Ch'ing and Early Republican Eras*, ed. Liu Ts'un-yan (Hong Kong: Chinese University Press, 1984), 199–240. On Butterfly literature and alternative modernities, see Rey Chow, "Mandarin Ducks and Butterflies: An Exercise in Popular Readings," in *Woman and Chinese Modernity: The Politics of Reading Between West and East* (Minnesota: University of Minnesota Press, 1991), 34–83; also Link, *Mandarin Ducks*; Gimpel, *Lost Voices*; and Chen Jianhua, "Repressed Popularity" and *Cong geming dao gonghe*.

18. See especially Michel Hockx, *Questions of Style: Literary Societies and Literary Journals in Modern China, 1911–1937* (Leiden: E. J. Brill, 2003); and Michel Hockx, "Is There a May Fourth Literature? A Reply to Wang Xiaoming," *Modern Chinese Literature and Culture* 11, no. 2 (1999): 40–52.

19. While the title of the piece uses the generic "monkey" (*hou'er* 猴兒), the text here specifies "macaques" (*husun* 猢猻, a variant of *misun* 獼猴). Various species of macaque (genus *Macaca*) are the most common types of monkeys in China.

20. Xiang Kairan 向愷然, "Sange houer de gushi" 三個猴兒的故事 [Three monkey tales], *Hong zazhi* 紅雜誌 [Scarlet Magazine] 1, no. 50 (July 27, 1924).

21. For a sense of the extent to which these remarks draw on well-established tropes and a familiar narratorial posture, compare Ling Mengchu's 凌濛初 1632 foreword to a collection of vernacular tales: "From time to time I would playfully select one or two marvelous incidents that I had heard of, ancient or contemporary, that were worthy of recording, and elaborate them into tales, casually easing the burdens of my breast. This is not to say that they are of any lasting import; I simply took them as sport to lighten my mood." Ling Mengchu 凌濛初, *Erke Pai'an jingqi* 二刻拍案驚奇 [Slapping the table in amazement at the marvels, second collection] (Nanjing: Jiangsu guji chubanshe, 1990), 787.

22. I use the masculine pronoun not because a narrator is necessarily male but because the narrators in Xiang Kairan's texts are consistently gendered as such.

23. Xiang Kairan 向愷然, "Quanshujia Li Cunyi zhi si" 拳術家李存義之死 [The death of boxing master Li Cunyi], *Zhentan shijie* 偵探世界 [Detective world] no. 24 (1924).

24. Xiang Kairan [Buxiaosheng 不肖生], "Bianse tan" 變色談 [Turning pale], *Shehui zhi hua* 社會之花 [Flowers of society] no. 1 (January 5, 1924).

25. Xiang Kairan 向愷然, "Wo yanjiu quanjiao zhi shidi lianxi" 我研究拳腳之實地練習 [My hands-on experience in the study of the martial arts], *Xingqi* 星期 [The Sunday] no. 50 (March 4, 1923).

26. Xiang Kairan [Pingjiang Buxiaosheng 平江不肖生], *Jianghu xiaoxia zhuan* 江湖小俠传 [Young gallants of the rivers and lakes] (Beijing: Zhongguo youyi chuban gongsi, 2012), 1. The distinction between the anonymous narrator and the diegetic character Buxiaosheng blurs yet is still maintained at the point in the text where the frame story leads into the embedded narrative: "When Buxiaosheng heard Zhu Baocheng's account of the events of sixty years ago, he was struck dumb with astonishment. Had he not heard Zhu Baocheng's words with his very own ears, and seen Zhu Baocheng's mother with his very own eyes, he would never have believed that such a thing could happen. As to just what occurred, please listen to the next chapter of this book, which shall spell it out starting from the beginning, offering it to the readers for their consideration" (14).

27. Patrick Hanan, "The Narrator's Voice Before the 'Fiction Revolution,'" in *Chinese Fiction of the Nineteenth and Early Twentieth Centuries* (New York: Columbia University Press, 2004), 9–32.

28. Henry Y. H. Zhao characterizes the phenomenon as a "generic mixture" contributing to "the final demolition of the traditional generic hierarchy." Zhao, "Historiography and Fiction," 83.

29. Xiang Kairan [Kairan 愷然], "Wulai chanshi" 無賴禪師 [The reverend Wulai], *Xiaoshuo hai* 小說海 [Ocean of fiction] 2, no. 8 (August 1916).

30. Xiang Kairan [Xiake shanren 俠客山人], *Banye feitou ji* 半夜飛頭記 [The flying head at midnight] (Shanghai: Wuqiang shuju, 1923), 1–2.

31. Hanan, "The Narrator's Voice," 10. As Hanan makes clear, this list covers the functions typically marked with formulaic language; the narrator's purview more broadly speaking includes the entire delivery of the text.

32. Hanan, "The Narrator's Voice," 21.

33. The downplaying of personal accomplishments resonates with the author-narrator's deprecation of his career as a professional writer. The latter, however, is additionally informed by, one the one hand, literati disdain for (or pose of disdain for) the world of commerce—a deeply traditional stance that nonetheless informs May Fourth progressives' attacks on "literary beggars" as well—and, on the other, by an ambivalence about the value of *xiaoshuo* as a genre—an ambivalence I will explore further on.

34. Bao Tianxiao, *Chuanying lou*, 458.

35. For a monographic study of the issue see Lu, *From Historicity to Fictionality*. See also Zeitlin, "*Xiaoshuo*"; and Zhao, "Historiography and Fiction."

36. Andrew H. Plaks, "Towards a Critical Theory of Chinese Narrative," in *Chinese Narrative: Critical and Theoretical Essays*, ed. Andrew H. Plaks (Princeton, NJ: Princeton University Press, 1977), 318.

37. Sarah M. Allen, *Shifting Stories: History, Gossip, and Lore in Narratives from Tang-Dynasty China* (Cambridge, MA: Harvard University Asia Center, 2014), 4–8.

38. Zhao, "Historiography and Fiction," 72–76.

39. Xiang Kairan 向愷然, "Li Cunyi xunji echuan" 李存義殉技訛傳 [The unfounded rumor of Li Cunyi's taking his art to the grave], *Hong meigui* 紅玫瑰 [Scarlet rose] 1, no. 6 (September 6, 1924).

40. Xiang Kairan, *Quanshu jianwen lu* (1919), 79–80.

41. Xiang Kairan [Kairan 愷然], "Wan Luo" 皖羅 [Luo of Anhui], *Xiaoshuo hai* 小說海 [Ocean of fiction] 2, no. 12 (December 1916).

42. We need not imagine that such claims of facticity are meant to be taken at face value. In 1948 the Buddhist periodical *The Enlightenment* (*Jue you qing* 覺有情) published an article by Xiang Kairan entitled "How I Became a Buddhist" ("Wo touru Fomen de jingguo" 我投入佛門的經過). Recalling his initial studies with a Buddhist teacher in Shanghai in the 1920s, the author notes that "at that time I was relying on selling my writings to make a living. In order to cater to the psychology of my many readers, what I wrote were for the most part preposterous supernatural tales, and I had no awareness that I was doing anything wrong." He tells how he received a letter from a reader who had learned of his interest in Buddhism and urged him to observe the religious injunctions; since "writing fiction couldn't help but violate the injunctions against falsehood, lewd words, bad language, duplicity, and so on," he should turn his brush to writings that promoted Buddhism. Xiang Kairan relates that he was affected by the letter but unable to follow its advice, constrained as he was by the need to make a living and limited moreover in his understanding of the Buddhist dharma. Although the moralizing perspective here may be a projection by the Xiang Kairan of 1948 upon his earlier life, conditioned as well by the context of his remarks, the comments make clear that invention was a conscious element of his work as an author. Assertions to the contrary may in some cases reflect a sincere commitment to recording objective truth. We may imagine this commitment to obtain with particular force in cases such as the Li Cunyi tales, which touch upon the teaching and historical transmission of the Chinese martial arts, an enterprise of concern to the author outside his career as a writer of fiction. And it is probably significant in this regard that the 1948 article refers to his mendacious writings not as martial arts fiction but as supernatural fiction (*shenguai xiaoshuo* 神怪小說). Chapter 4 of this study will return to the questions of *shenguai* and of facticity and fabrication in *Rivers and Lakes*. Fundamentally, however, we should understand these texts' persistent self-representation as records of actual events to be a declaration of literary identity. The claims to authenticity, like the narratorial persona that gives voice to them, are modeled on the conventions of premodern Chinese *xiaoshuo*. They are not so much an unreflective imitation of those conventions as a conscious deployment of them within the changing discursive and institutional contexts of mass-market publishing, an expression of the author's understanding of his literary affiliations, offered to readers who might recognize and appreciate them as such.

43. Plaks, "Towards a Critical Theory," 312–13; emphasis in the original.

44. Allen, *Shifting Stories*, 27–36.

45. Judith T. Zeitlin, *Historian of the Strange: Pu Songling and the Chinese Classical Tale* (Stanford, CA: Stanford University Press, 1993), 5–7.

46. The reference is to *Analects* (*Lunyu* 論語) 7:21: "The Master did not speak of the strange, feats of strength, disorder, or the spirits" (子不語怪力亂神).

47. Rania Huntington, "The Weird in the Newspaper," in *Writing and Materiality in China: Essays in Honor of Patrick Hanan*, ed. Judith T. Zeitlin and Lydia H. Liu (Cambridge, MA: Harvard University Asia Center, 2003), 341–96.

48. Shi, *Reconstructing the Historical Discourse*, 72.

49. Robert Ford Campany, *Strange Writing: Anomaly Accounts in Early Medieval China* (Albany: SUNY Press, 1996).

50. The perception of affinities between humans and other simians is evidently universal. Cultures around the world and across recorded history have recognized that of all the sentient beings with whom humans share the earth, monkeys and apes are closest to humans in physiognomy and behavior; the taxonomy that ranks humans among the apes and places apes and monkeys within the order of primates defines the relationship within the system of modern scientific knowledge but can claim no monopoly on the recognition of some form of fundamental kinship. A variety of nonhuman primates was and is native to the part of the world in which Chinese cultures developed. It is no surprise to find monkeys and apes, and various expressions of their relationship with humans, present in Chinese language, folklore, religion, scientific systems, and literature, beginning from the earliest records. It is beyond the scope of the present discussion to survey the roles of monkeys and apes in Chinese culture; an early but still invaluable study of the topic is Robert Hans van Gulik, *The Gibbon in China: An Essay in Chinese Animal Lore* (Leiden: E. J. Brill, 1967). And though the vast heritage of monkey lore often provides analogs or precedents for the plots and themes of Xiang Kairan's monkey stories, neither is the identification of these precedents this study's main concern. My focus here is simply on the ways in which apes and monkeys exemplify certain concerns of Xiang Kairan's fiction.

51. The issue of *Scarlet Magazine* in which "Three Monkey Tales" is published also includes an installment of the ongoing serialization of *Marvelous Gallants*—the second half of chapter 15, "A Young Gallant Travels by Night and Loses His Trousers, an Old Hero Captures Thieves and Makes a Gift of Silver" (小俠客夜行丢褲, 老英雄捉盜贈銀). The incident of Xiang Leshan's 向樂山 arrest for stealing a pair of woman's pants after losing his own is an excellent example of how the burlesque comedy characteristic of monkey tales can inform episodes in which no monkeys are present.

52. Xiang Kairan [Buxiaosheng 不肖生], *Huitou shi an* 回頭是岸 [Repent and be saved], *Xin Shanghai* 新上海 [New Shanghai] no. 1 (May 1925): 98: "If you wish to know about Lord Qu's history, please read the story proper beginning in the second chapter of *Repent and Be Saved*."

53. The following chapter begins the story of the five Qu brothers of Yuezhou, their tyrannical abuse of their martial skills, and the heroes and heroines who resist them. It is impossible to divine from the extant chapters the exact arc of the ensuing plot or the identity of the woman spotted by the narrator in the introduction.

54. It is probably not coincidental that these episodes appear soon after the author's resumption of the novel after a five-year hiatus. The divergence of the Liu Ti'an and Hu Zhizai

episodes from the tone of the previous portions of the novel is also betokened by the excision of the bulk of chapters 67 through 70 from the edition of *Modern Times* published in the People's Republic of China in 1984; it seems likely that the omitted chapters offended the orthodoxy of the day not only by the prominence of supernatural elements but also by their representing Liu Ti'an and Hu Zizhai as mystical bodyguards of none other than the historical Sun Yatsen 孫逸仙. On the 1984 edition, see chapter 6 of this study, note 26.

55. The female acrobat as an object of lust (and sometimes an engine for its chastisement as well) is a common trope in traditional fiction on martial themes. See, for example, the character Hua Bilian 花碧蓮 in the early-nineteenth-century linked-chapter novel *Lü mudan quanzhuan* 綠牡丹全傳 [Green peony]. The first story in Xiang Kairan's own 1919 *Matters Pugilistic, Seen and Heard* features a similar character and begins with the author-narrator's witnessing her performance.

56. Xiang Kairan [Buxiaosheng 不肖生], *Huitou shi an* 回頭是岸 [Repent and be saved], *Xin Shanghai* 新上海 [New Shanghai] no. 1 (May 1925): 98.

57. Glen Dudbridge, *The Hsi-yu chi: A Study of Antecedents to the Sixteenth-Century Chinese Novel* (Cambridge: Cambridge University Press, 1970), 114–28.

58. Xiang Kairan 向愷然, "Gaolan chenglou shang de baiyuan" 皋蘭城樓上的白猿 [The white ape in the Gaolan gate-tower], *Hong zazhi* 紅雜誌 [Scarlet Magazine] 2, no. 3 (August 24, 1923).

59. Xiang Kairan 向愷然, "Haoqi yu haose yu" 好奇歟好色歟 [Curiosity or lust?], *Zhentan shijie* 偵探世界 [Detective world] nos. 3–4 (1923).

60. Quoted in Lu, *From Historicity to Fictionality*, 52.

61. Zhao, "Historiography and Fiction," 78–83.

62. Lu Xun refers to novels of the demimonde as "textbooks on whoring" (*piaoxue jiaokeshu* 嫖學教科書) in his 1931 "A Glance at Shanghai Literature" (上海文藝之一瞥). Dong Bingyue 董炳月 points out that *Sojourners*, although not named, is clearly among the works intended: see *Guomin zuojia de lichang: Zhong Ri xiandai wenxue guanxi yanjiu* 國民作家的立場: 中日現代文学関系研究 [The standpoint of the national writer: studies in modern Sino-Japanese literary relations] (Beijing: Sanlian shudian, 2006), 63. The attacks on *The Burning of Red Lotus Temple* (i.e., *Rivers and Lakes*) will be discussed in chapter 4 of this study.

63. Maram Epstein, *Competing Discourses: Orthodoxy, Authenticity, and Engendered Meanings in Late Imperial Chinese Fiction* (Cambridge, MA: Harvard University Asia Center, 2001); 54; see her first chapter generally for an illuminating discussion of the relationships between Ming-Qing *xiaoshuo* and the rhetoric of orthodoxy.

64. See Nga Li Lam, "New World, *New World Daily*, and the Culture of Amusement in Early Republican China," PhD diss., Hong Kong University of Science and Technology, 2015.

3. THEMATIC SUBGENRE: MARTIAL ARTS FICTION

1. Manmiao [Bao Tianxiao], "Zhuiyi Buxiaosheng."

2. Edward H. Schafer, "The Table of Contents of the *Tai p'ing kuang chi*," *Chinese Literature: Essays, Articles, Reviews* 2 (1980): 258–63.

3. Translation by Clara Yu in *Chinese Civilization: A Sourcebook*, ed. Patricia Buckley Ebrey, 2nd ed. (New York: The Free Press, 1993), 182.

4. He Genmin 贺根民, "Wan Qing baokan xiaoshuo de fenlei he shenmei quxiang" 晚清报刊小说的分类和审美趋向 [The classification of fiction and aesthetic trends in late Qing periodicals], *Tangdu xuekan* 唐都学刊 23, no. 2 (March 2007): 120.

5. Wenkang 文康, *Ernü yingxiong zhuan* 兒女英雄傳 [A tale of romance and heroism], 2 vols. (Jinan: Qi Lu shushe 齊魯書社, 1989). The preface in question, signed Guanjian-wozhai 觀鑑我齋 and dated 1734, is generally held to be a fabrication by the author, Feimo Wenkang 費莫文康 (c. 1798–1866/1877).

6. I make these same points in my review of *Sound Rising from the Paper: Nineteenth-Century Martial Arts Fiction and the Chinese Acoustic Imagination* by Paize Keulemans, in *Harvard Journal of Asiatic Studies* 76 (2016): 241–42.

7. Ziying 紫英, "Xin'an xieyi" 新庵諧譯 [Harmonious renditions from the new cloister], *Yueyue xiaoshuo* 月月小說 [The All-Story Monthly] 5 (1907); reprinted in Chen Pingyuan 陈平原 and Xiao Xiaohong 夏晓虹, eds., *Ershi shiji Zhongguo xiaoshuo lilun ziliao, di yi juan (1897–1916)* 二十世纪中国小说理论资料·第一卷 (1897–1916) [Materials on twentieth-century Chinese fiction theory: volume 1 (1897–1916)] (Beijing: Beijing daxue chubanshe, 1989), 253–54. The passage is also cited and discussed in Chen Pingyuan 陈平原, "Zhongguo gudai xiaoshuo leixing guannian" 中国古代小说类型观念 [Premodern Chinese notions of fictional genres], in *Xiaoshuo shi: lilun yu shijian* 小说史：理论与实践 [The history of fiction: theory and practice] (Beijing: Beijing daxue chubanshe, 1993), 143; and Wang Xiangyuan 王向远, "Jindai Zhong Ri xiaoshuo de ticai leixing ji qi guanlian" 近代中日小说的题材类型及其关联 [Thematic categories of fiction in early modern China and Japan and their relationship], *Qi Lu xuekan* 齐鲁学刊 no. 3 (1997): 81.

8. Liang Qichao, "Zhongguo weiyi zhi wenxue bao *Xin xiaoshuo*" 中國唯一之文學報新小說 [China's only literary journal: *New Fiction*], *Xinmin congbao* 新民叢報 14 (1902); reprinted in Chen and Xiao, *Liliun ziliao*, 41–47.

9. Originally published in *Qingyi bao* 清議報, 1898; reprinted in Chen and Xiao, *Liliun ziliao*, 21–22; translated by Gek Nai Cheng in Denton, *Literary Thought*, 71–73.

10. Catherine Vance Yeh, *The Chinese Political Novel: Migration of a World Genre* (Cambridge, MA: Harvard University Asia Center, 2015), offers a transnational history of the genre and, more broadly, models the understanding of a fictional genre as a defined by a combination of formal, thematic, and ideological features.

11. "Xiaoshuo conghua" 小說叢話 [Miscellaneous remarks on fiction], *Xin xiaoshuo* 新小說 [New fiction] 2, no. 3 (1905); reprinted in Chen and Xiao, *Lilun ziliao*, 83.

12. "Xiaoshuo conghua 小說叢話 [Miscellaneous remarks on fiction], *Xin xiaoshuo* 新小說 [New fiction] 7 (1903); reprinted in Chen and Xiao, *Lilun ziliao*, 67. The remarks preceding this passage make clear that Liang adds his third category, the supernatural, to supplement Yan Fu 嚴復 and Xia Zengyou's 夏曾佑 earlier characterization of narrative (*shuobu* 說部) as concerned with the two fundamental themes of heroism (*yingxiong*) and sentiment (*ernü*); he also converts their generally positive evaluation of these categories into a limitation. Yan and Xia's schematization is of course a direct inheritance

from that described earlier in this chapter. Their 1897 "Ben guan fuyin shuobu yuanqi" 本館附印說部緣起 [Announcing our policy to print a supplementary fiction section] is reprinted in Chen and Xiao, *Lilun ziliao*, 1–12.

13. Liang Qichao, "Preface to the Translation and Publication of Political Novels," in Denton, *Literary Thought*, 72.

14. He Genmin, "Wan Qing baokan," 122. For more on the distinctions between short-form and chaptered fiction, see the next chapter of this study.

15. Guan Daru 管達如, "Shuo xiaoshuo" 說小說 [On fiction], *Xiaoshuo yuebao* 小說月報 [The Short Story Magazine] 3, nos. 3, 5, 7–11 (1912); reprinted in Chen and Xiao, *Lilun ziliao*, 371–387. Gimpel analyzes Guan's essays in *Lost Voices*, 137–46, and late-Qing fictional subtypes more broadly on 115–27.

16. Zhang Gansheng 张赣生, *Minguo tongsu xiaoshuo lun gao* 民国通俗小说论稿 [A draft study of Republican-era popular fiction] (Chongqing: Chongqing chubanshe, 1991), 28–30.

17. Link, *Mandarin Ducks*, 90: "The purpose of the 'type' label became, in fact, less one of placing a story in context than of previewing its contents."

18. On the proliferation of categorizers and their relation to the commercialization of Republican publishing, see Chen, *Lilun yu shijian*, 166–67; and Li Xingyang 李兴阳, "Wan Qing xiaoshuo leixing lilun de liubian yu yiyi" 晚清小说类型理论的流变与意义 [The development and significance of late Qing theories of fictional types], *Hubei shifan xueyuan xuebao (zhexue shehui kexue ban)* 湖北师范学院学报 (哲学社会科学版) 26, no. 4 (2006): 46.

19. Eva Hung, "Giving Texts a Context: Chinese Translations of Classical English Detective Stories, 1896–1916," in *Translation and Creation: Readings of Western Literature in Early Modern China, 1840–1918*, ed. David E. Pollard (Amsterdam: J. Benjamins, 1998), 158.

20. Liang Qichao, "Zhongguo weiyi zhi wenxue bao," in Chen and Xiao, *Lilun ziliao*, 45.

21. Guan Daru 管達如, "Shuo xiaoshuo," in Chen and Xiao, *Lilun ziliao*, 376.

22. On the influence of translated detective fiction on Chinese fiction generally, see Fan Boqun, *Jin- xiandai*, 1:769–80; and Jeffrey Kinkley, *Chinese Justice, the Fiction: Law and Literature in Modern China* (Stanford, CA: Stanford University Press, 2000), 170–240. On the progressive accommodation to new narrative techniques in the earliest translations, see Hung, "Giving Texts a Context," 160–63.

23. Hung, "Giving Texts a Context," 155–56; see also Kinkley, *Chinese Justice*, 194–208, for discussion of the progressive elements in detective fiction.

24. Chen, *Lilun yu shijian*, 174–75.

25. Wang Yunzhang 王蘊章, "Zuanshi an" 鑽石案 [The case of the diamond], *Xiaoshuo yuebao* [The Short Story Magazine] 1, no. 1 (August 29, 1910). The text is evidently a translation or adaptation of a Western story. British and American fiction periodicals of the early twentieth century featured several detectives surnamed Grey or Gray, but I have not been able to pinpoint a source text.

26. Fan Boqun, *Jin- xiandai*, 1:748–57.

27. Fan Boqun, *Jin- xiandai*, 1:758.

28. On the tension between the "progressive" and "popular" aspects of detective fiction, see Hung, "Giving Texts a Context," 151–54.

29. See for example Zhang Shewo's 張舍我 "Zhentan xiaoshuo zatan" 偵探小說雜談 [Miscellaneous remarks on detective fiction] in *Banyue* 半月 [The Half Moon Journal] 1, no. 6 (November 29, 1921): "Detective fiction can increase people's knowledge and awaken their intelligence, cultivating the practice of skillful investigation and observation; for this reason we cannot say that it is of no benefit to readers." Zhang goes on to refute allegations of detective fiction's pernicious effects, adducing the higher level of social order in Western nations with a more developed tradition of the genre.

30. For overviews, see Chen Pingyuan, *The Development of Chinese Martial Arts Fiction*, trans. Victor Petersen (Cambridge: Cambridge University Press, 2016); also Hamm, *Paper Swordsmen*, 11–23 and the additional references listed on 262n13.

31. Chen Pingyuan 陈平原, "Wan Qing zhishi de youxia xintai" 晚清志士的游侠心态 [The knight-errant mentality of late-Qing men of purpose], in *Zhongguo xiandai xueshu zhi jianli: yi Zhang Taiyan, Hu Shizhi wei zhongxin* 中国现代学术之建立—以章太炎、胡适之为中心 [The establishment of modern Chinese scholarship: with a focus on Zhang Taiyan and Hu Shizhi] (Beijing: Beijing daxue chubanshe, 1998), 275–319; Xu Sinian 徐斯年 and Liu Xiang'an 刘祥安, "Wuxia huidang bian" 武侠会党编 [Martial arts and secret societies], in Fan Boqun, *Jin- xiandai* 1:450–61; and Cai Aiguo 蔡爱国, *Qingmo Minchu xiayi xiaoshuo lun* 清末民初侠义小说论 [On late-Qing- and early-Republican-era chivalric fiction] (Beijing: Jiuzhou chubanshe, 2016), 12–20.

32. See Andrew D. Morris, *Marrow of the Nation: A History of Sport and Physical Culture in Republican China* (Berkeley: University of California Press, 2004), 185–229; Peter A. Lorge, *Chinese Martial Arts: From Antiquity to the Twenty-First Century* (Cambridge: Cambridge University Press, 2012), 212–25; Xu and Liu Xiang'an, "Wuxia huidang bian," 500–512; Cai Aiguo, *Xiayi xiaoshuo*, 20–39.

33. See Shi Juan 石娟, "Minguo wuxia xiaoshuo de fuwenben jiangou yu yuedu shichang shengcheng: yi Pingjiang Buxiaosheng *Jianghu qixia zhuan* wei hexin 民国武侠小说的副文本建构与阅读市场生成——以平江不肖生《江湖奇侠传》为核心 [Paratextual construction and the rise of the readership market for Republican-era martial arts fiction: with a focus on Pingjiang Buxiaosheng's *Marvelous Gallants of the Rivers and Lakes*], *Xinan daxue xuebao (shehui kexue ban)* 西南大学学报(社会科学版) 42, no. 5 (September 2016): 134.

34. On Oshikawa's fiction, see Okazaki Yumi 岡崎由美, "Wuxia yu ershi shiji chuye de Riben jingxian xiaoshuo" 武俠與二十世紀初葉的日本驚險小說 [*Wuxia* and early twentieth-century Japanese adventure fiction], in *Jin Yong xiaoshuo yu ershi shiji Zhongguo wenxue guoji xueshu yantaohui lunwen ji* 金庸小說與二十世紀中國文學國際學術研討會論文集 [Collected papers from the international conference on Jin Yong's fiction and twentieth-century Chinese literature], ed. Lin Lijun 林麗君 (Xianggang: Minghe she, 2000), 211–25.

35. Juewo 覺我, "Yu zhi xiaoshuo guan" 余之小說觀 [My views on fiction], *Xiaoshuo lin* 小說林 [Forest of fiction] 9 (1908); reprinted in Chen and Xiao, *Lilun ziliao*, 313.

36. Dingyi 定一, "Xiaoshuo conghua" 小說叢話 [Miscellaneous remarks on fiction], *Xin xiaoshuo* 新小說 [New fiction] 15 (1905); reprinted in Chen and Xiao, *Lilun ziliao*, 83.

37. On the history of the term in the twentieth century, see Zhang Gansheng, *Minguo*, 338; Ma Youyuan 馬幼垣 (Y. W. Ma), "*Shuihu zhuan* yu Zhongguo wuxia xiaoshuo de chuantong" 水滸傳與中國武俠小說的傳統 [*The Water Margin* and China's tradition of martial arts fiction], in *Shuihu lunheng* 水滸論衡 [On *The Water Margin*] (Taibei: Lianjing chuban shiye gongsi, 1992), 188n7; Ye Hongsheng 葉洪生, "Zhongguo wuxia xiaoshuo shi lun" 中國武俠小說史論 [On the history of Chinese martial arts fiction], in *Ye Hongsheng lun jian: wuxia xiaoshuo tan yi lu* 葉洪生論劍: 武俠小說談藝錄 [Ye Hongsheng speaks of the sword: talks on the art of martial arts fiction] (Taipei: Lianjing chuban shiye gongsi, 1994), 11–14; and Han Yunbo 韩云波, "Lun Qingmo Minchu de wuxia xiaoshuo" 论清末民初的武侠小说 [On late-Qing and early-Republican-era martial arts fiction], *Sichuan daxue xuebao (zhexue shehui kexue ban)* 四川大学学报 (哲学社会科学版) no. 4 (1999): 108–9.

38. Liang Qichao, "Fiction and the Government of the People," in Denton, *Literary Thought*, 80.

39. Liang Qichao, "Zhongguo weiyi zhi wenxue bao," in Chen and Xiao, *Lilun ziliao*, 45.

40. *The Water Margin* was a focus of late-Qing and Republican-era debates on fiction, the martial spirit, and related topics, and the views expressed here by Liang Qichao, though influential, were far from universally shared. For overviews, see Fan Boqun, *Jin- xiandai*, 1:452–56; also the relevant portions of Hongyuan Yu, "*Shuihu zhuan* as Elite Cultural Discourse," PhD diss., Ohio State University, 1999; Gao Rihui 高日晖 and Hong Yan 洪雁, *Shuihu zhuan jieshou shi* 水浒传接受史 [The reception history of *The Water Margin*] (Jinan: Qi Lu shushe, 2006); and Zhang Tongsheng 张同胜, *Shuihu zhuan quanshi shi lun* 《水浒传》诠释史论 [On the history of the interpretation of *The Water Margin*] (Jinan: Qi Lu shushe, 2009). Worthy of notice in the context of the present discussion is the preface to a 1908 edition of the novel (quoted in Fan Boqun, *Jin- xiandai*, 454), which declares that *The Water Margin* should be considered a social novel, a political novel, a military novel, a detective novel, a novel of human relations, *and* an adventure novel. The intent here is clearly to employ the prestige inherent in the array of new fictional categories to elevate the status of this novel and of the Chinese fiction tradition in general. What is striking about this strategy is the fact that it overrides the possibility that *The Water Margin* might serve as a model for a sui generis thematic genre of fiction. Even here, where one might most reasonably expect to find the coalescence of the identity of *wuxia xiaoshuo*, the (retrospectively) anticipated genre fails to come into focus.

41. Lengxue 冷血, "Xiake tan: Daoyusheng zhuan" 俠客談: 刀餘生傳 [Tales of knights-errant: the biography of Spared-the-Blade], *Xinxin xiaoshuo* 新新小說 [New new fiction] 1, no. 1 (1904): 22.

42. "Benbao tebai" 本報特白 [Special announcement], *Xinxin xiaoshuo* 新新小說 [New new fiction] no. 3 (January 1905).

43. On "Tales of Knights-Errant" and *New New Fiction* see Cai Aiguo, *Xiayi xiaoshuo*, 108–20; Fan Boqun, *Jin- xiandai*, 2:537–40; Fan Boqun 范伯群, "'Cuixingshu:' 1909 nian fabiao de 'Kuangren riji'" 《催醒术》: 1909年发表的"狂人日记" ["The Way of Awakening": A Lunatic's Diary Published in 1909], *Jiangsu daxue xuebao (shehui kexue ban)* 江苏大

学学报 (社会科学版) 6, no. 5 (September 2004): 1–8; and Xin Tinting 辛亭亭, "Chen Jing-han zhubian shenfen kaozheng ji *Xinxin xiaoshuo* 'duanming' yuanyin tanjiu" 陈景韩主编身份考证及《新新小说》"短命"原因探究 [Verification of Chen Jinghan's role as editor-in-chief and an inquiry into the reasons for the "brief lifespan" of *New New Fiction*], *Suzhou jiaoyu xueyuan xuebao* 苏州教育学院学报 33, no. 5 (October 2016): 19–24.

44. For overviews of the period, see Cai Aiguo, *Xiayi xiaoshuo*; Xu and Liu, "Wuxia huidang bian," 456–59, 461–67; Han Yunbo, "Qingmo Minchu de wuxia xiaoshuo"; and Lujing Ma Eisenman, "Fairy Tales for Adults: Imagination, Literary Autonomy, and Modern Chinese Martial Arts Fiction, 1895–1945," PhD diss., UCLA, 2016, 24–74.

45. See Cai Aiguo, *Xiayi xiaoshuo*, 86–107 for an overview and inventory of these tales and 121–142 on *Wuxia congtan* 武侠叢談. On the publication of Lin Shu's collection, see Lin Wei 林薇, "Lin Shu zizhuan de wuxia xiaoshuo: *Jiji yuwen* zui zao banben bianzheng" 林纾自撰的武侠小说—《技击余闻》最早版本辨正 [Lin Shu's martial arts fiction: verifying the earliest edition of *Anecdotes of the Combat Arts*], *Xin wenxue shiliao* 新文学史料 no. 3 (1999): 195–96.

46. I base this claim on a review of advertisements in Shanghai's *Shen bao* 申報; Shi Juan, "Fuwenjian jiangou," details several examples of similar advertisements from the *Xin-wen bao* 新聞報.

47. Hu Jichen 胡奇塵, "Xia shaonian" 俠少年 [A chivalrous youth], *Xingqi* 星期 [The Sunday] no. 50 (March 4, 1923).

48. The most influential such figure was Su Feiya 蘇菲亞, a fictionalized version of the Russian revolutionary Sophia Perovskaya, celebrated in the 1902 novel *Heroines of Eastern Europe* (*Dong Ou nühaojie* 東歐女豪傑). See the discussion of this figure in Ying Hu, *Tales of Translation: Composing the New Woman in China, 1899–1918* (Stanford, CA: Stanford University Press, 2000).

49. Zhen Zhang, "The Anarchic Body Language of the Martial Arts Film," in *An Amorous History of the Silver Screen: Shanghai Cinema, 1896–1937* (Chicago: University of Chicago Press, 2005), 199–243.

50. Bao Tianxiao [Tianxiao 天笑], "Shijie nüxia" 世界女俠 [A female gallant for the world], *Xingqi* 星期 [The Sunday] no. 50 (March 4, 1923).

51. Yao Gengkui 姚賡夔, "Guaixia" 怪俠 [The strange gallant], *Xingqi* 星期 [The Sunday] no. 50 (March 4, 1923).

52. Figures from Fan Boqun, *Jin- xiandai*, 2:554–55, 607–9.

53. For an overview of Shanghai publishing from 1912 to 1937, a period of "cutthroat print capitalism," see Christopher Reed, *Gutenberg in Shanghai: Chinese Print Capitalism, 1876–1937* (Honolulu: University of Hawai'i Press, 2004), 203–56.

54. On Shen Zhifang and World Books, see Reed, *Gutenberg in Shanghai*, 241–53.

55. For overviews of the World Books and Great Eastern periodicals, see Fan Boqun, *Jin-xiandai*, 2:616–44; also Link, *Mandarin Ducks*, 258–60.

56. Link, *Mandarin Ducks*, 91.

57. The story's Luo Ping is of course, as the introduction to the text makes clear, a Chinese version of Sherlock Holmes's counterpart and rival, the gentleman-thief Arsène Lupin; see Kinkley, *Chinese Justice*, 227–38.

58. Tang Zhesheng 汤哲声, "Zhentan tuili bian" 偵探推理編 [Fiction of detection and deduction], in Fan Boqun, *Jin- xiandai*, 1:782–84.

59. Tang Zhesheng 汤哲声, "Zhentan tuili bian." *Zhentan shijie*'s nonfiction material includes fillers and short articles of various sorts: anecdotes of real-life crime cases at home and abroad, articles on criminology (e.g., the science of fingerprints, the design of model prisons), columns on detective films, and frequent notes and discussions on the art of writing detective stories. These "secondary" texts on the science of detection and the art of detective fiction are numerous in the early issues, wane somewhat thereafter, and are then given new life with Zhao Tiaokuang's energetic restructuring of the magazine beginning with no. 13.

60. Shi Juan, "Fuwenben jiangou," 130, citing *Xinwenbao* 新聞報 of March 9, 1922.

61. See, e.g., Cheng Xiaoqing 程小青, "Zhentan xiaoshuo he kexue" 偵探小說和科學 [Detective fiction and science], *Zhentan shijie* 偵探世界 [Detective world] no. 13 (1923).

62. Shen Zhifang 沈知方, "Xuanyan" 宣言 [Manifesto], *Zhentan shijie* 偵探世界 [Detective world] no. 1 (1923).

63. Lu Dan'an 陸澹盦, "Jiyu zhuimo" 輯餘贅墨 [Post-editorial addenda], *Zhentan shijie* 偵探世界 [Detective world] no. 1 (1923). The colophon of the first issue of *Detective World* lists as editors Yan Duhe 嚴獨鶴, Lu Dan'an 陸澹安, Cheng Xiaoqing 程小青, and Shi Jiqun 施濟群. With Yan Duhe's involvement largely ceremonial, it was Lu Dan'an who actually took the helm for the early issues, signing the editorial comments included in each number. In issue 9, Shi Jiqun 施濟群 announced Lu's departure and his own temporary assumption of editorial responsibilities; with issue 13 Zhao Tiaokuang 趙苕狂 formally assumed the role of chief operating editor (Yan Duhe still retaining nominal pride of place).

64. Cai Aiguo, *Xiayi xiaoshuo*, 151.

65. "Zhentan xiaoshuo" 偵探小說 [Detective fiction] (advertisement), *Zhentan shijie* 偵探世界 [Detective world] no. 2 (1923). Cai Aiguo, *Xiayi xiaoshuo*, 152, likewise discusses this ad.

66. The category of "adventure" here denotes tales of nationalistically or patriotically motivated deeds of derring-do in foreign lands. Liang Qichao's 1902 "China's Only Literary Journal: *New Fiction*" characterized "adventure fiction" as "[works] such as *Robinson Crusoe* and the like, devoted to encouraging the people's spirit of exploration and adventure." Oshikawa Shunrô's *bukyô* fiction dealt with similar themes. In the editor's notes for *Detective World* no. 15, Zhao Tiaokuang declares that the upcoming issue's publication of Gu Mingdao's 顧明道 "The Secret Kingdom" ("Mimi zhi guo" 祕密之國) represents the first appearance of adventure fiction in the magazine, "despite the fact that it [i.e., this type of fiction] falls within the parameters of our publication." In no. 16, he characterizes the tale as one of "a chivalrous man's accomplishments in an alien land." Gu Mingdao's opening remarks in this story and its sequel, "Desperate Battle on an Ocean Isle" ("Haidao aobing ji" 海島鏖兵記) in no. 21, stress that the tales are meant to inspire his countrymen and correct the misconception that the Chinese people cannot match the West's record of adventure, exploration, and conquest.

67. "Waves on the Sea of Bitterness" ("Yuanhai bo" 怨海波) in nos. 1–6; "Room Number Two" ("Di er hao shi" 第二號室) in nos. 7–15; "The Hairy Lion" ("Mao shizi" 毛獅子) in nos. 16–21; "A Strange Meeting in the Dancehall" ("Wuchang qiyu ji" 舞場奇遇記) in nos. 22–24.

68. In addition to *Modern Times*, Xiang Kairan frequently contributed short fiction, almost all in the martial arts genre, to *Detective World*. Additional martial arts fiction was contributed by Gu Mingdao 顧明道, Yao Min'ai 姚民哀, Zhang Mingfei 張冥飛, Shen Yuzhong 沈禹鍾, and others. On the detective side, Cheng Xiaoqing likewise supplemented his primary serialized contributions with additional original works and translations; among the many other authors were Lu Dan'an, Zhao Tiaokuang, Xu Zhuodai 徐卓呆, Sun Liaohong 遜了紅, Zhao Zhiyan 趙芝岩, and Yu Tianfen 俞天憤.

69. The one piece that might qualify as an analog for the martial arts genre is Mang Gai's 茫勻 "Caravan Guards and Bandits" ("Biaohang yu lülin" 鏢行與綠林), published in nos. 9 and 10, a purportedly nonfictional account of the late-Qing protection agencies that provide the setting for many martial arts tales.

70. Shen Zhifang, "Xuanyan," 1923.

71. Shi Juan, "Fuwenben jiangou." One of the strengths of her argument is the extent to which it engages the problem of the oft-noted weaknesses of Xiang Kairan's long-form fiction.

4. FORM AND MEDIUM: THE SERIALIZED LINKED-CHAPTER NOVEL AND BEYOND

1. In the first chapter (第一回); see Cao Xueqin 曹雪芹, *Honglou meng* 紅樓夢 [Dream of the Red Chamber], 4 vols. (Beijing: Renmin wenxue chubanshe, 1959), 1:4.

2. Chen Meilin 陈美林 et al., *Zhanghui xiaoshuo shi* 章回小说史 [History of the linked-chapter novel] (Hangzhou: Zhejiang guji chubanshe, 1998), 1–9.

3. Plaks, *Four Masterworks.*

4. See Martin W. Huang, ed., *Snakes' Legs: Sequels, Continuations, Rewritings, and Chinese Fiction* (Honolulu: University of Hawai'i Press, 2004), in particular the discussion of the definition of sequels and continuations in Huang's introduction.

5. Paize Keulemans, *Sound Rising from Paper: Nineteenth-Century Martial Arts Fiction and the Chinese Acoustic Imagination* (Cambridge, MA: Harvard University Asia Center, 2014); on series fiction and commercial publishing, see esp. 169–76.

6. See Keulemans, *Sound Rising from Paper*; and on Ji Gong, see Meir Shahar, *Crazy Ji: Chinese Religion and Popular Literature* (Cambridge, MA: Harvard University Asia Center, 1998).

7. "Benshe zhengwen qi" 本社徵文啟 [Call for contributions], *Xin xiaoshuo* 新小說 [New fiction] 1, no. 1 (1902).

8. Here from the end of the fourth chapter of *Haidi lüxing* 海底旅行, the last chapter in the first issue of a translation (via Japanese) of Verne's *Vingt mille lieues sous le mers* [Twenty Thousand Leagues Under the Sea].

9. Alexander Des Forges, "Building Shanghai, One Page at a Time: The Aesthetics of Installment Fiction at the Turn of the Century," *Journal of Asian Studies* 62, no. 3 (2003): 782.

10. Des Forges, "Building Shanghai," 790.

11. On the emergence of the short story see Chen Pingyuan 陈平原, *Ershi shiji Zhongguo xiaoshuo shi: diyi juan (1897–1916)* 二十世纪中国小说史: 第一卷 (1897–1916) [The history of twentieth-century Chinese fiction, volume 1: 1897–1916] (Beijing: Beijing daxue chubanshe, 1989), 171–79.

12. Hu Shi 胡適, "Lun duanpian xiaoshuo" 論短篇小說 [On the short story], *Xin qingnian* 新青年 [New youth] 4, no. 5 (May 1918).

13. Hu Shi, "Lun duanpian xiaoshuo."

14. See Fan Boqun, *Jin- xiandai*, 1:52–60.

15. It must be noted that criticism of the linked-chapter novel and promotion of short fiction as the form most suitable for modern readers were not exclusive to the May Fourth New Literature camp. Xu Zhuodai 徐卓呆, a master of comic short fiction and a prominent contributor to entertainment-oriented fiction magazines, made claims in some ways comparable to Hu Shi's in "Xiaoshuo wuti lu" 小說無題錄 [Untitled notes on fiction], *Xiaoshuo shijie* 小說世界 [The Story World] 1, no. 7 (1923); see also the comments on this piece in Christopher Rea, *The Age of Irreverence: A New History of Laughter in China* (Oakland: University of California Press, 2015), 118–19.

16. Shen Yanbing 沈雁冰, "Ziranzhuyi yu Zhongguo xiandai xiaoshuo" 自然主義與中國現代小說 [Naturalism and modern Chinese fiction], *Xiaoshuo yuebao* 小說月報 [The short story magazine] 13, no. 7 (July 10, 1922).

17. It soon begins to reappear, though not in the form of *zhanghui xiaoshuo*; vol. 12, no. 3 (March 10, 1921) begins serial publication of a translation of Turgenev's short story collection *Sketches from a Hunter's Diary* under the title *Lieren riji* 獵人日記.

18. Fan Boqun, *Jin- xiandai*, 2:603–12.

19. Theodore Huters discusses *The Shanghai Tide* (I borrow his translation of the title) in the chapter "Swimming Against the Tide: The Shanghai of Zhu Shouju," in *Bringing the World Home: Appropriating the West in Late Qing and Early Republican China* (Honolulu: University of Hawai'i Press, 2005). See also Fan Boqun 范伯群, "Zhu Shouju lun" 朱瘦菊论 [On Zhu Shouju], *Xin wenxue shiliao* 新文学史 no. 1 (2013): 103–24.

20. Lu Xun coins the term *qianze xiaoshuo* and sketches a history of decline in the final chapter of his 1923 *Zhongguo xiaoshuo shi lüe* 中國小說史略 [A Brief History of Chinese Fiction]; see *Zhongguo xiaoshuo shi lüe* (Taipei: Fengyun shidai, 1989); and Lu Hsun, *A Brief History of Chinese Fiction*, trans. Yang Hsien-yi and Gladys Yang (Peking: Foreign Languages Press, 1976). David Wang offers a revisionist look at this genealogy in the chapter "Abject Carnival: Grotesque Exposés," in *Fin-de-Siècle Splendor: Repressed Modernities of Late Qing Fiction, 1849–1911* (Stanford, CA: Stanford University Press, 1997).

21. Prominent New Literature critiques of Black Curtain fiction are collected in Rui Heshi, *Wenxue ziliao*, 755–66. For a discussion of the genre and its place in literary history see Fan Boqun 范伯群, "Heimu zhengda, heimu xiaoshuo, jiehei yundong" 黑幕征答·黑

幕小说·揭黑运动 [Black curtain debates, black curtain fiction, whistle-blowing movements], *Wenxue pinglun* 文学评论 no. 2 (2005): 57–64.

22. Haishang shuomengren 海上說夢人, *Xin Xiepu chao*新歇浦潮 [New Shanghai tides], *Hong zazhi* 紅雜誌 [The Scarlet Magazine] 1, no. 1 (August 1922).

23. Unlike many periodicals of the time, the early volumes of *Scarlet* did not regularly feature a selection of illustrated plates at the front of each issue.

24. Some minor alterations were necessary. The verso of the last page of the serialized text, though included in the overall pagination, is occasionally occupied by notices, advertisements, or other material that is omitted from publication of the text in book form. See, e.g., chapter 38: the text ends on p. 607, and the verso, p. 608, carries an advertisement in the magazine but is empty in the first printing of the book edition in June 1924.

25. I have not had the opportunity to examine later volumes of the World Books book edition and do not have precise information on the dates of the book publication of the remaining chapters, nor can I verify how the book edition adjusted the magazine's pagination of the text.

26. Jiqun 濟群, "Bianji zhe yan" 編輯者言 [Editor's remarks], *Hong zazhi* 紅雜誌 [The Scarlet Magazine] 2, no. 40 (May 7, 1924).

27. The coordination of the accompanying illustrations also becomes slightly irregular. The illustrations for chapter 87, for instance, are absent from the head of that chapter in issue 87 but then printed at the beginning of chapter 88 in the subsequent issue.

28. Chen Jianhua, "Canon Formation," 59, *passim*.

29. The novels are *Shijing taowu shi* 市井檮杌史 [The monster of the marketplace], serialized in Bao Tianxiao's short-lived *Xiaoshuo huabao* 小說畫報 [Illustrated Novel Magazine] in 1918, and *Shengfen canzhi lu* 剩粉殘脂錄 [Traces of powder, remnants of rouge], serialized in *Banyue* 半月 [The Half Moon Journal] from 1921 to 1924. On the latter novel and the reasons for its cessation, see Fan Boqun, "Zhu Shouju lun," 117–18.

30. Some sources state or imply that the five *ji* were published consecutively, but Xu Sinian's chronology states that publication was simultaneous; Xu Sinian, "Nianbiao," 7. I have not seen the colophon(s) of the first edition.

31. Other related titles of uncertain authenticity also appeared, such as an *Amorous History of Sojourners in Japan* (*Liudong yanshi* 留東豔史).

32. Ikeda Tomoe 池田智惠, "*Jindai xiayi yingxiong zhuan* yu *Guoji daguan*: guanyu Minguo wuxia xiaoshuo he jindai wushu de chengli" 《近代俠义英雄传》与《国技大观》—关于民国武侠小说和近代武术的成立 [*Chivalric Heroes of Modern Times* and the *Panorama of National Skills*: on Republican-era martial arts fiction and the establishment of the modern martial arts] 华东师范大学中国现代文学资料与研究中心 (Center for Modern Chinese Literature Studies, East China Normal University), July 8, 2005.

33. "Duzhe zhuyi" 讀者注意 [Readers take note], *Hong zazhi* 紅雜誌 [The Scarlet Magazine] 1, no. 21 (January 1923).

34. Jiqun 濟群, "Bianji zhe yan" 編輯者言 [Editor's remarks], *Hong zazhi* 紅雜誌 [The Scarlet Magazine] 1, no. 22 (January 1923).

35. The only exception before vol. 2, no. 41, is vol. 1, no. 28, which prints the fourth chapter in its entirety.

36. The commentary disappears entirely after chapter 39 in vol. 2, no. 44.

37. In the printing of the texts, those pages dedicated to short-form fiction employ, as before, a smaller typeface than that used for the long-form pieces. But the organization of short-form texts now varies between one, two, and even three registers, and in many cases each item, even when textually distributed into upper and lower registers, occupies its own span of pages. There is more limited use of the vertical splitting of the page between two different texts characteristic of the first year's issues.

38. The illustrations for *Rivers and Lakes* lag behind and briefly become confused in their numbering, catching up only in issue 100. We may surmise that while the editor had enough chapters of the text in hand at this point to be flexible with the publication schedule, the illustrator was supplying his work on an as-needed basis and required some time to adjust to the new demands.

39. *Hong zazhi* 紅雜誌 [The Scarlet Magazine] 2, no. 50 (July 18, 1924).

40. With volume 4 in 1928 the magazine switches to thirty-six-issue volumes, publishing once every ten days.

41. Yan Duhe served as honorary editor for both magazines; the bulk of *Scarlet*'s editorial duties were shouldered by Shi Jiqun 施濟羣, and of *Scarlet Rose*'s by Zhao Tiaokuang 趙苕狂. For a history and overview see Fan Boqun, *Jin- xiandai*, 2:616–25.

42. In *Scarlet* 2, no. 50, the text of *Rivers and Lakes* ends on a recto numbered 917; the unnumbered verso, which would be page 918, is occupied by an ad.

43. Li Hanqiu's original *Yangzhou Tides*, originally titled *A Mirror of the Changes* (*Guodu jing* 過渡鏡), was serialized in a succession of newspapers beginning in 1909 and published in book form in 1919. See Fan Boqun 范伯群, "Yi yinqin wei niudai, yi shidai wei tuishou: xiandai Yangpai tongsu jingdian xiaoshuo *Guanglingchao* yanjiu" 以姻亲为纽带 以时代为推手——现代扬派通俗经典小说《广陵潮》研究 [Family ties and the force of the times: a study of the classic modern Yangzhou popular novel *Yangzhou Tides*], *Hanyu yanwenxue yanjiu* 汉语言文学研究 no. 1 (2016): 4–15; Yuan Jin 袁进, "Shilun *Guanglingchao* yu Min chu shehui xiaoshuo" 试论《广陵潮》与民初社会小说 [A tentative discussion of *Yangzhou Tides* and the early Republican social novel], *Xiandai Zhongwen xue kan* 现代中文学刊 7, no. 4 (2010): 22–26; and for an introduction and translation of an excerpt, Stefan Kuzay, "A Tale of Five Families Between Empire and Republic: Li Hanqiu's Novel *The Tides of Guangling* (*Guangling chao*, 1909–1919)," in *Yangzhou: A Place in Literature*, ed. Roland Altenburger et al. (Honolulu: University of Hawai'i Press, 2015), 282–307.

44. This is the end of chapter 106 in the editions commonly circulated today. On the divergence between editions in the division and numbering of the chapters, see further in this chapter. My discussion of the novel's publication history is deeply indebted to Gu Zhen, "*Jianghu qixia zhuan* banben kao."

45. Buxiaosheng 不肖生, *Jianghu qixia zhuan* 江湖奇俠傳 [Marvelous gallants of the rivers and lakes], *Hong meigui* 紅玫瑰 [Scarlet rose] 2, no. 32 (July 10, 1926); cf. 106:4, 208 in the 2003 edition.

46. Tiaokuang 苕狂, "Bianyu suohua" 編餘瑣話 [Idle editorial remarks], *Hong meigui* [Scarlet rose] 2, no. 32 (July 10, 1926).

47. Buxiaosheng 不肖生, *Jianghu qixia zhuan* 江湖奇俠傳 [Marvelous gallants of the rivers and lakes], *Hong meigui* 紅玫瑰 [Scarlet rose] 3, no. 1 (1 January 1927); cf. 107:4, 209–210 in the 2003 edition.

48. Alexander Des Forges gives a valuable overview and critique of "the reading of installment publication as a form of commodification that has significant effects on the narratives published, including a reduction in their aesthetic value" in "Building Shanghai, One Page at a Time."

49. Tiaokuang 苕狂, "Huaqian xiaoyu" 花前小語 [Remarks before the flowers], *Hong meigui* 紅玫瑰 [Scarlet rose] 3, no. 7 (March 5, 1927).

50. Tiaokuang 苕狂, "Huaqian xiaoyu" 花前小語 [Remarks before the flowers], *Hong meigui* 紅玫瑰 [Scarlet rose] 3, no. 10 (March 26, 1927).

51. [Tiaokuang 苕狂], "Huaqian xiaoyu" 花前小語 [Remarks before the flowers], *Hong meigui* 紅玫瑰 [Scarlet rose] 4, no. 35 (January 1, 1929).

52. The first issue of the fifth volume reprints the first *hui* of Yao Min'ai's *Dragons* and adds the second.

53. For an overview of Yao Min'ai's career and oeuvre, see Fan Boqun, *Jin- xiandai*, 1:533–61.

54. In the Lincheng Train Robbery or Lincheng Incident of May 1923, which aroused international attention, a force of bandits attacked the Pukou–Tianjin Express as it passed through Lincheng, Shandong, and kidnapped hundreds of passengers, including twenty-some foreigners, among whom were the Shanghai journalist J. B. Powell and the sister-in-law of the billionaire John D. Rockefeller Jr. Philip Billingsley's *Bandits in Republican China* (Stanford, CA: Stanford University Press, 1988) examines the incident in detail. Primary sources are collected in Wang Zuoxian 王作賢 et al., eds., *Minguo diyi an* 民国第一案 [The Republic's most notorious case] (Jinan: Shandong renmin chubanshe, 1990).

55. The six segments of *Highwaymen* appeared in *Detective World* nos. 6, 8, 9, 18, 19, and 22.

56. *Longju zouxue ji* 龍駒走血記 [Blood of the stallion] was published in *Scarlet Rose* 2, nos. 16 through 19 (four installments totaling 102 pages); *Sanfeng zhengchao ji* 三鳳爭巢記 [The war of the three phoenixes] in vol. 2, nos. 33 through 36 (four installments, 111 pages); *Duyan dadao* 獨眼大盜 [The one-eyed bandit] in vol. 3, nos. 18 through 29 (twelve installments, 120 pages); and *Xiagu enchou ji* 俠骨恩饞記 [Grace and Vengeance] in vol. 4, nos. 11 through 20 (ten installments, 137 pages). Yao Min'ai published several shorter stories on similar themes in *Scarlet Rose* before the commencement of this interlinked series.

57. Yao Min'ai 姚民哀, *Danghui xiaoshuo Longju zouxue ji* 黨會小說龍駒走血記三 [Secret-society novel: blood of the stallion, part 3], *Hong meigui* 紅玫瑰 [Scarlet magazine] 2, no. 18 (April 3, 1926).

58. Yao Min'ai 姚民哀, *Danghui xiaoshuo Longju zouxue ji* 黨會小說三鳳爭巢記 [Secret-society novel: the war of the three phoenixes], *Hong meigui* 紅玫瑰 [Scarlet magazine] 2, no. 33 (July 17, 1926).

59. *Jingji jianghu* 荆棘江湖 [Thorns and brambles of the rivers and lakes], serialized in Great Eastern's *Ziluolan* 紫羅蘭 [Violet], edited by Zhou Shoujuan 周瘦鵑, from December 1926 through June 1930.

60. *Dragons'* thirty-six *hui* are printed in nos. 1 through 35 of *Scarlet Rose*'s fifth volume (February through December 1928). Its sequel, *Ruomao shanwang* 箬帽山王 [The bandit king in a bamboo hat], also thirty-six *hui*, runs in vol. 6, nos. 1 through 34 (March 1930 through January 1931). A further sequel, *Shengsi pengyou* 生死朋友 [Friends through life and death], begins in the first issue of vol. 7 (March 1931) but ends unfinished at the twenty-third *hui* in no. 23 (November 1931), interrupted by the author's illness.

61. Shanghai: Shijie shuju, 1924; sixteen *hui*.

62. Shanghai: Shijie shuju, 1929: fifty *hui*.

63. Yao Min'ai 姚民哀, *Ruomao shanwang* 箬帽山王 [The bandit king in a bamboo hat], *Hong meigui* 紅玫瑰 [Scarlet rose] 6, no. 1 (March 11, 1930).

64. A "Brief Announcement" ("Xiao baogao" 小報告) in the tabloid *Pictorial Shanghai* (*Shanghai huabao* 上海畫報) no. 450 (March 24, 1929): 3, reported that World Books had received word of Xiang Kairan's death. On April 3 *The Crystal* (*Jingbao* 晶報) published (under the pen name Manmiao 曼妙) Bao Tianxiao's "Remembering Buxiaosheng" ("Zhuiyi Buxiaosheng" 追憶不肖生), which noted that the details of Xiang Kairan's reputed demise were unclear but took the occasion to survey his career and relate a number of anecdotes. Thereafter the rumor circulated more widely. See Xu Sinian, "Nianbiao," 15–16, for an overview of events and further references.

65. Gu Zhen, "*Jianghu qixia zhuan* banben kao," 31, quotes the *Qiongbao* article in full.

66. Pingping 平平, "Xiang Kairan qisu Shihuan shuju" 向愷然起訴時還書局 [Xiang Kairan sues Shihuan shuju], *Shanghai huabao* 上海畫報 [Pictorial Shanghai] no. 528 (November 18, 1929), 2.

67. On copyright in China, see William P. Alford, *To Steal a Book Is an Elegant Offense: Intellectual Property Law in Chinese Civilization* (Stanford, CA: Stanford University Press, 1995); and Fei-Hsien Wang, "Creating New Order in the Knowledge Economy: The Curious Journey of Copyright in China, 1868–1937," PhD diss., University of Chicago, 2012.

68. Gu Zhen, "*Jianghu qixia zhuan* banben kao," 21–32. My account here of the history of the novel's book publication summarizes and comments on Gu Zhen's study.

69. Although reports of Xiang Kairan's death seem to have appeared in print only in April 1929, several months after the serialization's unheralded cessation, it is possible that prior circulation of such rumors and the questions they raised might have influenced the magazine's decision to end the novel's serialized run. On the other hand, Shi Juan, "Fuwenben jiangou," 135–36, points out that the rumors of his death may well have buoyed sales of the final *ji* of the book publication and speculates on the possibility that World Books might even have fostered such rumors with just such an intent.

70. An ironic pun; the pseudonym can be interpreted as "The Unworthy Student Has Gone." Altenburger, "Xiang Kairan," 238.

71. The film was directed by Zhang Shichuan from a screenplay by Zheng Zhengqiu. For an account of the film and the wave it inspired, see Li Suyuan 郦苏元 and Hu Jubin 胡菊彬, *Zhongguo wusheng dianying shi* 中国无声电影史 [A history of silent film in China] (Beijing: Zhongguo dianying chubanshe, 1996), 222–44.

72. For basic information on *The Gallant's Revenge* see Zhongguo dianying ziliaoguan 中国电影资料馆, ed., *Zhongguo yingpian dadian: gushipian, xiqupian, 1905–1930* 中国影片大典: 故事片·戏曲片: 1905–1930 [Encyclopedia of Chinese film: narrative and theatrical films, 1905–1930] (Beijing: Zhongguo dianying chubanshe, 1996), 159. The film tells the story of the Ma assassination, on which see the discussion in chapter 5 of this study. Its failure relative to the spectacular success of *Red Lotus Temple* may speak to the appeal of the fantastic elements of the latter, on which see chapter 5 as well.

73. Weihong Bao, *Fiery Cinema: The Emergence of an Affective Medium in China, 1915–1945* (Minneapolis: University of Minnesota Press, 2015), 39: "These films, modeled after *The Burning of the Red Lotus Temple*, all assume a similar narrative pattern: a group of heroes and heroines meet at a site of evil—a temple, a village, a mansion, a town, or a nunnery—where feverish bodies struggle and compete in swordsmanship, magical sorcery, or other forms of battle. The success of the fiery films, according to surviving documents and images, was due to the physicality of the action, the excess of special effects, and the marvelous trick setting (*jiguan bujin*), culminating in the fire scene, where the most thrilling action takes place. Much of the attraction of these films seems to have come from the burning scenes, characteristically placed at the end."

74. Zhang, *Amorous History*, 199–200.

75. Li and Hu, *Zhongguo wusheng dianying shi*, 225.

76. Plot summaries of the various installments of *Red Lotus Temple* given in Zhongguo dianying ziliaoguan, *Yingpian dadian*, suggest that the films were a series rather than a serialization. It is not clear, however, what sources this volume uses for its summaries of lost films.

5. MARVELOUS GALLANTS OF THE RIVERS AND LAKES

1. Wang Chaoguang 汪朝光, "Sanshi niandai chuqi de Minguodang dianying jiancha zhidu" 三十年代初期的国民党电影检查制度 [The film censorship system of the Nationalist Party in the early 1930s], *Dianying yishu* 电影艺术 3 (1997): 63. For overviews of the Nationalists' film censorship, see also Zhang, *Amorous History*, 235–43; and Zhiwei Xiao, "Film Censorship in China, 1927–1937," PhD diss., University of Chicago, 1994.

2. Wang Chaoguang, "Jiancha zhidu," 63.

3. Portions of Zhang Shichuan's appeal, and a detailed list of content to be excised or revised, can be found in the proclamation "Xiuzheng *Honglian si* yingpian qingdan" 修正紅蓮寺映片清單 [Itemized list for the revision of the film *Red Lotus Temple*], published in various official organs, e.g., *Jiangxi jiaoyu xingzheng xunkan* 江西教育行政旬刊 [Ten-day bulletin of the Jiangxi Educational Administration] 1, no. 3 (March 21, 1932): 8–11.

4. "Neizhengbu xunling" 內政部訓令 [Order of the Ministry of the Interior], *Neizheng gongbao* 內政公报 [Bulletin of the Ministry of the Interior] 5, no. 28 (July 15, 1932): 4.

5. For the promotion of "science, patriotism, and adventure," see Xiao, "Film Censorship," 233. The forbidden categories are specified in Article II of the Film Censorship Statute

(Dianying jiancha fa 電影檢查法), published in *Dianying jiancha weiyuanhui gongbao* 電影檢查委員會公報 [Bulletin of the Film Censorship Committee] 1, no. 1 (August 1, 1932): 8–10; Xiao, "Film Censorship," 292–93 provides a translation.

6. On the campaign, see Xiao, "Film Censorship," 98–110; on the links with the prohibition of *shenguai* films, see 230–38; and Zhang, *Amorous History*, 235–43.

7. Cheng Xiaoqing 程小青, "Wo zhi shenguai yingpian guan" 我之神怪影片觀 [My views on fantasy films], *Shanghai* 上海 no. 4 (1927).

8. Lei Gao 壘高, "Jiuju he shenguai dianying de fandong" 舊劇和神怪電影的反動 [The reactionary nature of old-style drama and fantasy film], *Xinsheng xunkan* 新聲旬刊 [New voice] no. 3 (January 22, 1931): 9–10.

9. See Vincent Goossaert and David A. Palmer, *The Religious Question in Modern China* (Chicago: University of Chicago Press, 2011), 19–63; and Prasenjit Duara, *Rescuing History from the Nation: Questioning Narratives of Modern China* (Chicago: University of Chicago Press, 1995), 85–113.

10. Liang Qichao, "Fiction and the Government of the People," in Denton, *Literary Thought*, 79.

11. Mark R. E. Meulenbeld, *Demonic Warfare: Daoism, Territorial Networks, and the History of a Ming Novel* (Honolulu: University of Hawai'i Press, 2015); see esp. chap. 1, "Invention of the Novel: From Stage Act and Temple Ritual to Literary Text."

12. Huang Yichuo 黃漪磋, "Guochan yingpian de fuxing wenti" 國產影片的復興問題 [The question of the revival of Chinese cinema], *Yingxi zazhi* 影戲雜誌 [The Film Magazine] 1, no. 7–8 (June 1, 1930): 24.

13. "Neizhengbu xunling," 4.

14. The distinction holds even though printed texts were not infrequently shared or read aloud.

15. Bao, *Fiery Cinema*.

16. Shen Yanbing 沈雁冰 [Mao Dun 茅盾], "Fengjian de xiaoshimin wen yi" 封建的小市民文藝 [The feudal literature and art of the petty bourgeoisie], *Dongfang zazhi* 東方雜誌 [The Eastern Miscellany] 30, no. 3 (February 1, 1933): 17–18.

17. Shen Yanbing, "Fengjian de xiaoshimin wen yi"; Li Changjian 李昌鑑, "Shenguai pian zhen hairen" 神怪片真害人 [Fantasy films are truly harmful], *Yingxi shenghuo* 影戲生活 [Movie Weekly] 1, no. 7 (February 20, 1931): 14–16; Huang Yichuo, "Guochan yingpian," 24. Such portrayals were one of the inspirations for Zhang Tianyi's 張天翼 1936 satire *Yangjingbang qixia* 洋涇浜奇俠, translated by David Hull as *The Pidgin Warrior* (London: Balestier, 2017).

18. Zeitlin, *Historian of the Strange*, 15–42.

19. Zeitlin, *Historian of the Strange*, 3. Zeitlin refers here to "the atmosphere that prevailed in the People's Republic of China beginning in the 1950s," but as we have seen the rejection of supernatural content can be traced back at least to the late Qing.

20. Haiyan Lee, *The Stranger and the Chinese Moral Imagination* (Stanford, CA: Stanford University Press, 2014), 38.

21. Xiang Kairan [Pingjiang Buxioasheng 平江不肖生], *Jianghu guaiyi zhuan* 江湖怪異傳 [Strange phenomena of the rivers and lakes] (Shanghai: Shijie shuju, 1923). Citations will be to this edition, by page number.

22. "With regard to information about the story, the following homology must be observed: 'author : reader = criminal : detective.'" Tzvetan Todorov, "The Typology of Detective Fiction," in *The Poetics of Prose*, 49.

23. Xiang Kairan 向愷然, "Heimao yu qi'an" 黑貓與奇案 [A black cat and a strange case], *Hong meigui* 紅玫瑰 [The scarlet rose] 1, no. 21 (December 20, 1924). Timothy C. Wong translates it as "The Black Cat" in *Stories for Saturday: Twentieth-Century Chinese Popular Fiction* (Honolulu: University of Hawai'i Press, 2003), 147–57. I use Wong's translation here, citing his page numbers, and inserting the Chinese text from the serialization for certain key phrases.

24. Han Yunbo 韩云波, "Lun Pingjiang Buxiaosheng de 'qixia' luxiang" 论平江不肖生的奇侠" 路向 [On the tendency of Pingjiang Buxiaosheng's "marvelous gallants"], *Chongqing Sanxia xueyuan xuebao* 重庆三峡学院学报 27, no. 2 (2011): 42–47.

25. Zhang, *Amorous History*, 199–43.

26. On the strange and the *chuanqi* tradition as the novel's inspirations, see Xu Sinian 徐斯年, "Xiang Kairan de 'xiandai wuxia chuanqi huayu'" [Xiang Kairan's "discourse of modern chivalric romance"] 向愷然的"现代武侠传奇话语," *Zhongguo xiandai wenxue yanjiu congkan* no. 4 (2012): 88–97; also Xu and Liu, "Wuxia huidang bian."

27. Han Yunbo, "'Qixia' luxiang," also comments on the significance of this passage.

28. The wording of the title also echoes two particular texts frequently identified as among *Rivers and Lakes*' literary ancestors: the "Youxia lie zhuan" 遊俠列傳 [Biographies of the wandering gallants] chapter from Sima Qian's 司馬遷 foundational work of historiography, *Shi ji* 史記 [Records of the Historian]; and the vernacular novel *Shuihu zhuan* 水滸傳 [The Water Margin].

29. Hamm, *Paper Swordsmen*, 17–19, *passim*. For a characterization of the notion of the Rivers and Lakes from a historian's perspective, see Hanchao Lu, *Street Criers: A Cultural History of Chinese Beggars* (Stanford, CA: Stanford University Press, 2005), esp. 13–15.

30. Taking a master or a disciple establishes a vertical relationship, swearing brotherhood a horizontal (though still hierarchical) one. Sworn brotherhood is at the heart of the sagas of *Three Kingdoms* and *Water Margin*. These works' echoes in the episode of the Ma assassination will be discussed toward the end of this chapter.

31. See Shi Jiqun's commentary on the first chapter, 1:1, 14.

32. Xiang Kairan [Kairan 愷然], "Bianse tan" 變色談 [Turning pale], *Minquan su* 民權素 [Elements of people's rights] no. 16 (March 1916). A note at the end of the piece indicates that the text is to be continued in a future issue, but no such continuation appears in the subsequent number, which is the last of the periodical's run. The text is included in the anthologies *Minquan su cui bian* 民權素粹編 [The best of *Elements of People's Rights*] (Shanghai: Minquan chuban bu 民權出版部, 1926) and *Minquan su biji huicui* 民權素筆記薈萃 [Collected short prose from *Elements of People's Rights*] (Taiyuan: Shanxi gu ji chu ban she 山西古籍出版社, 1997).

33. "Lieren ou ji" 獵人偶記 [A hunter's miscellany] was published in six parts in *Xingqi* 星期 [The Sunday] 27–30, 32, and 35 (August through October 1922), under the name Xiang Kairan. The title echoes 1852 Turgenev's *Sketches from a Hunter's Album*, a translation

of which by Geng Jizhi 耿濟之 began serialization in *Xiaoshuo yuebao* 小說月報 [Short Story Magazine] under the title "Lieren riji" 獵人日記 [A hunter's diary] in March 1921. The two parts of "Tales of the Reverend Lan" ("Lan fashi ji" 藍法師記) appeared in *Xingqi* 星期 [The Sunday] 34 and 36 (October and November 1922), also under the name Xiang Kairan.

34. Xiang Kairan 向愷然, "Hama yao" 蝦蟆妖 [The toad demon], *Hong zazhi* 紅雜誌 [Scarlet Magazine] 2, no. 31 (March 7, 1924).

35. As the narrator points out, chapters 4 through 55 function in the same way, as an extended, multilevel analepsis; see 55:2, 439–40.

36. On the novel's narrative structure and its indebtedness to the aesthetics of the traditional vernacular novel see Xu Sinian, "Xiandai wuxia chuanqi huayu," 89–91.

37. For details see Ding Xianshan 丁贤善, "Lun *Jianghu qixia zhuan* de xushu yishu" 论《江湖奇侠传》的叙述艺术 [On the narrative art of *Marvelous Gallants of the Rivers and Lakes*], in *Pingjiang Buxiaosheng yanjiu zhuanji* 平江不肖生研究专辑 [Collected studies on Pingjiang Buxiaosheng], ed. Zeng Pingyuan 曾平原 and He Linfu 何林 (Shanghai: Fudan daxue chubanshe, 2013), 180–200.

38. "[Lan's] vigorous mettle was such that if someone in low spirits were to see it, they would immediately thrill with enthusiasm, and if someone cowardly were to see it, they would promptly feel their valor soar to the heavens. Yet despite his sturdy frame and pitch-black skin, his appearance was not at all uncouth. His bearing and movements revealed an air of refinement, not at all that of a Miao ignorant of culture and the Confucian teachings, and the clothes upon his body were those of a Han scholar" (58:3, 13).

39. Shi Juan, "Fuwenben jiangou," 133–36.

40. Advertisement for World Books' publication of the eleventh volume (*ji*) of *Rivers and Lakes* in *Xinwen bao* 新聞報, June 27, 1929, as quoted in Shi Juan, "Fuwenben jiangou," 134–35.

41. The local currency of accounts, including this example, is also cited by the ads for the novel in testimony to its facticity; see Shi Juan, "Fuwenben jiangou," 135.

42. Chapter 28's story of Zhou Dunbing 周敦秉 capturing a demon occasions a similar conflict between the narrator's use of the word *mixin* 迷信 and the presentation of spirits as a diegetic reality: "The character of the Hunanese is such that they possess an unshakeable superstitious belief in spirits and anomalies. Even those who have never seen anything like a ghost or spirit in their entire lives will unanimously insist that ghosts and spirits exist. And now that Zhou Dunbing had chained up a ghost in broad daylight for everyone to see, the level of superstition increased to an exceptional degree" (28:1, 399).

43. Han Yunbo, "'Qixia' luxiang," 42–44, discusses the significance of these and related passages in terms of Karl Popper's notion of "falsifiability."

44. See Arthur W. Hummel, *Eminent Chinese of the Ch'ing Period (1644–1912)* (Washington: U.S. Government Printing Office, 1943), 554–56. Lin Baochun's 林保淳 forthcoming "Cong 'Ci Ma an' dao *Toumingzhuang*: you lishi dao wenxue de zhuanzhe" 從「刺馬案」到《投名狀》—由歷史到文學的轉折 [From 'the Ma assassination case' to *The Warlords*: the shift from history to literature] examines both historical materials and literary and

cinematic renditions of the story, including the 1973 Shaw Brothers film *Ci Ma* 刺馬 [Blood Brothers] and the 2007 Jet Li vehicle *Touming zhuang*投名狀 [The Warlords].

45. The explanation of Minister Zheng's earlier encounter with Zhang is given at the tail end of the Ma assassination episode, across chapters 105–106.

46. In chapter 81 the author-narrator answers his audience's anticipated doubts about the plausibility of the Red Lotus Temple story by citing its currency in a play from the Han-diao 漢調 opera repertoire popular in Hunan some thirty years in the past. The appeal here is to source, precedent, and common knowledge, not to historicity as such.

47. See in particular chapters 37 and 48.

48. This explanation for the popularity of martial arts fiction is common in Chinese literary historiography and is echoed in E. Perry Link Jr., "Traditional-Style Popular Urban Fiction in the Teens and Twenties," in *Modern Chinese Literature in the May Fourth Era*, ed. Merle Goldman (Cambridge, MA: Harvard University Press, 1977), 333. Bao, *Fiery Cinema*, 57, notes its similar currency in the historiography of Republican-era martial arts film: "The canonical *History of the Development of Chinese Cinema* describes martial arts films as popular articulations of alternative justice and representations of struggle amid drastic social change, emerging when the nationalist war of the Northern Expedition that ended years of factionalist warlordism gave way to Chiang Kai-shek's massacre of the communists in April 1927."

6. CHIVALRIC HEROES OF MODERN TIMES

1. The film was also released in the United States under the title *The Chinese Connection*.

2. For a comparison of some of the early accounts see Han Yisong 韩倚松 [John Christopher Hamm], "Wei Jindai xiayi yingxiong zhuan zhong zhi Huo Yuanjia shi zhuigen" 为《近代侠义英雄传》中之霍元甲事追根 [An investigation of the sources of the Huo Yuanjia material in *Chivalric Heroes of Modern Times*], *Suzhou jiaoyu xueyuan xuebao* 苏州教育学院学报 29, no. 1 (January 2012): 12–17; reprinted in *Pingjiang Buxiaosheng yanjiu zhuanji* 平江不肖生研究专辑 [Collected studies on Pingjiang Buxiaosheng], ed. Zeng Pingyuan 曾平原 and He Linfu 何林福 (Shanghai: Fudan daxue chubanshe, 2013), 249–61.

3. I discuss some of the cinematic adaptations in "From the Boxers to Kung Fu Panda: The Chinese Martial Arts in Global Entertainment," in *Chinese Martial Arts and Media Culture: Global Perspectives*, ed. Tim Trausch (London: Rowman and Littlefield International, 2018), 101–18. See also Jason K. Halub, "Wushu Nationalism: Tracing the Invention of the Huo Yuanjia Story," *Journal of Chinese Martial Arts* 4, no. 1 (2015): 1–18.

4. My translation of the *jindai* of the novel's title as "modern" obviously differs from the "recent (-era)" I use for the same term in rendering, e.g., Fan Boqun's *Zhongguo jin- xian-dai tongsu wenxue shi* 中国近现代通俗文学史. In the latter case *jindai* refers to post-1949 mainland Chinese scholarship's periodization of 1842–1911 as *jindai* and 1911–1949 as *xiandai*; in the case of Xiang Kairan's title I understand *jindai* to refer more broadly to the recent events as distinct from the historical past and to signal the novel's thematic interest in the problems of the modern experience.

5. Han Yunbo 韩云波, "Zhuchiren yu" 主持人语 [Editor's remarks] to Fan Boqun, "Lun Minguo wuxia xiaoshuo dianji zuo," 37. See also Han Yunbo 韩云波, "Pingjiang Buxiaosheng yu xiandai Zhongguo wuxia xiaoshuo de neizai jiujie" 平江不肖生与现代中国武侠小说的内在纠结 [Pingjiang Buxiaosheng and the internal tension of modern Chinese martial arts fiction], *Xi'nan daxue xuebao (shehui kexue ban)* 西南大学学报 (社会科学版) 37, no. 6 (November 2011): 33–39; and Xu Sinian, "Xiandai wuxia chuanqi huayu," 88.

6. Fan Boqun, "Lun Minguo wuxiao xiaoshuo dianji zuo," 40. A version of this article with slight variations appears as "Minguo wuxia xiaoshuo dianji daibiaozuo: *Jindai xiayi yingxiong zhuan*" 民国武侠小说奠基代表作—《近代侠义英雄传》 [*Chivalric Heroes of Modern Times*—the foundational representative work of Republican-era martial arts fiction], in Zeng and He, *Pingjiang Buxiaosheng yanjiu zhuanji*, 226–31. See also, in the same volume, the contributions by Zhang Tangqi 张堂锜, 232–48; Zhang Yuelin 张乐林, 262–74; and Tong Lijun 童李君, 275–80.

7. The strategy corroborates Hockx's observation that the modern Chinese literary field is structured not merely by a simple tension between autonomous literary value and heteronomous economic value but also by the presence of a third, political axis that provides an additional mode of valuation even for works and authors deemed deficient in purely symbolic capital. See Hockx, *Literary Field*, 12, 17.

8. Prominent among recent reconsiderations of the novel are those in Dong Bingyue 董炳月, *Guomin zuojia de lichang: Zhong Ri xiandai wenxue guanxi yanjiu* 国民作家的立场: 中日现代文学关系研究 [The standpoint of the national writer: studies in modern Sino-Japanese literary relations] (Beijing: Sanlian shudian, 2006), 1–76; and Li Zhaozhong 李兆忠, *Xuannao de luozi: liuxue yu Zhongguo xiandai wenhua* 喧闹的骡子—留学与中国现代文化 [A braying mule: overseas study and modern Chinese culture] (Beijing: Renmin wenxue chubanshe, 2010), 27–38.

9. References to the text will cite Buxiaosheng 不肖生, *Liudong waishi* 留東外史 [The unofficial history of sojourners in Japan] (Shanghai: Minquan chubanbu 民權出版部, 1916; fourth printing, 1924), by chapter and page number (1:1 = chapter 1, p. 1). There are several modern editions, including that contained in *Zhongguo jindai xiaoshuo da xi* 中国近代小说大系 (Nanchang: Baihua zhou wenyi chubanshe, 1991); this simplified-character edition of the original ninety chapters and the seventy-chapter continuation includes the original interlinear and chapter commentaries.

10. Wang, *Fin-de-Siècle Splendor*, 183–251. *Sojourners*' affiliation with the exposé tradition is also suggested by the title's *waishi*, a common element in novelistic titles but one that may acknowledge a particular debt to Wu Jingzi's 吳敬梓 (1701–1754) *Rulin waishi* 儒林外史 [The unofficial history of the scholars], the early-Qing novel of social satire widely regarded as the ancestor of the end-of-the-dynasty exposés.

11. Wang, *Fin-de-Siècle Splendor*, 183–91. As Wang points out, the name and received conception of the category derive from Lu Xun's 1925 *A Brief History of Chinese Fiction*.

12. On the chronotope of the depravity novel, see Wang, *Fin-de-Siècle Splendor*, 53–61; the locus classicus on the genre is again Lu Xun's *Brief History*. See also Chloë F. Starr, *Red-Light Novels of the Late Qing* (Leiden and Boston: Brill, 2007); and Catherine Vance

Yeh, *Shanghai Love: Courtesans, Intellectuals, and Entertainment Culture, 1850–1910* (Seattle: University of Washington Press, 2006), esp. chap. 6.

13. Des Forges, "Building Shanghai, One Page at a Time." See also his expanded treatment in *Mediasphere Shanghai: The Aesthetics of Cultural Production* (Honolulu: University of Hawai'i Press, 2007).

14. Despite Lu Xun's continuing influence, other scholars have also traced the posthistory of the late Qing exposé. Particularly useful is the account in Fan Boqun, *Jin- xiandai*, 1:100–245.

15. The inescapable reference is again to Wang, *Fin-de-Siècle Splendor*, 252–312. For a recent study, see Nathaniel Isaacson, *Celestial Empire: The Emergence of Chinese Science Fiction* (Middletown, CT: Wesleyan University Press, 2017).

16. See Kirk A. Denton, "The Distant Shore: Nationalism in Yu Dafu's 'Sinking,'" *Chinese Literature: Essays, Articles, Reviews* 14 (1992): 107–23, for analysis of the story and a review of earlier scholarship.

17. Shu-mei Shih, *The Lure of the Modern: Writing Modernism in Semicolonial China, 1917– 1937* (Berkeley: University of California Press, 2001). See 16–30 on Japan's mediating role; 110–27 on "the libidinal and the national" in Yu Dafu and other writers; 129–31 on the distinction between the late-Qing and May Fourth varieties of "Occidentalism"; and 136–44 for the psychological parameters of "loving the other via Japan."

18. In chapter 23 of Jin Shengtan's 金聖嘆 edition; see Chen Xizhong 陈曦钟 et al., eds., *Shuihu zhuan huiping ben* 水浒傳会评本 [*The Water Margin*: collected commentaries edition] (Beijing: Beijing daxue chubanshe, 1981), 454–55.

19. See my translation of this episode in Buxiaosheng, "*The Unofficial History of Sojourners in Japan* (excerpt)," *Renditions* 87 & 88 (Spring and Autumn 2017): 155–64.

20. Though see also Wang, *Fin-de-Siècle Splendor*, 215, on the more widespread trope of the systematization and textual transmission of vice in late-Qing exposé fiction.

21. See C. T. Hsia, *The Classic Chinese Novel: A Critical Introduction* (New York: Columbia University Press, 1968), 88, 105–6; and for a more recent treatment, Martin W. Huang, *Negotiating Masculinities in Late Imperial China* (Honolulu: University of University of Hawai'i Press, 2006), 107–11.

22. See Huang, *Negotiating Masculinities*, 113–34, 155–82.

23. Dong Bingyue reads Huang Wenhan's sexual chauvinism as a manifestation of his broader cultural chauvinism and understands him as a stand-in for the author and his views; see *Guomin zuojia de lichang*, 36–45. Li Zhaozhong sees a stark contrast between the novel's reactionary chauvinism and the more progressive perspectives of New Literature writers associated with the Creation Society (Chuangzao she 創造社); see *Xuannao de luozi*, 31–33.

24. Any sense of Chinese triumph is further mitigated by the narrative's sympathetic treatment of the Russian strongman. The text describes the feats that constitute his performance—flexing and posing, breaking a steel chain, lifting an enormous barbell— in exhaustive detail and with apparent admiration. It briefly employs the Russian as the narrative focus and recounts with seeming empathy his frustration with the unprecedented clamor and unruliness of the Chinese audience. Although his spiel is

insultingly dismissive of the Chinese, both Huo Yuanjia within the diegesis and the novel's extradiegetic commentator admit to the essential justice of his remarks on the state of physical culture in China, and his proposition of friendship and collaboration seems, on the face of things, more rational and constructive than Huo's obdurate insistence on a duel to the death.

25. Immediately preceding the episode of the Russian strongman is that of Huo Yuanjia's encounter with the renowned martial artist Li Fudong 李富東. The episode both confirms Huo's eminence in the traditional martial world and highlights the cruelty of that world's rivalries; although the match between Huo and Li is collegial, Huo's victory sparks the tragic suicide of Li's disciple.

26. See in particular the well-known exchange between Lu Xun 魯迅 and Chen Tiesheng 陳鐵生 on the pages of *Xin Qingnian* in 1918–1919, discussed in Morris, *Marrow of the Nation*, 193–95; and in Paul A. Cohen, *History in Three Keys: The Boxers as Event, Experience, and Myth* (New York: Columbia University Press, 1997), 230–33. As Cohen's book details, historiography in the People's Republic of China exalted the Boxer uprising as an anti-imperialist movement. *Modern Times*' negative portrayal of the Boxers prompted the excision of chapters 14–19 from the edition published by Yuelu shushe in 1984 under the title *Dadao Wang Wu Huo Yuanjia Xiayi yingxiong zhuan* 大刀王五霍元甲侠义英雄传 [The chivalric heroes Broadsworder Wang Wu and Huo Yuanjia]. Fan Boqun included the Boxer chapters in his 2000 selection of Xiang Kairan's writings: see *Pingjiang Buxiaosheng* 平江不肖生, selected by Fan Boqun 范伯群, edited by Zhongguo xiandai wenxueguan 中国现代文学馆 (Beijing: Huaxia chubanshe, 2000), 259–315.

27. The news reports of Huo Yuanjia's deeds are described as casting him in roles familiar from fiction: "The newspapers in Beijing, Tianjin, Shanghai, and Hankou all published the facts of how Huo Yuanjia protected the converts. Some called Huo Yuanjia a knighterrant (*xiake* 侠客), some even called him a sword-immortal (*jianxian* 劍仙); the time had already come when the renown of the name Huo Yuanjia shook the whole world with astonishment" (19:2, 33–34).

28. Jing Tsu, *Failure, Nationalism, and Literature: The Making of Modern Chinese Identity, 1895–1937* (Stanford, CA: Stanford University Press, 2006).

29. By way of example: In chapter 6, Wang Wu, after making Huo Yuanjia's acquaintance in Tianjin, takes his leave and goes off to visit his friend Li Fudong 李富東, "Li the Nose" (Bizi Li 鼻子李). To talk about Li, the narrator declares, he must first introduce Li's teacher, Wang Donglin 王東林, and so we hear about Wang's background, martial education, and his match against the Shaolin monk Haikong 海空. Wang is later challenged by Li, who becomes his disciple and his successor (chapters 6–7). Li, in turn, is challenged by one Liu Muer 柳木兒, and we hear first about Liu's background, then about how he loses to Li because of a stumble. The narrative now returns to Wang Wu's visit (chapter 8). Li the Nose, hearing from Wang Wu of Huo Yuanjia's prowess, sends Huo an invitation to a friendly contest. Huo sets off to visit Li but is intercepted on the road by one Zhao Yutang 趙玉堂. We accordingly hear about Zhao's background and about how as a youth he was kidnapped by a monk who kept him in a cave and instructed him in the esoteric arts. Returning home after many years, Zhao takes up banditry to

support his widowed mother. His brazen exploits force him to flee to Harbin, where he runs afoul of a Russian police inspector, Rostov, who brings Zhao to the side of the law by holding his mother hostage (chapters 8–11). After various other adventures, Zhao hears of Huo Yuanjia and decides to go pay him a visit, resulting in chapter 8's encounter on the road. Huo entertains Zhao, then proceeds with his visit to Li the Nose (chapter 12). Arriving at Li's, he finds that another visitor has preceded him: "Geezer Wang," Wang Laotou'r 王老頭兒, and so we must hear about Geezer Wang's background, his service to kiln-master Yao 窰 (姚) 師父, an encounter with an itinerant female warrior, and a cure that requires eating cow dung (chapters 12–13). "Extraordinary matters (*xiang zhezhong xiqi de shi* 像這種希奇的事) such as this are precisely the sort of thing that the idle and curious love to relate" (13:1, 163). With all this out of the way, the narrative finally presents the match between Huo and Li, in which Li stumbles and loses (chapter 13). Huo then returns to Tianjin, where he will encounter the Russian muscleman (chapter 14). A single incident in the protagonist's story—his meeting with Li Fudong—has been stretched out over eight chapters and elaborated to include biographies and anecdotes of some half-dozen other martial artists.

CONCLUSION: THE UNWORTHY SCHOLAR FROM PINGJIANG

1. Xu Sinian, who dates Xiang Kairan's arrival in Japan to 1906, understands "this place" in the passage "since arriving in this place in Meiji 40" (自明治四十年即来此地) as referring to Tokyo as distinct from Japan in general; see his discussion of the various dates assigned to Xiang Kairan's arrival in "Nianbiao," 3–4.

2. Cf. the citations in the 1987 *Hanyu da cidian* 漢語大詞典 1:412–13.

3. *Sheng* 生 denotes a scholar or student in the particular sense of a junior and so still marginal member of the aspirational hierarchy of knowledge and status that stood at the center of premodern Chinese society. The term was an element in the pen names of many late-Qing- and early-Republican-era literary men, so much so that Lu Xun mocks the affectation in his 1922 "Erge de 'fandong'" 兒歌的"反動" ["Reaction" to a nursery rhyme]; see Dong Bingyue, *Guomin zuojia de lichang*, 63.

4. See Lin Xi 林熙, "Pingjiang Buxiaosheng Xiang Kairan" 平江不肖生向愷然, *Wanxiang* 萬象 2 (August 1975): 43; reprinted in *Minguo jiupai wenyi yanjiu ziliao* 民國舊派文藝研究資料 [Materials for the study of Republican-era old-school literature] (Jiulong: Shiyong shuju, 1978). Lin Xi cites a 1957 newspaper article, the original of which I have not seen. The Laozi passage is from *Dao de jing* 道德經, 67; translation by James Legge in *The Sacred Books of China: The Texts of Tàoism, Part I* (Oxford: Clarendon, 1891), 110 (Romanization revised).

5. Cf. the discussion in Fan Boqun, *Zhongguo xiandai tongsu wenxue shi*, 293.

6. Liang Qichao 梁啟超, "Gao xiaoshuo jia" 告小說家 [An indictment of the fiction writers], *Zhonghua xiaoshuojie* 中華小說界 (*Chung Hwa Novel Magazine*) 2, no. 1 (1915); see Huters, *Bringing the World Home*, 114–15.

7. Andreas Huyssen, *After the Great Divide: Modernism, Mass Culture, Postmodernism* (Bloomington: Indiana University Press, 1986), vii.

8. Fan Boqun, "Xulun" 绪论 [Preface], in *Jin- xiandai* 1:1–36.

9. Pierre Bourdieu, *The Rules of Art: Genesis and Structure of the Literary Field*, trans. Susan Emanuel (Stanford: Stanford University Press, 1996).

10. Hockx, *Questions of Style*; also "Theory as Practice: Modern Chinese Literature and Bourdieu," in *Reading East Asian Writing: The Limits of Literary Theory*, ed. Michel Hockx and Ivo Smits (London: Routledge Curzon, 2003), 220–39.

11. Hockx, "Theory as Practice," 229.

12. Michel Hockx, "Introduction," in *Literary Field*, 1–20.

13. Huters, "Cultivating the 'Great Divide,'" 18.

Bibliography

Please see the "Notes on Conventions" at the front of this volume.

Alford, William P. *To Steal a Book Is an Elegant Offense: Intellectual Property Law in Chinese Civilization*. Stanford, CA: Stanford University Press, 1995.

Allen, Sarah M. "Narrative Genres." In *The Oxford Handbook of Classical Chinese Literature (1000 BCE–900CE)*, ed. Wiebke Denecke, Wai-yee Li, and Xiaofei Tian, 273–87. New York: Oxford University Press, 2017.

Allen, Sarah M. *Shifting Stories: History, Gossip, and Lore in Narratives from Tang Dynasty China*. Cambridge, MA: Harvard University Asia Center, 2014.

Altenburger, Roland. *The Sword or the Needle: The Female Knight-Errant (*xia*) in Traditional Chinese Narrative*. Bern: Peter Lang, 2009.

Altenburger, Roland. "Xiang Kairan." In *Dictionary of Literary Biography*, vol. 328: *Chinese Fiction Writers, 1900–1949*, ed. Thomas Moran, 235–40. Detroit: Thomson Gale, 2006.

Altenburger, Roland, Margaret B. Wan, and Vibeke Børdahl, eds. *Yangzhou, a Place in Literature: The Local in Chinese Cultural History*. Honolulu: University of Hawai'i Press, 2015.

Bao Tianxiao 包天笑. *Chuanying lou huiyi lu* 釧影樓回憶錄 [Memoirs of bracelet shadow chamber]. 3 vols. Taibei: Longwen chubanshe, 1990.

Bao Tianxiao 包天笑 [Tianxiao 天笑]. "Shijie nüxia" 世界女俠 [A female gallant for the world]. *Xingqi* 星期 [The Sunday] no. 50 (March 4, 1923).

Bao Tianxiao 包天笑 [Chuanying 釧影]. "Xiang Kairan jia zhi hou" 向愷然家之猴 [The monkey in Xiang Kairan's home]. *Xingqi* 星期 [The Sunday] no. 46 (January 14, 1923).

Bao Tianxiao 包天笑 [Manmiao 曼妙]. "Zhuiyi Buxiaosheng" 追憶不肖生 [Remembering Buxiaosheng]. *Jingbao* 晶報 [The Crystal], April 3, 1929.

Bao Weihong. *Fiery Cinema: The Emergence of an Affective Medium in China, 1915–1945*. Minneapolis: University of Minnesota Press, 2015.

"Benshe zhengwen qi" 本社徵文啟 [Call for contributions]. *Xin xiaoshuo* 新小說 [New fiction] 1, no. 1 (1902).

Billingsley, Philip. *Bandits in Republican China*. Stanford, CA: Stanford University Press, 1988.

Bourdieu, Pierre. *The Rules of Art: Genesis and Structure of the Literary Field*. Trans. Susan Emanuel. Stanford, CA: Stanford University Press, 1996.

Cai Aiguo 蔡爱国. *Qingmo Minchu xiayi xiaoshuo lun* 清末民初侠义小说论 [On late-Qing- and early-Republican-era chivalric fiction]. Beijing: Jiuzhou chubanshe, 2016.

Campany, Robert Ford. *Strange Writing: Anomaly Accounts in Early Medieval China*. Albany: State University of New York Press, 1996.

Cao Xueqin 曹雪芹 and Gao E 高鹗. *Honglou meng* 紅樓夢 [Dream of the Red Chamber]. 4 vols. Beijing: Renmin wenxue chubanshe, 1959.

Cawelti, John G. *Adventure, Mystery, and Romance: Formula Stories as Art and Popular Culture*. Chicago: University of Chicago Press, 1976.

Chard, Robert L. "Transcendents, Sorcerers, and Women Warriors: Huanzhulouzhu's *Mountain Sword-Warriors of Sichuan*." *Chinoperl Papers* 20–22 (1997–1999): 169–95.

Chen Jianhua. "An Archaeology of Repressed Popularity: Zhou Shoujuan, Mao Dun, and Their 1920s Literary Polemics." In *Rethinking Chinese Popular Culture: Cannibalizations of the Canon*, ed. Carlos Rojas and Eileen Cheng-yin Chow, 91–114. London: Routledge, 2009.

Chen Jianhua. "Canon Formation and Linguistic Turn: Literary Debates in Republican China, 1919–1949." In *Beyond the May Fourth Paradigm: In Search of Chinese Modernity*, ed. Kai-Wing Chow et al., 51–67. Lanham, MD: Lexington Books, 2008.

Chen Jianhua 陈建华. *Cong geming dao gonghe: Qingmo zhi Minguo shiqi wenxue, dianying yu wenhua de zhuanxing* 从革命到共和: 清末至民国时期文学, 电影与文化的转型 [From revolution to republic: the transformation of literature, film, and culture from the late Qing to the Republican era]. Guilin: Guangxi shifan daxue chubanshe, 2009.

Chen Meilin 陈美林 et al. *Zhanghui xiaoshuo shi* 章回小说史 [History of the linked-chapter novel]. Hangzhou: Zhejiang guji chubanshe, 1998.

Chen Pingyuan. *The Development of Chinese Martial Arts Fiction*. Trans. Victor Petersen. Cambridge: Cambridge University Press, 2016.

Chen Pingyuan 陈平原. *Ershi shiji Zhongguo xiaoshuo shi: diyi juan (1897–1916)* 二十世纪中国小说史: 第一卷 (1897–1916) [The history of twentieth-century Chinese fiction, vol. 1: 1897–1916]. Beijing: Beijing daxue chubanshe, 1989.

Chen Pingyuan 陈平原. "Wan Qing zhishi de youxia xintai" 晚清志士的游侠心态 [The knight-errant mentality of late-Qing men of purpose]. In *Zhongguo xiandai xueshu zhi jianli: yi Zhang Taiyan, Hu Shizhi wei zhongxin* 中国现代学术之建立—以章太炎、胡适之为中心 [The establishment of modern Chinese scholarship: with a focus on Zhang Taiyan and Hu Shizhi], 275–319. Beijing: Beijing daxue chubanshe, 1998.

Chen Pingyuan 陈平原. *Xiaoshuo shi: lilun yu shijian* 小说史: 理论与实践 [The history of fiction: theory and practice]. Beijing: Beijing daxue chubanshe, 1993.

Chen Pingyuan 陈平原. "Zhongguo gudai xiaoshuo leixing guannian" 中国古代小说类型观念 [The concept of genre in premodern Chinese fiction]. In *Xiaoshuo shi: lilun yu shijian* 小说史: 理论与实践 [The history of fiction: theory and practice], 142–58. Beijing: Beijing daxue chubanshe, 1993.

Chen Pingyuan 陈平原 and Xiao Xiaohong 夏晓虹, eds. *Ershi shiji Zhongguo xiaoshuo lilun ziliao, di yi juan (1897–1916)* 二十世纪中国小说理论资料·第一卷 (1897–1916) [Materials on twentieth-century Chinese fiction theory: vol. 1 (1897–1916)]. Beijing: Beijing daxue chubanshe, 1989.

Cheng Xiaoqing 程小青. "Wo zhi shenguai yingpian guan" 我之神怪影片觀 [My views on fantasy films]. *Shanghai* 上海 no. 4 (1927).

Cheng Xiaoqing 程小青. "Zhentan xiaoshuo he kexue" 偵探小說和科學 [Detective fiction and science]. *Zhentan shijie* 偵探世界 [Detective world] no. 13 (1923).

Chen Xizhong 陈曦钟, Hou Zhongyi 侯忠义, and Lu Yuchuan 鲁玉川, eds. *Shuiyu zhuan huiping ben* 水浒傳会评本 [The water margin: collected commentaries edition]. Beijing: Beijing daxue chubanshe, 1981.

Chow, Kai-Wing, Tze-ki Hon, Hung-yok Ip, and Don C. Price, eds. *Beyond the May Fourth Paradigm: In Search of Chinese Modernity*. Lanham, MD: Lexington Books, 2008.

Chow, Rey. "Mandarin Ducks and Butterflies: An Exercise in Popular Readings." In *Woman and Chinese Modernity: The Politics of Reading Between West and East*, 34–83. Minnesota: University of Minnesota Press, 1991.

Cohen, Paul A. *History in Three Keys: The Boxers as Event, Experience, and Myth*. New York: Columbia University Press, 1997.

Denton, Kirk A. "The Distant Shore: Nationalism in Yu Dafu's 'Sinking.'" *Chinese Literature: Essays, Articles, Reviews* 14 (1992): 107–23.

Denton, Kirk A. "Lu Xun, Returning Home, and May Fourth Modernity." In *The Oxford Handbook of Modern Chinese Literatures*, ed. Carlos Rojas and Andrea Bachner, 19–38. New York: Oxford University Press, 2016.

Denton, Kirk A., ed. *Modern Chinese Literary Thought: Writings on Literature, 1893–1945*. Stanford, CA: Stanford University Press, 1996.

Des Forges, Alexander. "Building Shanghai, One Page at a Time: The Aesthetics of Installment Fiction at the Turn of the Century." *Journal of Asian Studies* 62, no. 3 (2003): 781–810.

Des Forges, Alexander. *Mediasphere Shanghai: The Aesthetics of Cultural Production*. Honolulu: University of Hawai'i Press, 2007.

Des Forges, Alexander. "Street Talk and Alley Stories: Tangled Narratives of Shanghai from *Lives of Shanghai Flowers* (1892) to *Midnight* (1933)." PhD diss., Princeton University, 1998.

DeWoskin, Kenneth. "The Six Dynasties *Chih-kuai* and the Birth of Fiction." In *Chinese Narrative: Critical and Theoretical Essays*, ed. Andrew H. Plaks, 21–52. Princeton, NJ: Princeton University Press, 1977.

"Dianying jiancha fa" 電影檢查法 [Film censorship statute]. *Dianying jiancha weiyuanhui gongbao* 電影檢查委員會公報 [Bulletin of the Film Censorship Committee] 1, no. 1 (August 1, 1932): 8–10.

Ding Xianshan 丁贤善. "Lun *Jianghu qixia zhuan* de xushu yishu" 论《江湖奇侠传》的叙述艺术 [On the narrative art of *Marvelous Gallants of the Rivers and Lakes*]. In *Pingjiang Buxiaosheng yanjiu zhuanji* 平江不肖生研究专辑 [Collected studies on Pingjiang Buxiaosheng], ed. Zeng Pingyuan 曾平原 and He Linfu 何林福, 180–200. Shanghai: Fudan daxue chubanshe, 2013.

Doleželová-Velingerová, Milena. Review of Perry Link, *Mandarin Ducks and Butterflies*. *Harvard Journal of Asiatic Studies* 44, no. 2 (December 1984): 578–86.

Doleželová-Velingerová, Milena, and Oldrich Král, eds. *The Appropriation of Cultural Capital: China's May Fourth Project*. Cambridge, MA: Harvard University Asia Center, 2001.

Dong Bingyue 董炳月. *Guomin zuojia de lichang: Zhong Ri xiandai wenxue guanxi yanjiu* 国民作家的立场: 中日现代文学关系研究 [The standpoint of the national writer: studies in modern Sino-Japanese literary relations]. Beijing: Sanlian shudian, 2006.

Duara, Prasenjit. *Rescuing History from the Nation: Questioning Narratives of Modern China*. Chicago: University of Chicago Press, 1995.

Dudbridge, Glen. *The Hsi-yu chi: A Study of Antecedents to the Sixteenth-Century Chinese Novel*. Cambridge: Cambridge University Press, 1970.

"Duzhe zhuyi" 讀者注意 [Readers take note]. *Hong zazhi* 紅雜誌 [The Scarlet Magazine] 1, no. 21 (January 1923).

Ebrey, Patricia Buckley. *Chinese Civilization: A Sourcebook*. 2nd ed. New York: The Free Press, 1993.

Eisenman, Lujing Ma. "Fairy Tales for Adults: Imagination, Literary Autonomy, and Modern Chinese Martial Arts Fiction, 1895–1945." PhD diss., UCLA, 2016.

Epstein, Maram. *Competing Discourses: Orthodoxy, Authenticity, and Engendered Meanings in Late Imperial Chinese Fiction*. Cambridge, MA: Harvard University Asia Center, 2001.

Fairbank, John K., ed. *The Cambridge History of China*. Vol. 12: *Republican China, 1912–1949, Part 1*. Cambridge: Cambridge University Press, 1983.

Fairbank, John K., and Kwang-ching Liu, eds. *The Cambridge History of China*. Vol. 11: *Late Ch'ing, 1800–1911, Part 2*. Cambridge: Cambridge University Press, 1980.

Fan Boqun 范伯群. "'Cuixingshu:' 1909 nian fabiao de 'Kuangren riji'" 《催醒术》: 1909年发表的"狂人日记" ["The Way of Awakening": A Lunatic's Diary Published in 1909]. *Jiangsu daxue xuebao (shehui kexue ban)* 江苏大学学报 (社会科学版) 6, no. 5 (September 2004): 1–8.

Fan Boqun 范伯群. "Heimu zhengda, heimu xiaoshuo, jiehei yundong" 黑幕征答·黑幕小说·揭黑运动 [Black curtain debates, black curtain fiction, whistle-blowing movements]. *Wenxue pinglun* 文学评论 no. 2 (2005): 57–64.

Fan Boqun 范伯群. "Lun Minguo wuxia xiaoshuo dianji zuo Jindai xiayi yingxiong zhuan" 论民国武侠小说奠基作《近代侠义英雄传》 [An Analysis of "The Legends of Modern Chivalric Heroes"—Foundation of Martial Arts Fiction in the Period of the Republic of China]. *Xi'nan daxue xuebao (shehui kexue ban)* 西南大学学报 (社会科学版) 37, no. 1 (January 2011): 37–40.

Fan Boqun 范伯群. "Yi yinqin wei niudai, yi shidai wei tuishou: xiandai Yangpai tongsu jingdian xiaoshuo *Guanglingchao* yanjiu" 以姻亲为纽带 以时代为推手—现代扬派通俗经典小说《广陵潮》研究 [Family ties and the force of the times: a study of the classic modern Yangzhou popular novel *Yangzhou Tides*]. *Hanyu yanwenxue yanjiu* 汉语言文学研究 no. 1 (2016): 4–15.

Fan Boqun 范伯群, ed. *Zhongguo jin- xiandai tongsu wenxue shi* 中国近现代通俗文学史 [A history of recent- and modern-era Chinese popular literature]. 2 vols. Nanjing: Jiangsu jiaoyu chubanshe, 1999.

Fan Boqun 范伯群. *Zhongguo xiandai tongsu wenxue shi* 中国现代通俗文学史 [A history of modern Chinese popular literature]. Beijing: Beijing daxue chubanshe, 2007.

Fan Boqun 范伯群. "Zhu Shouju lun" 朱瘦菊论 [On Zhu Shouju]. *Xin wenxue shiliao* 新文学史料 no. 1 (2013): 103–24.

Gao Rihui 高日晖 and Hong Yan 洪雁. *Shuihu zhuan jieshou shi* 水浒传接受史 [The reception history of *The Water Margin*]. Jinan: Qi Lu shushe, 2006.

Genette, Gérard. *The Architext*. Trans. Jane E. Lewin. Berkeley: University of California Press, 1992.

Gimpel, Denise. *Lost Voices of Modernity: A Chinese Popular Fiction Magazine in Context*. Honolulu: University of Hawai'i Press, 2001.

Goossaert, Vincent, and David A. Palmer. *The Religious Question in Modern China*. Chicago: University of Chicago Press, 2011.

Gu Guohua 顾国华, ed. *Wentan zayi quanbian* 文坛杂忆全编 [Reminiscences of the literary world]. 6 vols. Shanghai: Shanghai shudian chubanshe, 2015.

Gu, Mingdong. *Chinese Theories of Fiction: A Non-Western Narrative System*. Albany: State University of New York Press, 2006.

Gu Zhen 顾臻. "Guanyu Xiang Kairan suo zai sanshi liu jun jiben qingkuang" 关于向恺然所在第三十六军基本情况 [On the circumstances of the Thirty-Sixth Corps to which Xiang Kairan was attached]. *Suzhou jiaoyu xueyuan xuebao* 苏州教育学院学报 27, no. 3 (September 2010): 13–14.

Gu Zhen 顾臻. "*Jianghu qixia zhuan* banben kao ji xiangguan wenti yanjiu" 《江湖奇侠传》版本考及相关问题研究 [A study of the editions of *Marvelous Gallants of the Rivers and Lakes* and related issues]. *Suzhou jiaoyu xueyuan xuebao* 苏州教育学院学报 30, no. 3 (June 2013): 21–32.

Guan Daru 管達如. "Shuo xiaoshuo" 說小說 [On fiction]. *Xiaoshuo yuebao* 小說月報 [The Short Story Magazine] 3, nos. 3, 5, 7–11 (1912).

Halub, Jason K. "Wushu Nationalism: Tracing the Invention of the Huo Yuanjia Story." *Journal of Chinese Martial Arts* 4, no. 1 (2015): 1–18.

Hamm, John Christopher. "From the Boxers to Kung Fu Panda: The Chinese Martial Arts in Global Entertainment." In *Chinese Martial Arts and Media Culture: Global Perspectives*, ed. Tim Trausch, 101–18. London: Rowman and Littlefield International, 2018.

Hamm, John Christopher. "Genre in Modern Chinese Fiction: *Righteous Heroes of Modern Times*." In *The Oxford Handbook of Modern Chinese Literatures*, ed. Carlos Rojas and Andrea Bachner, 531–45. New York: Oxford University Press, 2016.

Hamm, John Christopher. *Paper Swordsmen: Jin Yong and the Modern Chinese Martial Arts Novel.* Honolulu: University of Hawai'i Press, 2005.

Hamm, John Christopher. Review of *Sound Rising from the Paper: Nineteenth-Century Martial Arts Fiction and the Chinese Acoustic Imagination*, by Paize Keulemans. *Harvard Journal of Asiatic Studies* 76 (2016): 237–49.

Han Yisong 韩倚松 [John Christopher Hamm]. "Wei Jindai xiayi yingxiong zhuan zhong zhi Huo Yuanjia shi zhuigen" 为《近代侠义英雄传》中之霍元甲事追根 [An investigation of the sources of the Huo Yuanjia material in *Righteous Heroes of Modern Times*]. *Suzhou jiaoyu xueyuan xuebao* 苏州教育学院学报 29, no. 1 (January 2012): 12–17. Reprinted in *Pingjiang Buxiaosheng yanjiu zhuanji* 平江不肖生研究专辑 [Collected studies on Pingjiang Buxiaosheng], ed. Zeng Pingyuan 曾平原 and He Linfu 何林福, 249–61. Shanghai: Fudan daxue chubanshe, 2013.

Han Yunbo 韩云波. "Lun Pingjiang Buxiaosheng de 'qixia' luxiang" 论平江不肖生的"奇侠"路向 [On the tendency of Pingjiang Buxiaosheng's "marvelous gallants"]. *Chongqing Sanxia xueyuan xuebao* 重庆三峡学院学报 27, no. 2 (2011): 42–47.

Han Yunbo 韩云波. "Lun Qingmo Minchu de wuxia xiaoshuo" 论清末民初的武侠小说 [On late-Qing- and early Republican-era martial arts fiction]. *Sichuan daxue xuebao (zhexue shehui kexue ban)* 四川大学学报 (哲学社会科学版) no. 4 (1999): 108–12.

Han Yunbo 韩云波. "Pingjiang Buxiaosheng yu xiandai Zhongguo wuxia xiaoshuo de neizai jiujie" 平江不肖生与现代中国武侠小说的内在纠结 [Pingjiang Buxiaosheng and the internal tension of modern Chinese martial arts fiction]. *Xinan daxue xuebao (shehui kexue ban)* 西南大学学报 (社会科学版) 37, no. 6 (November 2011): 33–39.

Hanan, Patrick. *Chinese Fiction of the Nineteenth and Early Twentieth Centuries.* New York: Columbia University Press, 2004.

Hanan, Patrick. "The Narrator's Voice Before the 'Fiction Revolution.'" In *Chinese Fiction of the Nineteenth and Early Twentieth Centuries*, 9–32. New York: Columbia University Press, 2004.

He Genmin 贺根民. "Wan Qing baokan xiaoshuo de fenlei he shenmei quxiang" 晚清报刊小说的分类和审美趋向 [The classification of fiction and aesthetic trends in late-Qing periodicals]. *Tangdu xuekan* 唐都学刊 23, no. 2 (March 2007): 120–23.

Hegel, Robert E. *Reading Illustrated Fiction in Late Imperial China.* Stanford, CA: Stanford University Press, 1998.

Hockx, Michel. "Is There a May Fourth Literature? A Reply to Wang Xiaoming." *Modern Chinese Literature and Culture* 11, no. 2 (1999): 40–52.

Hockx, Michel, ed. *The Literary Field of Twentieth-Century China.* Honolulu: University of Hawai'i Press, 1999.

Hockx, Michel. *Questions of Style: Literary Societies and Literary Journals in Modern China, 1911–1937.* Leiden: E. J. Brill, 2003.

Hockx, Michel. "Theory as Practice: Modern Chinese Literature and Bourdieu." In *Reading East Asian Writing: The Limits of Literary Theory*, ed. Michel Hockx and Ivo Smits, 220–39. London: Routledge Curzon, 2003.

Hsia, C. T. *The Classic Chinese Novel: A Critical Introduction.* New York: Columbia University Press, 1968.

Hsia, C. T. "Hsü Chen-ya's *Yü-li hun*: An Essay in Literary History and Criticism." In *Chinese Middlebrow Fiction from the Ch'ing and Early Republican Eras*, ed. Liu Ts'un-yan, 199–240. Hong Kong: Chinese University Press, 1984.

Hu Jichen 胡寄塵. "Xia shaonian" 俠少年 [A chivalrous youth]. *Xingqi* 星期 [The Sunday] no. 50 (March 4, 1923).

Hu Shi 胡適. "Lun duanpian xiaoshuo" 論短篇小說 [On the short story]. *Xin qingnian* 新青年 [New Youth] 4, no. 5 (May 1918).

Hu, Ying. *Tales of Translation: Composing the New Woman in China, 1899–1918*. Stanford, CA: Stanford University Press, 2000.

Huang, Fu-ch'ing. *Chinese Students in Japan in the Late Ch'ing Period*. Tokyo: Centre for East Asian Cultural Studies, 1982.

Huang, Martin W. *Desire and Fictional Narrative in Late Imperial China*. Cambridge, MA: Harvard University Asia Center, 2001.

Huang, Martin W. *Negotiating Masculinities in Late Imperial China*. Honolulu: University of Hawai'i Press, 2006.

Huang, Martin W., ed. *Snakes' Legs: Sequels, Continuations, Rewritings, and Chinese Fiction*. Honolulu: University of Hawai'i Press, 2004.

Huang Yichuo 黃漪磋. "Guochan yingpian de fuxing wenti" 國產影片的復興問題 [The question of the revival of Chinese cinema]. *Yingxi zazhi* 影戲雜誌 [The Film Magazine] 1, no. 7–8 (June 1, 1930): 24–25.

Hummel, Arthur W. *Eminent Chinese of the Ch'ing Period (1644–1912)*. Washington: U.S. Government Printing Office, 1943.

Hung, Eva. "Giving Texts a Context: Chinese Translations of Classical English Detective Stories, 1896–1916." In *Translation and Creation: Readings of Western Literature in Early Modern China, 1840–1918*, ed. David E. Pollard, 151–76. Amsterdam: J. Benjamins, 1998.

Huntington, Rania. "The Weird in the Newspaper." In *Writing and Materiality in China: Essays in Honor of Patrick Hanan*, ed. Judith T. Zeitlin and Lydia H. Liu, 341–96. Cambridge, MA: Harvard University Asia Center, 2003.

Huters, Theodore. *Bringing the World Home: Appropriating the West in Late Qing and Early Republican China*. Honolulu: University of Hawai'i Press, 2005.

Huters, Theodore. "Cultivating the 'Great Divide': Urban Literature in Early Twentieth-Century China." *Renditions* 87 and 88 (Spring and Autumn 2017): 7–18.

Huyssen, Andreas. *After the Great Divide: Modernism, Mass Culture, Postmodernism*. Bloomington: Indiana University Press, 1986.

Ikeda Tomoe 池田智惠. "*Jindai xiayi yingxiong zhuan* yu *Guoji daguan*: guanyu Minguo wuxia xiaoshuo he jindai wushu de chengli" 《近代俠义英雄传》与《国技大观》—关于民国武侠小说和近代武术的成立 [*Chivalric Heroes of Modern Times* and the *Panorama of National Skills*: on Republican-era martial arts fiction and the establishment of the modern martial arts]. 华东师范大学中国现代文学资料与研究中心 (Center for Modern Chinese Literature Studies, East China Normal University), July 8, 2005.

Isaacson, Nathaniel. *Celestial Empire: The Emergence of Chinese Science Fiction*. Middletown, CT: Wesleyan University Press, 2017.

Jiang Zhuchao 蔣箸超, ed. *Minquan su cui bian* 民權素粹編 [The best of *Elements of People's Rights*]. 4 vols. Shanghai: Minquan chuban bu, 1926.

Keulemans, Paize. *Sound Rising from Paper: Nineteenth-Century Martial Arts Fiction and the Chinese Acoustic Imagination*. Cambridge, MA: Harvard University Asia Center, 2014.

Kinkley, Jeffrey. *Chinese Justice, the Fiction: Law and Literature in Modern China*. Stanford, CA: Stanford University Press, 2000.

Kuzay, Stefan. "A Tale of Five Families Between Empire and Republic: Li Hanqiu's Novel *The Tides of Guangling* (*Guangling chao*, 1909–1919)." In *Yangzhou: A Place in Literature*, ed. Roland Altenburger et al., 282–307. Honolulu: University of Hawai'i Press, 2015.

Lam, Nga Li. "New World, *New World Daily*, and the Culture of Amusement in Early Republican China." PhD diss., Hong Kong University of Science and Technology, 2015.

Lee, Haiyan. *The Stranger and the Chinese Moral Imagination*. Stanford, CA: Stanford University Press, 2014.

Legge, James, trans. *The Sacred Books of China: The Texts of Tâoism*. Part 1: *The Tâo Teh King, The Writings of Kwang-sze, Books I–XVII*. Oxford: Clarendon, 1891.

Lei Gao 壘高. "Jiuju he shenguai dianying de fandong" 舊劇和神怪電影的反動 [The reactionary nature of old-style drama and fantasy film]. *Xinsheng xunkan* 新聲旬刊 [New voice] no. 3 (January 22, 1931): 9–10.

Lengxue 冷血 [Chen Jinghan 陳景韓]. "Xiake tan: Daoyusheng zhuan" 俠客談：刀餘生專 [Tales of knights-errant: the biography of Spared-the-Blade]. *Xinxin xiaoshuo* 新新小說 [New new fiction] 1, nos. 1–2 (1904).

Li Changjian 李昌鑑. "Shenguai pian zhen hairen" 神怪片真害人 [Fantasy films are truly harmful]. *Yingxi shenghuo* 影戲生活 [Movie Weekly] 1, no. 7 (February 20, 1931): 14–16.

Li Suyuan 酈苏元 and Hu Jubin 胡菊彬. *Zhongguo wusheng dianying shi* 中国无声电影史 [A history of silent film in China]. Beijing: Zhongguo dianying chubanshe, 1996.

Li Xingyang 李兴阳. "Wan Qing xiaoshuo leixing lilun de liubian yu yiyi" 晚清小说类型理论的流变与意义 [The development and significance of late-Qing theories of fictional types]. *Hubei shifan xueyuan xuebao (zhexue shehui kexue ban)* 湖北师范学院学报 (哲学社会科学版) 26 (2006, no. 4): 45–48.

Li Zhaozhong 李兆忠. *Xuannao de luozi: liuxue yu Zhongguo xiandai wenhua* 喧闹的骡子—留学与中国现代文化 [A braying mule: overseas study and modern Chinese culture]. Beijing: Renmin wenxue chubanshe, 2010.

Liang Qichao 梁启超. "Gao xiaoshuo jia" 告小說家 [An indictment of the fiction writers]. *Zhonghua xiaoshuojie* 中華小說界 [Chung Hwa Novel Magazine] 2, no. 1 (1915).

Liang Qichao. "On the Relationship Between Fiction and the Government of the People." Trans. Gek Nai Cheng. In *Modern Chinese Literary Thought: Writings on Literature, 1893–1945*, ed. Kirk A. Denton, 74–81. Stanford, CA: Stanford University Press, 1996.

Liang Qichao 梁啓超. "Zhongguo weiyi zhi wenxue bao *Xin xiaoshuo*" 中國唯一之文學報新小說 [China's only literary journal: *New Fiction*]. *Xinmin congbao* 新民叢報 14 (1902).

Lin Baochun 林保淳. "Cong 'Ci Ma an' dao *Toumingzhuang*: you lishi dao wenxue de zhuanzhe" 從「刺馬案」到《投名狀》—由歷史到文學的轉折 [From "the Ma assassination case" to *The Warlords*: the shift from history to literature]. Forthcoming.

Lin Wei 林薇. "Lin Shu zizhuan de wuxia xiaoshuo: *Jiji yuwen* zui zao banben bianzheng" 林纾自撰的武侠小说—《技击余闻》最早版本辨正 [Lin Shu's martial arts fiction: verifying the earliest edition of *Anecdotes of the Combat Arts*]. *Xin wenxue shiliao* 新文学史料 no. 3 (1999): 195–96.

Lin Xi 林熙. "Pingjiang Buxiaosheng Xiang Kairan" 平江不肖生向愷然. *Wanxiang* 萬象 2 (August 1975): 40–43. Reprinted in *Minguo jiupai wenyi yanjiu ziliao* 民國舊派文藝研究資料 [Materials for the study of Republican-era old-school literature] (Jiulong: Shiyong shuju, 1978).

Ling Mengchu凌濛初. *Erke Pai'an jingqi* 二刻拍案驚奇 [Slapping the table in amazement at the marvels, second collection]. Nanjing: Jiangsu guji chubanshe, 1990.

Link, E. Perry, Jr. *Mandarin Ducks and Butterflies: Popular Fiction in Early-Twentieth-Century Chinese Cities*. Berkeley: University of California Press, 1981.

Link, E. Perry, Jr. "Traditional-Style Popular Urban Fiction in the Teens and Twenties." In *Modern Chinese Literature in the May Fourth Era*, ed. Merle Goldman, 326–49. Cambridge, MA: Harvard University Press, 1977.

Liu, Petrus. *Stateless Subjects: Chinese Martial Arts Literature and Postcolonial History*. Ithaca, NY: Cornell University East Asia Program, 2011.

Liu Ts'un-yan, ed. *Chinese Middlebrow Fiction from the Ch'ing and Early Republican Eras*. Hong Kong: Chinese University Press, 1984.

Lorge, Peter A. *Chinese Martial Arts: From Antiquity to the Twenty-First Century*. Cambridge: Cambridge University Press, 2012.

Lu Dan'an 陸澹盦. "Jiyu zhuimo" 輯餘贅墨 [Post-editorial addenda]. *Zhentan shijie* 偵探世界 [Detective world] no. 1 (1923).

Lu, Hanchao. *Street Criers: A Cultural History of Chinese Beggars*. Stanford, CA: Stanford University Press, 2005.

Lu Hsun. *A Brief History of Chinese Fiction*. Trans. Yang Hsien-yi and Gladys Yang. 3rd ed. Peking: Foreign Languages Press, 1976 (2nd printing, 1982).

Lu, Sheldon Hsiao-peng. *From Historicity to Fictionality: The Chinese Poetics of Narrative*. Stanford, CA: Stanford University Press, 1994.

Lu Xun. *Diary of a Madman and Other Stories*. Trans. William A. Lyell. Honolulu: University of Hawai'i Press, 1990.

Lu Xun 魯迅. *Zhongguo xiaoshuo shi lüe* 中國小說史略 [A Brief History of Chinese Fiction]. Taipei: Fengyun shidai, 1989.

Luan Meijian 欒梅健. *Tongsu wenxue zhi wang: Bao Tianxiao zhuan* 通俗文學之王—包天笑傳 [The king of popular literature: a biography of Bao Tianxiao]. Taipei: Yeqiang chubanshe, 1996.

Ma, Y. W. "Fiction." In *The Indiana Companion to Traditional Chinese Literature*, ed. William H. Nienhauser Jr., 31–48. Bloomington: Indiana University Press, 1986.

Ma Youyuan 馬幼垣 (Y. W. Ma). "*Shuihu zhuan* yu Zhongguo wuxia xiaoshuo de chuantong" 水滸傳與中國武俠小說的傳統 [*The Water Margin* and China's tradition of martial arts fiction]. In *Shuihu lunheng* 水滸論衡 [On *The Water Margin*], 187–210. Taibei: Lianjing chuban shiye gongsi, 1992.

McKeon, Michael, ed. *Theory of the Novel: A Historical Approach.* Baltimore, MD: Johns Hopkins University Press, 2000.

Meulenbeld, Mark R. E. *Demonic Warfare: Daoism, Territorial Networks, and the History of a Ming Novel.* Honolulu: University of Hawai'i Press, 2015.

Morris, Andrew D. *Marrow of the Nation: A History of Sport and Physical Culture in Republican China.* Berkeley: University of California Press, 2004.

"Neizhengbu xunling" 内政部訓令 [Order of the Ministry of the Interior]. *Neizheng gongbao* 内政公报 [Bulletin of the Ministry of the Interior] 5, no. 28 (July 15, 1932): 4.

Okazaki Yumi 岡崎由美. "Wuxia yu ershi shiji chuye de Riben jingxian xiaoshuo" 武俠與二十世紀初葉的日本驚險小說 [*Wuxia* and early twentieth-century Japanese adventure fiction]. In *Jin Yong xiaoshuo yu ershi shiji Zhongguo wenxue guoji xueshu yantaohui lunwen ji* 金庸小說與二十世紀中國文學國際學術研討會論文集 [Collected papers from the international conference on Jin Yong's fiction and twentieth-century Chinese literature], ed. Lin Lijun 林麗君, 211–25. Hong Kong: Minghe she, 2000.

"Pingjiang Buxiaosheng Xiang Kairan, feiju tuoxian jingguo xiangji" 平江不肖生向愷然, 匪窟脫險經過詳記 [A detailed account of Pingjiang Buxiaosheng Xiang Kairan's experiences in escaping the perils of the bandits' lair]. *Yisiqi huabao* 一四七畫報 [One-four-seven pictorial] 17, no. 7 (December 4, 1947).

Pingping 平平. "Xiang Kairan qisu Shihuan shuju" 向愷然起訴時還書局 [Xiang Kairan sues Shihuan shuju]. *Shanghai huabao* 上海畫報 [Pictorial Shanghai] no. 528 (November 18, 1929), 2.

Plaks, Andrew H. *The Four Masterworks of the Ming Novel.* Princeton, NJ: Princeton University Press, 1987.

Plaks, Andrew H. "Towards a Critical Theory of Chinese Narrative." In *Chinese Narratives: Critical and Theoretical Essays*, ed. Andrew H. Plaks, 309–52. Princeton, NJ: Princeton University Press, 1977.

Pollard, David E., ed. *Translation and Creation: Readings of Western Literature in Early Modern China, 1840–1918.* Amsterdam: J. Benjamins, 1998.

Radway, Janice. *Reading the Romance.* Chapel Hill: University of North Carolina Press, 1984.

Rea, Christopher. *The Age of Irreverence: A New History of Laughter in China.* Oakland: University of California Press, 2015.

Reed, Christopher A. *Gutenberg in Shanghai: Chinese Print Capitalism, 1876–1937.* Honolulu: University of Hawai'i Press, 2004.

Reynolds, Douglas Robertson. *China, 1898–1912: The Xinzheng Revolution and Japan.* Cambridge, MA: Council on East Asian Studies, Harvard University, 1993.

Rojas, Carlos, and Andrea Bachner, eds. *The Oxford Handbook of Modern Chinese Literatures.* New York: Oxford University Press, 2016.

Rolston, David L., ed. *How to Read the Chinese Novel.* Princeton, NJ: Princeton University Press, 1990.

Rui Heshi 芮和师 et al., eds. *Yuanyang hudie pai wenxue ziliao* 鸳鸯蝴蝶派文学资料 [Materials on mandarin duck and butterfly literature]. 2 vols. Fuzhou: Fujian renmin chuban she, 1984.

Rui Heshi 芮和师 et al., eds. *Yuanyang hudie pai wenxue ziliao* 鸳鸯蝴蝶派文学资料 [Materials on mandarin duck and butterfly school literature]. 2 vols. Beijing: Zhishi chanquan chuban she, 2010.

Schafer, Edward H. "The Table of Contents of the *Tai p'ing kuang chi*." *Chinese Literature: Essays, Articles, Reviews* 2 (1980): 258–63.

Shahar, Meir. *Crazy Ji: Chinese Religion and Popular Literature*. Cambridge, MA: Harvard University Asia Center, 1998.

Shen Yanbing 沈雁冰 [Mao Dun 茅盾]. "Fengjian de xiaoshimin wen yi" 封建的小市民文藝 [The feudal literature and art of the petty bourgeoisie]. *Dongfang zazhi* 東方雜誌 [The Eastern Miscellany] 30, no. 3 (February 1, 1933): 17–18.

Shen Yanbing 沈雁冰. "Ziranzhuyi yu Zhongguo xiandai xiaoshuo" 自然主義與中國現代小說 [Naturalism and modern Chinese fiction]. *Xiaoshuo yuebao* 小說月報 [The Short Story Magazine] 13, no. 7 (July 10, 1922).

Shen Zhifang 沈知方. "Xuanyan" 宣言 [Manifesto]. *Zhentan shijie* 偵探世界 [Detective world] no. 1 (1923).

Shi Jiqun 施濟羣 [Jiqun 濟群]. "Bianji zhe yan" 編輯者言 [Editor's remarks]. *Hong zazhi* 紅雜誌 [The Scarlet Magazine] 1, no. 22 (January 1923).

Shi Jiqun 施濟羣 [Jiqun 濟群]. "Bianji zhe yan" 編輯者言 [Editor's remarks]. *Hong zazhi* 紅雜誌 [The Scarlet Magazine] 2, no. 40 (May 7, 1924).

Shi Juan 石娟. "Cong *Jianghu qixia zhuan* dao *Huoshao Hongliansi*" 从《江湖奇侠传》到《火烧红莲寺》 [From *Marvelous Gallants of the Rivers and Lakes* to *The Burning of Red Lotus Temple*]. In *Pingjiang Buxiaosheng yanjiu zhuanji* 平江不肖生研究专辑 [Collected Studies on Pingjiang Buxiaosheng], ed. Zeng Pingyuan 曾平原 and He Linfu 何林福, 174–79. Shanghai: Fudan daxue chubanshe, 2013.

Shi Juan 石娟. "Minguo wuxia xiaoshuo de fuwenben jiangou yu yuedu shichang shengcheng: yi Pingjiang Buxiaosheng *Jianghu qixia zhuan* wei hexin 民国武侠小说的副文本建构与阅读市场生成——以平江不肖《江湖奇侠传》为核心 [Paratextual construction and the rise of the readership market for Republican-era martial arts fiction: with a focus on Pingjiang Buxiaosheng's *Marvelous Gallants of the Rivers and Lakes*]. *Xinan daxue xuebao (shehui kexue ban)* 西南大学学报(社会科学版) 42, no. 5 (September 2016): 127–38.

Shi, Liang. *Reconstructing the Historical Discourse of Traditional Chinese Fiction*. Lewiston, NY: Edwin Mellen, 2002.

Shih, Shu-mei. *The Lure of the Modern: Writing Modernism in Semicolonial China, 1917–1937*. Berkeley: University of California Press, 2001.

Starr, Chloë F. *Red-Light Novels of the Late Qing*. Leiden: Brill, 2007.

Su Manshu 蘇曼殊 et al. *Minquan su biji huicui* 民權素筆記薈萃 [Collected short prose from *Elements of People's Rights*]. *Minguo biji xiaoshuo daguan* 民國筆記小說大觀 series 3, no. 8. Taiyuan: Shanxi gu ji chu ban she, 1997.

Todorov, Tzvetan. *The Poetics of Prose*. Translated by Richard Howard. Ithaca, NY: Cornell University Press, 1977.

Tsu, Jing. *Failure, Nationalism, and Literature: The Making of Modern Chinese Identity, 1895–1937*. Stanford, CA: Stanford University Press, 2006.

van Gulik, Robert Hans. *The Gibbon in China: An Essay in Chinese Animal Lore*. Leiden: E. J. Brill, 1967.

Wang Chaoguang 汪朝光. "Sanshi niandai chuqi de Guomindang dianying jiancha zhidu" 三十年代初期的国民党电影检查制度 [The film censorship system of the Nationalist Party in the early 1930s]. *Dianying yishu* 电影艺术 3 (1997): 60–66.

Wang, David Der-wei. *Fin-de-Siècle Splendor: Repressed Modernities of Late Qing Fiction, 1849–1911*. Stanford, CA: Stanford University Press, 1997.

Wang, Fei-Hsien, "Creating New Order in the Knowledge Economy: The Curious Journey of Copyright in China, 1868–1937." PhD diss., University of Chicago, 2012.

Wang Li 王立. "Pingjiang Buxiaosheng wuxia xiaoshuo zhong de 'shifu qiu xiantu' muti" 平江不肖生武侠小说中的'师傅求贤徒'母题 [The theme of 'the master seeking a worthy student' in Pingjiang Buixiaosheng's martial arts fiction]. In *Pingjiang Buxiaosheng yanjiu zhuanji* 平江不肖生研究专辑 [Collected studies on Pingjiang Buxiaosheng], ed. Zeng Pingyuan 曾平原 and He Linfu 何林福, 154–65. Shanghai: Fudan daxue chubanshe, 2013.

Wang Xiangyuan 王向远. "Jindai Zhong Ri xiaoshuo de ticai leixing ji qi guanlian" 近代中日小说的题材类型及其关联 [Thematic categories of fiction in early modern China and Japan and their relationship]. *Qi Lu xuekan* 齐鲁学刊 no. 3 (1997): 81–86.

Wang Yunzhang 王蘊章. "Zuanshi an" 鑽石案 [The case of the diamond]. *Xiaoshuo yuebao* [The Short Story Magazine] 1, no. 1 (August 29, 1910).

Wang Zuoxian 王作贤 et al., eds. *Minguo diyi an* 民国第一案 [The Republic's most notorious case]. Jinan: Shandong renmin chubanshe, 1990.

Wei Shaochang 魏紹昌. *Wo kan yuanyang hudie pai* 我看鴛鴦蝴蝶派 [My view of the Mandarin Ducks and Butterflies school]. Taibei: Taiwan shangwu yinshu guan, 1992.

Wei Shaochang 魏紹昌, ed. *Yuanyang hudie pai yanjiu ziliao* 鴛鴦蝴蝶派研究資料 [Research materials on the mandarin duck and butterfly school]. Shanghai: Shanghai wenyi chubanshe, 1962; repr., Hong Kong: Sanlian shudian, 1980.

Wenkang 文康. *Ernü yingxiong zhuan* 兒女英雄傳 [A tale of romance and heroism]. 2 vols. Jinan: Qi Lu shushe, 1989.

"Wenzhang zengming zhi Xiang Kairan" 文章憎命之向愷然 [Xiang Kairan, abhorring the writer's fate]. *Laoshi hua* 老實話 [Straight talk] no. 35 (1935): 10–11.

Wong, Timothy C. *Stories for Saturday: Twentieth-Century Chinese Popular Fiction*. Honolulu: University of Hawai'i Press, 2003.

Xiang Kairan 向愷然 [Xiake shanren 俠客山人]. *Banye feitou ji* 半夜飛頭記 [The flying head at midnight]. Shanghai: Wuqiang shuju, 1923.

Xiang Kairan 向愷然 [Kairan 愷然]. "Bianse tan" 變色談 [Turning pale]. *Minquan su* 民權素 [Elements of people's rights] no. 16 (March 1916).

Xiang Kairan 向愷然 [Buxiaosheng 不肖生]. "Bianse tan" 變色談 [Turning pale]. *Shehui zhi hua* 社會之花 [Flowers of society] no. 1 (January 5, 1924).

Xiang Kairan. "The Black Cat." In *Stories for Saturday: Twentieth-Century Chinese Popular Fiction*, ed. Timothy C. Wong, 147–57. Honolulu: University of Hawai'i Press, 2003.

Xiang Kairan 向愷然 [Pingjiang Buxiaosheng 平江不肖生]. *Dadao Wang Wu Huo Yuanjia Xiayi yingxiong zhuan* 大刀王五霍元甲侠义英雄传 [The chivalric heroes Broadsworder Wang Wu and Huo Yuanjia]. 2 vols. Changsha, Yuelu shushe, 1984.

Xiang Kairan 向愷然 [Kairan 愷然]. "Danchi xue" 丹墀血 [Blood on the palace steps]. *Xiaoshuo hai* 小說海 [Ocean of fiction] 2, no. 11 (November 1916).

Xiang Kairan 向愷然. "Danfeng chao yang" 丹凤朝阳 [The phoenix greets the sun]. Wenshi shiyi 文史拾遗.

Xiang Kairan 向愷然. "Gaolan chenglou shang de baiyuan" 皋蘭城樓上的白猿 [The white ape in the Gaolan gate-tower]. *Hong zazhi* 紅雜誌 [Scarlet Magazine] 2, no. 3 (August 24, 1923).

Xiang Kairan 向愷然. "Hama yao" 蝦蟆妖 [The toad demon]. *Hong zazhi* 紅雜誌 [Scarlet Magazine] 2, no. 31 (March 7, 1924).

Xiang Kairan 向愷然. "Haoqi yu haose yu" 好奇歟好色歟 [Curiosity or lust?]. *Zhentan shijie* 偵探世界 [Detective world] nos. 3–4 (1923).

Xiang Kairan 向愷然. "Heimao yu qi'an" 黑貓與奇案 [A black cat and a strange case]. *Hong meigui* 紅玫瑰 [The scarlet rose] 1, no. 21 (December 20, 1924).

Xiang Kairan 向愷然 [Buxiaosheng 不肖生]. *Huitou shi an* 回頭是岸 [Repent and be saved]. *Xin Shanghai* 新上海 [New Shanghai] 1, no. 1 through 2, no. 3 (May 1925–December 1926).

Xiang Kairan 向愷然 [Pingjiang Buxiaosheng 平江不肖生]. *Jianghu guaiyi zhuan* 江湖怪異傳 [Strange phenomena of the rivers and lakes]. Shanghai: Shijie shuju, 1923.

Xiang Kairan 向愷然 [Pingjiang Buxiaosheng 平江不肖生]. *Jianghu qixia zhuan* 江湖奇俠传 [Marvelous gallants of the rivers and lakes]. Changsha: Yuelu shushe, 1986.

Xiang Kairan 向愷然 [Pingjiang Buxiaosheng 平江不肖生]. *Jianghu xiaoxia zhuan* 江湖小俠传 [Young gallants of the rivers and lakes]. Beijing: Zhongguo youyi chuban gongsi, 2012.

Xiang Kairan 向愷然 [Buxiaosheng 不肖生]. *Jindai xiayi yingxiong zhuan* 近代俠義英雄傳 [Chivalric heroes of modern times]. 4 vols. Jindai Zhongguo wuxia xiaoshuo mingzhu daxi 近代中國武俠小說名著大系, ed. Ye Hongsheng 葉洪生. Taibei: Lianjing chuban shiye gongsi, 1984.

Xiang Kairan 向愷然 [Pingjiang Buxiaosheng 平江不肖生]. *Jindai xiayi yingxiong zhuan* 近代俠義英雄傳 [Chivalric heroes of modern times]. 5 vols. Taipei: Shijie shuju, 2004.

Xiang Kairan 向愷然 [Buxiaosheng 不肖生]. "Kou hun" 寇婚 [Stolen wedding]. *Cunxin* 寸心 [Heart] no. 3 (July 1917).

Xiang Kairan 向愷然. "Lan fashi ji: Lan fashi da hu" 藍法師記: 藍法師打虎 [Reverend Lan fights a tiger]. *Xingqi* 星期 [The Sunday] no. 36 (November 1922).

Xiang Kairan 向愷然. "Lan fashi ji: Lan fashi zhuo gui" 藍法師記: 藍法師捉鬼 [Reverend Lan catches a ghost]. *Xingqi* 星期 [The Sunday] no. 34 (October 1922).

Xiang Kairan 向愷然. "Li Cunyi xunji echuan" 李存義殉技訛傳 [The unfounded rumor of Li Cunyi's taking his art to the grave]. *Hong meigui* 紅玫瑰 [Scarlet rose] 1, no. 6 (September 6, 1924).

Xiang Kairan. "Li Zongren Yang Du tong yi wenzi xianzhi yu Yuan Shikai" 李宗仁楊度同以文字現知于袁世凱 [Li Zongren and Yang Du display their learning to Yuan Shikai]. *Xin xuefeng* 新學風 [New scholarship] no. 1 (1946).

Xiang Kairan 向愷然. "Lieren ou ji" 獵人偶記 [A hunter's miscellany]. *Xingqi* 星期 [The Sunday] nos. 27–30, 32, 35 (August–October 1922).

Xiang Kairan 向愷然 [Buxiaosheng 不肖生]. *Liudong waishi* 留東外史 [The unofficial history of sojourners in Japan]. Shanghai: Minquan chubanbu, 1916; 4th printing, 1924.

Xiang Kairan 向恺然 [Buxiaosheng 不肖生]. *Liudong waishi* 留东外史 [The unofficial history of sojourners in Japan]. Zhongguo jindai xiaoshuo da xi 中国近代小说大系. 3 vols. Nanchang: Baihua zhou wenyi chubanshe, 1991.

Xiang Kairan 向愷然 [Buxiaosheng 不肖生]. *Liudong waishi bu* 留東外史補 [Supplement to the unofficial history of sojourners in Japan]. Shanghai: Dadong shuju, 1926.

Xiang Kairan 向愷然 [Xiang Kui Kairan 向逵愷然]. *Longhu chunqiu* 龍虎春秋 [Annals of the dragon and tiger]. Shanghai: Jiaotong tushuguan, 1919.

Xiang Kairan 向愷然 [Pingjiang Buxiaosheng平江不肖生]. *Pingjiang Buxiaosheng* 平江不肖生. Comp. Fan Boqun 范伯群, ed. Zhongguo xiandai wenxueguan 中国现代文学馆. Beijing: Huaxia chubanshe, 2000.

Xiang Kairan 向愷然. "Quanshu" 拳術 [The art of pugilism]. *Zhonghua xiaoshuo jie* 中華小說界 [Chung Hwa Novel Magazine] 2, nos. 7–12 (July–December 1915).

Xiang Kairan 向愷然 [Buxiaosheng 不肖生]. *Quanshu* 拳術 [The art of pugilism]. Taibei: Hualian chubanshe, 1983; reprint of 1926 printing (11th printing) of 1916 ed.

Xiang Kairan 向愷然 [Xiang Kui Kairan 向逵愷然]. "Quanshu jianwen lu" 拳術見聞錄 [Matters pugilistic, seen and heard]. *Zhonghua xiaoshuo jie* 中華小說界 [Chung Hwa Novel Magazine] 3, nos. 3–5 (March–May 1916).

Xiang Kairan 向愷然 [Xiang Kui Kairan 向逵愷然]. *Quanshu jianwen lu* 拳術見聞錄 [Matters pugilistic, seen and heard]. Shanghai: Taidong tushu ju 泰東圖書局, 1919.

Xiang Kairan 向愷然. "Quanshujia Li Cunyi zhi si" [The death of boxing master Li Cunyi] 拳術家李存義之死. *Zhentan shijie* 偵探世界 [Detective world] no. 24 (1924).

Xiang Kairan 向愷然. "Sange houer de gushi" 三個猴兒的故事 [Three monkey tales]. *Hong zazhi* 紅雜誌 [Scarlet Magazine] 1, no. 50 (July 27, 1924).

Xiang Kairan 向愷然 [Buxiaosheng 不肖生]. "*The Unofficial History of Sojourners in Japan* (excerpt)." Trans. John Christopher Hamm. *Renditions* 87–88 (Spring/Autumn 2017): 155–64.

Xiang Kairan 向愷然 [Kairan 愷然]. "Wan Luo" 皖羅 [Luo of Anhui]. *Xiaoshuo hai* 小說海 [Ocean of fiction] 2, no. 12 (December 1916).

Xiang Kairan 向愷然 [Pingjiang Buxiaosheng 平江不肖生]. "Wo touru Fomen de jingguo" 我投入佛門的經過 [How I became a Buddhist]. *Jue you qing* 覺有情 [The Enlightenment] 9, no. 8 (August 1, 1948): 23–24.

Xiang Kairan 向愷然. "Wo yanjiu quanjiao zhi shidi lianxi" 我研究拳腳之實地練習 [My hands-on experience in the study of the martial arts]. *Xingqi* 星期 [The Sunday] no. 50 (March 4, 1923).

Xiang Kairan 向愷然 [Kairan 愷然]. "Wulai chanshi" 無賴禪師 [The reverend Wulai]. *Xiaoshuo hai* 小說海 [Ocean of fiction] 2, no. 8 (August 1916).

Xiang Kairan 向愷然. "Xiang Kairan xiansheng lian taijiquan de jingyan" 向愷然先生練太極拳的經驗 [Mr. Xiang Kairan's experience practicing *taijiquan*]. In Wu Zhiqing 吳志青, *Taiji zhengzong* 太极正宗 [The orthodox tradition of *taiji*]. Shanghai: Dadong shuju, 1936; repr., Hong Kong, Jinhua chubanshe, n.d.

Xiang Kairan 向愷然 [Kairan 愷然]. "Zhu Sangongzi" 朱三公子 [Third master Zhu]. *Xiaoshuo hai* 小說海 [Ocean of fiction] 2, no. 10 (October 1916).

Xiang Yixue 向一学. "Huiyi fuqin de yisheng" 回忆父亲的一生 [Remembering my father's life]. In Pingjiang Buxiaosheng 平江不肖生, *Jianghu qixia zhuan* 江湖奇侠传. Changsha: Yuelu shushe, 1986.

Xiao, Zhiwei. "Film Censorship in China, 1927–1937." PhD diss., University of Chicago, 1994.

Xin Tinting 辛亭亭. "Chen Jinghan zhubian shenfen kaozheng ji *Xinxin xiaoshuo* 'duanming' yuanyin tanjiu" 陈景韩主编身份考证及《新新小说》"短命"原因探究 [Verification of Chen Jinghan's role as editor-in-chief and an inquiry into the reasons for the "brief lifespan" of *New New Fiction*]. *Suzhou jiaoyu xueyuan xuebao* 苏州教育学院学报 33, no. 5 (October 2016): 19–24.

"Xiuzheng *Honglian si* yingpian qingdan" 修正红莲寺映片清单 [Itemized list for the revision of the film *Red Lotus Temple*]. *Jiangxi jiaoyu xingzheng xunkan* 江西教育行政旬刊 [Ten-day bulletin of the Jiangxi Educational Administration] 1, no. 3 (March 21, 1932): 8–11.

Xu Sinian 徐斯年. "Xiang Kairan de 'xiandai wuxia chuanqi huayu'" [Xiang Kairan's "discourse of modern chivalric romance"]. 向恺然的"现代武侠传奇话语". *Zhongguo xiandai wenxue yanjiu congkan* no. 4 (2012): 88–97.

Xu Sinian 徐斯年 and Liu Xiang'an 刘祥安. "Wuxia huidang bian" 武侠会党编 [Martial arts and secret societies]. In *Zhongguo jin xiandai tongsu wenxue shi* 中国近现代通俗文学史 [A history of recent-era and modern Chinese popular literature], ed. Fan Boqun, 1:439–735. Nanjing: Jiangsu jiaoyu chubanshe, 1999.

Xu Sinian 徐斯年 and Xiang Xiaoguang 向晓光. "Pingjiang Buxiaosheng Xiang Kairan nianbiao" 平江不肖生向恺然年表 [Chronological table for Pingjiang Buxiaosheng Xiang Kairan]. *Xinan daxue xuebao (shehui kexue ban)* 西南大学学报 (社会科学版) 38, no. 6 (November 2012): 95–109.

Xu Sinian 徐斯年 and Xiang Xiaoguang 向晓光. "Xiang Kairan (Pingjiang Buxiaosheng) nianbiao (buding gao)" 向恺然 (平江不肖生) 年表 (补订稿) [Chronological table for Xiang Kairan (Pingjiang Buxiaosheng): revised and corrected version]. In *Pingjiang Buxiaosheng yanjiu zhuanji* 平江不肖生研究专辑 [Collected studies on Pingjiang Buxiaosheng], ed. Zeng Pingyuan 曾平原 and He Linfu 何林福, 325–55. Shanghai: Fudan daxue chubanshe, 2013.

Xu Sinian 徐斯年, Xiang Xiaoguang 向晓光, and Yang Rui 杨锐. "Pingjiang Buxiaosheng Xiang Kairan nianbiao: zengbu gao" 平江不肖生向恺然年表 (增补稿) [Chronological table for Pingjiang Buxiaosheng Xiang Kairan: expanded and revised version]. *Pinbao* 品报 31 (July 2015): 2–28.

Xu, Xueqing. "The Mandarin Duck and Butterfly School." In *Literary Societies of Republican China*, ed. Kirk A. Denton and Michel Hockx, 47–78. Lanham, MD: Lexington Books, 2008.

Xu Zhuodai 徐卓呆 [Zhuodai 卓呆]. "Fagao hou" 發稿後 [Post-production]. *Xin Shanghai* 新上海 [New Shanghai] 2, no. 4 (January 1927).

Xu Zhuodai 徐卓呆. "Xiaoshuo wuti lu" 小說無題錄 [Untitled notes on fiction]. *Xiaoshuo shijie* 小說世界 [The Story World] 1, no. 7 (1923).

Yao Gengkui 姚賡夔. "Guaixia" 怪俠 [The strange gallant]. *Xingqi* 星期 [The Sunday] no. 50 (March 1923).

Ye Hongsheng 葉洪生. "Zhongguo wuxia xiaoshuo shi lun" 中國武俠小說史論 [On the history of Chinese martial arts fiction]. In *Ye Hongsheng lun jian: wuxia xiaoshuo tan yi lu* 葉洪生論劍: 武俠小說談藝錄 [Ye Hongsheng speaks of the sword: talks on the art of martial arts fiction], 3–110. Taipei: Lianjing chuban shiye gongsi, 1994.

Yeh, Catherine Vance. *The Chinese Political Novel: Migration of a World Genre*. Cambridge, MA: Harvard University Asia Center, 2015.

Yeh, Catherine Vance. *Shanghai Love: Courtesans, Intellectuals, and Entertainment Culture, 1850–1910*. Seattle: University of Washington Press, 2006.

Young, Ernest P. "Ch'en T'ien-hua (1875–1905): A Chinese Nationalist." *Papers on China* 13 (1959): 113–62.

Yu, Hongyuan. "*Shuihu zhuan* as Elite Cultural Discourse: Reading, Writing, and the Making of Meaning." PhD diss., Ohio State University, 1999.

Yuan Jin 袁进. "Shilun *Guanglingchao* yu Min chu shehui xiaoshuo" 试论《广陵潮》与民初社会小说 [A tentative discussion of *Yangzhou Tides* and the early Republican social novel]. *Xiandai Zhongwen xue kan* 现代中文学刊 7, no. 4 (2010): 22–26.

Yuan Jin 袁进, ed. *Zhipian zhanzheng: Hong zazhi, Hong meigui cuibian* 纸片战争—《红杂志》《红玫瑰》萃编 [Paper wars: selections from *Scarlet Magazine* and *Scarlet Rose*]. Shanghai: Shanghai guji chubanshe, 1999.

Yuan Jin 袁进. *Zhongguo wenxue de jindai biange* 中国文学的近代变革 [The early-modern transformation of Chinese literature]. Guilin: Guangxi shifan daxue chubanshe, 2006.

Yuan Jin 袁進. *Zhongguo xiaoshuo de jindai biange* 中國小說的近代變革 [The early-modern transformation of Chinese fiction]. Beijing: Zhongguo shehui kexue chubanshe, 1992.

Zeitlin, Judith T. *Historian of the Strange: Pu Songling and the Chinese Classical Tale*. Stanford, CA: Stanford University Press, 1993.

Zeitlin, Judith T. "*Xiaoshuo*." In *The Novel*, vol. 1: *History, Geography, and Culture*, ed. Franco Moretti, 249–61. Princeton, NJ: Princeton University Press, 2006.

Zeng Pingyuan 曾平原 and He Linfu 何林福, eds. *Pingjiang Buxiaosheng yanjiu zhuanji* 平江不肖生研究专辑 [Collected studies on Pingjiang Buxiaosheng]. Shanghai: Fudan daxue chubanshe, 2013.

Zhang Gansheng 张赣生. *Minguo tongsu xiaoshuo lun gao* 民国通俗小说论稿 [A draft study of Republican-era popular fiction]. Chongqing: Chongqing chubanshe, 1991.

Zhang Shewo 張舍我. "Zhentan xiaoshuo zatan" 偵探小說雜談 [Miscellaneous remarks on detective fiction]. *Banyue* 半月 [The Half Moon Journal] 1, no. 6 (November 29, 1921).

Zhang Tianyi. *The Pidgin Warrior*. Trans. David Hull. London: Balestier, 2017.

Zhang Tongsheng 张同胜. *Shuihu zhuan quanshi shi lun* 《水浒传》诠释史论 [On the history of the interpretation of *The Water Margin*]. Jinan: Qi Lu shushe, 2009.

Zhang, Yingjin. "The Institutionalization of Modern Literary History in China, 1922–1980." *Modern China* 20, no. 3 (July 1994): 347–77.

Zhang, Zhen. *An Amorous History of the Silver Screen: Shanghai Cinema, 1896–1937*. Chicago: University of Chicago Press, 2005.

Zhao, Henry Y. H. "Historiography and Fiction in Chinese Culture." In *The Novel*, vol. 1: *History, Geography, and Culture*, ed. Franco Moretti, 69–93. Princeton, NJ: Princeton University Press, 2006.

Zhao Tiaokuang 趙苕狂 [Tiaokuang 苕狂]. "Bianyu suohua" 編餘瑣話 [Idle editorial remarks], *Hong meigui* 紅玫瑰 [Scarlet rose] 2, no. 32 (July 10, 1926).

Zhao Tiaokuang 趙苕狂 [Tiaokuang 苕狂]. "Huaqian xiaoyu" 花前小語 [Remarks before the flowers]. *Hong meigui* 紅玫瑰 [Scarlet rose] 3, no. 7 (March 5, 1927).

Zhao Tiaokuang 趙苕狂 [Tiaokuang 苕狂]. "Huaqian xiaoyu" 花前小語 [Remarks before the flowers]. *Hong meigui* 紅玫瑰 [Scarlet rose] 3, no. 10 (March 26, 1927).

Zhao Tiaokuang 趙苕狂 [Tiaokuang 苕狂]. "Huaqian xiaoyu" 花前小語 [Remarks before the flowers]. *Hong meigui* 紅玫瑰 [Scarlet rose] 4, no. 35 (January 1, 1929).

Zhongguo dianying ziliaoguan 中国电影资料馆, ed. *Zhongguo yingpian dadian: gushipian, xiqupian, 1905–1930* 中国影片大典: 故事片·戏曲片: 1905–1930 [Encyclopedia of Chinese film: narrative and theatrical films, 1905–1930]. Beijing: Zhongguo dianying chubanshe, 1996.

Ziying 紫英. "Xin'an xieyi" 新庵諧譯 [Harmonious renditions from the new cloister]. *Yueyue xiaoshuo* 月月小說 [The All-Story Monthly] 5 (1907).

Index

Banye feitou ji (*The Flying Head at Midnight*) (Xiang Kairan), 22, 45–47, 51, 131, 234n14

Banyue (*Half Moon Journal*), 89–90, 112, 125, 251n29

Bao Tianxiao, 115, 158; on death rumors, 28, 254n64; "A Female Gallant for the World" by, 85–86; as *The Grand Magazine* editor, 23, 73, 79, 84; martial arts fiction promotion of, 84–85; Xiang Kairan introduction to, 22–23; on Xiang Kairan's contribution to martial arts fiction, 12, 48–49, 66–67; on Xiang Kairan's monkeys, 32–33. *See also Sunday, The*

"Bianse tan" (Xiang Kairan). *See* "Turning Pale"

birth (of Xiang Kairan), 16

Bi Yihong, 86, 111

"Black Cat and a Strange Case, A" ("Heimao yu qi'an") (Xiang Kairan), 146–48

Black Curtain fiction (*heimu xiaoshuo*), 120; critics and commentators on, 106, 108, 182, 223, 250n21; linked-chapter novels dominated by, 106, 108; New Fiction movement relation to, 223; *Sojourners* relation to, 114–15

Blood of the Stallion (*Longju zouxue ji*) (Yao Min'ai), 126, 127–28, 253n56

Bourdieu, Pierre, 225, 226, 232n11

Boxer Uprising, 80; martial arts in China relation to, 198–201; May Fourth movement and, 198–99; *Modern Times* portrayal of, 192–93, 198–201, 208–9, 215, 262n26

brotherhood. *See* sworn brotherhood

Buddhism, 24–25, 48, 57, 154, 240n42

Burning of Red Lotus Temple (*Huoshao honglian si*), 255n76; banning of, 136–40; martial arts popularity relation to, 67; opening of, 132–33;

reception of, 140, 142, 255nn72–73; *Rivers and Lakes* inspiration for, 13, 94, 132–34, 136–40, 176, 254n71

Butterfly fiction: as commercial fiction, 38–39; concept of, 7; critiques and defenses of, 6, 38–41, 64, 88, 105, 231n4, 237n9; entertainment focus of, 38; literary field place for, 41, 64; May Fourth movement on, 40–41, 88; New Literature movement on, 6, 39, 41, 105, 231n4; vernacular modernity relation to, 6

Buxiaosheng (pen name of Xiang Kairan), meaning of, 221–22. *See also* Xiang Kairan

Cai Aiguo, 92

Campany, Robert Ford, 53–54, 141–42

career (of Xiang Kairan); administrative writing, 34; approach to writing, 237n8; best-known works of, 2–3; breaks in, 25–27; context for, 8, 11; critics on long-form writing, 249n71; early works in, 2, 18–19, 20–21, 22, 34, 83, 114–15, 157–58; education influence on, 34; final works of, 30–31, 34; financial support from writing, 34; influences on writing, 227–28; Japan importance in, 179, 190–91, 263n1; literary society membership in, 24, 235n21; as literature teacher, 30; martial arts employment in, 17–18, 19, 22, 29, 30; research sources and approach to, 233n1; self-reflections on writing, 35–37, 40, 215–16, 239n33, 240n42; serialization impact on, 23–24; Shen Zhifang impact on, 12. *See also specific works*

"castigatory fiction" (*qianze xiaoshuo*), 106, 182, 250n20, 260n11

Cawelti, John, 9, 232n16

Changsha: early career of Xiang Kairan in, 18–19; education of Xiang Kairan in, 16–17

Cheng Xiaoqing, 89, 248n63; detective
fiction leadership of, 76; serialization of
works of, 92, 112, 127, *127*, 249n68; on
shenguai films, 138
Cheng Zikai, 20
Chen Jianhua, 113
Chen Jinghan (Lengxue), 81–82, 85
"Chenlun" ("Sinking") (Yu Dafu), 184–85
Chen Tianhua, 17
Chiang Kaishek, 26–29, 35
childhood (of Xiang Kairan), 16
chivalric fiction (*xiayi xiaoshuo*), 66, 67, 79,
87, 91, 178. *See also* martial arts fiction
Chivalric Heroes of Modern Times
(*Modern Times*) (*Jindai xiayi yingxiong
zhuan*) (Xiang Kairan), 121; author-
narrator in, 193–94, 200–201, 213–16,
228; Boxer Uprising portrayal in,
192–93, 198–201, 208–9, 215, 262n26;
completion of, 29; Confucian discourse
and orthodoxy in, 59–60; in *Detective
World*, 12, 23, 25–26, 68, 88, 92–93, *93*,
115; formatting and illustrations of, *93*,
93, *196*; Huo Yuanjia inspiration for and
portrayal in, 176–77, 179, 191–218,
262n25, 262n29; impact/influence of,
14, 176–78, 219, 228–29; Japan/Japanese
treatment in, 203, 205, 206–7; martial
arts cinema influence of, 176–77;
martial arts fiction influence of,
177–78, 219, 228–29; martial arts in,
14–15, 58, 78, 191–219, 262n25, 262n29;
martial arts influenced by, 14, 176;
modernity/modern world treatment in,
177–78, 195–201, 211; monkeys in,
58–60; narrative structure of, 193–94;
nationalism treatment in, 35–36,
191–94, 207–11, 261nn23–24; on
political engagement, 35–36;
publication starts and stops for, 123,
241n54; *Rivers and Lakes* compared
with, 94, 177–78; Rivers and Lakes
(place) use and portrayal in, 195, 198,

210–11; Russian strongman character
in, 195–98, *196*, 200–208, 261n24;
serialization of, 1, 12, 13, 23, 24, 25–26,
68, 88, 92–93, *93*, 97, 115; Shanghai
setting and portrayal in, 201–7, 208;
Sojourners contrasted with, 203–4, 205;
state censorship of, possible, 241n54;
titling and translation significance of,
177, 259n4; transmission of martial arts
in, 191–92, 194–95, 207–10, 217–19;
urban dystopia explored in, 14
civil war, 30, 35
comic books, 10, 134
commercial fiction, 5–6, 34, 65; authenticity
debates and, 50–51; authorial persona in
marketing, 48, 95, 166; Butterfly fiction
as, 38–39; genre and marketing of, 11, 73,
232n16; literary field relation with, 225;
political value of, 226–27; publishing
competition for, 23, 88–90, 228; serial
publications commodification and,
253n48; transmission of tales in, 50–52;
Xiang Kairan on producing, 35–37, 40,
215–16, 240n42
commercial imperative, 38–39
Commercial Press, 50, 73, 88, 104–5
Communist Party: detention of Xiang
Kairan, 30, 34–35, 235n30; opinion of,
Xiang Kairan's, 30–31
Confucian discourse and orthodoxy, 53,
58, 77, 187, 199, 222; in *Modern Times*,
59–60; in *Rivers and Lakes*, 151, 154,
165; the strange relation with, 59–60;
on superstition, 138–39; topics
shunned in, 69
copyright infringement, 130–31
cultural-commodity economy, 11
"Curiosity or Lust?" ("Haoqi yu haose yu")
(Xiang Kairan), 62–63

Dahan bao (newspaper), 19
"Danfeng chao yang" ("The Phoenix Greets
the Sun") (Xiang Kairan), 30–31, 34

dao (the Way), 135; author-narrator on, 222; defining, 154; *Rivers and Lakes* treatment of, 14, 151, 153–57, 163, 164, 172; sexual desire and, 163; transmission of, 14, 39, 151, 153–57, 163, 164

Darwinism, social, 81

Daxia fuchou ji (*The Gallant's Revenge*), 133, 255n72

death (of Xiang Kairan); actual, 31; rumors of, 28–29, 67, 130, 254n64, 254n69

"Death of Boxing Master Li Cunyi, The" ("Quanshujia Li Cunyi zhi si") (Xiang Kairan), 43, 50

depravity: novel, genre of, 182, 260n12; *Sojourners* addressing, 180, 184–85, 186–88, 220–21

Des Forges, Alexander, 100–101, 182–83, 253n48

detective fiction: adventure fiction relation to, 91–92, 248n66; characteristics and influences for, 75–76, 145, 247n57, 248n59; Cheng Xiaoqing as leader in, 76, 138; critics and commentators on, 74–75, 76, 245n29; in *Half Moon Journal*, 89–90; martial arts fiction emergence relation to, 12, 73–74, 79, 83, 90–92, 94–95; New Culture movement on, 76; New Fiction movement and birth of, 74–75, 76; reader/audience role in, 145, 257n22; *Strange Phenomena of the Rivers and Lakes* influenced by, 143, 145; as thematic subgenre, 73–76, 89–90, 94–95; Western traditions of, 75, 244n25, 245n29

Detective World (*Zhentan shijie*), 74; adventure fiction in, 91–92, 248n66; close of, 23, 25–26, 115; contributions to, 12, 23, 24, 25–26, 248n63, 249n68; cover, 93; *Highwaymen of Shandong* in, 125–26, 127, 253n55; launch of, 23, 89, 90; martial arts fiction promotion in, 91–92, 94; *Modern Times* in, 12, 23,

25–26, 68, 88, 92–93, *93*, 115; thematic subgenre influence of, 90

"Diary of a Madman" (Lu Xun), 3, 104, 223

didacticism: of *Repent and Be Saved*, 57; of *Sojourners*, 221; supernatural themes and, 147; *xiaoshuo* characteristics and, 15, 39, 64–65, 211

Doyle, Arthur Conan, 75

Dragons of the Four Seas (*Sihai qunlong ji*) (Yao Min'ai); illustrations and formatting for, 126–27, *127*, 129; linked-chapter novel form for, 124–30, 254n60; sequel, 128

Dream of the Red Chamber, The (*Honglou meng*), 69, 71

Dudbridge, Glen, 62

education (of Xiang Kairan); career relation to, 34; in Changsha, 16–17; in Japan, 17–18, 20

entertainment: Butterfly fiction focus on, 38; as category in periodical publications, 116, 118; detective fiction value as, 75, 76; early works of Xiang Kairan on pleasure of, 19; facticity role in, 50, 165; martial arts value beyond, 216–17, 229; *Rivers and Lakes* value as, 37–38; "Three Monkey Tales" as, 54, 165; *xiaoshuo* as, 15, 42, 64–65, 211

Ernü yingxiong zhuan (*Tale of Romance and Heroism, A*) (Wenkang), 69, 243n5

events, recording of: Ling Mengchu on approach to, 238n21; *Rivers and Lakes* and, 168–72; *xiaoshuo* and, 12, 42, 49–54, 168, 170, 212–14

exposé fiction, 182–83, 191, 223, 260n10, 261n14, 261n20. *See also* Black Curtain fiction; "castigatory fiction"

Extensive Records from the Taiping Reign (*Taiping guangji*), 68

facticity: entertainment function of, 50, 165; *Rivers and Lakes* claims of,

karma, 148, 163–64

Kobun Institute, Japan, 17–18

Kuaihuo (Merry Magazine), 24, 89, 111

Laozi, 222

lawsuit, copyright infringement, 130–31

Lee, Bruce, 14, 176–77, 179

Lengxue (Chen Jinghan), 81–82, 85

Liang Qichao: on "adventure fiction," 80, 248n66; on detective fiction, 74; on fiction genre reform, 70–71, 74, 76, 80, 81; on fiction's power, 139, 140; heroic fiction of, 77; on indigenous narrative traditions, 70–71; New Fiction manifestos of, 7, 35, 69–72, 74, 76, 139, 222–23, 246n40

Liang Yusheng, 94, 96

Liao Lei, 27, 28, 29–30

Liaozhai's Records of the Strange (Liaozhai zhiyi) (Pu Songling), 53, 141

"Lieren ouji" ("A Hunter's Miscellany") (Xiang Kairan), 23, 157–58, 234n17, 257n33

Li Fudong, 262n25, 262n29

Li Hanqiu, 111, 120, 252n43

Lincheng train robbery (1823), 125, 253n54

Ling Mengchu, 53, 238n21

linguistic registers: martial arts fiction employment of, 96; thematic subgenres and, 68, 69; xiaoshuo employment of, 4, 5, 39, 45, 96

linked-chapter novel (zhanghui xiaoshuo); Black Curtain fiction role in, 106, 108; as category of fiction, 72, 97; critics and commentators on, 13, 103–5, 106, 108, 113–14, 128–29, 228, 250n15; Dragons of the Four Seas (Yao Min'ai) as, 124–30, 254n60; formatting and structure for, 107, 108–19, 109, 126–28, 127; history and evolution of, 97–101; martial arts fiction association with, 13, 97, 121, 129, 135; May Fourth critics

on, 103–5, 113, 114, 250n15; narratorial voice in, 98; New Culture movement on, 113; New Fiction promotion of, 99–100, 100; New Literature movement on, 13, 104–5, 113, 228, 250n15; New Shanghai Tides (Zhu Shouju) as case study for, 97, 106–14, 107, 109, 116; "old-style" fiction relation to, 104, 129; Sojourners as, 114–15; valuation differences of, 228; Yao Min'ai on, 128–29

Lin Shu, 79, 82

literary field: Butterfly fiction place in, 41, 64; commercial fiction/publishing relation to, 225; establishment of modern, 225–27; Great Divide in, 224–27; New Literature movement status in, 39; political principles role in, 226–27, 260n7; xiaoshuo influence on, 5

literary genre: defining, 8–10; xiaoshuo as, 3–4, 10, 40–41, 68–73, 223

literature (wenxue), xiaoshuo compared with, 3, 40

Liudong waishi (Xiang Kairan). See Unofficial History of Sojourners in Japan, The

Liu Xing, 27, 28

long-form fiction: critics on Xiang Kairan ability for, 249n71; for martial arts fiction, tradition of, 96–97; short-form distinction from, 101–3, 106, 107, 107, 108, 111, 116, 118, 252n37

Longhu chunqiu (Annals of the Dragon and Tiger) (Xiang Kairan), 22, 234n14

Longju zouxue ji (Blood of the Stallion) (Yao Min'ai), 126, 127–28, 253n56

"low" and "high" literature debate, 224–27

Lu Dan'an, 91–92, 93, 248n63, 249n68

"Luo Seven" ("Luo Qi") (Xiang Kairan), 50

Lu Weichang, 87

Zhifang role in creation of, 12, 23, 24, 66, 67, 68, 87–89, 93–95, 96; *The Sunday* issue dedicated to, 83–87; as thematic subgenre, evolution of, 6, 9–10, 12, 76–95, 97, 228–29; World Book Company promotion of, 88–90, 92, 129, 177; Xiang Kairan role in birth of, 1–2, 7–8, 12, 23, 24, 48–49, 66–68, 87–88, 92–95, 96. *See also* chivalric fiction; "secret society" novels; *specific works*

marvelous, the. *See* strange or marvelous, the

Marvelous Gallants of the Rivers and Lakes (Rivers and Lakes) (Jianghu qixia zhuan) (Xiang Kairan); advertising campaign for, 165, 166; author-narrator on starts and stops of, 121–23; author-narrator on transmission of tale in, 170–71; *Burning of Red Lotus Temple* films adaptation of, 13, 94, 132–34, 136–40, 176, 254n71; Confucian discourse and orthodoxy in, 151, 154, 165; *dao* in, 14, 151, 153–57, 163, 164, 172; death rumors of Xiang Kairan and, 132, 254n69; *Dragons of the Four Seas* (Yao Min'ai) replacing serialization of, 124–25, 126, 127, 129–30; facticity claims of, 166–68, 175, 240n42, 259n46; final chapters/publications of, 121, 132, 172–75; formatting and illustrations of, 93, 116–19, 117, 120, 252n38; historicity in, 168–72, 174–75; impact and influence of, 1, 13, 67, 94, 119–20, 125–29, 132–40, 176, 177–78; Ma assassination significance in, 152, 155, 168–72, 175, 257n30, 259n45; martial arts cinema impacted by, 13, 94, 132–34, 136–40, 176; martial arts fiction role of, 67, 78, 120, 134, 228–29; master-disciple relationships in, 14, 135, 155–56, 159–60; *Modern Times* compared with, 94, 177–78; monkey tales influence in, 162, 241n51; narrative content and structure overview, 150–52; narratorial voice in, 161; *New Shanghai Tides* (Zhu Shouju) serialization compared with, 115–19; outlawry in, 168–70; political engagement in final chapters of, 173–75; publication in book form, 119, 235n24; publication stops and starts of, 25–26, 120–25, 130, 132; Reverend Lan character in, 157–65, 166–67, 258n38; self-reflection on purpose of, 37–38, 122–23; serialization of, 1, 13, 23, 24, 25–26, 29, 84, 93–94, 97, 109, 114–25, 131–32, 158, 172, 235n24, 252n44; serialization transition to *Scarlet Rose*, 119–25, 172; setting of, 152–54; sexual desire in, 162–65, 169–70; social life while writing of, 37–38; the strange addressed in, 14, 53, 153–54; supernatural in, 135–36, 154–55, 258n42; sword-immortals in, 135, 154–55, 165; sworn brotherhood in, 155, 168–70, 171; temporal manipulations in, 160–61; tigers in, 158–59, 162, 163; title translation and meaning, 149–50, 177; transmission centrality for, 150–51, 154–57, 162–65, 169–71; unauthorized portions of, 29, 130, 131–32; Yao Min'ai works compared with, 126–28

Marxist thought, 225, 235n30

master-disciple relationships: alternatives to, 78, 207, 209–10, 217–18; in *Modern Times*, 207, 214; in *Rivers and Lakes*, 14, 135, 155–56, 159–60; sworn brotherhood compared to, 257n30. *See also* transmission

"Matters Pugilistic, Seen and Heard" ("Quanshu jianwen lu") (Xiang Kairan), 20, 21, 50, 83, 114

May Fourth fiction, 7; literary modernity in response to, 224; *Sojourners* contrasted with, 184–85, 189

May Fourth movement, 22, 76; Boxer
Uprising and, 198–99; Butterfly fiction
critiques from, 40–41, 88; fiction
categorization by, 101–2; on linked-
chapter novel, 103–5, 113, 114, 250n15;
New Literature movement relation to,
3; questioning paradigm of, 41. *See also*
New Culture movement
medicine, Chinese, 204–7
Merry Magazine (Kuaihuo), 24, 89, 111
military service (of Xiang Kairan), 20, 26,
27–28, 29
modernism, birth of, 224–25
modernity/modern world: Butterfly fiction
and, 6; Chinese martial arts in, role of,
14–15, 77, 78, 87, 197–201; Great Divide
of art and culture in, 224–27; literary
field establishment and, 225–27;
Modern Times treatment of, 177–78,
195–201, 211; New Culture movement
and literary, 224, 226; supernatural and
fantasy in, 140–49
Modern Times (Xiang Kairan). *See*
Chivalric Heroes of Modern Times
monkey mind, 60–61
monkeys: anthropomorphizing of, 56–57,
61, 241n50; female abduction and rape
by, tales of, 61–62; as gatekeepers, 57–59,
63; in *Modern Times*, 58–60; motif of,
11, 41–42, 55–65, 238n19, 241nn50–51; in
Repent and Be Saved, 57–58, 60–61, 63;
in Rivers and Lakes (place/society), 59;
Rivers and Lakes and, 162, 241n51; Xiang
Kairan raising of, 32–34, *33. See also*
"Three Monkey Tales"
morality: New Fiction movement and, 71,
81; supernatural themes and debates
on, 138–39; *xiaoshuo* and debates on,
63–64; *xiaoshuo* poetics and, 185.
See also depravity
"My Hands-On Experience in the Study of
the Martial Arts" ("Wo yanjiu quanjiao
zhi shidi lianxi") (Xiang Kairan), 44, 48

narratorial voice: approach to, 238n21,
239n31; authenticity relation to,
240n42; in linked-chapter novel, 98;
in *Rivers and Lakes*, 161; in "Three
Monkey Tales," 41–43, 48, 50, 54–55.
See also author-narrator
National Film Censorship Committee
(NFCC), 136–37
nationalism: "adventure fiction" relation
to, 79, 248n66; martial arts as vehicle
for, 30, 78, 178, 191–94, 207–10; martial
arts fiction and cultural, 175, 178,
184–85, 188–89, 191–94, 207–10,
259n48; *Modern Times* treatment of,
35–36, 191–94, 207–11, 261nn23–24;
sexual desire relation with, 184–85,
188–89, 261n23; *Sojourners* treatment
of, 184–85, 188–89
Nationalist Party (China), 18, 19, 26–27;
civil war between Communists and, 30,
35; film censorship by, 136–40; martial
arts adopted by, 78
New Culture movement: on detective
fiction, 76; fiction categorization by,
101–2; fiction reform mission of, 223;
on linked-chapter novel, 113; literary
modernity in response to, 224, 226;
on martial arts organizations, 78;
New Literature movement relation to,
3. *See also* May Fourth movement
New Fiction (Xin Xiaoshuo); on genres and
thematic subgenres, 69–70, 71–72, 73,
74, 80; influence of, 71–72; linked-
chapter novels in, 99–100, *100*
New Fiction movement (1902 movement),
91, 99; Black Curtain fiction relation
with, 223; detective fiction and, 74–75,
76; on genres and subgenres, 69–73, 74,
76, 80–81; on indigenous narrative
tradition, 70–71; Liang Qichao
manifestos of, 7, 35, 69–72, 74, 76, 139,
222–23, 246n40; linked-chapter novel
and, 98; martial arts fiction and, 79,

works on hunting, 20, 23, 48, 157–58, 234n17

Trackless Art, 194, 195, 210, 214

traditional fiction. *See xiaoshuo*

transmission: of ancestral line, 151, 155–57, 158, 164, 169, 194–95; of *dao*, 14, 39, 151, 153–57, 163, 164; endorsement implication in, 52; of martial arts, 191–92, 194–95, 207–10, 217–19; *Modern Times* treatment of, 191–92, 194–95, 207–10, 217–19; popular culture circulation and, 51–52, 139; in *Rivers and Lakes*, centrality of, 150–51, 154–57, 162–65, 169–71; of sexual desire, 63, 162–65; of the strange or marvelous, 52–54; of tales/stories, 47, 49–52, 168–72; as *xiaoshuo* feature, 12, 14, 15, 42, 49–54, 63, 146, 168, 178

Turgenev, Ivan, 250n17, 257n33

"Turning Pale" ("Bianse tan") (Xiang Kairan), 21–22, 114, 234n17, 257n32; author-narrator feature of, 43–44, 45, 48; Reverend Lan character in, 157, 158

Unofficial History of Sojourners in Japan, The (Sojourners) (*Liudong waishi*) (Xiang Kairan), 37, 66; author-narrator in *Modern Times* compared with, 228; author-narrator motivations in, 220–21, 223; Black Curtain fiction relation to, 114–15; categorization debates, 182; characters and key themes of, 179–82, 186, 220–21; critics and commentators on, 64, 242n62; didacticism of, 221; exposé fiction affiliation of, 182–83, 191, 260n10; Japan/Japanese settings and treatment in, 179–91; linked-chapter novel form of, 114–15; martial arts in, role of, 186–91, 203–4; May Fourth fiction contrasted with, 184–85, 189; *Modern Times* contrasted with, 203–4, 205; nationalism and sexual desire relation

in, 184–85, 188–89; publication history for, 115; reputation built on, 14, 21, 22, 34; sequels to, 23, 24, 115; serialization of, 112, 115; setting for, significance of, 183; sexual desire and depravity addressed in, 180, 184–85, 186–89, 220–21; "Sinking" (Yu Dafu) compared with, 184–85; women's rights in, 187–88

"urban fiction," 182, 232n8

Wang, David, 182, 250n20

Wang Dungen, 106

Wang Houzhe, 86

Wang Zhiqun, 17–18, 19, 22

warlords/warlordism, 26, 28, 35, 86, 175, 259n48

War of Resistance, 35, 37

Water Margin, The (*Shuihu zhuan*); genre spanning nature of, 246n40; influence of, 71, 79, 83, 170, 193, 214, 246n40; New Fiction movement on genre of, 80–81; sexual desire in, 62, 187

Way, the. *See dao*

Wenkang, Feimo, 69, 243n5

wenxue (literature), *xiaoshuo* compared with, 3, 40

Western traditions: Chinese martial arts competition with, 191, 192–93, 204, 206; Chinese medicine compared with, 204–5; detective fiction in, 75, 244n25, 245n29; literary genre in, 9

women's rights, 187–88

World Book Company, 13, 24, 25, 66, 142; Great Eastern Books competition with, 23, 88–90; linked-chapter novel promotion by, 97, 129; linked-chapter novel structure by, 111; martial arts fiction promotion by, 88–90, 92, 129, 177; *Rivers and Lakes* marketing by, 165, 166; *Rivers and Lakes* unauthorized publications by, 132. *See also Detective World*; *Scarlet Magazine/Scarlet Rose*; Shen Zhifang

"Wo touru Fomen de jingguo" ("How I Became a Buddhist") (Xiang Kairan), 240n42

"Wo yanjiu quanjiao zhi shidi lianxi" ("My Hands-On Experience in the Study of the Martial Arts") (Xiang Kairan), 44, 48

Wuchang Uprising, 18–19

Wu Lingyuan, 86

wuxia xiaoshuo. See martial arts fiction

"Xiake tan" ("Tales of Knight-Errantry") (Chen Jinghan), 81–82, 85

Xiang Kairan (Buxiaosheng); birth, 16; childhood, 16; father, 16, 25, 29; marriage, 29–30; military service, 20, 26, 27–28, 29; pen name, meaning of, 221–22; photographic portrait, 33, 33, 37, 41, 42; Pingjiang county, birth in, 16; social life in Shanghai, 24–25, 37–38; teaching position, 30. *See also* career; Changsha; death; education; reputation; *specific works*

Xiangshan Temple, 30

xiaoshuo: author-narrator as feature of, 11–12, 26, 40, 42–49; category distinctions and evolution for, 3–7, 40, 97, 102; commercial imperative of, 38–39; critiques and defenses of, 4, 12, 39–40, 49–50, 63–64, 106, 149; didacticism as feature of, 15, 39, 64–65, 211; as entertainment, 15, 42, 64–65, 211; fabrication as feature of, 49, 54, 146–47, 170, 240n42, 243n5; facticity of, 14, 39, 49–51, 167, 240n42; historicity of, 39, 49–51, 142, 168–69, 212–14; linguistic registers (classical and vernacular) employed by, 4, 5, 39, 45, 96; literal translation of, 3; literary field influenced by, 5; as literary genre, 3–4, 10, 40–41, 68–73, 223; morality debates on, 63–64; narratorial voice of, 11–12, 42–43; nature and characteristics of,

10–11, 41–54, 63–64, 229; New Literature critiques of, 39–40; New Literature movement birth and, 3, 7; "old-style" fiction relation to, 5–6, 216–17; poetics of, 10–11, 12, 41, 54, 148–49, 185, 216; recording events as feature of, 12, 42, 49–54, 168, 170, 212–14; sexual desire relation to nature of, 63–64; the strange and marvelous as feature of, 12, 13–14, 49, 52–54, 136, 141, 168; transmission as feature of, 12, 14, 15, 42, 49–54, 63, 146, 168, 178; *wenxue* (literature) compared to, 3, 40; Xiang Kairan works in understanding, 7–8, 11–12, 41, 54–65, 223, 228–29. *See also* linked-chapter novel; martial arts fiction; *specific works*

Xiaoshuo daguan (*The Grand Magazine*), 23, 73, 79, 84

Xiaoshuo shijie (*The Story World*), 24, 104–5

Xiaoshuo yuebao. See Short Story Magazine, The

xiayi xiaoshuo (chivalric fiction), 66, 67, 79, 87, 91, 178

Ximen Qing (fictional character), 186, 187

Xingqi. See Sunday, The

Xinhai Revolution, 18, 20

Xin qingnian (*New Youth*), 3, 104, 223

Xinwen bao, 24, 25, 29, 89, 115, 165, 247n46

Xin Xiaoshuo. See New Fiction

Xin Xiepu chao (Zhu Shouju). *See New Shanghai Tides*

Xin xin xiaoshuo (*New New Fiction*), 72, 81–82

Xu Sinian, 28, 233n1

Xu Zhenya, 111

Xu Zhuodai, 250n15

Yan Duhe, 89, 105, 110, 120, 124, 248n63, 252n41

Yangzhou Tides (*Guangling chao*) (Li Hanqiu), 120, 252n43

Yao Gengkui, 87

The Collected Essays of
CHRISTOPHER
Hill

The Collected Essays of
CHRISTOPHER
Hill

Volume Two
Religion and Politics in
17th Century England

THE UNIVERSITY OF MASSACHUSETTS PRESS
Amherst

First published in the United States of America
in 1986 by the University of Massachusetts Press
Box 429 Amherst Ma 01004

Printed in Great Britain by Anchor Brendon Ltd, Tiptree, Essex

Library of Congress Cataloging in Publication Data
(Revised for vol. 2)

Hill, Christopher, 1912-
  The collected essays of Christopher Hill.

  Includes bibliographical references and index.
  Contents: 1. Writing and revolution in 17th-century
England — v. 2. Religion and politics in seventeenth-
century England.
  1. Great Britain — History — Stuarts, 1603-1714 —
Collected works. 2. English literature — 17th century —
History and criticism — Collected works. 3. Literature
and society — Great Britain — Collected works. I. Title.
DA375.H54 1985   941.06   84-16446

ISBN 0-87023-467-6 (v. 1)
ISBN 0-87023-503-6 (v. 2)

Contents

For Victor Kiernan
—wit, provocateur and
generous friend for
fifty years

Preface

As with a preceding volume, *Writing and Revolution in 17th Century England*, the pieces collected here are based on lectures, articles and reviews written over the past twenty years or so. Some have been substantially rewritten, and I have tried to remove repetitions and contradictions. I hope allowance will be made for the diverse origins of these occasional pieces. I should like to think I have been fairly consistent in my attitude towards the relationship of religion, economics and politics in seventeenth-century England. When I first started working on the period it was necessary, many of us thought, to challenge the then dominant concept of "the Puritan Revolution" and to establish, with the help of Marx, Weber and Tawney, that sixteenth- and seventeenth-century religious beliefs were related to the societies in which they arose.

But in the nineteen-fifties, with the gentry controversy, religion was abruptly thrown out of the window; and it became necessary to recall that those who lived through the Revolution thought religion more important than economics; to recall that Independency and Roman Catholicism were not just beliefs which gentlemen took up when their debts overwhelmed them, that the ecclesiastical patronage of peers was at least as important as their ownership of manors. But now, predictably, hemlines are coming down again. We are told, rightly, that when gentlemen had to choose sides in the civil war which started in 1642, religion was probably more decisive than any other single cause. What happened in the mid-century, Dr Morrill tells us, was not the first of the great revolutions but the last of the wars of religion.[1] Well, yes of course, in a sense; I think German Marxist historians are saying something similar when they call the Peasants' Revolt of 1525 the first bourgeois revolution.

But in stressing the importance of religion in both upheavals we should beware of isolating "religion" as a self-sufficient factor unrelated to this-worldly concerns. In a society in which church and state were one, where many ecclesiastics were great landowners and

vii

all incumbents collected tithes from their unwilling parishioners, where church courts punished "sin" — in such a society "religion" meant something fundamentally different from what it means today. It is important that we should not forget the sociological insights which have helped recent historians to recapture a richer and more all-round understanding of the German Reformation and the English Revolution, an understanding closer to that of contemporaries. Brian Manning has argued (to me convincingly) that the civil war came to look like a religious war only when the middling sort began to play a larger part on the Parliamentarian side. This was both consequence and cause of the deepening of the Revolution.[2] If I appear to labour this point in the present volume, it is because I think it may be forgotten in the excitement of rediscovering that those who lived and strove and suffered in the seventeenth century were not statistical automata. We must not go back to the facile anachronism of "the Puritan Revolution": though at least that phrase did recognize that there was a revolution.

Many people have helped me in preparing this volume. I have tried to acknowledge specific debts in the notes. I am especially grateful for help and encouragement to Norman O. Brown, Leland Carlson, Patrick Collinson, Penelope Corfield, Margot Heinemann, Ann Hughes, James Jacob, Margaret Jacob, Richard Popkin, Barry Reay, Judith Richards, David Taylor, Mayir Vereté and David Zaret. Joyce Appleby very kindly sent me a copy of her *Capitalism and a New Social Order* just in time to make me see (or think I saw) connections between themes in my own book which I hadn't fully appreciated. John Morrill and Geoffrey Nuttall were generous with their time and patience in helping me to avoid repeating errors I have made in previous books. None of these is responsible for what I have obstinately persisted in saying. I am very grateful to the staff of Harvester Press for the courtesy and skill with which they handled a difficult typescript. Bridget encouraged, consoled and stimulated all the time, and crowned everything by helping with the index.

I have modernized spelling, capitalization and punctuation except in titles of books. All books quoted were printed in London unless otherwise stated.

3 January 1985.

NOTES

1. J.S. Morrill, "The Religious Context of the English Civil War", *T.R.H.S.*, fifth series, 34 (1984), p. 178.
2. Manning, "Religion and Politics: the Godly People", in *Politics, Religion and the Civil War* (ed. Manning, 1973), pp. 83-123.

Acknowledgments

Earlier versions of many of the pieces collected in this volume were originally published elsewhere. I am grateful for permission to include them in this collection.

"History and Denominational History" appeared in *The Baptist Quarterly* (XXII, 1967). "From Grindal to Laud" incorporates material from reviews which appeared in *Economic History Review*, New Series, XX (1967), *Journal of Religious History*, 11 (1981), *The Times Literary Supplement*, 18 March 1983, *Journal of Ecclesiastical History*, 35 (1984). "Dr. Tobias Crisp" was originally published in *Balliol Studies* (ed. J. M. Prest, Leopard's Head Press, 1982). "The Religion of Gerrard Winstanley" appeared as *Past and Present Supplement*, No.5 (1978); for "John Reeve, Laurence Clarkson and Lodowick Muggleton" I have drawn on material from a discussion in *Past and Present*, No.104 (1984): these are reprinted with the permission of the Past and Present Society. "From Lollards to Levellers" was originally published in a Festschrift for A.L. Morton, *Rebels and their Causes* (ed. M. Cornforth, Lawrence and Wishart, 1978). "Occasional Conformity" first appeared in a Festschrift for Geoffrey Nuttall, *Reformation, Conformity and Dissent* (ed. R.B. Knox, Epworth Press, 1977). "God and the English Revolution" was printed in *History Workshop Journal*, 17 (1984).

Abbreviations

The following abbreviations have been used in the notes:

C.S.P.D. (Ven.)(Scottish)	*Calendar of State Papers, Domestic (Venetian) (Scottish)*
D.N.B.	*Dictionary of National Biography.*
H.M.C.	Historical Manuscripts Commission
M.E.R.	C. Hill, *Milton and the English Revolution* (1977; Penguin edn., 1979).
M.C.P.W.	Ed. D.M. Wolfe, *Complete Prose Works of John Milton* (Yale U.P., 8 vols., 1953-82).
P. and P.	*Past and Present*
T.R.H.S.	*Transactions of the Royal Historical Society*
U.P.	University Press
V.C.H.	*Victoria County History.*
W.T.U.D.	C. Hill, *The World Turned Upside Down* (Penguin edn., 1975). First published 1972.

I   *Introductory*

1. *History and Denominational History*[1]

"The Church of England hath three main divisions: the Conformist, the Non-Conformist, and the Separatist." *

The principal headache of the historian — at least of the sixteenth and seventeenth century historian — is not too few documents but too many predecessors. Much of his work consists in sifting and criticizing the writings of previous scholars, whose conclusions have often ceased to carry conviction with professional historians by the time they have become commonplace in the school text-books. Now there is, of course, an element of academic show-off here: demonstrating the folly of your elders and betters is always a good way to earn a reputation, even if a transient one. But there is more to it than that. Each generation naturally and necessarily questions the assumptions of its predecessors, assumptions which spring from and change with the society in which historians, like everyone else, live. Fresh questions are asked about the present, and things which one generation took for granted are called in question by its successor. It is difficult, in this healthy process, to avoid the appearance of ingratitude towards the great historians of the past. But we can see further, if we do see further, only because we pygmies are standing on the shoulders of giants. Anything I say here must be premised by this apology.

With that premise, many historians today would I think agree that, especially in the sphere of the religious history of Europe in the sixteenth and seventeenth centuries, there is some criticizing to be done. Considerable confusion was caused by historians, great historians in some cases, writing the history of their own sect, looking for its origins, and so tending to draw dividing lines more sharply

*Lord Brooke, *A Discourse opening the Nature of that Episcopacie, which is Exercised in England* (1642), p. 87.

than contemporaries would have done. Having assumed that their predecessors held (or ought to have held) the same views as they did, these historians rebuked the men of the sixteenth and seventeenth centuries for failing to live up to nineteenth-century standards.

To the nineteenth-century historian protestants were protestants and Catholics were Catholics; the criteria for distinguishing between them seemed perfectly clear, even if there was some blurring towards the centre. But when we are considering English history between, say, 1530 and 1560, it is much less certain how many English men and women thought of themselves as either "protestants" or "Catholics". If they asked such questions at all, most would probably think of themselves as members of a Church of England whose doctrine and discipline were at times subject to changes from on top, the full import of which would not be obvious in the localities. This was true of clergymen as well as of the laity: it is much the most satisfactory explanation of the fact that the overwhelming majority of the clergy who survived from 1545 to 1560 held on to their livings in a church which (in our modern terminology) was successively Anglo-Catholic, protestant, radical protestant, Roman Catholic, and then again protestant — if that is the word for the Elizabethan settlement! They were not chameleons, nor were most of them any less high-principled than we are: the lines of division were not so clear-cut for most contemporaries as they seem to the historian looking through his end of the telescope. There were of course men who did feel that profound issues of principle were involved, like the Marian martyrs and some of those who condemned them to the flames. But the vast majority of the martyrs were laymen, not clerics: it is arguable that most of them were backward-looking Lollards rather than forward-looking protestants. Many of them would certainly have won Elizabeth's disapproval.

The same consideration applies equally strongly to the next period of rapid development and transformation, the years between 1600 and 1660. Patrick Collinson emphasized that the search for sectarian origins may impose a retrospective strait-jacket on a struggling reality. "To make the problem of denominational history one of simple genealogy is to face difficulties in the period 1604-40, where it is hard to trace much continuity of either leadership or ideas. It is at least equally desirable to conduct the search in the half-formed attitudes and positions adopted in the inchoate groups of the godly-minded which never acquired a label through separation".[2] Environment is more important than heredity in the evolution of ideas. Sectarian lines of division begin to be clearly drawn only when the possibility and the necessity of the co-existence of different religious bodies has been accepted: it certainly had not been accepted by more than a tiny minority of Englishmen before 1640. Most of the small groups of émigrés in Holland and New England, even those who had most self-consciously separated from what they regarded as the corruptions of the Church of England, still hoped for the total reformation of the state church. Robert Browne's slogan, "reformation without tarrying for any", implied that men separated in order to reunite. It is easy for historians looking backwards to think they see sharper lines of division than contemporaries could. Before 1640, as Professor Haller warily pointed out, a congregation was much more likely to be swayed by the personality — often the developing personality — of its preacher than by attachment to any theological "-ism" [3] We should see diversity in a united opposition to Laudian control of the state church rather than an alliance of consciously differing religious communities.

When after 1640 the sectaries emerged from their underground existence in England, or returned from exile, their new freedom kept the situation fluid. Congregations expanded rapidly, and account had to be taken of the views of the newcomers; there were many "sermon-tasters", or "seekers", who went from congregation to congregation, some genuinely questing for truth, others out of curiosity or a desire to make mischief. It was long indeed before clear-cut lines of sectarian division were imposed on this flux. Bunyan's Bedford congregation, looking back to the early sixteen-fifties, said that its members "neither were nor yet desired to be embodied into fellowship according to the order of the Gospel; only they had in some measure separated themselves from the prelatical superstition, and had agreed to search after the nonconformity-men, such as in those days did bear the name of Puritans". [4] The Broadmead Baptist church at Bristol started in the sixteen-thirties as a meeting of "awakened souls and honest-minded people" with no doctrinal allegiances. They were all laymen, who separated "from the worship of the world" but were willing to listen to carefully selected ordained ministers. They so continued for over twenty years. [5] It was such non-sectarian congregations that George Fox found waiting for him all over the north of England when he rode thither in 1651-2.

Presbyterians from Queen Elizabeth's time to 1640, and indeed to

1662, were never willingly sectarian. They hoped for the transformation of the Church of England into a Presbyterian church. They wanted to change its management, not to abolish it.[6] It is therefore absurd, as well as anachronistic, to differentiate before 1640 between "Puritans" and "Anglicans". "Puritans" were just as much Anglicans as the "episcopalians" or "Laudians" or whatever we choose to call them. To place "Puritans" in opposition to "Anglicans" suggests that the latter held the "true" tradition and the former are odd men out: it assumes the hindsight of after 1660.[7] The early history of the Church of England had been one of permanent reformation; there was no reason to suppose that this process had come to an end in 1559. Even if it had, the Elizabethan settlement contained room for Puritans as well as conformists. The word "Anglican" is appropriate as a sectarian label only after 1662, when "dissenters" had withdrawn and "nonconformists" had been extruded from the national church.

Henry Burton, for instance, whom historians call an Independent, thought it was the Laudian bishops who were disrupting the unity of the state church. "They have laboured to bring in a change in doctrine; in discipline; in the civil government; in the prayer-books set forth by public authority; in the rule of faith, and in the customs".[8] Many who were to remain within the church agreed with him in regarding Laudianism as a brief aberration. Lord Brooke thought the Laudian prelates had been the true schismatics.[9] So did two preachers of Fast Sermons in 1644, as well as Francis Cheynell in 1648 and John Milton in 1660.[10] For long after 1640 such men hoped for a reformed Church of England which would be acceptable to many of those who had felt forced to separate. Before 1662, at earliest, most of those whom we call Presbyterians and Independents, and some of those whom we call Baptists, still believed in a national church, and their ministers were prepared to accept its livings and its tithes. A circular signed by Independents among other divines of the Westminster Assembly, for instance, urged "all ministers and people ...to forbear, for a convenient time, the joining of themselves into church societies of any kind whatsoever, until they see whether the right rule will not be commended to them in this orderly way". (The Five Dissenting Brethren were rebuked by the nineteenth century historian of Congregationalism as having "much to learn in relation to religious freedom".)[11] The necessity of a state church was still being expounded in the Independent Savoy Declaration of 1658;

Yarmouth Independents in 1659 defended tithes against Quaker criticisms, and professed their "utter dislike and abhorrence of a universal toleration, as being contrary to the mind of God in His word". ("It is very evident", commented another nineteenth century historian, "that though they had learned much, they were not already perfect; . . . it was necessary that they should again go into the school of affliction.")[12]

The Cromwellian state church of the sixteen-fifties included men whom we should today, no doubt, label "Anglican", "Presbyterian", "Congregationalist" and "Baptist". But it also included many men, and indeed many leaders, whom it is difficult to pigeonhole in this way at all. The disagreements among historians as to the exact sectarian classification of an individual or a congregation is the best evidence that what they are trying to do is unsatisfactory because anachronistic. Richard Baxter rejected in advance the label "Presbyterian" which historians continue to put upon him during this period. As late as 1672 John Bunyan registered himself and his congregation as Congregationalist; in the sixteen fifties many congregations could be described equally well as Congregationalist or Baptist. They practised intercommunion. Who knows what label to attach to Oliver Cromwell, John Milton, Major-General Fleetwood, John Ireton, Colonel John Hutchinson and Lucy his wife? If we cannot classify such well-documented figures as these, it is absurd to try to be more precise about men who have left fewer traces.

In time those sects whose community of believers was united by covenant or adult baptism lost hope of recapturing the state church from which they had seceded; they accepted the permanent status of sectaries. The unique freedom of the forties and fifties hastened this process by enabling far more national organisation on a sectarian basis than had ever before been possible. The Particular Baptists for instance organized themselves sufficiently to have evolved a Confession by 1644. But in the sixteen-fifties Baptists were still quarrelling among themselves about the lawfulness of taking tithes — which means about the lawfulness of a state church,[13] and some few Baptists actually held livings in, and acted as Triers for, the Cromwellian church. The Quakers I think were the first sect organised on a national scale which rejected any possibility of compromise with the state church. They consistently denounced its "hireling priests" and its "steeple-houses". But the Quakers themselves embraced many trends of thought, bellicose as well as pacifist,

political as well as quietist, until George Fox united them into a
sect after 1660.

Quaker influence may have helped to harden Baptist attitudes. By
the end of the fifties Quakers, General and Particular Baptists were
nationally organized as sects. After 1662 they were joined, extremely
reluctantly, by Congregationalists and Presbyterians. The latter
were deliberately excluded from the restored episcopalian church,
which rejected the idea, put forward by Baxter and others, of
returning to something like the pre-Laudian state church in which
there had been many mansions. In 1672 John Owen spoke of those
"who separate, or rather are driven from, the present public
worship". He claimed that dissenters were the true Church of
England.[14]

Occasional conformity, the habit of going to the services of the
Church of England once a year or so, was often practised in the later
seventeenth and eighteenth centuries as a means by which nonconformists could qualify themselves for state office. For this reason it
has been denounced as a hypocritical practice, and so no doubt it
often became in the eighteenth century. But occasional conformity
sprang from the logic of John Owen's position, and indeed has a very
respectable intellectual ancestry.

Before 1640 only a very small minority were separatists on fixed
principle, and they almost certainly hoped that their separation
would lead to reunion — either as a consequence of the abolition of
bishops, or of the rule of the saints or of the personal appearance of
Jesus. Men like Henry Jacob and the New England Independents
wished to retain some communion with the national church. Even
Robert Browne in 1588 had envisaged something not unlike the
Cromwellian state church when he said: "The civil magistrates have
their right in all causes to judge and set order, and it is intolerable
presumption for particular persons to scan of every magistrate's gifts
or authority, or to deny them the power of judging ecclesiastical
causes. ...If again it be said that while men might take and refuse
their ministers as they list, all factions and heresies might grow, I
answer that the civil magistrate must restrain that licentiousness.
But the way to restrain it is prescribed of God. ...None be suffered
to have their voice or right in choosing church offices and officers but
only such as are tried to be sufficiently grounded and tried to be able
to give a reason of their faith and religion. And that the civil
magistrates may, if they will, be both present and directors of the

choice, yet permitting any man to make just exceptions against them which are to be chosen."[15]

Congregationalists and some Baptists participated in Cromwell's state church, side by side with Episcopalians and Presbyterians, and many whose views were indeterminate by our standards. This confusion (as it seems to us) immensely strengthened the hand of the bishops after 1660. Take John Tombes, for instance. Doctrinally he was a Baptist. But he is not usually claimed by Baptist historians because he held a living from 1630 to 1662, and in his licence under the Indulgence of 1672 he described himself as a Presbyterian. On his death-bed he declared that he dared not separate from communion with the Church of England "any farther than by going out of church whilst that office [baptism] was performed, and returning in again when it was ended".[16] Thomas Grantham, who is accepted as a Baptist by Baptist historians, was buried in St. Stephen's Church, Norwich, by the vicar of that church, who was later himself buried in the same grave.[17] The Presbyterian Philip Henry was also buried in his parish church.[18]

When popery threatened again under James II the firm stand of the Seven Bishops no doubt contributed to Presbyterian willingness to consider comprehension once more in 1689. So though the practice of occasional conformity may ultimately have degenerated into a device by which dissenters dishonestly qualified themselves for government office, it was in origin the outward sign, among those forced into separation, of the continuing hope that a church uniting all protestant Englishmen might still be realizable. Oliver Cromwell's state church deserves more attention from those interested in protestant reunion: so too does the maligned practice of occasional conformity.[19]

Above all we need continual vigilance to preserve a historical attitude towards the evolution of bodies of worshippers who after 1662 became dissenters. We must neither attribute to them views which crystallized only later, nor criticize them too severely for not knowing what their successors were going to think. "We are the men of the present age!" cried the Leveller Richard Overton; he and his contemporaries must be studied as they were, warts and all, in relation to the society in which they lived: just as the assumptions and beliefs of our generation will one day be the subject of (one hopes) charitably relativistic historical enquiry.

NOTES

1. A lecture to the Baptist Historical Society, printed in *The Baptist Quarterly*, XXII (1967).
2. Collinson, *The Elizabethan Puritan Movement* (1967), p. 372; *Godly People: Essays on English Protestantism and Puritanism* (1983), p. 14; cf. pp. 15-17 and Chapter 20 *passim*.
3. W. Haller, *The Rise of Puritanism* (1938), pp. 179-80.
4. Ed. G.B. Harrison, *The Church Book of Bunyan Meeting, 1650-1821* (1928), p. 1.
5. Ed. R. Hayden, *The Records of a Church of Christ in Bristol, 1640-1687*, Bristol Record Soc., XXVII (1974), pp. 83-8.
6. See p. 305 below.
7. The title of J.F.H. New's *Anglican and Puritan: the Basis of their Opposition, 1558-1640* (Stanford U.P., 1964) makes my point. But I am sad to see that even Collinson falls into the same error, referring to those whom "we are bound, for want of a less anachronistic label, to call Anglicans" (*Godly People*) p. 1. It seems to me wrong as well as anachronistic, as no one has demonstrated better than Patrick Collinson. Contrast Barbara Lewalski, *Protestant Poetics and the Seventeenth-Century Religious Lyric* (Princeton U.P., 1979) p. 434.
8. Burton's sermon, *God and the King*, is quoted by J. Waddington, *Congregational History, 1567-1700* (1874), p. 338.
9. *A Discourse ... of ... Episcopacie*, pp. 92-5.
10. John Strickland, *Immanuel, or The Church Triumphing in God with Us* (1644), p. 32; Thomas Hill, *The Right Separation Encouraged* (1644), p. 65; Milton, *Brief Notes Upon a late Sermon* (1660), in *M.C.P.W.*, VII, p. 486. For Cheynell see pp. 80, 302 below.
11. Waddington, *op. cit.*, pp. 426, 430.
12. J. Browne, *History of Congregationalism ... in Norfolk and Suffolk* (1877), pp. 167, 225-6.
13. B.R. White, "The Organisation of the Particular Baptists, 1644-1660", *Journal of Ecclesiastical History*, XVII, pp. 211, 223-4.
14. J. Owen, *Discourse on Christian Love and Peace* (1672), in Works (ed. W.H. Goold, 1850-3), XV, p. 102; *The Nature and Causes of Apostacy* (1676), *Works*, VII, p. 74; cf. p. 133, XV, pp. 184-5, 345-58. See Chapter 14 below.
15. Robert Browne, *An Aunswere to Mr. Floweres letter*, in *The Writings of Robert Harrison and Robert Browne* (ed. A. Peel and L.H. Carlson, 1953), pp. 521-2. See Avihu Zakai, *Exile and Kingdom: Reformation, Separation and the Millennial Quest in the Formation of Massachusetts and its Relationship with England* (Ann Arbor, 1984), *passim*, for the continuing acceptance of this principle by New England divines.
16. A.C. Underwood, *A History of the English Baptists* (1947), pp. 69-70.
17. *Ibid.*, p. 111.
18. Ed. M.H. Lee, *Diaries and Letters of Philip Henry* (1882), pp. 379-82.
19. See Chapter 14 below.

2. *The Necessity of Religion*[1]

"Take away kings, princes, rulers, magistrates, judges and such estates of God's order, no man shall ride or go by the way unrobbed, no man shall sleep in his own house or bed unkilled, no man shall keep his wife, children and possessions in quietness, all things shall be common. . . . Wherefore let us subjects do our bounden duties, giving hearty thanks to God, and praying for the preservation of this godly order."*

Whether or not we think of the sixteenth and seventeenth centuries as "an age of faith", there can be no doubt that contemporaries thought of religion as necessary to the maintenance of civil order and of the state power which defended that order. William Thomas, Clerk of the Council in Edward VI's reign, asked the King "whether religion, besides the honour of God, be not also the greatest stay of civil order? And whether the unity thereof ought not to be preserved with the sword and rigour?"[2] "How vile a treason is heresy", declared a pamphlet against Wyatt.[3]

This note runs throughout the *Homilies*. Whitgift told Elizabeth that "religion is the foundation and cement of human societies", a commonplace which he used to urge that ministers should not be "exposed to poverty", lest "religion itself ... be exposed to scorn and become contemptible".[4] The free-thinking Christopher Marlowe agreed with the Archbishop: "the first beginning of religion was only to keep men in awe".[5] Robert Burton the anatomist, a parson and not an irreligious man, wrote, disapprovingly but realistically, "it hath ever been a principal axiom with them [politicians] to maintain religion or superstition, which they determine of, alter and vary upon all occasions, as to them seems best; they make religion a mere policy, a cloak, a human invention. ... No way better to curb than superstition, to terrify men's consciences and to keep them in awe: they make new laws, statutes, invent new religions, ceremonies,

---

* *An Exhortation concerning Good Order and Obedience to Rulers and Magistrates*, in *Sermons or Homilies appointed to be read in churches in the time of Queen Elizabeth of famous memory* (Oxford U.P., 1802, p. 88).

11

as so many stalking horses to their ends.... What devices, traditions, ceremonies have they [priests] not invented in all ages to keep men in obedience, to enrich themselves?"[6]

Helen White noted that "the maintenance of religion and the maintenance of the existing civil social order were viewed as interdependent by the preachers, both those who were fairly well satisfied with the existing religious settlement, and those who wished to see it substantially changed".[7] Neither group, that is to say, envisaged a society in which inequalities of property did not exist, nor the state power necessary to maintain them. Crowley with some simplicity expressed the view that preachers taught the poor:

> "To pay all with patience
>   That their landlords demand;
> For they for their sufferance
>   In such oppression
> Are promised reward
>   In the resurrection".[8]

When the Revolution came, this useful function of religion was noted on both sides. The Marquis of Newcastle impressed on his pupil, the future Charles II: "Were there no heaven or hell you shall see the disadvantage for your government. ... If no obedience to God, then none to your Highness". Newcastle disliked sermons; he much preferred homilies, which should limit themselves to preaching (1) that Christ is our saviour; (2) the desirability of living a godly life and (3) instruction to the people in "their obedience to their superiors and governors, with all the respects that may be".[9] Peace, thought the gentle Izaak Walton, can "never be expected till God shall bless the common people of this nation with a belief *that schism is a sin — and they not fit to judge what is schism*".[10]

There was thus nothing new in the view of the pamphleteer who expected "those that say in their heart there is no God" nevertheless to be ready to "allow the political convenience of persuading the people otherwise".[11] Sir William Petty in his cold scientific way drew up a balance between the social advantages of religion — making men behave well even when not under observation, making the poor cheerful and patient, giving strength to oaths — and its costs and disadvantages to science. He concluded "civil laws may for the most part effect what religion pretendeth to do".[12] Charles II, pupil of both Newcastle and Hobbes, continued to believe that "an implicit-ness in religion is necessary for the safety of government, and he looks upon all inquisitiveness into those things as mischievous to the state". This, Burnet tells us, was "an odd opinion".[13] How did the commonplaces of the Book of Homilies become "odd opinions" for a Whig bishop? Religion still continues to play a social role; but it is no longer an authoritarian, undiscussable creed. Something has happened to society which makes relatively free discussion even of fundamental philosophical problems possible within the framework of the existing law and order. The wild peasant revolts and communist heresies of the Middle Ages have been tamed. Religion was — or seemed to be — a prime mover in the sixteenth century; it certainly was not in the eighteenth century.

Not only was religion held to be indispensible to society, the church to the state, but before 1640 it was difficult to distinguish between them. Even before he became Head of the English church Henry VIII issued in 1530 a proclamation against "blasphemous and pestiferous English books" which were being sent to England with the dual object of perverting the people from the true Catholic faith and of stirring them to sedition against their prince. The 39 Articles of the Church of England come right down into the political arena, pronouncing on the subject of the civil magistrate, the righteousness of private property and the legitimacy of oaths demanded by the magistrate. John Selden pointed out that many of the 39 Articles "do not contain matter of faith. Is it matter of faith how the Church should be governed? Whether infants should be baptized? Whether we have property in our goods?"[14] But if not articles of faith, all these matters were of key importance to the state as it existed before 1640. The Homilies are even more manifestly political, notably the Homily against Disobedience and Wilful Rebellion, originally aimed at Papists but couched in the most general terms:

"All kings, queens and other governors are specially appointed by the ordinance of God", and therefore should be obeyed, good or bad, just as servants must obey their masters. "What a perilous thing were it to commit unto the subjects the judgment, which prince is wise and godly, and his government good, and which is otherwise; as though the foot must judge of the head". Only "the worst men" even raise such questions. Rebellion is "worse than the government of the worst prince"; since opinions are bound to differ, freedom in this respect would mean that "no realm should ever be without rebellion".[15]

Since it was assumed on all sides that in England there could be only one church, control of this church was a highly political question, a question of power. By the circumstances of England's Reformation, church and monarchy were inextricably linked. Bishop Bancroft believed that Puritan demands for modification of the settlement of the church in 1559 were in effect demands for a change of government in the state.[16] Elizabethan judges regularly accused Puritans who had conscientious scruples about the forms of discipline established in the church of being "rebels", to their extreme indignation.[17]

If religion is necessary to any government, bishops are especially necessary to monarchy. Sir Robert Cecil, for instance, said in 1605 that Puritans "dream of nothing but a new hierarchy, directly opposite to the state of a monarchy". They wish "to break all the bonds of unity to nourish schism in the church and commonwealth".[18] "The discipline of the Church of England by bishops etc.", wrote Bacon, "is fittest for monarchy, of all others. ... It is most dangerous in a state to give ear to the least alterations in government". The existing government of the church could scarcely be abandoned without "perilous operation upon the kingdom". Reformation was necessary, but it must proceed from the state and not from the people.[19] Sectaries are inconsistent with monarchy, he advised the future Duke of Buckingham.[20] So Cottington was not making a new point when he declared: "The truth is, Mr. Prynne would have a new church, a new government, a new King; for he would make the people altogether offended with all things at present".[21]

Hooker is the most theoretically respectable exponent of the hierarchical view. The title of *The Laws of Ecclesiastical Polity* illustrates the point I am labouring. When Hooker published his first five books few indeed of his opponents would have disputed his starting position, that all who are born in England are automatically members of the English church. Sir John Eliot expressed himself with some vigour: "Religion only it is that fortifies all policy. ... The strength of all government is religion. ... Religion it is that keeps the subject in obedience, as being taught by God to honour his vicegerents". Eliot perhaps thought this view more important to be taught to the mass of the people: in the same treatise he spoke of the excitability of the House of Commons on religious matters as a weakness which he did not share; but went on to explain for the benefit of posterity that the security of the state was involved in such questions.[22]

By 1640 Rudyerd on the Parliamentarian side, no less than Laud on the government's, strikes a more urgent note: "If we secure our religion, we shall cut off and defeat many plots that are now on foot. ... They who would introduce another religion into the church must first trouble and disorder the government of the state, that so they may work their ends in a confusion".[23]

This interest, common to both sides in the civil war, in religion as the buttress of a society founded on property, helped to make possible the restoration. Those who defended bishops in 1640-2 defended them for fear lest other institutions, including their own property, might next be attacked. Many who opposed bishops opposed them as the instruments of a political régime: once that régime had been destroyed, this reason for hostility to bishops ceased to exist. Nor should we forget the body of men who frankly recognized the political function of religion. We have no idea of their numbers, since (apart from Marlowe) for the most part they remained prudently silent. Hobbes is the great exemplar; but more typical, and certainly more influential on the Parliamentarian side, was Selden: "When a man has no mind to do something he ought to do by his contract with man, then he gets a text and interprets it as he pleases, and so thinks to get loose". "If men would say they took arms for anything but religion, they might be beaten out of it by reason; out of that they never can, for they will not believe you whatever you say".[24]

Lord Brooke's starting point, according to Haller, was that the clergy owed their authority and their property solely to their ability to secure the obedience of the people to political powers which represented the oppressive weight of vested interests in society.[25] Thomas Taylor put the point more naively: "If Christian religion confirm civil authority, then the way to bring men to become subject to superiors is to plant the gospel. ... It is not power, it is not policy, that will still, subdue and keep under a rebellious people without the power of the Word and their consciences".[26]

An important part of the church's function was to control the people. Once consensus between the court and the bulk of the landed ruling class broke down the question arose, Who controls the church? The early sixteen-forties revealed that the crown could not control it without the gentry: but in the revolutionary conditions which followed it became equally clear that many of the middling and poorer sort no longer accepted gentry control unquestioningly. Under stable circumstances religion could subdue people and keep them under. But it could also be used for rebellious purposes when their superiors were not united in support of a state church. The question, W'ıere was your church before Luther? had focused attention on mediaeval lower-class heresies, to which Foxe looked back with pride: they ran riot in the sixteen-forties and fifties.

Restoration of the church in 1660, complete with bishops and our most religious King Charles II at its head, demonstrated that the natural rulers had learnt their lesson. Robert South, former panegyrist of Oliver Cromwell, reminded the lawyers of Lincoln's Inn early in 1660 that "if there was not a minister in every parish you would quickly find cause to increase the number of constables". Churches would be needed as prisons if they ceased to be places of worship.[27] Winstanley and Bunyan also saw the established clergy as aggressive defenders of the privileged social order.[28] Samuel Parker, former Cromwellian and future bishop, was unsubtle but clear: "Put the case, the clergy were cheats and jugglers, yet it must be allowed they are necessary instruments of state to awe the common people into fear and obedience. Nothing else can so effectively enslave them as the fear of invisible power and the dismal apprehensions of the world to come".[29] It was no doubt with such arguments that the Latitudinarian and Whig Gilbert Burnet convinced the libertine Earl of Rochester that Christianity's social usefulness should stop him attacking it publicly.[30] Jeremy Collier spelt out Parker's point in 1698: "if eternity were out of the case, general advantage and public reason and secular policy would oblige us to be just to the priesthood. For ... religion is the basis of government". Even supposing "a scheme of infidelity" could be demonstrated, "they had much better keep the secret. The divulging it tends only to debauch mankind, and shake the securities of civil life".[31] "General advantage, public reason and secular policy": these are a far cry from Divine Right and the sacred Scriptures. I hope this book may help to illuminate the transition from one set of ideas to the other.

NOTES

1. Chapters 2 to 5 derive from lectures which I gave in the Theological Faculty of University College, Cardiff, in 1966-7. I am grateful to the audience for helpful discussions, and particularly to Dr Archie Cochrane for usefully caustic comments.
2. H. Ellis, *Original Letters Illustrative of English History* (1825-7), second series, II, p. 190.
3. Cf. an edict of Charles IV of Spain, published in 1789: "Everything which tends towards the crime of propagating revolutionary ideas contains the crime of heresy" (H.T.Buckle, *History of Civilization in England*, World's Classics, 1903-4, II, p. 112; cf. pp. 198-9).
4. Izaak Walton, *Lives* (World's Classics, 1927), p. 194.
5. P.H.Kocher, *Christopher Marlowe* (Chapel Hill, 1946), Chapters 2-3.
6. Burton, *Anatomy of Melancholy* (Everyman edn.), III, pp. 328-9, 331.
7. H.C.White, *Social Criticism in Popular Religious Literature of the Sixteenth Century* (New York, 1944), p. 188.
8. R. Crowley, *Select Works* (Early English Text Society, 1872), p. 41.
9. Ellis, *op. cit.*, first series, III, p. 289.
10. Walton, *op. cit.*, p. 207. Walton's italics.
11. [Anon.], *A Memento* (n.d., ? early 1660s), p. 206.
12. Ed. the Marquis of Lansdowne, *The Petty Papers* (1927), I, pp. 116-18.
13. Ed. H.C.Foxcroft, *A Supplement to Burnet's History of My Own Time* (Oxford U.P., 1902), p.50.
14. Selden, *Table Talk* (1847), p. 4. Selden's point was that the clergy were bound by Act of Parliament to subscribe only to Articles which contained matters of faith: it was Bancroft who had extended this to subscription to all the Articles.
15. *Sermons or Homilies appointed to be read in churches.* pp. 471-3.
16. Ed. A. Peel, *Tracts ascribed to Richard Bancroft* (Cambridge U.P., 1953), pp. 47, 78, 81-3, 90-3, 105. Cf. a Puritan petition of 1585, in *Select Statutes and . . . Documents* (ed. G.W.Prothero, Oxford U.P., 3rd. edn., 1906), pp. 219-21.
17. Prothero, *op. cit.*, pp. 442-3; cf. D.Neal, *History of the Puritans* (revised edn., 1837), I, pp. 209-10.
18. Quoted by W.K.Jordan, *The Development of Religious Toleration in England (1603-1640)*, I (1936), p. 28.
19. [Anon.], *Cabala, Mysteries of State* (1654), II, p. 46; Bacon, *Certaine considerations touching the better pacification and edification of the Church of England*, in *Works* (ed. J.Spedding, R.L.Ellis and D.D.Heath, 1857-72), X, pp. 107-9.
20. Bacon, "Matters of religion and the church . . . in these times are become so intermixed with considerations of estate" *(Advice to Sir George Villiers)*.
21. H.R.Trevor-Roper, *Archbishop Laud, 1573-1645* (1940), p. 164.
22. Eliot, *Negotium Posterorum* (ed. A.B. Grosart, 1881), I, pp. 70-1; J. Forster, *Sir John Eliot* (1865), I, pp. 11, 213.

23. Forster, *op. cit.*, I, p. 60.
24. Selden, *Table Talk*, pp. 196-7.
25. *Tracts on Liberty in the Puritan Revolution, 1638-1647* (ed. W.Haller, Columbia U.P., 1934), I, p. 20.
26. T.Taylor, *A Commentary Upon the Epistle of St. Paul Written to Titus* (1658), pp. 398-9. Taylor died in 1633, but his writings could not be published because of "the iniquity of those times" (title-page to *Works*, 1653).
27. South, *Sermons Preached Upon Several Occasions* (1737), I, p. 131.
28. See chapter 11 below.
29. Quoted by Marvell, *The Rehearsal Transpros'd* (ed. D.I.B.Smith, Oxford U.P., 1971), p. 139. Marvell's comments are agreeable.
30. G.Burnet, *Some Passages of the Life and Death of the ...Earl of Rochester* (1774), p. 58. First published 1680.
31. J.Collier, *A Short View of the Immorality and Profaneness of the English Stage* (4th edn., 1699), pp. 129, 190.

II *The First Century of the Church of England*

The first century in which England had a separate national church may be taken either from the fifteen-thirties to 1640 or from 1559 to 1660. Such a perspective attaches great importance to the Reformation as the turning point in the history of religion in England. But with a slight shift in perspective we could equally well call the period The last century of the Church of England. In the thousand or so years between the Synod of Whitby and the English Revolution there had been, in theory always, and in practice nearly all the time, a single Christian church in England. But it had always been part of an international organization. During the first century after the Reformation, uniquely, there was a single national church, dependent on nobody. The existence of a large Roman Catholic minority introduced an element of fiction into the legal theory that all English men and women were members of this state church: but it was still a plausible aspiration. But after 1640 it rapidly became obvious that there was no longer a single English protestant church; the restoration of the Anglican Church to a privileged position in 1660 highlighted the fact that it was one church among many. The first century of the Church of England was also the last in which it could claim to be *the* English church.

The absence of international controls meant that this was a century of instability for the church: the rapid changes of direction made under Henry VIII, Mary and Elizabeth encouraged many to see the Reformation as a beginning, not an end. However hard Henry VIII and Elizabeth tried to insist that their church settlements were final, there remained those who called for continuous reformation. Lord Brooke in 1641 referred, provocatively, to "the first reformation".[1] Some even thought that a second reformation should be financed by confiscations of bishops and dean and chapter

19

lands, as Henry's Reformation had been financed by monastic lands. Impropriated tithes in the possession of lay successors of the monasteries tempted reformers to suggest using them to finance preaching.

This church, then, to which all English men and women belonged by virtue of having been born in England, was created in the fifteen-thirties and collapsed in the sixteen-forties. But though the institutions of the hierarchical church collapsed, protestantism did not. Religion, as Sir Lewis Namier used to say, is a sixteenth-century word for nationalism. After as before 1640, any threat, real or imagined, to protestantism at once rallied national unity, as Laud, Charles I and James II all found to their cost. During the Revolution many English men and women showed they were attached to the rhythms and rituals of the prayer book.[2] But no one seems to have expressed much regret for the passing of bishops. Whereas in Scotland and Ireland it was the Kirk and the Roman Catholic church which focused national unity, in England protestantism, not the episcopal church, was associated with patriotism.

This sets us two problems. How do we account for the collapse of the state church in 1640? How do we account for its restoration in 1660?

The occasional pieces that follow manifestly do not deal systematically with these problems. But some of them, approaching from several different angles, may help to suggest the form that answers should take. Over all of them broods the majestic figure of Patrick Collinson, with whom I occasionally venture to disagree, but whose powerful presence can never be forgotten.

NOTES

1. Brooke, *A Discourse... of Episcopacie, passim.*
2. John Morrill, "The Church in England, 1642-9", in *Reactions to the English Civil War* (ed. Morrill, 1982), pp. 89-114.

3. *The Protestant Nation*

King James upon the conference at Hampton Court did absolutely conclude, "No bishops, no king, no nobility"; which as you see, hath lately fallen out according to his prediction. It is the church which supports the state, it is religion which strengthens the government; shake the one, and you overthrow the other. Nothing is so deeply rooted in the hearts of men as religion, nothing so powerful to direct their actions; and if once the hearts of the people be doubtful in religion, all other relations fail, and you shall find nothing but mutinies and sedition. Thus the church and the state do mutually support and give assistance to each other; and if one of them change, the other can have no sure foundation.*

I

The great changes of the sixteenth century — renaissance, new astronomy, consciousness of great non-Christian societies revealed by long-distance trade — were accompanied by the rise of a lay learned intelligentsia. Before the Reformation schools were being founded under the auspices of merchant companies rather than of the church. The monarchy increasingly employed lay civil servants and patronized humanists whose speculations were as much secular as spiritual.

Yet urban civilization produced great insecurity. The obverse of the wealth of urban patriciates was unemployment, vagabondage, crime and disease. The village community, at a very low economic level, had produced some sort of social security, an equality in poverty; it was to the advantage of landlords, to say no more, to keep their tenants and labourers alive in time of famine. But big towns were impersonal: a man could starve there unknown to his neighbours. By the seventeenth century many London parish churches could not possibly have held all their parishioners at one time. Ultimately sectarian congregations were to replace the parish as community centre and social security agency in the towns; but

---

*Bishop Godfrey Goodman, *The Court of King James I* (1839), I, p. 421. Goodman died in 1656.

that was far ahead. Meanwhile masterless men were by definition a menace to order: the Tudor poor law, the protestant emphasis on the wickedness of the mass of mankind and the Hobbist war of every man against every man, all seemed to make sense in this society. So too did the Puritan stress on discipline and hard work for the good of the commonwealth, which saw England through the economic crisis of the sixteenth and seventeenth centuries, performing a social role similar to that of Marxist theories in the Soviet Union and China in our own day.[1] Protestantism lumped idle monks and idle beggars together as reprobates: some radicals threw in idle gentlemen for good measure. Sir Francis Drake was never a better Protestant than when he said he would have the gentleman to haul and draw with the mariner — and executed the highest ranking gentleman on board to reinforce the point. Having done its job, the ideology lost its leading role when political and economic stability were established in the Lockist state after 1688.

Dryden summed up the sociological approach to the Reformation, looking back from a century and a half later:

> "In times o'ergrown with rust and ignorance
> A gainful trade their clergy did advance;
> When want of learning kept the laymen low
> And none but priests were authorized to know:
> When what small knowledge was in them did dwell,
> And he a God that could but read or spell;
> Then Mother Church did mightily prevail;
> She parcelled out the Bible by retail,
> But still expounded what she sold or gave,
> To keep it in her power to damn or save.
> Scripture was scarce, and as the market went,
> Poor laymen took salvation on content,
> As needy men take money, good or bad;
> God's Word they had not, but the priest's they had ..."

After the Reformation each man read the Bible for himself, "And saved himself as cheap as e'er he could".[2] (The "cheap church" was a familiar jibe. Sir Thomas Overbury's "devilish usurer" "likes our religion best because 'tis best cheap".[3] Sir Benjamin Rudyerd in the Commons' Committee on Religion in 1628, apropos the need to establish a well-paid preaching ministry, feared lest "this backwardness of ours will give the adversary occasion to say that we choose our religion because it is the cheaper of the two")[4] The appeal to the

business classes reached caricature form in verses summarizing the
covenant theology prefixed to a volume of sermons printed in 1622:

> "No desperate debts or bankrupts in this trade,
> God is the creditor, Christ surety made,
> And both have bound themselves to pay for us
> The principal, with gracious overplus".[5]

Already the connection between gain and godliness was presenting
the problem which was to worry John Wesley. Thomas Adams
lamented that "religion gives us riches, and riches forget religion. . . .
Poverty makes us religious, religion rich, and riches irreligious".[6]

II

The Reformation left the believer and his conscience alone in the
world with no help except from divine grace. Looking back over the
centuries, we can see how this theological attitude could be adapted
to a society of rugged individualists, wrestling with God and their
consciences, recognizing no superiors, whether priests or feudal
lords. Church courts making money out of the people's sins would
seem to such men as iniquitous as the sale of indulgences. The
payment of tithes to non-preaching ministers would seem sacrilege.
So would popish vestments, whose object was to differentiate the
priest, however ungodly, from any layman, however godly. "Now I
can make no more holy water", said Latimer with heavy irony when
he was forcibly disrobed as part of his degradation from the priesthood.[7] "Conjuring garments of popery", a separatist called a
bishop's cope and surplice in 1567.[8] The *Admonition to Parliament*
of 1572 said that in primitive times ministers were "known by voice,
learning and doctrine: now they must be discerned from other by
popish and antichristian apparel".[9]

Protestants demanded communion in both kinds, for laymen as
well as for priests, to emphasize their equality. Holy communion was
not a mystery, a miracle in which the priest — and only the priest —
actually turned bread and wine into body and blood; through shades
of opinion protestants came increasingly to think of communion as a
commemoration, a reminder of a miracle that had once taken place.
Further consequences followed. Bishop Joseph Hall was to justify
kneeling at communion on the analogy of kneeling to kiss the King's
hand,[10] and Elias Ashmole bowing to the altar because men bowed in

the royal presence.[11] But for Puritans these were not merely polite gestures, but an acknowledgment of the real presence. ("Papists kneel to the corporal presence", said a Newcastle merchant caustically in the late seventeenth century; "but protestants kneel to they know not what").[12] Those who denied transsubstantiation felt it a point of principle to withhold such gestures. "Altar-worship is idolatry", said Pym in the Long Parliament.[13] Railing off the altar at the east end of the church emphasized not only the real presence but also the mediating role of the priest. Puritans wanted the communion table to be in the centre of the church, with the *minister* attending on seated communicants, not the *priest* mediating the miracle of the mass.

So two utterly different conceptions of religion are concealed behind quarrels over vestments, altar rails and the position of the communion table. The protestant approach was at once less sacramental and less materialistic: it stressed the moral state of the worshipper, not the correct performance of ceremonies on his behalf. Again the question of human responsibility, of the equality of laymen with priests, was involved. "The table of communion", said Milton in 1641, "now become a table of separation, stands like an exalted platform, . . . fortified with bulwark and barricado to keep off the profane touch of the laics, whilst the obscene and surfeited priest scruples not to paw and mammock the sacramental bread as familiarly as his tavern biscuit". In Milton's eyes, the believer is "more sacred than any dedicated altar or church".[14]

These are commonplaces, but I emphasize them to recall that the issues at stake even in vestiarian disputes were not trivial. As the *Admonition to Parliament* declared, "Neither is the controversy betwixt them and us (as they would bear the world in hand) as for a cap, a tippet or a surplice, but for great matters concerning a true ministry and regiment of the church according to the Word".[15] When the Long Parliament met in November 1640 the House of Commons insisted on receiving communion at a table placed in the middle of the church. It was a political gesture.

Puritans said that they were trying to return to the practice of the primitive church, just as common lawyers and Levellers said they wished to return to the customs of their free Anglo-Saxon ancestors. In both cases one advantage of appealing to earlier, allegedly less corrupt, practices was that the appeal could be highly selective. Texts were applied, with no historical sense, to a context in which they were quite inappropriate. The reformers looked back to a church which owned no lands, which was in no position to persecute or censor, which indeed was out of sympathy with the then existing political order, not part and parcel of it. They found very few of the institutions of mediaeval society mentioned in the Bible. The reformers, like the early Fathers, abhorred the concessions which any established church has to make to the social and political order which maintains it. Hence the attraction of the simplicity of early Christianity as against "the subtleties of the schoolmen", those painful adaptations of the New Testament to the needs and standards of mediaeval society. This society was being transformed by geographical discoveries and industrial developments: forward-looking thinkers were correspondingly impatient with the old ideas. This is one of the points at which Renaissance and Reformation, intellectual criticism and theological protest, met. Erasmus and Luther agreed in their hostility towards scholasticism.

Hence the primary importance for reformers of getting the Bible translated into the vernacular, for which so many of them paid with their lives. The fortunate coincidence (or divine providence, Foxe thought) that the craft of printing had just been discovered made possible the mass circulation of Bibles and pamphlets, so that all who could read were open to the influence of the new ideas (and, in towns especially, many who could not read but listened to discussion). But literacy confined the main impact of the vernacular Bible to the middling classes, not the very poorest. As Thomas Münzer asked of Luther in the fifteen-twenties, "Doesn't he realise that men whose every moment is consumed in the making of a living have no time to read the Word of God?"[16]

Mediaeval heretics had relied on the Bible in opposing the miracle of the mass, confessions, images, church courts and ceremonies. But their Bibles were laboriously copied out by hand or learnt by heart. Printing made protestantism possible because it facilitated the rapid spread of popular theology among the literate, mainly in towns. Where the Lollard Bible had circulated in tens of copies, Tyndale's New Testament circulated in hundreds, and the Geneva Bible in thousands. But printing also ruined protestantism as a single coherent creed, because the reading of books is even harder to control than the reading of manuscripts. The portable Geneva Bible could be privately digested, privately interpreted, and discussed in small clandestine groups. The protestant appeal to the mind through the

Word, rather than the traditional appeal to the eye through symbols and ceremonies, may again have limited the range of its original spread in a society where the peasant majority was not only largely illiterate, but addicted to concrete visual symbols. The Homilies declared that "all images ... set up publicly have been worshipped of the unlearned and simple sort shortly after they have been publicly so set up. .... Images in churches and idolatry go always both together. ... The nature of man is none otherwise bent to the worshipping of images (if he may have them and see them) than it is bent to whoredom and adultery in the company of harlots".[17] Iconoclasm was educational, as Burnet realised.[18]

The Reformation, just because of this return to the primitive sources of Christianity, gave a great impetus to scholarship. It was vital to be sure what the Bible said, to have a certain text: and printing made this possible. The Reformation brought an advance in controversial methods and textual criticism, just because there were two sides (at least), each passionately convinced the other was wrong. Busy attacking papal forgeries and suppressions, men like Jewell, Hooker, William Crashawe, Chillingworth, laid the foundations of a new critical method. Protestants were convinced that Catholics believed ignorance to be the mother of devotion, and this made many wish to act on the opposite principle. In *Areopagitica* Milton could find nothing worse to say of censorship than that it was of popish origin. In fact an important part of Milton's argument for responsible freedom had been anticipated eighty years earlier in the Elizabethan Homily *Exhorting to the reading and knowledge of holy Scripture*: "If you will not know the truth of God ... lest you fall into error; by the same reason you may then lie still and never go, lest, if you go, you fall into the mire; nor eat any meat, lest you take a surfeit; nor sow your corn, nor labour in your occupation, nor use your merchandize, for fear you lose your seed, your labour, your stock".[19] As late as 1691 Richard Baxter tried to make the gentry's flesh creep by suggesting that if monastic lands were recaptured by the church, many landlords would repent that they did not spend more on educating the poor.[20]

The Bible was in the parish church for all to read, and the church was still a real community centre. The early reformers encouraged men not only to read but also to study and discuss the Scriptures. They thought that once the Bible was available in English, all men would agree on what it said. But many of those who in sixteenth-century England were encouraged to study the Bible were poorly educated, had little critical or historical sense, and regarded every word of the Scripture as divinely inspired. Their daily lives were filled with mysterious and inexplicable events which they accounted for in magical or miraculous terms. They tended to take the Bible entirely literally, and to apply its texts as a standard of criticism of the world about them. They found denunciations of the rich and powerful and praise of the poor and lowly, together with threatenings of wrath to come, which fitted well into the mood of rebellious despair that the crisis of their society was producing. In 1643 the Rev. John Jegon, an Essex parson, was accused of saying "'twas pity that ever the Bible was translated into English, for now every woman and beggarly fellow think themselves able to dispute with reverend divines".[21] He has our sympathy.

III

The first century of the Church of England saw the emergence of new loyalties to replace that to one's feudal overlord, which over most of Europe was losing its point. The newly consolidating national states were trying to subsume feudal and religious loyalties: the new Messiah, some said, was the King. But kings do not cut very inspiring figures in the Bible. For all their devotion to the godly prince, early reformers like Calvin, Tyndale and Becon found in the Bible the command "that we ought to obey God more than man".[22] Knox is very quotable on the subject. Preaching in 1559 he recalled "when we were a few number in comparison of our enemies, when we had neither earl nor lord — few excepted — to comfort us, we called upon God and took him for our protector, defence and only refuge".[23] "Who dare enterprise to put silence to the spirit of God, which will not be subject to the appetites of wicked princes?"[24] Even more ominously, he remarked "the prophet of God sometimes may teach treason against kings".[25]

Direct loyalty to God should bypass all mediators and mesne lords. "If earthly lords and masters will defend their servants", argued Bishop Pilkington in 1562, "much more He that [is] King of heaven and earth".[26] Archbishop Grindal warned Elizabeth that, though she was a mighty princess, yet "He that dwelleth in heaven is mightier".[27] The separatist John Penry was even less tactful: "He that hath made you and me", he told Elizabeth, "hath as great authority to send me of his message unto you, as he had to place you over me".[28] "These heretics neither fear God nor obey their betters", observed the Spanish ambassador, apropos the 1566 Parliament.[29]

Such doctrines could be socially as well as politically subversive. "Glory not that thou hast a gentleman to thy father", counselled Silver-Tongued Smith; "glory not that thou hast a knight to thy brother, but glory that thou hast a Lord to thy brother. . . . Seemeth it a light thing to you to be the sons of the King of kings, seeing you are poor men and of small reputation?"[30] "Shall your loyalty towards men excuse your treasons against the Lord?" Joseph Hall asked.[31] Sir Henry Slingsby in 1628 told the Earl of Huntingdon that "he cared not for any lord in England except the Lord of Hosts".[32] If conscience bids us, declared the preacher of an assize sermon in the same year, we should denounce "a neighbour, a kinsman, a landlord".[33]

How such attitudes could affect political action is shown by Oliver Cromwell's preference for a godly yeoman over a gentleman who is "nothing more". When the defenders of Taunton were called on to surrender in October 1644, they declared they would not "prefer the honour and reputation of gentlemen before the goodness and power of the almighty Saviour".[34] At a different social level we may compare the Baptist Henry Denne's answer to a man who felt he could not cease "to hear the priests of England" because "he hired a farm of Mr. Bendich, and if he should know he was baptized he would turn him out". Denne told him "the earth was the Lord's and the fullness thereof, and wished him to trust God, and he would be a better landlord than Mr. Bendich".[35] The Diggers in June 1649 told Fairfax that they had "chosen the Lord God Almighty to be our king and protector".[36] "The whole world", Colonel Daniel assured Monck in 1657, "is governed by superiority and distance in relations, and when that's taken away unavoidably anarchy is ushered in".[37] The future Duke of Albemarle hardly needed the warning.

So personal feudal loyalty was replaced by loyalty to God, to a cause. Treason was in origin a breach of *personal* fealty owed to an overlord; but Martin Marprelate in 1589 spoke of those who were "obedient subjects to the Queen and disobedient traitors to God and the realm".[38] Such distinctions were ominous: sixty years later Charles I was condemned for high treason against the people of England. Loyalty to God was the mediating term between loyalty to the person of the King and loyalty to the abstraction of the state.

Stephen Marshall in 1644 had said "The question in England is, whether Christ or Antichrist shall be lord or king?"[39] By 1649 Milton could write, with enviable simplicity, "the kings of this world have both ever hated and instinctively feared the church of God", since this church's doctrine "seems much to favour two things to them so dreadful, liberty and equality".[40] Loyalty to God came in practice to mean loyalty to conscience, the inner voice. "Greater is *he that is in you*", Margaret Fell assured her husband in 1653, "than he that is in the world".[41]

Loyalty to the king was replaced by loyalty to the commonwealth, to the nation. Dr Firth has argued that neither Bale nor Foxe saw an apocalyptic role for England, and she even suggests that Haller was wrong to see any conception of England as an elect nation before 1640.[42] But J. W. McKenna argues that "God became an Englishman" as early as the fourteenth century.[43] Latimer wrote in 1537 God "hath shown himself God of England, or rather an English God". The dying Edward VI was said to have called on God to "save thy chosen people of England".[44] Haller quoted Bishops Aylmer and Parker proclaiming that "God is English".[45] Richard Fitz's congregation in 1571 assumed a merciful relation of God to England and the English church, like that to Israel — a mercy dependent on the obedience of the people to his revealed will.[46] Philip Stubbe thought that the English were a chosen people.[47] "Passing by many other nations", wrote a Puritan who may have been Thomas Cartwright, "thou hast trusted our nation" with the gospel.[48] John Rolfe in 1616 described England as "a peculiar people marked and chosen by the finger of God" to possess North America.[49] Richard Bernard in 1619, Alexander Leighton in 1628, thought that the English were "the Lord's own people".[50] George Wither between 1625 and 1628 wrote an exceptionally long poem whose object was to call to repentance the land which God had "elected from among the heathen isles".

> "Thou wert as often warned and furnished
> As Judah was ...
> The Jewish commonwealth was never deigned
> More great deliverance than thou hast gained"

in 1588 and 1605.[51]

After 1640 such comments are of course even more frequent — in Fast Sermons[52] and in almanacs, for instance.[53] In 1681 George Hickes said sneeringly that the Puritans "made the common people

of Great Britain consider themselves as the people of Israel and . . .
act like enthusiasts and follow their leaders like the Jews of latter
times, to commit such execrable treasons as are not to be mentioned
without horror and tears"; he went on to compare the execution of
Charles I with the crucifixion.[54] But it was not only Puritans: Fuller
in 1655 argued that "England is God's on several titles".[55] Charles II
spoke of the English as "His own chosen people", and throughout
Dryden's *Annus Mirabilis* the parallel between Londoners and Jews
is maintained.[56]

Foxe depicted Englishmen defending the truth throughout the
centuries, now against Antichrist personified by the Pope and the
King of Spain. Catholicism lost Calais, Bishop Pilkington recalled;
the preaching of Jesus Christ, thought Knox, would bring about a
perpetual concord (for the first time in history) between England and
Scotland. [57] So the rather vulgar nationalism which we find among
the Elizabethans was sublimated and idealized. Puritans, as the most
anti-Catholic and anti-Spanish of Englishmen, seemed also to be the
most patriotic, especially during the two great crises of the fifteen-
eighties and the sixteen-twenties.

IV

Calvinism moreover was an *international* movement, like Catholicism. Even if its adherents came to despair of the English church,
they could still hope that our brethren in the Netherlands, France,
Scotland, would help against the common enemy. From the reign of
Edward VI to that of James I connections with continental protestantism were close. Bucer and Peter Martyr, John à Lasco,
Bernardino Ochino and many others played an important part in
establishing the faith of the English church under Edward. Marian
exiles fled to Frankfort, Strasburg, Basle, Geneva, Zürich. Under
Elizabeth epistolary contacts were kept up with leading continental
protestant divines, and Bullinger's *Decades* were compulsory reading
for non-graduate English clergy. Essex ministers in the fifteen-
eighties regarded it as a powerful argument against unqualified
acceptance of the English prayer book that it would put them out of
step with continental reformed churches.[58] English theology was
heavily dependent on the continent, Patrick Collinson reminds us.
Covenant theology "derived from the theological tradition of the
Zwinglian reform in Zürich". Sabbatarianism was not invented by
English Puritans either: it was well-known in Zürich, Geneva,

Heidelberg and the Netherlands.[59] Only after the rise of William Perkins in the last decade of the century was the debt repaid. Over fifty editions of Perkins's works were printed in Switzerland, nearly sixty in Germany, and over a hundred in the Netherlands, as well as smaller numbers in France, Bohemia and Hungary.[60]

The hierarchy came to stress the nationalism of the English church rather than the internationalism which appealed to Puritans and the first generation of bishops.[61] Grindal had friendly relations with the foreign churches, in London and on the continent: the former contributed to the development of prophesyings.[62] But Whitgift challenged the ordinations of non-episcopal churches, and cited in defence of the hierarchy the practice of the fourth and fifth centuries, when the church was fitting itself into the institutional framework of the Roman Empire. The decisive break came with Bancroft and his "Babylonian faction".[63] Bancroft thought French Huguenots as seditious as English Puritans.[64] He was, Andrew Melville thought, "the capital enemy of all the reformed churches of Europe".[65] His sharp distinction between bishops and the other ranks of the clergy made the former a superior order by Divine Right, with the sole power of ordination and of discipline. This justified a graded hierarchical concept of the church, with authority descending from above, thus isolating England from continental Calvinism. It was naturally accompanied by an elevation of the parson over the congregation.

This is reflected in the vicissitudes of the word "minister". It was normally used even in official documents in the later sixteenth century. When in 1606 an M.P. objected that "the old and usual word is clerk", the House of Commons agreed that "the word minister ... hath been used and is now usual and well understood, and an apt and good term".[66] It was ground for complaint against John Cosin in 1628 that "he hath changed the word 'minister' into the word 'priest'".[67] The ultimate compromise was "clergyman".

As James VI restored episcopacy in Scotland, as the Edict of Nantes registered acceptance in 1598 by the French Huguenots of the position of tolerated minority, as the victory of the Dutch struggle for independence created a national church in the Netherlands, the trend towards national isolation was strengthened. At the same time English and Dutch victories over Spain, and the succession of Henri IV of France rather than the Spanish candidate, removed the danger of a restoration of Catholicism in England by

Spanish arms, and so reduced the government's need for Puritan support.

The Synod of Dort in 1618-19 was the first and last international Calvinist council. England was represented at Dort, but the experience did nothing to reassure James I that Calvinism and monarchy were compatible. There followed the disastrous attempt of the Elector Palatine to seize the Bohemian crown. Frederick's defeat, and the failure of England and the Netherlands to combine in support of his cause, showed that the Calvinist international was in ruins. James turned to negotiations for a marriage alliance with Spain; Richelieu seized the opportunity to abolish Huguenot territorial power in France. The fatuous diplomacy of Buckingham and Charles I, intervening first against and then for the Huguenots, showed that English foreign policy had no firm ideological commitment; when the Habsburgs were checked in Germany, it was by Lutheran Sweden and Catholic France. The Calvinist international had failed.

Laud passed over to the offensive against it. He harried foreign protestant churches in England, nearly ruining the Wealden and Norwich clothing industries in the process. The English ambassador in Paris ceased to attend Huguenot worship. Laud tried to bring under his control both the English merchant churches overseas and the chaplains of English regiments in the service of the Netherlands, thus endangering relations with the Dutch republic and driving many English refugees from the Netherlands to a further emigration across the Atlantic. He tried to force conformity on Presbyterian Scots. At all points he seemed to be stressing the insularity of the English church. Small wonder that men suspected his little Englandism of being a cover for schemes to reunite with the Roman church. A papal agent appeared in England in 1636 for the first time since the reign of Mary Tudor. It was reported to Rome, *teste* Bishop Montagu, that Laud and several other bishops "held the opinions of Rome on dogma, and especially on the authority of the Pope".[68] Laud believed in the real presence, turned communion tables into altars, repaired broken images. We know, as contemporaries did not, that Laud refused a cardinal's hat. But the important thing may be that the Pope thought the offer worth making. The theories of monarchical absolutism prevalent in Counter-Reformation countries were entirely congenial to Charles I, Laud and the "Arminian" party. It was not unreasonable to suspect them of favouring the theology of the Counter-Reformation too. We know now that Laud disliked and was embarrassed by the "Popish Plot" carried on by Henrietta Maria and her courtiers, perhaps with the connivance of the King.[69] But the fact that such a plot existed had disastrous consequences for monarchy and episcopacy in England. When Henrietta Maria appealed to Rome for help in February 1641, explaining that her husband could not embrace Catholicism or he would lose his crown, Cardinal Barberini drily replied that Charles had lost his crown already.[70]

NOTES

1. Cf. M.Walzer, "Puritanism as a Revolutionary Ideology", *History and Theory*, III (1963), *passim*.
2. Dryden, *Religio Laici* (1682), in *Poetical Works* (Globe edn.), p. 200.
3. Overbury, *Characters* (1616), in *Miscellaneous Works* (ed. E.F. Rimbault, 1890), p. 135.
4. *Memoirs of Sir Benjamin Rudyerd* (ed. J.A.Manning, 1841), p. 137. Cf. William Chillingworth: "The late slovenly profaneness, (commonly called worshipping in the spirit, but intended to be worship without cost)" (*Works*, Oxford U.P., 1838, III, p.171).
5. John Wing, *The Best Merchandise* (Flushing, 1622), introductory verses.
6. T.Adams, *The Souls Sickness*, in *The Sermons of Thomas Adams* (ed. J.Brown, 1909), p. 215.
7. W.Pierce, *An Historical Introduction to the Marprelate Tracts* (1908), p. 9.
8. J. Strype, *Life... of... Edmund Grindal* (Oxford U.P., 1821), p. 175.
9. In *Puritan Manifestoes: A Study of the Origin of the Puritan Revolt* (ed. W.H.Frere and C.E.Douglas, 1907), p. 11.
10. Hall, *Works* (Oxford U.P., 1837), X, p. 69.
11. Ed. C.H.Josten, *Elias Ashmole (1617-1692)* (Oxford U.P., 1966), III, p. 819.
12. Ed. W.H.D.Longstaffe, *Memoirs of the Life of Mr. Ambrose Barnes* (Surtees Soc., 1867), p. 124.
13. Ed. J.Bruce, *Verney Papers: Notes of Proceedings in the Long Parliament* (Camden Soc., 1845), p. 123.
14. *M.C.P.W.*, I, pp. 547-8.
15. Frere and Douglas, *op.cit.*, p. 36.
16. Quoted by V.H.H.Green, *Luther and the Reformation* (1964), pp. 150-1.
17. *Homilies*, pp. 186, 206. Cf. Chapters 8-10 below for "natural man".
18. G.Burnet, *History of the Reformation of the Church of England* (1825), I, pp. 314-17.
19. *Homilies*, p. 5. "Like the man that would keep all wine out of the

country lest men should be drunk" was how Cromwell put the same point to the Governor of Edinburgh Castle in September 1650 (ed. W.C. Abbott, *Writings and Speeches of Oliver Cromwell*, Harvard U.P., 1937-47, II, p.339).

20. Baxter, *The Poor Husbandman's Advocate to Rich Racking Landlords* (ed. F.J.Powicke, Bulletin of the John Rylands Library, X, 1926), pp. 178-9.

21. J.W.Davids, *Annals of Evangelical Nonconformity in ... Essex* (1863), p. 236; Hobbes repeated the point (*English Works*, ed. Sir W.Molesworth, 1839-45), VI, pp.190-1.

22. J.Calvin, *A Commentary on Daniel* (trans. and ed. T.Myers, 1966), I, p. 382 (first published 1561, English translation 1570); W.Tyndale, *The Obedience of a Christian Man* (1527-8), in *Doctrinal Treatises* (Parker Soc., 1848), pp. 202-4; Thomas Becon, *Prayers and other pieces* (Parker Soc., 1844), pp. 302-4.

23. J.Knox, *The History of the Reformation of Religion in Scotland* (ed. W.M'Gavin, Glasgow, 1832), p. 172.

24. *Ibid.*, p. 150; cf. pp. 252-3, 290 and *passim*.

25. Knox, *Works* (ed. D.Laing, 1864), III, p. 184.

26. J. Pilkington, *Works* (Parker Soc., 1842), p. 191.

27. Grindal. *Remains* (Parker Soc., 1843), pp. 376-90; cf. Collinson, *The Elizabethan Puritan Movement*, pp. 29, 94, 107, 135.

28. J. Strype, *Life... of John Whitgift* (Oxford U.P., 1822), II, p. 181. Cf. *Writings of Robert Harrison and Robert Browne* (ed. A. Peel and L.H.Carlson, 1953), p. 413.

29. J.E.Neale, *Elizabeth I and her Parliaments, 1559-1581* (1953), p. 139.

30. H.Smith, *Three Sermons* (1632), p. 34; cf. my *Economic Problems of the Church* (Panther edn., 1971), p. 23; John Goodwin, *God a Good Master* (1641); Richard Sibbes, *The Soules Conflict* (1635), in *Works* (Edinburgh, 1862-4), I. p.123.

31. J.Hall, *Works*, X, p. 66.

32. Quoted by L.Stone, *The Crisis of the Aristocracy* (Oxford U.P., 1965), p.265. Conrad Russell rather oddly suggests that this remark may not show declining respect for the aristocracy but for the militia (*Parliament and English Politics, 1621-1629*, 1979, p. 376). Possibly; but it is not what the words say.

33. Robert Harris, *Two Sermons* (1628), quoted by M.Walzer, *The Revolution of the Saints: A Study in the Origins of Radical Politics* (Harvard U.P., 1965), pp. 233-4.

34. Quoted in C.D.Curtis, *Blake, General-at-Sea* (Taunton, 1934), p. 46.

35. Ed. E.B.Underhill, *Records of the Churches of Christ Gathered at Fenstanton, Warboys and Hexham, 1644-1720* (Hanserd Knollys Soc., 1854), p. 82. Note the reference to "the priests of England" in 1653. The Church of England, like landlords, still existed. See p.6 above.

36. Ed. G.H.Sabine, *The Works of Gerrard Winstanley* (Cornell U.P., 1941), p. 284

37. Ed. C.H.Firth, *Scotland and the Protectorate* (Scottish History Soc., XXXI, 1899), pp. 362-3.

38. M.Marprelate, *The Epitome* (1588), Sig.E iv. An analogous distinction had been drawn by some of the followers of Sir Thomas Wyatt (John Proctor, *The History of Wyatt's Rebellion*, 1555, in *An English Garner*, ed. E. Arber, 1896-7, VIII, p.54).
39. S.Marshall, *A Sacred Panegyric* (1644), p. 21.
40. *M.C.P.W.*, III, p. 509; cf. W.Dell, *Several Sermons and Discourses* (1709), p. 18. First published 1652.
41. Isobel Ross, *Margaret Fell, Mother of Quakerism* (1949), p. 119. My italics.
42. K.R.Firth, *The Apocalyptic Tradition in Reformation Britain, 1530-1645* (Oxford U.P., 1979), pp. 108, 252-3.
43. In *Tudor Rule and Revolution: Essays for G.R.Elton* (ed. D.J.Guth and J.W.McKenna, Cambridge U.P., 1983).
44. D.M.Loades, *The Oxford Martyrs* (1970), p. 26; J.N.King, *English Reformation Literature: The Tudor Origins of the Protestant Tradition* (Princeton U.P., 1982), p. 410.
45. W.Haller, *Foxe's Book of Martyrs and the Elect Nation* (1963), pp.87-8; cf. *Correspondence of Archbishop Parker* (Parker Soc., 1853), pp. 418-19.
46. B.R.White, *The English Separatist Tradition: From the Marian Martyrs to the Pilgrim Fathers* (Oxford U.P., 1971), pp. 30-2.
47. W.T.MacCaffrey, "The Anjou Match and the making of Elizabethan foreign policy", in *The English Commonwealth, 1547-1640: Essays in Politics and Society presented to Joel Hurstfield* (ed. P. Clark, A.G.T. Smith and N.Tyacke, Leicester U.P., 1979), p.66.
48. Ed. A.Peel and L.H.Carlson, *Cartwrightiana* (1951). pp. 143-4.
49. Rolfe, *A True Relation of the State of Virginia Lefte by Sir Thomas Dale Knight in May Last 1616* (ed. H.C. Taylor, New Haven, 1951), pp.33-41.
50. R. Bernard, *A Key of Knowledge* (1619), pp.127-9, 279; Leighton, *Sions Plea against the Prelacie* (Amsterdam, 1628), quoted by S.Foster, *Notes from the Caroline Underground* (Hamden, Conn., 1978), p. 263; B.S.Capp, *The Fifth Monarchy Men: A Study in Seventeenth-Century English Millenarianism* (1972), p. 34.
51. Wither, *Brittans Remembrancer*, 1628 (Spenser Soc., 1880), pp. 37-8, 46, 64-5, 314, 325-30, and *passim; cf.* Sibbes, *Works*, VII, pp.396-7. Professor McGiffert collected much evidence on England as chosen nation in "God's Controversy with Jacobean England", *American Historical Review*, 88 (1983), pp.1151-74; *ibid.* 89 (1984), pp.1217-18; cf. Carol Z. Wiener, "The Beleaguered Isle: A Study of Elizabethan and Early Jacobean Anti-Catholicism", *P. and P.*, 51 (1971), esp. p. 124.
52. S.Marshall, *A Peace-Offering to God* (1641), pp. 3, 40, 45-6; J. Burrough, *Sions Joy* (1641), pp. 38-9, 43-4, 49-50.
53. N.Culpeper, *An Ephemeris for the Year 1652*, p. 21.
54. Hickes, *Peculiam Dei* (1681), pp. 21-2.
55. T.Fuller, *Church History of Britain* (1842), I, p. 221.
56. M.McKeon, *Politics and Poetry in Restoration England* (Harvard U.P., 1975), pp. 63, 68, 159, 232.
57. Pilkington, *Works*, pp. 70, 86.

58. W.Hunt, *The Puritan Moment: The Coming of Revolution in an English County* (Harvard U.P., 1983), p. 97.
59. P.Collinson, *Godly People,* pp. 433-7.
60. I.Breward, "The Significance of William Perkins", *Journal of Religious History,* 4 (1966-7), p. 113.
61. See Peter Lake, *Moderate puritans and the Elizabethan church* (Cambridge U.P., 1982), pp. 208-10, 220-1, and *passim.* See pp.67-9 below.
62. Collinson, *Godly People,* Chapter 9 *passim.*
63. See pp.76, 80 below.
64. Bancroft, *Dangerous Positions* (1593), Book I, Chapters 3-5, Book II, Chapter 1.
65. N.Sykes, *Old Priest and New Presbyter* (1956), p. 57.
66. Ed. D.H.Willson, *The Parliamentary Diary of Robert Bowyer, 1606-1607* (Minnesota U.P., 1931), p.149.
67. *The Proceedings and Debates of the House of Commons in ... 1628. ... Taken and Collected by ... Sir Thomas Crewe* (1707), p. 73. I benefited from being able to listen to Wallace Notestein on this subject.
68. S.R.Gardiner, *History of England, 1603-1642* (1883-4), VIII, pp. 138-9.
69. On this see the valuable book by Caroline Hibbard, *Charles I and the Popish Plot* (North Carolina U.P., 1982).
70. Ed. Wallace Notestein, *The Journal of Sir Simonds D'Ewes* (Yale U.P., 1923), p. 321.

4. *The Problem of Authority*

"With God, if we have belief, [there is not] any porter to keep any man out."*

The age-old problem of authority came into sharper prominence with the Reformation. Lollards had challenged the authority of the Pope; if they had won Parliamentary backing, as at one time seemed just possible, the royal supremacy might have been instituted a century and a half before the Reformation Parliament.[1] Henry VIII's Reformation publicly and stridently rejected the Pope's authority, and that of the international church, replacing them by the royal supremacy. There had been mediaeval precedents for the lay power limiting that of the church; in the sixteenth century many Catholic monarchies were to establish a great deal of control over churches within their dominions. But such actions were taken with the agreement of the papacy. This agreement might be reluctantly conceded to *force majeure*; but its existence sharply differentiated Gallicanism from Anglicanism. A great war of words followed England's Reformation, in which fundamental questions were asked about the grounds on which religious authority was justified. The rapid changes in England from Henry to a nine-year-old boy and two women showed that it was difficult merely to replace the authority of the Pope by that of the monarch without raising vast problems about the nature of authority and allegiance. So what authority was there?

Protestants thought that the answer was to be sought in the Bible, now for the first time officially translated into the vernacular and so made available for popular discussion. But the original protestant hope that all men would agree in their interpretation of the Bible proved unfounded. The Bible said different things to different people: who was to decide between rival interpretations? Even if it was agreed that "the church" should decide, who is the church? Civil service bishops appointed by the government? and dependent on it

---

* William Tyndale, *The Obedience of a Christian Man* (1527-8), in *Doctrinal Treatises* (Parker Soc., 1848), p. 291.

for promotion? Bishop Jeremy Taylor in the seventeenth century taught that denial of the Apostolic Succession would be "a plain path and inlet to atheism and irreligion; for by this means it will not only be impossible to agree concerning the meaning of Scripture, but the Scripture itself, and all the records of religion, will become useless, and of no efficacy or persuasion".[2] That sounded like popery to radicals: conversely the extreme position of Milton seemed anarchy to conservatives, yet it was only an extension of Luther's logic: "Every believer is entitled to interpret the Scriptures . . . for himself. He has the Spirit who guides truth, and he has the mind of Christ. Indeed, no one else can usefully interpret them for him, unless that person's interpretation coincides with the one he makes for himself and his own conscience".[3] The essence of protestantism — the priesthood of all believers — was logically a doctrine of individualist anarchy. "Here I stand, so help me God, I can no other"; in that cry Luther rejected the authority of Pope, church and secular power.[4]

By proclaiming that the church is composed of all believers, and not a privileged corporation of clerics, protestantism undermined the authority of the church as a self-sufficient institution. By denying the immunity of the priesthood as a separate caste, and by denying the Pope's right to pronounce authoritatively in secular affairs, Luther by implication justified the intervention of the secular power in the internal affairs of the church. Luther had no hesitation in calling on the secular power against Anabaptists, just as Henry VIII martyred Catholics and Anabaptists impartially.[5] By what authority? It was not long before Parliament was determining what was and what was not heresy, and imposing its views on all subjects as a test of political reliability. They have "made laws", Sir Thomas Wilson noted, "that every man that hath voice in the Parliament or any state of possession in the land shall take his corporal oath for the maintenance of the religion now established".[6] The road runs straight from Luther to *Leviathan*.

Thomas Hall illustrated the point vividly in a sermon preached at the election of the Lord Mayor in 1644. Frederick Duke of Saxony "was almost discouraged by the popish doctrine about magistracy". But on reading Luther's *De Magistratu* the Duke "lifts up his hands to heaven, thanking God that at last he was convinced the state of magistracy he lived in to be pleasing to God, and that he might in it do him a great deal of service".[7] Yet the protestant emphasis on conscience, the inner light, leads logically on to anarchism. Once a constraining authority exists, be it state or bishops or presbytery, it is bound at some stage or other to come up against dissenting consciences.

Hobbes faced, and thought he had solved, the problem of authority. The absolute natural rights of individuals necessitate the absolute power of the sovereign; the only alternative is anarchy. This was a wholly protestant solution to a wholly protestant paradox. Tyndale for instance, wrote that "the king is in this world without law; and may at his lust do right or wrong and shall give accounts but to God only". James I had little to add to that: no wonder Henry VIII thought *The Obedience of a Christian Man* a book fit "for him and all kings to read". Tyndale is quite clear about the social functions of the monarchy: it gets rid of the Pope on the one hand; on the other, "it is better to suffer one tyrant than many".[8] The point was hammered home in the *Homily against Disobedience and Wilful Rebellion.* "Perfect submission to kings" is "the glory of the protestant cause", Jeremy Taylor wrote, with some justification.[9]

But though the Mortal God triumphed in the short run, the paradox remained. Protestant doctrine was primarily concerned with the inner man. Luther taught individuals to stand on their own feet and question authority. Yet he (and the English reformers) had to shelter behind the temporal authority both against the power of the international church and against those of the unprivileged who carried the appeal to conscience further than suited their betters. But this was a political necessity, not a logical consequence of the reformers' teaching.

Tyndale, unlike Hobbes, left the paradox wholly unresolved. "The most despised person in his realm is the king's brother and fellow-member with him and equal with him in the church of God and of Christ".[10] John Knox was to address stern words to Mary Queen of Scots on that theme. The same arguments that prevailed against the absolute authority of the Pope could be used against the absolute authority of the King: authority having once been challenged, the logical road to theories of democracy in church and state was clear — and not only with the hindsight of the historian. Whether and when any given community would travel down that road depended less on logic than on the development of social forces within that community.

The point was made by a critic of Henry Barrow, who had written "To our prince we are humble and obedient subjects in all things which are not repugnant to God's laws". His contemporary critic added the marginal comment: "in all things that you fancy".[11] Barrow thought that if "the estate of these prelates, clergymen, ministers and their proceedings ... be found repugnant unto the Testament of Christ, then are they ... for the safety of the state to be abolished", lest they draw down the wrath of God.[12] Barrow found no warrant in the Bible for fasting on ember days, the eve of saints' days or in Lent.[13] Robert Browne told Burghley that "the Word of God doth expressly set down all necessary and general rules of the arts and all learning", and that the universities should be reformed in accordance with these rules.[14] The antinomian separatist John Traske came to require express instructions from the Bible for everything that was done.[15] More subtly, Stephen Marshall in 1646 found social mobility and the career open to the talents justified by the lives of Moses, Issachar, Gideon ("a private gentleman, it may be but a yeoman's son"), Saul ("a private gentleman's son"), David, Amos and the fishermen of the New Testament. So God had taken "gentlemen from following their hawks and hounds, and tradesmen from their shops, and husbandmen from their ploughs" to command the New Model Army.[16] The Marquis of Newcastle was not absurdly exaggerating when he warned the young Charles II that "if any be Bible-men, ... they may think it a service to God to destroy you and say the spirit moved them".[17]

There is thus a tension between any state church and protestant individual consciences. Some consciences some time are likely to feel called upon to obey the God within them rather than the state or its church. Such clashes occur more often, and affect larger numbers of people, at times of social, economic or political crisis than when all is going relatively peacefully and normally: under Edward VI and Charles I rather than under Elizabeth, at least before the fifteen-nineties.

In 1656 Francis Osborne pointed out that "if faith is not allowed to be taken implicitly from the authority of any church, a freedom of choice will result to all. ... And since so considerable a falsehood is thought to be discovered by our governors in the clergy's tenet for the impunity of kings, why may not their poor subjects be unsatisfied about heaven and hell?[18] It was a powerful argument for the restoration of king, bishops and parochial clergy to interpret the Scriptures to their congregations.

Before the Reformation, first-hand knowledge of the Bible was normally confined to those who could read Latin. Lollards produced their own illicit translations into the vernacular, with the democratic intention of allowing all Christians to have access to the sacred text. After the Reformation the Bible was available for popular discussion. Henry VIII's attempt to confine Bible-reading to those of the rank of yeoman and above, and to abolish "diversity of opinions" by statute, were both unsuccessful. The circulation of an English Bible had been authorized in order to fortify Henry VIII's Reformation against Rome, which as all protestants knew preferred ignorance.[19] After 1525 Luther recognized the dangers of unsupervised and uncontrolled Bible-reading by the lower classes and their spokesmen. He tried to replace, or to control, Bible-reading by the use of catechisms. Since the answers were intended to be learnt by rote, catechisms could be used for indoctrinating the illiterate as well as the literate.[20]

In England the protestant emphasis on the importance both of preaching and of a learned clergy testifies to a similar anxiety to have qualified experts ready to undertake the ticklish job of interpreting the Bible. But the ethos of protestantism itself bred resistance to expert (and upper-class) interpreters. The Bible — in part perhaps thanks to Lollardy — proved a time-bomb which humbler protestants used against their betters. Whitgift discouraged Bible-reading in households, where there would be no university-trained divine handy to interpret "difficult" passages.[21] One of the objects of the Authorized Version of 1611 was to produce an approved official version to supplant the Geneva Bible, which was popular with Puritans but which James thought of all translations the worst because of its subversive marginal notes.

William Bradshaw had written in 1605: "The Word of God contained in the writings of the Prophets and Apostles is of absolute perfection, given by Christ the head of the church to be unto the same the sole canon and rule of all matters of religion and the worship and service of God. ... Whatsoever done in the same service and worship cannot be justified by the said Word is unlawful".[22] Nor was this just a separatist emphasis. Thomas Cartwright thought that the Bible called for the elimination of all remnants of popery, and that society could not be properly ordered or stable until this had been done. Until then everything would be topsy-turvy: "the water should go to the stream, the scholar should teach his master, the sheep control their pastor". The possibility of short-term disorder must be faced, in order to establish the right order permanently.[23] Whitgift on the other hand saw Cartwright's approach as permanently disorderly, since it called for aristocratic or democratic government of the church — and so was incompatible with monarchy.[24]

The point was summed up nicely by William Sanderson. If men seek "direct warrant from the written Word of God" for everything they do, "all human authority will soon be despised". The orders of princes no less than of parents and masters "shall be taken into slow deliberation, and the equity of them sifted by those that are bound to obey, though they know no cause why, so long as they know no cause to the contrary".[25]

So the original protestant hope that the conclusions to be drawn from the Bible were self-evident and incontestable proved woefully false. Officialdom assumed that the protestant clergy would continue to be the official interpreters of the Bible, under guidance from above. Hence insistence on a learned clergy, on a university education which would include Latin and theology, and which might include Greek, Hebrew and other languages. But — apart from the fact that most of the clergy fell short of the desired educational standard — if all believers are priests, why should officially ordained clergymen have a special capacity to interpret the Scriptures? The point was made forcefully by the Leveller William Walwyn. "Since the Scriptures are now in English, which at first were in Hebrew, Greek or Syriac or what other language; why may not one that understands English only both understand and declare the true meaning of them as well as an English Hebrician or Grecian or Roman whatsoever? . . . I pray you, what are you the better for having the Scripture in your own language? When it was locked up in the Latin tongue by the policy of Rome, you might have had a learned friar at any time to have interpreted the same. . . . Now . . . you must have a university man to interpret the English, or you are in as bad a case as before — but not in worse; for, for your money, you may have plenty at your service, and to interpret as shall best please your fancy".[26]

This is looking rather far ahead. Under Elizabeth attempts had been made, through prophesyings and classes, to arrive at an agreed consensus of clerical opinion. But these meetings were discouraged, to put it mildly, by Elizabeth, and were suppressed by her bishops. In any case, after the invention of printing, with literacy increasing, not only for economic reasons but also because lay protestants strove to read the Bible for themselves, it was difficult to preserve a clerical monopoly. The protestant and later Puritan emphasis on preaching as necessary for salvation was a way of maintaining clerical supremacy whilst allowing the laity to think for themselves within limits laid down by the clergy. But repetitions of sermons in families and among groups of the godly could easily develop into conventicles in which the laity usurped the authority of priests, some of whom were still dumb dogs. So preaching — and gadding to sermons when one's incumbent was a non-preacher — could lead to conventicles, conventicles to separatism.[27] In separatist congregations the whole body of believers, not merely the minister or the elders, joined in discussions and the administration of discipline.[28]

Professor Collinson has shown how compatible Puritanism was with the interests of the gentry — offering a diminution of episcopal control over the clergy and the substitution of the influence of the propertied laity.[29] It would have been a *via media* between democratic sectarianism and monarchical episcopacy: the example of the Scottish kirk, in which aristocratic lay elders played a prominent part, was always attractive. Hence the failure of attempts by Presbyterian ministers to build up classes of ministers within the state church. Such attempts foundered on the opposition of the secular power, whether Elizabeth working through her civil service bishops or the Long Parliament asserting its supremacy over the classes which it set up.

Separatism was one answer, though a very hazardous choice before 1640, since it involved exile or a risky illegality. Separatism signified among other things a rejection of the specialized, educated priests of the established church as fitting interpreters of the Bible or expounders of God's will. Against them appeal was made to the congregation of believers.[30] But even when separatism became easier after 1640, the ideal of a national church still retained its hold, as was demonstrated by the practice of occasional conformity when dissenters were excluded from the national church after 1660.[31] Tensions remained, between individual consciences and the state church before 1640, between individual consciences and all churches after 1660. For in order to survive after the restoration the sects had to organize, to define their beliefs, to expel or disown those who would not or could not accept what the majority accepted. Splits and schisms among the Quakers in the fifties and sixties show that most anarchical of all the religious groupings having to accommodate itself to the needs of organization and discipline. The sense of the meeting was a more democratic authority than that of bishops; but it was authority, and the Society of Friends became something like a church. The minutes of Baptist meetings in this period would almost suggest that excommunication was the main business of the congregations.[32] Hobbism prevailed.

Different tensions were felt between 1640 and 1660, but they too related to the problem of authority. Free trade in ideas replaced monopoly. Attempts to preserve or restore a group of professional expert interpreters roused intense hostility. Walwyn in his *Prediction of Mr. Edwards His Conversion* (1646) made that great persecutor confess to "base fear that plain unlearned men should seek for knowledge any other way than as they are directed by us that are learned". For "if they should fall to teach one another ... we should lose our domination in being sole judges of doctrine and discipline, whereby our predecessors have overruled states and kingdoms. Or lastly, that we should lose our profits and plenteous maintenance by tithes".[33]

A state church depended on the clergyman's legal right to collect tithes from his parishioners. If ministers were dependent on the voluntary contributions of their parishioners, Sir Walter Mildmay reflected in 1587, they would have but "a bare and uncertain" living. Abolition of tithes would have meant the end of a national church as it had hitherto existed: here again we can cite Bancroft, in agreement with interregnum radicals.[34] Milton thought abolition of tithes essential to religious liberty; the Master of Gonville and Caius, William Dell, shared Milton's hostility. In Winstanley's ideal commonwealth preaching for hire was one of the few offences which merited the death sentence. For most beneficed clergymen it was a bread and butter question, but there were strong traditional arguments in favour of the national community being organized within a single church.

The radical attack on Oxford and Cambridge must be seen in the context of the problem of authority. The universities trained clergymen with special linguistic skills which were thought to fit them to interpret the Scriptures. Those who believed that any layman could interpret the Bible for himself, and that mechanic preachers gifted with God's grace could interpret it far better than the most learned cleric lacking divine grace, had no use for the universities as they existed in the early seventeenth century. And indeed there is ample evidence that the behaviour of undergraduates and dons was often far from godly. In *An Almond for a Parrot* (1590) Nashe had accused Puritans of wanting to abolish the universities. Winstanley and other reformers hoped to get rid of them as seminaries training the clergy, to get rid of a special clerical caste altogether. "From Oxford and Cambridge come hireling priests", declared Edward Byllynge, speaking for many within and outside the Quaker movement.[35] Some would have been happy to see reformed universities surviving to give a secular education, with greater emphasis on science and modern subjects.[36] Restoration of a single state church and tithes, and preservation of the universities for training a learned clergy, were major achievements of 1660. Bishops lost their political power, but the exclusion of dissenters from the universities ensured a clergy more loyal to the established church than before 1640.

But there was too a long-standing popular hostility to education as a source of privilege, of class distinctions. The most obvious example of this was benefit of clergy, which allowed anyone who could stumble through the neck verse to escape the major penalties of his first criminal conviction. Originally this privilege had been restricted to the clergy; but with the extension of literacy it became a social privilege. Not until 1692 was it extended to women.[37] Jack Cade in *2 Henry VI* complained "because they could not read thou hast hanged them". "Away with him. He speaks Latin" (IV. vii 42-3, 55-6). Henry Barrow made the point rather differently when he spoke of the universities as guardians of Antichrist's throne and Latin as the language of the Beast.[38] "Cobblers and tinkers" in Chelmsford in 1642 were alleged to preach "that learning hath always been an enemy to the Gospel and that it were a happy thing if there were no universities, and all books burnt except the Bible".[39] "The common cry of the multitude", a preacher told the House of Lords in May 1647, was "down with learning": "ye may see what good learning did in the bishops' time".[40]

The Bible of course had to be interpreted. Calvin himself had done a good deal by way of interpreting the letter to mean what he wanted, as Milton was to do later.[41] Calvin developed the useful idea that the Holy Ghost spoke to the capacity of his audience. "Moses wrote in a popular style things which, without instruction, all ordinary persons endued with common sense are able to understand". He did not write for professional astronomers when describing the creation, for example. "Because he was ordained a teacher as well of the unlearned and rude as of the learned, he could not otherwise fulfil his office than by descending to this grosser method of instruction". Similarly Moses "was not ignorant of geometry", but in describing the building of the ark he "spoke in a homely style, to suit the capacity of the people".[42] This idea that God "accommodated" his Scriptural revelation to the capacity of the unlearned vulgar was to prove useful for seventeenth-century scientists like Galileo (under threat from the Inquisition) and a Puritan turned Latitudinarian like John Wilkins.[43]

A further advance was actually to criticize the Biblical text in the process of interpreting it. Ralegh did this frequently in his *History of the World*.[44] So did Milton, and Jeremy Taylor.[45] The profane had long pointed out the Bible's contradictions and inconsistencies. In Ralegh's dashingly advanced circle in the fifteen-nineties men agreed that religion had been invented "to keep the baser sort in fear".[46] Such ideas caused alarm even when limited to this restricted group of intellectuals. But in James's reign ordinary people were expressing scepticism about the Bible.[47] A Lancashire assize sermon of 1632 insisted that a ministry was essential to "keep the consciences of men in awe".[48]

During the Revolution Walwyn and Clement Wrighter were free to discuss publicly the contradictions and inconsistencies of the Bible, treating it as a historical document to which normal scholarly techniques should be applied. Samuel Fisher argued with much learning that a text so corrupt and self-contradictory could not possibly be the Word of God. His book was appropriately named *The Rusticks Alarum to the Rabbies: Or, The Country correcting the University, and Clergy*. It threatened to put interpreters of Scripture out of a job; and the suggestion that it came from the rustics who composed the mass of tithe-payers did not make it any more welcome to the rabbis. But Fisher's book was not published until 1660, and so made its main impact on scholars including, it appears, Spinoza.[49] If it had appeared earlier, when it could have been discussed by rustics and artisans, the undermining effect on the status of the Bible might have been more serious.[50] The restoration came just in time. Characters in restoration comedy made jokes about "faults in the translation" when faced with an inconvenient Biblical prohibition.[51] To the argument that women owed obedience to men because God created Adam before Eve Mary Astell — a serious and pious lady—retorted that God had created animals before Adam: what conclusion should be drawn from that?[52] The whole tone of intellectual discussion had changed.

The important thing for our purposes is not the conclusion reached, or not reached, to the problem of authority, but the process of discussion which the appeal to the Bible unleashed. Matthew Arnold was utterly wrong when he wrote "the one who says that God's Church makes him believe what he believes, and the other who says that God's Word makes him believe what he believes, are for the philosopher perfectly alike in not really and truly knowing, when they say 'God's Church' and 'God's Word', what it is they say or whereof they affirm".[53] They may be alike for the philosopher, but for the historian the one accepts an external and (for him) arbitrary authority, the church, the other an internal authority, whose validity he can test in discussion with other believers. That distinction is what the Reformation had been about. The mere fact of accepting the Bible as ultimate arbiter forced Biblical criticism upon protestants.

Desperate attempts were made to reassert the authority of Scripture by providing a convincing overruling authority, whose dicta would win acceptance. John Reeve's announcement that God had appointed him sole interpreter of the Bible was one such attempt; but Reeve won relatively few adherents. For Quakers the inner light within all men and women was to provide the answer; but new inner light proved to be but old conscience writ more extensively. "The Lamb's War" of the Quakers, Professor Bauman says, "was in one major outward sense a struggle between the charismatic prophets of Quakerism and the upholders of the priestly tradition of established religion, as rival claimants to exclusive religious legitimacy as spokesmen of the divine word".[54]

So all roads lead to Hobbes. His insistence that the sovereign and only the sovereign could interpret the Bible was unpopular among theologians, but it proved more acceptable to ordinary citizens and—in practice if not in theory—to governments. In 1676 Chief Justice Hale ruled that to say religion was a cheat was an offence punishable in the common-law courts.[55] Authority, which in the sixteenth century had belonged to the Pope, or to a divine king, or to the Apostolic Succession of bishops, now rested with the King in Parliament, and with the common law, taking over the functions of the declining ecclesiastical courts. After 1688 even Tories recognized that toleration must be extended to nonconformists. The Church of England kept rural congregations under control, with the aid of the gentry; but the help of dissenters was needed to check urban speculation. The Societies for the Reformation of Manners were one form of co-operation between the state church and nonconformists for social purposes.[56] "If the common people are induced to lay aside religion," wrote Charles Davenant in 1698, "they will quickly cast off all fear of their rulers."[57] It was worth expending time and money to avert that double catastrophy.

NOTES

1. K.B. McFarlane, *John Wyclif and the Origins of Nonconformity* (1952), pp. 51-2, 61, 92.
2. J. Taylor, *The Whole Works* (1836), II, p. 33. See p. 322 below.
3. *M.C.P.W.*, VI, pp. 583-4.
4. Cf. *The Reformation Crisis* (ed. J. Hurtsfield, 1971), p. 1: "in the profoundest sense a crisis of authority".
5. See p. 163 below, and a valuable paper by Robert Weimann, "Shakespeare und Luther", in *Shakespeare Jahrbuch*, Band 120 (1984), esp. pp. 20-4. For the crisis of authority in general see his "Autorität und Gesellschaftliche Erfahrung in Shakespeares Theater", *ibid.*, Band 119 (1983), esp. pp. 92-4. See also A. Sinfield, *Literature in Protestant England, 1560-1660* (1983), pp. 138-9.
6. Ed. F.J. Fisher, Thomas Wilson, *The State of England Anno Dom. 1600*, p. 41, in *Camden Miscellany*, XVI (1936).
7. T. Hall, *The Magistrates Commission from Heaven* (1644), p. 2.
8. Tyndale, *Doctrinal Treatises*, pp. 178-80.
9. Taylor, *The Whole Works*, II, p. 62; cf. p. 47, and III, p. 717.
10. Tyndale, *Doctrinal Treatises*, p. 125.
11. Ed. L.H. Carlson, *The Writings of Henry Barrow, 1587-1590* (1962), p. 125.
12. *Ibid.*, p. 241.
13. Ed. Carlson, *The Writings of Henry Barrow, 1590-1591* (1960) p. 68.
14. Ed. A. Peel and L.H. Carlson, *The Writings of Robert Harrison and Robert Browne*, p. 530.
15. B.R. White, "John Traske (1585-1636) and London Puritanism", *Trans. of the Congregational Historical Soc.*, XX (1968), p. 225.
16. Stephen Marshall, *The Right Understanding of the Times*, a sermon preached to the House of Commons, 30 December 1646 (1647), pp. 4-5.
17. In Ellis, *Original Letters Illustrative of English History*, first series, III, p. 289.

18. F. Osborne, *Advice to a Son,* in *Miscellaneous Works* (11th edn., 1722) I, p. 99. See chapter 8 below.
19. *Homilies,* pp. 501-2, 507-8.
20. R. Gawthrop and R. Strauss, "Protestantism and Literacy in Early Modern Germany", *P. and P.,* No. 104 (1984), pp. 31-55.
21. Ed. H. Gee and W.J. Hardy, *Documents Illustrative of English Church History* (1896), p. 481.
22. W. Bradshaw, *English Puritanism* (1605), p. 1.
23. Lake, *Moderate Puritanism and the Elizabethan Church,* pp. 90-1.
24. Strype, *Life of Whitgift,* I, pp. 114, 504. Cf. I, pp. 72-3 for the even greater subversiveness of Anabaptists.
25. Sanderson, *XXXV Sermons* (7th edn., 1681), pp. 61, 65.
26. [William Walwyn], *The Power of Love* (1643), pp. 46-8, in Haller (ed.), *Tracts on Liberty in the Puritan Revolution,* II. Cf. Brian Manning, "The Levellers and Religion", in *Radical Religion in the English Revolution* (ed. J.F. McGregor and B. Reay, Oxford U.P., 1984), p. 66.
27. D. Zaret, "Ideology and Organization in Puritanism", *Archive for European Sociology,* XXI (1980), pp. 93-5.
28. Cf. M. James, *English Politics and the Concept of Honour (P. and P.* Supplement, 83, 1978), pp. 82-3.
29. See pp. 67-9 below.
30. *W.T.U.D.,* pp. 371-3.
31. See Chapter 14 below.
32. *W.T.U.D.,* pp. 373-8; cf. my *The Experience of Defeat* (1984), pp. 290-4.
33. Walwyn, *A Prediction of Mr. Edwards His Conversion and Recantation* (1646), p. 9, in Haller, *Tracts on Liberty,* III. Cf. [Walwyn], *The Compassionate Samaritane* (1644), pp. 2-3, *ibid.;* [Lilburne], *Englands Birth-Right Justified* (1645), pp. 8-9, *ibid.*
34. S.E. Lehmberg, *Sir Walter Mildmay and Tudor Government* (Texas U.P., 1964), p. 289; ed. E.R. Foster, *Proceedings in Parliament, 1610,* I, *The House of Lords* (Yale U.P., 1966), p. 224.
35. E.B., *A Word of Reproof, and Advice to my late Fellow-Soldiers and Officers* (1659), pp. 19-20.
36. See my *Change and Continuity in Seventeenth-Century England* (1974), Chapters 5 and 7.
37. Susan Staves, *Players' Scepters: Fictions of Authority in the Restoration* (Nebraska U.P., 1979), p. 184.
38. Quoted in my *Antichrist in Seventeenth-Century England* (1971), pp. 138-42.
39. [Bruno Ryves], *Angliae Ruina* (1647), p. 27. Cf. Robert South: "Latin was with them a mortal crime, and Greek ... the sin" against the Holy Ghost *(Sermons,* 1692, I, p. 160).
40. William Hussey, *The Magistrates Charge for the Peoples Safetie* (1647), p. 28.
41. See for example Calvin, *A Commentary on Daniel* (trans. and ed. by Thomas Myers, 1966), II, p. 78. First published 1561. Cf. Milton's divorce pamphlets.

42. Calvin, *A Commentary on Genesis* (trans. and ed. John King, 1965), I, pp. 85-7, 256; cf. pp. 141, 177. First published 1534.
43. B.J. Shapiro, *John Wilkins, 1614-1672: An Intellectual Biography* (California U.P., 1969), pp. 51, 268-9.
44. Cf. for example *The History of the World* (Edinburgh, 1820), I, pp. 63, 75-9, 87-9, 158, 237, 257; II, pp. 130, 222-3, 278-82, 369; III, pp. 214, 266-7; IV, pp. 572-3, and *passim.*
45. J. Taylor, *The Whole Works*, I, pp. 218-21.
46. See p. 131 below. Cf. George Chapman, *Bussy D'Ambois*, in *Comedies and Tragedies* (1873), II, p. 39; *W.T.U.D.*, p. 163.
47. M.J. Ingram, *Ecclesiastical Justice in Wiltshire, 1600-1640, with especial reference to cases concerning sex and marriage* (Oxford D. Phil. thesis, 1976), pp. 81, 91, 104.
48. R. Richardson, *Puritanism in north-western England: A Regional Study of the Diocese of Chester to 1642* (Manchester U.P., 1972), p. 145.
49. R.H. Popkin, "Spinoza and the Conversion of the Jews", in *Spinoza's Political and Theological Thought* (ed. C. De Deugd, Amsterdam, 1984), p. 174.
50. *W.T.U.D.*, Chapter 11.
51. E.g. Sir John Vanbrugh, *The Provok'd Wife* (1697), I, i.
52. M. Astell, *Reflections upon Marriage* (3rd edn., 1706), Sig. a2. I am grateful to Bridget Hill for drawing my attention to this point.
53. Arnold, *Culture and Anarchy* (Nelson, n.d.), p. 256.
54. R. Bauman, *Let your words be few: Symbolism of speaking and silence among seventeenth-century Quakers* (Cambridge U.P., 1983), p. 41. Cf. B. Reay, "Quakerism and Society", in McGregor and Reay, *op. cit.*, pp. 145-7.
55. See p. 338 below.
56. See p. 335 below.
57. *The Political and Commercial Works of Charles Davenant* (1967), pp. 45-7.

5. *The State-Ecclesiastical*

"These differences ... arose originally solely from the constitution of an authoritative national church-state, consisting solely in the power and interest of the clergy – wherein the people, either as Christians, protestants or subjects of the kingdom, are not concerned. ...

"It is no less glorious in the sight of God ... to suffer in giving testimony against the abominations of the apostate, antichristian church-state, than to suffer for the Gospel itself in opposition to idolatrous paganism".*

The idea of the English nation was bound up with protestantism. The state-ecclesiastical, as Owen makes clear, was something distinct from the nation and from the civil state. The clergy formed an estate of the realm, yet although bishops sat in the House of Lords, the lower clergy were not represented in the House of Commons. The Convocations of Canterbury and York legislated for the clergy; but unless the canons passed by them were confirmed by Parliament their authority over the laity was uncertain. Bishops thus occupied a curious constitutional position; the only members of the clerical estate who sat in Parliament.

A besetting problem for historians is the survival of names describing things which have totally changed their nature. It took several reform bills to convince historians that Parliaments in the seventeenth century did not represent the people of England. It is difficult for historians even today to appreciate that seventeenth century radicals often use the word "people" whilst, consciously or unconsciously, excluding "the poor". Similarly with the word "bishop". To us the word conjures up genial rosy-faced old gentlemen patting children on the head; or learned scholars. It comes as a salutory shock to find Milton concluding his first prose pamphlet, *Of Reformation Touching Church-Discipline in England*, by consigning all bishops, apparently *ex officio* and regardless of their

---

*John Owen, *Some considerations about union among protestants* (1680), and *A brief and impartial account of the nature of the protestant religion* (1682), both in *Works* (1850-3), XIV, pp. 520, 555.

51

individual merits, to "the deepest and darkest gulf of hell", there to remain to all eternity. This is an attitude repugnant to twentieth-century liberal ideas. But before we get too one-sidedly self-righteous, let us recall another judgment of Milton's more congenial to twentieth-century liberalism: "It is disgraceful and disgusting that the Christian religion should be supported by violence".[1] And let us remember that Archbishop Laud normally favoured imposing the most severe corporal sentences on his enemies; when others suggested a flogging, he would add branding or loss of ears. Bishops aroused intense passions because they were vigorous partisans, wielding political power in an age of revolutionary crisis.

Patrick Collinson's splendid Ford Lectures depict conscientious and hard-working Jacobean and Caroline bishops presiding over a broadly-based church which won general acceptance.[2] One problem with this is the volume of literary evidence attesting to the unpopularity of bishops and the clergy. My object in this chapter is to collect evidence on attitudes towards bishops and the church in the two generations before 1640. This was an age of fierce Puritan and separatist attacks on bishops. These are of course biassed and not to be used in isolation. Instead of quoting them, I shall cite almost exclusively defenders of the hierarchy. Whatever allowances we make, it is quite clear from their evidence that "episcopacy had few defenders", as Collinson himself writes.[3] Statements by bishops themselves cannot be lightly brushed aside.

The opening words of the future Bishop Cooper's *Admonition to the People of England* (1589) speak of "the loathesome contempt, hatred and disdain that *the most part* of men in these days bear ... toward the ministers of the church of God. ... He who can most bitterly inveigh against bishops and preachers ... thinketh of himself, *and is esteemed of other*, as the most zealous and earnest furtherer of the gospel".[4]

Cooper put a hypothetical case against the hierarchy, that God has shown judgment against them for their wickedness, "because he hath made them so contemptible, so vile and despised before all the people: for (say they) we may see how all men loathe and disdain them". Cooper's answer is not to deny the contempt, but to deny that it is "always an unfallible token of evil priests and ministers, or a certain sign of God's displeasure toward them, when the people do hate, disdain and contemn them. ... It may be surely, and indeed I think it to be very true, that God hath touched our bishops and preachers with the scourge of ignominy and reproach for their slackness and negligence in their office". "The whole state ecclesiastical ... is grown into hatred and contempt, and all inferior subjects disdain in any point to be ruled by them". "The people ... have conceived an heathenish contempt of religion, and a disdainful loathing of the ministers thereof".[5] That is no doubt hyperbole; but Archbishop Sandys said something very similar: "the ministers of the word, the messengers of Christ, ...are esteemed *tamquam excrementa mundi*".[6] "Our estimation is little", Aylmer confirmed, "our authority is less; so that we are become contemptible in the eyes of the people".[7] The clergy themselves, in a formal document of 1586, remarked "with how great hatred the common sort of men are influenced against the ministers of the church";[8] and the Puritan Richard Greenham spoke of the "great hatred" which had "sprung up from the people" against the clergy because they were more diligent in collecting tithes than in dispensing hospitality.[9] Bancroft was sure that if congregational elections were allowed, candidates favoured by the hierarchy would be rejected because of "the sinister affections of the people".[10] In the Parliament of 1628 Sir Humphrey May argued that "juries of poor freeholders" could not be trusted to be fair to the clergy".[11] Cooper had been alarmed by the dangerous argument that bishops should be deposed and their lands confiscated merely because "our bishops and ministers are evil men". He did not deny the allegation, but suggested that the same argument could be turned against princes and magistrates.[12]

Francis Godwin, in his *Catalogue of the Bishops of England* (1601), admitted that "in the vulgar sort ... is bred a conceit not only that the men [he is speaking of pre-Reformation clergy] were wicked, and so their doctrines corrupt, but also their functions and callings to be utterly unlawful and antichristian".[13] Even Burghley was shocked to see "such worldliness in many that were otherwise affected before they came to cathedral chairs."[14]

Now many of these statements are to be discounted: they were propagandist special pleading by men on the defensive. But their cumulative effect is remarkable; and special pleading pleads in vain if it is recognizably incorrect. The social argument in favour of episcopacy, used by Cooper, had already become familiar. Archbishop Parker had observed that "how secure soever the nobility were of these Puritans, and countenanced them against the bishops, they themselves might rue it at last". Puritans "tended towards a popularity".[15] "If you had once made an equality ... among the clergy", Whitgift told Puritans, "it would not be long or you attempted the like among the laity".[16] "Men", he declared in 1583, "are naturally prone to speak ill of two kinds of persons, viz. of bishops and magistrates". The original cause of this, he thought, was the devil.[17] Hooker pointed out that the title of bishops to their livings was as good as any lay title to property.[18] When in the Long Parliament Oliver Cromwell attacked the great properties of bishops, the answer came pat: parity in the church will lead to parity in the state.[19]

The judicious Hooker was on the defensive about the ecclesiastical establishment. "If we maintain things that are established, we have ... to strive with a number of heavy prejudices deeply rooted in the hearts of men, who think that herein we serve the time and speak in favour of the present state because thereby we either hold or seek preferment".[20] Brightman in 1615 confirmed the unpopularity of bishops with "the people and multitude", and the popularity of Marprelate's attack on them twenty-six years earlier.[21]

This evidence appears to confict with Collinson's scholarly reconstruction of the virtues of many Jacobean bishops. Perhaps there had been a rapid improvement? Perhaps bishops, then as now, varied in their tastes and performance? But we cannot ignore the views I have quoted, however exaggerated. Hostility towards bishops seems to be more prominent under the primacies of Whitgift, Bancroft and Laud. Yet the clergy were not immune from criticism even under James. In 1610 the Bishop of Lincoln said in the House of Lords that the lower House "loved not bishops" — a charge which Lord Saye and Sele sharply denied.[22] Marten in the same year attacked parsons for preaching up a prerogative right to taxation, and both he and Sir Roger Owen in 1614 accused the clergy of supporting absolutism. Bishop Neile was said to have committed a greater treason than killing a judge when he attacked the House of Commons:[23] and there was "murmuring against the bishops" for urging payment of a benevolence after the dissolution of Parliament and then contributing inadequately themselves.[24] The sordid scandal of the Essex divorce, in which the saintly Lancelot Andrewes was involved as well as Laud,[25] also brought discredit on the hierarchy. There were allegations that money was offered for bishoprics.[26] There was the Archbishop of Dublin who, Bishop Bedell's biographer reports, had only one sermon, on the text "Touch not mine Anointed", which he preached every year upon the King's accession day. It was in 1640

that Bishop Atherton was "condemned for iniquities far above all
that is kept upon record concerning Sodom".[27]

In the anecdote of James I admitting that he made bad men
bishops, his explanation was that "no good men would take the
office on them".[28] Hooker had anticipated the point: "Herod and
Archelaus are noted to have sought out purposely the dullest and
most ignoble that could be found amongst the people, preferring
such to the High Priest's office" in order to discredit it. "It may be
there hath been partly some show and just suspicion of like practice
in some" in England.[29] Weighty words from the church's most
distinguished defender. Even a loyal church and king man like Ralph
Knevet wrote, probably in the sixteen-forties:

> Now the English crown
> And mitre must go down;
> Forth of his temple Christ will throw
> Those greedy money-changers now.
>
> A clergy proud and too licentious,
> Ever more ready tithes to gather
> Than to preach truths, and rather
> Conformable than conscientious,
> Neglecting for to give
> Bread truly nutritive
> To hungry souls, may chiefly own
> The troubles of this realm and crown.[30]

The necessity of a hierarchical state church to monarchy was
admitted on all sides. Cooper claimed to be afraid that the Presbyterian platform would "bring the government of the church to a
democracy or aristocracy", and this would spread "to the government of the common weal".[31] "No monarchy being able to stand
when the church is in anarchy", as the Earl of Salisbury put it in
1607.[32] Parity amongst ministers cannot agree with monarchy, James
said. "Whensoever the ecclesiastical dignity shall be turned in contempt", he told Salisbury, "and begin to evanish in this kingdom, the
kings thereof shall not long prosper in their government and the
monarchy shall fall in ruin". "Revolt in the Low Countries... began
first by a petition for matter of religion; and so did all the troubles in
Scotland".[33] Innumerable statements could be cited of the necessity
of the church to the state, and of episcopacy to monarchy — by
Laud, Charles I and the Canons of 1640.[34] But they were not alone.

In the Parliament of 1628 Sir Walter Earle declared "Never was there ... a more near conjunction between matter of religion and matter of state, in any kingdom in the world, than there is in this kingdom at this day".[35] "It is necessary to have a religion to preserve the commonwealth", said Calibute Downing in the early thirties. Aristocracy is more convenient for this state at this time than democracy: the nobility and clergy are the main pillars of a monarchy.[36] "The civil magistrate is a church officer in every Christian commonwealth", added Sir Benjamin Rudyerd.[37]

If episcopacy was necessary to monarchy, presbytery was necessary to aristocracy. Richard Overton observed that "without a powerful compulsive presbytery in the church, a compulsive mastery or aristocratical government over the people in the state could never long be maintained".[38] But links are also suggested between parsons and the ruling class in general. Cobbler How declared that the clergy must be dressed and maintained like "men of honour, and such as be distinct from others"; "reproach and nakedness and living on mere alms they cannot brook".[39] There were to be many such denunciations from radicals during the revolutionary decades. The church's social links are confirmed by Richard Baxter: "If any would raise an army to extirpate knowledge and religion, the tinkers and sowgawters and crate-carriers and beggars and bargemen and all the rabble that cannot read, nor ever use the Bible, will be the forwardest to come into such a militia".[40] Clergymen were "the black guard of Satan", said Buckinghamshire Levellers in 1648;[41] "redcoats and blackcoats" maintained order for Diabolus in Bunyan's Mansoul.

Not unexpectedly, hostility to bishops and the clergy generally was expressed with renewed vigour after the breakdown of ecclesiastical controls in 1640-1. In *The World Turned Upside Down* I gave a good deal of evidence for popular hostility towards bishops and clergy during and immediately after the Laudian régime.[42] "So generally peevish and fanaticized were the people that not any particular discontent or personal quarrel with any private clergyman but 'these bishops, these parsons' (the whole coat)". Chestlin stressed the political connection. Just as Elizabeth's Bishop Aylmer defended the surplice as "the Queen's livery", so Chestlin referred to "episcopal government in England being indeed the King's spiritual militia, and the most powerful as commanding the consciences of subjects".[43] Charles himself had said in 1646 "I am most confident that religion will much sooner regain the militia than the militia will religion".[44] I might have quoted Bishop Warner of Rochester,[45] or Peter Barwick's *Life of Dr. John Barwick*,[46] or Bruno Ryves[47], all defenders of episcopacy.

Those who attacked bishops did so on what were (or what they said were) religious grounds. Those who defended them often defended them as necessary parts of the social order, or of the constitution of the kingdom. Thus a petition in defence of bishops in 1641 declared that "government of the church by episcopacy is most suitable to the form and frame of the civil government here in this kingdom. ... We conceive it may be of dangerous consequence for men of settled fortunes to hazard their estates by making so great an alteration and overturning upon a new form of government." "Every great alteration in church or state must needs be dangerous". The petitioners claimed the support of "many, and those of the better sort, of the inhabitants" of London.[48] Falkland echoed these words. "Since all great changes in government are dangerous, I am for trying if we cannot take away the inconveniences of bishops and the inconveniences of no bishops".[49] Strangeways and Waller expressed the same anxiety more robustly.[50]

In a valuable recent book Dr Joyce Malcolm wrote of the civil war "to the Parliamentarians it was a religious as well as a political war, to the royalists essentially a political and socio-economic conflict".[51] This simple observation clears up some of the confusion caused by an either/or attitude towards the causes of the war. Why should we assume that both sides had the same motivation? Some might be thinking of the dangers of international popery whilst others were concerned with social stability. "Putting religion first" might mean many things which are not "religious" in the modern sense — questions of foreign policy, social grievances, the right of self-expression for those normally denied it.

The conservative position was summed up with all the wisdom of hindsight by Clarendon. Of Laud's activities in Scotland his protégé wrote that it was "almost impossible that any new discipline could be introduced into the church which would not much concern the government of the state. ... It was now easy ... to suggest to men of all conditions that here was an entire new model of government in church and state".[52] "The ecclesiastical and civil state was so wrought and interwoven together ... [that it was unlikely that] the law itself would have the same respect and veneration from the people when the well-disposed fabric of the church should be rent asunder". "Many ... cordially and constantly opposed that [clerical disabilities] act, as friends rather to monarchy than religion", who however after Charles's acceptance of the act "never considered or resisted any attempt or further alteration in the church, looking upon the bishops as useless to sovereignty".[53] Digby said "I do not think that a king can put down bishops totally with safety to monarchy",[54] a point which Clarendon later elaborated in his *History of the Rebellion:* removing the bishops out of the House of Lords was "removing landmarks, and not a shaking ... but dissolving foundations".[55] Clarendon contrasted his own conscientious position on these questions with that of Sir John Colpeper, who "in matters of religion ... was in his judgment very indifferent; but more inclined to what was established, to avoid the accidents which commonly attend a change, without any motives from his conscience".[56] The distinction between Clarendon's conscience and Colpeper's lack of it is perhaps of greater importance to the recording angel than to the historian trying to disentangle the causes of the civil war.

Sir Henry Slingsby, who wanted to curb the political power of bishops, nevertheless feared lest "the common people ... would think themselves loose and absolved from all government when they should see that which they so much venerated so easily subverted".[57] "Episcopacy", said Charles I in 1648, who by that time had learnt Hyde's lesson, "was so interwoven in the laws of the land, that we apprehended the pulling out of this thread was like to make the whole garment ravel".[58] "They that hate bishops have destroyed monarchy" was Jeremy Taylor's brief summing up.[59] But James I had said it long ago: "No bishops, no King, no nobility".[60]

Bishops came back in 1660 primarily for the social reasons that had led middle-of-the-road Anglicans to defend them in 1641.[61] Isaac Barrow noted that the Church of England enjoys "the favour of the almost whole nobility and gentry".[62] But in November 1663 Robert Blackburne, Secretary to the Admiralty Committee, observed to Pepys that "the present clergy ... are hated and laughed at by everybody." Pepys agreed that they "will never heartily go down with the generality of the commons of England, they have been so used to liberty and freedom and they are so acquainted with the pride and debauchery of the present clergy".[63] Samuel Butler likewise spoke of the "general ill will and hatred they have contracted from the people of all sorts... These officers and commanders of the

Church Militant are like soldiers of fortune that are free to serve on any side that gives the best pay".[64] Barrow, Blackburne and Butler could all be right: that was what the national church had come to. Archbishop Sheldon, Burnet wrote, spoke of religion "most commonly as of an engine of government and matter of policy". This led Charles II "to look on him as a wise and honest clergyman that had little virtue and less religion".[65]

But experience of the scorpions of Presbyterian discipline had perhaps made some of the lower orders less hostile to the whips of the Anglican establishment. Add to this the failure of the sects to sink their differences sufficiently to unite against a restoration. 1660 saw the end of hopes of a broad protestant church, the beginning of the two nations. But protestant patriotism remained. When the second Popish Plot revived fears of foreign-backed absolutism, protestant Englishmen united to bring about 1688,[66] and toleration of a limited sort in 1689. The Non-Jurors were isolated as effectively as the Laudians had been between 1640 and 1660, and this time they had to accept the changes. The Act of Settlement of 1701 finally guaranteed security from a Catholic succession. Attempts to recreate a broad Grindalian church failed after 1688, despite efforts; a limited toleration was established, which survived Tory attempts to repeal it. Protestant England was saved, despite the failure of the protestant international: Catholic allies proved useful in the wars of William and Anne against Louis XIV. The chosen nation became the England whose manifest destiny it was to rule lesser breeds.[67]

NOTES

1. *M.C.P.W.*, I, pp.616-17, VI, p.123. The tolerant Lord Brooke was almost equally virulent about bishops in his *Discourse . . . of Episcopacie.*
2. Collinson, *The Religion of Protestants, passim.*
3. Collinson, *Godly People*, p.346; cf. p.148.
4. *Op. cit.*, p.9. My italics.
5. *Ibid.*, pp.102-5, 175; cf. pp.118-19, 139, 144-5, 148, 159.
6. Quoted by Stone, *The Crisis of the Aristocracy*, p.406.
7. Quoted by Waddington, *Congregational History, 1567-1700*, p.8.
8. Petition of the clergy, in Strype, *Life of Whitgift*, p.500.
9. R. Greenham, *Works* (1612), p.698.
10. *Tracts Ascribed to Richard Bancroft.*, p.83.

11. *Commons Debates, 1628* (ed. R.C. Johnson, M.J. Cole and others, Yale U.P., 1977), III, p.432.
12. Cooper, *op. cit.*, pp.168-9.
13. Godwin, *op. cit.*, Sig. A3 v. The common people came to believe bishops to be Antichrist, Izaak Walton confirmed (*Lives*, p.185).
14. W.T. MacCaffrey, *Queen Elizabeth and the Making of Policy, 1572-1588* (Princeton U.P., 1981), p.107.
15. Strype, *Life of Parker* (Oxford U.P., 1821), II, p.323.
16. Whitgift, *Works* (Parker Soc., 1851-3), II, p.398.
17. Strype, *Life of Whitgift*, III, p.78.
18. Hooker, *Works* (1836), III, p.402.
19. The point had been made by Laud in a sermon to the Parliament of 1626 (Laud, *Works*, Oxford U.P., 1847-60, I, pp.82-3); cf. J.L. Malcolm, *Caesar's Due: Loyalty and King Charles, 1642-1646* (1983), pp.139-48.
20. Hooker, *Of the Laws of Ecclesiastical Polity* (Everyman edn.), I, p.148; cf. II, p.7. Cf. Bowyer's *Parliamentary Diary*, p.169. For parity cf. T. Case, *Gods Rising, His Enemies Scattering*, a sermon preached to the House of Commons, 26 October 1642 (1644), p.12; Francis Woodcock, *Christs Warning-piece*, preached before the House of Commons, 30 October 1644 (1644), p.2.
21. T. Brightman, *The Revelation of St. John Illustrated* (4th edn., 1644), pp. 139, 149: "Yea, and the nobility hath of a long time smelt out this rub".
22. Foster, *Proceedings in Parliament, 1610*, I, p.102.
23. *Ibid.*, II, p.328; T.L. Moir, *The Addled Parliament of 1614* (Oxford U.P., 1958), pp.116-17.
24. *Letters of John Chamberlain* (ed. N.E. McClure, Philadelphia, 1939), I, pp.542, 546.
25. Laud had already blotted his copybook by marrying (illegally) the divorced Penelope Rich to his patron, the Earl of Devonshire. See p.75 below.
26. Chamberlain, *Letters*, II, pp.154, 157.
27. Ed. E.S. Shuckburgh, *Two Biographies of William Bedell* (Cambridge U.P., 1902), pp.146, 149.
28. Lord Brooke, *A Discourse opening the Nature of ... Episcopacie*, p.138. "Shall I make a man a prelate ... who hath a flagrant crime upon him?" asked James, referring to Laud's illegally marrying Lady Rich to his patron. The answer was "yes" (Sylvia Freedman, *Poor Penelope: Lady Penelope Rich*, 1983, p.168).
29. Hooker, *Works*, III, p.389; cf. my *Economic Problems of the Church*, pp.308-10, for further examples of reprehensible behaviour by Jacobean and Caroline bishops.
30. Ed. A.M. Charles, *The Shorter Poems of Ralph Knevet* (Ohio State U.P., 1966), p.80.
31. L.H. Carlson, *Martin Marprelate, Gentleman: Master Job Throkmorton laid open in his Colors* (San Marino, 1981), p.14.
32. R.G. Usher, *The Reconstruction of the English Church* (1910), II, p.142 — letter of 7 July to Secretary Lake.
33. D.H. Willson, *King James VI and I* (1956), pp.259, 209.

34. See C. Hill and E. Dell (eds.), *The Good Old Cause* (1949), pp. 167-8, 171-3, 178, 181-2.

35. Crewe, *Proceedings and Debates of the House of Commons in ... 1628*, p. 31.

36. Calibute Downing, *A Discourse of the State-Ecclesiasticall of this King-dome, in relation to the Civill* (2nd edn., revised and enlarged, 1634), pp. 2, 63.

37. Quoted by H. Hensley Henson, *Studies in English Religion in the 17th century* (1903), p. 107.

38. R. Overton, *A Remonstrance of Many Thousand Citizens* (1646), p. 12, in Haller, *Tracts on Liberty*, III.

39. S. How, *The Sufficiency of the Spirits Teaching* (1639), pp. 26-7; Walwyn, *A Prediction of Mr. Edwards his Conversion and Recantation* (1646), in Haller, *op. cit.*, III.

40. Baxter, *The Poor Husbandman's Advocate to Rich Racking Landlords*, p. 182.

41. [Anon.], *Light Shining in Buckinghamshire*, in Sabine, *op. cit.*, p. 622.

42. *W.T.U.D.*, pp. 29-34.

43. Pierce, *Historical Introduction to the Marprelate Tracts*, p. 78; [R. Chestlin], *Persecutio Undecima* (1681), pp. 4, 7. First published 1648.

44. Ed. Sir C. Petrie, *The Letters ... of King Charles I* (1935), pp. 200-6.

45. E. Lee Warner, *The Life of John Warner, Bishop of Rochester* (1901), p. 33.

46. P. Barwick, *Life of Dr. John Barwick* (ed. and abridged by G.F. Barwick, 1903), p. 177.

47. [Bruno Ryves], *Angliae Ruina* (1647), *passim*.

48. Quoted in [Anon.], *The Petition for the Prelates Briefly Examined* (1641), pp. 1v, 4.

49. Quoted by Neal, *History of the Puritans*, II, p. 45.

50. See p. 313 below.

51. Joyce L. Malcolm, *op cit.*, p. 163. Cf. J. Morrill, "The Religious Context of the English Civil War", *T.R.H.S.* (1985), pp. 176-7, though he seems to me to employ a very narrow definition of "religion". I am very grate-ful to Dr Morrill for allowing me to read this article in advance of publication.

52. Edward Hyde, Earl of Clarendon, *History of the Rebellion and Civil Wars in England* (ed. W.D. Macray, Oxford U.P., 1888), I, pp. 138-9, 142.

53. Clarendon, *op. cit.*, I, pp. 406-7, 568.

54. J. Nalson, *An Impartial Collection of the Great Affairs of State* (1682), I, p. 752.

55. Clarendon, *op. cit.*, I, p. 407; cf. Hyde's letter to Hopton of 2 May 1648 about bishops and aristocracy in Scotland (*Calendar of Clarendon State Papers*, II, p. 403).

56. Clarendon, *The Life* (Oxford U.P., 1759), I, p. 94.

57. *Diary of Sir Henry Slingsby* (ed. D. Parsons, 1886), pp. 67-9.

58. R.W. Harris, *Clarendon and the English Revolution* (1983), p. 179.

59. J. Taylor, *The Golden Grove* (1655), in *The Whole Works*, III, p. 717.

60. G. Goodman, *The Court of King James I* (1839), I, p. 421. On "parity

in the church" leading to "parity in the state", see Joyce Malcolm, *op. cit.*, pp.139-48.

61. See *W.T.U.D.*, p.347.
62. P.H. Osmond, *Isaac Barrow: His Life and Times* (1944), p.77. See also p.318 below.
63. S. Pepys, *Diary*, 9 November 1663.
64. S. Butler, *Characters and Passages from Note-Books* (ed. A.R. Waller, Cambridge U.P., 1908), p.318.
65. Burnet, *History of My Own Time*, I, pp.313-14.
66. See p.316 below.
67. See my *Experience of Defeat*, Chapters 6(4) and 10(5).

6. *From Grindal to Laud*[1]

The personal independency of kings
Is mere state-popery in several things;
That kings have absolute command of fate
Is transsubstantiation in the state;
The senses this new doctrine can't receive,
But what we cannot see we must believe. ...

That kings can be accountable to none,
And he can do no wrong that wears the crown,
Makes monarchs popes, and civil tyranny
Be furnished with infallibility.*

I

The Reformation gave birth to a new vested interest in protestantism which henceforth forced a *via media* upon successive governments, simply because a return to Catholicism was politically impossible. The Reformation also contributed to the enhancement of royal authority, the centralization and concentration of political power. This again was a long-term process, necessary (among other things) for defence of the landed class against peasant revolt, as well as against the great monarchies forming on the continent. The Commons and the temporal peers were calling for a royal supremacy before Luther produced his *95 Theses*.[2]

The Reformation and the royal supremacy broke the bonds of Rome, supplied the cash needed for building a substantial fleet, provided windfalls for a large number of courtiers and other government supporters at a time of economic difficulty, and enabled the revolts of 1536 and 1549 to be suppressed (the latter with foreign mercenaries). Henry VIII's French war was a failure, as was Somerset's attempt to conquer Scotland; but land-grabbing in Ireland was to keep a section of the aristocracy happily occupied for years to come. After Mary's reign had tested and proved the strength of the

*Daniel Defoe, *Jure Divino: A Satyr* (1706), Book VI, pp. 6-7.

vested interest, Elizabeth continued her father's and brother's policy, though with sadly diminished assets: the plunder of bishops', deans' and chapter lands was all she had to offer the growing army of hungry courtiers.

The royal supremacy, then, was a necessary price to pay for the economic and other advantages which lay property owners secured from the Reformation, and for the reduction of clerical privileges and immunities. It was a price worth paying, just as the Tudor peace was worth the "Tudor despotism". But the royal supremacy as a fact, and the Divine Right of Kings as an idea, were as riddled with contradictions as was the protestant cause. First, the elevation of the king to headship of the church, as the conduit through which the landed class tapped the church's wealth, in fact gave the monarch a certain independence. The machinery of the church, now entirely at the disposal of the crown, offered itself as an instrument of government independent of Parliamentary control, and with a long tradition of prestige and authority behind it. Conversely it became the interest of the upper ranks of the clergy to cry up the crown's independent power, and with it their own independence of Parliament. The king was the new Pope rather than the new Messiah.[3]

The royal supremacy appealed to many interests — parson and King, spoliators and Puritans anxious to use church property for educational reform or augmentation of parish livings, Catholics needing protection.[4] A paper offered to Elizabeth, and later to James, asking for representation of the lower clergy in the House of Commons, said that "it concerneth the clergy most of all men in England that the present state be continued ... without any alteration".[5]

Secondly, the royal supremacy originally involved the humiliating submission of the clergy, the reduction of ecclesiastical wealth: and yet if the church was to be of any use to the crown as an instrument of government its prestige must be restored and maintained. Plunder of the church created the royal supremacy: but this supremacy was ultimately used to halt the plunder of the church. The Reformation degraded the priesthood and exalted the Supreme Head; yet the Supreme Governor in her own interest wished always to maintain the dignity of the clergy, and especially of the hierarchy. Created by the Reformation, the Head of the Church was always trying to deny his maker. Sir Francis Knollys stated the dilemma neatly when he said that from the Divine Right of bishops preached by Bancroft it would follow that the Queen was not Supreme Governor over the clergy: bishops, he thought, must be under-governors to the Queen, not claim to be superior governors over their brethren by God's ordinance.[6]

Thirdly, the royal supremacy itself contradicted the logical principles of the Reformation. Even Elizabeth, certainly her two successors, always found the Counter-Reformation ideal of monarchy more attractive than did even their greatest subjects, lumbered as they were with monastic lands. This contradiction was felt in its acutest form just before and during the civil war, when Charles I would gladly have employed Irish or foreign Catholic military force, but most of his supporters feared them almost as much as they feared the Parliamentarian revolutionaries.[7] The *via media* turned out to be a *cul de sac*.

The same illogicality appeared when the royal supremacy was looked at from below. Every argument used against the authority of the Pope could be used against the Defender of the Pope's Faith. (The retention of the title conferred before the Pope's authority was repudiated is itself an example of the crown's contradictory position). The Tudor theory of Divine Right was a Divine Right of government: it was powerful so long as the governing class was united.[8] James I's personal theory of divine hereditary right, though it had its uses as an additional justification of the Stuart succession, was a poor makeshift as soon as it no longer expressed this solidarity, as soon as it came up against divine right of the gentry which, according to Fuller, John Ball had denied.[9]

On the one hand, then, the Reformation encouraged discussion and criticism — the Bible in English in every church, denunciations of the Pope and of the miracle of the mass; on the other hand the government tried to limit this criticism to specific objectives. This contradiction led to a division in the ranks of the clergy; as the hierarchy and the government tried to call a halt, to set the clock back to before the Reformation, so a section of the preachers turned increasingly to "the people", to educated and self-confident gentry, yeomen, merchants and artisans who valued the independence which the Reformation had conferred on laymen of status.

A final contradiction derives from the great divide in the landed classes which our period sees. Some become involved in commercial activities, whether in privateering or trade, in the conquest of Ireland, or in industrial or agricultural production. Others remain rentiers and look mainly to the court for economic favours. A growing minority patronizes Puritan ministers, associating through them with the middling sort of laymen to whom they appeal; others flirt dangerously with Catholicism and Arminianism, and wish to see discussion of religious matters suppressed. For the first group the royal supremacy has served its turn. For the conservative group the royal supremacy has come to occupy the position of papal supremacy in the early sixteenth century: a bulwark against change, an ally against movements from below. Protestantism and the royal supremacy were twin births in England. Yet a century later the Parliamentarians attacked the royal supremacy in the interests of advanced protestantism; Laudians and their lay supporters defending the royal supremacy come near to rejecting the principles of the Reformation, and would no doubt have gone further had not most of them been receivers of stolen goods.

These contradictions are reflected in the 39 Articles. But we can see them most clearly in the relations of Parliament to the crown. In the Elizabethan Acts of Supremacy and Uniformity the royal supremacy is affirmed as a defence against "foreign power and bondage", but at the same time attempts are made to subordinate the church to the crown in Parliament rather than to the crown alone. Elizabeth was not opposed to Parliamentary action on religious questions, any more than Henry VIII had been. Her objection was to losing the initiative, to having the running made by Puritan laymen rather than by the bishops.[10]

Nevertheless, and naturally enough, the attitude of members of the hierarchy, because of their office, was different from that of MPs. "I have heard from old Parliament-men", said Peter Wentworth in 1572, "that the banishment of the Pope and the reforming true religion had its beginning from this House, but not from the bishops; few laws for religion had their foundation from them".[11] Peter Wentworth looked back; but the full significance of the activities of the Wentworths and their group can be grasped only if we also look forward, to the period when the House of Commons took command. The divisions were only accidentally constitutional: they were in origin political. They concerned policy for the church, by whom the church was to be controlled. They became constitutional conflicts only as two parties slowly polarized, one grouped around the crown and the bishops, the other entrenched in the House of Commons.

II

The dilemma of the monarchy was manifested during the Archbishopric of Edmund Grindal (1576-83), which Patrick Collinson sees as a climacteric. The crucial issue was preaching, which "godly Maṣter Dering" called an essential mark of the church. "If ye will be saved", he told the gentry of Norfolk, "get you preachers into your parishes". The "prophesyings" — day schools for preachers — "were probably the most effective means that had been found for propagating the reformed religion in the rural areas of Elizabethan England".[12]

But they were more than that. "The kind of ecclesiastical reform to which the prophesyings and exercises were a pointer was much to the liking of the protestant nobility and gentry". The effect of these and other Puritan reforms would have been "to reduce still further both the powers of the unpopular ecclesiastical courts and the social status of the higher clergy"; their tendency was "to make the shire rather than the diocese the working unit of church administration and to bring into close harmony, if not to unify, the spiritual discipline of the ecclesiastical courts and the government of the magistrates".[13] The church would have been subordinated more effectively to the "county communities" of the gentry. "A partnership of ministry and magistracy . . . was a real alternative to clericalism on the one hand and naked erastianism on the other". It might well have been a first step to the gentry domination of the church which was established after 1660.[14]

In Elizabethan market towns there was a "firm alliance between 'magistracy and ministry' ", and between both and the neighbouring gentry. "The superstructure of the presbyterian movement had been erected on a foundation of market-town exercises, fasts and informal conferences". Bishops were tolerable if their powers were small and if they never "set themselves against the gentry". Grindal's successor Whitgift was accused of being the first Archbishop to do this. The Parliament of 1584-5, which wanted prophesyings restored, proposed to make a commission of laymen the arbiters of the fitness of the clergy. "The essence of the problem was social — the bishop against the gentry".[15] Work published since *The Elizabethan Puritan Movement* has reinforced Collinson's case by emphasizing the appeal of Puritanism not only to magistrates drawn from the gentry but also to parish élites — constables, churchwardens, overseers of the poor, drawn from yeomen and craftsmen — who had to administer the villages, looking after the poor law, vagabonds, squatters on commons and wastes, etc. They might well find the Puritan ethic congenial to their ideals of social discipline.[16]

Many early Elizabethan bishops had been exiles under Mary, sharing the aims of those who came to be called Puritans. For the first two decades of Elizabeth's reign Puritans were relatively leniently treated by bishops, and might reasonably hope that the Reformation would still be pushed further in the direction they desired. They had strong support from gentlemen and towns, expressed in the House of Commons. In Leicester and Walsingham they had powerful patrons at court. Through prophesyings and lectureships, and through the universities, Puritan influence was steadily extending. In Grindal they had an Archbishop who (unlike his predecessor and successor at Canterbury) had been an exile himself and was more sympathetic to their cause than Parker had been. Grindal represents a suppressed tradition in the history of the Church of England, but one that might have preserved a truer *via media*. John Milton, no friend to bishops in general, thought Grindal "the best of them".[17] The Mayor of Bridgewater in 1685 confirmed this from the opposite point of view by describing those who electioneered against James II's government as "Grindallizing self-willed humourists".[18] Until Collinson published his biography Grindal was consistently under-rated by historians, either because they succumbed to the post-humous charms of the Queen who suspended him from office, or because the fact that nonconformists were ultimately ejected from the church led to the hindsight assumption that attempts to create a broad protestant church could never have succeeded.

The immediate cause of Grindal's downfall was the "prophesyings" Many of the clergy badly needed the training in preaching which the prophesyings offered. The north and west of England, and still more Wales, were not yet securely protestantized; in the south and east hundreds of the clergy fell short of the exacting standards of the educated laity. Puritan preachers were needed if the "rustic Pelagianism"[19] of the mass of the population was to be overcome. The prophesyings were held under a moderator, often in the presence of the laity. They were indeed often lay-sponsored, out of the control of the bishops.[20] This last fact rendered them particularly obnoxious to the Queen.[21] She, like Archbishops Parker and Whitgift, deplored any activities that allowed "the people to be orderers of things". She ordered Grindal to suppress the prophesy-ings. Imprudently, he made no attempt to find a compromise formula, but bluntly refused to obey. "I cannot marvel enough", he wrote to the Queen, "how this strange opinion should once enter into your mind, that it should be good for the church to have few preachers". He added, in a very conventional protestant sentiment, "public and continual preaching of God's word is the ordinary mean and instrument of the salvation of mankind". It was also a means of holding subjects in obedience: London, where there was "continual preaching", overflowed with loving loyalty. The ignorant north had risen in rebellion in 1569; but Halifax, a centre of preaching, had rallied to the Queen.[22]

Grindal concluded "I am forced, with all humility, and yet plainly, to profess that I cannot give my assent to the suppressing of the said exercises. . . . Bear with me, I beseech you, Madam, if I choose rather to offend your earthly majesty than to offend the heavenly majesty of God". It was magnificent; but it was not the way to handle Elizabeth. There was no doubt at court of the popularity of Grindal's stand, "the people addicted to that matter as they were", in the words of Sir Walter Mildmay.[23]

But, as Collinson shows, there were wider considerations. Prophesyings, household religion, repetition of sermons, "were a solvent of the ecclesiastical parish, and ultimately of the national church grounded on the parochial principle". They were part of the lay initiative which Collinson saw as essential to Puritanism. They brought the godly into closer voluntary union with one another — "a religion tending towards Independency". "The religious exercises which filled the leisure hours of godly professors literally took the place of what Baxter called 'the old feastings and gossipings'. . . . The godly supplied one another with the love and mutual support which they might otherwise have looked for among kindred and neigh-bours".[24] They came near to forming Independent congregations within the state church of a sort which the Cromwellian church was later to embrace. "Non-separating congregationalism" had deep roots.[25] It helped to forge the godly party of the sixteen-forties.

"Grindal was the victim not simply of a specific issue of conscience but of courtly intrigue. His fall was recognized to be a portent of reaction against the progressive protestantism which he symbolized, at a time when protestant and conservative, even crypto-catholic, forces were in contention for the mastery, at Court and in the direction of domestic and foreign policy". Contemporaries were aware of the relation of the Grindal affair to "the great issues of the day".[26] In the late fifteen-seventies a series of new appointments to bishoprics "led to a rift between the episcopate and the protestant nobility and gentry which was scarcely more marked in the years of Archbishop Laud's ascendancy".[27] In the dangerous international situation many protestants thought the safety of the country depended on support for the Netherlands in their revolt against Spain, close understanding with protestant Scotland, and (as Sir Francis Knollys put it) "the timely preventing of the contemptuous growing of the disobedient papists here in England". "If the Bishop of Canterbury shall be deprived", he added, "then up starts the pride and practice of the papists". Grindal was a symbol of a protestant policy, at home and abroad.[28] The conservatives, under Sir Christopher Hatton's influence, were not strong enough to get Grindal deprived; but he was kept suspended from his duties till his death in 1583. He was succeeded by John Whitgift, "the first Archbishop to set himself against the gentry of Kent"[29] and far more hostile to Puritans than Grindal.

Elizabeth had come to regard Grindal as a thoroughly unsatisfactory primate, whom she by-passed and sequestrated. But after the first year of her reign she never went further than threatening to unfrock a prelate. The prestige of the hierarchy was necessary to the independence of the crown. Elizabeth wanted both to elevate the authority of bishops as against the mass of the clergy and to maintain the prestige of the church and its hierarchy, in their own sphere, as against her lay councillors, some of whom, she may have thought, were aspiring to interfere in an area of administration which was none of their business. An independent *jure divino* episcopacy was a prop of an independent *jure divino* crown. A Puritan councillor like Knollys positively wanted the bishops to be forced to admit that their authority over other clergy derived from royal grant and had nothing divine about it. The deposition of Grindal would have made the bishops' lay dependency clear. Elizabeth therefore was torn. Personally, no doubt, she would have deposed Grindal as cheerfully as she would have had Mary Queen of Scots put to death. But as a politician she had to think of the consequences of her actions. So Grindal remained nominal primate, and Mary's execution was delayed and finally extorted greatly against the Queen's will.

In both these matters Elizabeth had a majority of her councillors against her. Grindal had been Burghley's nominee for the primacy. Councillors did not share the Queen's inhibitions about anointed monarchs. Between 1567 and 1586 there were no churchmen on the Council. We may contrast either the reign of Henry VIII, or the Laudian régime. In between the ecclesiastical hierarchy reached its nadir; and bishops made their way back to positions of political influence not as great magnates but as servants devoted to and dependent on the crown.

During this period many councillors appear normally to have sympathized with Puritans more than with bishops. The Council often reversed its own instructions once the Queen's back was turned, and protected Puritan ministers.[30] Leicester, Walsingham and Essex were well-known patrons of Puritans; but Penry thought it worth while also to make a personal appeal from the bishops to Burghley:[31] and the Lord Treasurer exercised a curious protection over his kinsman Robert Browne. When Whitgift had succeeded Grindal and began to suspend nonconforming ministers, it was to Burghley that Sir Francis Knollys wrote a letter of protest in June 1584: "I do think it to be a dangerous matter to her Majesty's safety that the politic government of matters of state, as well concerning forms and accidents of and to religion as otherwise, should be taken from all Councillors of her Majesty's estate and only to be given over to the rule of bishops that are not always indifferent in their own cases of sovereignty".[32] Within a month Burghley wrote his famous letter to Whitgift comparing the Court of High Commission to the Spanish Inquisition. Yet only two years later the Archbishop himself was made a Councillor at Burghley's instance in order to counteract the influence of Leicester. Divisions inside the ruling group were sharpening; and the conservatives were henceforth to feel the need for support from the ecclesiastical hierarchy.

III

Social consequences followed from this reversal of Elizabethan policy. Edmund Freke, Bishop of Norwich, "found the only course open to him in making common cause with conservative and crypto-catholic elements who for one reason or another opposed the ascendancy of Puritan teachers and justices". The High Commission was used to counteract Privy Council support for the Puritan gentry. "The decline of Puritan influence at court and its steady progress in the country were developments full of portent for the political as well as the religious history of the coming half-century".[33]

The regrouping took place mainly over questions of foreign policy but it was accelerated by Martin Marprelate's appeal to popular opinion against the bishops, encouraging rank-and-file laymen to discuss religious matters, to scoff at their superiors and the government by law established.[34] The proclamation of 13 February 1588-9 against seditious and schismatical books said that they aimed at "the abridging or rather the overthrow of her Highness's lawful prerogative", and at dissolving "the estate of the prelacy, being one of the ancient estates under her Highness".[35] The Marprelate Tracts, Elizabeth thought, tended to the subversion of all government under her charge, both in church and state. Bancroft, in his sermon at Paul's Cross, also in February 1589, echoed these sentiments: "Her majesty is depraved, her authority is impugned". "The interest of the people in kingdoms is greatly advanced".[36]

Bishop Cooper followed up loyally: "If this outrageous spirit of boldness be not stopped speedily, I fear he will prove himself to be not only Mar-prelate but Mar-prince, Mar-state, Mar-law, Mar-magistrate and all together until he bring it to an Anabaptistical equality and community. ...Their whole drift, as it may seem, is to bring the government of the church to a democracy or aristocracy. The principles and reasons whereof, if they be once by experience familiar in the minds of the common people, and that they have the sense and feeling of them: it is greatly to be feared that they will very easily transfer the same to the government of the commonweal".[37] Nashe (or some other propagandist for the hierarchy) pretended to fear that Marprelate would provoke a rising of the masses, who needed no help from him "to increase their giddiness".

> Yes, he that now saith Why should bishops be?
> Will next cry out: Why kings? The saints are free.[38]

In 1590 another pamphleteer accused Martin of betraying the gentry by encouraging "the commons to cast off the yoke of obedience".[39] Some aristocrats at least took the point. "As they shoot at bishops now", wrote the Earl of Hertford, "so will they do at the nobility also if they be suffered".[40] To scare the "Puritan" nobility was perhaps one of the most serious long-term consequences of the Marprelate Tracts.

Puritan ministers too were alarmed by Marprelate's success. Cartwright wrote to Burghley disowning him. Martin himself said: "The Puritans are angry with me; I mean the Puritan preachers. And why? Because I am too open; because I jest. ... I am plain; I must needs call a spade a spade, a Pope a Pope".[41] The hierarchy's defenders were quick to seize their opportunity. Bancroft's police work stopped the tracts. Numbers of separatists were arrested. Cooper published a lengthy and reasoned exposition of the social dangers of popular Puritanism. The defeat of the Armada came opportunely for the government's prestige. The deaths of Leicester and Walsingham weakened resistance to Whitgift's policies on the Council. Field's death deprived the Puritans of a leader who had not been afraid to appeal to "the multitude and people".[42] The absurd plot of Hacket and Coppinger in 1590 was heavily written up, and every effort was made to associate Cartwright and his coadjutors with the plotters.[43] Bancroft's *Dangerous Positions* (1593) reinforced Cooper's social criticism, and advanced into a general attack on Calvinism as an international revolutionary movement.[44] The judicious Hooker completed the work of consolidation for his generation. The reprinting of Marprelate's works after 1640 showed both how timely the government's suppression and campaign of counter-propaganda had been, and that it had failed to achieve its ultimate objective.

Elizabeth and Hatton wrecked the chance of an all-embracing protestant national church. James I at the Hampton Court Conference was only confirming decisions taken by his predecessor. Hatton, who was Whitgift's patron as Leicester had been Grindal's, tried in the House of Commons to "appeal to the self-interest of the property-owning laity", arguing that "the Presbyterian revolution would be at their expense. It would deprive them of their ecclesiastical patronage, while the cost of maintaining the fourfold [Presbyterian] ministry in every parish would require the resumption of secularized church property, impropriate tithes and perhaps even abbey lands. ... 'It toucheth us all in our inheritances'".[45]

The combination of government successes against Marprelate and social panic temporarily frightened off most of the Puritans' influential patrons. But Puritanism was not destroyed by being driven underground and losing support from peers and councillors. When John of Gaunt and his like deserted the Wycliffites, Lollardy found a refuge among humbler people. But now there was a very different social basis for the reforming movement. The agitation for reform through Parliament having failed, many of its supporters turned to establishing independent congregations, inside or outside the church. The Marprelate Tracts were Puritan, not separatist. Yet Penry, who was closely associated with their production, died a Brownist.

Presbyterianism was primarily a clerical movement, with some support from Parliament and gentry. There was however a tension between the land-grabbers, always prepared to work the episcopal system provided they got enough spoil from it, and doctrinaire Presbyterians. Presbyterianism was, in Collinson's words, "strong medicine, impossible to contemplate apart from a general instit-utional and social revolution from which all but the strongest stomachs shrank".[46] Clerical Presbyterianism was routed. But its lay backers, less committed to the "ism", preserved what Collinson calls "presbytery in episcopacy", or congregational independency in epis-copacy. Gentlemen and corporations used patronage or the creation of lectureships to continue the provision of Puritan preaching (and bishops winked at it in the papist north of England).[47] When Presbyterianism revived in England in the sixteen-forties it was again primarily a clerical movement, looking for support from Scotland against the English House of Commons — though by then it had also won some conservative support as a lesser evil than sectarianism.[48]

Increasing government reliance on conservative elements, crypto-papist peers and gentlemen, had consequences both for home and foreign policy. Under James it led to the rise of the Howards, appeasement of Spain, the execution of Ralegh, strained relations with the House of Commons. Bancroft revived theories of the Divine Right of bishops. All these developments made their contribution to the atmosphere in which the breakdown of 1640 became possible.

Bancroft rose to influence, Collinson tells us, in a way "which may recall for the modern reader the methods of Senator Joseph McCarthy in our own time".[49] We may recall the list of qualities which, in Whitgift's view, qualified Bancroft for appointment as Bishop of London. His conduct had never been the subject of complaint; he had the usual academic degrees; he was a resolute opponent of popery and of all "sects and innovations"; he had held various governmental and ecclesiastical posts, and had served for twelve years on the High Commission; he did useful detective work against the Marprelate printing press and in organizing counter-propaganda; he took the lead against Cartwright, Penry and the classis movement; he had been engaged for fifteen or sixteen years in the public service, during which period "seventeen or eighteen of his juniors (few or none of them being of his experience) have been preferred — eleven to deaneries and the rest to bishoprics".[50] It was an unanswerable case for civil service promotion. As a commentary upon it we may recall that Archbishop Bancroft, adjudicating in the Rich divorce in 1605, "chid my Lord Rich very much" for his Puritanism, "and gave my Lady great commendations for her noble birth", observing that her error (adultery) was *"error venialis"* by comparison with Rich's Puritanism.[51]

But pressures for a Grindalian policy continued. When James appointed the Calvinist George Abbott (1610-33) to succeed Bancroft, a revival of Grindal's "first hundred days" even seemed possible. Abbott became one of the main advocates of a protestant foreign policy. Under his genial tolerance bishops like Montague, Lake and Morton allowed prophesyings again, though now they were prudently called "exercises".[52] But with Abbott's disgrace (over foreign policy, in effect) and the succession of Laud, historical tragedy repeated itself as farce. The Kentish gentry loved Abbott and hated Laud, as they had loved Grindal and hated Whitgift.[53] John Chamberlain in 1616 distinguished between Abbott and "the court bishops and other courtiers", whose views "commonly prevail".[54] In 1633 a Puritan — soon to be deprived — was recalling the days when an Archbishop of York — Grindal — had actually favoured preaching.[55] "Such bishops [as Grindal] would have prevented our contentions and wars", declared Richard Baxter in 1656. One argument for supposing that the English Revolution had long-term causes is the fact that Abbott failed no less than Grindal: the victim, like Grindal, of court intrigue. He was effectively succeeded by William Laud long before the latter was appointed Archbishop in 1633. "It was the Laudian successors of such [Grindalian] bishops who believed, with how much justification is a matter to be discussed rather than assumed, that by making itself beholden to the laity and by working with the grain of provincial society the church placed itself at risk".[56] So Collinson sums up.

IV

Whitgift's promotion had marked a turn away from spoliation and towards greater care for the prestige of the hierarchy. The steady move towards conservatism began with economics under Whitgift, tackled organization under Bancroft, and ended with doctrine under Laud. But there was no lasting reconstruction. Each success brought new problems. The church's revenues could be recovered or expanded only at the expense of the politically decisive landed class, far too many of whom were themselves in economic difficulties to be prepared to make sacrifices on behalf of the church, however much their appreciation of its services to their social order may have been growing. Usher's two large volumes on Bancroft's *Reconstruction of the English Church* show how little reconstruction there could be without a frontal attack on the protestant vested interest.[57]

The economic and political retreat from the Reformation led to a theological retreat. Whitgift himself was a sound Erastian Calvinist; but his proceedings against advocates of a Presbyterian discipline, together with the hardening of Genevan positions under Béza's influence, no doubt stimulated a reconsideration of Calvinism in general. Hooker's work of consolidation proved no more final than Whitgift's and Bancroft's. Liberal Calvinism, reasonableness, the attempt to marry protestantism with Catholic tradition: within less than a generation the leading Anglican figures had rejected all this, and had been won for "Arminianism". Laud was trying to get rid of the Lambeth Decrees on predestination which Whitgift promoted and Hooker approved.[58] Calvinism, essential to promotion in the last decade of Elizabeth's reign, was the way to Ireland or a country vicarage under Charles I. In 1595 the University of Cambridge demanded public recantation from a preacher of anti-Calvinist views.[59] Thirty-one years later it was the House of Commons, not the university, which took the offensive against Mr Adams of Cambridge who asserted the expediency of confession.[60] Hooker's reputation was not continuous: it was recreated (by Locke, among others) in the very different social context of the late seventeenth century.

A change in attitudes towards Catholics was harbinger of changes in Anglican theology. Already Sir Christopher Hatton, Whitgift's ally against the Puritans, was advocating lenience towards Catholics. His mother's family adhered to the old religion, and he himself was probably brought up a Catholic. Bancroft was Hatton's chaplain. His leniency towards Catholics is no doubt to be explained by anxiety to preserve their loyalty whilst England was at war with Spain; but it points forward to the days when a papal agent was received by Charles I at Whitehall, when conversion was fashionable at court, and when it was all that £1500 a year could do to prevent Bishop Goodman declaring himself a Catholic.[61]

Bancroft's major achievement was the canons of 1604. Previously no serious attempt had been made to resolve the contradictions of the Elizabethan settlement and of the royal supremacy. But the canons of 1604 codified and excluded ambiguities. They proclaimed the autonomy of the church under the crown, its independence of Parliament. They also represent the culminating point in the campaign against Puritans in insisting on a doctrinal test before admission to any eccesiastical office. Explicit penalties were prescribed for separatists and non-communicants, and for churchwardens who failed to present them. The sacraments were not to be refused if offered by a non-preaching minister. The hands of the ecclesiastical courts were strengthened. The canons make an interesting parallel to James I's attempt to give precision to the theory of the royal prerogative. In each case ambiguous or conflicting precedents were being sharply defined.[62]

The canons were passed by Convocation only, and ratified by letters patent under the Great Seal. Parliament was not asked to ratify them. So in attacking the canons the Commons found themselves attacking one conception of the royal supremacy. "Your Majesty should be misinformed", the Commons kindly explained to James, "if any man should deliver that the kings of England have any absolute power in themselves to alter religion (which God defend should be in the power of any mortal man whatseover) or to make any laws concerning the same otherwise than as in temporal causes, by consent of Parliament".[63] The Commons tried to invalidate all canons affecting the life, liberty or property of laymen which had not received the consent of Parliament. Twenty-three canons were singled out as fit to be voided.[64] But their bill was rejected, thanks to the bishops' vote in the Lords. Only after 1640 did the judges accept the Commons' view that ecclesiastical canons were not binding on the laity unless confirmed by Parliament. That one decision prevented the restoration in 1660 of "the church as Bancroft had left it".[65]

Collinson's main strength as a historian lies in his judicious (and unusual) combination of a theological with a sociological approach. "No form of church polity can be considered apart from the structures of the secular society in which it is set, or from its values", he wrote in 1965. "The policies and actions of Archbishops Whitgift and Bancroft, as later of Laud, seem to have been based on the assumption that ... the Church must defend itself against lay interference by the reinforcement of its ancient claims of spiritual government. ... It is not the historian's place to condemn the ends pursued by Whitgift or Laud, but he may feel bound to declare them unattainable".[66] Such an appraisal should help us to avoid a recent tendency to blame Laud exclusively for the Revolution of 1640.

All conscientious members of the church hierarchy worked under severe restraints. They lived in a rapidly changing society. They had to take account of the wishes, policies and whims of the sovereign. They were subject to ever-present pressures from the gentry. They were conscious of the threat to their church, at home and abroad, from popery; and at home from Puritans and sectaries. Like the crown, they could not rule without the co-operation of parish élites: parishes may not have been able to choose their parsons, but they did elect their churchwardens. The co-operation of the latter was essential to the proper functioning of church courts, and it was unlikely to be willingly given when their communities resented episcopal policies. Collinson used to emphasise, more perhaps than in his later books, lay initiatives in Puritanism — objections to "the surplice, the cross in baptism, and other celebrated dregs of Antichrist still entertained in the English church".[67] This was one approach to "independency within the church." In Grindleton Roger Brearley's congregation seems to have pressed further towards antinomianism than their minister.[68] Collinson's insight helps us to understand such a phenomenon; it received confirmation from a number of subsequent researchers,[69] and helps to account for the transition from non-separating Puritanism to sectarianism in which the laity predominated.[70] It may even help us better to understand the New England way.[71]

Collinson's sociological approach will also help us to keep theological questions in perspective. Naturally his enemies pilloried Laud's "Arminianism", and equated it with popery. Whether Laud actually was an Arminian has exercised historians recently, but it matters not much. The real enemy for Parliamentarians (as opposed perhaps to Puritans) was not Laud's theology but the defence by him and his supporters of what were held to be absolutist tendencies. Most of Laud's theological "innovations", Usher argued, can be found in the canons of 1604.[72] James I's sympathy for Arminians after the Synod of Dort seems to have sprung from a belief that the Calvinist position could lead to rebellion against the higher powers. More important for our purposes, Laud seemed to be putting into effect claims for the royal prerogative which had got Harsnett into trouble in 1610, Neile in 1614.[73] Sibthorpe, Manwaring and Montagu may have been theological innocents; but there was no mistaking their support for Divine Right monarchy. Abbott on the other hand is said to have told James I that he could grant toleration to papists only through Parliament "unless he was prepared to throw down the law of the land".[74] The Grand Remonstrance said that the bishops and the corrupt part of the clergy had tried to subvert the fundamental laws and principles of government of the kingdom.[75]

Just as it has been said that the trouble with Charles I was that he lacked his father's saving laziness, so the trouble with Laud was his seriousness and conscientiousness in carrying out the traditional policies of Whitgift and Bancroft, and the fact that he had Charles's ear as they never had the full confidence of their wiser sovereigns. Laud remembered Udall and Penry when dealing with Prynne, Burton and Bastwick.[76] John Cook in 1652 thought the execution of Charles I was God's revenge for the blood of Prynne and Bastwick.[77] Laud's theological position was however far more provocative than Whitgift's had ever been. He was driven to a fiercer onslaught on Puritans, to a break with international Calvinism and to a total breach with Parliaments. He was met by a concerted opposition of gentlemen and townsmen which brought down the monarchy as well as bishops. Again the roots of the civil war are to be found in Elizabeth's reign.

Church and crown faced similar economic and political problems in the century before 1640. In each case the only possible solutions appeared to threaten the gentry and Parliament — Divine Right of Kings, Divine Right of bishops, Divine Right to tithes, recovering impropriations.[78] The Laudian clergy "have claimed their calling immediately from the Lord Jesus Christ, which is against the laws of this kingdom": the Root and Branch Petition made the point succinctly.[79] The options of both church and crown steadily narrowed and so forced new problems on Parliament and gentry. The fall of Grindal led to enhanced Catholic influences; the fall of Abbott much more so. The York House Conference in 1626 removed the last hope that Buckingham might play the role of a new Northumberland, Leicester or Essex. In 1643 Cheynell looked back to "Bishop Bancroft and the Babylonian faction" in the church.[80] Laud carried much further Bancroft's policy of severing relations with continental protestants; and so he was wide open to accusations of popery, although he seems to have been no party to the court Popish Plot which Professor Hibbard has revealed.[81]

There are many ways in which Laudian policies had been anticipated under Whitgift and Bancroft. The rift between the episcopate and the protestant nobility after the fall of Grindal recalled for Collinson that of the sixteen-thirties.[82] It was James I who first issued the Book of Sports and forbade preachers to discuss predestination and reprobation. James commended bishops for suppressing "popular lecturers", and approved of the "beauty of holiness". The ideological polarization which derived from anxieties about foreign policy dates from the fall of Grindal, and intensified from James's reign.[83] James first promoted Arminians, who were to be virtually the only proponents of a theory of absolutism, derived from French Catholic thinkers.[84] Hooker's synthesis, as Usher pointed out, was based on Bancroft.[85] Hooker's dedication of Book V of The Laws of Ecclesiastical Polity to Whitgift reads almost like a prophecy of the Long Parliament: the threat of Presbyterianism "to erect a popular authority of elders, and to take away episcopal jurisdiction" has gained "many helping hands, ... contented (for what intent God doth know) to uphold opposition against bishops" to the disadvantage of Her Majesty's service.[86]

Collinson's picture is of ex-émigré radical protestant bishops settling under Elizabeth for a possibilist second best, less than they had hoped for, better than they had feared. They heroically squeezed as much as they could — prophesyings, lectureships, itinerant preachers in the North — out of the immobile social structure, in the hope of slowly converting the pagan-Catholic mass of the population. So they spurned the radical Lollard-Anabaptist-Familist trend, which for a moment it seemed they might have headed, and drove the radicals into separation and exile.[87] It was not the virulent Laud who forced extremism on the sects; that had been done earlier by the worthiest middle-of-the-road Elizabethan and Jacobean bishops.

Laud reaped the whirlwind they had sown. The case against Laud is not so much innovation, still less "revolution", but that he presided over the upsetting of a balance which had long been becoming more and more precarious. It was his use of his powerful position to monopolize ecclesiastical patronage that was the real innovation, plus the savagery with which he silenced his enemies. I find myself in agreement here with Avihu Zakai, who emphasizes the equally provocative stance of the minority of convinced Puritans.[88]

After Grindal and Abbott one more Archbishop found himself out on a limb. John Williams was a successful courtier and civil servant under James. He was among the first to demand Abbott's suspension and the forfeiture of his estate. A pluralist, whose religion sat lightly on him, he regarded Bohemian protestant refugees as rebels deserving no sympathy. Despite all these well-timed views, he found himself out-manoeuvred by Laud, beaten to the bishopric of London,[89] not for lack of any theological suppleness, but simply because he was late in realizing how important theological politics could be to a court churchman. In disgrace he attached himself to opponents of the court, confident that he could win their sympathy as Abbott had done, and that the next turn of the tide would bring the great territorial magnates back to their proper positions of influence, and himself, in alliance with them, to a dominant position in the church.[90]

It was indeed evidence of the weakness in the position of those who defended "moderate episcopacy" in 1640-1 (and who proposed to solve the King's financial problems by a reorganization of taxation) that Williams became their candidate for high ecclesiastical office. Whatever one may think of Laud, no one has ever challenged his adherence to a principled Christian position. But Williams? As Professor Trevor-Roper pointed out, he was never in the cathedral of which he was bishop for twenty years; during three years in the Tower he never took the sacrament, never indeed attended church service.[91] He was a secularist of the secularists: not even King Log to Laud's King Stork. He would no doubt have made a successful eighteenth-century primate. But in between lay a revolution with which he was temperamentally unfitted to cope. He was neither a De Retz nor a Talleyrand. He could play the game of politics within the old restricted circle well enough, but he was twice defeated — first by Laud's passionate and unscrupulous pursuit of principle, then by a new phenomenon even further outside Williams's range of vision:

effective political action by humble laymen such as those whom
Marprelate had addressed fifty years earlier.

NOTES

1. This chapter incorporates material from reviews of four books by
   Patrick Collinson — *The Elizabethan Puritan Movement* (1967); *Arch-
   bishop Grindal, 1519-1583: The Struggle for a Reformed Church* (1979);
   The Religion of Protestants: The Church in English Society, 1559-1625
   (Oxford U.P., 1982); *Godly People: Essays on English Protestantism*
   (1983). They appeared respectively in *Economic History Review*, N.S.,
   XX (1967); *Journal of Religious History*, II, (1981); *Times Literary
   Supplement*, 18 March, 1983; *Journal of Ecclesiastical History*, 35
   (1984).
2. A. Ogle, *The Tragedy of the Lollards' Tower* (Oxford, 1949),
   pp. 144-54.
3. Cf. Defoe, cited as epigraph to this Chapter.
4. Cf. H. White, *op. cit.*, pp. 132-7, 150-5, 169.
5. Burnet, *History of the Reformation of the Church of England*, IV, p. 145.
6. Strype, *Life of Whitgift*, I, pp. 559-65.
7. Cf. royalists cited in John Adair's *By the Sword Divided: Eyewitnesses
   of the English Civil War* (1983), pp. 37-8, 131.
8. Cf. David Mathew, *The Celtic Peoples and Renaissance Europe* (1933),
   pp. 53, 75.
9. Fuller, *Church History of Britain*, I, p. 451.
10. M. M. Knappen, *Tudor Puritanism: A Chapter in the History of Ideal-
    ism* (Chicago U.P., 1939), p. 227.
11. Strype, *Annals of the Reformation ... during Queen Elizabeth's Happy
    Reign*, (Oxford U.P., 1824), II, p. 12.
12. Collinson, *Godly People*, pp. 297-9, 59-60.
13. Collinson, *The Elizabethan Puritan Movement*, p. 187.
14. *Godly People*, pp. 78-9, 175-80, 187.
15. *The Elizabethan Puritan Movement*, pp. 188-9, 203, 259, 285, 437.
16. K. Wrightson, *English Society, 1580-1680* (1982), *passim*; William Hunt,
    op. cit., *passim*.
17. M.C.P.W., I., pp. 539-40.
18. R. Clifton, *The Last Popular Rebellion* (1984), pp. 71, 157; cf. p. 302
    below.
19. *The Elizabethan Puritan Movement*, p. 37; cf. W.T. MacCaffrey, *Queen
    Elizabeth and the Making of Policy, 1572-1588* (Princeton U.P., 1981),
    pp. 38, 83.
20. *Ibid.*, Part Four, Chapters 2, 4 and 5 *passim*; *Godly People*, pp. 59-60.
21. Elizabeth may have been more right than Collinson admits. In Scotland
    in the fifteen-seventies an easy transition was made from "exercises"

to presbyteries. "The exercise may be judgit a presbytery" (Duncan Shaw, *The General Assemblies of the Church of Scotland, 1560-1600*, Edinburgh, 1964, pp. 176-7). Cf. Aylmer on the "boldness in the meaner sort" that exercises bred in Leicestershire (quoted by Claire Cross, *The Puritan Earl: The Life of Henry Hastings, Third Earl of Huntingdon*, 1966, pp. 137-8).

22. *Grindal*, pp. 247-8, 289, 240.
23. *Grindal*, pp. 242, 260.
24. *Godly People*, pp. 8-9, 11-15, 422, 446, 539-40, 547-8; *The Elizabethan Puritan Movement*, pp. 92-7, 173, 202, 223, 375-82, and *passim*; *Grindal*, pp. 177-8. I use the word "saw" as Collinson has shifted his position on this point. See p. 78 below.
25. *The Elizabethan Puritan Movement*, pp. 82-91, 229-31, 334-5, 343-4, and *passim*. Cf. Strype, *Life of Whitgift*, I, p. 229; B. R. White, *The English Separatist Tradition*, pp. 84-6, 90, 94; T. H. Breen, *Puritans and Adventurers* (Oxford U.P., 1980), p. 198; R. Richardson, *op. cit.*, pp. 37, 86-97; cf. L. Ziff, *Puritanism in America* (New York, 1973), p. 50.
26. *Grindal*, pp. 256-7.
27. *The Elizabethan Puritan Movement*, p. 201.
28. *Grindal*, pp. 257-8.
29. *Ibid.*, p. 286; *The Elizabethan Puritan Movement*, Part 4, Chapter 4; Part 8, Chapter 1. Peter Clark suggests that in the short run Grindal's suspension actually helped the radicals (*English Provincial Society from the Reformation to the Revolution: Religion, Politics and Society in Kent, 1500-1640*, (Hassocks, Sussex, 1977, pp. 167-9).
30. Knappen, pp. 261-2, 275.
31. Ed. A. Peel, *The Notebook of John Penry, 1593* (Camden third series, 1944), pp. 53-77.
32. Knappen, *op. cit.*, p. 275.
33. *The Elizabethan Puritan Movement*, pp. 202-5, 444.
34. One of the charges that led to the condemnation of Protector Somerset had been that he encouraged the common people to have ideas of their own about politics.
35. A. Sparrow, *A Collection of Articles* (1684), p. 173.
36. Pierce, *An Historical Introduction to the Marprelate Tracts*, p. 161, 175.
37. Cooper, *Admonition*, pp. 31, 70.
38. *The Returne of the Renowned Cavaliero Pasquill* (1589), Sig. B i-iii; *A Whip for an Ape*. The attribution to Nashe is in each case uncertain. Field, it will be remembered, had said "seeing we cannot compass these things by suit nor dispute, it is the multitude and people that must bring the discipline to pass which we desire" (Collinson, *Godly People*, p. 370).
39. L. Wright, *A Friendly Admonition to Martine Marprelate and his Mates* (1590), p. 2, quoted in Pierce, *op. cit.*, p. 236.
40. Ed. E. Arber, *An Introductory Sketch to the Martin Marprelate Controversy* (1895), p. 114.
41. *An Epitome* (1588), To all the Cleargie masters.
42. *Grindal*, pp. 314, 397.

43. Cf. Hooker, *Of the Laws of Ecclesiastical Polity*, Dedication to Book V (Everyman edn., II, pp.5-7), and R. Cosin, *Conspiracy for pretended Reformation* (1591), *passim*.
44. Knappen, *op. cit.*, p. 497. Recalling Marprelate's description of the activities of government *agents provocateurs* among members of underground congregations, and their attempts to snare them into compromising statements or actions (Pierce, *op. cit.*, p. 192), it is perhaps legitimate to wonder whether there may not have been something of the sort behind Hacket's "plot".
45. *The Elizabethan Puritan Movement*, p. 314.
46. *Godly People*, p. 168.
47. *The Elizabethan Puritan Movement*, pp. 405-7; *Godly People*, p. 348. Richardson and Haigh confirm the continuance of prophesyings in Lancashire (Richardson, *op. cit.*, pp. 65-9; Haigh, *Reformation and Resistance in Tudor Lancashire*, Cambridge U.P., 1975, pp. 301-4). Cf. Cross, *op. cit.*, pp. 259-60 (Yorkshire); R.O'Day, "Thomas Bentham: A Case Study in the Problems of the Early Elizabethan Episcopate", *Journal of Ecclesiastical History*, XXIII (1972), p. 153 (Staffordshire).
48. I have benefited from discussing this point with David Zaret.
49. *The Elizabethan Puritan Movement*, p. 397.
50. Pierce, *op. cit.*, pp. 118-19; C. Burrage, *The Early English Dissenters* (Cambridge U.P., 1912), II, pp. 132-3.
51. Freedman, *Poor Penelope*, p. 164.
52. *Grindal*, pp. 291-2.
53. *Ibid*, p. 286, Cf. Clark, *English Provincial Society*, pp. 306-366.
54. Chamberlain, *Letters*, II, p. 44.
55. See p.302 below.
56. *Grindal*, p. 292.
57. Bancroft was less impressed by the stability of his work than Usher. He cancelled a will leaving his library to Lambeth Palace and left it to Cambridge University, "suspecting an impression of popular violence on cathedrals" (Fuller, *The History of the Worthies of England*, 1840, II, p. 200). If Fuller's account of Bancroft's motives is correct, his was an interestingly exact forecast. In the sixteen-forties the property of bishops' sees was confiscated, but not that of the universities. But learning did not, as forecast, fall together with bishops.
58. P. Heylyn, *Cyprianus Anglicus* (1671), p. 256; Hooker *op. cit.*, II, pp. 542-3.
59. Fuller, *History of the University of Cambridge* (1655), pp. 150-1.
60. Neal, *op. cit.*, I, p. 598.
61. S.R.Gardiner, *History of England, 1603-1640*, IX, p. 279.
62. J.W. Allen, *English Political Thought, 1603-1644* (1938), pp.123-4.
63. The Apology of the House of Commons, 1604, in Prothero, *op. cit.*, pp. 290-1.
64. Faith Thompson, *Magna Carta: Its role in the making of the English Constitution, 1300-1629* (Massachusetts U.P., 1948), p. 248.
65. Usher, *op. cit.*, II, p. 266.
66. *Godly People*, pp. 187-8; contrast pp. 433-7.

67. *Godly People* p. 541; cf. pp. 11-15, 422, 446, and *English Puritanism* (Historical Association Pamphlet, 1983), pp. 30-1.

68. See pp.149, 163 below.

69. See for instance R.W.Ketton-Cremer, *Norfolk in the Civil War* (1969), p. 72 and *passim*; F.G.Emmison, *Early Essex Town Meetings* (1970), p. vii; B.R.White, *The English Separatist Tradition*, pp. 76-9; R. Richardson, *op. cit.*, pp. 16-17, 27, 97-108; E.J.I.Allen, *The State of the Church in the Diocese of Peterborough, 1601-1642* (Oxford B.Litt. Thesis, 1972), esp. pp. 118-20, 134-42, 153-4; C.Haigh, *op. cit.*, p. 298; A.Fletcher, *A County Community in Peace and War: Sussex 1600-1660* (1975), pp. 74, 90-3, 108; P. Clark, *English Provincial Society*, pp. 170, 174-8, 326-7, 335, 370-2, 389, 440; W.J.Sheils, *The Puritans in the Diocese of Peterborough, 1558-1610* (Northants Record Soc., 1979), *passim*; K.Wrightson and D.Levine, *Poverty and Piety in an English Village: Terling 1525-1700* (1979), p. 161; D. Zaret, *The Heavenly Contract* (Chicago U.P., 1985), *passim*, fully documents his view that lay initiative was central to Puritanism. Cf. J.W. Martin, "The Protestant Underground Congregations of Mary's Reign," *Journal of Ecclesiastical History*, 35 (1984), *passim; Barrington Family Letters*, p. 70; Lake, *op. cit.,* 89-90, 132; Hunt, *op. cit.*, pp. 92, 255-7, 296 and *passim*; Helena Hajzyk, "Household, Divinity and Covenant Theology in Lincolnshire, c. 1595-c. 1640", *Lincolnshire History and Archeology*, 17 (1982), pp. 45-9; J.Y. Cliffe, *The Puritan Gentry*, p. 188; P. Gura, *A Glimpse of Sion's Glory: Puritan Radicalism in New England, 1620-1660* (Wesleyan U.P., 1984), pp. 8, 238. The exodus to New England was primarily a lay initiative.

70. Adam Martindale's experience of the sixteen-forties is relevant: "the enslaving of the ministers" by congregations "to the will of the people", to such an extent that sometimes ministers "have been forced with disgrace to retract" (*The Life of Adam Martindale*, ed. R. Parkinson, Chetham Soc., 1845, pp. 66-7).

71. Zakai, *Exile and Kingdom, passim*.

72. Usher, *op. cit.*, I, p. 382; cf. New, *Anglican and Puritan*, pp. 70, 74.

73. See p.54 above; cf. Foster, *Notes from the Caroline Underground*, p. 108.

74. Lambeth MS 943 f. 79. This document's authenticity has been questioned.

75. Ed. S.R.Gardiner, *Constitutional Documents of the Puritan Revolution, 1625-1660* (Oxford U.P., 3rd edn., 1906), pp. 206-7.

76. Laud, *Works*, VII, p. 329.

77. Cook, *Monarchy no Creature of Gods making* (1652), Sig b.

78. See my *Economic Problems of the Church, passim*.

79. Gardiner, *Constitutional Documents*, p. 137.

80. Francis Cheynell, *Sions Memento and Gods Alarum* (1643), p. 30.

81. C. Hibbard, *Charles I and the Popish Plot, passim*.

82. See pp.69-70 above.

83. See pp.70-5 above.

84. Hunt, *op. cit.*, pp. 175-80, 214; cf. P. White, "The Rise of Arminianism

Reconsidered", *P. and P.*, No. 101 (1983), *passim*.

85. Usher, *op. cit.*, I, pp. 73-4.
86. Hooker, *op. cit.*, II, p. 7.
87. Cf. chapter 7 below.
88. Zakai, *Exile and Kingdom*, pp. 67-8 and *passim*. Dr Zakai stresses that Brightman had the same sense that Winthrop and his colleagues had — that England was a doomed nation; and suggests that this witnesses to a long-term crisis in England *(ibid.,* p. 131).
89. *Cabala, Mysteries of State*, I, pp. 45, 85; Heylyn, *Cyprianus Anglicus*, p. 324. Cf. Zachary Catlin, *Dr Sibbs his Life* (1652), p. 263, and *The Knyvett Letters* (ed. B.Schofield, 1949), p. 30.
90. Lambeth MS. 1030 ff. 38, 94-106.
91. Trevor-Roper, *Archbishop Laud*, p. 137.

III *Heresy and Radical Politics*

7. From Lollards to Levellers [1]

"Heresies are like leaden pipes in the ground. They run on still, though we do not see them, in a commonwealth where they are restrained. Where liberty is they will discover themselves, and come to punishment." *

"If God be a Father, and we are brethren, it is a levelling word. . . . If they be great in the world, brethren of high degree; yet 'brother' levelleth them." †

In the sixteen-forties, when the censorship broke down and church courts ceased to function, a whole host of radical ideas popped up and were freely expressed. The question I want to ask is how far these ideas had had an underground existence before 1640, so that the novelty is only in the freedom to express them: or were they novel ideas, the product of novel circumstances? I shall do no more than throw out a few suggestions: I have no completed thesis to put forward, only a few working hypotheses, a list of questions I am asking myself.

My point of departure was a book that I wrote called *The World Turned Upside Down*, in which I tried to analyse some of the more extreme ideas of the radical minority of the sixteen-forties and sixteen-fifties. I sent a copy of this book to G.R.Elton, with an apologetic remark that I knew it was not his sort of book, but it was what I had written. Professor Elton replied, courteously but trenchantly: "the ideas you find put forward are awfully old hat — commonplaces of radical and heretical thinking since well before the Reformation". I had already noticed some parallels between late Lollard ideas, as described by J.A.F.Thomson and A.G.Dickens, and my seventeenth-century radicals. What began to interest me was the possibility of continuity, and its mechanisms.

---

* Lord Strickland, 9 December 1656 (*Parliamentary Diary of Thomas Burton*, ed. J.T.Rutt, 1828, I, p. 88).

† Richard Sibbes, *A Heavenly Conference* (1656), in *Works*, VI, p. 458. Sibbes died in 1635.

Now of course there are very special problems in attempting to trace continuities of underground ideas. A successful underground leaves no traces. Before the nineteenth century we rarely hear the lower orders speaking for themselves in a natural tone of voice. We hear instead what JPs in Quarter Sessions, judges in ecclesiastical courts, heresy-hunting pamphleteers, thought their inferiors were thinking, with all the dangers of distortion by such sources. ("Who writ the history of the Anabaptists but their enemies?" asked the Leveller Richard Overton; and the Leveller William Walwyn spoke of "that lying story of that injured people ... the Anabaptists of Münster".)[2] Alternatively, we have to rely on inference, from the survival of particular doctrines in particular areas. In putting together scraps of evidence, which have survived by chance, we are unlikely to arrive at decisive conclusions. The problems are perennial whenever we try to reconstruct the history of the common man, still more of the common woman. Nearly all our history is upper-class and male. One of the delights of the English Revolution is the exceptional nature of the surviving evidence, thanks to the exceptional political liberty and the relative cheapness of printing.

Let us remind ourselves how very radical some of the ideas were which surfaced in the sixteen-forties and sixteen-fifties. Levellers advocated political democracy, a republic with a widely extended franchise, abolition of the House of Lords, election of magistrates and judges, drastic legal and economic reforms. Diggers and others carried the Leveller emphasis on natural rights to advocacy of a communist society. Sectaries and Milton extended the Puritan attack on bishops to rejection of the whole idea of a state church — its courts, its tithes, its fees, its control of education and the censorship, the very distinction between clergy and laity. They carried anti-sacramentalism to the point of regarding worship as discussion. Spiritual equality and the doctrine of the inner light were extended to rejection of the idea of "sin", to a belief in human perfectibility on earth. Many denied the divinity of Christ, the immortality of the soul. Some ceased to believe in a local heaven or hell; the gospel story was treated as an allegory. Winstanley found the word Reason preferable to God. The protestant ethic, the dignity of labour, monogamous marriage, all came under attack.

Many of the proponents of these ideas looked back to Lollards and Marian martyrs as their ancestors. Foxe had of course accustomed

Englishmen to this pedigree, to this answer to the question "Where was your church before Luther?" England differed from most continental countries in having a "respectable" pre-reformation heresy to appeal to. But Foxe, we know, often played down the radicalism of his heretics.[3] Many of the views of Lollards and Marian martyrs would have been punishable under Elizabeth — which did not stop her making political capital out of Foxe's book. In the seventeenth century Levellers like Lilburne, Overton, Walwyn, a reformer like William Dell, emphasized the more radical elements in the heretical heritage. The point was regularly made from the other side. John Cleveland spoke of "Presbyter Wyclif" and "Tyler's toleration"; the sneer was repeated by other poets, Abraham Cowley and John Collop. Charles I, in his answer of 18 June 1642 to the Parliament's 19 Propositions, warned that, if opposition to him continued, "at last the common people ... [will] set up for themselves, call parity and independence liberty, ... destroy all rights and properties, all distinctions of families and merit, and by this means this splendid and excellently distinguished form of government end in a dark, equal chaos of confusion, ... in a Jack Cade or a Wat Tyler"[4] This Answer of Charles's became the classic royal statement of "mixed monarchy", the King's acceptance of a Parliamentary share in government. Charles did not hold consistently to this doctrine, but he repeated it at his trial in 1649, and it played its part in preparing for the restoration of 1660.

Continuities certainly exist between fifteenth- and seventeenth-century radicals. Some are doctrinal, some geographical. I shall try to look at both. Joan Thirsk and Alan Everitt have distinguished between champaign arable areas of the country, with stable docile communities subordinated to parson and squire, on the one hand, and pastoral, forest, moorland and fen areas on the other. In the latter, parishes were often very large, so that ecclesiastical control was less tight, there were fewer lords of manors, and vagrants could squat in relative security ("out of sight or out of slavery", as Gerrard Winstanley put it). In the seventeenth century these forest cottagers formed a pool of labour for the new industries that were developing. Both Lollardy and later heresy are found especially in clothing counties, and in pastoral, forest, moorland and fen areas.

Let us look at some areas where continuities can be seen. The Weald of Kent and Sussex was a region of forests, with few gentlemen and few manors. Parishes were large, and many families rarely attended church. It was a heavily populated and industrialized area (clothing and iron); the population was mobile and wayfaring, with "multitudes of rogues and beggars", since there were many opportunities for casual labour.[5] Masterless men abounded who were fodder for conscription in time of war. The Lollard areas can be roughly correlated with those that produced the most Marian martyrs, and with later Baptist and Quaker regions. Heresy was widespread in Kent in the fifteen-thirties, not only in the Weald; Peter Clark speaks of protestant pressure coming from below in Kentish towns. There were anti-Trinitarians in the fifteen-thirties and among the many Marian martyrs. Rye was especially Puritan, or worse. Its poorer townsmen, their pastor said in 1537, "reeked of Lollardy and ribaldry". There were "free-willers" under Edward VI, and what Patrick Collinson calls "rustic Pelagianism" under Elizabeth.[6]

Radical heresy continued later in the century. Robert Master of Woodchurch denied the resurrection. Another man "maintains . . . usury and says there is no hell". In the sixteen-twenties there were Brownists. There were political rebels in Kent in 1381, 1450, 1549 and 1554. There were food riots in 1630, and the Weald produced the largest single contingent of emigrants to Massachusetts later in the decade. Both John Taylor the Water-Poet, a man of conservative sympathies, and the radical George Wither thought it necessary to distinguish between Christendom and Kent. This tribute to the county's heretical reputation goes back at least to Sir Thomas Wyatt's time.[7]

In 1638 ten labourers from the old Lollard centre of Tenterden were up before the church court for refusing to pay tithe on wages. "What care we for his Majesty's laws and statutes?" the church-wardens of Little Horsted in the Sussex Weald were asking. The Kent and Sussex Weald was firm in support of Parliament during the civil war, unlike the western area of Sussex. A host of sectaries appeared in the forties, at Tenterden among other centres. Kent was one of the earliest areas to have women preachers.[8] The county looms large in Thomas Edwards's Gangraena of 1646. Kentish radicalism produced a strong Leveller movement, culminating in a Digger colony and a near-Digger pamphlet. It was a General Baptist and Muggletonian centre of some significance. Samuel Fisher, who evolved from a Baptist into a Quaker, and who argued in a scholarly folio that the Bible was not the Word of God, operated around

Ashford. After the restoration the Weald was "a receptacle for distressed and running parsons.[9]

Essex, my next county, was another woodland region, especially in the north, the traditional radical area. Itinerants and squatters abounded. The cottage clothing industry of this region was described as a breeding ground for Lollardy; John Ball had preached in Colchester. Essex participated in the Lollard revolt of 1414, and heresy survived into the sixteenth century.[10] There were major disturbances in the county in 1549, the year of Kett's rebellion. There were more Marian martyrs from Essex than from any other county except Kent (and London). In 1566 there was an abortive rising in the clothing towns of the north-east of the county. Under Edward VI there had been groups of "free-willers", under Mary lower-class conventicles, and under Elizabeth Familists, in Essex just as in Kent. The Legate brothers, one of whom was burned in 1612, the other dying in prison, came from Essex: they denied the existence of any true church on earth. In 1581 there was an illegal preaching place in the woods at Ramsey, with straw and moss for seating, "and the ground trodden bare with much treading".[11]

Essex was also a county in which there was an unusually large number of indictments for witchcraft in the sixteenth and seventeenth centuries. Here I can only hint at the possible connections which caused Lollards, Anabaptists and early Quakers to be denounced as witches.[12] When the famous Puritan William Ames was expelled from Christ's College, Cambridge, in 1610, he was promptly offered a city lectureship at Colchester. But the bishop ensured that he was not allowed to accept it.[13] Men spoke of "Colchester the Zealous", "the city upon a hill." The Puritan Thomas Shepard thought Essex the best county in England, John Hampden agreed that it was the place of most religion in the land. The Familist John Everard held a living at Fairstead in Essex.[14]

Essex is a county in which economic developments to the disadvantage of the poor are particularly well documented. Parish vestries and élites are busy imposing social discipline. There was an enormous increase after 1600 both in poor rates and in presentation of cottagers and lodgers. In the fifteen-eighties and nineties revolt was being foretold there. Some would even have welcomed a Spanish invasion. "What can rich men do against poor men if poor men rise and hold together?" artisans were asking in 1594. Next year there were threats to hang sellers of victuals — a simple popular remedy against inflationary price increases. In 1629 there were two riots in Maldon, led by Anne Carter, a butcher's wife. She was hanged, with two others.[15] Charles I's enforcement of forest laws in the sixteen-thirties hit small and large cultivators in Essex particularly hard. The Venetian ambassador said that the total composition fines to be levied on the county's forest lands would have amounted to at least £300,000 — more than ten times the total collected in Ship Money. So it did not need the Earl of Warwick's encouragement for Essex to be the earliest and most outstanding of the counties defaulting on Ship Money payments. When "intelligencers' news" was read in Colchester streets on market days, "zealants" flocked to hear "as people use when ballads are sung". In 1637 a parson at Maldon, where Anne Carter had been hanged eight years earlier, was said to have preached that the King's sins were being visited upon the kingdom. He prayed for Charles's conversion, and urged the people to arm themselves if all else failed. Next year he prayed that God would "utterly destroy those that are enemies to the plantations" because these offered a refuge in America to the godly.[16]

After 1638 Essex was the scene of violent anti-clericalism. The common people pulled down altar rails and images. In 1640 Laudian clergy were rabbled. Much popular iconoclasm was *social*, directed against the coats of arms of noble families depicted in churches. At the county elections in 1640 "rude vulgar people", "fellows without shirts" (the English equivalent of sans-culottes?) threatened to "tear the gentlemen to pieces" if the popular candidate were not elected.[17] "Many thousands" turned out to sack the papist Countess of Rivers's house. When manorial documents and evidences were destroyed at Colchester in 1641 the jury gave an ignoramus verdict against the plunderers. They were indicted again at the assizes, but the sheriff could not get a jury to convict. At Milford, "no man appeared like a gentleman but was made a prey to that ravenous crew". "The rude people are come to such at head", said a Colchester gentleman, "that we know not how to quiet them". There were enclosure and other riots in 1641-2. They "must take advantage of these times", said an Essex enclosure rioter in 1642, "lest they never have the like again". "There was no law settled at this time that he knew", declared a poacher in the same county in the same year.[18]

Essex men "were with the first ... for recovering of liberty". In January 1642 6,000 Essex freeholders signed a petition against bishops. Thousands from Essex marched on London after the arrest of the Five Members. Bruno Ryves's account of the principles held by the lower classes of Chelmsford around 1642 is prophetic of much that was to be developed later: but it also recalls much that had gone before. Kings are burdens. The relation of master and servant has no ground in the New Testament; in Christ there is neither bond nor free. Ranks such as those of the peerage and gentry are "ethnical and heathenish distinctions". There is no ground in nature or Scripture why one man should have £1000 per annum, another not £1. The common people have long been kept under blindness and ignorance, and have remained servants and slaves to the nobility and gentry. "But God hath now opened their eyes and discovered them their Christian liberty". Gentlemen should be made to work for their living, or else should not eat. Learning has always been an enemy to the Gospel; it would be better if there were no universities, and all books except the Bible were burned. Any gifted man may be chosen by the congregation as its minister. Essex plays almost as big a part in Edward's *Gangraena* as does Kent. Baptists, Ranters and Muggletonians were all to be found there in the forties and fifties. The main Quaker strength was in North Essex, the new drapery region, an area of arable small holdings. After 1660 Essex was the third county in numbers of ejected ministers.[19]

The Chiltern hills of Buckinghamshire formed another Lollard area, where there was a revolt in 1413-14. Again heresy survived. In 1521 more were persecuted for heresy in Buckinghamshire than in all the rest of England. A century later Isaac Penington, the Long Parliament's Lord Mayor of London, came of a family resident in Buckinghamshire since the fifteen-fifties. There were many refusals to pay Ship Money in the county, including John Hampden's. In 1640 payment of coat and conduct money was almost universally refused, and the elections of High Wycombe and Great Marlow provided classic examples of class conflict. County freeholders elected John Hampden, and rode up to London in their thousands to defend the Five Members against Charles I's attempt to impeach them in January 1642. Buckinghamshire Levellers sponsored anti-enclosure riots, and produced two pamphlets — *Light shining in Buckinghamshire* and *More Light Shining in Buckinghamshire* — which are close to the Diggers in sentiment, though both were published before digging started at St George's Hill. Winstanley's colony was endorsed by a third pamphlet from the Chiltern

Hundreds, *A Declaration of the Well-Affected in the County of Buckinghamshire* (May 1649). Like Kent, Buckinghamshire had a Digger colony, at the old Lollard centre of Iver, with its own pamphlet (May 1650). There had been Baptists in Buckinghamshire in the sixteen-twenties, and Mr Watts sees General Baptist strength in the county (and in Kent) as a Lollard legacy.[20] Quakers found an early welcome in the county of Pennington and Penn: High Wycombe was one of the centres of the near-Ranter Story-Wilkinson separation.

Readers of Dickens's admirable *Lollards and Protestants in the Diocese of York* will remember that many of the most savoury Lollard remarks came from the moorland and clothing areas of the West Riding of Yorkshire, another remote region of huge and uncontrolled parishes. Christopher Shuter, vicar of Giggleswick, a nominee of Archbishop Grindal, opened up or revived a radical tradition in the area. In the sixteen-twenties the Pennine valleys produced Grindletonians, who put the spirit before the letter of the Bible, and thought that heaven was attainable in this life; in the sixteen-forties the lower classes in the West Riding forced the gentry to take up arms for Parliament. John Webster, religious radical and would-be reformer of the universities, came from the Grindleton region; George Fox found his first congregations there in 1651, including James Nayler and many other subsequent Quaker leaders. The Grindletonians were to be associated retrospectively with Coppinger (who had Kentish connections) and the Yorkshire gentleman Arthington, disciples of William Hacket who in the fifteen-nineties believed he was the Messiah. Giles Wigginton, Marprelate suspect and disciple of Hacket, founded a separatist congregation at Sedbergh when he was suspended from his living there. There were Familists in Bradford in the sixteen-thirties, Ranters later.[21]

From another Lollard area, Gloucestershire, the reformers William Tyndale and Robert Crowley came in the sixteenth century, the anti-Trinitarians John Bidle and John Knowles a century later. John Rogers of Colesbourn in 1636 told an audience of young people that women had no souls and therefore could commit any sin without fear of damnation; men could live as wickedly as they wished, confident that they could repent at leisure. The Forest of Dean was an area in which "people of very lewd lives and conversations" found greater freedom for "their villanies" than elsewhere; and this too was a heretical region. "Those tried notorious foresters of Dean" were "constant friends of the Parliament", "ever ready to rise against his Majesty's forces".[22] Levellers and Quakers found their greatest support in south-western England in Bristol. There were anti-nomians, Brownists and enclosure riots in Gloucestershire in the sixteen-thirties, forties and fifties. There was a Digger colony: later there were Ranters.

The clothing towns of Berkshire (Newbury, Reading) nourished heresy from the fifteenth to the seventeenth century. There had been Lollards in Salisbury in 1443, Brownists and Barrowists in Salisbury and elsewhere in Wiltshire in the late sixteenth century. Mr Watts believed he could trace continuity in Somerset between late fifteenth-century Lollards and seventeenth-century Baptists. Mr Evans saw similar continuity between Lollardy and nonconformity in Norwich. East Anglia generally was a Lollard area. There were Lollards in Ely in 1457, Familists under Elizabeth and Quakers in the mid-seventeenth century. Ely was well known as a haunt of sectaries in the forties, and a recruiting ground for Oliver Cromwell. In the Isle of Axholme there were Anabaptists in the sixteen-twenties, Levellers in the fifties, Fifth Monarchists, Quakers and republicans in the sixties. There had been East Anglian anti-Trinitarians in the fifteen-seventies and eighties. There were Quakers in the sixteen-fifties in parts of Cambridgeshire where there had been Familists eighty years earlier.[23]

In Lincolnshire, Leicestershire and Warwickshire Professor Jordan suggested continuities between Lollards and Baptists. The Midlands industrial region around Coventry produced Lollards in the fifteenth century, heretics in the early sixteenth and again in the early seventeenth centuries, Ranters in the sixteen-forties and fifties. Celia Fiennes at the end of the century noted Coventry as a dissenting town. In London the parish of St Stephen's, Coleman St., harboured heretics from Lollards to Foxe's martyrs and beyond. It had close links with Buckinghamshire and Essex heretics in the fifteen-thirties; in 1628 it produced libels on the Duke of Buckingham; after 1629 many emigrated thence to New England, and in the forties it was London's most notorious radical centre, housing its own secret printing press. Venner's Fifth Monarchist revolt started from there in 1661. Ayrshire, traditionally radical in religion in the seventeenth century, had been one of the few Lollard areas in Scotland. There were "Lollards" in Kyle in 1494; there were anti-clerical demonstrations in the county in 1511; heretics were being hunted there in 1637.[24]

I do not want to impose too much organizational coherence upon those who transmitted the ideas I have been discussing: that is one of the dangers of historical hindsight. In the fifteenth and early sixteenth centuries the orthodox spoke of "Lollards"; under Elizabeth of "Anabaptists" or "Familists". There were indeed Lollard and Anabaptist groups, and the Family of Love also had some sort of organization. We do not know much about any of them yet: more research is needed. But I suspect that clerical inquisitors imposed classifications, "-isms", for their own convenience. They started with some idea of what "Lollards", "Anabaptists" or "Familists" ought to believe, just as they started with assumptions about what "witches" believed. Leading questions would then encourage suspects to conform to the expected type.

So though there were "Lollard", "Anabaptist" and "Familist" trends in popular thought, we should not necessarily postulate the existence of an organized underground. But there are tantalizing hints. A heretical meeting in Colchester in 1555 was so widely advertised that a servant attended from Cambridgeshire. If there was underground organization, itinerants necessarily played a considerable part in it. The clothier Thomas White, involved in Dudley's conspiracy in 1556, carried on treasonable activities under cover of "collecting the wool". Humphrey Newman, a cobbler at one time attached to the household of Sir Richard Knightley, was the principal distributor of the Marprelate Tracts in the Midlands and London. A travelling clothier from Berkshire was alleged to be spreading sedition in Chichester in the late sixteen-thirties. Elizabethan Familists are said to have been linked by itinerant weavers, basket-makers, bottle-makers, musicians, joiners. In 1622 Thomas Shepard in Essex knew about the Grindletonian Familists, lurking in the obscurity of a Yorkshire Pennine valley. The clothing industry linked Essex and the West Riding.[25]

Familists — like Lollards before them — tended when challenged to recant, but to remain of the same opinion still. This unheroic attitude was related to their dislike of all established churches, whether protestant or Catholic. Their refusal of martyrdom no doubt helped their beliefs to survive, but it increases the historian's difficulty in identifying heretical groups with confidence. Only after the excitement of the reign of Edward VI were lower-class heretics for a brief period prepared to court martyrdom: after 1660 one suspects that many former Ranters and Baptists reverted to the ways of their Familist predecessors and returned formally and unbelievingly to the national church. The Ranters "would have said as we said and done as we commanded, and yet have kept their own principle still", said Durant Hotham, stressing this Lollard and Familist way of acting as the main difference between Ranters and Quakers.[26]

Before 1640 the traditions I have been describing circulated verbally. Historians, themselves the products of a literary culture, relying so much on written or printed evidence, are always in danger of underestimating verbal transmission of ideas. Men did not need to read books to become acquainted with heresy: indeed censored books were the last place in which they would expect to find it. Again and again the great heresiarchs deny being influenced by their predecessors. Luther was astonished to find that he was reproducing Hus's heresies: Milton was astonished and delighted to find that many protestant divines had anticipated his views on divorce.

With all these reservations, let me now suggest some continuing lower-class traditions which burst into the open in the sixteen-forties. There is no need to produce further evidence of the point I have already stressed, class hatred, since this has been fully documented in Mr Brian Manning's magnificent *The English People and the English Revolution*. Illustrations of more generalized hostility to social subordination are refusal to remove the hat in the presence of magistrates or social superiors, and addressing them as "thou" in symbolic assertion of equality. (Compare Coke's insult to Ralegh at his trial: "Lo! I thou thee, thou traitor!" Treason demoted a gentleman from his own class to equality with the lower orders: "thouing" a social superior marked an attempt to escape from the social and political contempt to which "thou" condemned those to whom it was addressed). The Quakers inherited a long-standing lower-class rejection of deference here. The fifteenth-century Lollard William Thorpe kept his hat on in presence of authority. So did Marian martyrs, Essex heretics in 1584, William Hacket in 1591, John Traske in 1618, an oatmeal-maker up before the High Commission in 1630, the future Leveller John Lilburne in 1638, John Saltmarsh in 1647, and very many others. John Lewis, burnt at Norwich in 1583 for anti-Trinitarianism, "did thou each wight".[27]

Refusal to take an oath is also a rejection of political authority: we find it among Norwich and Essex Lollards, some Anabaptists,

Barrowists, Lilburne. Some Lollards rejected all judicial proceedings, and any form of deliberate killing, whether in warfare or by execution of criminals. Again these positions were inherited by Quakers. The myth of the Norman Yoke enshrines a similar anti-authoritarian and anti-aristocratic attitude, rejection of the ruling class and its law. So does the 1381 question, "When Adam delved and Eve span/Who was then the gentleman?" quoted in the reign of Edward VI, in 1593, and often after 1640 — "this levelling lewd text", Cleveland called it. Sneers about Jack Straw, Wat Tyler and Jack Cade were frequent. Fuller said the rebels of 1381 were "pure Levellers". Sir Thomas Aston referred in 1641 to "the old seditious argument, that we are all the sons of Adam, born free; some of them say, the Gospel hath made them free. . . . They will plead Scripture for it, that we should all live by the sweat of our brows". Nor was it only via Scripture that human equality was asserted. In 1310 a peasant pleaded (through his lawyer) that "in the beginning every man in the world was free".[28]

The Digger community at St George's Hill, we now know, was only one of ten or more such experiments; communist ideas are found in writers not directly associated with the Diggers — the Ranters Abiezer Coppe and George Foster, and the author of *Tyanipocrit Discovered;* they were attributed to the Leveller Walwyn. John Ball, and Essex, Norwich and Worcestershire Lollards were alleged to have said that property should be common. Similar charges were made against participants in Cade's rebellion in 1450.[29] Such accusations may be the product of the alarmed imagination of the rich; but since community of property is commended in the New Testament it is unlikely that no lower-class Bible-reader would take the point. An Essex man did, late in Henry VIII's reign: Chelmsford radicals a century later were said to have done so. Tyndale came dangerously near to justifying community of property, and such ideas occurred in the mid-sixteenth century often enough for one of the 42 Articles of 1552 and of the 39 Articles of 1562 to be directed against them. The Presbyterian John Field found it necessary in 1572 to denounce communist theories.[30]

Turning to more specifically religious matters, Essex Lollards said that priests should marry and work, and attacked non-preachers. Pluralism was as bad as bigamy, asserted an Essex Lollard burnt in 1440. Another in the same county seventeen years later said that the best man was the best priest, and that confession should be made only to God — anticipating the lay initiative in Puritanism and the sects. John Ball taught that tithes should be paid only by men richer than the priest. Many Lollards opposed tithes. Ministers should not be paid, said Augustine Draper of Essex in 1587; he also denied the immortality of the soul. Opposition to tithes and church courts became standard among the radicals of the revolutionary decades. Wyclif had thought that the exercise of civil jurisdiction by ecclesiastics, and in particular the use of force, was antichristian. So did many seventeenth-century radicals, including John Milton.[31]

The seventeenth-century view that a layman is as good as a parson, that the whole ecclesiastical hierarchy is antichristian, that tithes and a state church should be abolished, together with universities as training centres for the clergy; advocacy of "mechanic preachers" who enjoy the spirit of God, so much more important than academic education: all these ideas are so familiar from Wyclif and the Lollards through Anabaptists and Familists to Levellers and sectaries that documentation would be superfluous. Some Lollards seem to have accepted that all believers were priests. Familist ministers were itinerant craftsmen, and indeed the conditions of underground sectarianism forced the emergence of mechanic preachers. Anti-sacerdotalism was a necessity as well as an ideology. Some Lollards, and the reformer William Tyndale, even thought that women might preach.[32]

Secondly comes a strong emphasis on study of the Bible, and use of its texts — as interpreted by the individual conscience — to criticize the ceremonies and sacraments of the church. Worship of images, for instance, was denounced as idolatry. Sacredness was denied to church buildings: worship and prayer could take place anywhere. Lollards as well as Edwardian radicals anticipated the iconoclasm of the mid-seventeenth century. Essex and Norwich Lollards were accused of scorning infant baptism; so did Francis Kett and Edward Wightman. This looks forward to Samuel Oates, weaver and button-maker, dipping in Essex in 1645 as well as begetting Titus. Millenarianism, familiar in lower-class underground movements, was found among the later Lollards.[33] Around 1580 Familists were alleged to believe that the saints were to judge the world, doctrine repeated by Thomas Collier, Gerrard Winstanley, George Fox, Fifth Monarchists. Ludlow, like John Cook and John Milton, saw regicide as an anticipation by the saints of the Last Judgment.[34]

Arminianism, the doctrine that men may save themselves by their own efforts, does not seem a particularly dangerous heresy to us today. But it did to orthodox sixteenth- and seventeenth-century Puritans. (We must distinguish between radical Arminianism, rejecting the sacraments of the church as aids to salvation, and Laudian Arminianism). Many sixteenth-century English heretics rejected predestination, attached greater value to works than to faith, emphasized human freedom and effort — a sort of pre-Arminianism, which can be found among Familists as well as among continental Anabaptists, from one or other of whom it was taken over by the English General Baptists. A Kentish heretic, Henry Hart, a "froward freewill man", who wrote a treatise against predestination in 1554, anticipated Milton in saying that human freedom to choose between good and evil was essential if God was to be absolved of responsibility for evil. There were "free-will men" in London in 1560. An Essex heretic in 1592 thought that "all the world shall be saved"; Thomas Edwards in 1646 attributed the idea of universal salvation to Familists and other radicals. It was certainly held by Winstanley, and under the 1648 Blasphemy Ordinance was made an offence carrying the penalty of life imprisonment. Thomas Shepard's interest in the Yorkshire Grindletonians led him in 1622 to ask "whether that glorious state of perfection might not be the truth?" The belief that perfection could be attained in this life had been held by London tradesmen in 1549 and 1631, and by many Familists in between. In the sixteen-forties Saltmarsh, Everard and Winstanley believed that Christ would not appear in the flesh but in the saints. Mrs Attaway and William Jenny did not think it could stand with the goodness of God to damn his creatures eternally: Walwyn was to say that eternal punishment was too great for "a little sinning".[35]

Another recurrent heresy is anti-Trinitarianism. Some Lollards denied the divinity of Christ and the Holy Spirit. The rapid spread of anti-Trinitarianism both in the liberty of Edward VI's reign and in prisons under Mary gave rise to great alarm among orthodox protestants — so much so that the godly John Philpot had to apologize for "spitting upon an Arian". In 1549 an Arian said Christ was a prophet, the Son of God, but only the first-begotten amongst many brothers.[36] This gives rise to thoughts about the connection of anti-Trinitarianism with attacks on primogeniture, familiar later among the Levellers.

In 1555 denial of the divinity of Christ by an itinerant joiner, later a well-known Familist, was the subject of illegal discussions in a Colchester tavern, to which servants and husbandmen travelled long distances from outside the county. Some of the Marian martyrs were probably anti-Trinitarians, and between 1548 and 1612 at least eight persons were burnt in England for heresies concerning the Trinity. Among them was Marlowe's friend Francis Kett, grandson of the leader of the Norfolk rebels in 1549, who was also a mortalist, an opponent of infant baptism and of the death penalty for heresy; he rejected the authority of ministers to excommunicate. Marlowe, himself from Kent, was said to have called Christ a bastard; in 1560 a Kentish man had said that those who believed Christ sat on the right hand of the Father were fools.[37] The Legate brothers from Essex, one of whom was burnt in 1612, were anti-Trinitarians: so was Wight-man, the last Englishman to be burnt for heresy, also in 1612. Their courage made the common people, Fuller tells us, "ready to entertain good thoughts even of [their] opinions". When Archbishop Neile in 1639 wished to revive the practice of burning heretics his chosen victim would have been John Trendall, anti-Trinitarian stonemason of Dover.[38]

Anti-Trinitarianism was associated especially with Familists, who rejected the whole theology of the Atonement, Christ's vicarious sacrifice: some abandoned belief in the historical existence of Christ. For them the word Christ was a metaphor for the divine spark which exists in every man. William Pynchon of Essex carried anti-Trinitarianism to Massachusetts in the sixteen-thirties; John Bidle of Gloucestershire, John Milton and very many others proclaimed it in England in the forties and fifties. Quakers and Muggletonians were accused of the heresy.[39] The humanity of Christ enhanced the dignity of man.

Another heresy which recurs among underground groups was mortalism, the doctrine that the soul either sleeps from death until the general resurrection or dies with the body. Professor N.T. Burns has so thoroughly demonstrated the continuous existence of *Christian Mortalism from Tyndale to Milton* that I refer to him for evidence, though with a caution that mortalism existed in England well before the Reformation — among Essex Lollards, for example. Tyndale was a mortalist.[40] The 42 Articles of 1552 condemned mortalism, though the condemnation was omitted in the 39 Articles of 1562. Elizabethan Familists were alleged to be mortalists, be-lieving that the resurrection occurred in this life. In the fifteen-sixties in Surrey and in the fifteen-eighties in Wisbech and Wiltshire there were those who believed that the soul was annihilated at death, with no ultimate resurrection. Among mortalists was Augustine Draper of Essex, who also thought the clergy should not be paid, and the anti-Trinitarians Francis Kett and Edward Wightman. Christopher Marlowe was said to be a mortalist; Donne — like Sir Thomas Browne — appears to have toyed with the heresy in his younger days. Mortalism too travelled to New England, where Mrs Anne Hutchinson and Samuel Gorton were accused in the sixteen-thirties of being mortalists as well as Familists. In the forties and fifties William Bowling of Kent, Richard Overton, Clement Wrighter, Henry Marten, Lodowick Muggleton and John Milton were some of a large number of adherents to the belief. The Quakers and Henry Stubbe were also accused of the heresy.[41]

Mortalism was often accompanied by, or led to, a species of materialism. Wyclif, like some troubadours, was said to believe in the eternity of matter. In 1428 the Lollard Margery Backster anticipated Milton in a crude reference to the ultimate physical fate of bread eaten in the eucharist, in order to show that it could hardly be the body of Christ. Dickens quotes many similar remarks. A man from north-west Kent in 1538 denied that God had created him,[42] and many early heretics believed — like Ranters in the sixteen-fifties and the rebel angels in *Paradise Lost* — that "all comes by nature". Ranters, like Milton, held that matter is good in itself. Such doctrines can by a natural progression lead to anti-asceticism, glorification of the body, a belief that life is to be enjoyed here and now. This may be expressed as an antinomian libertinism: the elect are exempt from the moral law since God is in them; they partake of God's nature. A Lollard lay "priest" in 1389 was said to believe himself free from the possibility of sin. Such doctrines in England were denounced by Thomas Rogers in 1607. They surfaced in the sixteen-forties. Baxter said in 1649 and 1654 that all men were naturally antimonians, especially the vulgar. Arminianism on the other hand was a heresy of the learned.[43] John Milton is an example of a learned antinomian.

If at death the body returns to its elements, as a drop of water taken out of the ocean returns to it again, mortalism can also lead to scepticism about heaven and hell, which become states of mind rather than geographical locations. Some Lollards denied their existence, and placed purgatory in this world. The devil too was internalized. This could combine with allegorical interpretations of the Bible to make the whole Christian myth describe conflicts which take place only within the believer. Familists were said to hold that Christ and Antichrist were not real persons, heaven and hell not real places. Francis Kett the mortalist thought there would be no hell before the Last Judgment. In Wiltshire and in Somerset in the early seventeenth century men were denying the existence of a local heaven or hell. A preacher in Lancashire appointed by the Bishop of Chester early in James I's reign thought hell a mere delusion, invented to oppress and torment the consciences of men. In 1619 a Wiltshire heretic was accused of doubting whether the writings of the apostles and prophets were true. Saltmarsh and Everard treated the Scriptures as an allegory, though Everard added "I deny not the history". For Winstanley "it matters not much" whether the Bible was true or not; from his earliest pamphlets he concentrated on their allegorical meaning. James Nayler more cautiously said "there is no knowledge of heaven or hell". In the sixteen-twenties the Grindle-tonians, like Thomas Müntzer before them and Gerrard Winstanley after them, emphasized the spirit as against the letter of Scripture, a doctrine not unknown to Milton. A Norfolk anti-Trinitarian in 1579 anticipated the Ranters by saying that the New Testament was "a mere fable".[44]

The poet Gower in the fourteenth century described labourers who were not satisfied with the bread and water on which they had been brought up but demanded good food and drink — and did not believe in God. There were "libertines" in Essex in 1551, and later men who denied the existence of "sin" and criticized the Bible in a way that looks forward to Clement Wrighter and Samuel Fisher in the sixteen-fifties. One described himself as an atheist.[45] Antinomianism led to sexual heresies. Whenever suspected Lollards were up before the Norwich church courts in 1428-31 they were asked, in a standard formula, if they believed in church marriage. Clearly the answer expected was No. Miss Hudson confirms this from other regions. Some Norwich suspects were accused of advocating community of women — a recurrent charge long before Münster. "Marriage is superfluous", the Venetian ambassador reported heretics as saying in 1499. "A lewd fellow out of Essex" in 1457 thought marriage should be a civil ceremony; Buckinghamshire heretics taught this in the first decades of Henry VIII's reign, Barebone's Parliament enacted it in 1653. In 1548 it was thought necessary to issue a royal proclamation attacking seditious preachers who advocated divorce. Sixteenth-century Familists married and divorced by a simple declaration before the congregation. The Yorkshire custom of "handfast marriages" was taken up by Ranters and Quakers. Some Lollards may have advocated polygamy, though the evidence is doubtful. It was defended in 1548, in Kent in 1572, and by Milton. In 1592 Nashe referred to "adulterous Familists". Drunken Barnabee repeated the slander against Bradford Familists in the sixteen-thirties. It was entirely in keeping that James Nayler should be accused of saying that "he might lie with any woman that was of his judgment". Similar accusations were more plausibly made against Abiezer Coppe and Laurence Clarkson, who in the sixteen-forties advocated free love. Underlying these radical theories of marriage and divorce was the widely attested fact that lower-class attitudes towards matrimony were much more casual and fluid than the ethic which middle-class Puritans wished to impose. Evidence for *de facto* marriage and easy divorce is overwhelming, especially — but by no means exclusively — among vagrants.[46]

We isolate heresies for the purpose of analysis, but they normally came in combination. Sir Thomas More linked anti-Trinitarianism with advocacy of common ownership of property.[47] Edmund Leach has suggested that anti-Trinitarianism, millenarianism and social revolt go together, among the early Christians and in seventeenth-century England. Radical Arminianism, rejection of infant baptism, antinomianism, mortalism and materialism were frequently linked with Leach's heresies in England, as Thomas Edwards noted in *Gangraena* in 1646. In the same year the respectable inhabitants of Great Burstead, Essex, saw similar connections. They petitioned against "a dangerous sect" which had arisen in their parish, admitting and rebaptizing all comers, "setting up mechanics for their preachers, denouncing the order and ministry of the Church of England as antichristian". They taught "unsound opinions" like universal grace, the abrogation of the law, the sinfulness of repentance. Their name was legion, and they had a long pedigree.[48]

Looking back to Lollards and Familists helps to emphasize that, if there was a continuing heretical underground, it was essentially composed of laymen. This fits in with what we are coming to know about the initiative in Puritanism of lay members of congregations in refusing to allow their minister to wear the surplice or to conform to other ceremonies. The Puritan clergy were moderate reformers, safely educated at Oxford or Cambridge. They naturally had not much use for lay mechanic preaching. There were initially some

Lollard hedge priests, but they counted for less and less with time. Familist ministers seem normally to have been craftsmen.

The church was the official meeting place; and it belonged to the official clergy. The meeting place of the unorthodox was the tavern or ale-house, from Lollards to Familists and on to Baptists, Levellers and Ranters. The only other popular meeting place was the open air; Quakers preached there. Laurence Clarkson said that a tavern was the house of God.[49] The popularity of the ale-house, apart from the obvious reason, was partly due to the evolution of a new itinerant working-class, which sought social intercourse and information about jobs in ale-houses. JPs deeply resented any attempt to remove control of ale-houses from their hands, whether by Buckingham's protégés Mitchell and Mompesson or by Oliver Cromwell's Major-Generals.

So I suggest as a hypothesis for further investigation that there may have been a continuing underground tradition — not necessarily organization — in which we can identify certain heretical and seditious beliefs. Professor Elton's notorious statement that there was no connection between Lollardy and the Reformation is true only if we interpret the Reformation in the narrowest sense as Henry VIII's act of state. But if we ask why England became a protestant country we cannot leave Lollardy out of account, though it was the more radical protestants who looked back to the Lollards. Bruce McFarlane was right to call his book *John Wyclif and the Origins of Nonconformity*. We may be able to trace direct links in ideas from Lollards through Familists and Anabaptists to the radical sectaries, the Levellers, Diggers, Ranters and Quakers of the mid-seventeenth century. The author of *Semper Iidem: Or, a Parallel betwixt the Ancient and Modern Fanaticks* (1661) certainly thought so.[50]

This leads to a final question. What happened after 1660? It took some time to realise that defeat was final, that the above-ground decades had been a mere interlude. In 1678-81 something surfaced again in London. But the defeat of the radicals in 1685 facilitated the coup of 1688, when Whigs and Tories united against the radicals no less than against James II. Some emigrated to the West Indies, New England and the continent. There were Ranters on Long Island and Rhode Island in the sixteen-eighties and nineties.[51] Some of those who remained in England no doubt lapsed into silent bloody-mindedness. Some became sectaries; the Quakers cast off their radical wing and became pacifists. All sects were purged by the fierce

persecution of the three decades after 1660. They had to recognize
that Christ's kingdom was not to be built on earth, but was to be
expected in heaven at a date later to be announced.

But the Levellers were never wholly forgotten. Goldsmith praised
them. Jefferson quoted William Rumbold, who had been para-
phrased by Defoe and cited in an almanac of 1708. There were men
who called themselves Levellers in revolt in Worcestershire in 1670,
in anti-enclosure riots in 1724, in Ledbury in 1735, in the Lowlands
of Scotland in the seventeen-twenties, in the Hudson valley in 1760,
other American rebels under William Prendergast in 1765.[52] Beau
Nash, rather unexpectedly, spoke of Levellers in Bath in 1742.[53] The
Leveller sea-green colours had reappeared on the streets of London
in 1681; the Whig Green Ribbon Club took its name from them.
London weavers in 1675 had rioted in green aprons, and green aprons
soon came to be "almost regarded as a badge of Quakerism".[54] The
French prophets in London in Anne's reign were accused of "levelling" and "Ranterism"; they wore long green ribbons. The fact that
the Chartist flag was green is usually attributed to Irish influence;
but why did Irish protestants adopt the colour in the first place? In
1690 William III's troops in Ireland wore green, and some are said to
have chosen the Leveller sea-green, so there may be continuity here
from Levellers through Whigs to United Irishmen and Chartists. At
all events the Levellers were still remembered in the Chartist movement.[55] Was it only because of Robespierre's complexion that
Carlyle dubbed him "sea-green?" Pamphlets by Winstanley were in
the library of Benjamin Furly, who linked radical Quakers with deist
free-thinkers like Anthony Collins — who also possessed pamphlets
by Winstanley. In the mid-eighteenth century the radical Thomas
Hollis gave a copy of *The Law of Freedom* to Henry Fielding.[56]

Nor is it only a matter of politics. A.L. Morton showed that Blake
was aware of the Ranter past, and Burns may have been.[57] How the
ideas were transmitted is more difficult to document. A lay clerk of
Norwich cathedral about 1700 was alleged to think that "there is no
heaven but a quiet mind, and no hell but the grave" — almost a literal
quotation from many Ranters. There were people called Ranters in
the Midlands, Nottingham, Cumberland, near Inverness and elsewhere at the turn of the century. Wesley in the seventeen-forties met
antinomian preachers in the Black Country — an old Lollard/Ranter
area — who believed in community of property and did not believe in
monogamy.[58] The future bishop George Horne also knew Ranters in

the mid-century, as well as anti-monarchist Presbyterians.[59] The linked doctrines of mortalism, millenarianism and the perfectibility of man on earth were still being discussed in a Kentish General Baptist congregation in the middle of the eighteenth century.[60] In 1756 the Robin Hood Society met every Monday night at a pub in Butchers' Row, London. Here deists, Arians, Socinians, papists and Jews aired their doubts about the resurrection, the incarnation, the Trinity ("their everlasting butt"), the authenticity of the Scriptures, of the gospel miracles. They were a set of mechanics — tailors, barbers, butchers and shoemakers.[61] Where did the millenarian revivalism come from which accompanied the American as it had accompanied the English Revolution? What about the New England antinomians of the eighteen-twenties and eighteen-thirties, whose belief that perfection was attainable on earth led to sexual eccentricities and experiments as it had done in old England nearly two centuries earlier? If we look for them, I think we can find other traces, before 1640 and after 1660. One of the objects of this chapter is to encourage others to look. With that in mind I have documented it pretty fully.

NOTES

1. Originally published in *Rebels and their Causes: Essays in honour of A.L. Morton* (ed. M. Cornforth, 1978); reprinted, slightly revised, in Bulletin Nos. 12 and 13 of *Documenta Anabaptistica Neerlandica* (Amsterdam, 1980-1), and in abbreviated form in *Religion and Rural Revolt* (ed. J.M. Bak and G. Benecke, Manchester U.P., 1984).
2. *W.T.U.D.*, p. 120; G.F. Nuttall, "The Lollard Movement after 1384, its Characteristics and Continuity", *Transactions of the Congregational Historical Soc.*, XII (1935), pp. 243-50.
3. I.B. Horst, *The Radical Brethren* (Nieuwkoop, 1972), pp. 146-8.
4. J. Cleveland, *The Rustic Rampant*, in *Works* (1687), p. 506; A. Cowley, *The Civil War* (ed. A. Pritchard, Toronto U.P., 1973), pp. 88, 103; J. Collop, *Poems* (ed. C. Hilberry, Wisconsin U.P., 1962), p. 48; J. Rushworth, *Historical Collections* (1659-1701), V, p. 732.
5. A. Fletcher, *op. cit.*, pp. 3, 21, 61, 165-6, 193, 200.
6. J. Foxe, *Acts and Monuments* (ed. J. Pratt, n.d.), IV, pp. 123, 181, 619; V, pp. 16, 647-52, 841; VII, pp. 287-321, 329-41, 383, 604, 750-2; VIII, pp. 130-1, 151-6, 243-7, 253-5, 300-3, 320-77, 394, 430-3, 504-6, 549-50, 566-8, 576, 695, 729-30, appendix VI; Collinson, *The Elizabethan Puritan Movement*, p. 37; cf. pp. 96-7; *Godly People*, p. 12, Chapter 15 *passim;*

Horst, *op. cit.*, pp. 122-40; Fletcher, *op. cit.*, pp. 62, 91, 124; J.W. Martin, "English Protestant Separatism at its Beginnings: Henry Hart and the Free-Will Men", *Sixteenth Century Journal*, VII (1976), pp. 58, 66-7; Claire Cross, *Church and People, 1450-1660* (1976), pp. 25, 28, 37-9, 73-4, 98-9, 112, 114, 170; P. Clark, *English Provincial Society*, pp. 23, 30-1, 56, 60, 63, 67, 77, 101, 156, 399, 401-2, 444 and *passim*; "Reformation and Radicalism in Kentish Towns, c. 1500-1553", in *The Urban Classes, the Nobility and the Reformation* (ed. W.J. Mommsen, Stuttgart, 1979), p. 124; M.R. Watts, *The Dissenters from the Reformation to the French Revolution* (Oxford U.P., 1978), pp. 283-4, 354-5; B. Reay, "Quaker Opposition to Tithes, 1652-1660", *P. and P.*, No. 86 (1980), p. 102. For the geography of surviving Lollardy see J.F. Davis, *Heresy and Reformation in the South-East of England, 1520-1559* (1983), pp. 2, 58, 102, 141 and *passim*.

7. J. Walter and K. Wrightson, "Dearth and Social Order in Early Modern England", *P. and P.*, No. 71 (1976), p. 27; P. Clark, "Popular Protest and Disturbance in Kent, 1558-1640", *Economic History Review*, XXIX (1976), pp. 365-82; *English Provincial Society*, pp. 156, 335, 381, 389, 393; C. Burrage, *Early English Dissenters*, II, pp. 202-3; J. Taylor, *All the Works* (1973 reprint), II, p. 114 (rightly 124); G. Wither, *Fragmenta Prophetica* (1669), p. 130, in *Miscellaneous Works* (Spenser Soc., 6th collection, 1878); Sir T. Wyatt, *Complete Poems* (ed. R.A. Rebholz, Penguin), p. 189.

8. Fletcher, *op. cit.*, p. 22; Manning, *The English People and the English Revolution* (1976), p. 41; my *Society and Puritanism in Pre-Revolutionary England* (Panther edn., 1969), p. 298; D. Underdown, "Clubmen in the Civil War" *P. and P.*, No. 85 (1979), p. 42. Peter Clark helped me with Tenterden.

9. Edwards, *Gangraena* (1646), I, p. 75 and *passim*; *W.T.U.D.*, pp. 46-7, 124-7, 239; *V.C.H., Kent*, II (1926), p. 100; J.F. McGregor, "The Baptists: Fount of All Heresy", in *Radical Religion in the English Revolution*, p. 35.

10. Foxe, *op. cit.*, IV, pp. 214-17, 584-6, 695, 706-7; V, pp. 29-34, 38-42, 251; VI, pp. 729-40; VII, pp. 86-90, 97-123, 139-42, 329, 370, 605, 718-30; VIII, pp. 107-21, 138-41, 303-10, 381-94, 420-3, 433-6, 467-8, 525-6, appendix VI; Horst, *op. cit.*, pp. 122-3; Collinson, *The Elizabethan Puritan Movement*, p. 223; Collinson, "The Godly: Aspects of Popular Protestantism in Elizabethan England", *Papers Presented to the Past and Present Conference on Popular Religion* (1966), p. 16; Martin, *op. cit.*, p. 66; Cross, *op. cit.*, pp. 25, 37-9, 73-4, 77, 98-9, 112.

11. A. Gordon, *Heads of English Unitarian History* (1895), pp. 16-17; D.D. Wallace, "From Eschatology to Arian Heresy: the Case of Francis Kett", *Harvard Theological Review*, No. 67 (1974), p. 467. A.G. Dickens, "Heresy and the Origins of English Protestantism", in *Britain and the Netherlands*, II (Ed. J.S. Bromley and E.H. Kossmann, Groningen, 1964), pp. 53-5, 60; Cross, *op. cit.*, pp. 28-32.

12. C.L.E. Ewen, *Witch Hunting and Witch Trials* (1929), pp. 100, 302; A. Macfarlane, *Witchcraft in Tudor and Stuart England* (1970), *passim*;

W. Hunt, *Bath and Wells* (Diocesan Histories, 1885), pp. 140, 146.

13. K.L. Sprunger, *The Learned Doctor William Ames* (Illinois U.P., 1972), pp. 24-5.

14. *Rump; or an Exact Collection of the Choycest Poems and Songs relating to the Late Times* (1662), I, p. 354; T. Shepard, *God's Plot* (ed. M. McGiffert, Massachusetts U.P., 1972), p. 47; Hunt, *The Puritan Moment*, pp. 87-90 and *passim*.

15. Walter and Wrightson, *op. cit.*, p. 36, and *passim*; K.V. Thomas, *Religion and the Decline of Magic* (1971), pp. 406, 422; Hunt, *The Puritan Moment*, pp. 60-1, 147-8 and *passim*.

16. *C.S.P.D., 1634-5*, pp. 216, 227; *1636-7*, pp. 223, 483; *C.S.P. Ven., 1632-6*, pp. 299-300; *1636-8*, p. 269; *V.C.H., Essex*, II, p. 228. I owe these references and much of this and the following paragraphs to Hunt, *The Puritan Movement*, esp. Chapters 10 and 11.

17. J. Gruenfeld, "The Election for Knights of the Shire for Essex, Spring 1640", *Essex Archaeological Soc. Trans.*, II (3rd series, 1967), pp. 145-6; J.A. Sharpe, "Crime and Delinquency in an Essex Parish, 1600-1640", in *Crime in England, 1500-1800* (ed. J.S. Cockburn, 1977), pp. 90-109.

18. C. Holmes, *The Eastern Association in the English Civil War* (Cambridge U.P., 1974), pp. 33-6, 43-4.

19. [Anon.], *A New Found Stratagem* (1647), p. 4; Marie Gimelfarb-Brack attributes this pamphlet to Richard Overton (*Liberté, Egalité, Fraternité, Justice! La Vie et l'Oeuvre de Richard Overton, Niveleur*, Berne, 1979, pp. 402-3); *W.T.U.D.*, pp. 37, 263; Watts, *op. cit.*, p. 277. I owe North Essex to Barry Reay's Oxford D. Phil. thesis, *Early Quaker Activity and Reactions to it, 1652-1664* (1980).

20. Foxe, *op. cit.*, IV, pp. 123-6, 211-43, 580-6; V, p. 434; P. Gregg, *King Charles I* (1981), pp. 302, 313; K.V. Thomas, "Another Digger Broadside", *P. and P.*, No. 42 (1969), pp. 57-68; *W.T.U.D.*, pp. 21, 117, 126; A.G. Dickens, "Heresy and the Origins of English Protestantism", pp. 53-6; Cross, *Church and People*, pp. 28-32, 35, 42, 73, 98; Edwards, *Gangraena*, I, p. 64; Burrage, *op. cit.*, I, p. 274; Watts, *op. cit.*, pp. 283-4; McGregor, *op. cit.*, p. 35.

21. Dickens, *Lollards and Protestants in the Diocese of York, 1509-1558* (Oxford U.P., 1959), *passim*; Collinson, *Grindal*, pp. 205-12; R. Braithwait, *Barnabae Itinerarium or Barnabees Journal* (ed. W.C. Hazlitt, 1876), Sig. C.

22. C.E. Hart, *The Free Miners of the Royal Forest of Dean* (Gloucester, 1953), pp. 174-5; Buchanan Sharp, *In Contempt of All Authority: Rural Artisans and Riot in the West of England, 1586-1660* (California U.P., 1980), *passim*; B.L. Beer, *Rebellion and Riot: Popular Disorder in England during the Reign of Edward VI* (Kent State U.P., 1982), Chapter 6; B.S. Capp, *The Fifth Monarchy Men*, p. 35, for millenarianism in fifteenth-century Gloucestershire. I owe John Rogers to the kindness of Dr Andrew Foster, citing Gloucester Diocesan Register.

23. A. Hudson, "A Lollard Compilation and the Dissemination of Wycliffite Thought", *Journal of Theological Studies*, No. 23 (1972), pp. 79-80;

"A Lollard Mass", *ibid.*, p.410; M.J. Ingram, *Ecclesiastical Justice in Wiltshire, 1600-1640, with Special Reference to Cases Concerning Sex and Marriage* (Oxford University D. Phil. thesis, 1976), p.70; Watts, *op. cit.*, p.355; J.T. Evans, *Seventeenth-Century Norwich: Politics, Religion and Government, 1620-1690* (Oxford U.P., 1979), p. 84; Claire Cross, "'Great Reasoners in Scripture': the Activities of Women Lollards, 1380-1530", in *Medieval Women* (ed. D. Baker, Studies in Church History Subsidium, I, 1978), pp. 373-5; Reay, Thesis, Chapter 2; Wallace, *op. cit.*, p. 464; W.K. Jordan, *The Development of Religious Toleration in England, 1603-1640* (1936), p. 267; M. Spufford, *Contrasting Communities; English Villages in the Sixteenth and Seventeenth Centuries* (Cambridge U.P., 1974), p. 351. For Newbury I am indebted to an unpublished paper by Mr C.G. Durston. See also Capp, *op. cit.*, p. 35, for millenarianism in fifteenth- and early sixteenth-century Newbury and Wiltshire; K. Lindley, *Fenland Riots and the English Revolution* (1982), pp. 195-6, 234; C. Holmes, *Seventeenth-Century Lincolnshire* (Lincoln, 1980), pp.45, 112, 205. For Wiltshire see also pp.141-2, 151-3 below.

24. *W.T.U.D.*, pp.83, 121, 124-5, 218, 226-8, 234, 239; Manning, *op. cit.*, pp.210-16; A. Hassell Smith, *County and Court: Government and Politics in Norfolk, 1558-1603* (Oxford U.P., 1974), p.203; Foxe, *op. cit.*, IV, pp.133-5, 243, 557-8; VI, p.612; VII, pp.384-402, 799 sqq.; VIII, pp.163-202, 256, 401-5, appendix VI; Cross, *Church and People*, pp.27-8, 35-7, 73, 75, 112; I. Laxton, "The Reformation and Popular Culture", in *Church and Society in England, Henry VIII to James I* (ed. F. Heal and R. O'Day, 1977), pp.66-7; Cross, "'Great Reasoners'", pp.365-8; J.F. Davis, "Lollard Survival and the Textile Industry in the South-East of England"', *Studies in Church History*, II (ed. C.J. Cumming, Leiden, 1966), p.194; A. Hudson, "A Lollard Compilation", pp.79-80; *The Journeys of Celia Fiennes* (ed. C. Morris, 1947), p.113; D.A. Kirby, "The Radicals of St. Stephen's, Coleman St., London, 1624-1642", *Guildhall Miscellany*, III (1970), pp.98-119; J.N. King, *English Reformation Literature*, p.253; I.B. Cowan, *Regional Aspects of the Scottish Reformation* (Historical Association Pamphlet, 1978), pp. 7-8, 25.

25. Spufford, *op. cit.*, pp.247, 351; *W.T.U.D.*, pp.26-7, 45, 83-4; G.F. Nuttall, *The Holy Spirit in Puritan Faith and Experience* (Oxford, 1946), pp.178-9; L.H. Carlson, *Martin Marprelate*, pp.9, 23, 32-5, 214; K.V. Thomas, *op. cit.*, pp.134-6; D.M. Loades, *Two Tudor Conspiracies* (Cambridge U.P., 1965), pp.206-7; Leona Rostenberg, *The Minority Press and the English Crown (1558-1625)* (Nieuwkoop, 1971), p.181. I am grateful to Peter Clark for information about Coppinger. See also p.73 above.

26. *W.T.U.D.*, p.257; A. Hamilton, *The Family of Love* (Cambridge, 1981), Chapter 6.

27. Foxe, *op. cit.*, VIII, p.314; J. Strype, *Annals of the Reformation* (Oxford U.P., 1824), IV, p.97; F.G. Emmison, *Elizabethan Life: Morals and Church Courts* (Chelmsford, 1973), pp.309-10; *W.T.U.D.*, p.29. For

Traske see p.164 below; ed. H.E. Rollins, *Old English Ballads, 1552-1625*, (Cambridge U.P., 1920), p. 56.

28. Emmison, *op. cit.*, p. 126; J. Cleveland, *Works* (1687), p. 402; Fuller, *Church History of Britain*, I, p. 451; Sir T. Aston, *A Remonstrance Against Presbytery* (1641), Sig. I 4v; O. Lutaud, *Winstanley: socialisme et Christianisme* (Paris, 1960), p. 10; *Selections from English Wycliffite Writings* (ed. A. Hudson, Cambridge U.P., 1978), pp. 20, 28, 161; R.H. Hilton, *The Decline of Serfdom in Medieval England* (Studies in Economic and Social History, 2nd edn., 1983), pp. 28-9. For the Norman Yoke see my *Puritanism and Revolution* (Panther edn., 1968), pp. 58-125.

29. Hudson, "The Examination of Lollards", in *Bulletin of the Institute of Historical Research*, No.46 (1973), pp.146, 154-5. I owe Cade to Mr Robin Jeffs.

30. L.B. Smith, *Henry VIII* (Panther edn., 1973), pp.144, 149; W. Tyndale, *Doctrinal Treatises*, pp.97-9; Horst, *op. cit.*, p.147; *Heresy Trials in the Diocese of Norwich, 1428-31* (ed. N.P. Tanner, Camden 4th series, No.20, 1977), *passim*; ed. A. Peel, *The Seconde Parte of a Register* (1915), I, p.87. See Chapter 11 below.

31. Emmison, *op. cit.*, p.110; cf. my *Economic Problems of the Church* (Panther edn., 1971), pp.121, 133; Foxe, *op. cit.*, IV, p.178; Hudson, "The Examination of Lollards", pp.153, 155.

32. Foxe, *op. cit.*, IV, pp.213, 234, 580; Tanner, *op. cit., passim*; Hudson, "The Examination of Lollards", p.151.

33. Ed. H.E. Rollins, *Cavalier and Puritan* (New York 1923), pp.171-8; J.A.F. Thomson, *The Later Lollards, 1414-1520* (Oxford U.P., 1965), pp.240-1; Thomas, *op. cit.*, p.144; Tanner, *op. cit.*, pp.10-13 and *passim*; Cross, *Church and People*, pp.76-8; Wallace, *op. cit., passim*.

34. Jean Moss, "Variations on a Theme: The Family of Love in Renaissance England", *Renaissance Quarterly*, XXX: (1976), p.190; ed. A.S.P. Woodhouse, *Puritanism and Liberty* (1938), p.390; G. Winstanley, *The Breaking of the Day of God* (2nd edn., 1649), p.30; J. Nayler, *Sauls Errand to Damascus* (1654), pp.2-6, 10-11; E. Ludlow, *A Voice from the Watch Tower* (ed. B. Worden, Camden Soc., 4th series, No.21, 1978), p.235.

35. Martin, *op. cit.*, pp.55-74, and *passim;* Horst, *op. cit.*, pp.122-40; Emmison, *op. cit.*, p.101; *W.T.U.D.*, pp.83-4, 147-8, 184; Thomas, *op. cit.*, pp.133-4; Cross, *Church and People*, pp.98-9, 114, 170; Collinson, *The Elizabethan Puritan Movement*, pp.238-9; Winstanley, *The Mysterie of God* (2nd edn., 1649), p.15. I am indebted to discussions with Professors Joseph Martin and Jean Moss about sixteenth-century Familism. For Grindleton see pp.149, 163 below.

36. I owe the last point to Mr John Fines of the West Sussex Institute of Higher Education. I am also grateful to Professor Martin for drawing my attention to Philpot. Cf Clark, *English Provincial Society*, p.101; Tanner, *op. cit.*, p.91.

37. Thomson, *op. cit.*, pp.36, 82, 106, 196, 248; J. Jewell, *An Apology for the Church of England* (Parker Soc., 1848-50), II, p.1241; Spufford, *op.*

cit., p.247; Wallace, *op. cit.*, pp.461-2. The last point I owe to Mr Peter Clark.

38. T. Fuller, *op. cit.* (1842), III, pp.252-6; *C.S.P.D., 1639*, pp.455-6. I owe this reference to the kindness of Dr Andrew Foster.
39. H.J. McLachlan, *Socinianism in Seventeenth-Century England* (Oxford U.P., 1951), p.234; Nayler, *op. cit.*, p.5.
40. N.T. Burns, *Christian Mortalism from Tyndale to Milton* (Harvard U.P., 1972), *passim;* cf. Cross, *Church and People*, p.95.
41. Burns, *op. cit.*, pp.57-8, 69-72, 133-4; Moss, *op. cit.*, pp.191, 194; Emmison, *op. cit.*, p.110; Wallace, *op. cit.*, pp.461-2, 473; J. Carey, "Donne and Coins", in *English Renaissance Studies Presented to Dame Helen Gardner* (ed. Carey, Oxford U.P., 1980), p.162; J.R. Jacob, *Robert Boyle and the English Revolution* (New York, 1977), pp.171-2.
42. Tanner, *op. cit.*, p.45; J. Lindsay, *The Troubadours and Their World* (1976), p.225; Fuller, *op. cit.*, I, p.445; Foxe, *op. cit.*, III, pp.594-5. I owe the last point to Mr Peter Clark. Cf Thomas, *op. cit.*, p.170.
43. T. Rogers, *The Faith, Doctrine and Religion Professed and Protected in... England* (Cambridge U.P., 1681), p.39: first published 1607; Hudson, "A Lollard Mass", p.409; W. Lamont, *Richard Baxter and the Millennium* (1979), pp.128, 143. For antinomianism, see Chapter 10 below.
44. My *Antichrist in Seventeenth-Century England* (Oxford U.P., 1971), pp.142-3; *W.T.U.D.*, p.66; Thomson, *op. cit.*, pp.36, 184; Thomas, *op. cit.*, p.169; Wallace, *op. cit.*, pp.461, 465; Clark, *English Provincial Society*, pp.56, 156, 178, 199; J. Everard, *The Gospel-Treasury Opened* (2nd edn., 1659), I, pp.355-6; G.R. Quaife, *Wanton Wenches and Wayward Wives* (1979), p.64; Ingram, Thesis, pp.81, 104; my *Change and Continuity in Seventeenth-Century England*, p.15; Nayler, *op. cit.*, p.14; cf. Chapter 11 below, *passim.*
45. R.H. Hilton, *The English Peasantry in the Later Middle Ages* (Oxford U.P., 1975), p.24; Horst, *op. cit.*, p.134.
46. Ed. G.L. and M.A. Harriss, *John Benet's Chronicle for the Years 1450 to 1462* (Camden Miscellany, XXIV), p.166; Foxe, *op. cit.*, IV, p.243; D.M. Loades, *The Oxford Martyrs* (1970), p.95; *Politics and the Nation, 1450-1660* (1974), p.147; Dickens, *op. cit.*, p.19; Thomson, *op. cit.*, pp.64-6, 78, 127, 130, 159, 177; Tanner, *op. cit.*, *passim;* Cross, "Great Reasoners in Scripture", p.363; Hudson, "The Examination of Lollards", p.151; 'A Lollard Mass', pp.409-10; Thomas Nashe, *The Unfortunate Traveller and Other Works* (Penguin, 1972), p.68; Richard Brathwait, *Barnabees Journal*, Sig. C.; Thomas Harman, *A Caveat for Common Cursetors* (1567), in *Coney-Catchers and Bawdy-Baskets* (ed. G. Salgado, Penguin), pp.101, 121; W. Saltonstall, *Picturae Loquentes* (1635), p.39; R. Younge, *The Poores Advocate* (1655), pp.10-11; J.A. Sharpe, *op. cit.*, pp.99-100; K. Wrightson and D. Levine, *Poverty and Piety in an Essex Village*, p.133; Ingram, Thesis, pp.152-3, 216, 370.
47. More, *Refutation of Tyndale* (1532), quoted by G.R. Elton, *Reform and Reformation* (1977), p.44; *W.T.U.D.*, Chapter 25.
48. E. Leach, "Melchisedech and the Emperor: Icons of Subversion and Orthodoxy", *Proceedings of the Royal Anthropological Institute*, 1972,

pp.5-14; A.C. Edwards, *English History from Essex Sources* (Chelmsford, 1957), pp.77-8.

49. M.H. Keen, *England in the Later Middle Ages* (1973), p.243; L.B. Smith, *Henry VII*, p.150; *W.T.U.D.*, p.200; Cross, *Church and People*, pp.21, 73, 79; Clark, *English Provincial Society*, pp.63, 156, 181, 405; Hudson, "A Lollard Mass", p.411. For ale-houses as centres of sedition, see *Mercurius Politicus*, No.305 (1656), pp.6899-901; No.315 (1656), pp.7053-5; P. Clark, *The Alehouse: A Social History, 1200-1850* (1983), esp. Chapters 6 and 7; D. Underdown, "The Problem of Popular Allegiance in the English Civil War", *T.R.H.S.* (1981), esp. p.90; J.F. Davis, *Heresy and Reformation*, pp.58, 76.

50. In *Harleian Miscellany* (1744-6), VII, pp.376-85.

51. For Long Island see D.S. Lovejoy, "'Desperate Enthusiasm': Early Signs of American Radicalism", in *The Origins of Anglo-American Radicalism* (ed. M. Jacob and J. Jacob, 1984), pp.235, 240; John Whiting, *Persecution Exposed* (1714), a reference I owe to the kindness of Peter Linebaugh.

52. D.M. Wolfe, *The Image of Man in America* (Dallas, 1957), p.19; *V.C.H.*, *Worcestershire*, IV, p.192; G.P. Gooch, *The History of English Democratic Ideas in the Seventeenth Century* (Cambridge U.P., 1898), p.359; E.P. Thompson, *Whigs and Hunters* (1975), p.256; W.A. Speck, *Stability and Strife: England 1714-1760* (1977), p.181; J.H. Lawson, "Parrington and the Search for Tradition", *Mainstream* (Winter, 1947), p.395; *A Journal of the Life of Thomas Story* (Newcastle upon Tyne, 1747), p.192; B.S. Capp, *Astrology and the Popular Press, p.249. See ibid.*, pp.96, 266-7 for almanacs and radical ideas. For Joyce, Cromwell and other English republicans in the folklore of the American Revolution see A.F. Young, "English Plebeian Culture and Eighteenth-Century American Radicalism", in *Origins of Anglo-American Radicalism*, pp.194-204.

53. Quoted by P.J. Corfield, *The Impact of English Towns, 1700-1800* (1982), p.65.

54. E.M. Dunn, "The London Weavers' Riot of 1675", *Guildhall Studies*, I, p.17; ed. N. Penney, *The Short Journal and Itinerary Journals of George Fox* (Cambridge U.P., 1925), pp.350-1, where many examples are given; Hillel Schwartz, *The French Prophets: The History of a Millenarian Group in Eighteenth-Century England* (California U.P., 1980), pp.128, 131, 143. For the Green Ribbon Club see J.R. Jones's article in *Durham University Journal*, December 1956. M.C. Jacob suggests that the Green Ribbon Club had links with early freemasonry (*The Radical Enlightenment: Pantheists, Freemasons and Republicans*, 1981, p.117).

55. T.A. Jackson, *Ireland Her Own* (1946), p.63. Penelope Corfield has drawn my attention to a broadsheet of 1795 addressed *To the Poor of Norwich* by "a Leveller, Jacobin and Revolutioner". Dr Morrill points out to me that later use of the name does not necessarily demonstrate continuity of aims: it may have been merely a convenient smear-word. This may be true of some of the instances I cite — notably Beau Nash. But the Levellers were remembered down to the nineteenth century, and, in many of my examples, remembered with approval.

116 *Heresy and Radical Politics*

56. *Biblioteca Furliana* (Rotterdam, 1714); T. Bullard, *Biblioteca Antonij Collins, Arm.* (1731); C. Robbins, "Library of Liberty", *Harvard Library Bulletin*, 5 (1951), p.17; see p.339 below. I am grateful to Margaret Jacob for this reference.
57. A.L. Morton, "The Everlasting Gospel", in *The Matter of Britain* (1966), pp.85-121; cf. *W.T.U.D.*, p.382; J. Kensley, "Burns and the Peasantry, 1785", *Proceedings of the British Academy*, LII (1968), p.136. Professor Pocock thinks "there is much to be done with the notion" of an occultist scientific underground from the restoration to the late eighteenth century ("Authority and Property: The Question of Liberal Origins", in *After the Reformation: essays in honor of J.H. Hexter*, ed. B.C. Malament, Manchester U.P., 1980, p.343). See also J.R. Jacob, *Henry Stubbe*, p.213.
58. *W.T.U.D.*, pp.380-1; *Life of Thomas Story*, pp.70-2, 676-7; G.F.S. Ellen, "The Ranters Ranting: Reflections on a Ranting Counter Culture", *Church History*, XL (1971), p.92.
59. Quoted by M.C. Jacob, *op. cit.*, p.98.
60. Burns, *op. cit.*, p.121.
61. Richard Lewis, *The Robin Hood Society, A Satire by Peter Pounce* (1756), pp.v-vi, 19, 79. I owe this reference to the kindness of Dr Vincent Caretta.

8. Sin and Society[1]

"The belief in heaven and the fiery pit makes the simple folk give obedience to their governors, and behave with great care, so that they may avoid torment after death and enjoy bliss". *

"Continually preaching to the rest their duty towards God ... is the most effectual way to dispose them to obedience to man. For he that truly fears God cannot despise the magistrate. ... There is nothing more apt to induce men to a suspicion of any religion than frequent innovation and change".†

I

In seventeenth-century England there were revolutionary changes in politics, economics and science. Almost as important a turning-point was the emergence of new ideas of sin and hell, of man's fate in the after life and consequently of the way in which he should behave in this life. At the beginning of the century the conviction prevailed among the articulate that a minority was predestined to eternal life, the vast majority to an eternity of torture. By the end of the century we are on the verge of the Enlightenment, of deism, of rationalism. Human effort and morality, based on the demands of the individual conscience, now appear more important than the arbitrary decisions of an omnipotent God. How did this transition come about?

We should not assume that it just happened, that it was a slow triumph for reason, for sensible, middle-of-the-road moderation. Nor do I think that the apparently new ideas were in fact new. They were often traditional ideas which had been submerged by the imposition from on top of what we call "the protestant ethic", though it existed in Catholic countries too: a theology emphasizing the duty of hard and regular work in one's calling, labour discipline, austerity, thrift, monogamy: the bourgeois virtues. It was imposed

*Thomas Hariot, *A Brief and True Relation of the New Found Land of Virginia* (1588), in *The New World* (ed. S. Lorant, 1954), p. 268.

†Robert South, *Sermons Preached Upon Several Occasions* (1737), pp. 132, 140. Preached at Lincoln's Inn in 1660.

117

on populations accustomed to spasmodic bouts of labour punctuated by saints' days, populations accustomed to consume rather than to accumulate their meagre surplus and regarding marriage as a much less binding contract than it became in an economy dominated by the working household partnership.

Throughout human history sin has been associated with scarcity. The legend of the Fall of Man reflects this. Adam and Eve were expelled from a Paradise of abundance, and Adam was condemned to hard agricultural labour: "in the sweat of thy face shalt thou eat bread", just as women were to perform their productive functions in labour and sorrow. The existence of a landed ruling class was for long justified by its duty of alleviating hardship in time of dearth, of dispensing hospitality to the poor, of remitting rent to the victims of natural disasters. No doubt these functions had not always been performed, and by the sixteenth century they were slipping badly as monasteries were abolished, big households disbanded, and the hospitality of aristocracy and clergy proved incapable of coping with growing mass poverty. But the idea of a paternalistic landed élite presiding over a moral economy and exercising some control over the production and distribution of food — this idea still made some sort of sense. It was the basis for hierarchical doctrines of society and claims to obedience and deference on religious grounds. Such doctrines assume a community with shared needs in face of the constant danger of scarcity which threatened fallen humanity.

But the consequences of human sinfulness could only be mitigated, not cured. Too often rulers tended to succumb to sin themselves — greed, luxury, callousness when the poor were in want, failing to relieve their necessities from the superfluities which came to them by virtue of their presiding and organizing role. This role could be fundamentally challenged only when the possibility of abundance appeared, when the whole unprivileged population was no longer trapped in a poverty from which there seemed no escape.

The two generations before the civil war saw a great economic divide. The mass of the people was getting relatively and probably absolutely poorer; the poor were becoming a permanent part of the population. The fortunate few who were conveniently placed for the market, and who were skilful, industrious and lucky enough to seize their chances, might prosper by taking advantage of rapidly rising prices. So new and sharper class divisions were arising — no longer setting gentry against the rest, but gentry, some yeomen, some merchants, some artisans, against the poor. As Dr Morrill points out, this situation was so new that contemporaries had no word to describe the emerging new rich as a social group:[2] the term parish élites is an invention of historians. Artisans who had mastered more advanced techniques had greater confidence in their ability to stand on their own feet. The Calvinist preachers' covenant theology looks like an attempt to adapt traditional protestant doctrines to the assumptions of men who worked in a world of bargains and agreements enforceable by law.

The fact that some could better themselves whilst others sank into permanent rightless poverty seemed to justify belief in the wickedness of the poor, the righteousness of those who prospered, often through no merits of their own.[3] Responsibility for such poor relief as there was, and for labour discipline, was increasingly handed over to parish élites, those who by and large were themselves prospering. So the whole system began to seem less natural, less inevitable. If new techniques allowed some to prosper, why not all? Some bold spirits came to envisage prosperity not only for the elect, not only for lucky individuals, but for society as a whole.

Bacon glimpsed this possibility: so did Adolphus Speed and other agricultural improvers of the seventeenth century. Gerrard Winstanley made it the basis for his claim that the poor should have access to uncultivated land: "true religion and undefiled" is "to let every one quietly have earth to manure, that they may live in freedom by their labours". For now they were "kept poor by their brethren in a land where there is so much plenty for everyone". There is "land enough in England to maintain ten times as many people as are in it".[4]

Winstanley rejected the doctrine of original sin, as did many of the radicals. Men could be saved by their own efforts just as they could feed themselves by their own labour — provided the obstacles could be removed. For Winstanley these obstacles were the gentry who monopolized more land than they needed to feed their own families, the law and lawyers who protected this inequality, and "the subtle clergy" who charmed the people "to look after riches, heaven and glory when they are dead"; and so "their eyes are put out, that they see not what is their birthright, and what is to be done by them here on earth while they are living".[5]

Winstanley's was an extreme position. But conservatives were right to see radical Arminianism in general, and antinomianism, as containing a challenge to the whole social order.[6] Sin seemed to be essential to social cohesion. Winstanley, Ranters and early Quakers grasped the obverse — that those who preached up sin were in effect keeping the poor down.[7]

Beneath the veneer of official protestantism in England, the old beliefs continued: of this there is plenty of evidence. The ignorance of the common sort was agreed on all sides, by Whitgift and Lancelot Andrewes[8] no less than by George Giffard and Samuel Hieron.[9] Many Calvinist preachers in the early seventeenth century cried out that the common people are virtually pagans. By this I suspect they meant that they did not accept the Calvinist world outlook, that their attitudes were dominated by traditional magic mediated through Catholicism. For our purposes the important thing is rejection of the comfortable doctrines of original sin and of the predestination of a favoured few to salvation.

Perhaps one in a thousand is saved, thought Thomas Shepard, New England Puritan divine.[10] More generously, John Donne estimated it at one in three, the Fifth Monarchist John Spittlehouse at one in four.[11] John Bunyan varied between one in twenty and one in 5000.[12] The assumption that a merciful God fore-ordained the mass of mankind to hell was challenged in the seventeenth century, initially by religious and political radicals: it is the counterpart of their aspirations on earth.[13]

Calvinist preachers in Elizabethan and Jacobean England believed that most men, women and children were damned, and if they were honest they had to say so to their congregations. The doctrine was not always popular. The "ignorant rout" of Kidderminster did not appreciate being told, even by the saintly Richard Baxter, that their children before regeneration were loathesome in the eyes of God, and that if they died they would almost certainly go to hell.[14]

The doctrine of original sin, however, makes sense to the beneficiaries of a society in which inheritance is the rule. Heaven is not "the hire of servants or the booty of purchasers", explained Hieron; "it is the reward of sons, of inheritance". We receive it only as heirs, with no colour of desert.[15] Sir John Davies demonstrated God's justice from its congruence with human practice:

> Is it then just with us, to disinherit
> The unborn nephews for the father's fault?
> And to advance again for one man's merit
> A thousand heirs that have deserved naught?
>
> And is not God's decree as just as ours?[16]

Thomas Goodwin made a similar point: "It is a strange thing that you will not allow God that which kings and princes have the prerogative of.... They will have favourites whom they will love, and will not love others; and yet men will not allow God that liberty", but accuse him of cruelty and injustice.[17]

Original sin is the converse of divine hereditary right, as Dryden made very clear in *Absalom and Achitophel*:

> How then could Adam bind his future race ...
> If those who gave the sceptre could not tie
> By their own deed their own posterity?[18]

Inheritance of sin may first have begun to lose its immediately obvious inevitability among those living in the contract society which grew up within the world of inherited landed property. Seventeenth-century political theorists still assumed that men are to all eternity bound by contracts which may have been made (though not recorded) by their remote ancestors. This seems odd to us, but Hobbes and Locke were an advance on Filmer: their contracts are tacitly renewed as generation succeeds generation.

Protestant theology not only emphasizes the predestination of the elect. Even more important, it stresses the *freedom* of the elect. By divine grace they are singled out from the mass of humanity. Most men, like animals and the inanimate creation, are subject to and helpless before the forces of nature and society — famine, pestilence, war and death. They are sunk in sin. The elect alone are free, since to them the forces which govern the world are not blind. The elect understand and co-operate with God's purposes, and this sense of intimacy with the source of law gives them a confidence, an inner assurance, which helps them to prosper in this world as well as to inherit the next. Justification by works, by conformity with the ceremonies and sacraments of the church, is fitted to a relatively static civilization: rewards are to be attained not on earth but in the after life, merit is acquired by passive acquiescence. Justification by faith, paradoxically, is an active doctrine, active in this world. It rejected attempts to propitiate an angry God by ceremonies mediated by a priesthood. It preached the supremacy of elect individual consciences, boosting the morale of those who could believe that, against such heavy odds, they were of the number of the saved.[19]

Protestantism established democracy within the élite, as against the traditional hierarchies of mediaeval society and the mediaeval church. Since the elect were in direct communication with God they had no need for mediators; nor was the law for them. But protestant-ism never solved the problem of the relationship of the elect to the unregenerate. Even the identity of the elect could not be established on earth. At the same time that protestant churches emphasized the freedom of the elect, the protestant state had to keep the un-regenerate under control. All protestant state churches experience this dilemma. The elect, who in one sense are the only true members of the church, do not really need its laws and its discipline at all. The ungodly must be controlled and disciplined by church and state, but they were never fully members at least of the former.

So Calvinism stimulated an individualism in behaviour and thought against which it had no external, visible objective checks: it had only the individual conscience itself, and once it had been discovered that men were prepared to die for different truths, Calvinism could ultimately maintain itself only by violence. The burning of the heretic Servetus in mid-sixteenth-century Geneva was a portentous event.[20] Hence the tensions of the Elizabethan church, whose articles were drawn widely so as to include the maximum possible number of English men and women. Puritans called for further reformation, dividing between those who accepted the neces-sity of tarrying for the magistrate and those who separated in order to secure immediate reform.

From the time of the Lollards, at least, the dogma of original sin had been challenged. Theological distinctions should be drawn between Collinson's "rustic Pelagianism"[21] — the belief that men could be saved by their good works — and the Familist doctrine that men and women could attain to pre-lapsarian perfection in this life. But what matters for our purposes is that both rejected the division of mankind into an elect minority of sheep and the mass of reprobate goats. A husbandman in 1395 had suggested that "sinners and lay persons and simple souls" could understand the "mysteries and ... secrets of the Scriptures" better than the learned.[22] Mid-sixteenth-century London tradesmen claimed that "a man regenerate could not sin"; there were "free will men" in the capital. Henry Hart wrote a treatise denouncing predestination.[23] Bishop Ponet under Mary reported English Anabaptists who denied the doctrine of original sin, with the expected social consequences: they thought that "as when there was no sin, all things were common, so they ought now to be".[24] This conclusion would often be drawn later. In 1592 an Essex heretic held that "all the world shall be saved". John Smyth in James's reign called original sin "an idle term", and said that children dying in infancy are undoubtedly saved.[25] That these were more than isolated individuals is suggested by the fact that the English delegates to the Synod of Dort in 1618, on the insistence of the King, drew the attention of their Dutch brethren to the need for "great wariness and discretion in propounding to the common people the doctrine of predestination, and especially reprobation". John Hales, who was at Dort, thought that "the meaner sort may by no means be admitted" to "disputations and controversies concerning the profounder points of faith and religious mysteries"[26] — sound advice if it could have been followed. But in the free discussion of the sixteen-forties it became clear that there was no way of knowing on earth who were elect and who were reprobate,[27] and that those whom their social betters regarded as unregenerate might have views of their own on the subject.

For the orthodox, a coercive state was a consequence of the Fall too. "The nature of man", wrote Calvin, "is such that every man would be lord and master over his neighbours, and no man by good will be subject". "For we know that men are of so perverse and crooked a nature that everyone would scratch his neighbour's eyes out if there were no bridle to hold him in".[28] In England the *Homily against Disobedience and Wilful Rebellion* taught that after the Fall God "did constitute and ordain ... governors and rulers ... for the avoiding of all confusion which else would be in the world". Without the state "there must needs follow all mischiefs and utter destruction ... of souls, bodies, goods ...".[29] This was a doctrine which Henry Parker and Hobbes took over, together with so much else, from Calvinism. The masses must be held in subordination.

Such doctrines, so comfortable to the lucky few, were less acceptable to the many when they had the opportunity to think about them. And they led some Puritans to adopt a dual standard, together with a rather unpleasing contempt for the mass of mankind. William Perkins, high priest of English Puritanism, thought that the church exists for the elect.[30] He attributed to "the common sort of ignorant people, and all natural men" Collinson's "rustic Pelagianism". "Though in show they profess reformed religion, ... they look to be saved by their good serving of God, and by their good deeds".[31] They "conceive God made all of mercy, without his justice". They reason, "If I be chosen to salvation, I shall be saved;

therefore I may live as I list". "Our common people ... say they ever
kept God's law, and loved him with all their heart, and their
neighbours as themselves, and think hence all is well".[32] Even worse,
they "think, because they deal truly and justly before men, that they
are in as good a case as they that hear all the sermons in the world".[33]
The common people "hope well, because God is merciful, but to be
certain they think it impossible".[34] Perkins always associated ignorance of this kind with popery. It was much more culpable in his day,
he thought, than it had been at the beginning of Elizabeth's reign.[35]
"The doctrine and opinion of merit", Samuel Hieron confirmed in
the sixteen-twenties, "is graven in the tables of every natural heart".
He too was speaking of "the common people".[36] "The multitude of
our people", Perkins observed, "are justly blamed as enemies of
Christ".[37] "The common sort" found even Sabbath observance
difficult, claiming that "we shall not be able to maintain ourselves
and our families".[38]

The opinion of "the universal redemption of all and every man",
Perkins thought, "is a witless conceit, ... no better than a forgery of
man's brain": the Bible refutes it immediately. It "may fitly be
termed the school of universal atheism". For it "pulls down the pale
of the church, and lays it waste as every common field". "When as
men shall be persuaded that grace shall be offered to every one
effectually, whether he be of the church or not, ... wheresoever and
howsoever he live; as in the like case, if men should be told that
whether they live in the market town or not, there shall be sufficient
provision brought them, if he will but receive it and accept of it, who
would then come to market?"[39] The metaphors — the comparison of
grace to enclosure which shuts out the poor, or to a market — define
the audience for which Perkins is writing. Perkins concluded that the
very poor were wicked. "Rogues, beggars, vagabonds ... are (for the
most part) a cursed generation", because "they join not themselves
to any settled congregation".[40] (They did not join settled congregations, it may be added parenthetically, because when they attempted
to settle in any parish not that of their birth the poor law provided
that they should be flogged to the next one. Heads I win, tails the
poor lose. Perkins thought that the poor law of 1597 was "an
excellent statute, and being in substance the very law of God, is never
to be repealed". He only regretted that it was not more severely
enforced).[41]

The idea that most of the poor were wicked was self-validating:

the lower classes could not spare the labour of their children to give them the education without which they had no hope of bettering themselves; and their family life was inevitably less stable than that of godly householders.[42]

A generation after Perkins wrote, his disciple Richard Sibbes reiterated that many men and women "live miserable poor, ... without laws, without church and without commonwealth, irregular persons that have no order taken for them. ... They live as beasts or worse".[43] Another twenty-five years later, with the experience of the revolutionary decades behind him, Richard Baxter drew political conclusions. "The major part are not only likely but certain to be bad. ... It is in almost all places the smaller number that are converted to loyalty and subjection to God, ... so that ordinarily to plead for a democracy is to plead that the sovereignty may be put into the hands of rebels. ... That the major vote of the people should ordinarily be just and good is next to an impossibility".[44]

The future Bishop Gilbert Burnet, writing to the Marquis of Halifax in 1680, said charitably "For the herd, they are of so little consequence, that if their folly bring on them the punishment due for their sins, a man cannot lament it much".[45] John Winthrop in Massachusetts agreed that too many men "stand for your natural corrupt liberties, and will do what is good in your own eyes, you will not endure the least weight of authority; ... but if you will be satisfied to enjoy such civil and lawful liberties, such as Christ allows you, then will you quietly and cheerfully submit unto that authority which is set over you".[46] Fortunately in New England the godly were the authority. Perhaps that is why the power of sin seemed greater there, as it did in Geneva and Scotland.

II

The Fall then was central to seventeenth-century debates about the nature of the state and its laws, as well as about the justification of private property, social inequality and the subordination of women. "Had all been virtuous men", as George Chapman put it, "There never had been prince upon the earth".[47] The judicious Hooker declared that laws "are never framed as they should be ... unless presuming man to be in regard of his depraved mind little better than a wild beast".[48] In August 1632 the Recorder of King's Lynn told the grand inquest of his borough that "the sins we have are the causes of the laws we have. Sin is a transgression of the law of God, and whoever is a transgressor of the laws of God is also a transgressor of the laws of man".[49] John Pym repeated Hooker's point: "if you take away the law, all things will fall into a confusion, every man will become a law unto himself, which in the depraved condition of human nature must needs produce many great enormities".[50] The Independent divine John Owen in 1655 agreed that the majority of men must be "overpowered by the terror of the Lord" and "threats of the wrath to come", if mankind is to be preserved from "the outrageousness and immeasureableness of iniquity which would utterly ruin all human society".[51]

The sinfulness of the majority was regularly used — by mediaeval Catholics and seventeenth-century bishops as well as by Calvinists — as an argument against social reform, against any change in the direction of a less unequal society. In 1649 the Leveller William Walwyn was told that "a natural and complete freedom from all sorrows and troubles was fit for man only before he had sinned, and not since; let them look for their portion in this life that know no better, and their kingdom in this world that believe no other".[52] Bishop Godfrey Goodman put it more succinctly: "If Paradise were to be replanted on earth, God had never expelled man [from] Paradise".[53] It was the seventeenth-century equivalent of "you can't change human nature", not extinct today.

The tacit assumption, never clearly stated, still less theoretically justified, was that the elect roughly coincided with the ruling class. Once such matters could be freely discussed, the identity of the elect became a crucial question. How many are they? How do we recognize them? The coincidence of the spread of printing with the Reformation, and new translations of the Bible into the vernacular, let loose forces which challenged traditional assumptions on this as on so many other subjects. Supporters of the magisterial Reformation, some German princes and town oligarchies, the bourgeoisie of Swiss and Dutch cities, La Rochelle, London, found no difficulty in accepting that the elect were a minority. But things seemed different to peasants in revolt in Germany in the fifteen-twenties, to lower-class Anabaptists in Flemish towns in the fifteen-thirties, to English Lollards, Familists and Anabaptists throughout the sixteenth century, and to radical sectaries in the seventeenth century. The doctrine of the priesthood of all believers, of the sovereignty of informed consciences, became subversive when taken over by groups normally excluded from political life.[54]

The stark predestinarian theology of the early reformers presented difficulties for conscientious preachers. How could they undertake the pastoral care of congregations of whom they believed 99% to be damned? What was the point of preaching moral virtue to the reprobate, since nothing could change their fate? Calvinism drove many worried men and women to despair and suicide because of their statistically plausible doubts about their eternal state. The covenant theology offered a way out. God covenants with the elect to give them eternal salvation in return for faith. Although it is difficult to be certain that I am one of the believing minority, there are certain plausible signs, notably leading a pious and moral life. The elect are not saved because of their good works — perish the thought — but good works and a moral life offer presumptive evidence that I am in a state of grace. Serious concern about my soul's condition in itself suggests that divine grace is at work. God, in Perkins's famous phrase, accepts the will for the deed.[55] It was a doctrine particularly apt to appeal to parish élites, self-confident men accustomed to a relatively prosperous world of contracts and bargains.

The Laudians went even further, back to a theology of works and ceremonies. But as fear of popery intensified in England during the Thirty Years War, Laudian Arminianism seemed to many protestants a half-way house back to the old religion. A group of clerics whom we call antinomians began to point out that the covenant theology itself led to "works-mongering". The true covenant of faith must surely be unconditional? The gap between the omnipotence of God and the filthiness of fallen men can be bridged only by divine intervention. God saves some men and women of his own mere volition. But since God is omniscient and all-powerful, he must know his elect from all eternity: they are chosen, in Tobias Crisp's vivid phrase, from the womb.[56] But how can they be known on earth, to themselves and to others? One man's conviction of grace may be another man's evidence of total damnation. So long as a punitive state church existed, those who carried antinomian convictions to their logical conclusion could be punished and silenced. But not after 1640.

Crucial was the breakdown of censorship. Lower-class sects emerged from underground and rapidly expanded in numbers; liberty could no longer be restricted to those whom respectable Puritans regarded as the elect. The great deterrent, sin, no longer controlled the lower classes. A ferment of religious discussion ensued in the forties, which Milton and the radicals hailed enthusiastically as the way to truth and the establishment of Christ's kingdom on earth, and which Thomas Edwards and London oligarchs deplored. Religious toleration is the greatest of evils, said Edwards. It disrupts the family, and deference generally.[57]

Popular rejection of the oligarchy of the elect, and a common-sense suspicion that perhaps all morally good men might be saved, could now be discussed freely, side by side with the writings of more intellectual antinomian theologians who concentrated on demanding complete moral freedom for the elect without troubling to ask how they were to be known. This opened a door to a sort of *de facto* universalism. If all believers were prophets as well as priests, and all men might be saved, where were we?

Universalism, as we would expect, was widespread among the middling and poorer sort. A bricklayer at Hackney "maintained that all men should be saved". So did Mrs Attaway, a woman preacher who earned notoriety by practising the divorce for incompatibility which Milton had preached.[58] "One Lamb, a soap boiler", preached universal grace; so did a trooper in Northamptonshire, and very many others.[59] The Socinian John Bidle held that "there is no such thing as original sin"; he was defended by Sir Henry Vane and Levellers.[60] For Samuel Oates, father of Titus, predestination was "damnable doctrine".[61] One preacher, addressing a crowd of what he called "Levellers", deliberately emphasized absolute reprobation "because this is a doctrine not often insisted upon and at this time denied".[62]

In 1648-9 Gerrard Winstanley and Richard Coppin independently proclaimed, for the first time in print, that all mankind would be saved. Winstanley set up a communist colony, and rejected the state and its laws. "They were the laws of a conqueror", he wrote, "to hold the people in subjection". "All laws that are not grounded upon equity and reason, not giving a universal feedom but respecting persons", should have been "cut off with the King's head".[63] Coppin declared that "to deny that there is a full end of sin for all men" is "damnable heresy".[64] Such doctrines proved popular. Coppin, we are told, wound "himself into the bosoms of (a many-headed monster), the rude multitude" in Kent.[65] John Saltmarsh and Clarkson also preached free grace; many radicals announced that sin was abolished.[66] The anonymous author of *Tyranipocrit Discovered* (1649) believed that all men had the grace to be saved if they only looked for

God within them. Teachers of absolute predestination were defenders of inequality: "he that teacheth a partial God, loveth partiality".[67] Even so respectable a preacher as Peter Sterry believed in universal salvation.[68]

What did Milton think? In *Paradise Lost* Sin sprang fully born from Satan's head, as Athene from Zeus's. This is one way of exonerating God from responsibility for evil, but it raises a host of other problems. Sin was born in heaven. If Sin is Satan's brainchild, does this mean that Sin does not really exist, that it is a figment of Satan's imagination? That is what Clarkson had said. But it is not what Milton's *Of Christian Doctrine* says.[69]

The radical Arminianism of John Goodwin led in the same direction. George Fox thought that God's light was in everyone, without exception.[70] He knew that his inner voice was from God, as clearly as he knew that his opponents were agents of the devil: an impasse was reached, from which there was no escape on the assumptions of either side. The homogeneity of Calvinism in normally tranquil times stems from its discipline and from fundamental agreement among those who administer that discipline, drawn from propertied social groups. Calvinist leadership in opposition can focus attention upon those aspects of the old régime to which all save the narrow ruling group are opposed. But in times of social crisis and revolution the propertied lost their grip. As was discovered in the French Revolution, the third estate is not a homogeneous class. In the English Revolution those who were least satisfied with the condemnation of the mass of mankind to eternal torment were able to preach what God had said to them, to cast out Calvinism by the inner light. They found an audience in the social groups whom respectable Calvinists regarded as unregenerate, because their standards and outlook on life were different. Samuel Fisher in his Baptist days confirmed that there was much popular hostility to the doctrine of original sin, though the gentry accepted it.[71]

Strong evidence of the contempt in which "the looser sort" held the religion of their betters came when the Long Parliament instituted monthly fasts to deplore the sins of the nation and to urge God to continue his favour towards England. "God punisheth national sins with national punishments", John Downame had written.[72] National fasts and days of national humiliation were attempts to appease God. For month after month from November 1640 the two Houses duly listened to denunciations of idolatry, profanation of the Sabbath, contempt for ministers, sectarian preaching, etc.; and to prayers to God to continue his favour to England. But it soon became clear that outside Parliament the fasts were not taken as seriously as might have been wished. Already in 1642 Cornelius Burges was complaining that they were not observed by the populace.[73] "Are there not multitudes of people", Edmund Calamy asked in October 1644, "even in the City of London, ... carried away with grace-destroying and land-destroying opinions", such as "that God sees no sin in his elect children? ... and that God is never displeased with his people, though they fall into adultery or any other sin?"[74] It was "the looser sort", Cheynell and others argued in the same year, who "refuse to observe the monthly fast".[75]

Perhaps Calamy was right. In New England John Wheelwright, accused of antinomianism, outraged his fellow-ministers by using the occasion of a fast-day sermon to say "If he [Christ] be present with his people, then they have no cause to fast; ... when he is taken away, then they must fast". "Those that do not know the Lord Jesus", he added provocatively, "they are usually most given to fasting".[76]

The Act of 23 April 1649 repealing the Act for monthly Fasts admitted that they had been wholly neglected for divers years in most parts of the Commonwealth. One last fast day was held in May to ask God to pardon "the iniquities of the former monthly fast days".[77] Yet still in 1666 Dryden could make Charles II say to God "we all have sinned, and thou hast laid us low."[78] It was more convenient to blame the sins of the nation than the incompetence and corruption of court and government. It was also not illogical, since the merrie monarch had attributed his unexpectedly easy restoration to "his own chosen people" in 1660 to "divine providence."[79]

III

Parliament's Blasphemy Ordinance of May 1648 picked out the doctrine that all men should be saved as an offence carrying the penalty of life imprisonment.[80] Throughout the sixteen-fifties conservative preachers tried to restore some sort of ecclesiastical control over obstreperous parishioners and visiting prophets, either by pressurizing Parliament for legislation or by forming organizations like Baxter's Worcestershire Association.[81] The debates on the Nayler case in Parliament in 1656 show how panic-stricken conservatives were.[82] But as long as the Army remained united and regularly paid nothing could be done. Success was achieved only after

1660, when the Army was disbanded and church courts returned in order to restore social discipline, to restore sin.

In the forties and fifties it had been possible for innumerable English men and women to think of themselves as members of the elect, enjoying the moral liberty hitherto reserved for the predestined minority. Democracy of salvation went hand in hand with the political democracy of the Levellers, the economic democracy of the Diggers. It was a remarkable turning-point. Which came first in men's thinking, the democracy of grace or political democracy, is perhaps a meaningless question. The critique of sin and hell accompanied the criticism of oligarchy; the restoration of oligarchy after 1660 was cause and consequence of a revived acceptance of sin.

In Sir Walter Ralegh's circle in the fifteen-nineties men had said that hell was only a bugbear, and religion invented "to keep the baser sort in fear" in order to protect private property, the family and the state: sin was "a monster/ Kept only to show men for servile money".[83] For a brief moment in the sixteen-forties and fifties such ideas were proclaimed more widely. "Many thousands in these three nations", wrote John Reeve disapprovingly in 1656, "count the Scriptures mere inventions of wise men, to keep the simple in awe under their rulers".[84] But once the censorship had been with difficulty restored in the early fifties such ideas could no longer be expressed in print. After 1660 we hear no more of them, though this does not necessarily mean that they ceased to be held. Already the dissidence of dissent was working against the radicals. No unity could be found among the individual consciences which had agreed in rejecting a state church. Milton deplored this:

> O shame to men! Devil with devil damned
> Firm concord holds, men only disagree
> Of creatures rational, though under hope
> Of heavenly grace (*Paradise Lost*, II. 496-9).

The other side learnt unity from their interregnum experience.[85] By 1660 consensus had been restored on this issue.

Robert Boyle in the sixteen-fifties, and the Royal Society after 1660, saw it as the task of scientists to combat "enthusiasm" and what they saw as a tendency towards atheism in the sects; to insist that science demonstrated the existence of God and so contributed to his glory. The quintessential aristocratic rake, the Earl of Rochester, was convinced of the social usefulness of Christianity, and therefore that he should not attack it publicly, well before his death-bed "conversion".[86]

1660 saw a return to what some historians call "normality", by which I think they mean restoration of censorship. But nothing was ever quite the same again. The Latitudinarians who came to pro-minence in the restored Church of England after 1660, and who dominated it after 1688, quietly shed both the Calvinism of their Puritan predecessors and the Laudian ceremonial which had split the Church in the thirties. Just as Daniel Scargill in 1668 was expelled from his Fellowship at Corpus Christi College, Cambridge, for Hobbism, and was only restored after he had recanted, so in 1670 John Edwards was forced to resign from St John's College, Cam-bridge, for preaching too predestinarian a Calvinism. He did not recant, but by the end of the century he was a unique and isolated figure in the state church.[87]

Latitudinarians were closely associated with the scientists of the Royal Society. They evolved a broad Anglicanism with the minimum of theology, which performed useful social functions in the villages. Sin still remained the great deterrent, but the rigours of predesti-narianism were abated, and a non-ceremonial Arminianism led imperceptibly on to rational religion, Socinianism, deism. At the opposite end of the spectrum, the defeated sectaries re-introduced sin as they abandoned politics. George Fox had written of ministers of the state church that they "roar up for sin in their pulpits": "it was all their works to plead for it".[88] But after the restoration, when Robert Barclay systematized Quaker theology, sin returned.[89] Per-fectibility had been a dream of the heady forties and fifties.

Yet although sin returned and church courts were restored in 1660, the High Commission was not, and so there was no power behind ecclesiastical censures. By the end of the century church courts had virtually ceased to function. The only 'sins" now prosecuted were those which led to charges on rate-payers: J.Ps. punished those who bore bastards, and the societies for reformation of manners strove to carry on some of the supervision which church courts had formerly exercised. The later seventeenth century saw a progressive decline of belief in hell, in magic whether black or religious.[90] But the sinfulness of the mass of humanity was no longer a subject for discussion: it seemed somehow irrelevant to the problems of the Age of Reason. Less than a century after the English Revolution so unoriginal a thinker as Bolingbroke, speaking of predestination to damnation, refused to "impute such cruel injustice to the all-perfect Being. Let Austin and Calvin and all those who teach it be answerable for it alone. You may bring Fathers and Councils as evidences ...but reason must be the judge ... in the breast of every Christian that can appeal to her tribunal".[91] So yesterday's persecuted heresy becomes today's self-evident orthodoxy. We are all Pelagians now.

Bolingbroke seems to me to be right, but he is profoundly unhistorical. When his great-grandfathers looked into their breasts they found nothing there about universal grace. Bolingbroke's "reason" has taken into itself the results of two centuries of bitter struggle. And even so, was he quite as liberal as he sounds to us today? What does he mean by "every Christian that *can* appeal to reason's tribunal"? Whom does he exclude? Has he not his own category of those who are outside the pale? Exclusion based on differential rationality, which itself derives from educational opportunity, or lack of it, is not so very different from predestination to damnation.

Rustic Pelagianism leading on to Arminianism — Socinianism — deism was one route into the modern world. Another was from Luther to antinomianism and beyond, to the doctrine that God does not intervene in the day-to-day running of individual lives. If the elect are known from all eternity, then their relationship to God is fixed, and cannot be changed for the worse by their sins nor for the better by their prayers. This led to a new, self-sufficient morality.[92]

Hobbes pushed miracles back into the age of the Apostles; Thomas Mun, writing in the sixteen-twenties but not published till 1664, envisaged a market society in which the hidden hand of supply and demand preserved order; economists began to think that to act according to self-interest was rational, not sinful.[93] Newtonian scientists saw God as the supervisor of a mechanical universe. Socinians, deists and some antinomians virtually abolished a personal God to be propitiated. They based human morality neither on expectation of reward nor on fear of punishment in the after life, but on purely human laws of reason and of nature.[94] Supernatural sanctions were in effect abolished. Man is the measure of all things, and has to solve his moral problems in the light of God's Word but with no more divine guidance than he finds in his own conscience. The saints, the Virgin and priestly mediators had disappeared in protestant countries at the Reformation: now the belief that God exists in all of us undermined belief in divine or Satanic intervention in everyday human affairs.[95]

Hence concern about "atheism", which led Swift in 1708 to say "I look upon the ... body of our people ... as free-thinkers, that is to say, as staunch unbelievers as any of the highest rank".⁹⁶ "Atheism" of course was not dangerous because of one man, even so great a man as Hobbes. Nor was it dangerous because aristocratic wits made sceptical jokes about the Bible and the clergy: they had been doing that since Ralegh's time and no doubt earlier. The dangerous atheism was "mechanic atheism", the philosophy of the rude mechanicals, who had learnt about it in the no-holds-barred discussions of the sixteen-forties and fifties. Some of the sects, as we have seen, appear to be driven by a kind of inner logic to denial of the external, personal God of orthodox Christianity.

Saint Evremond, who knew his post-restoration England, noted this tendency in protestantism. "The Catholic might, indeed, spare some ceremonies; yet that hinders not, but that men of understanding may see well enough through them. The Reformed use too little, and their ordinary worship is not sufficiently distinguished from the common functions of life. ... Where it rules, it produces only an exact compliance with duty, such as either the civil government or any other obligation might do. ... The danger is lest after having retrenched all that appears superfluous, religion itself should be cut off".⁹⁷

That was indeed the danger. This illuminating passage helps to explain why "men of understanding" in 1660 welcomed the Church of England back again with its authorized interpreter of the Scriptures in every parish, and why the great Calvinist theologies, Presbyterianism and Independency, which played such a leading role in the Revolution, retained relatively so little hold, losing ground first to non-Calvinist Baptists and Quakers, later to Unitarianism and Wesleyanism. The danger here was that sin, which the Ranters and early Quakers had failed to abolish, might die a natural death. Hence the almost hysterical concern of Boyle and the early Royal Society, Newton and Newtonians, to preserve rewards and punishments in the after life, God and the devil (and perhaps witches too).⁹⁸ How else could the enormity of natural man be restrained?

"The great business of religion", said John Fell in a sermon preached before Charles II in 1675, "is to oblige its votaries to present duty by the awe and expectation of future retribution".⁹⁹ A die-hard like Henry Sacheverell clung on to sin and hell. "The great sanction of the gospel", he declared in a notorious sermon preached before the Lord Mayor of London in 1709, is "the eternity of hell torments".[100] More sophisticated was Dr John North. An Arminian by conviction, he thought Calvinism, "with respect to ignorant men, to be more politic, and thereby in some respects fitter to maintain religion in them, because more suited to their capacity. But that is referred to art, and not to truth, and ought to be ranked with the *piae fraudes* or holy cheats".[101]

Calvinism, with its stress on God's power and justice, was always more acceptable to the middling sort, concerned about maintaining law, order and property against an unpredictable multitude. A theology of good works, emphasizing God's love and mercy, appealed more to those who had no power and did not expect justice. They looked to the after life to redress the injustice of this. That the number of the elect should be very small made less sense to them than to the ruling minority of their betters. But theirs was *radical* Arminianism, not related to the ceremonies and sacraments of a church which was also a great property owner, and a collector of tithes at their expense.[102]

The rulers of society acted on the assumption that the mass of mankind was sinful; they did not really want the lower orders to discuss the subject at all. It may not have been the object of the censorship and of the discipline both of church courts and of presbyteries to frighten off ordinary people from having ideas above their station, but this seems to have been the effect. The sects' demand for the democratization of salvation offered the possibility of self-respect to the middling and some of the lower sort: salvation was potentially accessible to all, perhaps even especially accessible to the poor and humble. This emerges very clearly in the teaching even of the Calvinist John Bunyan, who was not deferential to ungodly gentlemen.[103] Such a comfortable community religion survived political defeat, and after 1660 helped to create a sense of purpose for likeminded men and women below the privileged classes.[104]

During the revolutionary decades men had dreamt that the world could be turned upside down — by the establishment of Leveller political democracy and of the same security of tenure for copyholders as the gentry had won in their holdings; by the abolition of sin and recognition that all men were sons of God: a move towards secularization. Wildman looked forward to deist freethinking: "If a man consider that there is a will of the Supreme Cause, it is an hard thing for him by the light of nature to conceive how there can be any sin committed; and therefore the magistrate cannot easily determine what sins are against the light of nature and what not".[105] But the radical political and social revolutions failed. In the last resort the middling sort of people followed Oliver Cromwell rather than Levellers or True Levellers. A few yeomen prospered, the majority of husbandmen ultimately sank to the position of wage labourers. Such men had to accommodate themselves to the market society, just as the restored Church of England did: the sects abandoned radical political ideas, and agreed that the millennium was not imminent, indeed that Christ's kingdom was not of this world. When the Licensing Act lapsed in 1695 "normality" had re-established itself; the censor had been internalized by members of the political nation; sectaries were excluded from participation in public life. Prophets were honoured, if at all, only within the enclosed world of their own sects. It was not what Milton or Dell had hoped for, still less Walwyn or Clarkson. Their objectives still had to be fought for a century and a half later when Blake proclaimed that "every honest man is a prophet".[106] But then Blake remembered the seventeenth-century radicals as few did by the early nineteenth century. By his time most democrats talked in secular terms. Religion continued to defend the *status quo*, even when the attack was no longer mounted in religious idiom. Methodism, declared Jabez Bunting, was opposed to democracy because Methodism was opposed to sin.

NOTES

1. An earlier version of this paper was delivered at a Conference on Religion and Revolution held at the University of Minnesota in November 1981. The papers of this conference are to be published in 1985.
2. J.S. Morrill, *Seventeenth-Century Britain, 1603-1714* (1980), pp. 108-9.
3. See p. 123-5 above.
4. Sabine, *op. cit.*, pp. 428, 507, 558; cf. pp. 414, 428. For Speed see *Biographical Dictionary of British Radicals*, III (1984), p. 194. Cf. *Petty Papers* (ed. the Marquis of Lansdowne, 1927), II, p. 232. I have drawn heavily for these paragraphs on Joyce Appleby's *Capitalism and a New Social Order*, esp. pp. 26-9.
5. Sabine, *op. cit.*, pp. 523-4.
6. Not of course Laudian "Arminianism", whose doctrine of justification by works did not reverse the Fall, and whose "works" were associated with the ceremonies and sacraments of the church.
7. *W.T.U.D.*, p. 169.

8. Strype, *Life of Whitgift, III*, p. 268; Andrewes, *XVI Sermons* (2nd edn., 1631), p. 459, contrasting "the common sort" with "true Christians".
9. G. Giffard, *The Country Divinity*, quoted by Hunt, *The Puritan Moment*, p. 87; cf. pp. 151-2; S. Hieron, *Sermons* (1624), pp. 122, 132, 297, 536. Cf. G.B. Harrison, *The Elizabethan Journals* (New York, 1965), I, pp. 184-5: ignorance and anti-clericalism in Devon in 1600.
10. C.M. Andrews, *The Colonial Period of American History* (Yale U.P., 1964), I, p. 48; cf. Walker, *The Decline of Hell*, pp. 35-40, for a general assumption that the majority are damned. Cf. L. Andrews, *Works* (Oxford U.P., 1841), VI, p. 191.
11. Donne, *Sermons* (ed. G.R. Potter amd E.M. Simpson, Berkeley, 1953-62), VIII, p. 372; Capp, *Fifth Monarchy Men*, p. 173.
12. Bunyan, *Works* (ed. G. Offor, 1860), I, pp. 105, III, pp. 20-1.
13. Walker, *op. cit., passim.*
14. Ed. M. Sylvester, *Reliquae Baxterianae* (1696), p. 24.
15. S. Hieron, *Sermons*, p. 373.
16. Sir John Davies, *Nosce Teipsum* (1599), in *Silver Poets of the Sixteenth century* (Everyman edn.), pp. 369-9; cf. John Davies of Hereford, *Complete Works* (ed. A.B. Grosart, 1878), I. p. 471.
17. T. Goodwin, *An Exposition of the Second Chapter of the Epistle to the Ephesians, Verses 1-11*, in *Works* (Edinburgh, 1861-3), II, p. 163.
18. *Op. cit.*, lines 769-71. Cf. William Chillingworth, *Works*, II, p. 426.
19. W. Perkins, *Works* (1609-13), I, p. 563; II, pp. 19-24; III, pp. 270-3. See also my *Puritanism and Revolution*, p. 214.
20. Cf. pp. 37-8 above.
21. Collinson, *The Elizabethan Puritan Movement*, p. 37.
22. C. Cross, *Church and People, 1450-1640* p. 23.
23. Burnet, *History of the Reformation*, III, p. 146; cf. p. 102 above.
24. J. Ponet, *A Shorte Treatise of Politike Power* (1556), Sig. E8, quoted by H.C. White, *Social Criticism in Popular Religious Literature in the Sixteenth Century*, p. 125.
25. R. Barclay, *The Inner Life of the Religious Societies of the Commonwealth* (1876), Appendix to Chapter 6, p. viii; cf. Burrage, *The Early English Dissenters*, II, p. 188, and pp. 101-2 above.
26. J. Hales, *Golden Remains* (1659), I, p. 32; *Letters from the Synod of Dort, ibid.*, III, pp. 18, 31.
27. Cf. Henry Robinson, *Liberty of Conscience* (1644), pp. 37-8, in Haller, *Tracts on Liberty*, III, pp. 153-4.
28. Calvin, *Sermons Upon the Book of Job* (English translation, 1574), p. 718; *Sermons Upon the Fifth Book of Moses* (English translation, 1583), p. 872, both quoted by J. DiSalvo, *War of Titans: Blake's Critique of Milton and the Politics of Religion* (Pittsburgh U.P., 1983), p. 256; cf. Calvin, *Institutes of the Christian Religion* (trans. H. Beveridge, 1949), I, p. 518; and p. 178: the poor must endure patiently.
29. *Homilies*, pp. 468-9; cf. pp. 87-8, *An Exhortation concerning Good Order and Obedience to Rulers and Magistrates*.
30. Perkins, *Works*, I, p. 298.
31. *Ibid.*, II, p. 300; III, p. 500.

32. *Ibid.*, III, pp. 493-5.
33. *Ibid.*, II, p. 290.
34. *Ibid.*, III, p. 498; cf. I, pp. 537, 631; III, pp. 583, 595.
35. *Ibid.*, III, p. 585.
36. Hieron, *op. cit.*, p. 122. Cf. p. 174-5 below for natural man's confidence in good works.
37. Perkins, *op. cit.*, III, p. 595.
38. *Ibid.*, II, p. 109, cf. Alan Sinfield, *Literature in Protestant England* (1983), pp. 151-2.
39. Perkins, *op. cit.*, I, pp. 295-6.
40. *Ibid.*, III, p. 191 (second pagination); cf. I, p. 755; III, pp. 92 (second pagination), 539; cf. my *Puritanism and Revolution*, pp. 223-4.
41. Perkins, *Works*, I, p. 755.
42. Jackie DiSalvo, *op. cit.*, Chapter 9.
43. R. Sibbes, *Works* (Edinburgh, 1862-4), III, pp. 40-1; cf. *Puritanism and Revolution*, p. 224.
44. Baxter, *The Holy Commonwealth* (1659), pp. 92-4.
45. Ed. H. C. Foxcroft, *Some Unpublished Letters of Gilbert Burnet* (Camden Miscellany, XI, 1907), p. 21.
46. Quoted in Perry Miller, *The New England Mind: the Seventeenth Century* (New York, 1939), pp. 426-7, 455-6.
47. Chapman, *Dramatic Works* (1873), I, p. 331.
48. R. Hooker, *Of the Laws of Ecclesiastical Polity*, I, p. 188.
49. Quoted by W. R. Prest, *Professors of the Law: A social history of the English Bar, 1590-1640* (forthcoming).
50. Pym, speech at the trial of Strafford, in J. Rushworth, *Trial of Strafford* (1680), p. 662.
51. J. Owen, *Works*, XII, p. 587.
52. [Anon], *Walwins Wiles* (1649), in *The Leveller Tracts, 1647-1653* (ed. W. Haller and G. Davies, Columbia U.P., 1944), p. 312.
53. G. Goodman, *The Two Great Mysteries of Christian Religion* (1653), p. 90.
54. See Chapter 10 below.
55. Perkins, *Works*, II, pp. 19-24, 44-5, 629; cf. I, p. 43, and M. McGiffert, "God's Controversy with Jacobean England", *American Historical Review*, 88 (1983), pp. 1161-7, and pp. 143-5 below.
56. See p. 146 below.
57. Edwards, *Gangraena*, I, pp. 121-2, 156; III, pp. 268-70. See pp. 174-5 below.
58. *Ibid.*, I, pp. 80, 87. There is much more evidence to be found here.
59. *Ibid.*, I, p. 92, III, pp. 9-10, 107, 173.
60. Quoted by John Owen, *Works*, XII, p. 164; *The Second Part of Englands New-Chains Discovered* (1649), in Haller and Davies, *op. cit.*, p. 175.
61. Edwards, *Gangraena*, I, p. 94.
62. H. Schultz, *Milton and Forbidden Knowledge* (New York, 1955), p. 128.
63. Winstanley, *The Mysterie of God* (1648), pp. 17, 35-6, 56-8; *The Breaking of the Day of God* (1648), p. 15; *The Law of Freedom* (1652),

Dedication to Oliver Cromwell; Sabine, *op. cit.*, p. 286. See Chapter 11 below.

64. Coppin, *Man's Righteousness Examined* (1652), pp. 9-10, 16. See pp. 146-8, 170 below.

65. Coppin, *Truths Testimony* (1655), pp. 21, 31; Walter Rosewell, *The Serpents Subtilty Discovered* (1656), Sig. A 3; *W.T.U.D.*, p. 222.

66. J. Saltmarsh, *Free Grace* (10th edn., 1700), esp. pp. 47, 67, 86, 104, 111 (first published 1645; by 1649 it had reached its sixth edition); Clarkson, *A Single Eye* (1650), pp. 8-12, 16; P. Gura, *A Glimpse of Sion's Glory: Puritan Radicalism in New England, 1620-1660* (Wesleyan U.P., 1984), p. 85. For Clarkson see *W.T.U.D.*, esp. pp. 213-17.

67. *Tyranipocrit Discovered*, in *British Pamphleteers*, I (ed. G. Orwell and R. Reynolds, 1948), esp. pp. 110-12.

68. Walker, *The Decline of Hell*, p. 108.

69. See esp. Book I, Chapters xi-xii.

70. Fox, *Journal* (1902), I, pp. 28, 34; cf. *M.C.P.W.*, VI, *passim*.

71. S. Fisher, *Baby-Baptism meer Babism* (1653), pp. 27-9, 34-8, 44, 105-6.

72. Downame, *Lectures upon the Four First Chapters of the Prophecy of Hosea* (1608), quoted by M. McGiffert, "God's Controversy with Jacobean England", p. 1161.

73. Burges, *Two Sermons Preached to the House of Commons* (30 March 1642 and 30 April 1645) (1645), p. 33.

74. Calamy, *Englands Antidote, Against the Plague of Civil Warre*, 22 October 1644, pp. 18-19.

75. Quoted by A. Fletcher, *A County Community in Peace and War: Sussex, 1600-1660*, p. 113.

76. Ed. D. D. Hall, *The Antinomian Controversy, 1636-1638* (Wesleyan U.P., 1968), pp. 154, 157.

77. Trevor-Roper, *Religion, the Reformation and Social Change*, p. 140.

78. Dryden, *Annus Mirabilis*, lines 265-6.

79. Quoted by McKeon, *Politics and Poetry in Restoration England*, p. 232.

80. Ed. C. H. Firth and R. S. Rait, *Acts and Ordinances of the Interregnum* (1911), I, pp. 133-6.

81. See R.B. Schlatter, *Richard Baxter and Puritan Politics* (Rutgers U.P., 1957), esp. pp. 45-67.

82. Burton, *Parliamentary Diary*, I, *passim*.

83. *W.T.U.D.*, pp. 163, 175, quoting Marlowe and Chapman among others.

84. J. Reeve, *A Divine Looking-Glass* (1719), p. 94. First published 1656: cf. p. 165.

85. Cf. pp. 57-9 above.

86. Gilbert Burnet, *Life of the Earl of Rochester* (1774), pp. 47, 58. First published 1680.

87. S. I. Mintz, *The Hunting of Leviathan: Seventeenth-Century Reactions to the Materialism and Moral Philosophy of Thomas Hobbes* (Cambridge U.P., 1962), pp. 50-2; R. Stromberg, *Religious Liberalism in Eighteenth-Century England* (Oxford U.P., 1954), p. 11.

88. G. F. Nuttall, *The Welsh Saints, 1640-1660* (Cardiff, 1957), p. 59; R. B.

Schlatter, *The Social Ideas of Religious Leaders, 1660-1688* (Oxford U.P., 1940), p. 242.

89. R. M. Jones, Introduction to W. C. Braithwaite, *The Second Period of Quakerism* (1919), esp. pp. xliv-vii.

90. Walker, *op. cit., passim*; K.V. Thomas, *op. cit., passim*. See pp. 330, 333-4 below.

91. Lord Bolingbroke, *Letters to Sir William Windham and Mr. Pope* (1894), pp. 178-9.

92. See pp. 146, 170-1 below.

93. Joyce Appleby, *Economic Thought and Ideology in Seventeenth-Century England* (Princeton U.P., 1978), Chapters 2-4, 8-9, pp. 115-17, 198 and *passim*. The point had been made by Tawney (*Religion and the Rise of Capitalism*, Penguin edn., p. 152.

94. Cf. Boyle: "Piety was to be embraced not so much to gain heaven, as to serve God with" (quoted by J. R. Jacob, *Robert Boyle and the English Revolution: A Study in Social and Intellectual Change*, New York, 1977, p. 39).

95. I have benefited here by reading in advance of publication an article by Peter Elmer on John Webster's *The Displaying of Supposed Witchcraft* (1677).

96. Swift, *An Argument to prove that the Abolishing of Christianity in England may ... be attended with some inconveniences*, in *Works* (1814), VIII, p. 194.

97. Ed. John Hayward, *The Letters of Saint Evremond* (1930), p. 140. Sir William Petty made a similar observation, though with more pleasure and less apprehension (*Petty Papers*, II, pp. 116-18, 190-1).

98. J. R. Jacob, *Robert Boyle and the English Revolution*, *passim*; M. C. Jacob, *The Newtonians and the English Revolution*, *passim*.

99. J. Fell, *The Character of the last Daies* (1675), p. 1.

100. Sacheverell, *The Perils of False Brethren* (1709), p. 9.

101. D. North, *Lives of the Norths* (1826), III, p. 344. First published 1740-2.

102. See Sinfield, *op. cit.*, esp. p. 108 and Chapter 7 *passim*.

103. E.g. Bunyan, *Works*, I, pp. 88-102; cf. p. 606, III, p. 130 and *W.T.U.D.*, pp. 405-6.

104. I have discussed this point at greater length in my *Society and Puritanism in Pre-Revolutionary England*, Chapter 14.

105. Woodhouse, *op. cit.*, p. 161. Wildman however still believed in fairies (K. V. Thomas, *op. cit.*, pp. 236-7).

106. W. Blake, *Poetry and Prose* (Nonesuch edn., 1927), p. 961.

9. *Dr Tobias Crisp, 1600-43*[1]

*"He that fears God is free from all other fears."**

I

Tobias Crisp was born in 1600 in Bread St., London, a prosperous area where Milton was born eight years later. Tobias was the third son of "one of the richest families in the City". His merchant father had been sheriff of London. Tobias's elder brother was Sir Nicholas Crisp (1598-1666), who was "the driving force behind the [West African gold] trade for most of the period 1625-44", and who was also engaged in the slave trade between West Africa and the West Indies. He too became sheriff of London, was a trained band captain and M.P. in both the Short and the Long Parliaments of 1640. He had imprudently become a customs farmer in that year, that is to say one of the very unpopular government financiers. He was also a monopolist, and for this he was expelled from the House of Commons in February 1641. He was perforce a royalist during the civil war, equipping a privateering vessel for the King. He survived to become a baronet in 1665.[2]

Tobias's connections and outlook seem to have been very different from his brother's. He was educated at Eton, which did not then mean quite what it means now. In 1624 he took his B.A. at Christ's College, Cambridge, the year before Milton entered the College as an undergraduate. Crisp incorporated at Balliol to take his M.A. in 1626.[3] His D.D. followed much later. He married the daughter of Rowland Wilson of the Vintners' Company, another prominent London merchant. Wilson commanded a City regiment for Parliament during the civil war, was alderman and sheriff of London and a Trustee for crown lands when they were sold in 1649. He was a recruiter M.P. for Calne, Wiltshire, and a member of the Commonwealth's Council of State. He became a friend of Bulstrode White-

*William Dell, *Sermons*, p. 18.

locke, who married his widow after Wilson died in 1650.[4] From the start Tobias seems to have had Puritan leanings. In 1627 he was deprived of his first living, the rectory of Newington Butts, on a charge of having entered into a simoniacal contract. This may be less reprehensible than it sounds: Crisp had been presented to the rectory only a few months earlier by a group which had leased the presentation from the Bishop of Worcester. They may have incurred the wrath of the hierarchy as a Puritan group trying to present Puritan ministers, like the Feoffees for Impropriations, who flourished between 1625 and 1633 before being suppressed by Archbishop Laud.[5]

In the same year, 1627, Crisp was presented to the vicarage of Brinkworth, Wiltshire — the county with which his father-in-law was associated. Here Crisp became famous for his lavish hospitality: "a hundred persons, yea and many more, have been received and entertained at his house at one and the same time, and ample provision made for man and horse". His substantial fortune enabled him to refuse "preferment or advancement", and Crisp stayed at Brinkworth until in 1642 persecution by royalist soldiers drove him back to London, where he died a year later.[6] His preaching appears however to have left memories behind him in Wiltshire.[7]

In the year before his death Crisp preached in London. Among others Laurence Clarkson the future Ranter heard him hold forth against all existing churches — Anglican, Presbyterian, Independent, Baptist (the last three of which had appeared publicly only since 1640). "Be in society or no, though walked all alone, yet if he believed that Christ Jesus died for him, God beheld no iniquity in him". The prose style is Clarkson's but the sentiments are unmistakably Crisp's. Clarkson read all his books as they came out.[8] He was to carry Crisp's antinomian doctrines well beyond anything Crisp advocated.

Crisp's sermons were published posthumously in 1643 and later: it is unlikely that they could have been published before 1640. "Taken in short writing and compared with his notes", their genuineness is attested by his son.[9] But we must recall that they were delivered at a time of rigid ecclesiastical censorship and control, so he had to be careful what he said.

II

Crisp is primarily concerned with the problem of reconciling predestination and free will, God's omnipotence and human freedom — not a new problem. His starting point seems to have been dissatisfaction with traditional Calvinist predestination which — he thought — led many to despair because they could not believe in their election. His initial reaction in the sixteen-twenties was towards Arminianism, then becoming fashionable at court and soon to win control of the Church of England through the Laudians. But Crisp had been brought up to have a strong gut-hatred of popery, and as the Thirty Years War progressed the danger of Roman Catholic domination on the continent (and then in England) alarmed him as it did many other English protestants. Laudian Arminianism revived sacramental emphases which Crisp disliked and which he — again like many others — saw as a reversion to popery.

He expresses himself cautiously, but he makes pretty clear his anxiety about both the foreign and the domestic situation. "Look upon the present time, now you may see what sadness fills the hearts and faces of men, yea even of God's own people. . . . They look every hour when they shall be cut off by the sword". There is no certainty "that our lives and estates shall be spared".[10] "How many among you, yea and of the uppermost form (bishops) have warped of later times and have turned their faces to return back to the fleshpots of Egypt".[11] Thomas Goodwin expressed similar anxieties in 1639 — more openly because he was writing in exile. He foresaw the subjugation of protestantism in its last refuge in Europe, Britain, because of the connivance with popery of men like the Laudian bishops. "It were happy for other states professing the Calvin[ist] religion if they could wash their hands of the blood of the churches not only not assisted but betrayed by them".[12] Because we know that nothing came of such fears, we perhaps underestimate their strength in forging the near-unanimity with which in 1640-1 the Long Parliament set about destroying the power of the Laudian clergy, and of royal ministers in whom they had no confidence. Events in Germany in the sixteen-twenties had created a real and lasting fear of popery; the sixteen-thirties bred suspicions that members of Charles I's government were its accomplices.[13]

Crisp's aversion from justification by works spills over into anxiety about the covenant theology which, thanks to preachers like William Perkins, John Preston and Richard Sibbes, had become almost orthodox among Anglican protestants until the Laudian challenge of the sixteen-twenties. The covenant theology attempted to smuggle works back into Calvinism by arguing that God contracted to save those who kept his covenant. Their good works would not earn the elect salvation, but would testify to their state of grace. It was an understandable attempt by harassed clergymen to preserve their flocks from the despair to which Calvinism was apt to lead. Perkins argued that a sincere and strong desire for grace is presumptive evidence that grace is at work in the soul: God accepts the will for the deed. Crisp thought that sincerity and good intentions were not enough,[14] and that the covenant theology led to presumption. Those who looked for assurance of salvation in the good works that they performed came to rely on their own merits rather than on Christ.

Crisp's own solution was to go back to pristine Calvinist theology before Theodore Béza and the covenant theologians had watered it down.[15] In Crisp's view the elect are ordained to salvation from all eternity; they cannot fall from grace. This, as we shall see, seemed to his critics to run the risk of antinomianism, of encouraging those who believed that their election was secure to indulge in all manner of licentious practices. Crisp's answer was that *no* person is capable of works pleasing to God; all — elect and reprobate alike — are sinful and filthy. We are saved only because "the Lord hath laid on him [Christ] the iniquity of us all" (Isaiah 53.6). This was the text for sermons III to XVII of the 1643 volume. (The association of this passage with the Messiah was commonly accepted by seventeenth-century theologians.)

Crisp's onslaught on the covenant theology arose from his dislike of its legalism, its implied bargaining with God: "you give me salvation, and I will give you faith, and works too". "Even true faith", Crisp wrote, "is no condition of the covenant".[16] "The new covenant is without any conditions whatsoever on man's part". Man "is first justified before he believes, then he believes that he is justified".[17] Crisp was anxious to emphasize that the elect were saved before they were born. Christ himself "is not so completely righteous but we are as righteous as he was; ...Christ became ...as completely sinful as we". Crisp insists with almost monotonous repetition that "as soon as ever [a believer] hath committed this sin, ... the Lamb of God ... hath already taken away this very sin".[18] To restrict justifica-ion until after a man believes in Christ is to bring to life again the covenant of works, to trouble the consciences of those who are convinced that they are under the hatred of God.[19]

The source of all this is Crisp's determination to relieve believers of "horror in their consciences", of the superstition of scarecrow sins which Milton deplored. Stand "fast in the liberty wherein Christ hath made you free, and do not again entangle yourselves with such yokes of bondage that neither you nor your fathers were able to bear".[20] He was against preaching the terrors of the law, the wrath of God, damnation and hell-fire. The object of such sermons, if preached at all, should be not to terrify but to reassure believers that they are secure from damnation.[21] Crisp strongly disapproved of preachers who "fetch blood at the hearts of children with their causeless cautions, and then rejoice to see them in their spiritual afflictions, which methinks is an inhuman cruelty ... Children must not want their food for fear of dogs".[22] In 1643, the year when Crisp's sermons were first published, the future Leveller William Walwyn was also concerned lest "fears and terrors may abound" in those who have been terrified by the fear of sin. Like Crisp, Walwyn attacked the doctrine that God accepts "our wills for our performance".[23]

Crisp was worried about those who "are apt to think their peace depends on this subduing of sin" which they find impossible. "Fetch peace where it is to be had", was his advice. "Let subduing alone for peace".[24] "Sadness in any believer whatsoever ... in respect of his jealousy of his present and future estate", shows that he is "out of the way of Christ". "I believe many poor souls have been held under hatches the longer because some have withheld Christ from them, or themselves have not dared to think Christ belongs to them". "Christ doth not look for your pains; he came to save those that could not tell which way to turn themselves". Believers "must not fear their own sins". "The Father forces open the spirit of the man, and pours in his Son, in spite of the receiver".[25] "This grace of the Lord's laying of iniquities upon Christ is applicable to persons even ... before they have mended their ways", Crisp insisted again and again, though he recognized that it is a view which "will find great opposition in the world", because it gives "way to looseness".[26]

Crisp's continuing concern was to escape from the formal self-righteousness of those who believed that their election was demonstrated by their good works. "Even the most blameless walking according to God's law, not only before but also after conversion, is truly counted but loss and dung".[27] "Righteousness is that which puts a man away from Christ".[28] Good works should be performed only because they are profitable to others, not with any idea that they confer merit on the doer. Loving mankind anyway "is no evidence of our being in Christ. For publicans and harlots love one another".[29] "When we labour by our fasting and prayer and seeking the Lord ...

to take away his displeasure, ... do you serve God or no? Do you not serve yourselves?" "Is there not much self mixed in your performances?"[30] Men must be taken off "from performing duties to corrupt ends", from "idolizing their own righteousness".[31]

Since the elect are saved from the womb, Crisp logically concludes that neither prayers, tears, fasting, mournings, reluctancy and fighting against our corruptions have "the least prevalency with the Lord". "They move God not a jot. ... God is moved only from himself".[32] God hears only Christ's prayers.[33] It was a doctrine later adopted by the Muggletonians. I have argued elsewhere that they derived it from Clarkson, who joined the sect in the late fifties. Clarkson was preaching the doctrine in 1650; so was another Ranter, Jacob Bauthumley. Clarkson almost certainly derived the doctrine from Crisp, whom he had heard preach, and all of whose books he read as they came out.[34]

For all Crisp's hostility to the covenant theologians, he could be as unpleasantly legalistic as any of them. "The Lord's justice", he wrote, must "be satisfied to the full"; "reparation must be had".[35] This recalls Milton concerning Christ's sacrifice on the cross: "Die he or justice must".[36] But Crisp dwells quite unnecessarily on the pleasure which Christ's sufferings give God. "It is Christ's personal bearing of iniquity upon the cross once for all that gives unto the Lord the full pleasure and content to his own heart's desire". Nor does this pleasure and content derive from the salvation of mankind. "Christ's main aim is at the giving his Father content"; that "poor sinners are saved ... is a subordinate thing".[37] Crisp's use of the word "purchase" to describe Christ's sacrifice caused uneasiness to his nineteenth-century editor.[38]

III

I think we should assume that Crisp did not believe that all men were saved. But his rhetoric in insisting that God applies "the laying of iniquities upon Christ" to the ungodly, to the worst of sinners, long before they repent, exposed him to accusations of preaching universal grace. However ungodly a sinner may be, "what hinders but that thou mayst have as good a portion in him as thy heart can wish?[39] It is rash to speak of those who are still unconverted as damned: their names may be in the Book of Life though they do not yet know it.[40] "There is no man under heaven ..., if he do but come to Christ, ... shall be rejected of him". "There is no better way to know your portion in Christ than upon the general tender of the gospel to conclude absolutely he is yours; and so without any more ado to take him as tendered to you, on his word; and this taking of him, upon a general tender, is the greatest security in the world that Christ is yours".[41] Crisp is anxious here to assure the worst sinner that there is still hope: he may have a better chance of salvation than the formally righteous. But his way of expressing it laid him open in the seventeenth-century to the charge of preaching universal redemption: even his nineteenth-century editor annotates such passages uneasily.

To contemplate the possibility that divine grace might be offered to all does not seem terribly shocking in our liberal age: but to the orthodox in the seventeenth century it seemed horrific. Private property, social inequality, and the state which protected both, were all accepted as the consequence of the wickedness of the mass of fallen mankind, of the fact that God's grace was limited to the few whom he had chosen. Reject the comfortable doctrine of original sin, and the floodgates might be opened — to ideas of human equality such as the Quakers were to preach, to democratic theories such as the Leveller Walwyn advocated, to the communism of the Diggers.[42]

Above all, it seemed to Crisp's contemporaries that licentious and immoral conclusions might be drawn from his theology. The orthodox had always known that the heresy "they can commit no sin offensive to God" appealed especially to "some of the meaner ignorant sort of people"[43] But with the breakdown of ecclesiastical control and of censorship in the revolutionary sixteen-forties such creatures were able to express themselves freely. As a horrified poet put it:

> No teaching now contents us the old way;
> The layman is inspired every day,
> Can pray and preach *ex tempore*; the priest
> With all his learning is despis'd and hiss'd
> Out of the church ...
> The world is a great Bedlam, where men talk
> Distractedly, and on their heads do walk,
> Treading antipodes to all the sages
> And sober-minded of the former ages.[44]

In the forties and fifties the world was temporarily turned upside down: ideas previously unthinkable were freely expressed. Coppe and Clarkson, whom their contemporaries called Ranters, preached against monogamy and in favour of free love. ("Polygamy's no sin/In a free state", Washbourne growled.)⁴⁵ And Clarkson at least had listened to Crisp.

Crisp died too early to see the full and scandalous development of popular antinomianism in England, but he certainly contributed to it, however innocent his intentions may have been. It is easy to pick out sentences in his sermons which might reasonably alarm the orthodox. "To be called a libertine is the most glorious title under heaven; take it for one that is truly free by Christ."⁴⁶ Sin, Crisp declared, is finished. To the question "Is thy conscience Christ?" he replied in the affirmative.⁴⁷ "Suppose a believer commit adultery and murder?" Crisp asked himself. And he replied that before he even confesses his sin "he may be as certain of the pardon of it as after confession". "I know the enemies of the gospel will make an evil construction of it", Crisp admitted.⁴⁸ He had earlier recognized that some believed "this kind of doctrine opens a gap to all manner of licentiousness and presumption". His answer was "only such as are rejected and given up of God" would so abuse the doctrine.⁴⁹ "Nothing doth more establish a restraint from sin", he asserted. "The children must not want their bread because dogs abuse it".⁵⁰ Like Milton, Crisp was so concerned with the freedom of the elect that he virtually ignored the existence of the unregenerate.

It was to the elect that Crisp addressed himself when he declared "If you be freemen of Christ, you may esteem all the curses of the law as no more concerning you than the laws of England concern Spain or the laws of Turkey an Englishman". "I am far from imagining any believer is freed from acts of sin," Crisp expostulated; "he is freed only from the charge of sin. ... God doth never punish any believer, after he is a believer, for sin". "You are in as true a state of salvation, you that are believers, as they that are now already in heaven".⁵¹

Crisp regarded it as "a gross, notorious and groundless slander that I should affirm that an elect person should live and die a whoremonger and an adulterer ... and be saved." But it was hardly enough in the sixteen-forties merely to assert that the elect "person is changed in conversation."⁵² "Good works or inherent righteousness are necessary attendants on free grace."⁵³ No one can "out-sin the death of Christ."⁵⁴

Crisp counter-attacked. "People are afraid to speak out of things that are Christ's, for fear of giving liberty." Milton might have echoed the phrase. "And in the mean while other things shall be set up above Christ", Crisp continued with growing irony; "the divine rhetoric of repentance and humiliation, the prevalency of tears to wash away sin, and our conscionable walking, will commend us to God at the last day. Here must be a magnifying of man's righteousness; and when these come to be examined they are but rhetorical expressions."[55] By Crisp's theology "the freeman of Christ is let loose to enjoy the free spirit."[56]

If Crisp had survived to see what some who thought themselves Christ's freemen did with the free spirit, he might have realized the inadequacy of his perfunctory assurances that it could not be used to undermine traditional morality.

IV

Crisp's views were not unprecedented. Roger Brearley, curate first of Grindleton, then of Kilwick, in the West Riding of Yorkshire, taught not dissimilar doctrines from 1615 to 1631. His hearers, as often happened, carried his doctrines further than he did.[57] The collapse of censorship in the early forties, which allowed Crisp's sermons to be printed, also led to the printing of writings by other antinomians — John Eaton, Robert Towne, Henry Denne, William Walwyn. Eaton died in 1641. His *The Discovery of the most dangerous dead Faith* was published in that year, "set forth ... (as they say) by Dr. Crisp".[58] Eaton's *The Honey-comb of Free Justification by Christ alone* was also published posthumously, in 1642, edited by Robert Lancaster, who was to edit Crisp's sermons. Eaton's, Denne's and Crisp's books were all condemned by the Westminster Assembly of Divines in August 1643.[59] The Assembly had "an eminent Christian ... secured in gaol for promoting the publishing of Dr. Crisp his works",[60] though the Prolocutor of the Assembly, Dr Twisse, was said to have remarked that opposition to Crisp's sermons arose from the fact that "so many were converted by his preaching and (said he) so few by ours".[61]

In 1643 Abraham Cowley listed antinomians together with libertines and Arians among the most enthusiastic supporters of Parliament in London.[62] The Scots Presbyterian Robert Baillie reported that the number of antinomians was growing even faster than the number of Independents and Anabaptists.[63] By 1643 the House of Commons, egged on by the Assembly, was becoming worried about antinomianism. A succession of sermons preached to the House on the occasion of its monthly fast kept the subject before the attention of M.Ps. In January the Scots Presbyterian Samuel Rutherford denounced antinomianism: he named Crisp in the margin when he printed the sermon.[64] Rutherford's Scottish colleague Robert Baillie took up the cry a month later, followed by Herbert Palmer in August.[65] In October Edmund Calamy attacked those who preached against days of national humiliation on the ground that "God is never displeased with his people", and that "the very being of their sins is abolished out of God's sight".[66] He did not name Crisp, but the allusion seems fairly clear. "National sins", Crisp had preached, "bring about national judgments, yet all the sins of the times cannot do a member of Christ a jot of hurt (even though you have had some hand in them)".[67]

In 1643 John Sedgwick published *Antinomianisme Anatomized*. Thomas Bakewell in 1643-4 directed a series of pamphlets against antinomianism, attacking especially Crisp but also naming Lancaster and Giles Randall. Baillie followed up his sermon by *A Disswasive from the Errours of the Time* (1645). Three fat volumes of Thomas Edward's *Gangraena* appeared in 1646. In one of them he reported an apparently antinomian lady who told a minister that "to kill a man, to commit adultery, or steal a man's goods" were no sins.[68] Thomas Bedford's *An Examination of the chief points of Antinomianism* (1647) devoted two chapters to Crisp.[69] Samuel Rutherford too returned to the fray in *A Survey of the Spirituall Antichrist* (1648), naming Crisp among others on his title-page; and there were many others.[70] In 1644 Stephen Geree, elder brother of the better-known John Geree, had directed *The Doctrine of the Antinomians ... Confuted* specifically against Crisp, "so magnified of many".[71] Antinomianism, Geree observed, was "most plausible and pleasing to flesh and blood": and he referred to Crisp in this connection.[72] He paid tribute to the popular appeal of Crisp's theology in the new circumstances of the forties. Crisp's "strains of rhetoric ... do marvellously allure and ensnare the minds of many simple and unsettled souls". His doctrine "will most abundantly please the carnal palates of the worst men in the world, even atheists, drunkards, rioters and rankest rebels that can be". Geree associated Crisp with Brearley and Eaton, and accused him of preaching universal grace and election: for him Christ belongs "to all sinners without exception of any particulars".[73]

Others were contributing to what Geree called these "sweet

poisons".[74] Clarkson later wrote that Giles Randall ("a great antinomian", Edwards called him)[75] and Paul Hobson taught "such a
doctrine as Dr Crisp, only higher and clearer".[76] Edwards quoted
Hobson as saying "I am persuaded when I used all these duties" —
prayer, penitence — "I had not one jot of God in me" — a phrase of
Crisp's which his critics had made notorious.[77] John Saltmarsh,
William Dell, early Quakers and many others popularized the heresy.
William Erbery praised Crisp.[78] But the full libertine consequences of
antinomianism remained to be drawn by the Ranters.[79]

Robert Towne, from the Grindleton area, wrote an answer to John
Sedgwick in 1644. In this he declared "They that believe on Christ
are no sinners".[80] Abiezer Coppe in 1649 repeated Crisp's and
Towne's announcement that sin was finished. God's service, Coppe
said, is "perfect freedom and pure libertinism", a word that Crisp had
used. Coppe claimed that God was "that mighty Leveller".[81] Laurence Clarkson systematized the ideas which Edwards's antinomian
lady had so shamelessly put forward, and in sexual matters at least
Clarkson practised what he preached. Jacob Bauthumley proclaimed
that God is "glorified in sin"; many others alarmingly suggested that
sin had been invented by the ruling classes to keep the lower orders in
place.[82]

V

In 1655 Richard Baxter introduced a tract against antinomianism
by Thomas Hotchkis, "minister at Stanton-by-Highworth, Wiltshire", who "liveth not far from the place where Dr Crisp did
exercise his ministry". After naming Eaton, Towne, Randall, John
Simpson and Saltmarsh, Baxter concluded "but the man that most
credited and strengthened their party was Dr Crisp". In consequence
antinomianism was stronger in Wiltshire than elsewhere.[83] Hotchkis
had written (but not published) an *Examen* of Crisp's Third Volume
(1648).[84] Henry Pinnell, who wrote a preface to the 1648 volume,
knew Crisp personally. "Upon mine own experience and more than
twelve years' knowledge" he vindicated the author "from all vicious
licentiousness of life, and scandalous aspersions cast upon him".[85]
Pinnell's antinomianism was more plebeian than Dr Crisp's. "All the
learning I had at Oxford", he observed, "I laid out and improved in
opposing the truth". He was no "whit the fitter to be a minister
because of the repute and notion of scholarship". "I got more from
simple country people, husbandmen, weavers, etc., about Brink-

worth, Southwick and those parts in Wiltshire, than ever I did or got here by books and preachers".[86] Brinkworth, where Pinnell was born in 1613, was the living held by Crisp from 1627 to 1642.

Pinnell, formerly chaplain in Colonel John Pickering's regiment, became a separatist preacher at Brinkworth after leaving the Army.[87] This he did in two stages. In December 1646, disillusioned with Parliament's policy, he resigned, but he rejoined in the summer of 1647 after the rank-and-file revolt led by the Leveller-influenced Agitators. But by the end of the year, when the generals had routed the Agitators, "the Army, which was once so beautiful and lovely in mine eye, is now become most black and ugly, God having made me ashamed of my fleshy confidence therein." After expostulating with Cromwell, who listened politely and thanked him for his plain dealing, Pinnell finally abandoned the Army.[88] In the fifties he published alchemical treatises and made an important translation of works by Croll and Paracelsus.[89]

The "cheese" area of north-western Wiltshire, which embraces Brinkworth, Highworth and Southwick, was an area of poorly-paid part-time cloth-workers, which in the early seventeenth century saw weavers' riots and religious heresy. It was strongly Parliamentarian at the beginning of the civil war; from it Clubmen favourable to Parliament later came.[90] There were antinomians there in the fifties, though it is not clear — in spite of Baxter — how far Crisp's teaching had influenced them. Richard Coppin preached "frequently in those parts", collecting "sundry disciples" from "the profane sort of people ... who do hold that there is no resurrection, no day of judgment, no salvation, no damnation, no heaven nor no hell but what it is in this life". ("I do less wonder", Hotchkis commented, "that the antinomian preachers are accounted by the ignorant and profane multitude the only comfortable preachers".)[91]

In the sixteen-fifties Ranters were said to be "building up their Babel of profaneness and community" in Wiltshire, though the writer cited only Thomas Webbe. Webbe, of an old Wiltshire clothing family, was rector of Langley Burhill. He was alleged to be "one of Lilburne's faction" (i.e. a Leveller), was friendly with Joseph Salmon and praised Abiezer Coppe. Webbe allegedly claimed to "live above ordinances, and that it was lawful for him to lie with any woman". His epigram, "there's no heaven but women, nor no hell save marriage" suggests a certain light-heartedness. It was in a letter to Webbe that Salmon wrote "the Lord grant we may know the worth of hell, that we may for ever scorn heaven".[92] William Eyre, minister of a gathered congregation in Salisbury, another son of an old Wiltshire family, published in 1654 a defence of antinomianism, *Justification without Conditions*, which Hotchkis, Baxter and others attacked.[93] In 1656 there was an antinomian group in Lacock, one of whose members echoed Coppin to say "there was neither heaven nor hell except in a man's conscience"; another thought "whatever sin he did commit, God was the author of them all and acted them in him".[94] Langley Burhill and Lacock are both in the "cheese" area of the county.

VI

The most interesting seventeenth-century antinomian, another undergraduate of Christ's College, was John Milton. Milton was in London during the last year of Crisp's life, when he was attracting a good deal of attention. Milton may or may not have heard him preach: it is very unlikely that he did not read the sermons when they were published. In 1645 Milton defended "the maids of Aldgate" who claimed to be incapable of sin because they were "godded with God". Milton believed, like Crisp, that "the entire Mosaic Law is abolished". "We are released from the decalogue". "Everyone born of God cannot sin". "The practice of the saints interprets the commandments". "The greatest burden in the world is superstition ... of imaginary and scarecrow sins", which "enslave the dignity of man". Apart from the last clause, all the above sentences might have been written by Crisp. Milton was careful, like Crisp, to stress that such ideas gave no authority for licence; but he too was denounced by his contemporaries as a libertine. Like Crisp, he was so concerned with the liberty of the elect that he hardly bothered about the consequences which the unregenerate might draw from his writings. The same is true of his doctrine of divorce, where he gave very great liberty to the husband to put away his wife in cases of incompatibility of temperament, oblivious apparently of the possibilities of abuse. And *The Doctrine and Discipline of Divorce* created scandal because it — like Crisp's sermons — was published in the vernacular. Most of Milton's antinomian ideas — like his acceptance of polygamy — were too dangerous to be published even veiled in the decent obscurity of a learned language.[95]

Crisp anticipates both Gerrard Winstanley and Milton in his interesting belief that "Christ is to be considered collectively: that is, he is not only Christ as he is one person of himself; but he is Christ as he himself in that one person is united to the persons of all the elect in the world. We and they make up but one collective body". To the union of the Father and the Son, and of the two natures in Christ, we must add the mystical union which makes "Christ the Mediator ... one, with all the members of Christ jointly".[96] The Godhead is too remote for man to approach, but when Christ's humanity is united to it, it becomes more accessible.[97] Winstanley associated a version of this doctrine with belief in the advent of a communist society, brought about by Christ rising in all men and women.[98] The evidence for the idea in Milton is less clear-cut: it is stronger in *Paradise Lost* than in Milton's theological treatise, the *De Doctrina Christiana*. I had set out the evidence for Milton holding some such doctrine before the possibility that he might have derived it from Crisp occured to me.[99] Some scholars have expressed scepticism of Empson's theory that at the end of time Milton's God will abdicate his power to this collective Christ, to all the saints.[100] The clear exposition of the "collective body of Christ" in Crisp — a more respectable source than Winstanley, and one which Milton is more likely to have read — perhaps reinforces the case for accepting some such doctrine in Milton.

VII

In 1690, when the press was again freer, Crisp's sermons were reprinted by his son. They caused a great scandal. Crisp's main critics now were Presbyterians, anxious to disavow antinomianism lest it bring discredit on the reputation of dissent. Daniel Williams's *Gospel-Truth Stated and Vindicated: Wherein some of Dr. Crisp's Opinions Are Considered and the Opposite Truths are Plainly Stated and Confirmed* (1692)[101] led to fierce controversies with Congregationalists. The furore ultimately broke up the recently-formed union between Congregationalists and Presbyterians. Isaac Chauncy, one of the first to withdraw from the union, declared that "according to the opinion of our modern divines", Luther "was an antinomian himself, and Calvin but a little better".[102] Richard Baxter now thought Crisp's views antichristian, and that opposition to them was a cause which "will endure no indifferency or neutrality".[103] An anonymous tract published in 1693, *Crispianism Unmask'd*, reverts to the social threat implied in Crisp's doctrine, with a dark reference to "Mr. Saltmarsh and such like men ... in those days". If only the learned read Crisp, no harm will be done. "But when I saw that the book was bought up, and read, and (which is more) applauded by the common readers, I thought it was time" to protest. Crisp's doctrine "cuts the sinews of all the duties and exercises of Christianity". Why should we bother to be good if nothing we do is acceptable to God?[104] "By means of Çrisp's book", we are told by the pious biographer of Bishop Bull, "the poison of antinomianism soon spread, not only in the country but infected London too".[105]

Congregationalists rallied to the defence of freedom of expression. Crisp's son Samuel wrote on behalf of his father in 1691 and 1693, pointing out that the Presbyterian attitude recalled the Westminster Assembly's attempt to suppress Crisp's sermons in 1643.[106] These sermons were again reprinted in 1791 : perhaps a significant date if we recall that they were first published in the revolutionary sixteen-forties, and reprinted after the revolution of 1688. There was a further republication in 1832: the editor was still nervously aware that controversial conclusions could be drawn from Crisp's doctrine.

VIII

A final question, to which I have no clear answer, is Was Tobias Crisp as simply innocent as he appears? When it was suggested to him that libertine conclusions could be drawn from his doctrine he protested with outraged incredulity; and so far I have assumed that he erred on the side of naiveté rather than of duplicity. Yet this raises worrying questions too. Crisp was no unsophisticated provincial; he was the son, brother and son-in-law of highly-powered London business men, all of them deeply involved in City and national politics. The circumstances in which Tobias was deprived of his first living suggest either that he committed the sin of simony or that he was deceiving the ecclesiastical authorities in the interests of what he thought a good cause — neither the act of a political innocent.

Crisp was certainly aware of the accusation that his doctrine opened a door to all licentiousness. But his answer was alarmingly inadequate for so clever a man. He said, in effect, the elect could by definition not indulge in licentious practices (as we may be pretty sure that he himself did not: he and his wife had thirteen children). He gave no indication at all of how we know who the elect are, how we differentiate between elect and unregenerate, how we distinguish those who wrongly believe themselves to be elect. He must have known that this was one of the crucial questions of seventeenth-century protestant theology. The covenant theologians answered it by saying that the visible elect could be known by their good works: they were not saved by their works but their works demonstrated that they were saved. Crisp utterly rejected works as evidence of salvation at the same time that he widely extended the freedom of the elect. Like Milton, Crisp appears to regard the unregenerate as totally unimportant; he says nothing about them at all. Curious for a man with fifteen years pastoral experience in Wiltshire.

The further question then arises, Who are the unregenerate? How many people are we talking about? If you believed that they were the vast majority of the population, could you just ignore them? Did Crisp believe that all men and women would be saved, as some Ranters did? Did he believe that salvation was offered to all who threw themselves on Christ, as Milton perhaps did, and as many were to suggest in the sixteen-forties? Did he believe in hell? Many came to regard hell as an inner state rather than a geographical location.[107] Crisp once wrote rather testily of those who were not satisfied with his doctrine: "for aught I know they may have their deserved portion in the lowest part of hell".[108] It is an ambiguous remark, committing him to nothing: could the ambiguity be deliberate?

I think it unlikely that Crisp was as unorthodox as Milton became: but the evidence does not exclude the possibility that he was moving in that direction. Men had to be very careful how they expressed themselves on such questions. The possibility of universal salvation was not raised in print in England till 1648, by Winstanley and Coppin: though almost certainly it had been discussed verbally much earlier. Most of Crisp's sermons were presumably delivered under the Laudian régime, when it would have been foolhardy in the extreme to commit oneself on paper to unorthodox opinions.

So the question must remain open. We just do not know what Crisp's attitude to Ranters and suchlike would have been if he had lived to see them. All we can say is that some of them looked back to him with respect. Crisp's ideas excited the lower orders in the sixteen-forties and again in the sixteen-nineties; they still caused discomfort to the orthodox two hundred years after his death. We all try to provoke: but which of us can hope to enjoy so long a posthumous life?

NOTES

1. Originally published in *Balliol Studies* (ed. J.M. Prest, 1982).
2. R. Porter, 'The Crispe Family and the African Trade in the Seventeenth Century", *Journal of African History*, IX (1981), pp. 57-74; D. Brunton and D. H. Pennington, *Members of the Long Parliament* (1954), pp. 54-7; M.F. Keeler, *The Long Parliament* (Philadelphia, 1954), p. 147.
3. H.W.C. Davis, *A History of Balliol College* (revised by R.H.C. Davis and Richard Hunt, Oxford, 1963), pp. 104-5.
4. Brunton and Pennington, *op. cit.*, p. 59; D. Underdown, *Pride's Purge: Politics in the Puritan Revolution* (Oxford U.P., 1971), p. 234; B. Worden, *The Rump Parliament, 1648-1653* (Cambridge U.P., 1974), p. 224.
5. D. Lysons, *The Environs of London*, I (1792), p. 394; my *Economic Problems of the Church* (Panther edn.), p. 64 and Chapter XI, *passim*. It is possible indeed that Crisp may have been presented to Newington Butts by the Feoffees.
6. *D.N.B.* The reference to Crisp's refusal of advancement may be intended as retrospective rebuttal of the charge of simony.
7. See pp. 151-3 above.
8. Clarkson, *The Lost sheep Found* (1660), p. 9. See p. 146 above.
9. T. Crisp, *Christ Alone Exalted: in Seventeene Sermons* (1643), title-page. Subsequently referred to as *Seventeene Sermons*. The title-page says the sermons were preached in London, but presumably many of them had first been delivered at Brinkworth. Cf. [Anon], *A Memorial To Preserve Unspotted to Posterity the Name and Memory of Dr Crispe* (1643).
10. *Seventeene Sermons*, pp. 386-7.
11. *Crisp's Christ Alone Exalted, Being the Complete Works of Tobias Crisp, ... containing Fifty-Two Sermons* (ed. J. Gill, 1832), pp. 406-7. Hereafter referred to as *Fifty-Two Sermons*. The word in brackets occurs in the printed version, though presumably Crisp was not so specific in his manuscript. Cf. Milton's addition of an anti-episcopal headnote to *Lycidas* when he reprinted it in 1645.
12. T. Goodwin, *An Exposition of the Revelation*, in *Works* III, p. 174.
13. For one example among many of such anxieties shared by a layman of the sixteen-twenties, see R. Cust and P.G. Lake, "Sir Richard Grosvenor and the Rhetoric of Magistracy", *Bulletin of the Institute of Historical Research*, LIV (1981), pp. 42-53. See now the authoritative book by C. Hibbard, *Charles I and the Popish Plot, passim*.
14. *Seventeene Sermons*, p. 443. For the covenant theology see pp. 119, 127 above.
15. R.T. Kendall, *Calvin and the English Calvinism to 1649* (Oxford U.P., 1979), Chapter 13.
16. *Seventeene Sermons*, p. 60; cf. pp. 43, 58; and *Fifty-Two Sermons*, pp. 174-7.
17. *Fifty-Two Sermons*, pp. 86, 91.
18. *Seventeene Sermons*, pp. 89, 146-7.

19. Crisp, *Christ Alone Exalted*, III (1648), pp. 273-8. Hereafter cited as Vol. III.
20. *Seventeene Sermons*, pp. 87, 156. For Milton see pp. 153-4 above.
21. Vol III, pp. 129-30, 136; *Fifty-Two Sermons*, p. 22.
22. *Fifty-Two Sermons*, p. 411.
23. W. Walwyn, *The Power of Love* (1643), pp. 19-22, reprinted in Haller, *Tracts on Liberty*, II. See p. 127 above and pp. 166-9 below.
24. *Fifty-Two Sermons*, p. 14.
25. *Ibid.*, pp. 55, 106, 137, 190; II, p. 137.
26. *Seventeene Sermons*, pp. 409, 412.
27. *Ibid.*, p. 6.
28. *Fifty-Two Sermons*, p. 104.
29. *Seventeene Sermons*, pp. 16-17, 28, 452-3.
30. *Ibid.*, pp. 391, 446. This was a point later to be made very forcibly by the Ranter Abiezer Coppe, *A Fiery Flying Roll* (1649), pp. 5-9 and *passim*.
31. *Fifty-Two Sermons*, p. 143.
32. *Seventeene Sermons*, p. 182; cf. pp. 283-4.
33. Vol. III, p. 185.
34. Clarkson, *A Single Eye* (1650) and *The Lost sheep Found*, both printed in *A Collection of Ranter Writings from the 17th Century* (ed. N. Smith, 1983); Bauthumley, *The Light and Dark Sides of God* (1650), *ibid.*, pp. 243, 246, 259; cf. pp. 260-2 below. Sir Thomas Browne flirted with the doctrine in *Religio Medici*, as he did with mortalism; cf. Hotchkis, *op. cit.*, pp. 151-2.
35. *Seventeene Sermons*, pp. 319-26, 329.
36. *Paradise Lost*, Book III, line 210; Book XII, lines 401-4.
37. *Seventeene Sermons*, pp. 324, 332. Bunyan was equally barbaric: God "will burn sinners in the flames of hell ... with delight ... for the easing of his mind and the satisfaction of his justice" (*Works*, II, p. 111).
38. *Fifty-Two Sermons*, p. 191.
39. *Seventeene Sermons*, pp. 409, 412, 425-6; cf. Vol. III, pp. 174-9.
40. Vol. III, pp. 179-81.
41. *Fifty-Two Sermons*, pp. 114, 213; cf. pp. 202-3.
42. For Walwyn, see pp. 166-7 above.
43. Richard Sibbes, *Works*, II, p. 316. See pp. 173-5 below.
44. Thomas Washbourne, *Poems* (ed. A. B. Grosart, 1868), pp. 182-4. Washbourne — like Crisp, a Balliol man — survived to publish *The Repairer of the Breach. A Sermon Preached at the Cathedral Church of Gloucester* on 29 May 1661, which he dedicated to Charles II in a shameless bid for preferment: "to share in your triumphs as we had done in your sufferings". Washbourne's sufferings did not extend to loss of his living (A. G. Matthews, *Walker Revised*, Oxford U.P., 1948, p. 178).
45. Washbourne, *op. cit.*, p. 227; cf. *M.E.R.*, pp. 136-9.
46. *Fifty-Two Sermons*, p. 122.
47. *Seventeene Sermons*, pp. 156-9, 87.

48. *Fifty-Two Sermons*, pp. 224-6; cf. p. 131: even "a scandalous falling into sin" does not bring a believer under the curse. Cf. Adam Squire, sixteenth-century Master of Balliol: the Holy Spirit does not desert the elect when they sin (Anthony Kenny, "Reform and Reaction in Elizabethan Balliol, 1559-1588", in *Balliol Studies*, ed. J. Prest, 1982, p. 38).
49. *Seventeene Sermons*, p. 164; cf. Vol. III, pp. 105, 110.
50. Vol. III, pp. 113, 119-32, 167-8. Cf. note 22 above.
51. *Fifty-Two Sermons*, pp. 10, 43, 132; cf. pp. 15-18.
52. Vol. III, p. 326.
53. *Fifty-Two Sermons*, p. 328.
54. Vol. III, p. 362.
55. *Ibid.*, p. 359.
56. *Fifty-Two Sermons*, p. 133.
57. For initiatives by congregations, see p. 163 below.
58. Stephen Geree, *The Doctrine of the Antinomians ... Confuted* (1644), p. 41. Geree referred to Eaton as Crisp's "master" — *ibid.*, p. 5. But there is no evidence that they ever met, and Crisp's ideas must have been settled long before Eaton's writings were published. Eaton was twenty-five years Crisp's senior.
59. Kendall, *op. cit.*, pp. 185-8. See also R. S. Paul, *The Assembly of the Lord: Politics and Religion in the Westminster Assembly and the 'Grand Debate'* (Edinburgh, 1985), pp. 82-4.
60. S[amuel] C[risp], *Christ Alone Exalted in Dr Crisp's Sermons* (1693), p. 7.
61. Tobias Crisp, *Christ Made Sin* (ed. S. Crisp, 1691), p. 4.
62. Cowley, *The Civil War* (ed. A. Pritchard, Toronto U.P., 1973), pp. 110-11.
63. R. Baillie, *Letters and Journals* (Edinburgh, 1775), I, p. 408.
64. Samuel Rutherford, *A Sermon Preached to the Honourable House of Commons* (1644), pp. 32-7; cf. *The Tryal & Triumph of Faith* (1645), pp. 56-9, 111-12, 132, 169-71 — against Crisp.
65. Robert Baylie, *Satan the Leader in chief to all who resist the Reparation of Sion* (1644), pp. 25-6; H. Palmer, *The Glasse of Gods Providence towards his Faithfull Ones* (1644), pp. 54-5.
66. Edmund Calamy, *Englands Antidote against the Plague of Civil Warre* (1645), pp. 18-19; cf. William Jenkyn, *A Sleeping Sicknes the Distemper of the Times* (1647), Sig. A3.
67. Vol. III, pp. 28-9.
68. Bakewell, *A short View of the Antinomian Errors* (1643); *A faithfull Messenger sent after the Antinomians* (1644), esp. pp. 28, 35; *The Antinomians Confounded* (1644), esp. pp. 1-16, 28, 33 sqq.; T. Edwards, *Gangraena*, II, p. 6; cf. II, p. 146, III, p. 107.
69. *Op. cit.*, pp. 50-64. Bedford also attacked Henry Denne, pp. 25-33, 60-70.
70. Rutherford attacked Eaton, Towne, Saltmarsh and Dell as well as Crisp.
71. *Op. cit.*, Sig. B 3.

72. *Ibid.*, Sig A 2.
73. *Ibid.*, pp.1-2, 5, 26, 41, 46-8, 127, 133-4. For Brearley see p.163 below.
74. *Ibid.*, Sig. A 2.
75. Edwards, *op. cit.*, I p.97.
76. Clarkson, *op. cit.*, p.9.
77. Edwards, *op. cit.*, I. p.90. See p.146 above.
78. *The Testimony of William Erbery* (1658), p.68. For Erbery see *W.T.U.D.*, pp.192-7.
79. For Ranters see A.L. Morton *The World of the Ranters* (1970), and Frank McGregor "Ranterism and the Development of Early Quakerism", *Journal of Religious History* (Sydney, 1978), pp.349-63.
80. R. Towne, *The Assertion of Grace* (n.d.? 1644), p.23. See also Rutherford "A modest Survey of the Secrets of Antinomianism", printed with *A Survey of the Spirituall Antichrist*, pp.25, 71. See p.165 below.
81. Coppe, *op. cit.*, I, pp.1-5, 11.
82. For Bauthumley see *W.T.U.D.*, pp.219-20; for sin generally see *ibid.*, Chapter 8 *passim.*
83. Thomas Hotchkis, *An Exercitation Concerning the Nature and Forgivenesse of Sin* (1655), Sig. B 2, B 3v.
84. *Ibid.*, p.152.
85. Crisp, Vol. III, Sig. A 8v.
86. H. Pinnell, *A Word of Prophecy concerning The Parliament, Generall and the Army* (1648), p.49.
87. C. Webster, *The Great Instauration: Science, Medicine and Reform, 1626-1660* (1975), p.184.
88. Pinnell, *op. cit.*, pp.2-4, 7-10, 17, 74.
89. Webster, *op. cit.*, p.280. Crisp's successor as rector of Brinkworth was the Presbyterian John Harding, an even more active translator of Paracelsus, *ibid.*, p.281. Harding was expelled after the restoration.
90. D. Underdown. "The Chalk and the Cheese: Contrasts among the English Clubmen", *P. and P.*, 85 (1979), esp. pp.30, 39-40; *W.T.U.D.*, pp.46-7, 77, 109; cf. Buchanan Sharp *In Contempt of All Authority: Rural Artisans and Riot in the West of England, 1586-1660* (California U.P., 1980), *passim*, and *V.C.H. Wilts*, III p.102.
91. Hotchkis, *op. cit.*, pp.239, 291-2. For Coppin, see pp.194-6 below, and *W.T.U.D.*, esp. pp.220-3.
92. E. Stokes, *The Wiltshire Rant* (1652), pp.4, 14, 53, 61. Former Levellers in Wiltshire were alleged to have become Ranters (*W.T.U.D.*, p.239). For Salmon see *ibid.*, esp. pp. 217-19.
93. Hotchkis, *op. cit.*, pp.172-6. Eyre's book (dedicated, rather late, to Barebone's Parliament) gave rise to an exceptionally tedious and long-winded controversy, in which Baxter mentioned Crisp as an antinomian of learning and judgment (*Richard Baxters Admonition to Mr William Eyre of Salisbury*, 1654, Sig. A3). John Graile (of Tidworth, Wilts.), another participant in the discussion, associated Eyre with Crisp's doctrines (*A Modest Vindication of the Doctrine of Conditions in the Covenant of Grace*, 1655, p.25; cf. pp.49, 57). I have not been able to

trace any relationship between the Rev. William Eyre and Colonel William Eyre the Leveller, also of Wiltshire. If there was any connection it was a distant one.

94. *W.T.U.D.*, p. 228.
95. M.E.R., pp. 303, 313-16.
96. Vol. III, pp. 346-7.
97. *Fifty-Two Sermons*, p. 27.
98. See chapter 11 below.
99. *M.E.R.*, pp. 303-5.
100. W. Empson, *Milton's God* (1961), pp. 130-46.
101. John Toland's first appearance in print arose from the Crisp controversy. Toland, still a very young man, rather unexpectedly "greatly liked" Daniel Williams's book, and made an abstract of it which Le Clerc published in his *Bibliothèque Universelle*, Tome XXIII, p. 505. Benjamin Furly, the Quaker patron of Toland and other radical thinkers, had three volumes of the first edition of Crisp's sermons in his famous library (*Bibliotheca Furliana*, Rotterdam, 1714, p. 143). The freethinker Anthony Collins had a copy of the 1690 edition of Crisp's works (T. Ballard, *Biblioteca Antonij Collins, Arm.*, 1731, pp. 36, 134).
102. Isaac Chauncy, *Neonomianism unmasked: or the ancient Gospel Pleaded* (1692), p. 2.
103. Quoted in W. M. Lamont, *Richard Baxter and the Millennium* (1979), p. 267; cf. *Reliquiae Baxterianae*, p. 43.
104. *Op. cit.*, pp. 3, 50, 54, 61. Crisp is (with Milton) one of the very few seventeenth-century Englishmen to have an '-ism' attached to his name (*M.E.R.*, p. 226n.)
105. Robert Nelson, *The Life of Dr George Bull, Late Lord Bishop of St David's* (1713), p. 260. John Mason, who proclaimed the millennium in Water Stratford in 1694, was "inclined to antinomianism" (H. Maurice, *An Impartial Account of Mr John Mason*, 1695, p. 27).
106. Tobias Crisp, *Christ Made Sin* (1691), Preface; S. C., *Christ Alone Exalted in Dr Crisp's Sermons* (1693), pp. 7-14.
107. *W.T.U.D.*, Chapter 8, *passim*; *M.E.R.*, Chapter 21, *passim*.
108. Volume III, p. 362.

10. *Antinomianism in 17th-century England*[1]

*"That old leaven of innovations, masked under the name of reformation, ... was never wont so far to infect the whole mass of the nobility and gentry of this kingdom, however it dispersed among the vulgar."** *

I

An unfriendly but moderately balanced anonymous pamphlet of 1644 summarized antinomian doctrines as: The elect are always beloved of God, who sees no sin in them even when by human standards they commit sin.[2] Antinomians stressed the complete freedom of the regenerate — restrained by no law, not even the Mosaic Law, by no rulings of churches, not even by the text of the Bible. The protestant concept of the priesthood of all believers abolished all mediators between man and God, whether the Virgin and the saints in heaven, or the hierarchy of the church on earth. The conscience of the individual believer was put in direct contact with God. This supremacy of the individual conscience facilitates ecclesiastical change in response to social pressures. In the first place it gives relatively little (if any) weight to the church and its ceremonies. Secondly, individual consciences are formed in a given society: what the conscience believes must bear some relation to the society in which it is formed. Believers living in the commercial strongholds of early protestantism found "the protestant ethic" written on their consciences — hard work in one's calling, frugality, accumulation, monogamy — the bourgeois virtues. It was to be different later when lower-class consciences also established a direct relationship with God.[3]

Antinomians carried this freedom for elect consciences to its

---

**Eikon Basilike*, *The Portraicture of His Sacred Majestie in His Solitude and Sufferings* (1649), p. 69. Attributed to Charles I, but almost certainly by John Gauden, later Bishop of Worcester. I cite from the edition of 1876.

extreme. For Luther the informed consciences of the godly were above the law — though of course because they were elect their consciences would be guided by God's will and so would *voluntarily* keep his commandments. But the important thing was their freedom of choice. "Whatsoever thou shalt observe of liberty and of love", Luther preached, "is godly; but if thou observe anything of necessity, it is ungodly". "If an adultery could be committed in the faith, it would no longer be a sin".[4] Luther no doubt intended this as a *reductio ad absurdum* for normal persons, though perhaps he had the difficult case of King David in mind too. Luther did after all authorize bigamy for Philip of Hesse. But seventeenth-century antinomian theologians pushed Luther's doctrine just a little bit further. Samuel Rutherford filled many score pages explaining away remarks by Luther which were susceptible of an antinomian interpretation.[5]

When antinomianism revived — or emerged from underground — in England, the urgent need seemed to be to liberate the consciences of the godly from external pressures, first of the Laudians, then of the Presbyterians. Antinomianism in England was a reaction against the alleged "works-mongering" of Laudians and covenant theologians, in the same way as Luther reacted against the formal ceremonial "works" of the Catholic church of his day. "The title of antinomian", said William Eyre sourly in 1654, "is by some of our new doctors appropriated to them who have most faithfully managed the protestant cause against the papists".[6]

It is difficult to estimate how much conscious antinomianism there had been in England before 1640. Roger Brearley's congregation at Grindleton was accused in 1617 of holding that "the Christian assured can never commit gross sin". It is indeed sinful to ask God's forgiveness, or to believe the Bible "without a motion of the spirit". The Christian assured "must never think of salvation".[7] Brearley's congregation seems to have carried his doctrines even further than he did. Thomas Shepard in 1622 was attracted by the Grindletonians, wondering "whether that glorious estate of perfection might not be the truth".[8] He decided it was not, and became a very orthodox New England divine; but Governor Winthrop attributed the heresies of Mistress Anne Hutchinson (which Shepard confuted) to Grindletonian doctrines.[9] Samuel Gorton, who carried another version of antinomianism to New England in 1636-7, came from Lancashire like Clarkson and Winstanley, but we do not know where he picked up his ideas.[10] John Cotton described them as "Familist".[11]

The almost immediate appearance of antinomianism in New England suggests that it may have been fairly widespread in England. Mrs Hutchinson was born in Lincolnshire, and returned there at the age of twenty-one after some years in London. In Lincolnshire she made contact with John Cotton, and followed him to New England in 1634. In England in 1607 Thomas Rogers was attacking antinomians.[12] Twenty-five years later a number of antinomians were brought before the High Commission. Samuel Pretty of London was charged with preaching that "a believer ought not to be sorrowful for his sins, nor to be grieved for anything". All the effects of sin are taken away for believers. He was imprisoned and degraded from the ministry.[13] Richard Lane, a conventicler, was alleged to have declared that "we are without sin", and that he himself was perfect God and perfect man. His group met at the house of one Westbrook, a tailor of Shoe Lane.[14] Another group of "plain men" were said to hold that justified persons cannot displease God, and that believers were justified before they had actual faith. "To the believer all things are pure": David when he committed adultery pleased God as well as when he danced before the Ark.[15]

In his *Antinomianisme Anatomized* of 1643 John Sedgwick begins his list of antinomians with the name of John Traske.[16] Traske obtained notoriety for his Judaizing opinions. For these Star Chamber in 1618 degraded him from the ministry, and ordered him to be whipped, nailed by the ear to the pillory, branded, fined £1000 and imprisoned for life. (By recanting he obtained his release in 1620, but his wife, made of sterner stuff, remained in jail till the sixteen-forties.)[17] Earlier and later Traske professed antinomian opinions: he was alleged to have said that the truly converted were "as free from sin as Jesus Christ". He ended life as a Baptist. While in prison he wrote a letter to the King in which he "thee'd" and "thou'd" him.[18]

The leading antinomian in this period seems to have been John Eaton, who was also the first antinomian whose works got into print after the liberation of the press in 1640. Eaton was born in Kent, and started his career as curate of St Catherine, Coleman St, a traditional radical area since Lollard times. Later he was vicar of Wickham Market, Suffolk. He was convicted in the High Commission "for preaching ... that God seeth no sin in his elect". In 1632, when John

Ettrall was up before the same court, Laud declared that Eaton was "your patriarch". Ettrall was certainly in touch with Eaton, who wrote urging him to resist — unlike Samuel Pretty, who was alleged to be wavering. In this letter Eaton sent greetings to "Mr. Towne" — possibly Robert Towne; and Laud stated that "one Townes" had held tenets similar to Pretty's.[19] John Cotton in 1635 or 1636 referred to "Mr. Townes of Nottinghamshire" as "a ring-leader of that sect" of Familists. The county is wrong, but it is difficult to see who else could have been meant.[20] Robert Towne's whole career was in fact spent on the Yorkshire-Lancashire border in which the Grindletonians flourished and which was to be a centre of Quakerism in the sixteen-fifties. He was ultimately buried in Haworth, the Bronte's parish.[21] Towne declared: "I am a sinner and no sinner. Daily I fall in myself and stand in Christ for ever. My works fail, his never can, and they are also mine". "To faith there is no sin, nor any unclean heart".[22]

II

Because the elect are saved from all eternity, they are uninfluenced by what conservatives saw as the main social function of religion, the maintenance of standards of conduct by fear of penalties or hope of rewards in the after life. The antinomian godly knew their eternal reward was secure. Some few drew libertine conclusions from this — and of course the possibility was always heavily emphasized in the propaganda of their enemies. Other antinomians, conscious of the enormous love God had shown in choosing them, wished to reciprocate by living on earth as God would wish them to live. But this was not from fear of hell or hope of heaven: it was to satisfy their own consciences.

John Eaton was clear on this point. "Where there is any moral work commanded to be done upon pain of punishment, or upon promise of any reward either temporal or eternal, there is to be understood the voice of the Law". Only where promise of salvation is offered freely and unconditionally do we hear the doctrine of the Gospel, whether such promises occur in the Old or the New Testament. "There is no sin in the sight of God".[23] Like Crisp, Eaton was concerned to escape from the revival of justification by works which he saw in the covenant theology, and in particular from "the popish rotten pillar that God accepts the will for the deed".[24]

As the careers of Luther and John Cotton show, the border line between orthodoxy and antinomian heresy was often difficult to draw. Crisp appealed to Calvin against latter-day Calvinists, and so did Cotton.[25] Crisp alleged the authority of William Twisse, Pro-locutor of the Westminster Assembly of Divines, the custodian of authority, for the claim that justification might precede faith.[26] Cotton, defending himself against the attacks of Robert Baillie, also cited "Dr. Twisse (not suspected for an antinomian, much less for a Familist)".[27] So did William Eyre, Wiltshire antinomian.[28] Crisp faced the possible abuse of his doctrine by the licentious, but was himself convinced that the elect could never willingly sin. "The grass and the pasture is so sweet that he [God] put a believer into, that though there be no bounds to keep in such a soul, yet it will never go out of this fat pasture to feed on a barren common".[29]

III

One of the more interesting antinomians is William Walwyn. Unlike most, he accepted the label. "I . . . had long been established in that point of doctrine (called then antinomian) of free justification by Christ alone".[30] Like Crisp, Walwyn emphasized that Christ died for sinners, the ungodly, all the world.[31] "Your present comfort depends upon your believing; . . . yet the work of Christ depends not on your believing". It comes freely to all sinners.[32] Like Crisp too, Walwyn denounced hell-fire preachers with their harrowing effect on sensitive consciences. "Many of you may, through sense of sin and of wrath due for sin, walk in a very disconsolate condition: fears and terrors may abound in you". They are the product of "the grossest antichristian error, to think righteousness comes by the law". Wal-wyn was later to speak of "those yokes of bondage unto which sermons and doctrine mixed of law and gospel do subject distressed consciences".[33] Like Crisp, Walwyn attacked Perkins's doctrine that God accepts the will for the deed. No one "should so much as doubt of your salvation".[34] Neither infidelity nor impenitence nor un-thankfulness nor denying Christ "can separate you from his love".[35] As soon as men realise this they will lead good lives,[36] and — a characteristic Walwyn touch — "will be inflamed to fight against injustice". "True Christians are of all men the most valiant defenders of the just liberties of their country, and the most zealous preservers of true religion".[37] So Walwyn's support for the Levellers seemed to him to follow naturally from his religious principles. Samuel Ruther-ford may have been referring to Walwyn when he said that "sundry antinomians say Irish papists ought to have liberty of conscience".[38]

Like Crisp, Walwyn is ambiguous on the question of whether salvation is offered to all men. In *The Power of Love* he spoke of those liable to eternal death.[39] In *A Whisper in the Eare of Mr. Thomas Edwards, Minister*, Walwyn denied the salvation of all.[40] Yet *The Vanitie of the Present Churches* (1649), which may not be by Walwyn, but which he cited approvingly, speaks of "the love of God which bringeth salvation unto all men".[41] In *Tyranipocrit Discovered* (1649), which some have attributed to Walwyn, we are told that "God accepteth any man that desireth to be good".[42] "Neither doth God give more grace unto one man to be saved than he doth to all and every man".[43] But other theological statements in *Tyranipocrit* make me think it cannot be by Walwyn. The author appears to approve of the doctrine that God accepts the will for the deed, which Walwyn had attacked in *The Power of Love*.[44] The author of *Tyranipocrit* speaks of "working out of their salvation in fear and trembling".[45] "God hath given unto man a free power to will, and till man hath used his willing power in leaving such sins as are in his power to leave, God will not help him".[46] "God's predestination is no forcing power, but a prescience".[47] "He that teacheth an absolute predestination in God of man, without man, he cannot honour God nor comfort man".[48] If Walwyn wrote *Tyranipocrit*, he had abandoned his antinomianism of 1643-4, of which he had spoken without disapproval in May 1649.[49]

Henry Denne is another antinomian who was closely associated with the Levellers, until his recantation after playing a leading role in the Army mutiny which ended at Burford in May 1649 led them to denounce him as "Judas Denne". Although an ordained minister of the Church of England, Denne ultimately became a Baptist preacher. In *The Doctrine and Conversation of John Baptist* (1643) — a visitation sermon "contradicted by many of the auditors" — Denne argued that "the safest way is to say No" when asked "whether a desire to believe be faith itself".[50] "The poor man can tell you that to be rich and to desire to be rich are two things".[51] Two years later he put forward a familiar antinomian position. "God is freely reconciled to the elect, and loveth them in Jesus Christ, without any previous dispositions, without any qualifications, without any performances or conditions on their parts, unless to be polluted and sinful be a previous condition or qualification".[52] Grace was given before the world began, and God's love is just as great before as after our conversion.[53] He did not love us because he foresaw that we would repent and believe.[54] Free grace is a doctrine of liberty. Those who think "it were better to hide this from the people, and to terrify them with hell-fire, with wrath and judgment" aim "to keep them in bondage".[55] (Again the image of political liberty, which the Levellers were to take up.)

Denne was aware that he might "to many seem guilty of that crime which was laid against the Apostle, to turn the world upside down".[56] But he was unconcerned. All false religions, Denne argued, those of Jews, Turks, papists, pharisaical protestants and heathen, all these "propound in some degree or other an angry God", who has to be propitiated. For them, "the world would be saved by doing", not by reliance on Christ. All ask, as Bunyan's Pilgrim was soon to ask, "What shall I do to be saved?" In Denne's view, "there cannot be greater idolatry committed than to conceive a possibility of gaining the love and favour of God by works wrought in the creature".[57] So his was not a religion of doing: one begins to see the force of Winthrop's remark, "most of their tenets tended to sloth-fulness, and quench all endeavour in the creature".[58] This is some-thing rather different from "the protestant ethic". But as early as 1643 Denne's was a socially conscious religion. In a dialogue he made a minister ask a man who claimed to be in a state of grace "Why have you not sold either the whole or half of your possessions and divided it among ... your brethren in great poverty?"[59] It was a theme which Abiezer Coppe and the author of *Tyranipocrit Discovered* were later to take up. Crisp similarly had argued that good works should be performed only because they are profitable to others, not with any idea that they confer merit on the doer.[60] Samuel Gorton asked indignantly "When and where have I lived upon other men's labours and not wrought with mine own hands for things honest in the sight of men?"[61] We recall Milton's slightly shame-faced admission that his "ease and leisure" came "out of the sweat of other men".[62]

In his own day John Saltmarsh, another Yorkshireman, had the greatest reputation of any antinomian. He conditionally accepted the label, though he himself preferred to speak of "free grace".[63] But his reputation was perhaps won by his literary qualities rather than by any novelty in his ideas: and I must say I prefer Walwyn as a writer. But Saltmarsh was also famous, or notorious, for his radical commitment, which culminated in his rising from his death bed and riding across southern England in December 1647 to denounce the generals for departing from God by dividing the Army and suppressing the Agitators.

It is indeed of Walwyn that Saltmarsh reminds us. "Love began all the work of salvation in God";[64] it is God's mercy, not his justice, that Saltmarsh stresses. Like Crisp, Saltmarsh was anxious to deny the allegation that "from free grace there will follow nothing but looseness and libertinism". "If any man sin more freely because of forgiveness of sins, that man may suspect himself to be forgiven".[65] Like Crisp, Walwyn and Denne, Saltmarsh had no use for the doctrine that God accepts the will for the deed: the preacher who "told me my desire to pray was a prayer" did not help him.[66] Saltmarsh had himself been in despair, with temptations to suicide, till he learnt that "no sin can make one less beloved of God or less in Christ".[67] "The promises of Christ are held forth to sinners as sinners, not as repenting sinners or humble sinners, as any condition in us upon which we should challenge Christ".[68] "A person justified, or in covenant, is as perfect in the sight of God as the righteousness of Christ can make him (though not so in his own eyes). ... No sin can make God love us less".[69] "There is no sin to be committed which Christ did not pay down the price of his blood for". A believer is "as free from hell, the law and bondage ... as if he were in heaven".[70]

William Dell's antinomianism is much less central to his thought, but he too proclaimed that we are free from the law and sin.[71] Dell was more interested in the independence of the congregational churches than anything else. "Our union with the church flows from our union with Christ", and not vice versa.[72] "The assemblies of the true church are all equal", and within them all believers are equal.[73] "If every free society hath power to choose its own officers, much more hath the true church, being ... the freest society under heaven".[74] Here we see how ideas about liberty and equality can be freely transferred from the spiritual to the secular sphere.

Thomas Collier, like Dell and Saltmarsh a former Army chaplain, was another man influenced by antinomianism. "As God writes his laws in the hearts of his people", he declared, "so shall they live above the Law in the letter, even of the gospel, yet not without it, for they have it within them, ... and so they are a law to themselves".[75] John Reeve, founder of what was later called Muggletonianism, held that "whosoever hath that true love of God in him, that man hath no need of man's law to be his rule, but he is a law to himself, and lives above all laws of mortal men". "And yet", he added, he "is obedient to all laws".[76] Milton held similar views.[77]

IV

Crisp had been aware that his doctrine could be interpreted as authorizing libertinism.[78] Thomas Shepard thought the ideas of New England antinomians were "mere fig-leaves to cover some distempers and lusts lurking in men's hearts".[79] In England in the mid-forties Samuel Rutherford and Robert Baillie,[80] the English Presbyterians Herbert Palmer, Edmund Calamy, John Sedgwick, Stephen Geree, Thomas Edwards and Thomas Bedford recognized that antinomian doctrines were "most plausible and pleasing to flesh and blood".[81] "Oh it pleaseth nature well, to have heaven and their lusts too", John Winthrop had said apropos New England antinomians in the sixteen-thirties.[82] The most frightening thing about antinomianism was indeed its appeal to natural man. It was, Richard Baxter argued, "so easy a way, which flesh and blood hath so little against, as being too consistent with men's carnal interest";[83] so "pleasing to the fleshly mind", said Thomas Symonds in 1657.[84]

Crisp announced that sin was finished.[85] Robert Towne declared in 1644 "if thou believe sin, death and the curse to be abolished, they are abolished".[86] Five years later the Ranter Abiezer Coppe repeated that sin was finished; God's service is "perfect freedom and pure libertinism". But he concluded from this that "I can ... love my neighbour's wife as myself, without sin". He claimed God as "that mighty Leveller".[87] When a very different character from Coppe, John Bunyan, declared that "no sin shall frustrate or make election void", he added: "the world, when they hear that God would have mercy offered in the first place to the biggest sinners, will be apt to think that this is a doctrine that leads to looseness and gives liberty to the flesh".[88] Bunyan had known Ranters in his younger days, and his ideas were perhaps sometimes closer to those of an antinomian like Crisp than is always recognized.

Laurence Clarkson was influenced by Crisp. He tried to become one of those in whom God saw no sin — or so he tells us.[89] In 1647 he wrote a Leveller tract. Two years later he was "Captain of the Rant", systematizing the ideas which critics of the antinomians had most feared. "There is no such act as drunkenness, adultery and theft in God", he wrote. "Sin hath its conception only in the imagination. . . . Which act soever is done by thee in light and love, is light and lovely, though it be that act called adultery. .... No matter what Scripture, saints or churches say, if that within thee do not condemn thee, thou shalt not be condemned".[90] He even claimed that "none can be free from sin till in purity it be acted as no sin".[91] The Ranter John Robins authorized his disciples to change their spouses, changing his own wife "for an example".[92] Samuel Gorton expressed a common Ranter view when he said that the clergy conspired "to press the poorer sort with the burdens of sins, and such abundance of servile obedience as to make them slaves to themselves and others".[93]

V

Now that we have seen the full development of antinomianism in the freedom of the sixteen-forties in England, it may be helpful to look back at its first appearance in New England in the thirties. "The late stirs in the New England churches, occasioned by Master Wheelwright, Master Hutchinson and their followers", an opponent of antinomianism declared, were greatly influenced by the "tenet 'No condition in the covenant', ... if it were not the main cause thereof".[94] Most English antinomian doctrines were present in embryo in the case of Anne Hutchinson — either taught by her or her adherents, or attributed to her by her enemies. She and her brother-in-law, the Rev John Wheelwright, "inveighed against all that walked in the covenant of works", among whom Mrs Hutchinson included many of the ministers.[95]

John Winthrop summarized "their opinions", clearly referring to wider circles than the supporters of Mrs Hutchinson and Wheelwright. Many of his points were to become familiar in England in the sixteen-forties. "No. 9: to question my assurance, though I fall into murder or adultery, proves that I never had true assurance".[96] "No. 18: God loves a man never the better for any holiness in him, and never the less, be he never so unholy. No. 19: Sin in a child of God must never trouble him".[97] Error 20 condemned by the New England churches was "to call in question whether God be my dear Father, after or upon the commission of some heinous sins (as murder, incest, etc.), doth prove a man to be in the covenant of works".[98] Among "unsavoury speeches" Winthrop cited: "I may know I am Christ's, not because I do crucify the lusts of the flesh, but because I do not crucify them, but believe in Christ that crucified my lusts for me". Unsavoury speech (2) suggested that "to evidence justification by sanctification or graces, savours of Rome".[99] One of Wheelwright's disciples was alleged to have said that the commandments "... were a dead letter ...".[100] Mrs Hutchinson was accused of holding that "the law is no rule of life to a Christian". "Not being bound to the law, it is not transgression against the law to sin, or break it, because our sins they are inward and spiritual ... and only are against Christ".[101] Error 49: "we are not bound to keep a constant course of prayer in our families or privately, unless the spirit stir us up thereunto".[102]

Winthrop did not fail to recall "the tragedy of Münster", which "gave just occasion to fear the danger we were in".[103] Peter Bulkeley provided this familiar slander with a theological basis by arguing that if our union with Christ were the only resurrection, "then all that are united are the children of the resurrection, and therefore are neither to marry nor to give in marriage, and so by consequence there ought to be community of women" — "that foul, gross, filthy and abominable opinion held by the Familists". It seems a far-fetched conclusion, but it shows the acute awareness of the ministers that a good man's theological theory may become a lewd man's immoral practice. Mrs Hutchinson, who did not deny that "we are united to Christ with the same union that his humanity on earth was with the deity",[104] indignantly repudiated the sexual consequences which Bulkeley asserted. But Cotton — once her friend — repeated it in his formal admonition to her on behalf of the church. That union with Christ amounted to a resurrection in this life was an "argument ... which the Anabaptists and Familists use" to "set an open door to all epicureanism and libertinism".[105]

A further charge against Mrs Hutchinson was the heresy of mortalism, shared in England by Richard Overton the Leveller, Milton, Ranters and Muggletonians. Mrs Hutchinson admitted this accusation. She also admitted to having revelations: "if she had not a sure word that England should be destroyed her heart would shake" when she saw the "meanness" of New England.[106] "These disturbances that have come among the Germans", commented Deputy-Governor Dudley, "have been all grounded upon revelation".[107]

Samuel Gorton, who survived to sum up New England antinomianism, thought that "every believer, Godded, deified and anointed with the spirit, is Christ".[108] Heaven was to be found on earth in the hearts of men.[109] He questioned the existence of sin, suggesting that it had been invented by the privileged in order to control the lower classes.[110]

VI

Antinomianism drew on strong protestant traditions going back to Luther; it was anti-catholic and anti-Laudian. Its appeal to the individual conscience of those who felt themselves to be the elect was well calculated to attract members of congregations which had just come up from underground, or were newly formed around some charismatic mechanic preacher. It was, as an anonymous pamphlet of 1644 put it, a "doctrine of liberty".[111] "The antinomians were commonly Independents" Baxter wrote — much later, it is true.[112]

Antinomianism indeed cannot be divorced from the context of mid-seventeenth century England. Its adherents faced political problems; and their theology led many of them to radical conclusions. Until the breakdown of 1640 consensus politics had prevailed, at least among those who were able to express opinions. Since there was no police force, no absolute monarchy whose policies could be enforced by an Army and a bureaucracy, society was held together by the consent of "the political nation", of those gentry and merchants whose wealth and status gave them authority in normal times.

But stresses had been developing with the great economic divide of the two generations before 1640. Among the unprivileged classes the rich were getting richer, the poor poorer. It may well be that Sir Thomas More was right to see all commonwealths as conspiracies of the rich to oppress the poor,[113] but the legal aspects of this tyranny became more obvious with the development of the poor law, laws against vagrants, cottagers, etc. The bland Richard Hooker could claim that "laws they are not which public approbation hath not made so",[114] but this was consensus among the beneficiaries of society, J.Ps. and parish élites, and even as Hooker wrote it was wearing thin. Mr Tim Curtis has spoken of Elizabeth's government as "a beleaguered garrison"; Ralegh called J.Ps. "the garrisons of good order throughout the realm".[115] Well and good, so long as the garrison held together; but the sixteen-twenties saw a polarization, not only for or against the King's government, but also on attitudes towards poverty.[116] The traditional political consensus no longer seemed to work. The ultimate answer was that of Hobbes: law is the command of the sovereign, who is sovereign because he has power; and later still when consensus was restored again, law derives from

the social contract agreed by "the people", who are sharply differentiated from the poor.[117] But such ideas were far ahead in 1640.
What had men to hold on to?

Respect for the law — perhaps for a purged and purified law, not
for the actual law administered by Charles I's judges — is something
which historians cite as characteristic of Englishmen in the seventeenth century, just as they speak of "ages of faith", meaning the ages
from which nearly all surviving records were written by churchmen.
But as soon as men were free to speak, this respect for law seems to be
confined to the possessing classes. "Our very laws were made by our
conquerors", said Wildman in the Putney Debates. "The old kings'
laws", Winstanley agreed, "were the laws of a conqueror to hold the
people in subjection".[118] The young Milton had longed to be rid of
"this Norman gibberish".[119] Hence the continued opposition of the
propertied classes to suggestions that the law might be reformed.
Any questioning of its immemorial authority seemed to them risky.

The keystone of the arch holding propertied society together, as
both James I and Wentworth pointed out, was the King — an
anointed, semi-divine figure, aloof and intangible, above the law
which he enforced. From this point of view the greatest error of the
revolutionaries was to execute Charles I when he refused to accept
the position of constitutional monarch. Charles played magnifi-
cently on this stop at his trial — if power without law can do this to
the King, who is safe? — and so ensured Charles II's restoration in
1660 as the sanction of a deferential society — though by now the
King had accepted that he was above neither the law nor those who
enforced it.

Not only the law of Moses but all human laws were inapplicable to
the elect. Antinomianism thus helped to undermine the mystique of
law and of power. Its attractiveness to the unprivileged, to "natural
man", was very early revealed. The speculative theology of Brearley,
Eaton and Crisp was soon transformed by these popular overtones,
which Traske had foreshadowed. With the breakdown of traditional
controls after 1640, antinomian doctrines easily fused with the
radical tradition, which certainly goes back to sixteenth-century
Familists and perhaps to fifteenth-century Lollards.[120] Perfection is
attainable on earth, believers can be in heaven in this life. All men can
be saved, God is in all men, all men are Sons of God.[121] Consequently
all men can be above the law.

Antinomianism could appeal to very different social groups, who had in common only a feeling that the existing law thwarted their activities. For Anne Hutchinson and her female adherents in New England, it has been suggested, antinomianism was "an ideology through which the resentments they [women] felt could be focused and actively expressed".[122] Bernard Baylin suggested that support for Mrs Hutchinson came predominantly from merchants, and it seems clear that, although she had lower-class supporters, some of her partisans were well-to-do men who opposed the regulation of commerce in the interests of consumers and farmers and wanted greater freedom to use their elbows.[123] We may recall that Tobias Crisp came from a very rich merchant family and that in Barbados planters equated Independency with free trade.[124]

The accusation which contemporaries brought against antinomians was rather different. Their doctrine provided an excuse for the "slothful" to escape the demands of the law, said Thomas Shepard.[125] Winthrop agreed: "their way of life was made easy; if so, no marvel so many like of it". Hence its popularity in London among "carnal and vile persons". "Oh, it pleaseth nature well to have heaven and their lusts too". Mrs Hutchinson's was "a very easy and acceptable way to heaven, to see nothing, to have nothing, but to wait for Christ to do all". It appealed to "many profane persons" as well as to women.[126] "In the ordinary course of [God's] dispensation", the New England Synod told Mrs Hutchinson, "the more we endeavour, the more assistance and help we find from him".[127] Rejection of "the protestant ethic" suggests a plebeian version of antinomianism, such as was to flourish in England. John Trapp tells an anecdote of an antinomian servant girl who denied any personal responsibility for stealing: it was sin in her.[128] "The antinomian doctrine", wrote Baxter, "is the very same in almost every point which I find naturally fastened in the hearts of the common profane multitude".[129]

VII

When liberty of conscience was affected, the antinomian impulse led men to associate with other groupings to achieve political ends. But in general antinomianism was a dissolvent rather than a positive political creed. There was never a sect of antinomians. Their doctrine imposed no external constraints on the way in which they should act; they had no predetermined or planned political programme. Their liberty, like Milton's, was a negative liberty.[130]

Walwyn decided that discussion was a more important part of religious worship than preaching; like the antinomian Milton he advocated liberty of the press.[131] With Clarkson and Denne he supported the Levellers. Richard Overton, later a Leveller like Walwyn, attacked the dogma of universal human depravity and insisted that Christ died for all.[132] The anonymous pamphlet *Vox Plebis*, variously attributed to Overton and to Henry Marten, near-Leveller M.P., affirmed that "God created every man free in Adam: so by nature are all alike freemen born, and since made free in grace by Christ".[133] "The interest of the people in Christ's Kingdom", wrote John Saltmarsh, "is not only an interest of compliancy and obedience and submission, but of consultation, of debating, counselling, prophesying, voting, etc. And let us stand fast in the liberty wherewith Christ hath made us free".[134] William Dell drew less democratic but more revolutionary conclusions. If "the things of God" are determined "by the plurality of votes, ... the greater part still overcomes the better". "According to our new or second birth ... there is exact equality"; to faith nothing is impossible.[135] So antinomianism justified military dictatorship. An intense urge to secure freedom for the consciences of the elect was combined with considerable pragmatism about the means by which this freedom was to be attained.

So although contemporaries often linked antinomians with Levellers, antinomians who did not believe that God is in all men could justify minority dictatorship. Fifth Monarchist insurrection, Digger communism, the petty Hobbism of the Muggletonians, could all be so defended. After 1649, as the radicals lost their basis of popular support, their only hope seemed to lie in giving power to a godly minority. "How can the kingdom be the saints' when the ungodly are electors and elected to govern?" one of them pertinently asked in 1649.[136] Barebone's Parliament in 1653 failed to provide a solution. Milton was still trying to grapple with the problem in 1659-60.

Part of the difficulty was something which Crisp and Milton at least always shirked. Who are the elect whose freedom must be guaranteed? How are the unregenerate to be controlled? Crisp and Walwyn often speak as if grace was offered to all men.[137] Did they mean it? There were those who argued, in the words of John Goodwin, that "Christ ... died intentionally to save all the posterity of Adam".[138] In controversies in Wiltshire in the sixteen-fifties antinomians and their opponents accused each other of opening the door to universal redemption.[139] Failure to ask such questions, still more to answer them, increased the liability of antinomianism to fragment when doctrines of universal grace and political democracy came to the fore. Intellectual antinomianism was essentially an élitist creed, calling for liberty for the elect. But the intensity of feeling about the necessity of such liberty tended to spill over into universal statements, just as many Parliamentarians called for liberty for "the people" when they were far from including the whole population in that undefined phrase.[140] So Milton in 1644 declared that "now the time seems come, wherein ... all the Lord's people are become prophets".[141] Nothing must be suppressed, lest God's truth should be lost. "The true church", wrote Dell in 1649, "is a kingdom of prophets", for Christ lives in his elect. In this church the learned have no advantage over the unlearned.[142]

Antinomianism was always potential within Puritan protestantism. It attended on Calvinism like a shadow. But the antinomian moment, like the universalist moment, was short-lived. The theoretical antinomianism of the theologians could fuse with traditional heretical doctrines only in conditions of upheaval, of revolution. Larzer Ziff suggested that New England antinomianism relied heavily on belief that the millennium was imminent.[143] Its supersession as millenarian hopes faded was perhaps natural, though the decline of popular antinomianism seems in fact to have occurred before Fifth Monarchism reached its peak. Richard Baxter modestly took some credit for this decline to "those ungrateful controversial writings of my own".[144]

Looking back, we can see why respectable contemporaries attached such importance to having only one religion in a society. More than one religion could lead to more than one centre of political power — as Hobbes noted. This was the case in France between the Edict of Nantes and Richelieu's suppression of the Huguenots' fortified towns: after that the Edict could be repealed whenever the government wished. This illuminates the importance which Bancroft, Elizabeth and James attached to getting the oath of allegiance accepted by as many papists as possible; it explains the danger seen in any foreign protection of recusants (or of Huguenots in France). It explains too the hostility of the radicals to the clergy who accepted a monopoly state church, and to the universities which trained them.[145]

The political and ideological exhaustion of the sixteen-fifties testifies to recognition of the magnitude of the task of totally reconstituting the ideas and institutions of society. It was too much for one generation. The changes ultimately came about by gradualist means after the revolutionaries had been defeated. They could come because the key institutions had been overthrown in 1641. There was insufficient agreement among those who criticized the old law, the old church. It was easier to unite the anti-revolutionaries than the revolutionaries.

The nonconformists' recognition that Christ's kingdom was not of this world was an acceptance of the fact that the elect could not be identified on earth, or at any rate that the visible elect would not challenge the laws of the state. The spiritual was segregated from the secular.[146] The restricted sphere of religion which this implied, the withdrawal of the clergy from aspirations to political power, brings us into the modern world.

Historians — myself included[147] — have perhaps been too apt to dwell on the sexual consequences of antinomianism — following too closely the emphases of contemporaries. Coppe and Clarkson are exceptionally quotable. But this is I think a mistake, comparable with the error which emphasizes the polygamy of the Münster Anabaptists to the exclusion of their other ideas and activities. Coppe and Clarkson, after all, were both highly political thinkers: sexual libertinism was only one part of their radical ideology. Such antinomians as Crisp, Walwyn, Denne and Saltmarsh (and many others) appear to have drawn no libertine conclusions from their similar starting point. The monogamous family was very important to the social stability of working householders. Immoralists were aristocratic rakes or the poor.

More important, perhaps, was the antinomian challenge to laws and institutions, though this lasted only as long as the political and social crisis lasted, whilst Cromwell was asking "What if a man should take it upon him to be King?" and others were looking to King Jesus to save them from King Oliver. When antinomians had an arbitrary sword in their hands, everybody else cried out for law. Harrington was right when he said that the call for restoration of monarchy in England was really a demand for restoration of known laws.[148] Popular antinomianism was permanent revolution reduced to the absurd: no accepted sanctions, no known authorities, no limits: and yet no agreement among the permanent revolutionaries. Antinomianism extended the principle of the priesthood of all believers to the kingship of all believers, the absolute sovereignty of the individual conscience. "Then every Christian in a common-wealth must be king and sheriff and captain and Parliament-man and ruler", snorted Edward Winslow.[149]

The question, as Albertus Warren put it, was not "whether we should be governed by arbitrary power, but in whose hands it should be".[150] "Better the Grand Turk than the rabble rout", an Independent observed in 1650.[151] The replacement of monarchy by military rule produced few lasting benefits for most of the population, and was much more expensive than any form of government previously known. The return to monarchy, to bishops, to the natural rulers, was also a return to belief in sin. Perfection, men discovered the hard way, was not to be found in this vale of tears.

NOTES

1. This piece is a by-product of Chapters 8 and 9 above.
2. [Anon], *A Declaration against the Antinomians and their Doctrine of Liberty* (1644), quoted by Gertrude M. Huehns, *Antinomianism in English History. With special reference to the period 1649-1660* (1951), p. 8. I have not always made specific references to this pioneering book, but I found it immensely useful in writing this essay, especially in directing me to sources.
3. See my *Change and Continuity in 17th-century England*, Chapter 3.
4. Martin Luther, *Thirty-four sermons* (trans. William Grace, 1747), p. 281; H. Haydn, *The Counter-Renaissance* (New York, 1950), p. 485. See pp. 170-1 above.
5. Rutherford, *A Survey of the Spirituall Antichrist* (1648), p. 87.
6. W. Eyre, *Vindiciae Justificationis Gratuitae: Justification without Conditions* (1654), Sig. a 3; cf. Sig. a 4v.
7. For the Grindletonians see p. 149 above, and *W.T.U.D.*, pp. 81-5. Baxter said there were links between William Hacket, executed in 1591, and the Grindletonians: see G.F. Nuttall, *The Holy Spirit in Puritan Faith and Experience* (Oxford, 1946), pp. 178-9. For Hacket see pp. 73, 84, 96 above.
8. "Autobiography of Thomas Shepard", *Publications of the Colonial Soc. of Massachusetts*, XXVII (1927-30), pp. 362-3.
9. Nuttall, *op. cit.*, p. 179.
10. Philip F. Gura, "The Radical Ideology of Samuel Gorton: New Light on the Relation of English to American Puritanism". *William and Mary Quarterly*, XXXVI (1979), pp. 80-1.
11. Hall, *The Antinomian Controversy*, p. 398.
12. T. Rogers, *The Faith, Doctrine and Religion, Professed and Protected in*

the Realm of England (Cambridge U.P. 1681), p. 39. First published 1607.

13. Ed. S. R. Gardiner, *Reports of Cases in the Courts of Star Chamber and High Commission* (Camden Soc., 1886), pp. 182-5, 275, 316-21.

14. *Ibid.*, pp. 191-4, 269, 275.

15. *Ibid.*, pp. 270-1, 313-14.

16. Sedgwick, *op. cit.*, p. 1; cf. p. 26.

17. *C.S.P.D.*, *1639*, pp. 466-7; cf. p. 40 above.

18. B. R. White, "John Traske (1585-1636) and London Puritanism", *Baptist Quarterly*, XX (1968), pp. 223-33; D.S. Katz, *Philo-Semitism and the Readmission of the Jews to England* (Oxford U.P., 1982), pp. 8-34.

19. *Ibid.*, pp. 316-21, 186. Wood says that Eaton died in 1641, but it was probably earlier. For Eaton see pp. 149-51 above, and Rutherford, *The Tryal &Triumph of Faith*, pp. 147-8; for Towne, *ibid.*, pp. 23-4, 114.

20. Hall, *op. cit.*, p. 32.

21. *W.T.U.D.*,p. 216; Nuttall, *op. cit.*, p. 179.

22. Towne, *The Assurance of Grace* (1644), pp. 40, 71; Rutherford, *A Modest Survey of the Secrets of Antinomianism*, p. 25, in *A Survey of the Spirituall Antichrist*. Cf. also p. 151 above.

23. Eaton, *The Honey-comb of free justification*, pp. 65-6, 62-3.

24. Eaton, *The Discovery of the most dangerous dead Faith* (1641), pp. 62-3.

25. Hall, *op. cit.*, p. 188; cf. E. Battis, *Saints and Sectaries: Anne Hutchinson and the Antinomian Controversy in the Massachusetts Bay Colony* (North Carolina U.P., 1962), pp. 18, 33. For departures from Calvinism by later "Calvinists", see Kendall, *Calvin and English Calvinists to 1649, passim.*

26. Cf. Crisp, *Fifty-Two Sermons*, pp. vi-vii.

27. Hall, *op. cit.*, p. 409; cf. Battis, *op. cit.*, p. 171.

28. Eyre, *op. cit.*, pp. 22, 174; T. Hotchkis, *An Exercitation Concerning the Nature and Forgiveness of Sin* (1655), p. 219. For Eyre see p. 153 above.

29. Crisp, *Christ Alone Exalted*, p. 39.

30. *Walwyns Just Defence* (1649), in Haller and Davies, *op. cit.*, p. 361; cf. *A Whisper in the Eare of Mr. Thomas Edwards, Minister* (1646), p. 6, in Haller, *Tracts on Liberty*, III, and *The Power of Love* (1643), Sig. A 5v., *ibid.*, II.

31. *The Power of Love*, pp. 24-5, 31.

32. *Ibid.*, pp. 32, 35; cf. *Walwyns Just Defence:* "God putteth away our sins out of his remembrance" (*op. cit.*, p. 378).

33. *The Power of Love*, pp. 19-22; *Walwyns Just Defence*, p. 361. He was replying to *Walwyns Wiles* (1649), in which he had been accused of rejecting prayer and Sabbath observance (Haller and Davies, *op. cit.*, p. 297).

34. *The Power of Love*, pp. 21, 27-8.

35. *Ibid.*, p. 30.

36. *Ibid.*, pp. 35-40.

37. *Ibid.*, pp. 39-41. Cf. *A Whisper in the Eare:* "I esteem it a high point of true religion to promote common justice" (p. 5).

38. S. Rutherford, *A Modest Survey of the Secrets of Antinomianism*, pp. 176-7.
39. *The Power of Love*, p. 18.
40. *Op. cit.*, in Haller, *Tracts on Liberty*, III, p. 327.
41. In Haller and Davies, *op. cit.*, p. 266.
42. *Op. cit.*, in *British Pamphleteers*, Vol. I, p. 94.
43. *Ibid.*, p. 110.
44. *Ibid.*, p. 92. Contrast *The Power of Love*, p. 21.
45. *British Pamphleteers*, p. 92.
46. *Ibid.*, p. 98.
47. *Ibid.*, p. 110.
48. *Ibid.*, p. 112. "He that saith that the mercy of God endureth for ever, and yet that it may fail a man in this life, *if he seeketh it*, maintaineth an absurd paradox" (*ibid.*, p. 111). The words I have italicized are hardly those of an antinomian.
49. *Walwyns Just Defence*, p. 361; cf. p. 378.
50. Denne, *op. cit.*, p. 51. Rutherford attacks Denne in *The Tryal & Triumph of Faith*, pp. 169, 287-91.
51. Denne, *A Conference Between a sick man and a minister*, p. 2.
52. Denne, *Grace, Mercy and Peace* (1645), printed in *Records of the Churches of Christ gathered at Fenstanton, Warboys and Hexham, 1644-1720* (ed. E. B. Underhill, Hanserd Knollys Soc., 1854), p. 378.
53. *Ibid.*, pp. 380, 384.
54. *Ibid.*, p. 388.
55. *Ibid.*, p. 398.
56. *Ibid.*, p. 422.
57. *Ibid.*, pp. 400-2.
58. Winthrop, *A Short Story of the Rise, raign and ruine of the Familists and Libertines* (1644), p. 32.
59. Denne, *A Conference Between a sick man and a minister*, p. 8.
60. See pp. 143-5 above.
61. Gura, *A Glimpse of Sion's Glory*, p. 93.
62. *M.C.P.W.*, I, p. 804.
63. Saltmarsh, *An End of One Controversie* (1646), p. 116; *Free Grace* (10th edn. 1700), Sig. A 3.
64. *Free Grace*, Epistle Dedicatory.
65. *Ibid.*, Sig. A 3.
66. *Ibid.*, pp. 22-3, 28-9.
67. *Ibid.*, pp. 47-8, 67.
68. *Ibid.*, p. 86.
69. *Ibid.*, p. 104.
70. *Ibid.*, p. 111. For Saltmarsh see A. L. Morton, *The World of the Ranters* (1970), pp. 45-69. Thomas Gataker's *Antinomianism Discovered and Captured* (1652) is directed against Saltmarsh: "Mr. Eaton's spirit seems to be revived in this man" (Sig. A2v, pp. 1, 35, and *passim*).
71. Dell, *The Crucified and Quickened Christian* (1652), in *Several Sermons*, pp. 316-18, 327-8.

72. Dell, *The Way of True Peace and Unity* (1649), in *Several Sermons*, p. 190.
73. *Ibid.*, pp. 192, 266-7.
74. *Ibid.*, pp. 246.
75. T. Collier, *The Marrow of Christianity* (1647), p. 68.
76. John Reeve, *A Divine Looking-Glass* (3rd edn., 1719), pp. 56-7. First published 1656.
77. See pp. 153-4 above. Cf John Smith: "It is not anything a man can do that makes him more or less beloved of God" (*Soul Reviving Influence of the Sun of Righteousness*, 1654, pp. 107-8, 160, 178-80).
78. See pp. 147-8, 155 above.
79. Gura, *A Glimpse of Sion's Glory*, p. 53.
80. Rutherford, *A Sermon Preached to the Honourable House of Commons* (1644), pp. 32-7; *A Survey of the Spirituall Antichrist, passim*: Baillie, *Satan the Leader in chief* (1643-4), pp. 25-6; *A Disswasive from the Errours of the Time, passim*.
81. Palmer, *The Glasse of Gods Providence* (1644), pp. 54-5; Calamy, *Englands Antidote*, pp. 1-19; John Sedgwick, *Antinomianism Anatomized, passim*; Edwards, *Gangraena, passim*; Bedford, *An Examination of the chief points of Antinomianism* (1647), *passim*; Geree, *The Doctrine of the Antinomians Confuted* (1644), Sig. A.2.
82. Winthrop, *A Short Story*, in Hall, *The Antinomian Controversy*, p. 204.
83. *Richard Baxters Confession of Faith* (1655), p. 3.
84. Symonds, *The Voice of the Just* (1657), pp. 3-4, quoted by Watts, *The Dissenters*, p. 202; cf. pp. 123-5, 147 above.
85. See pp. 144-5 above.
86. Towne, *The Assertion of Grace*, p. 73.
87. Coppe, *A Fiery Flying Roll*, I, pp. 1-5, 11. Cf Crisp, pp. 146-9 above, and pp. 329-30 below.
88. Bunyan, *Works*, I, p. 163.
89. Clarkson, *The Lost sheep Found*, p. 9.
90. Clarkson, *A Single Eye*, pp. 8-12, 16; Cf. *A Generall Charge* (1647), *passim*. This doctrine had been anticipated by a group of "plain men" in 1632 (see p. 164 above).
91. Clarkson, *The Lost sheep Found*, p. 24; cf. Bauthumley, quoted on p. 151 above.
92. J. Reeve, *A Transcendent Spiritual Treatise* (1711), p. 12. First published 1652.
93. Gorton, *An Antidote against the Common Plague of the World* (1655), quoted by Gura, *op. cit.*, pp. 298-9; cf. pp. 85-6. See p. 210 below.
94. John Graile, *A Modest Vindication of the Doctrine of Conditions in the Covenant* (1655), p. 93. Graile was minister at Tidworth, Wilts.
95. Hall, *op. cit.*, p. 7.
96. *Ibid.*, p. 202.
97. *Ibid.*, p. 203.
98. *Ibid.*, p. 224.
99. *Ibid.*, pp. 244. Cf. Crisp, p. 143 above.

100. *Ibid*, p. 278.
101. *Ibid.*, pp. 302-3, 352. Parallels could be found in almost any antinomian.
102. *Ibid.*, p. 232.
103. *Ibid.*, pp. 275, 304-5, 362-3.
104. *Ibid.*, p. 302.
105. *Ibid.*, pp. 363, 371-2.
106. *Ibid.*, pp. 216, 301, 304, 338. She also quoted Thomas Hooker's claim that "it was revealed to me that England should be destroyed", which derived from Hooker's *The Danger of Desertion: A Farewell Sermon* preached in 1641 before he left for New England. Revelations seem to have been no necessary part of English antinomianism; but Winstanley and Reeve also claimed to have had them, and Milton was visited nightly by his Muse.
107. Hall, *op. cit.*, p. 343. Dudley can hardly have thought this an explanation of the Thirty Years War. I suspect he was looking back to Münster again.
108. Gura, *op. cit.*, p. 294.
109. *Ibid.*, p. 89; cf. pp. 298-9.
110. *Ibid.*, pp. 85-6. Gorton's adherents were described as "not learned men" (L. Ziff, *Puritanism in America: New Culture in a New World*, New York, 1973, p. 95).
111. [Anon]. *A Declaration against the antinomians and their doctrine of liberty;* cf. Crisp, *Christ Alone Exalted*, Vol. III, p. 359.
112. *Reliquiae Baxterianae*, p. 111.
113. Sir T. More, *Utopia* (Everyman edn.), p. 112.
114. R. Hooker, *op. cit.*, I, p. 194.
115. I owe the phrase to discussions with Mr Curtis; Sir Walter Ralegh, *Works* (1751), II, p. 320.
116. Cf. B. Manning, *The English People and the English Revolution*, Chapter 6.
117. See my "The Poor and the People in 17th-century England", in *Political and Social Ideas in 17th-century England* (forthcoming).
118. Woodhouse, *op. cit.*, p. 65; Winstanley, *The Law of Freedom and Other Writings* (Cambridge U.P., 1983), p. 283.
119. See *M.E.R.*, pp. 100-1.
120. See Chapter 7 above.
121. Gura, *op. cit.*, p. 93. Gura notes that so well-informed a theologian as Roger Williams linked Gorton with the Familists (*ibid.*, p. 94), as Cotton did the Hutchinsonians (p. 164 above).
122. L. Koehler, "The Case of the American Jezebels: Anne Hutchinson and Female Agitation During the Years of the Antinomian Turmoils", *William and Mary Quarterly*, XXXI (1974), pp. 57-63.
123. B. Bailyn, *New England Merchants* (Harvard U.P. 1955), p. 40; L. Ziff, *Puritanism in America*, pp. 75-77; E. Battis, *Saints and Sectaries*, pp. 102-3. See G. F. Nuttall, *The Holy Spirit*, pp. 178-80, for links between the Hutchinsonians and the Quakers.
124. See my "Radical Pirates?", in *The Origins of Anglo-American Radicalism* (ed. M. and J. Jacob, 1984), Chapter 1.

125. Hall, *op. cit.*, p.18.
126. Hall, *op. cit.*, pp.204, 264.
127. Quoted by Perry Miller, *The New England Mind: from Colony to Province* (Harvard U.P., 1953), p.56.
128. J. Trapp, *Commentaries on the New Testament* (Evansville, 1958), p.501. First published 1647. For the appeal of "slothful" ideologies to those whom their betters believed to be the labouring classes, see *W.T.U.D.*, p.326.
129. *Richard Baxters Confutation of a Dissertation for the Justification of Infidels* (1654), p.288, quoted by Lamont, *op. cit.*, p.128; cf. p.143; Baxter, *The Holy Commonwealth*, pp.65, 92, 103, 203, 226-8.
130. *M.E.R.*, pp.262-7.
131. Walwyn, *The Vanitie of the Present Churches* (1649), in Haller and Davies, *op. cit.*, p.273.
132. R.O., *Mans Mortalitie* (Amsterdam, 1644). I quote from the reprint edited by H. Fisch (Liverpool U.P., 1968), pp.8-9.
133. *Vox Plebis* (1646), p.4.
134. Saltmarsh, *The Smoke in the Temple* (1646), p.184. Samuel Gorton published in 1655 *Saltmarsh Returned from the Dead*. Cf. A. L. Morton, *The World of the Ranters*, pp.60, 68.
135. Dell, *Sermons*, pp.253, 266, 342-3.
136. [Anon.], *Certaine Queries Presented by many Christian People* (1649), in Woodhouse, *Puritanism and Liberty*, p.246.
137. Crisp, *Fifty-Two Sermons*, pp.114, 213; cf. pp.202-3; for Walwyn see pp.166-9 above.
138. J. Goodwin, *Truths Conflict with Error* (1650), p.28.
139. Cf. W. Eyre, *op. cit.*, p.84.
140. See my "The Poor and the People", in *Political and Social Ideas in 17th-century England*.
141. *M.C.P.W.*, II, pp.355-6; cf. I, p.14.
142. Dell, *Sermons*, pp.275-6.
143. Ziff, *The Career of John Cotton* (Princeton U.P., 1962), p.156.
144. *Reliquiae Baxterianae*, p.111. In retrospect Baxter sounds almost sympathetic to antinomianism here. Perhaps he has been edited.
145. See chapters 2 and 4 above.
146. Woodhouse, *Puritanism and Liberty*, Introduction, *passim*.
147. Especially in *W.T.U.D.*
148. *The Political Works of James Harrington* (ed. J. G. A. Pocock, Cambridge U.P., 1977), p.49.
149. Winslow, *Hypocrisie Unmasked* (1646), p.44, quoted by Gura, *op. cit.*, p.81. Winslow was attacking Gorton.
150. Warren, *Eight Reasons Categorical* (1653), p.5.
151. John Price, *The Cloudie Clergy* (1650), p.14.

11. *The Religion of Gerrard Winstanley*[1]

"Some others of this age, by a new art of levelling, think nothing can be rightly mended or reformed unless the whole piece ravel out to the very end ... Say they, the law enslaves one sort of people to another. The clergy and gentry have got their freedom, but the common people are still servants to work for the other ... I wonder not so much at this sort of arguing as to find that they who have such sort of arguments should have spades in their hands ..." *

I

INTRODUCTION

There have been two approaches to the religion of Gerrard Winstanley. One has stressed the modernity of his ideas, relating them forward to nineteenth- and twentieth-century socialism. In this perspective his theology seems relatively unimportant, the main problem being to explain how he broke sufficiently loose from the religious ideas with which he started to arrive at conclusions which are unprecedented in the seventeenth century. The other approach stresses the continuity of Winstanley's ideas, and sees him primarily as a religious thinker, whose communist ideas were the result of a mystical experience and of his study of the Bible. The digging at St George's Hill was "symbolic" rather than political.[2]

Each approach removes Winstanley from his historical context. The first exaggerates the break between the early ("mystical") and the later ("rationalist") Winstanley.[3] Adherents of the second view have rightly denied that Winstanley was a "seventeenth-century Marxist", though I do not know that anyone ever suggested he was.

---

* Anthony Ascham, *Of the Confusions and Revolutions of Governments* (1649), pp. 18-19. This clear reference to the Diggers was contained in a chapter added to the first version of Ascham's pamphlet, *A Discourse Wherein is examined, What is particularly lawfull during the Confusions and Revolutions of Government* (1648). This chapter, significantly, was entitled "The Originall of Property".

The second approach fails to emphasize the profoundly heretical nature of Winstanley's religion, and the extent to which he threatened the traditional orthodoxy of his time; and it underestimates the seriousness of the Diggers' political motivation. It leads to what Professor Hudson called "a mystifying paradox": "if the new order was dependent on God's decision, why should Winstanley embark upon a programme of practical action?" Professor Hudson's rather weak explanation is that the digging was intended as a "sign" demanding attention from the Lord.[4] Each of these approaches seems to me unsatisfactory, because Winstanley is treated in isolation. My object is first to relate him to the radical and heretical ideas of his predecessors and contemporaries, and then to show in what respects he broke away from them and was truly original.[5]

Historians pay perhaps too little attention to Winstanley's earlier pamphlets, and indeed they must yield in interest to those which deal with the digging and Winstanley's communism. Nevertheless many of his later ideas are already present in the early theological tracts, which seem to have been the more popular. There were two editions each of *The Breaking of the Day of God, The Mysterie of God, The Saints Paradise* and *Truth Lifting Up its Head above Scandals*. These four together with *The New Law of Righteousness* were reprinted, with a separate introduction, in *Several Pieces Gathered into One Volume* (December 1649). Eight years later the same pamphlets (except for *Truth Lifting up its Head*) were listed by William London in his *Catalogue of the Most Vendible Books in England*, whose object was to bring culture to the north.[6]

Part II of what follows briefly summarizes Winstanley's ideas as they had matured in his first four tracts. Part III relates these ideas to those of Winstanley's radical contemporaries and predecessors. Part IV discusses his conversion to communism, and Part V the evolution of his ideas after that turning-point. Part VI discusses some points on which I disagree with others who have written about Winstanley, and Part VII attempts to draw some conclusions.

II

BEFORE THE END OF 1648

Winstanley's early thinking, like that of most of his radical contemporaries, is concerned with explaining the existence of evil, with the relationship of man to God, with the Fall of man. "Mankind is a garden which God hath made for his own delight to dwell and walk in". But selfishness, the Serpent, rose up in Adam's heart, in the middle of the living garden.[7] Since the Fall, good and evil struggle together within man. God is not to be found "without you", "at a distance", "in some particular place of glory beyond the skies", nor is he to be known only after we are dead. He is to be known here and now within each one of us. Before Winstanley understood this, he tells us, he worshipped a devil and called him God. And so do most Englishmen still. "While ... I looked after a God without me, I did but build upon the sand, and as yet I knew not the rock". "He that looks for a God without himself, and worships God from a distance, he worships he knows not what, but is ... deceived by the imagination of his own heart". Worship of anything external must be idolatry, devil-worship.[8] But "he that looks for a God within himself ... is made subject to and hath community with the spirit that made all flesh, that dwells in all flesh and in every creature within the globe" The universe was created out of the substance of God.[9] When the spirit of the Father finally prevails over the evil in man, then that man becomes a saint and is one with Christ.

God is the sun of righteousness, burning up the dross and evil in man in order that pure gold may emerge. "This dross and gold in man is so mixed together that nothing can separate them but the fiery orb, which is the Father himself, that tries all things". "All must be burned herein, more or less, before they lie down quietly in the lap of providence".[10] Burning is an unpleasant process, which men often attribute to the devil. But the devil does not exist: the Serpent is "my own invention". Like God, he is within men and women. "The devil which thou thinkest is a third power, distinct between God and thee", is nothing "but the declaration of the rigour of the righteous law of God laying hold upon the corruption that is in the creature". The sinner cannot look upon the law and live; only when "the law of love hath swallowed that law of works that required perfection from the creature" and has changed "the man to the same nature and glory" can man behold God and live. Then "your eyes being opened, you shall see the King of Righteousness sit upon the throne within yourselves, judging and condemning the unrighteousness of the flesh". The Father dwells bodily in every man and woman: they become perfect when they are taken up into this spirit and live in the light of Reason.[11]

Few so far, Winstanley thought, have attained to this knowledge, but it is accessible. The beginning of wisdom is to reject traditions and hearsay, together with the hireling clergy who preach from books and other men's words. The spirit is a teacher within each one of us: "when your flesh is made subject to him, he will teach you all things ... so that you shall not need to run after men for instruction". Winstanley himself did not aspire to be a teacher, only to draw men's attention to this teaching within each one of them. "You may teach me, for you have the fountain of life in you as well as I". The poor and ignorant ("in men's learning") can "become abundantly learned in the experimental knowledge of Christ". "The spirit of righteousness within yourselves ... will bring you into community with the whole globe"; and then you will have peace, and will be freed from covetousness and the slavery of the flesh.[12]

This is the age in which God is beginning to gather his elect, to appear in the flesh of the saints.[13] The day of Christ is begun, Winstanley proclaimed in *Truth Lifting up its Head*.[14] Relying apparently upon the text, "Touch not mine anointed", which Winstanley like Milton interpreted as meaning "Touch not my saints",[15] Winstanley referred regularly to "the anointing which the saints receive from the Father" and which "doth teach them all things"; "the anointing, or that Son of God ruling as King of Righteousness and peace within you, that sets you free". This is not a wholly original concept,[16] but Winstanley gave it an unusual emphasis. There are two witnesses, he tells us: "the word of God, or the anointing in the person of Christ after the flesh, and the spirit of God, or the anointing in the flesh of the saints".[17] If the "anointing, or power and wisdom of God dwell and rule in you", as it did in the prophets and apostles, then you "can speak the mind of the Scriptures, though you should never see, hear nor read the Scriptures from men". "Anointing unites Christ in the saints": "faith, or the anointing in you". The anointing is Christ, "the wisdom and power of the Father". "When the anointing hath made a oneness ... God dwells and rules in man, and man lives in God". "The Father and you become one".[18] It is "the same anointing or spirit that was sent down" into the body of the historical Jesus Christ, and which will ultimately fill all men and women.[19] It is "God himself in man". "This anointing is said to be the earnest of an inheritance, that as the power of God did dwell in Jesus, ... even so the same power in the Father's times and seasons will bruise the same Serpent's head in every son and daughter of Adam".[20]

"If you cast your eyes abroad among the sons and daughters of men, you shall see very few that are saved, and very few in whom Christ dwells". This was conventional doctrine. But Winstanley added a millenarian note: the Son of Righteousness is coming, and ere long "the sweet song that is sung in private shall be sung publicly upon the house tops, Rejoice, for the Lord God omnipotent reigns".[21] Both in *The Mysterie of God* and in the final chapter of *The Saints Paradise* Winstanley argued a wholly unorthodox case for universal salvation: at the last, "Jesus Christ ... will dwell in the whole creation" and "every man shall be saved ... without exception". The Father "is not simply angry with his creatures, but with this sin or curse in the creature". To sin, and to sin only, "the Father will ever be a consuming fire"; "yet he will make his creature, man, one with him when the curse is swallowed up of life". The everlasting fire in which sin is consumed is not really everlasting: it will merely last for a long time.[22]

The anointing is "the power, life and peace of the Father; ... this is Christ in you, which is the hope of glory, or the earnest of the future inheritance". Jesus Christ or the anointing of flesh sets us free from the Serpent. Anointing unites Christ and the saints, "and makes them but one mystical body". "The anointing of the Son of God" is not one man only; Christ and all his saints "makes up but one Son of God". "The Father and the saints, ... being but one body, one man, ... one Son of God": this composite Christ, "this complete man or seed of the woman, shall break the Serpent's head".[23] "God now appears in the flesh of the saints". "Every particular saint is a true heaven or place of glory": the Father dwells in "this his Son", and he is in the Father. "And this is God's kingdom". When the sin against the Holy Ghost is mentioned in Matthew 12.31, the Holy Ghost means "the anointing, or the spirit ruling in flesh, either in the flesh of Christ or in the flesh of his saints". The sin against the Holy Ghost is a sin against a Son in whom the Father dwells bodily. " Every creature ... is a Son to the Father"; "perfect man is the Son of the Father in perfect glory".[24]

The concept of the anointing thus virtually equates the saints with Jesus Christ: Christ is regularly spoken of as a man. Even when Winstanley was trying to defend his orthodoxy in *Truth Lifting up its Head* it is fairly clear that he did not believe in the Trinity in any normal sense. "Jesus Christ ... was the first in whom the Father did appear bodily to dwell".[25] "Men that are wholly taken up into God are called angels" — for example, Jesus Christ and Moses. Jesus Christ "was the great prophet", and "the same anointing or power and wisdom of God" that dwelt in the prophets and apostles can dwell in the saints.[26] "Jesus Christ ... is not a single man at a distance from you, but ... the wisdom and power of the Father ... dwelling and ruling King of Righteousness in your very flesh".[27] Christ "cannot properly be called a perfect man if he should be separated from the saints". To deny that the anointing is manifest in the flesh of the saints is to deny that Christ is come in the flesh.[28]

Not only does Winstanley reject the orthodox doctrine of the Trinity: he attaches more significance to his allegorical interpretation of the gospel story than to its historical truth. If you look for Christ "under the notion of one single man after the flesh to be your Saviour, ye shall never taste salvation by him". "His ascension, so called", is an allegory of the spirit of the Father rising up "from under the earthy imaginations and lusts of the sons of men, for mankind is the earth that contains him buried". To expect Christ to "come in one single person" is to "mistake the resurrection of Christ". "You must see, feel and know from himself his own resurrection within you, if you expect life and peace by him". "Everyone hath the light of the Father within himself, which is the mighty man Christ Jesus. And he is now rising and spreading himself in these his sons and daughters, and so rising from one to many persons". This "spirit and power ... dwells in every man and woman". We are not "saved by believing there was such a man that lived and died at Jerusalem". "A man filled with the power of God ... bears the name Christ".[29] "The Scripture", Winstanley declared, "is to me but the declaration of a historical truth pointing out this higher mystery".[30]

Similarly the devil's temptation of Christ in the wilderness is a dramatization of doubts and murmurings which appeared in the human nature of Jesus. "But Jesus Christ gave no consent therunto, as Adam the first man did".[31] The fall of the rebel angels occurs "when Adam (or indeed any man or woman) doth give way to self" and prefers it to the King of Righteousness in man. Milton too compared heaven and earth apropos the fall of the rebel angels. Winstanley refers to Adam's fall in the garden of Eden as "the history"; but he is more interested in "the mystery", the allegory. "We may see Adam every day before our eyes walking up and down the street".[32]

If God and Christ are within us, not external, the day of judgment is to be taken as a metaphor. It may be a single day at the end of time, but it is also a series of events that take place within the saints during their life on earth, over a long period, "till the power of Christ do make it appear to the man's clear knowledge that self and flesh is the devil". "The ... salvation which is pointed at in the letter of the Scripture doth lie in the restoring of the creature, mankind, from the power" of evil.[33] "If you desire to know the Beast that treads you and the holy city underfoot, look first into your own hearts, for there She sits". "Whersoever God dwells, ... that is called heaven". Heaven and hell signify the saints and the unregenerate.[34]

When in *Truth Lifting up its Head* Winstanley defended his belief in Jesus Christ, he treated the resurrection as an allegory; the "ascension, so called" was not a historical event but "was only a declaration in vision" to the apostles "of the spirit's rising up". Jesus was "*a man* [my italics] taken up to live wholly in the Father; or a meek spirit drawn up to live in the light of Reason". He appears to be everyman. When Christ rules in sons and daughters, then "the writings of the apostles and prophets ... are to cease", for they will be superseded by the internal spirit.[35]

What Winstanley has to say about God the Father is no less unorthodox. "This spirit or Father is pure Reason". Reason "gave being to all and ... knits all creatures together in peace". It "governs the whole globe in righteousness, ... and the light thereof discovers thy darkness".[36] Reason is the highest name that can be given to the Father. This Reason is to be found within every man and woman if only he or she will submit to it. "Let Reason rule the man, and he dares not trespass against his fellow-creature, but will do as he would be done unto. For Reason tells him, Is thy neighbour hungry and naked to-day, do thou feed and clothe him; it may be thy case tomorrow, and then he will be ready to help thee". The opposite of Reason is selfishness, the Serpent. In *Truth Lifting up its Head* Winstanley explained why he used the word "Reason" instead of the word "God". Partly it was because he had "been held under darkness" by the word "God". Reason is "that spiritual power that guides all men's reasoning in right order and to a right end ... It hath a regard to the whole creation, and knits every creature together into a oneness, making every creature to be an upholder of his fellow". Christ reconciles man to Reason.[37] In *Fire in the Bush* Winstanley equated God with universal love, righteous conscience and pure Reason.[38]

So, Winstanley concluded, we must always speak only from our own experience of God within us; the trade of preaching as practised by hireling parsons of the state church is useless and harmful. Indeed Winstanley rejected this church and its ordinances totally — prayer, preaching, holy communion, baptism, Sabbath observance.[39] Winstanley was to express anticlericalism more violently later; but from his earliest writings he seems to have held it as strongly as Milton did. It was wrong that "sharp punishing laws were made to prevent fishermen, shepherds, husbandmen and tradesmen from ever preaching of God any more", and that preaching was restricted to "scholars bred up in human letters".[40] Winstanley was already critical of the text of the Bible, and extended this to the antinomian position of rejecting the Ten Commandments as "the letter" to which the spirit is superior.[41] The Bible "shall cease" when the Lord rules in sons and daughters.[42]

It is hazardous to look for autobiography in Winstanley's theological writings, but let us see what we can find. His description of the inadequacy of Seekers, roaming in quest of religious fellowship, may well relate to his own experience.[43] So may his account of the satisfaction of being "taken off from either glorying in the presence or mourning in the absence of any creature-help or fruit. If you never see the faces of the saints, but live in prison, in a wilderness, or in some private place, yet you are at rest in God".[44] So may his description of the man who finds he cannot pray: "when people do not regard him for his preaching and praying, then he is troubled", though he will not yet accept that "he must cease praying and preaching and self-acting, and wait upon the Father for his pure teaching". (Winstanley may well have had a period of itinerant preaching.) He had been a cloth merchant, and this may be recalled in his account of the scruples of the man who asks "sometimes too little, as sometimes too much" for his wares.[45] He had been beaten out of this trade;[46] in 1660 he was still being sued for debts incurred before 1643, when he retired to Surrey to earn a difficult living as wage labourer. We may hear echoes of this when he writes of "sickness, frowns of friends, hatred of men, losses of his estate by fire, water, being cheated by false-spirited men, death of his cattle, or many such-like casualties whereby he becomes poor in the world" and has to endure "hard language, hungry belly, to be despised" and imprisoned. In April 1646 Winstanley with five others was in trouble at Cobham manor court for cutting peat from the waste.[47]

Winstanley was certainly no Fifth Monarchist. He had published all his pamphlets before the Fifth Monarchist movement started.[48] But with Milton and almost all the radicals he shared general millenarian expectations, foreseeing a time when God will reveal himself to "the despised, the unlearned, the poor, the nothings of this world". (Foxe's *Book of Martyrs*, the main source for such ideas, was the only book to which Winstanley referred.)[49] The very desperation of his own and England's plight suggested to Winstanley that the mystery of iniquity, the Beast, the Serpent who rules in flesh, was nearing the end of his reign; in his place God will dwell in flesh himself.[50] In May 1648, faced by "these uproar risings", when men sought to chain the Roundheads up under an ecclesiastical and state power, Winstanley believed that the last period of the Beast's reign had come — very hot but short.[51] The "wrath, bitterness and discontent that appears generally in men's spirits in England, one against another ... in the midst of these national hurly-burlies" suggested to him that "the Father hath cast England into the fire, and is purging the dross from the gold, that liberty is not far off, and that the plentiful pouring out of the anointing, even the spirit of love, truth and oneness is near at hand". England, Scotland and Ireland may be "the tenth part of the city Babylon that shall fall off first and bow down at the feet of the anointing, which is the wisdom and power of God that rules in flesh". Then national divisions will be swallowed up in brotherly oneness.[52]

Thus Winstanley's attitude towards millenarianism was complex. More specific than an expectation of the reign of Christ on earth in the near future, which was widespread in the exciting sixteen-forties, was the millenarian belief which often accompanied the heresies of the radical underground — that Christ would reign and judge the world in and through his saints.[53] "God the Father hath committed all judgment to the Son" is the same as saying he "hath engaged himself to subdue the Serpent's power under the feet of the saints".[54] Here too Winstanley's doctrine of Sonship was crucial. "The three days and a half or 42 months of the saints' captivity under the Beast" are "very near expired", declared the title-page of *The Breaking of the Day of God*. "Christ hath begun to reign in his saints". "Jesus Christ is upon his rising from the dead, and will rule King of Righteousness in flesh", treading "the powers of flesh under his feet". Since Christ is the saints and they are Christ, his "dominion over the nations of the world", we must suppose, would be exercised by them.[55] But Winstanley never envisaged the forcible rule of a godly minority, as the Fifth Monarchists (and perhaps William Erbery) were to do in the sixteen-fifties. For Winstanley believed that ultimately Jesus Christ "will dwell in . . . every man and woman without exception".[56]

III

THE HERITAGE OF RADICAL THEOLOGY

It is difficult to decide which writers during the revolutionary epoch are producing original ideas, and which are expressing or recombining commonplaces. Before 1640 the censorship prevented unorthodox ideas getting into print: we hear of them only through the distorting medium of their enemies' attacks. But it is clear from the writings of Robert Baillie, Ephraim Pagitt, Samuel Rutherford, Thomas Edwards and other propagandists against the radicals that, before Winstanley wrote a line, many of the ideas which he was to make his own were circulating in the world of Familists, Hermeticists, Behmenists, General Baptists and Seekers. It would be difficult to find a single heresy of Winstanley's which was not adumbrated, however crudely, by someone reported by Edwards in *Gangraena* (1646). From this milieu were to come the ideas of Ranters, Quakers, Muggletonians and many others, as well as of Winstanley and the Diggers.[57]

Winstanley rejected the doctrine of original sin. He has been classed with Richard Coppin as one of the first English universalists, who taught that all men would be saved.[58] They may have been the first to make the positive point in print; but the heresy was attributed to Elizabethan Familists, and John Penry said in 1587 that such beliefs were popular. They were held in Essex in 1592 and in 1646.[59] General Baptists preached universal redemption from at least the early seventeenth century. Belief that perfection could be attained in this life was attributed to London tradesmen in 1549, to Elizabethan Familists, and to Yorkshire Grindletonians in the 1620s. William Walwyn, Henry Denne, Mrs Attaway and William Jenny in the mid-sixteen-forties, were said to believe that it could not stand with the goodness of God to damn his creatures eternally. Tobias Crisp thought sin was finished; so did many Ranters.[60] The young Thomas Browne was a universalist as well as a mortalist. Giles Randall and

John Saltmarsh preached perfectibility on earth in the sixteen-forties, and Saltmarsh toyed with the idea of universal salvation.[61] Samuel Fisher tells us in 1653 that rejection of original sin was popular.[62] So when we find *Tyranipocrit Discovered* in 1649, Richard Coppin, Ranters and George Fox in the sixteen-fifties, and John Milton, holding similar beliefs, we need not attribute them to Winstanley's influence.[63] Even when Coppin and Milton speak of a Paradise within, happier far than the garden of Eden, to be attained in this life, we need not necessarily postulate Winstanley's influence, though we should note the similarity.[64]

The doctrine of perfectibility on earth is linked by Winstanley with the idea of the Sonship of all believers. This of course derives from the New Testament, and is to be found in orthodox Puritans. "If God be a Father and we are brethren", wrote Richard Sibbes, "it is a levelling doctrine".[65] In the sixteenth and seventeenth centuries Hermeticism contributed to the conception. *Pimander*, published in John Everard's translation in 1650, taught that men can again become like gods on earth;[66] Paracelsus held that man could become the Son of God and be united to God — a state higher than that of the angels.[67] So again the fact that — after Winstanley — Erbery, Morgan Llwyd, Ranters, Quakers and Milton held similar beliefs is no evidence of influence.[68] The idea that God was to be found within man was familiar to Familists, Boehme, John Everard, John Saltmarsh, Thomas Collier, Joseph Salmon, William Erbery, Jacob Bauthumley, Richard Coppin, John Pordage and Quakers.[69]

Fox proclaimed that he was the Son of God. As men became the Sons of God, "this would bring them into unity with the Son and with the Father".[70] James Nayler agreed that "the saints are all one in the Father and the Son". Nayler denied that Fox had claimed to be Christ, but did not query his assertion that, as a saint, he was "the judge of the world".[71] Fox spoke of "a teacher within thee, the anointing".[72] Samuel Rutherford attributed the phrase "the state of perfection or anointing" to the Familist leader Henry Niklaes.[73] A pamphlet of 1642 attacked those who "will turn a monarchy into a democracy" by claiming that the people are the Lord's Anointed.[74] George Wither and John Milton both referred to the elect as the Lord's Anointed.[75] In 1655 Richard Overton associated "the anointing" with anti-Trinitarianism.[76]

If the significant Christ is the Christ in us, then the Christ who died at Jerusalem diminishes in importance. Thomas Webbe made this point before Winstanley, and George Wither, John Pordage and many others after him.[77] Familists had long been accused of allegorizing the Scriptures, of making the Fall, the resurrection and the last judgment take place in this life only.[78] Mrs Anne Hutchinson was alleged to believe there was no resurrection but union to Christ Jesus.[79] John Everard, John Saltmarsh and Giles Randall before Winstanley, and William Erbery, Richard Coppin, Ranters and Quakers after him, taught similar doctrines. "Thou needest not go to Rome, Canterbury or Westminster", wrote Joseph Salmon in 1647, before Winstanley said something very similar, "but thou mayst find that Adam in thee, denying Jesus Christ to be come in thy flesh". "Thy heart is the temple where this great Whore sitteth". The day of judgment took place within each individual.[80] John Warr in 1648 thought that "the end of the world", "the resurrection from the dead" and "the world to come" all referred to changes in this life. "The highest pitch of a Christian life is Christ risen, or rather sitting at the right hand of God".[81] God "as really and substantially dwells in the flesh of other men and creatures as well as in the man Christ", declared Bauthumley in 1650. Where God dwells is "all the heaven I look ever to enjoy". At about the same time Richard Coppin taught that we come to a right knowledge of God through his resurrection in us, and then we have a fuller revelation than prophets and Apostles, returning to "a more excellent state" than the Paradise which Adam lost.[82]

Christ's coming in the flesh was but a figure, declared the Quaker Richard Hubberthorne. Bunyan in 1656-8 accused Ranters and Quakers of mocking the Second Coming.[83] For Collier and Erbery the Second Coming was "God appearing in the saints", who would rule on earth and judge the world.[84] John Cook argued that the court which sentenced Charles I "was a resemblance and representation of the great day of judgment, when the saints shall judge all worldly powers". John Canne and John Milton agreed with him.[85] For Ranters, Christ's Second Coming meant "his coming into man by his spirit", and that only.[86] Clarkson expected to "know nothing after this my being was dissolved".[87]

To men who thought along these lines, heaven and hell ceased to be geographical locations — an idea which the Copernican astronomy had already called in question. Elizabethan Familists had taught that heaven and hell were to be found in this world only, that the devil was not a real person.[88] Boehme also held that heaven and hell were in the conscience, doctrine later repeated by John Everard, Mrs Attaway, William Jenny, Richard Overton, William Walwyn and many others.[89] The young Thomas Browne disbelieved in a local hell.[90] In 1651 Henry Newcome in Cheshire was invoking the Rump's Blasphemy Act against an intruder who taught that God and hell existed only within the soul of man.[91] Clarkson rejected both God and the devil.[92] John Reeve thought that "the bottomless pit . . . is in a man and not without a man".[93] Jacob Bauthumley and Richard Coppin were accused of holding similar views.[94] Sir Henry Vane rejected the idea of a material hell.[95] "There is no knowledge of heaven or hell", said Nayler, in words which may echo Winstanley or Clarkson.[96] What was new in Winstanley was the vigour with which, in *The Law of Freedom*, he denounced the evil effects on men and women of the fear of hell and the hope of heaven.[97]

If Christ was within men, then either men were gods or Christ was not God. The logical conclusion of elevating man to Sonship was to stress the humanity of Christ to the exclusion of his divinity. Anti-Trinitarianism has a long history in England, going back to the Lollards, the Marian martyrs, Familists and the last two heretics to be burned in England, in 1612. In the sixteen-forties the heresy was common among Baptists. It was shared by Milton. Again Winstanley was only one of many.[98]

Another consequence of the doctrine of Sonship was rejection of a separate clerical caste, insistence that laymen (and sometimes women) may preach, that a godly mechanic preacher is better than a university-trained hireling, that "experience is a copy written by the Spirit of God upon the hearts of believers".[99] Consequently the tithes which maintained parish ministers should be abolished. Evidence of such anti-clericalism in the sixteen-forties and early sixteen-fifties is overwhelming.[100] Winstanley and Milton are two of the fiercest exponents of an attitude which extended from Oliver Cromwell to William Walwyn.[101]

Hence rejection of the state church and its ordinances. These matters were much discussed in the late sixteen-forties and in the sixteen-fifties.[102] Coppe, Clarkson, Muggleton and "Jock of Broad Scotland" agreed with Winstanley in rejecting prayers; Salmon, Reeve, Erbery, Colonel Hutchinson, Milton and early Quakers agreed with him in withdrawing from church worship.[103] Another consequence was the passionate belief in liberty of conscience which Winstanley shared with Milton, Walwyn, Overton, Reeve and so

many of the radicals.[104] Even when severely critical of the Ranters,
Winstanley insisted that they were to be reasoned with, not forcibly
repressed.[105] He had been attacking antinomian immoralism as early
as 1648 — those who say "that which was sin formerly ... is now no
sin while thou art under the law of love".[106] But rejection of the law of
Moses was often taught — by Saltmarsh and Milton as well as by
Winstanley, Coppe and Clarkson.[107]

Mortalism, the doctrine that the soul sleeps from death till the
general resurrection (or dies with the body) frequently accompanied
anti-Trinitarianism and rejection of a local hell. The heresy extended
from Lollards through Familists to Richard Overton, Clement
Wrighter, Mrs Attaway and William Jenny, Winstanley, Agricola
Carpenter, Ranters, Muggletonians and Milton. Winstanley seems
to me to imply mortalism in *The Mysterie of God*,[108] but his
expression of it was not specific until 1652.

The mortalist doctrine that at death the body returns to the
elements of which it was composed occurs in the Hermetic writings.
Richard Overton, Winstanley, Bauthumley, Clarkson and the
author of *Annotations upon All the Books of the Old and New
Testaments* (1657) may all have got it from this source. An extreme
version of mortalism was annihilationism — denial of any ultimate
resurrection. This doctrine was being taught in London in the early
sixteen-forties — long before Winstanley or Clarkson had written; in
1646 it was held by "some whole troops in the Army", Edwards
thought.[109] Bunyan accused Quakers of denying the resurrection of
the body.[110]

Another Hermeticist doctrine was that matter could not exist
apart from God, from which it derived. The visible universe was the
demiurge, the second God.[111] Winstanley, like Milton, believed that
matter was created *ex deo*, not *ex nihilo*. George Fox's desire for
unity with the creation, whether or not he got it via Winstanley, was
almost certainly Hermeticist. Fox admitted to having been tempted
to believe, as the Ranters did, that there is no God and that all comes
by nature.[112] Bacon had taught that "to look for a first cause beyond
the chain of natural causes is to abandon the principle of causation
and to fly from solid knowledge into a realm of fantasy" — words
which Winstanley appears to echo.[113] William Harvey recalls both
writers when he told men not to look beyond the elements of which
the body is compounded, nor "to fly up to heaven to fetch down I
know not what spirits", to whom they ascribe "these divine opera-

tions" of the blood.[114] Winstanley, like the Ranters, believed that God was in all things, that the creation was the clothing of God. But this did not lead him to the pantheistic emphasis of Servetus in the sixteenth century and Jacob Bauthumley in the seventeenth (God is in "dog, cat, chair, stool", as well as in men). Winstanley's interest was mainly in God in humanity: on the title-page of *The Mysterie of God* he equated "the whole creation" with "mankind".[115]

Winstanley may have got his doctrine that God is a purging fire, burning up the evil in men, from John Everard. Everard believed that God was the sun, and no doubt took the idea from Hermes Trismegistus, whom he translated.[116] It was repeated by Saltmarsh and Coppin, and hinted at by George Fox.[117] The equation of God and Reason was another Hermeticist doctrine which Winstanley was using as early as 1648, together with the idea that Reason in men is itself drawn from the substance of God, so that those men and women in whom it is found are approaching the divine.[118] Winstanley might also have found the identification of God and Reason in Richard Overton's *Mans Mortalitie*. The Ranters were said to identify God and Reason too.[119] In 1648, a very sophisticated version of this doctrine appeared in John Warr's *Administrations, Civil and Spiritual*. For Warr, Equity or Reason is a divine principle in a man, telling him to "do as thou wouldst be done unto". When Reason rules within, "man becomes a law unto himself". "Reason hath been long out of the throne", replaced by Form. But "God himself is on Reason's side". Reason "is content to tarry the Lord's leisure"; but when the time comes, "Reason shall ride in triumph in the spirits of men". "When Reason ... rises from the dead" it will mean "the destruction of the world, or the present state of things". "When Equity itself comes, then the order, government and majesty thereof shall command the spirits of all ... . This will be a glorious time indeed", when every man shall be "a complete resemblance of divine wisdom, goodness and love". Till then "we shall never attain to perfect freedom".[120] Although it is impossible to be confident who influenced whom, Winstanley seems to have developed Warr's ideas.[121]

Winstanley held that the rising of Christ in sons and daughters was the victory of Jacob over Esau, of Abel over Cain, of the younger over the elder brother. This picked up a traditional popular metaphor, which Boehme used and which George Smith employed in 1645.[122] Mrs Attaway and William Jenny distinguished between

Esau's world and Jacob's world. When the latter replaced the former, then all creatures would be saved.[123] Coppe in 1649, Bauthumley in 1650, Wither in 1653, Vane in 1658, George Fox, Lodowick Muggleton and John Bunyan, all made use of the metaphor.[124]

Thus although Winstanley's theology had led him to very radical positions before the end of 1648, these views came out of a common pool of heretical ideas. What was uniquely novel in Winstanley was his association of the doctrine of Sonship with community of property, and the way in which he combined other ideas from the radical heritage into a single coherent theory. There was of course nothing new in advocacy of communal ownership, from John Ball through sixteenth-century Anabaptists to Walwyn, Coppe, Foster, Pordage and the author of *Tyranipocrit Discovered*.[125] Sir Thomas More had thought that communist ideas went naturally with anti-Trinitarianism.[126] The Hermeticist literature frequently attacked property, and argued that communion or fellowship drives out cupidity.[127] John Everard thought that not only "selfness" but also "property must be taken away".[128] It was a commonplace in orthodox Puritan writings that Sonship gave a special right to earthly possessions. In Jesus Christ, wrote John Ball, the author of *A Treatise of Faith*, "a son-like right and title to the creatures is restored, which by sin and disobedience was forfeited". Milton insisted that "the liberty we have in Christ" restores us "in some competent measure to a right to every good thing, both of this life and the other".[129] But in Winstanley this becomes something very different.

We now turn to the tracts in which Winstanley expressed his communist ideas.

IV

WINSTANLEY'S TRANCE

Before 1648 Winstanley had been through a period in which he was "a blind professor and strict goer to church, as they call it, and a hearer of sermons". He then "believed as the learned clergy ... believed". At some stage he had joined a Baptist church, but did not find satisfaction there.[130] It was after his financial ruin and flight to the country that he took to writing theological pamphlets. He may perhaps have been excommunicated either from his parish church or by a gathered congregation.[131] Aware possibly of a lack of verbal fluency to expound the tumultuous and complex ideas that were welling up inside him, he started to write in an obsessive way.[132] He had had trouble with the clergy in the Cobham area well before the digging began. This was, we must recall, before the 1650 Act had accepted the fact that it was no longer possible to force people to attend their parish churches if they did not want to. *Truth Lifting up its Head* is Winstanley's reply to accusations of blasphemy, of denying God and the Trinity, the Scriptures and all ordinances, brought against him and William Everard. Such charges might have carried a death sentence under the Blasphemy Ordinance of 1648, which became ineffective only after the Army's seizure of power in December of that year.

In *The Saints Paradise* Winstanley tells us that God sometimes speaks inwardly to believers, by voice, vision, dream or revelation.[133] In *The New Law of Righteousness* he claimed to have received in a trance the messages "Work together, Eat bread together"; "Let Israel go free; Israel shall neither give nor take hire".[134] I have been taken to task for suggesting that this may have been a seventeenth-century way of referring to a moment of clarification in a process of deep meditation.[135] But the *Oxford English Dictionary* appears to confirm this interpretaiton, quoting seventeenth-century examples of *trance* as meaning "a state of mental abstraction from external things". Richard Baxter described exactly this state; Sir Isaac Newton had similar trance-like revelations.[136] I referred to Lord Herbert of Cherbury, Descartes and Pascal (as well as Fox and Bunyan), in order to indicate that such claims were commonly made by men who are not normally regarded as religious mystics. I might have added John Sadler, friend of Milton and member of the Council of State, who was said to have had "a vision and a trance for three days together", holding communion with angels.[137] The phenomenon is of course familiar to anthropologists.[138] The Whig politician and financier, Goodwin Wharton, willed himself to hear divine voices in 1686 and later. This was at a time of tension, when he had attempted to solve his problems by communicating with God through his mistress, Mary Parish. Wharton undoubtedly believed that God spoke to him, both in dreams and in "waking visions"; he was taken aback by God's use of four-letter words and by his recommendation that Wharton commit incest.[139]

I am not quite sure what alternative explanation is proposed. That

Winstanley did receive a direct divine message? That would be difficult to prove. For a man to say "God hath spoken to him in a dream", as Hobbes put it in 1651, "is no more than to say he dreamed that God spake to him".[140] Winstanley himself contrasted "speaking inwardly ... by voice, vision, dream or revelation" with speaking "by the voice of a material man, standing before him". Milton's muse, we must suppose, did not speak "by the voice of a material woman". The authors of "Winstanley: A Case for the Man as He Said He Was" go so far as to speak of "a dialogue" between Winstanley and "a real visible God who could appear and speak to him with a real visible voice". The passage to which they refer, so far from describing the miracle of a dialogue with "a real visible voice", has Winstanley conducting a monologue "within my heart".[141]

If we do not accept a supernatural explanation, it is not enough merely to say that Winstanley had a mystical experience, as though that ended the matter. It is pertinent to ask why Winstanley, why in the winter of 1648-9, why this particular message. We know that he had the habit of working very intensively, forsaking "my ordinary food whole days together", ignoring cold when "the power of that overflowing anointing" took hold of him.[142] Most of us know from our own experience that when one has wrestled with an intractable problem for some time it may suddenly appear to solve itself, as though in a flash of intuition. For Winstanley the peat-cutting incident of 1646 may have initiated, or may have been part of, an intellectual wrestle with the compatibility of private property and communal welfare. And, we might add, we have Winstanley's own later statement of the ways in which traditional religion could make people believe they had seen visions.[143]

We know too that Winstanley thought it important that significant truths should be "a free revelation" from within, not taken from books or at second hand from the mouth of any flesh. "I have writ nothing but what was given me of my Father", he assured his fellow-Lancastrians in 1648.[144] (The Father, let us recall, is Reason within each one of us). In so far as Winstanley thought of himself at this stage as a prophet of God, some such form of communication as a vision or trance was appropriate to give special authority to the words spoken.[145] He was after all announcing a *new* law of righteousness, "that is to be writ in every man's heart, and acted by every man's hand", and would supersede the traditional Scriptures. It was necessary to support so major an undertaking "by vision, voice and revelation"; the later choice of St George's Hill for the digging was similarly supported.[146]

There are also factors which may have a bearing on the time of the trance. In *The New Law of Righteousness*, dated 26 January 1648/9, Winstanley said that it had occurred "not long since".[147] The winter of 1648-9 was a particularly cruel one. The disruption of the civil war had been followed by a succession of bad harvests; men were said to be starving in London. The economic crisis exacerbated and was exacerbated by the political crisis. The Army seized power in December; Charles I was executed four days after Winstanley had signed his preface to *The New Law*. Leveller agitation was at its height; it was soon to lead to Army mutinies. Radical ideas for relieving the poor were expressed by the regiment of horse for the county of Northumberland at the beginning of December, and by many others.[148]

Also at the beginning of December *Light Shining in Buckinghamshire* had drawn on Winstanley's (or Warr's) theology to define Reason in all men as the principle of co-operation, of doing as you would be done by. If Winstanley read the pamphlet — as is surely likely — he could have learned from it that men had certain birthright privileges, which included enjoyment of "the creatures, without property one more than another"; and he would have noticed the phrase "kingly power", which he was to use to good effect later. He might also have observed a reference to "freeholders which had their freedom of the Normans" and to the desirability of using church, crown and forest lands for the poor.[149] *Light Shining* is much more specifically anti-monarchical than Winstanley's early writings, more explicitly pro-Leveller; and it attacks the privileges of corporations in the name of property rights in a way Winstanley never did. A later pamphlet from the same group of Buckinghamshire Levellers promised help to the Digger colony, which had then been in existence for a month.[150] The three Buckinghamshire pamphlets were almost certainly not written by Winstanley; but it is difficult to suppose that he did not read them. They were produced, after all, less than forty miles from Cobham.

The point I wish to stress is that, whatever we make of Winstanley's trance, it is unlikely that his ideas were as completely original as he wished to suggest. His theological emphasis on Sonship was almost a commonplace in the radical milieu; communist ideas had been floating around for some time, and were appearing in print in the starvation winter of 1648-9. Winstanley put the two together.

But the juxtaposition led to novel conclusions. Sonship extends to all men and women, and the title to the creatures (that is, the right to enjoy what God has made as a common treasury for all) is a "creation-right" to be exercised collectively rather than individually.[151] The privilege and benefit of Sonship is to have free access to cultivate the earth. "The glorious liberty of the Sons of God", the Iver Digger pamphlet put it, "is equality, community and fellowship with our own kind".[152] If Winstanley's communism is immanent in his early theological tracts, we shall have to ask whether it was also immanent in the writings of all those others whom I have cited, with whom Winstanley had so much in common. Was their failure to press on to Winstanley's conclusion due to a failure of nerve? Or did Winstanley's experience as an unsuccessful merchant pushed down into the ranks of wage labourers force conclusions upon him? Or must we attribute it all to the caprice of that "visible voice"? These are difficult, perhaps unanswerable questions.[153]

From *The New Law of Righteousness*, his first tract after his trance, it appears that Winstanley expected a transformation of society to come swiftly and peaceably as a consequence of Christ rising in sons and daughters. Poor men and women (and not only the poor) would see what was the reasonable way out of their desperate situation. Universal love, as Winstanley put it in *A New-Yeers Gift*, will "make mankind to be all of one heart and one mind, and make the earth to be a common treasury".[154]

The pamphlets which Winstanley poured out during the next eighteen months were almost all propagandist appeals to specific audiences — *Letters* to Fairfax for the Army, *An Appeal* to the House of Commons, *A Watch-Word* for London and the Army, *A New-Yeers Gift* for Parliament and Army. Most important for our purposes is *Fire in the Bush*, whose date has now been established as the middle of March 1650: that is to say, towards the end of the Digger colony's existence. This date has proved embarrassing for those who wish to play down the theological element in Winstanley's thought.[155] But from our perspective there is no problem. *Fire in the Bush* appeared shortly after Winstanley had reprinted his first five tracts, with a preface stressing the continuity between his theological and his communist writings.[156] *Fire in the Bush* was written for the churches. It is possible that it may have been drafted earlier,[157] but Winstanley may well have felt in March 1650 that his recent propagandist writings had become excessively preoccupied with historical and legal arguments. He no doubt wished to sort out and complete his fusion of theology with economics, at a time when he was becoming aware that the Digger colony might fail.

Fire in the Bush is in no sense a retreat to "merely" religious themes; it is as fiery and fierce as any of his pamphlets, from its introductory denunciation of hypocrisy, in terms worthy of Milton, and of "murdering property". Jesus Christ is "the true and faithful Leveller". The God whom priests and professors worship is the devil. Law is "but the declarative will of conquerors, how they will have their subjects to be ruled". Winstanley admits that his doctrine "will destroy all property and all trading", all existing government, ministry and religion.[158] The tract ends by defining the two greatest sins in the world. "First for a man to lock up the treasuries of the earth in chests and houses ... while others starve for want to whom it belongs, and it belongs to all". Secondly, "for any man or men first to take the earth by the power of the murdering sword from others; and then by the laws of their own making do hang or put to death any who takes the fruits of the earth to supply his necessaries". *Fire in the Bush* is not different in spirit from *An Appeale to All Englishmen*, issued at the end of March 1650 as a last broadside appeal to the common people, "whether tenants or labouring men", provocatively inciting them to illegal action. "Will you be slaves and beggars still, when you may be free men? Stand up for your freedom in the land by acting with plough and spade upon the commons".[159] If we read *Fire in the Bush* carefully, we can I think detect in it some of Winstanley's answers to the weaker brethren in the Digger commune who were tempted to despair. Defeat need not mean surrender: it was the theme of Milton's *Paradise Regained*, of Bunyan's *The Holy War*.[160]

Professor Hudson argued that the Diggers "did not conceive of their venture as a means of affecting social change"; "the peace they experienced in their hearts was the *final* justification of the digging" (my italics).[161] One wonders how he knew that. It is not what Winstanley said. "The first reason is this, that we may ... lay the foundation of making the earth a common treasury for all". To fail to act was to "consent still to hold the creation down under bondage". "I command thee, to let Israel go free".[162] "As the Scriptures threaten misery to rich men ...surely all those threatenings shall be materially fulfilled, for they shall be turned out of all".[163] Clearly the Diggers' enemies did not regard them as merely making symbolic gestures. From *The True Levellers Standard Advanced* onwards

Winstanley called for rejection of landlordism and an economic revolution. "That Scripture which saith 'The poor shall inherit the earth' is really and materially to be fulfilled", he told Parliament, Army and preachers in *A New-Yeers Gift*. The transition would be peaceful, for "the people shall all fall off from you", and follow the Levellers; but in the colony's last weeks Winstanley was inciting to disobedience, and ominously repeating the denunciation of idle gentry to be found in the *Light Shining* pamphlets.[164] In March 1650 a new colony had been started at Wellingborough, with some co-operation from local farmers and in contact with the Diggers. It produced its own pamphlet. In May another pamphlet appeared from the colony at Iver, Buckinghamshire, the title of which was almost identical with that from Wellingborough. It revealed that in all some ten colonies had been set up, with others in prospect; Digger emissaries met with a successful reception in many places in the midlands.[165] The movement was spreading: it was time to respond to the demands of local landowners by suppressing the headquarters at Cobham.

The message that Winstanley received in his trance was that men should break bread together and work together, and that they should not take hire. They should live and work in community, rejecting wage labour.[166] It is important to grasp the significance of the second part of the divine message, for it was essential to the first. Winstanley always proclaimed that the Diggers had no intention of expropriat-ing landlords: they should retain their enclosures, and the common people should cultivate the common lands, paying no rent for them.[167] But in so far as the ban on wage labour became effective — that is, as the spirit rose in sons and daughters — so the gentry would be unable to get their enclosures cultivated: they would effectively own no more than they could cultivate themselves, so living "freed from the straits of povety and oppression".[168] The point is spelt out most clearly by Robert Coster.[169] It was not expropriation, but it would have amounted to a piecemeal deprivation of the profits of ownership. So Winstanley's provision for the gentry to receive compensation if they wished to throw their lands into the common stock was a hard-headed realistic proposal: a life annuity in return for surrendering a capital asset on which no return could be expected.[170]

Moreover the Digger claim to common lands, for which no rent was to be paid, came to include the demand originally put forward in *Light Shining in Buckinghamshire* for confiscated church, crown and forest lands; and (in *The Law of Freedom*) for monastic lands too.[171] Realization of this claim would have amounted to a large-scale act of expropriation. To work "for another, either for wages or to pay him rent" lifts up the curse; "by denying to labour for hire ... men join hands with Christ, to lift up the creation from bondage" and restore "all things from the curse".[172] The common land is the due of the poor both "by right of creation and by the laws of a commonwealth".[173] Copyholds were "parcels hedged in and taken out of the common waste since the conquest"; the poor should be as free in them as lords of manors in their land after the abolition of feudal tenures.[174]

In *The New Law of Righteousness* the emphasis was still internal, but by April 1649 communal cultivation of the earth had for Winstanley become central to the overthrow of the curse. "All the prophecies, visions and revelations of Scriptures, of prophets and apostles, concerning the calling of the Jews, the restoration of Israel and making of that people the inheritors of the whole earth, doth all rest themselves in the work of making the earth a common treasury".[175] Private property in land is "rebellion and high treason against the King of Righteousness".[176] If they perished in the attempt, the Diggers told Fairfax, they would "die doing our duty to our Creator, by endeavouring from that power he hath put into our hearts to lift up his creation out of bondage". "True religion and undefiled is this, to make restitution of the earth".[177]

This conviction that they were about the Lord's work, and that Christ was already rising in sons and daughters, gave the Diggers a naïve confidence not only in the persuasiveness of their words and example, but also that, as they told Fairfax, the earth would be made fruitful when the curse was removed from the creation.[178] But manuring was part of cultivation: "true religion and undefiled", Winstanley came to think, "is to let everyone quietly have earth to manure, that they may live in freedom in their labours". To withhold it from them is sin.[179]

V

FROM RIGHTEOUSNESS TO FREEDOM

Winstanley devoted considerable attention to his titles: each contains something programmatic.[180] It is therefore not altogether without significance that his writings after his trance begin with *The New Law of Righteousness* and end with *The Law of Freedom*: a transition from theology to politics. In each case the law concerned is the law of Reason. Winstanley's intellectual evolution is towards a realization that lack of freedom impedes the rise of Reason within men and women. It is inadequate to say that "to Winstanley the only freedom that mattered was freedom from economic insecurity", or to deny to him any "respect for the individual" [181] and his freedom. This travesties the thought of the man who wrote "freedom is the man that will turn the world upside down"; "freedom is Christ in you and among you".[182] Like many thinkers after him Winstanley came to appreciate that it is not possible to be fully human so long as one is hungry, or indeed so long as anyone else is unnecessarily hungry. It is true Winstanley thought "there cannot be a universal liberty till this community be established". But freedom meant rather more than Mr Davis suggests. It is the rule of Reason, "the appearance of Christ in the earth". "When men are sure of food and raiment, their reason will be ripe, and ready to dive into the secrets of the creation".[183] In his final pamphlet Winstanley declared that "all the inward bondages of the mind" are "occasioned by the outward bondage that one sort of people lay upon one another".[184] It is a remarkable statement of apparent social determinism. This section attempts to explain how Winstanley's thinking about communism, which started from a vision, arrived at this anticipation of socialist materialism. The evolution, I believe, is less paradoxical than appears at first sight.[185]

In certain respects Winstanley's theology had advanced since his commitment to digging the commons. He made more precise his idea of the Second Coming as the rising of Christ in sons and daughters. The very extent of oppression and bondage was for him evidence that "it is the fullness of time for Jacob to arise. Extreme necessity calls for the great work of restoration". "We dig upon the commons to make the earth a common treasury", Winstanley told Fairfax, "because our necessity for food and raiment requires it".[186] Digging was no mere symbol: it was a political act, part of the rising of Christ in sons and daughters which would establish a just commonwealth on earth.[187] "Now the man of Righteousness shall take the kingdom". "The righteous judge will sit upon the throne in every man and woman", and this will be "the day of judgment". "The material earth shall be his possession".[188] "A few years now will let all the world see

who is strongest, love or hatred, freedom or bondage".[189] "Before
many years pass: ... I can set no time", wrote Winstanley less
confidently ten months later, in April 1650.[190]

> And to the Son the Father hath
> All judgment given now

sang Robert Coster, having made it clear that the Son is Jacob, the
younger brother. The Lord will make

> All tyrants servants to the Son
> And he the power will take.[191]

"The rising up of Christ in sons and daughters", Winstanley tells
us as explicitly as possible, "is his Second Coming". "His ... Second
Coming in the flesh ... is justice and judgment ruling in man". This
spirit in "whole mankind ... becomes the alone King of Righteousness", who is "not one single person". It is difficult to understand
how anyone who has read these passages can argue that Winstanley
postulated "a literal Second Coming" of "a real personal Christ",
"an external Christ" and "a God who existed beyond the realm of
men and nature", "whose intervention was essential".[192] If we must
use the technical terms of twentieth-century theology, Winstanley
knew no transcendent God, only immanent Reason. Only if we
forget that the Father is Reason and that Christ's Second Coming is
in sons and daughters can we slip into thinking of an external God.
We must continually pay close attention to what Winstanley says,
and especially to his definition of terms. Professor C.H. George has
demonstrated Winstanley's cavalier use of proof texts: they often
make his point only if we assume the very special meaning which he
gives to a term like the Second Coming, or to the liberation of the
Jews signifying the establishment of a communist society in England.
They make the point, that is to say, only if we assume it in advance.
Winstanley uses Scripture to bolster up a position which he has
already adopted.[193] The novelty came in *The True Levellers Standard
Advanced*, where Winstanley specifically equated the rising Christ
with Jacob the younger brother, "the poor people" who would be
"the Saviours of the land". It is repeated in *Fire in the Bush*: Christ
dwells among the poor, "Christ levelling".[194]

It is in this context that we must set Winstanley's conception of

himself as a prophet, the mouthpiece of God. Jacob, Moses and
David were Christ.[195] "Christ in that one body", the historical Jesus
Christ, was "a great prophet". So is the man today who has "the light
and power of Christ within".[196] Winstanley saw himself as one of the
Sons in whom Christ had risen in these last days. It was his duty to
proclaim the message of the Father, for the benefit of others in whom
Christ was still to rise. His duty was not to preach, as hirelings did;
but to testify, so that those who had the spirit of Reason within them
could try Winstanley's spirit.[197] ("Oh that all the Lord's people were
prophets!"). Hence the importance for Winstanley of stressing that
"what I have spoken I have not received from books nor study, but
freely I have received and freely I have declared what I have received".[198] for this was the *new* law of righteousness which would
replace the old: the message from Christ rising in sons and daughters,
before which Christ in one single person would fall back.

In *The New Law of Righteousness* and the pamphlets which
followed, Winstanley envisaged the day of judgment more clearly as
an internal event occurring to every man and woman during their
lifetime, rather than as the end of the world.[199] He rejected Biblical
history more firmly in favour of allegorical interpretations. "The
public preachers have cheated the whole world by telling us of a single
man called Adam, that killed us all by eating a single fruit called an
apple".[200] There is no need "to go up into heaven above the skies to
find Christ". In this world "few are saved, that is enter into rest and
peace". To say that all will be saved means that all will "live in peace
and rest". "The outward heaven ... is a fancy, which your false
teachers put into your heads to please you with while they pick your
purses". Heaven and hell are within us: we make our own hell.
Heaven is "a comfortable livelihood in the earth". "The glory of
Jerusalem" is not "to be seen hereafter, after the body is laid in the
dust": the Diggers expected "Glory here!" "Whether there was any
such outward things" as the Bible related "or no, it matters not
much".[201] The Fall, the Virgin birth, the resurrection, the ascension,
the Second Coming are likewise treated as allegories.[202] Professor
Pocock, whose asides on Winstanley are very much to the point, said
that for him "community of ownership of the earth and the resurrection of Christ are interchangeable concepts".[203] The War in Heaven
"wherein Michael and the Dragon fights the great battle of God
Almighty" takes place within "the living soul": we are reminded of
Milton's

> What if earth
> Be but the shadow of heaven, and things therein
> Each to other like, more than on earth is thought?[204]

Winstanley advances to a more secure Bibilical criticism, possibly based on Clement Wrighter but more probably drawing on general sceptical discussions in radical circles.[205] Whether the earth should be free for all men and women to cultivate, Winstanley told Fairfax, is a question "not to be answered by any text of Scripture, or example since the Fall, but the answer is to be given in the light of itself, which is the law of righteousness, or that word of God that was in the beginning, which dwells in man's heart and by which he was made, even the pure law of creation". Arguments drawn from Biblical texts thus cut no ice with Winstanley himself, though he used them for specific audiences whom they might influence, as in *An Humble Request*. He virtually abandoned them in *The Law of Freedom*, where he adopted the position of Henry Parker and Milton, that we must interpret the Bible by reason, and not attribute to the Creator intentions contrary to the good of man, including his temporal good.[206] Winstanley's patronizing phrase, "there are good rules in Scripture if they were obeyed and practised", reminds one of Milton's "I am not one of those who consider the decalogue a faultless moral code".[207]

The New Law of Righteousness is perhaps a little more specific than its predecessors in asserting that the spirit shall "in these last days be sent into whole mankind", that "there is not a person or creature within the compass of the globe but he is a Son of the Father". The blessing which lies hid in Jacob "must be the alone Saviour and joy of all men", Winstanley assured "the twelve tribes of Israel".[208] Jacob, Moses and David will rise and reign in sons and daughters, who will live in the kingdom of heaven on earth.[209] Then "as Moses gave way to Christ", so the historical Christ will give way to the spreading of the spirit in sons and daughters. This will be the true Second Coming. "The spreading power of righteousness and wisdom" is to be "set ... in the chair"; "the ministration of Christ in one single person is to be silent and draw back". "Perfect man shall be no other but God manifest in the flesh".[210]

In the day of Christ, Winstanley had written in *Truth Lifting up its Head*, all created flesh shall be made subject to Reason, "so that the Spirit, which is the Father, may become all in all, the chief ruler in flesh". "Those sons and daughters in whom the Spirit rests cannot be deceived, but judge all things".[211] When "the Spirit ... manifested in flesh ... draws all things back again into himself", then "the Son delivers up the kingdom to the Father; and he that is the spreading power, *not one single person*, becomes all in all in every person, that is the King of Righteousness in every one" (my italics). Then Moses and Christ will both yield place "as the earth grows up to be a common treasury for all", for the King of Righteousness will dwell in everyone, "the alone King in that living soul, on earth; or the five living senses".[212] The point could hardly be made more explicitly. As communist society develops, Christ and the Bible will be superseded, and there will be no authority greater than that of Reason in each human being, which alone can be called God.

What has been added to Winstanley's pre-1648 theology is the equation of the Second Coming with the establishment of a communist society on earth. In *Fire in the Bush*, when Winstanley writes "Christ the anointing spirit ... comes to set all free", he makes it quite clear that liberty includes free access to cultivate the earth.[213] But we must watch Winstanley's use of words rather carefully, since under the 1648 Blasphemy Ordinance he cannot express himself with complete freedom. In *Truth Lifting up its Head*, where he was defending himself against charges of blasphemy, for instance, he wrote: "I pray continually, calling upon the name of the Lord, in the manner I declared before". But the manner he declared before is in fact a rejection of prayer in the normal sense of the word. His statement, "I do walk in the daily practice of such ordinances of God as Reason and Scriptures do warrant", must be interpreted in the light of his rejection of prayer, preaching, holy communion, baptism, Sabbath observance.[214]

In *A New-Yeers Gift*, *Fire in the Bush* and *The Law of Freedom* Winstanley drew an analogy, which perhaps would not have occurred to him earlier, between the Calvinist doctrine that "some are elected to salvation, and others are reprobated" and the inheritance law of "the kingly power". But Christ, "the true and faithful Leveller", "will have all saved, that is, will have all live in peace and rest".[215] To speak of "Christ, the great prophet" only confirms the anti-Trinitarianism of the earlier tracts.[216]

"This particular property of mine and thine", Winstanley wrote in *The New Law of Righteousness*, "hath brought in all misery upon the people".[217] "When self-love began to arise in the earth, then man began to fall". "The Fall of man ... came in by the rising up of covetousness in the heart of mankind". "When mankind began to buy and sell, then did he fall from his innocency".[218] Winstanley's emphasis all through is on private property in land, on treating land as a commodity. "The first step of the Fall" came when "the stronger or elder brother" claimed a larger part of the earth than his younger brother; the second step was "to enclose parcels of the earth" as private property, which then were bought and sold. "When mankind began to quarrel about the earth, and some would have all and shut out others, forcing them to be servants: this was man's fall".[219] When Adam "consented to that serpent covetousness, then he fell from righteousness, was cursed, and was sent into the earth to eat his bread in sorrow; and from that time began particular property to grow in one man over another".[220] "The law of property is ... as far from the law of Christ as light from darkness".[221] This reverses the orthodox view that private property, inequality, and the state which protects them, were the consequences of eating an apple, however allegorically that action is interpreted. For Winstanley the establishment of private property in land, and freedom to buy and sell it, *was* the Fall; the abolition of private property was therefore necessary if prelapsarian freedom was to be restored. So long as landownership survives, "so long the creation lies under bondage". Any who will truly acknowledge Christ will set the earth free, "for the voice is gone out, freedom, freedom, freedom".[222] The government that maintains private property is "the government of imaginary, self-seeking Antichrist", and "shall be rooted out". "The government of highwaymen" is *The Law of Freedom*'s more succinct summary. "Buying and selling ... both killed Christ and hindered his resurrection" — that is, in sons and daughters. Freedom — "the man that will turn the world upside down" — "is Christ in you"; "this work of digging" is "freedom or the appearance of Christ in the earth".[223]

The New Law of Righteousness had proclaimed that "now the kingdom is delivered into the Father's hand, the one spirit that fills all and is in all"; and "this distinction of dominion in one single person over all shall cease". This is "the new heaven and earth", to be "seen by the material eyes of the flesh", not after death but "here in this earth while bodies are living upon earth".[224] "Kingly power is the old heaven and the old earth that must pass away", and be succeeded by community. The Diggers expected "glory here", on earth.[225]

After the Fall men who get riches and government into their hands aim to "suppress the universal liberty, which is Christ", to bring "the creation under the curse of bondage, sorrow and tears".[226] Landowners naturally become "justices, rulers and state governors, as experience shows". So one part of the creation is forced "to be a slave to another; and thereby the spirit is killed in both". The creation groans under this curse of "civil property", "waiting for deliverance". To maintain the curse, not to struggle against it, is to "sin against light that is given into us, and so through the fear of the flesh, man, lose our peace". Property derives from murder and theft, and is maintained by violence.[227] "By the law of righteousness ... the poorest man hath as true a title and just right to the land as the richest man", and "the earth ought to be a common treasury of livelihood for all, without respecting persons". This is our creation-freedom.[228]

In *The New Law of Righteousness*, Christ spreading himself "in multiplicities of bodies" makes them "all of one heart and mind", acting in righteousness one to another. This unanimity of Reason in community will make government unnecessary.[229] Punishments should be inflicted only in order "to make the offender to know his maker [Reason], and to live in the community of the righteous law of love one with another".[230] By the time of *Truth Lifting up its Head* it is "when once the earth becomes a common treasury again" and mankind has "the law of righteousness once more writ in his heart" that all will be "made of one heart and one mind". Then "the love of Christ in us constrains all men to do his will".[231] "True freedom ... lies in the community in spirit and community in the earthly treasury, and this is Christ, ... spread abroad in the creation".[232] "To live in the enjoyment of Christ", Winstanley put it in *Fire in the Bush*, "will bring in true community and destroy murdering property". The battle is between property or the devil on the one hand, and community, called Christ or universal love, on the other. "There is but bondage and freedom", Winstanley maintained in *The Law of Freedom*, "particular interest or common interest".[233]

From the significantly entitled *The True Levellers Standard Advanced*, the millenarian aspect of Winstanley's thought fades into the background; economics and politics loom larger — the Norman Yoke, the Solemn League and Covenant, kingly power.[234] Or — more correctly perhaps — millenarian theology and politics fuse. The Second Coming, Christ rising in sons and daughters, would be equivalent to establishing "the state of community".[235] "The cause of those they call Diggers is the life and marrow of that cause the Parliament hath declared for, and the Army fought for; the perfecting of which work will prove England to be the first of nations, or the tenth part of the city Babylon that falls off from the Beast first". So ran the title-page of *A New-Yeers Gift*.[236]

Winstanley thus fitted the traditional Leveller theory of the Norman Yoke into his own theology. Overton and other Levellers had already advanced from a claim that Englishmen should be liberated from Norman bondage to a claim that all men had rights as men.[237] This theory appeared in *Light Shining in Buckinghamshire*, which referred to "the whole Norman power" and to "freeholders which had their freedom of the Normans". More specifically, *More Light* referred to "the Norman and Beastly power" — that is, Antichristian power.[238] Three weeks later Winstanley used the theory of the Norman Yoke for the first time; and it is already fused with his doctrine of the English as the chosen people. "The last enslaving conquest which the enemy got over Israel was the Norman over England, . . . killing the poor enslaved English Israelites". Landlords are "the Norman power". In *A Declaration from the Poor Oppressed People*, six weeks later, the argument that the land belongs to the people because of the promises of the Solemn League and Covenant and Parliament's victory over the King is put before the arguments from Scripture and from "the righteous law of our creation", although Winstanley regarded the first two as "our weakest proofs", to be interpreted "in the light of Reason and Equity that dwells in all men's hearts".[239] At this stage he clearly regarded historical and constitutional arguments as secondary to theological, though useful for propaganda purposes.[240]

The stronger argument, for Winstanley, derived from "our privileges given us in our creation, which have hitherto been denied to us, and our fathers, since the power of the sword began to rule".[241] The reformation needed in England was "not to remove the Norman Yoke only" but to restore "the pure law of righteousness before the Fall, . . . and he that endeavours not that is a covenant-breaker". The right to cultivate the earth had been regained "by the law of contract", for all those who had contributed by fighting or by paying taxes "to recover England out of bondage" in the civil war.[242] In *An Appeal to the House of Commons* of July 1649 the emphasis was mainly on historical and legal arguments: tithes are a part of the Norman Yoke.[243]

In *A New-Yeers Gift*, where Winstanley referred to "true public-spirited men called Levellers", the incorporation of the Norman Yoke theory into Winstanley's theology is complete.[244] England has lain "under the power of the Beast, kingly property"; but "if England is to be the tenth part of the city Babylon that falls off from the Beast first", then kingly covetous property must be cast out, and the crown set upon "Christ's head, who is universal love or free community". To restore the creation calls first for "community of mankind, which is comprised in the unity of the spirit of love, which is Christ in you, or the law within the heart, leading mankind into all truth and to be of one heart and one mind"; secondly, for community of the earth. "These two communities, or rather one in two branches, is that true levelling which Christ will work at his more glorious appearance". "Jesus Christ the Saviour of all men is the greatest, first and truest Leveller that ever was spoke of in the world". "Christ comes riding upon these clouds", upon the True Levellers.[245] To restore the earth from the bondage of property to true community "is the work of the true Saviour to do, who is the true and faithful Leveller, even the spirit and power of universal love, that is now rising to spread himself in the whole creation". "His appearance will be with power, ... this great Leveller, Christ our King of Righteousness in us". "Righteous conscience or pure Reason ... is now rising up to bruise the Serpent's head ... He is called the restorer, Saviour, Redeemer, yea and the true and faithful Leveller".[246] So Christ rising in sons and daughters (the True Levellers) becomes Jesus Christ the Head Leveller.

The phrase "kingly power" occurs in *The Saints Paradise*,[247] but the concept was not developed there as fully as in *Light Shining* and *More Light Shining in Buckinghamshire*. The last-named pamphlet associated lawyers with kingly power. Winstanley did not use the phrase again until *A Watch-Word* of August 1649, where it referred especially to the royalist cause in the civil war.[248] Only in *A New-Yeers Gift* did he develop the notion of kingly power as "covetousness ... or the power of self-love" and equate it with the Norman Yoke and with property. This recognition that buying and selling, lords of manors, lawyers, priests and the state all form one kingly power differentiates Winstanley from the many radicals who attacked lawyers and priests. The law is "the strength, life and marrow of the kingly power", Winstanley wrote; the power of lawyers is "the only power that hinders Christ from rising".[249] Buying and selling killed Christ, but now he is rising up in sons and daughters, and kingly power in all its branches must be "shaken to pieces at the resurrection of Christ ... when righteous community rises". A government that "gives liberty to the gentry to have all the earth and shuts out the poor commoners from enjoying any part, ... this is the government of imaginary, self-seeking Antichrist. And every plant which my heavenly Father hath not planted shall be rooted out". It is "unreasonable men, who have not faith in Christ" who "uphold the kingly power" which Parliament has voted down.[250]

It is worth trying to sort out Winstanley's attitude towards the government of the Commonwealth, and to government in general, since this has caused confusion. Some have seen Winstanley as an anarchist who came to believe in the necessity of political action and political power. Mr Davis has argued, on the contrary, that Winstanley always respected power and was never an anti-authoritarian; and that in his ideal community "slavery replaced imprisonment".[251] Such views seem to me to err in using the blanket concepts "authority" and "political power". Winstanley was always opposed to the laws which upheld covetousness. He distinguished between laws which maintain the power of the Serpent and those which uphold the power of Reason.[252] Even in the early *Truth Lifting up its Head* he accepted the necessity of punishing a man who walked "unrighteously towards his fellow-creatures *in civil matters*" (my italics).[253] The commonwealth envisaged in *The Law of Freedom* differs from any form of kingly power by the fact that there would be no buying and selling, no lawyers, no state church or clergy. Even under kingly power, Winstanley accepted, some good laws had been passed — Magna Carta, for instance. Yet "that enslaving covetous kingly power ... runs in every man's and woman's veins, more or less, till Reason the spirit of burning cast him out".[254]

Winstanley "was always against the Cavaliers' cause", and the Diggers "have been ever friends to the Parliament"; their song treats Cavaliers as the personification of kingly power.[255] But "truly tyranny is tyranny in one as well as in another; in a poor man lifted up by his valour as in a rich man lifted up by his lands" — that is, in the Rump of the Long Parliament supported by the Army as well as in the Cavaliers. "Where tyranny sits, he is an enemy to Christ, the spreading spirit of righteousness". "Justices and most state officers doth more oppress than deliver from oppression". *The True Levellers Standard Advanced* accused "the powers of England" of restoring bondage; "all thy power and wit hath been to make laws and execute

them against such as stand for universal liberty".[256] Winstanley saw
the second civil war as Dragon against Dragon, one Beast against
another: "and the King of Righteousness hath been a looker on".
But now (June 1649) the battle is of Lamb against Dragon.[257]
Winstanley frequently expressed his abhorrence of violence, but he
expected "the government of Esau" to be beaten down "by wars,
counsels or hands of men". He told "lords of manors and Norman
gentry" that they would lose their kingdom of darkness. "The power
that is in" the Diggers "will take the rule and government from you
and give it a people that will make better use of it".[258] That sounds
like a transfer of political power, though it was to be brought about
by passive resistance, not by fighting. "The people shall all fall off
from you, and you shall fall on a sudden like a great tree that is
undermined at the root". "This falling off is begun already, divisions
shall tear and torture you till you submit to community". And in *An
Appeale to All Englishmen* Winstanley went a long way in inciting to
disobedience. Copyholders, he wrote, "are freed from obedience to
their lords of manors" by the Rump Parliament's Act declaring
England a free commonwealth, which "breaks in pieces ... the laws
of the conqueror"[259]

Winstanley attached great importance to this Act of 19 May 1649,
and to the Act abolishing monarchy (17 March 1649), as well as to the
Engagement to maintain the present Commonwealth. "You have set
Christ upon his throne in England", he told the "rulers of England,
... by your promises, engagements, oaths", and by those two Acts of
Parliament which he interpreted as giving Englishmen the right to
exercise their creation-freedom by cultivating the common land.[260]
What are we to make of his attitude towards the Rump, which had
also passed an Act "to maintain the old laws"? Winstanley referred
disparagingly to this latter Act as "made by a piece of the Parliament"
and warned his countrymen to beware of the danger of allowing the
Norman and kingly power to reassert itself.[261] Yet he wrote *Englands
Spirit Unfoulded* to urge support for the Commonwealth, specifically
on the ground that the Parliament's two Acts "declare plainly what
this state government aims at, and that is that all Englishmen may
have their freedom in and to the land, and be freed from the slavery of
the Norman Conquest". Professor Aylmer rightly sees this as a
realistic acceptance of the lesser evil.[262]

If we try to penetrate Winstanley's mental processes, it is I think
clear that he initially expected a sudden conversion to Reason, a

universal acceptance of community, as Christ rose everywhere in sons and daughters, and this Second Coming ended disagreement. Monarchy was abolished, we may recall, a fortnight before the digging started; the declaration that England was a free Commonwealth came two months later. In the euphoria of the moment this might seem to fortify the conviction that the digging was to initiate the Second Coming in England. But as the experience of the colony soon taught him, Winstanley had underestimated the institutional power of the Beast, the hold of the Serpent over the minds of men. What he must have found most upsetting of all was the hostility of many local tenants to the Diggers, as well as the antics of Ranters in the Cobham community which he attacked in *Englands Spirit Unfoulded*. Clearly a period of education was needed before Christ arose in a sufficient number of sons and daughters to overthrow kingly power.

Yet his experience also taught Winstanley that there were divisions among the ruling powers; sometimes the Army was less hostile than the local gentry. Charles I had after all been executed, and the Parliament had proclaimed a republic. The generals had at one stage allied with the Levellers; circumstances might force them to do so again. As late as January 1650 Winstanley still seems genuinely to have hoped for Army support.[263] Meanwhile divisions among the rulers could perhaps be exploited. Winstanley seems to have hoped that the Rump would fill up its vacant seats;[264] he expected "successive Parliaments", and seems to have suggested that "treacherous Parliament-men" might be recalled and replaced.[265] Whether Winstanley really believed that Parliament's two Acts aimed at granting all Englishmen their freedom in his sense matters not much; it was a good propagandist tactic to say so. His habit of interpreting Biblical texts in the sense he chose to give them might naturally lead him to read Acts of Parliament in the same spirit.[266]

Here the theory of the Norman Yoke was useful. Winstanley perhaps originally adopted its phraseology for propagandist reasons; but to denounce the gentry as Norman invaders drew on ideas which were widespread, especially in London, Buckinghamshire and among the rank and file of the Army; so did denunciations of lords of manors as representatives of Antichrist. As long ago as 1646 Christopher Feake was reported as saying that there was an "enmity against Christ" in aristocracy and monarchy.[267] Winstanley's equation of the rights of Englishmen with the creation liberties of all men, including the descendants of the free Anglo-Saxons, drew on the same traditions.

Pending the Second Coming, perhaps the Norman kingly power could be sapped piecemeal, since those in office differed in the extent of their readiness to compromise with it. Such an approach made co-operation with Parliament possible, even though many members of the Rump adhered to the Dragon. Some Quaker leaders were to pursue a similar tactic in 1659-60.[268] Popular pressure for Winstanley's interpretation of the two Acts could be used as a lever against conservatives in the government. Winstanley may have envisaged a period of dual power, in which Christ rising in sons and daughters would slowly hem the lords of manors into their enclosures, deprive them of labour, and so peacefully establish true freedom. In such circumstances, to call for the restoration of the creation liberties of all Englishmen was at once good propaganda and an accurate description of Winstanley's goal.

Hence by the time he came to write *The Law of Freedom* his emphasis had changed in relation to law. In *The New Law of Righteousness* he had envisaged the law of kingly power collapsing and being succeeded by the unanimous agreement of sons and daughters in whom Christ had risen — the *new* law. But *The Law of Freedom* is a more gradualist document. *Pace* Mr Davis, Winstanley did not anticipate a society "engaged in endless combat with sin and wickedness", nor did he return to the concept of original sin.[269] Mr Davis attributes far too great stability to the gentry power in Winstanley's Utopia, because he has failed to grasp what Winstanley expected to be the consequences of the withdrawal of labour from the enclosures. I think he is mistaken in supposing that Winstanley postulated, even in this transitional period, two systems of law and government existing side by side. Copyhold was to be abolished. So were the laws which favoured lords of manors.[270] Once wage labour became illegal, the only private property which could have survived for any length of time was peasant proprietorship, the farm worked by the labour of members of the family. One of the two greatest sins in the world, Winstanley had insisted in *Fire in the Bush*, was to hoard up more of the fruits of the earth than could be used by one particular family.[271]

Winstanley was concerned in *The Law of Freedom* with a transitional period. "In time ... this commonwealth's government ... will be the restorer of long lost freedoms to the creation". But meanwhile "the rudeness of the people", whether browbeaten tenants or pseudo-liberated Ranters, was a major obstacle to the Second Coming of Christ in sons and daughters. Winstanley's experience at St George's Hill and Cobham Heath must have convinced him that it was not possible to pass directly to a libertarian society: it would take time for Christ fully to rise in all. Winstanley's appeal to Cromwell shows an awareness, hinted at in *Englands Spirit Unfoulded*, of the importance of political power. So "because offences may arise from the spirit of unreasonable ignorance, therefore was the law added", Winstanley told "the friendly and unbiased reader"; it was "added ... against the rudeness and ignorance that may arise in mankind", he insisted in "A Short Declaration to take off Prejudice".[272] In the same way the law of Moses had been necessary against the hardness of the hearts of earlier Israelites. "The law was added ... to preserve common peace and freedom", "to limit men's manners, because of transgression one against another".[273] (Note the convenient Pauline phrase "was added", which Winstanley repeats in all these early references to the law.)[274] Whenever reasonable arbitration could "put a stop to the rigour of the law", it should do so, since the law is added as a "bridle to unreasonableness", to "regulate the unrational practice" of "covetous, proud and Beastly-minded men". Sentence for any offence which does not incur the death penalty may be mitigated by the judge, "for it is amendment not destruction that common-wealth's law requires".[275] Meanwhile the education both of innocent children (to help them "to govern themselves like rational men") and of unregenerate younger brothers is of the first importance.[276] Idleness is unreasonable because it hampers co-operation; so are extravagance and waste. Laws will be needed against them until this is understood.[277]

In this light I think we may conclude that Mr Davis exaggerated a little when he wrote that "flogging, judicial violence and torture" as well as capital punishment "were accepted by Winstanley as essential *and continuing* parts of the machinery of social discipline" (my italics).[278] We may think Winstanley's punishments unduly severe, but "torture" is an unnecessarily emotive word. In his earlier pamphlets Winstanley had totally rejected the law and its punishments; to execute a murderer was to commit another murder. His acceptance now of the necessity of some coercion was a reversal of this position in the light of the Diggers' political experience.

Winstanley was endeavouring to be realistic, and intended his punishments to be corrective. Given his desire "to prevent the cruelty of prisons", [279] what alternative was there in the seventeenth century to corporal penalties as a means of ensuring that the law was enforced? Whipping and burning in the hand were still so frequent that John Bunyan regarded them as minor punishments.[280] Mr Davis disregards the passage in *A Watch-Word to the City of London* where Winstanley tells "the Norman gentry" that "all the harm I would have you to have" is "that you my enemies may live in peace".[281] Mr Davis's word "continuing" suggests that Winstanley supposed that "the spirit of unreasonable ignorance" would last for ever. But that contradicts what he actually said. Such a denial of the Second Coming would be the sin against the Holy Ghost.[282]

Winstanley lived in the same world as Hobbes. His Reason has the same sort of universal validity, whether men recognize it or not, as the scientific laws of nature which Hobbes described in *Leviathan*. But Winstanley regarded co-operation as the law of the universe, whereas Hobbes saw competition and fear of death as the universal principles.[283] Winstanley's Reason, I have suggested elsewhere, also has its analogies with Rousseau's General Will. Its light is in all men, but will not completely dominate the thinking of any single individual until Christ has risen. "Many times men act contrary to Reason, though they think they act according to Reason". Winstanley's laws fulfil something like the function of "forcing to be free".[284]

In *The Breaking of the Day of God* Winstanley had described how the clergy cunningly juggled a corrupt power "out of the hands of the civil magistrates of the earth, which is God's ordinance ... for the government of the world". Magistracy must stand, but "this ecclesiastical power was always a troubler of godly magistrates.[285] Winstanley came to see closer connections between kingly power and the clergy power, and went beyond the traditional radical solution of separating church and state. He came to accept that "most laws are but to enslave the poor to the rich";[286] but "most" implies that some were not. Winstanley never wholly despaired of using state power in the cause of Reason against the kingly and clergy power.

In *Fire in the Bush* Winstanley recalled how Daniel had seen the Beast, kingly power, "lifted up from the earth and made to stand upon the feet like a man, and a man's heart was given to it; that is, this power should be the image of true magistracy, and while the Beastly power of self-love rules in the hearts of mankind this kingly power should be the preserver of the meek in spirit" for a transitional period until Christ comes to reign.[287] True magistracy was to be sought "among the poor despised ones of the earth, for there Christ dwells", rising up to unite the creation against false magistracy.[288]

"The great lawgiver in commonwealth government is the spirit of universal righteousness dwelling in mankind, now rising up to teach everyone to do to another as he would have another do to him". This spirit has been buried "for many years past". But we may hope, "because the name of commonwealth is risen and established in England", that "we or our posterity shall see comfortable effects". "It is the work of a Parliament to break the tyrants' bonds, to abolish all their oppressing laws, and to give orders, encouragements and directions unto the poor oppressed people of the land".[289] "All laws that are not grounded upon Equity and Reason", Winstanley told Fairfax, "not giving a universal freedom to all but respecting persons, ought ... to be cut off with the King's head".[290] He presumably hoped that Parliament would do the cutting.

Winstanley's position in *The Law of Freedom* signified something of a retreat. In *An Humble Request* and *Fire in the Bush* he had referred to the law of Moses as "but the moderation or curbing in of the Fall of mankind".[291] Moses "gave way to Christ" as Christ would now give way to the spreading power of righteousness.[292] But since in the England of 1652 the Second Coming clearly was not imminent, guidance was needed: the law was the schoolmaster to bring us to Christ. *The Law of Freedom* was subtitled *True Magistracy Restored*: it was pointing a radical way forward by removing the usurpations of kingly power, against which the Parliament had adopted two good laws.[293] It might be persuaded to pass more — if not the full programme of *The Law of Freedom*, at least part of it. Former monastic lands might be put at the disposal of the people, as well as church, crown and royalists' estates. Winstanley hoped that Parliament would legislate against tithes and copyhold services — both of which would have amounted to a form of expropriation.[294] It was a slim hope, but it was all there was. In realistic terms, all depended on winning over Oliver Cromwell.

In the years from the battle of Worcester to the dissolution of Barebone's Parliament Cromwell seemed the last hope of the radicals. It looks absurd to us now, knowing as we do that he was to

preside over the reunion of Cavalier and Roundhead gentry which
was ultimately to lead to the Restoration. But in these two years, as
anger and frustration grew in the Army, Cromwell may well have
appeared an ally. He had succeeded Fairfax, to whom as head of the
Army Winstanley had previously addressed appeals. In April 1653
Cromwell was associated with Harrison and the millenarians against
a conservative Rump. It was only his disillusionment with Barebone's
Parliament that finally allowed him to succumb to conservative
pressures. Winstanley can hardly have been very optimistic in 1652,
but there was no other hope left. "You have power, . . . I have no
power," he sadly wrote. Pending the Second Coming (in Winstanley's sense) power was the essential consideration. Kingly power
had defeated the Diggers; only commonwealth power could curb the
Norman and Antichristian gentry, as it had abolished the Norman
and Antichristian monarchy and House of Lords. "O power where
art thou, that must mend things amiss?" were almost Winstanley's
last printed words.[295]

Officers in Winstanley's commonwealth play a role similar to that
of the law: they bridge the gap between the present divided state of
England and the unanimity which will prevail after the Second
Coming. The law in the heart of every man will be a check on all
officers. So will the provision that officers are to be elected annually,
by all men aged twenty and over, and that they may not be
immediately re-elected. Laws will be fully discussed by all before
enactment, and will be "few and short and often read".[296] The
provision that judges are to apply, not to interpret, the law was
intended to have the same effect as the written constitutions put
forward by Levellers and others: to guard against the tendency of
power to corrupt, and to prevent judicial discretion being used to
achieve political and social ends.[297] We may think Winstanley's
solution to this problem unsatisfactory, but he provided a degree of
flexibility by the possibility of appeals to his County Senate and to
Parliament. The militia of citizens in arms — as unprofessional a
body as possible — existed to protect laws derived from Reason
against "the turbulency of any foolish or self-ended spirit that
endeavours to break their common peace".[298]

"All armies", as Winstanley rather pointedly told Oliver Cromwell, "make some poor, some rich, put some into freedom and others
into bondage". "In the days of a free commonwealth" there was to be
no professional army. The army was all the citizens, and would "be

used to resist and destroy all who endeavour to keep up or bring in kingly bondage again". If a land be "so enslaved as England was under the kings and conquering laws, then an army is to be raised with as much secrecy as may be, to restore the land again and set it free".[299] These circumstances would presumably arise if the republican government and the generals failed to carry out the Commonwealth programme. It is a significant modification of the passive resistance which Winstanley had advocated when writing about the period before a communist society had been established.

VI

SOME PROBLEMS

If the foregoing analysis is correct, the outspoken materialism of *The Law of Freedom* should not present the difficulties it does to some commentators. Those who see Winstanley using religious language as a cloak to conceal atheistic materialism suggest that he cast off the veil in *The Law of Freedom* — though this is rather surprising in a pamphlet which clearly aims at moderation of expression in order to win maximum support. Those who think Winstanley believed in a personal God outside the creation have a good deal to explain away in *The Law of Freedom*. Among the many relevant passages the most important are, first, the starting point — that freedom depends on use of the earth, since men cannot live without the fruits of the earth. Take these away "and the body languishes, the spirit is brought into bondage". "A man had better to have had no body than to have no food for it. ... Free enjoyment" of the earth "is true freedom".[300] This leads on, secondly, to the famous paean beginning "to know the secrets of nature is to know the works of God", for God cannot be known outside the creation, nor can we have any knowledge of life after death. The desire to seek for "spiritual things" elsewhere comes from the devil. Third is Winstanley's equally well-known denunciation of divinity, speculation about such unknowable matters; and his explanation of "this doctrine of a God, a devil, a heaven and a hell, salvation and damnation after a man is dead" in psychological terms.[301] Finally, Winstanley's flat statement "I am assured that if it be rightly searched into, the inward bondages of the mind, as covetousness, pride, hypocrisy, envy, sorrows, fears, desperation and madness, are all occasioned by the outward bondage that one sort of people lay upon another".[302]

This materialism in no way contradicts Winstanley's theology, rightly understood. As we saw, he shared the theological materialism of many radical heretics. The doctrine of creation *ex deo* (as opposed to the orthodox *ex nihilo*) was proclaimed as early as *Truth Lifting up its Head*, and was shared by Familists, Ranters and Milton.[303] The creation is the clothing of God. For Winstanley this doctrine *excludes* a personal God. There are no external Saviours, there is no God beyond the sky, no heaven or hell after death, no personal external devil.[304] This is the annihilationist mortalism shared by Clarkson and many others. Those who offer themselves as Saviours are personifications of the Serpent, varieties of kingly power.[305]

I have been upbraided for suggesting that Winstanley rejected a personal God: what he rejected was only "the clergy's version ... of a capricious, arbitrary God".[306] We are in agreement at least on this rejection: Winstanley's God was Reason. But what remains of a personal God in his system of ideas? A man who "thinks God is in the heavens above the skies ... worships his own imagination, which is the devil".[307] The spirit which will rule after the Second Coming is "not one single person".[308] Sincerity and love are God, "the King of Righteousness which is called conscience". "The same spirit that made the globe" is "the indweller in the five senses of hearing, seeing, tasting, smelling and feeling".[309] The "murdering God of the world", who defends property, who "appointed the people to pay tithes to the clergy" and is "the author of the creatures' misery" is "the God devil".[310] He sounds at times suspiciously like the God of the Old Testament.[311] "That God whom you serve, and which did entitle you lords, knights, gentlemen and landlords, is covetousness, the God of this world, ... under whose dark governing power you and all the nations of the world for the present are under".[312]

This, the clergy's God, is no more a real person than Winstanley's Reason is. It is a "dark power", which bears sway within professors and whom they call God and Christ. "Indeed, Imagination is that God which generally everyone worships and owns; ... they worship the devil and mere nothing".[313] "Your Saviour must be a power within you to deliver you from that bondage within; the outward Christ, or the outward God, are but men Saviours", comparable to Moses, Joshua and Judges; "and these Gods sometimes proves devils". Preachers who tell you "your God and Saviour is without" (not those who assert the capricious, arbitrary God of Calvinism) "are servants to the curse".[314] That is why the Diggers would "neither come to church nor serve their God".[315] Each man has "his God", his Reason, his conscience, which he must be free to follow to the best of his ability.[316] Winstanley associated himself with the man who is called an atheist "because he will neither preach nor pray"; he regarded punishment for denying God, Christ and Scriptures as totally wrong. Like "wise-hearted Thomas" men should "believe nothing but what they see reason for".[317]

Always in Winstanley's thought there is a dialectic between the inner spirit and the external world, as well as between Reason and the Serpent.[318] Property, kingly power and a state church are institutionalizations of the Serpent within man; but they also vigorously protect and defend the Serpent, propagate its values. The establishment of private property is the Fall, the institutionalization of evil which gives it lasting power. Hence the importance of setting men and women free from a state church[319] so long as it exists, and of abolishing a state church altogether in the society envisaged in *The Law of Freedom*. Here Winstanley called for righteous laws based on Reason, to guide and help the young, the weak and the wavering. Hence too the great significance which Winstanley attached to education, and to studying the secrets of nature experimentally; both fortify Reason, as surrender to external objects, improperly understood, or idle speculation, fortify the Serpent. For Winstanley, as for Milton, education was a means by which men could get back behind the Fall.[320]

From his own experience Winstanley knew that the rising of Christ in sons and daughters can be hindered and delayed by the power of institutions; outward bondage occasions the inward bondages. That is why it seems to me wrong to describe the digging on St George's Hill as a mere symbolic gesture.[321] The Serpent must be cast out "not in words only, as preachers do, but in action, whereby the creation shines in glory".[322] Every political concession extorted from kingly power makes it easier for Christ to rise in sons and daughters. The dialectic is similar to that of more orthodox Puritans who believed that God's omnipotent will could be furthered by keeping one's power dry. But Winstanley's Christ is no external Saviour: men's wills cannot be changed except by themselves. If Winstanley had succeeded in casting down the kingdom of darkness, he believed that this would also be to the advantage of the men of property who themselves suffered from the institutions of the Serpent, though they were not yet sufficiently ruled by Reason to appreciate the fact. It would "break the devil's bands asunder, wherewith you are tied, that you my enemies may live in peace".[323]

The authors of "Winstanley: A Case for the Man as He Said He Was" are quite right to argue that there is no reason for surprise if a day-to-day pamphleteer reacting to events is not absolutely consistent;[324] though in *The Law of Freedom*, when Winstanley is looking back in defeat, one might expect his position to be more rather than less self-consistent. But in fact, I am suggesting, a very great consistency of *attitude* can be traced as Winstanley's ideas developed, as he learned from events. He *experienced* the might of kingly power and its ideologists, priests and lawyers; he learned from *experience* that Christ rose slowly in sons and daughters, that many were seduced by false arguments. It is the devil who tells a man that he "must not trust his own experience".[325] Winstanley's incorporation into his theological system of the myths of the Norman Yoke and of Antichrist, with correspondingly greater emphasis on external institutions and powers, reflects the experience of the Diggers' struggle, the growing appreciation that Reason too must be institutionalized. Hence the laws in *The Law of Freedom*, the stress on education and on diffusion of scientific knowledge. But this is only a shift in emphasis, not a fundamental change. There is no inconsistency, no "paradox", once we grasp that the dialectic is there from the start, and that Winstanley's theology *precludes* external Saviours and a personal God.[326] He uses the Christian myth in the same manner as he uses the Norman Yoke — as a myth. God and Christ are no more persons for him than Antichrist. "God is an active power, not an imaginary fancy". In "the great battle of God Almighty, light fights against darkness, universal love fights against selfish power, life against death, true knowledge against imaginary thoughts".[327] Property, "called the devil or covetousness", fights against "community ... called Christ or universal love".[328]

Winstanley's relationship to the Quakers has often been discussed. I was long unconvinced by the attempt to identify him with the Gerrard Winstanley who was a corn-chandler in 1666, and died a Quaker ten years later.[329] But new evidence presented by James Alsop leaves no doubt, I think, that the man who received Quaker burial in 1676 was our Gerrard Winstanley.[330] Exactly what this fact signifies remains to be assessed. The Gerrard Winstanley who was sued for debts in 1660 did not use Quaker language. If Winstanley was an active Quaker in the sixteen-sixties and seventies, no evidence of this has been found. In 1659 he was appointed waywarden for Cobham parish. He occupied this office and those of overseer and churchwarden at various dates until 1668. In 1671 and 1672 he was one of two chief constables of Elmbridge Hundred. This suggests that he conformed to the state church during those years. The christening of three children born in the sixties is recorded in the Cobham parish register.[331]

In 1653 Francis Higginson, in 1655 Ralph Farmer, accused the Quakers of being "downright Levellers", well versed in the "learning of Winstanley and Collier".[332] Also in 1655 Francis Harris suggested that many Quakers had been Diggers, and others Levellers.[333] Thomas Comber in 1678, Thomas Tenison in 1683 and Thomas Bennett in 1700 all asserted that "Winstanley published the principles of Quakerism".[334] There are indeed analogies between Digger ideas and those of early Quakerism, but these may just as well derive from a common radical milieu as from direct influence — except perhaps for the Quaker adoption of Winstanley's phrase "the children of light".[335]

Winstanley's Quaker burial is often used to argue if not that he was a pacifist (as clearly he was not) at least that his approach to politics was primarily religious. But this was certainly not Comber's point, and it is to misunderstand the early Quakers. Before 1660 they were not pacifists and did not abstain from political action. As late as 1659 Edward Burrough was negotiating with the Rump of the Long Parliament with a view to Quaker support for and possible participation in the republican government.[336] Burrough was one of the activists among the Quaker leaders. The only direct evidence of contact between Winstanley and Quakers has recently been discovered by Dr Reay. In a letter to Margaret Fell, probably of August 1654, Burrough wrote: "Wilstandley [sic] says he believes we are sent to perfect that work which fell in their hands. He hath been with us".[337] At that date Quakers were being denounced as Levellers: Winstanley's remark is no evidence that he then held the doctrines which the Quakers espoused after 1660. But where else could he go after it became clear that Christ was not going to rise in Charles II's England?

VII

CONCLUSION

In what I have written my object has been strictly limited. If I had intended a full-scale reassessment of Winstanley's intellectual position I should have had to place much more emphasis on the political and economic ideas which he developed in and after *The True Levellers Standard Advanced*. I have confined myself to an attempt to assess the role of Winstanley's theology in the evolution of his ideas, since this I believe has been misinterpreted by too static an approach. Winstanley was not a crypto-atheist. Neither was he a traditional Christian. His theology was that of a very radical heretic, and can best be understood in relation to the thinking of his contemporaries, though ultimately it transcended their world of ideas.

A chronological approach makes it clear that Winstanley's conversion to communism antedates his adoption of the Leveller theory of the Norman Yoke, and his adoption of the name "Leveller". Before December 1648 he was relatively conventional in suggesting that God's people must learn by suffering and then wait patiently upon the Lord, expecting their consolation later. But Winstanley's conversion to communism included a new conviction that "action is the life of all; and if thou dost not act thou dost nothing". Action took the form of digging at St George's Hill, and the rest followed from that. In *The New Law of Righteousness* "the greatest combat is within a man".[338] But Winstanley learned that the external enemies of Christ rising were at least equally serious. His colony was opposed by local landlords, parsons, lawyers, ultimately by the power of the state: by kingly power. The Diggers were supported by the Levellers of Buckinghamshire; the Leveller newspaper, *The Moderate*, reprinted one of their declarations and echoed Winstanley's ideas on property as the cause of sin.[339] Perhaps support came from other radicals in the City and southern England. It was natural to take over Leveller political arguments in this context. In February 1649 Winstanley and another future Digger, Henry Bickerstaff, acted as arbitrators chosen by John Fielder, miller of Kingston-on-Thames, who had been imprisoned for holding a conventicle. In 1650 Lilburne took over Fielder's defence, using the same arguments as Winstanley had used. They can hardly have failed to meet. Fielder, like Lilburne, became a Quaker later in the sixteen-fifties: his house was used for Quaker meetings.[340]

What is interesting is the ease with which Winstanley combined his theology with the historical myth of the Norman Yoke and with Leveller doctrines of natural rights. Here Winstanley is unique only in the comprehensiveness and intellectual power of his synthesis. Walwyn, one suspects, had similar ideas, but he did not express them in writing. The Clarkson of *A General Charge, or, Impeachment of High-Treason, in the Name of Justice Equity, against the Commun-ality of England* (1647), the author of *Tyranipocrit Discovered* (1649), the Coppe of *A Fiery Flying Roll* (1649), combined some communist ideas with radical theology, but never synthesized them.[341] John Warr linked the radical theology with the Norman Yoke theory in an elegant synthesis, but does not seem to have thought that com-munism necessarily followed.[341] Winstanley's is the most complete and successful marriage of politics and economics to the radical theology, the key concept being that of kingly power — the institutionalized Serpent — and its representatives: landlords, law-yers, clergy.

The heretical theology, with its deep roots in English history, and the radical version of the Norman Yoke theory which evolved during the civil war, both circulated in the same circles of artisans and small producers. Communist ideas had flickered in the radical under-ground for a long time, but had never (so far as the record shows) been elevated to a theory. Winstanley linked the three. His extension of the symbolism contained in the word "hedge" shows how naturally they came together. The word was commonly used in the seventeenth century as a symbol for private property, which the Levellers were alleged by their enemies to wish to cast down. Marvell, probably at almost exactly the same time as Winstanley was writing *The Law of Freedom*, spoke of:

> ...this naked equal flat,
> Which *Levellers* take pattern at.

It was a slur which Oliver Cromwell was to repeat.[342]

"A hedge in the field is as necessary in its kind as government in the church or commonwealth", wrote the Reverend Joseph Lee in 1656.[343] Winstanley wanted to throw down hedges in the field. But he also saw that churches "in the Presbyterian, Independent, or any other form of profession ... are like the inclosures of land which hedges in some to be heirs of life, and hedges out others". So in a single phrase he linked, and dismissed, landlordism and the traditional "particular churches". In *The Law of Freedom* he extended the analogy to the doctrine of predestination which (he no doubt thought) protected landlordism. "This is the mighty ruler, that hath made the election and rejection of brethren from their birth to their death, or from eternity to eternity. He calls himself the Lord God of the whole creation".[344] The overt, explicit reference is to kingly power; but it is difficult not to suppose that Winstanley also intended a backhand blow at the orthodox "Lord God of the whole creation", who of course could not be explicitly attacked. So the hedge with which Norman freeholders shut us out of the earthly community has its analogue in the barriers with which priests try to prevent us realising the spiritual equality of all men and women. Both are cast down by Christ the true Leveller, simultaneously.

In Winstanley's mythology, then, the Norman Yoke, radical theology and his theory of communism came to be indissolubly linked. Landlords, kingly power and priests will be overthrown together as Christ rises in sons and daughters: there is no distinction between economic freedom, political freedom and spiritual freedom.

If we stress the theological origins of Winstanley's ideas, therefore, we must also emphasize the unorthodoxy of the theology. From the start it was barely compatible with traditional Christianity; it became little more than a metaphor when salvation meant that all will live in peace and rest on earth, with no after life; and Christ yields place to the spreading of Reason in men and women "as the earth grows to be a common treasury for all".[345] Once Winstanley had broken loose from orthodoxy his thinking developed rapidly. He took over Leveller political ideas, and his communism became steadily less theological and more materialist as he learned from the power of the enemies he was up against. By 1652 his message could be expressed in almost wholly secular terms. In his ideal commonwealth men called ministers were retained, but there was no state church, and the unpaid "ministers" were elected by all the parishioners for one year only, to perform secular educational functions. We cannot explain this development except by reference to the England in which he had hoped to see Christ rising. "Never has the tendency towards secularization been so clear as in the years 1649-52", wrote

Professor Lutaud, who knows Winstanley and his world better than most scholars.[346]

We have seen that Winstanley was not an isolated thinker, though he pushed on further and more consistently than most. Ideas such as his, if freely preached in the tense political climate of 1649-50, with no censorship or church courts, would threaten not only the existence of a state church but also the authority of traditional theology. Such a prospect might well terrify those contemporaries, whether former Roundheads or former Cavaliers, who had no wish to see a social revolution. Hence the successive forcible suppressions of the Levellers in 1649, of the Diggers in 1650, of the Ranters in 1651, and the savage sentence on James Nayler in 1656. The debates on Nayler in the second Protectorate Parliament reveal with great clarity the hysterical *social* anxieties of those who most feared the Quakers. Hence too the political philosophy of Hobbes, with its emphasis on the authority of the sovereign — any sovereign who protects established civil society — as the only safeguard against the fanatical enthusiasm of the proponents of the radical theology — against those who, like Winstanley, received subversive messages from what they held to be a divine authority. Hobbes was only one of many proclaiming such theories in the early sixteen-fifties.[347]

When Cromwell accepted the Petition and Advice, a state church with an orthodox theology (to be defined by Parliament) had apparently been established. But in the traumatic winter 1659-60 this control slipped again as the attack on tithes developed, as Levellers and Agitators reappeared, as Quakers were said to be taking to arms. Hence the panic rush to recall Charles II, a rush in which conservative Puritans joined traditional episcopalians.[348] At many points in the history of popular revolutions it has appeared that radical religion might lead to irreligion. In France in the fifteen-sixties the respectable in "communities that had finally driven out priests and smashed idols feared that the congregations were in danger of drifting into atheism or worse if pastors did not arrive promptly to reorganize religious life".[349] "Does one come to unbelief through the mediation of a religious sect?", Albert Soboul asked, apropos the French Revolution. Many were the pamphleteers after 1660 who claimed that, religion apart, the church was essential to the maintenance of social order.[350]

The failure of the millennium to arrive, and the futile Fifth Monarchist revolts of 1657 and 1661, made the former millenarians

John Owen and John Bunyan reconsider the time-table for the events prophesied in Daniel and Revelation.[351] The coming of Christ's kingdom was postponed to kingdom come, and any connection with "fanaticism" was disavowed. The sixteen-fifties brought a decisive change in the perspective of the radicals too; the Restoration totally and finally defeated their this-worldly hopes. The Quakers turned pacifist and abandoned any attempt to bring about by political means a better world on earth. The Muggletonians also gave up Reeve's millenarianism; whilst retaining much of the radical theology (and Reeve's pacifism) Muggleton recreated an arbitrary authoritarianism under the surviving prophet.[352] The Diggers had hoped for salvation and glory on earth, and their this-worldliness reinforced the secularizing trend of their theology. But after 1660 not only conservative but also radical dissenters — at all events, those who could be heard — abandoned earthly solutions. It is a very important turning-point, the exact mechanisms of which have not been fully explored. It was a symptom rather than a cause of the defeat of the radical revolution in England, but it ensured that that defeat lasted for a long time. For thirty-five years at least it was very risky to publish anything which would have continued the radical theological trend. When the press regained a measure of freedom after 1695, the new world had established itself. The old ideas had been firmly driven underground or into exile, perhaps out of existence altogether. Freer though England was after 1688, anti-Trinitarians still risked a death sentence. Eighteenth-century deism was so abstractly secular that it lacked the emotional appeal of Winstanley's ideas. Never again were serious revolutionary ideas to be expressed in religious form in England. With Winstanley the radical theology reached a peak at which it was trembling over into secularism; but the reaction was so strong that the advance to secularism was stopped short, abandoned and perhaps forgotten. Even Toland, who salvaged so much of the seventeenth-century radical heritage, nevertheless felt that he had to invent a new religion to express it. When radicalism revived in the later eighteenth century, theology had been left behind.[353]

The historical achievement of Christianity has been to provide western civilization with a moral code for living in society. Its main weaknesses have been its attempt to combine human equality with property rights, and its invocation of the after life to compensate for the consequent injustices of this world. So it has proved increasingly inadequate as society moved towards greater equality.

Winstanley did not look for consolations after death. His philosophy was designed for living in this world. But if supernatural sanctions and the authority of priests are abolished, how are standards of conduct to be maintained? Winstanley's original answer was by Reason in the conscience of every man and woman. But he came to realise that Reason can prevail only in an equal society; and that this must mean the abolition of private property and the wage relationship. Then free discussion in communities of equals can lead to acceptance of Reason's rule. (There is no space to do more than draw attention to Winstanley's very remarkable stress on sexual equality. Traditional orthodox emphasis on the Sonship of man becomes Christ rising in sons *and daughters.*)

The trouble about our unequal society, which has lost its belief in supernatural sanctions, is that there is no general acceptance of standards of right and wrong, and therefore no satisfactory means of enforcing them. Winstanley's intuition gives at least a possible answer: that in a non-exploitative society Reason might have a chance of rising in men and women, on the basis of their own social experience, and of being universally accepted as a guide to conduct. The weakness of his position is that, as Hobbes saw, "commonly they that call for right reason to decide any controversy do mean their own".[354] But it is arguable that in an equal society these disagreements might be soluble by rational discussion, since no vested interests would prejudice the debate. One could deny this *a priori* only by asserting a doctrine of original sin. Whether it is now too late to construct a society which shall be both non-exploitative and organized in communities small enough to conduct rational discussion (as Rousseau wished) is another matter. In Winstanley's time the possibilities were greater, as they may be today in parts of the Third World.

Winstanley, it seems to me, was groping his way towards a humanist and materialist philosophy, in which there were no outward Saviours, no heaven or hell or after life, but only men and women living in society. We should not underestimate the difficulties of this quest. There may have been philosophical atheists in the seventeenth century, though Bunyan doubted it.[355] It is at least as likely that those whom their contemporaries called atheists were either deists or "couldn't-care-less" non-philosophical hedonists. Until the concept of evolution had been established, it was not easy to account for the existence of the universe without postulating a creator. Theological materialists like Milton, philosophical materialists like Hobbes, took for granted the existence of a creator-God. The Bible had been accepted for so long as the source of all truth and wisdom that it was difficult to escape from its myths: popular radicalism indeed in the century since the Reformation had drawn on the Bible to criticize existing authorities and institutions. The fact that Winstanley left the historical veracity of the Bible an open question is evidence of very daring intellectual independence. His Reason, which is both the creator of the universe and the spirit which dictates co-operation to men and women living in society, is an attempt to maintain the unity of mankind and the cosmos.

So it is perhaps irrelevant to ask whether Winstanley "believed" the Christian myths, or whether he used them only as a convenient mode of expression, a metaphor. The question imposes twentieth-century assumptions on him. This was the idiom in which men thought: so were the Norman Yoke and Antichrist. Whether the myths were historically true "matters not much". What did matter — for Winstanley as for Milton — was that through the myths truths about man, society and the universe could be poetically expressed, in a way that would inspire to action. The battles of God Almighty between Christ and the Serpent could be described more prosaically, but I do not suppose that Winstanley thought in prose and then wrote in poetic myth. He used the myths because they were for him the most accessible way of expressing profound truths about humanity.

But these truths were very different from traditional orthodox Christianity, and in so far as they denied a human Saviour, a personal God, they were in opposition to orthodoxy. Winstanley's system of ideas could be rewritten in the language of rational deism; had he lived fifty years later he might have so expressed them. But a great deal of their force and immediacy derives from the poetic, mythopoeic style which came naturally to him. We should not classify him as a deist, still less as a seventeenth-century Marxist; but we should recognize the profound difference between the content of his ideas and that of traditional Christianity. His thinking was struggling towards concepts which were to be more precisely if less poetically formulated by later, non-theological materialisms.

NOTES

1. Originally published as *Past and Present Supplement*, No.5 (1978). It was followed by a discussion in *P. and P.*, No.89 (1980). This discussion raised no new issues, but I have incorporated in the present text a few passages from my "Rejoinder" (pp.147-51) to the comment by L. Mulligan, J.K. Graham and J. Richards (pp.144-6). Since this piece was written T. Wilson Hayes's *Winstanley the Digger: A Literary Analysis of Radical Ideas in the English Revolution* (Harvard U.P., 1979) has added greatly to our understanding of Winstanley in his radical heretical context.

2. W.S. Hudson, "Economic and Social Thought of Gerrard Winstanley", *Journal of Modern History*, XVIII (1946), pp.1-21; L. Mulligan, J.K. Graham and J. Richards, "Winstanley: A Case for the Man as He Said He Was", *Journal of Ecclesiastical History*, XXVIII (1977), pp.57-75.

3. George Juretic, "Digger no Millenarian: The Revolutionizing of Gerrard Winstanley", *Journal of the History of Ideas*, XXXVI (1975), pp.268-70, 274-6, 280.

4. Hudson, *op. cit.*, pp.7, 11, 21. Had the Quakers no practical intentions when they did things "for a sign"?

5. I have already written at some length on these matters in *W.T.U.D.*, in my Introduction to Winstanley's *The Law of Freedom and Other Writings* (Cambridge U.P., 1983; hereafter cited by title only), and in *M.E.R.*. Here I concentrate on Winstanley's religion in its historical context. Cf. also Chapter 7 above.

6. Gerrard Winstanley, *The Breaking of the Day of God* (1648; 2nd edn., 1649); Gerrard Winstanley, *The Mysterie of God, Concerning the Whole Creation, Mankind* (1648; 2nd edn., 1649); Gerrard Winstanley, *The Saints Paradise* (two editions, both undated, almost certainly 1648); Gerrard Winstanley, *Truth Lifting up its Head above Scandals* (1649; 2nd edn., 1650); Gerrard Winstanley, *The New Law of Righteousness* (1649); Gerrard Winstanley, *Several Pieces Gathered into One Volume* (December 1649); William London, *A Catalogue of the Most Vendible Books in England, Orderly and Alphabetically Digested* (1657). *Truth Lifting up its Head* and *The New Law of Righteousness* are both reprinted in *The Works of Gerrard Winstanley*, ed. G.H. Sabine (Cornell U.P., 1941; hereafter *Works*). Subsequent references to *The Breaking of the Day of God* and to *The Mysterie of God* are to the second editions of these works. I cite the edition of *The Saints Paradise* which has 134 pages. These last three works of Winstanley listed above are hereafter cited by title only.

7. *The Mysterie of God*, pp.2, 4.

8. *The Saints Paradise*, Sigs. B, D, pp.54-5, 89; cf. "Another Digger Broadside", ed. K.V. Thomas, *P. and P.*, No.42 (1969), pp.57-68 (hereafter *A Declaration ... [from] Iver*); *W.T.U.D.*, pp.113-14; *M.E.R.*, p.243.

9. *The Saints Paradise*, Sigs. B, C, pp. 85, 89-90, 98; *Works*, p. 107; cf. pp. 375, 441, and *M.E.R.*, Ch. 26. See p. 226 above.

10. *The Mysterie of God*, Sig. A 2v, pp. 14-15, 21; *The Breaking of the Day of God*, p. 130; *The Saints Paradise*, pp. 39, 88. For the Father as the sun, cf. *ibid.*, pp. 1, 17.

11. *The Mysterie of God*, pp. 10-11, 23, 26; *The Saints Paradise*, Sig. B, pp. 29-30, 32, 35-9, 44-54, 101, 105, 110-11.

12. *The Saints Paradise*, Sigs. A-B, D-E, p. 11; *The Mysterie of God*, pp. 33-5; *The Breaking of the Day of God*, pp. 22-3, 63-4, 79, 115, 123, 129-30.

13. *The Saints Paradise*, pp. 24, 27; *The Breaking of the Day of God*, pp. 10-12, 16; *The Mysterie of God*, pp. 31-2, 38, 41.

14. *Works*, p. 125.

15. Cf. *ibid.*, p. 332: "Doth the murderer's sword make any man to be God's Anointed?" See pp. 195-6 above.

16. *The Saints Paradise*, pp. 3, 6.

17. *The Breaking of the Day of God*, p. 16.

18. *The Mysterie of God*, pp. 33, 35, 38; cf. p. 40; *The Breaking of the Day of God*, Sig. A 3v, pp. 80, 120; *The Saints Paradise*, pp. 9, 14, 49-50, 111.

19. *Works*, pp. 112, 120-4.

20. *The Breaking of the Day of God*, p. 12; *The Saints Paradise*, p. 53; cf. *The Mysterie of God*, p. 28. For the anointing see *The Experience of Defeat*, pp. 304-6.

21. *The Saints Paradise*, pp. 120-1. For the meaning Winstanley was later to give to "salvation", see p. 210 above.

22. *The Mysterie of God*, Sigs. A 3-4, pp. 7-8, 15, 46-7, 50-1; *The Saints Paradise*, pp. 126-34.

23. *The Breaking of the Day of God*, pp. 10-11; cf. p. 6, and *The Mysterie of God*, p. 6; also *Works*, pp. 120, 166, 169. See *M.E.R.*, pp. 303-5, and pp. 153-4 above.

24. *The Saints Paradise*, pp. 118-19, 63-4, 132; *The Mysterie of God*, pp. 24-5, 31-2; *Works*, pp. 124, 131-2.

25. *Works*, pp. 112, 121, 131-2; cf. pp. 113, 118. For the radical doctrine of Sonship, see *M.E.R.*, Ch. 23; cf. pp. 203-4 above.

26. *The Saints Paradise*, pp. 66-7, 13-14. For Christ as the great prophet, see John Saltmarsh, *Sparkles of Glory, or Some Beams of the Morning-Star* (1648), p. 39; *M.E.R.*, pp. 392-3.

27. *Works*, p. 116; cf. p. 82.

28. *The Breaking of the Day of God*, pp. 34, 37; cf. p. 10.

29. *The Saints Paradise*, pp. 82-5; *The Mysterie of God*, pp. 67-9; *Works*, p. 114.

30. *The Saints Paradise*, p. 94; cf. *Works*, p. 116. On the familiar distinction between "the history" and "the mystery", see *The Mysterie of God*, pp. 3, 5, and *The Breaking of the Day of God*, p. 90; cf. *W.T.U.D.*, p. 261.

31. *The Saints Paradise*, pp. 51-3. It is not uninteresting to compare these pages with *Paradise Regained*, and Winstanley's doctrine of Sonship

with Milton's: *M.E.R.*, Ch. 23.

32. *The Saints Paradise*, pp. 68-9; *The Mysterie of God*, p. 4; *Works*, p. 120.
33. *The Saints Paradise*, pp. 72-3, 87; *The Mysterie of God*, pp. 8, 53, 82-3. Cf. pp. 209-10 above.
34. *The Breaking of the Day of God*, pp. 39, 62, 119; *The Saints Paradise*, pp. 76, 98. Cf. Joseph Salmon quoted on p. 196 above.
35. *Works*, pp. 112-15, 122, 127.
36. *The Saints Paradise*, pp. 93, 105-6.
37. *Ibid.*, pp. 122-5; *Works*, pp. 104-5, 109, 111, 124-5. Cf. *Light Shining in Buckinghamshire*: Reason in all men teaches them to do as they would be done by; and *More Light Shining in Buckinghamshire*: Reason equals co-operation: *Works*, pp. 611, 627. If Winstanley had any hand in these pamphlets, these passages might well have been written by him.
38. *Works*, pp. 451-3.
39. *The Saints Paradise*, p. 16; *Works*, pp. 136-44. One of the few respects in which Kevin Brownlow's admirable film *Winstanley* errs is in making Winstanley say grace before eating. In *The New Law of Righteousness* he rejects the practice: *Works*, p. 232.
40. *The Breaking of the Day of God*, pp. 79, 115, 123, 129-30.
41. *The Saints Paradise*, pp. 12, 30, 78; cf. *M.E.R.*, pp. 314-16, and pp. 210-12 above.
42. *Works*, p. 122.
43. *The Saints Paradise*, pp. 8, 15-16.
44. *Ibid.*, pp. 18-19. Did Winstanley feel that his move into Surrey had cut him off from some London congregation?
45. *Ibid.*, pp. 57-8; cf. p. 115, and *The Mysterie of God*, p. 59.
46. *Works*, p. 315.
47. *The Saints Paradise*, p. 60; cf. p. 33. I owe the peat-cutting to David Taylor, citing recently identified Cobham manorial court records for the period 1620-60.
48. Contrast Hudson, "Economic and Social Thought of Gerrard Winstanley", pp. 5, 7, 11, 17, 19. Professor Hudson believes that the dedicatory epistle to *The Law of Freedom* is "a clear indication that he had been converted to the Fifth Monarchy point of view", at least so far as methods were concerned. Having argued that "political action was irrelevant" for Winstanley, Professor Hudson had to find a way out of the "mystifying paradox" of his own invention. But there were no Fifth Monarchist methods in 1651, when Winstanley completed *The Law of Freedom*.
49. *The Breaking of the Day of God*, p. 133; cf. *Works*, p. 186. D.W. Petegorsky believed that Winstanley had read More and Bacon: Petegorsky, *Left-Wing Democracy in the English Civil War* (1940), p. 122. My guess would be the same; but he never mentions them. Cf. P. Zagorin, *A History of Political Thought in the English Revolution* (1954), pp. 53-4; and T.W. Hayes, "Gerrard Winstanley and Foxe's 'Book of Martyrs'", *Notes and Queries*, new series, XXIV (1977), pp. 209-12.
50. *The Saints Paradise*, pp. 21, 27; cf. *The Breaking of the Day of God*,

pp. 35, 50, 70, 91-2, 132-6, and *Works*, p. 188.

51. *The Saints Paradise*, Sig. A 2v-3, pp. 70, 86-9, 93, 106.

52. *Ibid.*, pp. 19, 62-3; *The Breaking of the Day of God*, Sig. A 3v-4v, pp. 79, 125-7.

53. Cf. *Antichrist in Seventeenth-Century England* (1971), *passim*. We might list William Aspinwall, John Brayne, Mary Cary, Collier, Erbery, Nathanael Homes, Robert Purnell, William Sedgwick, John Spittlehouse, Peter Sterry and many others.

54. *The Breaking of the Day of God*, pp. 1, 40; cf. p. 30. This tract takes the form of an exposition of Revelation XI, a favourite chapter with millenarians: cf. Lodowick Muggleton, *A True Interpretation of the Eleventh Chapter of the Revelation of St. John, and Other Texts* (1662); Hanserd Knollys, *An Exposition of the Eleventh Chapter of the Revelation* (1679).

55. *The Saints Paradise*, pp. 81-2; cf. *The Mysterie of God*, p. 6: "The mystery of iniquity will be subdued under the feet of his Son, the human nature".

56. *The Mysterie of God*, p. 7; *W.T.U.D.*, p. 193. See pp. 196, 211 above.

57. Thomas Edwards, *Gangraena*, I, pp. 87-8, II, p. 11, and III, pp. 26-7; *W.T.U.D.*, esp. pp. 35-8, 184-92; *M.E.R.*, Chs. 6, 8. Sabine is good on the religious flux from which Winstanley's ideas emerged: *Works*, pp. 22-39.

58. *Works*, pp. 493-4; Alexander Gordon's article on "Richard Coppin" in *D.N.B.*

59. John Penry, *Three Treatises concerning Wales* (ed. D. Williams, Cardiff, 1960), p. 33. See Chapter 7 above.

60. Burrage, *op. cit.*, I, Chapters 9-11; *W.T.U.D.*, pp. 165-6; cf. p. 102 above. Thomas Edwards and the 1648 Blasphemy Ordinance denounced universalism.

61. R.M. Jones, *Spiritual Reformers of the Sixteenth and Seventeenth Centuries* (1928), p. 254; *Works*, pp. 25-6, 29; Saltmarsh, *Sparkles of Glory*, pp. 145-6; cf. C.H. Firth, *Cromwell's Army* (1902), p. 400, and p. 128 above.

62. Samuel Fisher, *Baby-Baptism meer Babism* (1653), pp. 27-9, 105-6; cf. *W.T.U.D.*, p. 259.

63. [Anon.], *Tyranipocrit, Discovered with his Wiles, Wherewith He Vanquisheth* (Rotterdam, 1649); *W.T.U.D.*, pp. 166-7, 204-6, 220-1; George Fox, *Three General Epistles to be Read in all the Congregations of the Righteous* (1664), p. 5.

64. *W.T.U.D.*, pp. 220-1, 232; Milton, *Paradise Lost*, xii. 585-7; cf. *Works*, p. 481; Lutaud, *Winstanley*, pp. 270-1.

65. *W.T.U.D.*, p. 186; cf. Saltmarsh, quoted in *Works*, p. 31.

66. F. Yates, *Giordano Bruno and the Hermetic Tradition* (1964), pp. 8, 23; P.J. French, *John Dee: The World of an Elizabethan Magus* (1972), p. 74; W. Shumaker, *The Occult Sciences in the Renaissance* (California U.P., 1972), pp. 230-2.

67. *Philosophy Reformed and Improved in Four Profound Treatises* (by O. Croll and Paracelsus), trans. Henry Pinnell (1657), p. 65.

68. *W.T.U.D.*, pp. 233, 236; William Erbery, *The Testimony ... left upon Record for the Saints of Succeeding Ages* (1658), pp. 5-15, 23, 40; Fisher, *Baby-Baptism meer Babism*, pp. 511-13; for Morgan Llwyd see R. Tudor Jones, "The Healing Herb and the Rose of Love: the Piety of Two Welsh Puritans", in *Reformation, Conformity and Dissent* (ed. R.B. Knox, 1977), pp. 172, 175-6.
69. *W.T.U.D.*, pp. 188-97, 204-6, 217, 220-2, 224-5, 228, 236-7, 259, 264; cf. Winstanley, *Works*, pp. 28-30, 39; Jones, *Spiritual Reformers*, pp. 214-15; Saltmarsh, *Sparkles of Glory*, pp. 9-12, 18, and *passim; Short Journal and Itinerary Journals of George Fox* (ed. N. Penney, Cambridge U.P., 1925), pp. 13, 21, 41; John Everard, *The Gospel-Treasury Opened* (2nd edn., 1657-9), I, pp. 54-5, 60, 76-8; Collier, *A Discovery of the New Creation* (1647), in Woodhouse, *Puritanism and Liberty*, p. 390.
70. Fox, *Short Journal*, pp. 17, 31-2. The passages in which Fox made this claim on his own behalf were omitted from the *Journal* as printed in 1694.
71. Nayler, *Sauls Errand to Damascus* (1654), pp. 2, 5-6, 10-11; Nayler, *A Discovery of the Man of Sin* (1654), p. 14.
72. Fox, *Short Journal*, pp. 1, 16. (These passages were also omitted from the 1694 *Journal*).
73. Rutherford, *A Survey of the Spirituall Antichrist* (1648), pp. 59-68.
74. [Anon.], *The Sovereignty of Kings* (1642), Sig. A 1v, A 3.
75. Wither, *Fides Anglicana* (1660), p 22, in *Miscellaneous Works* (Spenser Soc.), V (1877); *M.C.P.W.*, IV, pp. 403, 499; *M.E.R.*, p. 302; Saltmarsh, *Sparkles of Glory*, pp. 155, 187-8.
76. R[ichard] O[verton], *Mans Mortalitie* (Amsterdam, 1644) (ed. H. Fisch, Liverpool U.P., 1968), p. 97, quoting Overton's *Man Wholly Mortal* (1655).
77. *W.T.U.D.*., pp. 224-7; cf. pp. 237-40, 261-2; Wither, *Fragmenta Prophetica* (1669), in *Miscellaneous Works*, VI (1878), p. 121.
78. William Perkins, *Works* (1609-13), III, p. 392; Rutherford, *A Survey of the Spirituall Antichrist*, pp. 9, 55-68; Ephraim Pagitt, *Heresiography* (2nd. edn., 1645), pp. 84-7; cf. pp. 104-5 above.
79. D.D. Hall, *op. cit.*, pp. 350-73, esp. pp. 361-2.
80. Jones, *Spiritual Reformers*, pp. 225, 245-6, 262; Erbery, *Testimony*, pp. 207, 217-20, 237; *M.E.R.*, pp. 312-13; Fisher, *Baby-Baptism meer Babism*, pp. 511-13; Saltmarsh, *Sparkles of Glory*, pp. 39, 187-8, 219 and *passim*.
81. Warr, *Administrations, Civil and Spiritual* (1648), pp. 28, 35-6, 40.
82. *W.T.U.D.*., pp. 178, 187, 219-22.
83. Nayler, *Sauls Errand to Damascus*, pp. 2, 8; Bunyan, *Works*, II, pp. 168, 177, 198, 210.
84. *W.T.U.D.*, pp. 193-4; *M.E.R.*, pp. 304, 309; Collier, in Woodhouse, *Puritanism and Liberty*, p. 390.
85. Cook, *King Charls His Case* (1649), p. 40; Canne, *A Voice from the Temple to the Higher Powers* (1653), p. 14; *M.E.R.*, p. 298. Cf. pp. 193-4 above.

86. *W.T.U.D.*, pp. 204-6; cf. Clarkson, *ibid.*, p. 338.
87. *M.E.R.*, p. 322.
88. *W.T.U.D..*, pp. 142-6; Winstanley, *Works*, p. 28; G. K. Hyland, *A Century of Persecution* (1920), pp. 103-12; cf. pp. 103-5 above.
89. *W.T.U.D.*, pp. 170-9, 191, 209, 225-6, 228; *M.E.R.*, p. 309; Jones, *Spiritual Reformers*, pp. 186-7, 251-2; Edwards, *Gangraena*, III, pp. 26-7; R.O., *Mans Mortalitie*, pp. 38-42; Haller and Davies, *op. cit.*, pp. 296-7.
90. J. N. Wise, *Sir Thomas Browne's 'Religio Medici' and Two Seventeenth Century Critics* (Missouri U.P., 1973), pp. 25-6, 149.
91. Henry Newcome, *Autobiography* (ed. R. Parkinson, Chetham Soc., 1852), II, p. 37.
92. Clarkson, *A Single Eye*, Sig. A lv.
93. *A Discourse between John Reeve and Richard Leader* (1682), p. 9.
94. *W.T.U.D.*, pp. 219-22.
95. F. J. C. Hearnshaw, *Life of Sir Henry Vane the Younger* (1910), p. 57.
96. Nayler, *Sauls Errand to Damascus*, p. 14.
97. *Works*, pp. 567-70; Lutaud, *op. cit.*, p. 367.
98. *M.E.R.*, pp. 72-3 and Chapter 23; Pagitt, *Heresiography*, pp. 84-7; cf. Emmison, *Elizabethan Life: Morals and the Church Courts*, p. 110, and p. 103 above.
99. V. Powell, quoted in Jones, "The Healing Herb and the Rose of Love", pp. 157-8; cf. George Starkey, quoted by R. L. Greaves, "The Nature of the Puritan Tradition", in Knox, *Reformation, Conformity and Dissent*, p. 272; Saltmarsh, *Sparkles of Glory*, pp. 79-101.
100. *M.E.R.*, pp. 71-2 and Chapter 8; Fisher, *Baby-Baptism meer Babism*, pp. 34-8, 553, 591-2; *W.T.U.D.*, Chapter 6, p. 214.
101. For more on Winstanley and the clergy see *Change and Continuity in Seventeenth-Century England*, pp. 142-8.
102. B. R. White, "Henry Jessey in the Great Rebellion", in Knox, *op. cit.*, pp. 142-3; Saltmarsh, *Sparkles of Glory*, pp. 280-2.
103. *W.T.U.D.*, pp. 187, 195-6, 209, 372; *M.E.R.*, pp. 112-13; Hill, *Irreligion in the "Puritan" Revolution* (Barnett Shine Foundation Lecture, 1974), p. 19; cf. pp. 212, 226-7 above. I cannot understand how Professor Hudson came to suppose that Winstanley made "provision for regular worship" in *The Law of Freedom*, nor for "sermons to deal with what we would call 'historical theology', 'natural theology' and 'philosophy of religion'": Hudson, "Economic and Social Thought of Gerrard Winstanley", pp. 19-20. This seems to me a very strained interpretation of the passages to which he refers: *Works*, pp. 562-4, 597.
104. John Reeve, *A Remonstrance from the Eternal God* (1653), p. 21; Reeve, *Sacred Remains* (1706), p. 46.
105. *Works*, p. 402.
106. *The Saints Paradise*, p. 7.
107. *M.E.R.*, pp. 211-16; Saltmarsh, *Sparkles of Glory*, p. 117; *Free Grace* (10th edn., 1700), p. 111: first published 1645. Cf. Chapter 10 above.
108. *The Mysterie of God*, pp. 18, 44-5; *Works*, pp. 565-6; N. T. Burns, *Christian Mortalism from Tyndale to Milton* (Harvard U.P., 1972),

pp. 232-3 and *passim*; *M.E.R.*, pp. 73-5 and chapter 25; Emmison, *op. cit.*, p. 110; D.E. Underdown, *Somerset in the Civil War and Interregnum* (Newton Abbot, 1973), p. 146; cf. pp. 103-4 above.
109. Edwards, *Gangraena*, III, p. 101; cf. I, p. 117; *W.T.U.D.*, pp. 207, 221; *M.C.P.W.*, VI, p. 409; R.O., *Mans Mortalitie, passim.*
110. Bunyan, *Works*, II, pp. 176-7, 200. Bunyan may have confused Quakers with Ranters or even Diggers: both were to be found in Bedfordshire in the early sixteen-fifties.
111. Shumaker, *The Occult Sciences in the Renaissance*, pp. 214, 223; Yates, *Giordano Bruno and the Hermetic Tradition*, p. 34; *M.E.R.*, pp. 330-1.
112. *W.T.U.D.*, pp. 179, 206, 209; Winstanley, *Works*, pp. 107-8; William Sewel, *The History of ... the ... Quakers* (1722), pp. 16-17; G.F. Nuttall, *The Puritan Spirit* (1967), pp. 194-203; cf. p. 104 above.
113. Francis Bacon, *Works* (ed. J. Spedding, R.L. Ellis and D.D. Heath, 1857-74), III, pp. 213, 377; cf. Winstanley, *Works*, p. 565.
114. Harvey, *Anatomical Exercitations Concerning the Generation of Living Creatures* (1653), pp. 456-7. This was the first English translation, so what Winstanley published in 1652 is unlikely to derive from Harvey: *Works*, p. 565.
115. See pp. 187, 226 above; *M.E.R.*, p. 330; *W.T.U.D.*, pp. 206, 219-20.
116. Everard, *The Gospel-Treasury Opened*, I, pp. 5-11, 71-7, 111-13; II, pp. 64, 361, 363, 373-5.
117. Saltmarsh, *Sparkles of Glory*, pp. 189-93; Richard Coppin, *Divine Teachings* (1653), II, *Antichrist in Man*, pp. 99-101; Fox, *Short Journal*, p. 4.
118. *W.T.U.D.*, pp. 148, 391-2.
119. John Holland, *The Smoke of the Bottomlesse Pit* (1651), p. 2; Edward Hyde, *A Wonder and Yet No Wonder* (1651), pp. 35 ff., both quoted by Theodor Sippell, *Werdendes Quäkertum* (Stuttgart, 1937).
120. Warr, *Administrations, Civil and Spiritual*, pp. 2, 5-6, 10-11, 13-15, 18.
121. See p. 223 above; and for Warr, see also *W.T.U.D.*, Chapter 12.
122. Jacob Boehme, *The Signature of All Things* (Everyman edn.; first published in 1621), pp. 218-19; George Smith, *Englands Pressures, or, The Peoples Complaint* (1645), pp. 4-5.
123. Edwards, *Gangraena*, III, pp. 26-7.
124. *W.T.U.D.*, pp. 146, 220; C.S. Hensley, *The Later Career of George Wither* (The Hague, 1969), p. 99; Sir Henry Vane, *The Retired Man's Meditations* (1655), p. 173; Lodowick Muggleton, *A True Interpretation ... of the Whole Book of the Revelation* (1665), pp. 66-7.
125. *W.T.U.D.*, pp. 114-21, 169, 223-7; see p. 100 above. An English translation of More's *Utopia* had been published in 1639.
126. See Sir Thomas More, *The Cofutacyon of Tyndales Answere* (1532), quoted in G.R. Elton, *Reform and Reformation* (1977), p. 44.
127. Shumaker, *The Occult Sciences in the Renaissance*, pp. 213, 231.
128. Everard, *The Gospel-Treasury Opened*, I, p. 293; cf. p. 236; II, pp. 159-211. Everard died in 1650.
129. John Ball, *A Treatise of Faith*, (2nd edn. 1632;), p. 363 (I owe this

reference to Dr David Zaret); *M.C.P.W.*, II, p.601. Cf.*W.T.U.D.*, 149-50 (Sibbes and Bolton).

130. *Works*, pp.101, 243, 141.
131. This is only an inference from *Works*, pp.209, 213, 232.
132. *Ibid.*, pp.139, 232; *The Law of Freedom and Other Writings*, pp.157-8.
133. *The Saints Paradise*, p.78.
134. *Works*, pp.190, 199.
135. By Mulligan, Graham and Richards, "Winstanley: A Case for the Man as He Said He Was", pp.65-7. At this and other points my critics might have been less severe if they had reflected that I was introducing Winstanley, as a Penguin *Classic*, to readers most of whom would be unfamiliar with seventeenth-century society.
136. Lamont, *Richard Baxter and the Millennium*, esp. pp.66-7, 298; F.E. Manuel, *A Portrait of Isaac Newton* (Harvard U.P., 1968), pp.29, 86-7. Cf. Thomas Patience, *The Doctrine of Baptism* (1654), Epistle to the Reader.
137. Ed. A. Macfarlane, *The Diary of Ralph Josselin* (1976), p.350
138. For a good example see Peter Webster, *Rua and the Maori Millennium* (Victoria U.P., New Zealand, 1979), p.63.
139. J. Kent Clark, *Goodwin Wharton* (Oxford U.P., 1984), pp.145, 164, 179, 182, 213 and *passim*.
140. Thomas Hobbes, *Leviathan* (Penguin, 1968), p.411.
141. *The Saints Paradise*, p.78; Mulligan, Graham and Richards, *op. cit.*, p.67; *Works*, pp.328-9.
142. *The Law of Freedom and Other Writings*, pp.155-7.
143. *Works*, pp.218, 567-8; cf. p.520. See p.192 above.
144. *The Mysterie of God*, Sig. A 2; cf. pp.9, 33. Are we to postulate "a visible voice" here too?
145. *Works*, pp.244, 315, 329; cf. *Fire in the Bush*, *Works*, p.445: "This following declaration of the word of life was a free gift to me from the Father himself; and I received it not from men". So he sent it to the churches.
146. *Works*, pp.195, 257, 260-2, 264; cf. p.164: visions and revelations have not ceased. John Reeve had a vision in February 1652 which differentiated him from other prophets (*A Divine Looking Glass*, 1719, p.111. This is a reprint of the original edition of 1656: Muggleton considerably altered it when he reissued it in 1661).
147. *Works*, p.190.
148. *W.T.U.D.*, pp.133-6, 146-8. See p.193 above.
149. *Works*, pp.611, 613, 622; cf. *More Light Shining in Buckinghamshire*, in *Works*, p.638 (30 March 1649). See pp.214-16, 223 above.
150. *Works*, pp.612-14, 619-20, 628, 636, 646-7.
151. *W.T.U.D.* pp.163, 393; cf. p.336 (Roger Crab in 1657).
152. *Works*, pp.185, 192, 198; *A Declaration ... [from] Iver*, p.62. See pp.211-15 above.
153. I elaborate these points in my "Rejoinder", pp.149-50.
154. *Works*, pp 380-1.
155. Keith Thomas, "The Date of Gerrard Winstanley's *Fire in the Bush*", *P*

and P., no. 42 (1969), pp. 160-2; Juretic, "Digger no Millenarian", p. 279.

156. *The Law of Freedom and Other Writings*, pp. 155-7.

157. "*England's Spirit Unfoulded, or An Incouragement to Take the 'Engagement':* A Newly Discovered Pamphlet by Gerrard Winstanley", ed. G. E. Aylmer, *P. and P.*, no. 40 (1968), pp. 3-15 (hereafter *England's Spirit Unfoulded*.

158. *Works*, pp. 448, 453-7, 464, 488, 471.

159. *Ibid.*, pp. 496, 408, 413-14.

160. *Ibid.*, pp. 460-3, 478-82, 494-7; cf. *M.E.R.*, Ch. 30.

161. Hudson, "Economic and Social Thought of Gerrard Winstanley", pp. 11, 21. Contrast pp. 227-8 above.

162. *Works*, pp. 257-8, 265; cf. pp. 260, 262-4, 271, 315-17, 395, and the passage cited at note 159 above.

163. *Ibid.*, p. 181.

164. *Ibid.*, pp. 260, 389, 432; cf. p. 378.

165. *Ibid.*, pp. 650, 439-41; *A Declaration* ... [from] *Iver*, p. 65.

166. *Works*, p. 194.

167. *Ibid.*, pp. 305, 513; cf. p. 597.

168. *Ibid.*, pp. 195, 262, 326.

169. *Ibid.*, pp. 656-7.

170. *Ibid.*, p. 266; cf. pp. 191, 205.

171. *Ibid.*, pp. 363-4, 513, 558; cf. pp. 616, 638, and *A Declaration* ... [from] *Iver*, p. 65 (refusal of rent). Fox took up the suggestion of using former monastic lands to relieve the poor, and added manorial fines, in his *To the Parliament of the Comon-Wealth of England* (1659), pp. 6-8.

172. *Works*, pp. 260, 262; cf. pp. 303, 505, 529, 568, and *A Declaration* ... [from] *Iver*, p. 65.

173. *Works*, p. 420; cf. *Change and Continuity in Seventeenth-Century England*, pp. 228-9.

174. *Works*, p. 387. "The conquest" is of course the Norman Conquest.

175. *Ibid.*, p. 260; cf. p. 253. Cf. also the dedication of *The New Law of Righteousness* "to the twelve tribes of Israel that are circumcised in heart", and Everard's and Winstanley's proclamation to Fairfax that they were "of the race of the Jews", that is of the chosen people: *ibid.*, p. 15.

176. *Ibid.*, p. 201; cf. p. 492. The words could hardly be stronger.

177. *Ibid.*, pp. 284, 373.

178. *Ibid.*, pp. 15, 186; cf. pp. 114-16, 221.

179. *Ibid.*, pp. 200, 373, 428; cf. *A Declaration* ... [from] *Iver*, p. 62.

180. The point is made in O. Lutaud, *Winstanley: socialisme et christianisme* (Paris, 1976), p. 448.

181. J.C. Davis, "Gerrard Winstanley and the Restoration of True Magistracy", *P. and P.*, no. 70 (1976), pp. 78, 92. "Respect for the individual" is Mr Davis's phrase, though he appears to attribute it to me, as he also appears to attribute to me the description of Winstanley as a "counter-cultural hero" — a phrase which I am so far from accepting that I am not sure that I know what it means: *ibid.*, pp. 76, 93.

182. *Works*, pp. 316-17.

183. *Ibid.*, *199*, 437, 580; cf. p. 225 above.
184. *Works*, p. 520; cf. pp. 225-6 above.
185. See p. 226 above.
186. *Works*, pp. 187-8, 344. Contrast Paul Elmen, "The Theological Basis of Digger Communism", *Church History*, XXIII (1954), p. 214.
187. See pp. 227-8 above.
188. *Works*, pp. 206-8, 217, 226; cf. p. 239.
189. *Ibid.*, pp. 254, 297; cf. pp. 263-4.
190. *Ibid.*, p. 432; cf. p. 532.
191. *Ibid.*, pp. 673-4. Professor Lutaud compared *Paradise Lost*, X 55-7: God transfers all judgment to the Son: Lutaud, *Winstanley*, p. 301. For Milton too the Second Coming meant an end to "all earthly tyrannies".
192. *Works*, pp. 162, 225, Mulligan, Graham and Richards, "Winstanley: A Case for the Man as He Said He Was", pp. 65, 68, 71, and *passim*. See my "Rejoinder", pp. 148-9, citing *Works*, pp. 385-6 and 487-8; cf. pp. 317, 496.
193. C.H. George, "Gerrard Winstanley: A Critical Retrospect", in C.R. Cole and M.E. Moody (eds.), *The Dissenting Tradition: Essays for Leland H. Carlson* (Athens, Ohio, 1975), pp. 215-16.
194. *Works*, pp. 264, 470-1, 473-4; cf. Coster, quoted on p. 209 above.
195. *Works*, p. 189.
196. *Ibid.*, p. 210; cf. p. 264.
197. *The Saints Paradise*, Sigs. A-B, D-E, p. 11; *The Mysterie of God*, pp. 33-5; cf. p. 188 above.
198. *Works*, pp. 204, 244.
199. *Ibid.*, pp. 206, 227. Only on p. 296 does he appear to speak of the day of judgment in the traditional sense.
200. *Ibid.*, pp. 176-7, 203, 210-12, 215-16. Cf. Satan's mockery in *Paradise Lost*, X 485-7.
201. *Works*, pp. 153, 211, 216-19, 223, 226-7, 377, 409, 454, 462-3, 484, 495. Cf. *The Saints Paradise*, pp. 21-3.
202. *Works*, pp. 480-8. The Bishop of Durham has recently announced a similar theological position.
203. Pocock, *The Political Works of James Harrington*, p. 96; cf. pp. 3, 80.
204. *Works*, p. 481; Milton, *Paradise Lost*, V., 574-6; cf. *M.E.R.*, p. 408.
205. *Works*, pp. 210, 255; cf. Elmen, "The Theological Basis of Digger Communism", pp. 209-10. But already in *Truth Lifting up its Head* Winstanley had commented on the uncertainty of the text of the Bible: *Works*, pp. 100, 128. See p. 192 above.
206. *Works*, pp. 289, 569; cf. *M.E.R.*, p. 247, and George, "Gerrard Winstanley: A Critical Retrospect", p. 216.
207. *Works*, p. 509; *M.C.P.W.*, VI, p. 711; cf. *M.E.R.*, p. 314.
208. *Works*, pp. 149, 168-9; cf. p. 175.
209. *Ibid.*, pp. 160-1, 189, 215-16, 234-5, 251, 460; cf. p. 484.
210. *Ibid.*, pp. 161-3, 166, 224-5; cf. pp. 204-5, 462-3.
211. *Ibid.*, p. 124.

212. *Ibid.*, pp. 162-4, 170, 486-7; cf. *M.E.R.*, pp. 304-5, for other examples of what Empson called the "abdication of God".
213. *Works*, pp. 447-8.
214. *Ibid.*, pp. 136-44; cf. pp. 223-4. See pp. 197-8 above.
215. *Works*, pp. 381, 445-6, 454, 530; cf. pp. 176-7, and pp. 231-2 above.
216. *Works.*, p. 160; cf. pp. 189-90 above.
217. *Works*, p. 201; cf. p. 204.
218. *Ibid.*, pp. 301, 323, 511; cf. pp. 253-4, 289-90, 376, 385, 531. I deal with Winstanley on the Fall at what may seem excessive length because the subject has been misunderstood: see *P. and P.*, 89, pp. 145-6, 150.
219. *Works*, p. 424; cf. my "Rejoinder", p. 150.
220. *Works*, pp. 289-90. Cf. Chapter 7 of *Fire in the Bush*, "How came man's fall at the first?" It starts from covetousness for outward objects (*Works*, pp. 489-97).
221. *Ibid.*, pp. 489-94; cf. pp. 197, 380, 423-4, 464-6, 655.
222. *W.T.U.D.*, p. 163; *Works*, p. 448; cf. p. 316. Anthony Ascham, almost certainly after reading Winstanley, wrote that Adam's "first sin was a sin against property and therefore theft, or at least a sin of ambition by theft" (*Of the Confusions and Revolutions of Governments*, pp. 21-2).
223. *Works*, pp. 316-17, 437, 472, 529, 580. Cf. T. Wilson Hayes: for Winstanley "the Fall constitutes the progressive destruction of innocence through the creation of private property" (*Winstanley the Digger*, pp. 201-3).
224. *Ibid.*, pp. 170, 153, 184, 410; cf. p. 406, and *The Saints Paradise*, p. 122.
225. *Works*, pp. 532; *The Law of Freedom and Other Writings*, p. 395.
226. *Works*, p. 158-9.
227. *Ibid.*, pp. 253-8, 309, 321, 329.
228. *Ibid.*, p. 508; cf. pp. 420, 529, and *Change and Continuity in Seventeenth-Century England*, pp. 228-9.
229. *Works*, pp. 183-4; cf. p. 455.
230. *Ibid.*, p. 193; cf. p. 197. Mr Davis thinks that Winstanley "always had a respect for power": Davis, "Gerrard Winstanley and the Restoration of True Magistracy", p. 78. I think Winstanley consistently rejected the government and laws of kingly power, but approved of laws which helped men "to live in the community of the righteous law of love". See pp. 223-4 above.
231. *Works*, pp. 253, 473; cf. pp. 380, 426.
232. *Ibid.*, pp. 316-17; cf. pp. 337 ("community and freedom which is Christ"), 427.
233. *Ibid.*, pp. 453, 493, 559; cf. p. 496.
234. See p. 203 above.
235. *Works*, pp. 76, 376-7. Cf. pp. 209-10 above.
236. *Works*, p. 74.
237. *Puritanism and Revolution*, pp. 58-125.
238. *Works*, pp. 613, 622, 637.
239. *Ibid.*, pp. 259-60, 276; cf. p. 285.
240. They are so used in the *Letter to Fairfax* delivered on 9 June 1649:

Works, p. 282; as well as in *A Declaration from the Poor Oppressed People*.

241. *Works*, pp. 271, 273; cf. p. 529: land is the younger brother's "creation birthright". The concept of "creation liberties" had been worked out by Lilburne in *The Free Mans Freedom Vindicated* (1646), pp. 11-12.

242. *Ibid.*, pp. 288, 292; cf. pp. 289-90, 370.

243. *Ibid.*, pp. 311-12. In *The New Law of Righteousness* Winstanley denounced tithes as "the greatest sin of oppression": *Works*, p. 238.

244. *Works*, pp. 332, 382.

245. *Ibid.*, pp. 385-6; cf. pp. 316-17. For England as the tenth part of the city Babylon, see p. 193 above.

246. *Works*, pp. 389-91, 453-4; cf. p. 471. Winstanley makes it clear that his reference is not to the fighting Levellers but to Christ levelling. In the French Revolution "Jésus était sans-culotte": R.C. Cobb, *Les armées révolutionnaires*, 2 vols. (Paris and The Hague, 1961-3), II, p. 679. See p. 339 below.

247. *The Saints Paradise*, p. 34: "The Power of my unrighteous flesh strives to maintain the kingly power in me".

248. *Works*, pp. 615, 630, 639, 645, 330; cf. p. 349.

249. *Ibid.*, pp. 353-7, 362, 364, 388; cf. pp. 238-41, 470, 527, 617, and *W.T.U.D.*, Chapter 12.

250. *Works*, pp. 369, 463-4, 466, 472, 488, 580.

251. Davis, "Gerrard Winstanley and the Restoration of True Magistracy", pp. 78-9, 90. See pp. 221-3 above.

252. Winstanley draws this distinction carefully in *Fire in the Bush: Works*, pp. 472-3.

253. *Works*, p. 130.

254. *Ibid.*, pp. 362, 303; *Englands Spirit Unfoulded*, p. 13. For Reason as the spirit of burning, see p. 187 above.

255. *Works*, pp. 301, 389; cf. pp. 360-1, 366-7; *The Law of Freedom and Other Writings*, pp. 393-5.

256. *Works*, pp. 198, 188, 255; cf. p. 258 for the corruption of these rulers.

257. *Ibid.*, p. 297; cf. p. 467: "Where you see army against army, it is but the kingly power divided, tearing and devouring itself". Cf. also *More Light Shining in Buckinghamshire*, in *Works*, p. 633.

258. *Works*, pp. 205, 333.

259. *Ibid.*, pp. 384, 390, 411-13, 429-30; cf. p. 456.

260. *Ibid.*, pp. 411-12, 386, 429-30; cf. pp. 353, 372, 507.

261. *Ibid.*, pp. 302, 330.

262. *Englands Spirit Unfoulded*, pp. 9-10, 5.

263. *Works*, pp. 395-6.

264. *Ibid.*, p. 289.

265. *Englands Spirit Unfoulded*, pp. 9-10, 12.

266. Cf. *Works*, p. 430.

267. Edwards, *Gangraena*, III, pp. 147-8.

268. See Reay, "The Quakers and 1659: Two Newly-Discovered Broadsides by Edward Burrough", *Journal of the Friends' Historical Soc.*, 54 (1977), pp. 101-11.

269. Davis, "Gerrard Winstanley and the Restoration of True Magistracy", pp. 92, 85. See pp. 221-2 above.
270. *Works*, pp. 83, 505-10, 533-5, 586-7, 592; cf. pp. 308, 387, and p. 220 above
271. *Ibid.*, pp. 496-7. Something rather similar took place in Russia in the nineteen-twenties.
272. *Works*, pp. 534-5, 515, 526-7; cf. the reference to Moses on p. 516.
273. *Ibid.*, pp. 536, 539.
274. Cf. *ibid.*, p. 539: "the unruly ones, for whom only the law was added"; p. 588: "this outward law ... is a whip for the fool's back, for whom only it was added".
275. *Ibid.*, pp. 545-8, 553, 583, 587-90, 594.
276. *Ibid.*, pp. 493-4, 576-80. See p. 227 above.
277. *Ibid.*, pp. 593-4, 599-600.
278. Davis, "Gerrard Winstanley and the Restoration of True Magistracy", pp. 78-9, 85, 90, 92. Cf. pp. 217, 220.
279. *Works*, pp. 553, 597-8. This was not new: cf. pp. 193, 197-8.
280. Bunyan, *Works*, II, p. 127; cf. *The Law of Freedom and Other Writings*, pp. 41-2.
281. *Works*, pp. 332-3.
282. See pp. 188-90 above.
283. See *W.T.U.D.*, Appendix I.
284. *Ibid.*, pp. 391-2; *Works*, p. 105.
285. *The Breaking of the Day of God*, pp. 88, 132-6.
286. *Works*, p. 388.
287. *Ibid.*, p. 465.
288. *Ibid.*, pp. 473-4. This makes very clearly the point that Mr Davis misses — that Winstanley was not for or against state power as such, but for and against particular kinds of state power. See pp. 214-18 above.
289. *Works*, pp. 534, 558.
290. *Ibid.*, p. 288. I suspect an echo of John Warr in the equation of Equity and Reason, as well as in the suggestion that the spirit of righteousness has been buried for many years. See p. 199 above.
291. *Works*, pp. 425, 490-1; cf. pp. 254-5.
292. *Ibid.*, pp. 161-2; cf. p. 516.
293. Cf. *A Declaration ...* [from] *Iver*, p. 63 (Parliament's three Acts).
294. *Works*, pp. 510, 587, 581.
295. *Ibid.*, pp. 510, 600: followed by "O death, where art thou?" Cf. p. 581.
296. *Ibid.*, pp. 537-41, 559, 590-1, 596; cf. Davis, "Gerrard Winstanley and the Restoration of True Magistracy", p. 86.
297. It appears to have been so used in Surrey (the Diggers' county) in the eighteenth century: those of whom the substantial members of the community did not approve fared worse in court than those for whom a gentleman or a parson put in a good word: J.M. Beattie, "Crime and the Courts in Surrey, 1736-1753", in *Crime in England, 1550-1800* (ed. J.S. Cockburn, 1977), pp. 170-86.
298. *Works*, pp. 554-6, 559, 562, 572-3.

299. *Ibid.*, pp. 513, 573. Perhaps the reading should be "king's and conquering laws".
300. *Ibid.*, pp. 519-20.
301. *Ibid.*, pp. 565-8.
302. *Ibid.*, p. 502. Cf. Sabine's comments on this: *ibid.*, p. 59. Contrast the embarrassed passages in Mulligan, Graham and Richards, "Winstanley: A Case for the Man as He Said He Was", pp. 71-3: "at most, this shows that Winstanley was capable of being inconsistent", and has shifted to a "new vision of the millennium".
303. See pp. 187, 198-9 above, and cf. *W.T.U.D.*, pp. 206-7 (Bauthumley, Coppin).
304. *Works*, pp. 451, 523, 565, 567-8. See pp. 187, 190-1 above.
305. *ME.R.*, Chapter 25; *Works*, pp. 362, 454-7, 496.
306. Mulligan, Graham and Richards, *op. cit.*, p. 71.
307. *Works*, p. 107; cf. pp. 168, 476.
308. *Ibid.*, pp. 162-4, 169-70; cf. pp. 208-10 above.
309. *Works*, p. 251.
310. *The Saints Paradise*, Sig. B, pp. 28, 75, 114, 118; *Works*, pp. 197, 219-20, 222, 532; cf. p. 327.
311. *Works*, p. 255: Aaron and the priests were the first that deceived the people: weakness of the Mosaic law.
312. *Ibid.*, p. 332; cf. p. 383.
313. *Ibid.*, pp. 447-8, 453-7; cf. p. 187 above.
314. *Works*, pp. 490-1, 496; cf. p. 530 (against predestination).
315. *Ibid.*, p. 434. Cf. the much earlier reference to "their God" in *Light Shining in Buckinghshire*, in *Works*, p. 614.
316. *Works*, pp. 129-30, 453, 591.
317. *Ibid.*, pp. 232, 509, 523.
318. Cf. T. Wilson Hayes: for Winstanley "no human act is caused by a mere inner compulsion or a simple outer force. He combines reference to internal and external forces whenever he gives causal explanations, and he holds to this dialectic throughout his writing career", starting from the theological pamphlets of 1648 (*op. cit.*, p. 15; cf. Lutaud, *Winstanley*, esp. Part 7). In my "Rejoinder", for the benefit of a member of the editorial board of *P. and P.* who pretended not to know what "dialectical" meant, I cited the *Oxford English Dictionary*: "pertaining to the process of thought by which contradictions are seen to merge themselves in a higher truth that comprehends them, and the world process which develops similarly" — though that is perhaps a too post-Hegelian definition ("Rejoinder", p. 151n.).
319. *Works*, pp. 238-41; cf. *Antichrist in Seventeenth-Century England*, p. 170.
320. *Works*, pp. 564, 576-80; cf. pp. 203, 238, 452-6, and *M.E.R.*, p. 158. See p. 221 above.
321. *Works*, p. 362. Cf. pp. 205, 208-9, 219-20 above.
322. *Works*, p. 290; cf. p. 475.
323. *Ibid.*, p. 333.
324. Mulligan, Graham and Richards, "Winstanley: A Case for the Man as

He Said He Was", p.73.
325. *Works*, p.566.
326. The authors of "Winstanley: A Case for the Man as He Said He Was" may have been misled by Professor Hudson's argument that for Winstanley "the power of Satan" (whose existence Winstanley specifically denied) could be extirpated "only by the direct action of a personal deity ... who intervened in the affairs of the world and who was tremendously concerned about the everyday actions of men". He would intervene "by sudden miracle" to establish the new order in society. Hudson, "Economic and Social Thought of Gerrard Winstanley", pp.5-6; cf. p.20. Careful attention to Winstanley's use of words shows all these statements to be incorrect.
327. *Works*, pp.579, 457; cf. pp.200, 315, 395, 409, 567.
328. *Ibid.*, p.493; cf. p.375.
329. R.T. Vann, "From Radicalism to Quakerism: Gerrard Winstanley and Friends" *Journal of the Friends' Historical Society*, 49 (1959-61), pp.42-4; R.T. Vann, "The Later Life of Gerrard Winstanley", *Journal of the History of Ideas*, 26 (1965), pp.133-6.
330. J. Alsop, "Gerrard Winstanley's Later Life", *P. and P.*, No.82 (1979).
331. D.C. Taylor, *Gerrard Winstanley in Elmsbridge* (1982), pp.4-5. I have benefited from discussing these matters with Mr Taylor.
332. F.H. Higginson, *A Brief Relation of the Irreligion of the Northern Quakers* (1653), p.16; R. Farmer, *The Great Mysteries of Godliness and Ungodliness* (1655), dedication. I owe Higginson and the following reference to Barry Reay.
333. F. Harris, *Some Queries* (1655), p.23.
334. Comber, *Christianity no Enthusiasm* (1678), pp.90-2, 181; Tenison, *An Argument for Union* (1683), p.8; Bennett, *An Answer to the Dissenters' Pleas for separation* (1700), p.4. I owe the reference to Tenison to Barry Reay.
335. *The Breaking of the Day of God*, Sig. A 2v; *Works*, p.127. But the phrase was used by Giles Randall (Jones, *Spiritual Reformers*, p.259) and no doubt by Familists.
336. Reay, "The Quakers and 1659".
337. Friends' Meeting House Library, William Caton MS., 3, p.147: I owe this reference to the kindness of Dr Barry Reay. For Quakers and politics, see *W.T.U.D.*, esp. Chapter 10.
338. *Works*, pp.315, 228.
339. *The Moderate*, 10-17 April, 31 July-7 August 1649; cf. Lutaud, *Winstanley*, pp.172, 178, 215-16.
340. L.F. Solt, "Winstanley, Lilburne and the Case of John Fielder", *Huntington Library Quarterly*, 47 (1984), pp.119-36.
341. Warr, *Administrations, Civil and Spiritual*, passim.
342. Marvell, *Poems* (ed. H.M. Margoliouth, Oxford U.P., 1971), p.76; *Writings and Speeches of Oliver Cromwell*, III, pp.435-6. The slur seems to modern historians very unfair; they distinguish sharply between Levellers and Diggers on the property issue. But the digging of the True Levellers was the last visible action of the radical groups,

and it would remain in the memory of conservative contemporaries because it confirmed their stereotype of "levelling". This would be reinforced perhaps by the opposition to fen drainage at the Isle of Axholme in 1651, in which Lilburne and Wildman played a part: J.D. Hughes, "The Drainage Disputes in the Isle of Axholme", *Lincolnshire Historian*, II (1954), pp. 13-14.

343. Joseph Lee, *A Vindication of a Regulated Inclosure* (1656), p. 28.
344. *Works*, pp. 445-6, 530. Cf. p. 212 above.
345. See pp. 210-11 above. "The religion expressed in *The Law of Freedom* was no longer Christian, despite its terminology", as Professor Zagorin rightly remarked: Zagorin, *A History of Political Thought in the English Revolution*, p. 57. Professor Zagorin seems to me to have understood Winstanley's religion much better than some of the later commentators whom I have cited. So did Petegorsky and Sabine.
346. Lutaud, *Winstanley*, p. 426.
347. Q. Skinner, "Conquest and Consent: Thomas Hobbes and the Engagement Controversy", in *The Interregnum: The Quest for Settlement, 1646-60* (ed. G.E. Aylmer, 1972), pp. 79-98, and references at pp. 208-9.
348. *W.T.U.D.*, pp. 344-8; *The Experience of Defeat*, pp. 282-8.
349. R.M. Kingdon, *Geneva and the Coming of the Wars of Religion in France, 1555-1563* (Geneva, 1956), p. 11.
350. Soboul, *Paysans, sans-culottes et jacobins* (Paris, 1966), p. 202; see chapters 2 and 4, pp. 131-4 above and p. 333 below.
351. *Antichrist in Seventeenth-Century England*, pp. 146-8.
352. See chapter 12 below.
353. *Change and Continuity in Seventeenth-Century England*, p. 268. Cf. chapter 15 below.
354. Hobbes, *The Elements of Law* (ed. F. Tönnies, Cambridge U.P., 1928), p. 150.
355. "If there be such a thing as an atheist in the world", he made his Mr Wiseman say: Bunyan, *Works*, III, p. 627.

IV *The Millennium and After*

Historians are coming more and more to appreciate the importance of millenarianism in the seventeenth century — for radical politics, for literature, for political ideas. The failure of Jesus Christ to arrive, and the re-establishment of censorship and a repressive political régime after 1660, marked the end of revolutionary millenarian activity. Henceforth discussion of the dating of the Second Coming appears to be restricted to innocent academics. But the absence of visible millenarian politics after 1660 may mean only that popular millenarianism was driven underground rather than destroyed. There is perhaps a book to be written on the subject from 1660 to the early nineteenth century.[1]

But organized political action to expedite the millennium certainly ceased. The small body of London Fifth Monarchists tried and failed in 1657 and 1661, and that was the end. Quakers, Muggletonians and other sects abandoned immediate millenarian expectations, and went in for a good deal of rewriting of their own history. Yet the millenarian rhetoric had given expression to forces in articulate English society which were too strong to be obliterated: in different forms a secularized millenarianism took their place.

1. Cf. J.F.C. Harrison, *The Second Coming: Popular Millenarianism, 1780-1850* (1979), *passim*.

12. John Reeve, Laurence Clarkson and Lodowick Muggleton[1]

> "Hail! prophets sublime,
>   Who hath brought truth divine
> From heaven's imperial throne;
>   Which the great prophet Reeve
>   In commission received
> And imparts to the faithful alone."*
>
> "When men of learning leave discerning,
>   Perfect truth then flourish shall,
> The laity then will be esteemed;
>   Now mark what then there will befall:
> No false speaking, no false seeking,
>   Will be heard any more at all;
> But upright dealing without stealing,
>   Evermore then flourish shall. ...
>
> Not many wise, not many noble,
>   E'er embraced Christianity;
> They gave the world the shadow of it,
>   But ever practised cruelty;
> The conscientious, not contentious,
>   Evermore were punished;
> No compassion, but proud passion,
>   Ever great men fancied."†

I

The reader finding the Muggletonians sandwiched between Winstanley and Marvell — one of the greatest political thinkers and one of the greatest poets of the seventeenth century — may well feel that my interest in the extreme radicals has destroyed all sense of

---

*James Miller, 86th Song (Tune: 'Young Nancy once more'), *Divine Songs of the Muggletonians* (1829), p. 240. Other references to Reeve alone will be found on pp. 142, 240, 281, 383, 432, 519.

†Thomas Turner, 46th Song, *Divine Songs*, pp. 136-7. For Turner see p. 257 below.

255

proportion. Yet in the sixteen-fifties the followers of Reeve and Muggleton attracted more support than the Diggers did; the Muggletonian sect lasted for 327 years, whilst the Diggers were suppressed after little more than 327 days. It is arguable that the *Divine Songs of the Muggletonians* may have enjoyed a wider readership in the early nineteenth century than Marvell's poems.

More seriously, the Muggletonians are of historical interest because they and the Quakers are the only sects which originated in the radical milieu of the late sixteen-forties and early fifties, in the world of Ranters and Seekers, to survive until the present century. (Baptists and Congregationalists had long pedigrees and were not all involved in the radical politics of the late forties and early fifties, as was shown by their repudiation of the Levellers in 1649). After 1660 the Quakers regarded the Muggletonians as their most dangerous rivals. Both Quakers and Muggletonians revised their doctrines in the period of the restoration, and substantially rewrote their history: historians have only recently begun to recover the history of the pre-pacifist Quakers.[2]

Unlike the Quakers, the Muggletonians retained sacred writings, by Reeve and Muggleton, and (after some rewriting of Reeve by the surviving Muggleton) these remained basic for the sect's theology. Consequently they give us a unique glimpse of the radical theology of the late forties and early fifties: the Quakers had no texts of comparable authority. But the Muggletonians in their first decade underwent crises, challenges and splits just as the early Quakers did. What follows is an attempt to recover some aspects of the history of these years.[3]

II

Muggleton is often spoken of as co-founder with John Reeve of the sect which later bore his name: they were the Two Last Witnesses. But every significant doctrine of the Muggletonians is to be found in writings properly attributed to Reeve alone, even though after Reeve's death in 1658 Muggleton tried to claim a share in these writings, and equality for his commission with Reeve's.[4] The record is against him.

It was to John Reeve alone that God spoke on 2-5 February 1652. Long after the event Muggleton claimed that he too had had a series of revelations "before John Reeve had any". So far as we know this was never mentioned before Reeve's death. The claim was hinted at in 1662, in Muggleton's first published work,[5] but it was not formally made in print until 1699, in Muggleton's posthumous *Acts of the Witnesses of the Spirit*. This was a polemical work, written to establish Muggleton's position as the equal if not the superior of Reeve. It was greatly to his advantage to claim precedence in revelations, and to hint that Reeve had been jealous of his priority in the period immediately before Reeve received his divine commission. There is every reason to be sceptical about Muggleton's claim.

Many others in the seventeenth century saw visions and heard voices; but none claimed quite the same authority as Reeve, to whom God gave "understanding of my mind in the Scriptures above all men in the world". The Bible was cited by every squabbling sect to support its case, but from February 1652 John Reeve became its sole authorized interpreter. "All men in the world" must include Muggleton, whom God gave to Reeve "to be thy mouth". The Holy Spirit reminded Reeve of Aaron's relationship to Moses. A glance at Exodus 4 will make clear Aaron's inferiority: "He shall be to thee instead of a mouth, and thou shalt be to him instead of God".

God's next command to Reeve was to curse "Theaureaujohn" (Thomas Tany), taking Muggleton and Thomas Turner with him. "If Lodowick Muggleton deny to go with thee, do thou from me pronounce him cursed to eternity". God seemed to be more sure of Thomas Turner (otherwise known only as author of the hymn used as epigraph to this Chapter) than of Muggleton. God was right: the threat of damnation had to be used before the latter agreed to accompany Reeve. Reeve's account of these matters, published whilst all parties concerned were still alive, was never challenged: Muggleton himself regarded *A Transcendent Spirituall Treatise*, our source for these events, as an inspired work. He must at the time have accepted his inferior status as therein recorded.

Confusion has been caused for historians by the addition of Muggleton's name to the title-page of Reeve's tracts: this was always done when Muggleton reprinted them after Reeve's death, and occasionally earlier. Cataloguers add to the confusion by citing Muggleton as co-author with Reeve, though *The Short-Title Catalogue* corectly attributes all "Muggletonian" pamphlets published in or before 1658 to Reeve alone.

Reeve published eight pamphlets in his lifetime:

A Transcendent Spirituall Treatise (1652)
A Letter presented unto Alderman Fouke, Lord Mayor of London (1653).
A General Epistle from the Holy Spirit (1653).
A Remonstrance from the Eternal God (1653).
An Epistle from the Prophet Reeve (1656).
An Epistle to a Quaker (1656).
A Divine Looking-Glass (1656).
Joyfull Newes from Heaven (1658).

Muggleton later claimed all but the fifth and last of these as "written by us",[6] but that is clearly untrue. There are in addition many pieces by Reeve subsequently published in *Sacred Remains* (1706), and others collected in *Spiritual Epistles* (1755). These confirm Reeve's claim to special status.

A Transcendent Spirituall Treatise is described on the title-page as "by the hand of his [God's] own prophet, being his last messenger and witness". Later on the page Muggleton's name is added, confusingly, but Muggleton himself admitted that Reeve was the sole author.[7] The treatise is written entirely in the first person singular: "The Lord Jesus spake unto me", "I am the messenger of the holy invisible Spirit", "I declare by revelation from the Holy Spirit", "by virtue of my commission": "unto me, John Reeve", "the third and last witness by commission from the Lord".[8]

When Reeve and Muggleton were examined by the Lord Mayor, it is clear from Muggleton's later account that Reeve did all the talking, though this is obscured by Muggleton using the first person when Reeve is speaking.[9] Muggleton also tells us that Reeve wrote the *Letter to Alderman Fouke* whilst they were in prison,[10] though this is described on the title-page as "from the Two Witnesses and prisoners of Jesus Christ in Newgate", "the two last spiritual witnesses and true prophets by commission from the holy Spirit of the true God". The tract begins "by our commission received by voice of words from ... the only true God, ... we declare"; "God sent us". But Reeve soon takes over: "I gave you a full account of the Lord Jesus speaking unto me"; "what I have been made to write in this paper". Only at the end does he change to "the Holy Spirit that sent us. ... We pronounce you".[11]

A General Epistle and *A Remonstrance from the Eternal God* both refer on the title-page to "the two Last Spiritual Witnesses", but the text of *A General Epistle* starts off firmly "by virtue of my commission ... I present this epistle", and continues "I declare by revelation from the Spirit ...". "God spake to me, John Reeve, his third and last witness".[12] In *A Remonstrance* both "I" and "we" are used.[13] *An Epistle of the Prophet Reeve* and *An Epistle to a Quaker* are throughout clearly by John Reeve, and signed by him only: "the light in me bears witness".[14]

The more important work, *A Divine Looking-Glass* begins "I being a poor layman, ... God spake unto me"; "by inspiration from the unerring Spirit I positively affirm ...". "We came forth" as the result of a message "by voice of words spoken unto me". God gave me "understanding above all men in the world" of "his mind in the Scriptures".[15] (Reeve repeated this claim, with emphasis, in *A Letter to William Sedgwick*, 1657).[16] In "Another Epistle Annexed" to *A Divine Looking-Glass* Muggleton claimed to share this gift of understanding the Scriptures — a claim he made specific in 1668.[17] But the text of *A Divine Looking-Glass* states flatly "I John Reeve am the last commissioned prophet". "I have both tasted and seen with my spirit a greater measure of the eternal glory and shame to come than any creature now living". "In the name and power of the Lord Jesus, by whose ... spirit I was inspiringly moved to write it". Muggleton's name is joined with Reeve's at the end — "the two last commissioned spirits or prophets".[18] To later editions Muggleton added his own Epistle, in which he claimed that God hath chosen "*us two* to be his last commissioned prophets".[19] But in an introductory epistle to the 1661 edition Muggleton himself attributed *A Divine Looking-Glass* to "the unerring spirit of God which was given unto John Reeve".[20]

The title-page of *Joyfull Newes* states that Reeve and Muggleton are "the last commissioned witnesses and prophets", but the tract was "printed for the author" in the singular and the text is in the first person singular throughout. "I shall write", "from an unerring spirit I confidently affirm".[21] "I say again from that God that sent me"; "when a man is chosen alone, having only but one companion given unto him".[22] At the very end the names of John Reeve and Lodowick Muggleton are appended. Only in editions published after Reeve's death did Muggleton put "by" before their names, but in *Acts of the Witnesses* he confirms that Reeve was the author.[23] Even *A Discourse between John Reeve and Richard Leader*, which purported to be "recited by Lodowick Muggleton" when it was printed (in 1682?), is also written in the first person singular by Reeve.[24]

III

Some time before Reeve's death in 1658 he converted Laurence Clarkson. Like Reeve and Muggleton, Clarkson was a former Ranter, and a much better-known — not to say notorious — figure in the world of radical religion.[25] In 1659-60 Clarkson published four tracts in which he assumed the role of spokesman for the sect, calling Reeve — as Reeve had called himself — "the last commissioned prophet of the Lord".[26] In *The Quakers Downfall* (1659) Clarkson claimed to have inherited Reeve's mantle. He styled himself "the alone true and faithful messenger of Christ Jesus", bearing "the last revelation and commission that ever shall be". The spirit was "more fully manifested" in Clarkson "than it was in the saints that gave forth the Scriptures".[27] His Quaker critic, John Harwood, reported that Clarkson, like Reeve before him and Muggleton after him, claimed to be "the judge of the Scriptures, and all must believe the meanings he gives unto them, yet would show no reason for it".[28]

In his autobiographical *The Lost sheep Found* (1660) Clarkson continued his bid for the succession to Reeve, claiming to have been "a fellow-labourer" with him "beyond all now living" — that is, beyond Muggleton, whom Clarkson did not even mention. Reeve, Clarkson said, had seen him as "a glorious instrument, ... the like should never come after me". Clarkson referred to "our last comission", meaning his and Reeve's, and declared that he was "the true and only bishop now living".[29] We should not take Clarkson's word about his relationship with Reeve, any more — I am suggesting — than we should take Muggleton's. But Clarkson did publish his version at the time: Muggleton's did not appear till forty years later.

A struggle followed, which lasted for four years. Muggleton excommunicated Clarkson, took away his power to pronounce sentence of damnation and cut off his allowance. Clarkson had joined the sect too recently to have acquired a significant following, and Muggleton finally won out. According to the latter, Clarkson repented and agreed not to write any more. He preserved silence until his death in 1667. Muggleton demonstrated his superiority by reversing a sentence of damnation which Clarkson had pronounced.[30] It is possible that Clarkson had been interested in the succession primarily for financial reasons, as well as from considerations of power. He made no bones about his readiness to lie and cheat on other occasions.[31] We do not know much about the Muggle-tonians' finances, but Muggleton may have stood to lose a good deal if Clarkson had ousted him.[32] That was the end of Clarkson, but it was not the end of Reeve.

With Reeve dead and Clarkson silenced, Muggleton ventured into print for the first time in 1662, with a 200-page *True Interpretation of the Eleventh Chapter of the Revelation of St. John*, in which he firmly placed himself at the centre of the picture as the survivor of the two Witnesses whom God had commissioned.[33] Three years later he followed it up with a still vaster tome, *A True Interpretation of all the chief texts ... of the Revelation of St. John*. "I can truly say with Moses, the prophets, apostles and saints blessed by the Lord God of truth, who hath revealed unto me the mystery of God" and many other mysteries "never revealed before unto prophet or apostle".[34]

In 1671 the self-elevated Muggleton had to face a more serious challenge from William Medgate and Walter Buchanan. Medgate, like Muggleton, called himself the prophet of the Lord. The rebels accused Muggleton of going about to overthrow John Reeve and substitute his own authority. Muggleton virtually admitted the charge, confidently claiming "John Reeve is dead, and those that wrote the Scriptures are dead, but ... God hath preserved [Muggleton] alive to be the judge of John Reeve's writings and of the writings of the prophets and apostles. ... I being chosen of God had power to contradict him [Reeve] in his judgment".[35]

The rebels challenged Muggleton's doctrine that God takes no notice even of believers, which they rightly saw as an innovation. The furthest Reeve had ever gone was to deny the value of outward (as against inward) prayer.[36] Later Muggleton claimed to have corrected Reeve on this point whilst he was still alive; but again we have no evidence to confirm this. The rebels associated the new doctrine with Clarkson.[37] The view that prayer was ineffective was familiar in the antinomian circles in which Clarkson had moved.[38] Clarkson first taught the doctrine, so far as we know, as long ago as 1650, in *A Single Eye*. He may well have got the idea from Tobias Crisp, whose sermons he had attended. But it was of long standing in radical circles, having been taught by Henry Niklaes.[39] Mrs Anne Hutchin-son and the New England antinomians of the sixteen-thirties were alleged to reject prayer.[40] Jacob Bauthumley, Joseph Salmon and John Smith all taught the doctrine.[41] Gerrard Winstanley thought prayer was useless.[42]

In 1659 Clarkson said that he could not "find that ever God did hear or give an answer to any private believer".[43] In *The Lost sheep Found* Clarkson asserted as "the highest pitch of revelation" that God does not hear even "us his last commissioners", let alone ordinary mortals.[44] That was printed in 1660, long before Muggleton publicly adopted the doctrine. It looks as though he took it over from Clarkson, a more experienced and sophisticated theologian, of whose abilities Muggleton remained in considerable awe long after Clarkson's death.[45]

The idea that God takes no notice of his creation may derive from Stoicism. Seneca was available in English translation from 1614.[46] Grotius had contemplated the possibility that God did not care about humanity.[47] We can find it in Fulke Greville and Robert South.[48] Rochester did not think "prayers were of much use", and he translated Lucretius to the effect that God was "not pleased by good deeds nor provoked by bad".[49] Stoical acceptance of the fact that God takes no notice may well have been reinforced by the experience of defeat, first by royalists, then by Parliamentarians, and by the waning of the millenarian hope in the years after Reeve's death. Muggleton assumed the role, attributed to Clarkson, of the prophet who would carry the burdens of the saints, provided they believed implicitly in him.[50]

If God takes no notice of our prayers, there is no check on the infallible interpreter of Scripture. Clarkson spotted this. "There is no going to God but by commissioners",[51] a point Muggleton was to use more crudély to his own advantage. He accused the rebels of 1671 of "minding God only and disobeying and rebelling against the prophet".[52] (In *The World of the Muggletonians* I compared, semi-seriously, Muggleton's rewriting of the history of the sect with Stalin's rewriting of the history of the Soviet Communist Party to put himself on an equality with Lenin.[53] I missed the further analogy that Muggleton had to overcome a challenge to his authority from a brilliant recent recruit to the sect, and then quietly took over some of Clarkson's ideas, as Stalin took over some of Trotsky's).

Another point which Muggleton held against the rebels of 1671 was that "they would make all the Lord's people holy if they were in the prophet's place".[54] Reeve indeed said that "God himself is the alone teacher of his elect only, by the immediate inspiration of his holy spirit", which was rather different from Muggleton's idea (and perhaps Clarkson's before him) that the prophet is the essential

mediator between God and the elect.[55] Reeve's position is close to
Ranterism and Quakerism. Perhaps Medgate thought all the Lord's
people were prophets.

IV

Among Reeve's doctrines which Muggleton dropped was the former's belief in the imminence of the end of the world. Reeve did not
expect a thousand-year rule of the saints.[56] But in 1656 he said that
"the day of the Lord" is "near at hand", and in *A Remonstrance from
the Eternal God* he had implied that "the dissolution of this vain
world" would occur during the lifetime of himself and Muggleton. In
private correspondence in 1656 he suggested that it was a matter of
months.[57] By the time Muggleton reprinted *A Divine Looking-Glass*
in 1661 it was fairly clear that the millennium was not coming: King
Charles rather than King Jesus had taken the throne. Anxious no
doubt — like Quakers and other sectaries — to dissociate the Muggletons from the few desperate Fifth Monarchists who revolted in
1657 and 1661, Muggleton deleted the millenarian passages: in 1665
he himself declared that the time of the end of the world was
uncertain.[58] But as late as 1674 Thomas Tomkinson could still assert
that "the time will not be long".[59] A century and a half later a poem
on the title-page of *Divine Songs of the Muggletonians* spoke of
"these last days". Millenarianism was not dead.

Reprinting *A Divine Looking-Glass*, Muggleton tells us, was "the
first thing I did after Clarkson was put down".[60] The massive
deletions were an exercise of power, though it was sensible to cut out
Reeve's dedication to "most heroic Cromwell", hoping that "thou
mayst in due season become ... a faithful defender and deliverer of all
suffering peoples upon a spiritual account within thy dominions".[61]
Muggleton also excised the passages in the text in which Reeve had
defended Cromwell and attacked "all those powers which endeavour
to exalt the Roman see of Charles's seed upon his throne again".
"Who can tell for what end the Protector of heaven and earth hath so
highly exalted [Cromwell]? It may be that God will "make use of
Oliver Cromwell to be an instrument of general good beyond thy
expectation". "I positively affirm, by an immediate commission
from the Holy Spirit, that the God of glory hath exalted Oliver
Cromwell ... into the throne of Charles Stuart, that the yoke of
Jesuitical persecution for conscience sake may be utterly taken off
the necks of his people in these three nations". God "hath delivered

his innocent people by thy [Cromwell's] hand out of their spiritual and natural tyranny in many places". "There is a secret hope in me of better things concerning thee". "Blessed are all spiritual warriors, for their crowns are immortal and eternal".[62] The qualified hope recalls Marvell's "If these the times, then this must be the man" in *The First Anniversary*: though the qualifications are perhaps a little surprising in an infallible prophet. Clarkson also recalled Cromwell's tolerance gratefully: "had it not been for the late Lord Protector, whose soul was merciful to tender consciences, O ... what a bloody persecuting day had been in England!"[63] Muggleton's distrust of human reason (greater than Reeve's) may derive from Clarkson,[64] though it no doubt also relates to the discomfiture of all radicals by the inability of their theories to cope with the events of the late fifties and of 1660.

V

Muggleton overcame the rebels of 1671, and started to write *The Acts of the Witnesses* to establish definitively his position as Reeve's infallible successor and equal if not superior. Hence the strong emphasis on the priority of his revelations and on his corrections of Reeve; hence his rather unpleasant attempts to denigrate Reeve.[65] There are interesting analogies between George Fox's reorganization of the Society of Friends after 1661 and Muggleton's takeover after defeating Clarkson. Neither Fox nor Muggleton had been in a position of sole authority earlier, but after the deaths of James Nayler and John Reeve, and after Fox had defeated the Story-Wilkinson revolt as Muggleton defeated Medgate and Buchanan, each stamped his personality on his sect at a time when rethinking was the order of the day for all radicals. The millenarian hope had proved delusive: Fox and Muggleton set about organizing their followers to face life as it was in the post-restoration world.

Muggleton's strengths were his pragmatic common sense as moralist and counsellor, and his organizing ability, to which we paid tribute in *The World of the Muggletonians*. He had an easy-going attitude towards the peccadilloes, and worse, of members of his sect, so long as they retained faith in his commission.[66] This laissez-faire tolerance, indeed laxity, undoubtedly contributed much to the survival of the Muggletonians: we do not know whether Reeve possessed such gifts, or could have acquired them.[67]

Contemporaries had no doubt that until his death Reeve was the important figure. Edward Burrough's *Answer to John Reeve's Epistle from the Mighty Jehovah* of 1654 makes no mention of Muggleton.[68] George Fox was well aware of Muggleton's attempt to exalt himself and demote Reeve. The idea that "a commission was given to him and John Reeve", Fox observed, was contradicted by the fact that Reeve called Muggleton merely his mouth. Reve claimed to be the last messenger and witness: how then could Muggleton be the last witness?[69] William Penn in 1672, in what Muggleton called "a wicked Antichristian pamphlet", reiterated the charge that Muggleton contradicted the infallible Reeve.[70] Thomas Tompkinson, the most significant Muggletonian spokesman after Muggleton himself, had virtually nothing to say about the two last witnesses, and refers only once to "this commission", which "will last to the end of the world".[71]

Divine Songs of the Muggletonians present an agreeable picture of a cosy, friendly, self-contained community, mainly of London artisans. The hymns were set to popular tunes — an old radical protestant tradition — and at least a score of them were written by women. These hymns provide interesting evidence of the survival of attitudes deriving from the radical milieu of the Revolution. There is much about liberty, which in one sense is the freedom given by consciousness of salvation, of the "peace of mind" which Muggleton said mortalism had given him.[72] But it is also political libertarianism, a class-conscious alignment with the poor against the rich and powerful. The hymns are fiercely anti-clerical ("the fat-gutted priest") and against that other enemy of interregnum radicals, lawyers.[73] The whole effect is of comradeship and solidarity, informal and jolly, notwithstanding the Muggletonians' predestinarian theology. Or rather perhaps because of this theology: knowing they were of the right seed, they could place the bishops in hell with the same confidence and relish as the young Milton had done.[74]

The survival of this non-proselytizing sect for so long owes much to Lodowick Muggleton's down-to-earth qualities. I do not wish to underestimate these in trying to establish Reeve's priority as leader and thinker, and to show how Muggleton successfully imitated Clarkson in deliberately setting out to appropriate Reeve's legacy. Despite Muggleton's efforts, "Reevonianism" remained alive. In 1719 and 1760 Reeve's original version of *A Divine Looking-Glass* was reprinted, with Muggleton's cuts restored. Whenever there was a crisis within the sect, whether in the seventeenth, eighteenth or nineteenth centuries, it was accompanied by a "back-to-Reeve" movement.[75]

NOTES

1. Based on my contribution to a discussion in *P. and P.*, No. 104 (1984).
2. W.A. Cole, *The Quakers and Politics, 1652-1660* (unpublished Thirlwall Prize Essay, Cambridge University, 1954); Barry Reay, *The Quakers and the English Revolution* (1985), *passim*.
3. See the discussion in *P. and P.*, No. 104.
4. C. Hill, B. Reay and W. Lamont, *The World of the Muggletonians* (1983), pp. 64-110, esp. pp. 91-3.
5. Muggleton, *A True Interpretation of the Eleventh Chapter of the Revelation of St. John* (1751-3), p. 47. First published 1662.
6. Ed. A. Delamaine and T. Terry, *A Volume of Spiritual Epistles ... by John Reeve and Lodowicke Muggleton* (1755), pp. 45-6.
7. *The Acts of the Witnesses of the Spirit* (1764), pp. 48-9. First published 1699.
8. *A Transcendent Spirituall Treatise*, pp. 1, 4, 7, 32, 35, 56, 58, 71 and *passim*.
9. *Acts of the Witnesses*, pp. 68-72.
10. *Ibid.*, p. 75.
11. *A Letter to Alderman Fouke*, pp. 1, 4-7.
12. *Op. cit.*, pp. 18-19, 22.
13. *Op. cit.*, pp. 3, 6, 10.
14. *An Epistle to a Quaker*, p. 8.
15. *Op. cit.* (1719), pp. 1, 5, 7, 9, 11, 17, 22, 26-7, and *passim*. The table of contents, presumably added by Muggleton when he reprinted the tract in 1661, says that p. 1 gives "the names of the two last witnesses and the time of their call", though it does nothing of the sort.
16. Reeve, *Sacred Remains*, p. 13.
17. *Spiritual Epistles*, p. 147.
18. *A Divine Looking-Glass*, pp. 183, 190, 194.
19. *Ibid.*, Sig. A 3. My italics.
20. *Ibid.*, (1661 edn.), Sig. A 4v. On p. 25 occurs what is described as "the Prophets prayer", on p. 99 "the Prophets interpretation" and on p. 199 "the Prophets heavenly conclusion". The absence of an apostrophe in the original leaves the faint possibility that "prophets'" rather than "prophet's" might be the correct spelling; but in later editions on p. 107 Muggleton changed "the Prophets great confidence" to "the last Witnesses'", which suggests that he understood the singular elsewhere.
21. *Op. cit.*, pp. 1, 11, 21, 32, 46.
22. *Ibid.*, pp. 33, 46.
23. *Acts of the Witnesses*, p. 79.
24. *Op. cit.*, p. 1.
25. B. Reay, "Laurence Clarkson", in *The World of the Muggletonians*.
26. Clarkson, *Look about you* (1659), Sig. B.
27. John Harwood, *The Lying Prophet Discovered and Reproved* (1659), title-page, Sig. A 2, p. 1, quoting *The Quakers Downfall*, p. 1.
28. Harwood, *op. cit.*, p. 15.

29. Clarkson, *The Lost sheep Found*, pp. 38, 42-6, 48, 50, 52-3, 59-60, 62-3.
30. Muggleton, *Acts*, pp. 81, 145; *The World of the Muggletonians*, pp. 97-8.
31. *The Lost sheep Found*, *passim*.
32. Reay, "The Muggletonians: an Introductory Survey", in *The World of the Muggletonians*, esp. pp. 36-7.
33. *Op. cit.*, esp. Chapters LXXIV-LXXXIV.
34. *Op. cit.*, p. 312.
35. *The Prophet Muggletons Epistle to the Believers of the Commission, Touching the Rebellion Occasioned by the Nine Assertions* (?1671), pp. 8-13, printed with Reeve, *Divine Looking-Glass* (1719 edn.); Muggleton, *Acts*, pp. vi, 144-52.
36. *Joyfull Newes*, p. 42.
37. *Muggletons Epistle to the Believers of the Commission*, pp. 2-5, 7-11.
38. *The World of the Muggletonians*, p. 95.
39. Cf. Jean Moss, "*Godded with God: Hendrik Niclaes and His Family of Love* (Transactions of the American Philosophical Soc., 1981), pp. 25-6, 58, 71. For Crisp see p. 146 above.
40. D.D. Hall, *The Antinomian Controversy*, p. 232. See p. 172 above.
41. Smith, *Ranter Writings*, pp. 243, 246, 257 (Bauthumley); 194 (Salmon); [John Smith], *Soule-Reviving Influences of the Sun of Righteousness* (1654), pp. 107-8, 160, 178-80.
42. See pp. 192, 239 above.
43. Harwood, *op. cit.*, p. 13, quoting *The Quakers Downfall*, p. 41.
44. *Op cit.*, p. 56: cf. pp. 59-62. See also *The World of the Muggletonians*, pp. 94-5, 141.
45. *Spiritual Epistles* (1755), pp. 467-8, 542, 555.
46. Seneca, *Naturales quaestiones, XXXV-XXXVI*, trans. T. Lodge, in *The Works of L.A. Seneca, Both Morall and Naturall* (1614).
47. R. Tuck, *Natural Rights Theories: Their origin and development* (Cambridge U.P., 1979), p. 76.
48. Greville, *Poems and Dramas* (ed. G. Bullough, Edinburgh, n.d., ?1939), I, p. 124; *The World of the Muggletonians*, p. 95.
49. G. Burnet, *Some Passages of the Life and Death Of the ... Earl of Rochester* (1774), p. 26: first published 1680; ed. D.M. Veith, *Complete Poems of ... Rochester* (Yale U.P., 1974), p. 35.
50. See p. 260 above.
51. *The Lost sheep Found*, p. 36; cf. *The World of the Muggletonians*, p. 94.
52. *Muggletons Epistle to the Believers of the Commission*, Sigs. A-Av.
53. *The World of the Muggletonians*, pp. 64, 101.
54. Lamont, "The Muggletonians, 1652-1979", *P. and P.*, No. 99 (1983), p. 30.
55. *Epistle to Believers*, pp. 11-13.
56. *A Divine Looking-Glass*, pp. 159-65; *The World of the Muggletonians*, p. 26.
57. *A Divine Looking-Glass*, p. 110; *A Remonstrance from the Eternal God*, p. 6; Lamont, "The Muggletonians, 1652-1979", p. 28.
58. *A True Interpretation of ... the Whole Book of the Revelation*, pp. 109-10.
59. Lamont, "The Muggletonians, 1652-1979", p. 28.

60. Muggleton, *Acts*, p. 82.
61. *A Divine Looking-Glass*, Sig. A 2v.
62. *Ibid.*, pp. 60, 62, 64-5.
63. Clarkson, *Look about you*, pp. 31-2.
64. *The World of the Muggletonians*, pp. 81, 176-8; Clarkson, *The Lost sheep Found*, pp. 54-8.
65. Muggleton, *Acts*, pp. 4-5, 7, 136-52; *Spiritual Epistles*, pp. 355-6; *The World of the Muggletonians*, pp. 98, 158.
66. *Op. cit.*, esp. pp. 34-46, 98-102, 142-53.
67. Lamont sees pragmatism on moral questions in *A Divine Looking-Glass*, though he is wrong in regarding it as "a joint work" ("The Muggletonians, 1652-1979", pp. 25, 38).
68. Burrough, *The Memorable Works of a Son of Thunder and Consolation* (1672), pp. 36-44; cf. Burrough and Francis Howgil, *Answers to Several Queries* (1654).
69. G.F., *Something in Answer to Lodowick Muggletons Book,* ... *"The Neck of the Quakers Broken"* (1667), p. 21.
70. W.P[enn], *The New Witnesses Proved Old Hereticks* (1672), pp. 43 sqq.; *Spiritual Epistles*, p. 367.
71. Tomkinson, *Truths Triumph: or, A Witness to the Two Witnesses* (1823), p. 421: written 1676; cf. *A System of Religion* (1729).
72. Muggleton, *Acts of the Witnesses*, p. 25. Reeve had proclaimed mortalism in *A Transcendent Spirituall Treatise* (pp. 71-6); it was the main theme of *Joyfull Newes*. Muggleton, as was to be expected, later claimed to have discovered the doctrine before Reeve (*Acts*, pp. 25-8).
73. See esp. 6th, 28th, 50th, 55th, 78th, 139th, 165th, 169th, 174th, and 193rd songs.
74. *M.C.P.W.*, I, pp. 616-17. Cf. pp. 51-2 above.
75. See Lamont in *The World of the Muggletonians*, pp. 128-9.

13. *"Till the conversion of the Jews"*[1]

> *"Had we but world enough, and time,*
> *This coyness, lady, were no crime.*
> *We would sit down and think which way*
> *To walk and pass our long love's day.*
> *Thou by the Indian Ganges side*
> *Shouldst rubies find: I by the tide*
> *Of Humber would complain. I would*
> *Love you ten years before the Flood;*
> *And you should, if you please, refuse*
> *Till the conversion of the Jews."**

I

Nearly thirty years ago I published a 350-page book dealing with economic problems of the Church of England during its first century. I described it, a bit wrily, as a footnote to *Lycidas*. My present subject is a footnote to the opening lines of Marvell's 'To his Coy Mistress'.

If you try just to read the words on Marvell's page, much of his wit will escape you. That happened to John Crowe Ransom, no mean critic in his day, who accused Marvell in this poem of "indeterminacies that would be condemned in the prose of ... College freshmen". He criticized "the tide of Humber", as though Marvell were indulging in mere periphrastic poetic diction.[2] In fact the Humber is the greatest of all English tidal rivers. John Taylor the Water-Poet, when he crossed it in 1622, had never seen anything like the waves that "like pirates board our boat and enter".[3] Marvell's father was drowned when crossing the Humber in 1641, a few years before the presumed date of the poem. Marvell had reason to complain of Humber's tide. Ransom also objected to "Indian Ganges", since "Ganges has little need of a defining adjective"; and suggested that it ought to be balanced by "English Humber". No doubt twentieth-century American readers know more about the

---

* Marvell, 'To his Coy Mistress'.

Ganges than about the Humber, but the reverse was true of seventeenth-century Englishmen, for whom the Ganges must have been incredibly exotic, whilst the Humber was one of the three greatest rivers in England.

Of the lines "And you should, if you please, refuse/ Till the conversion of the Jews", Ransom said "refuse brings out of the rhyming dictionary the Jews, which it will tax the poet's invention to supply with a context. ... The historical period from the Flood to the conversion of the Jews ... is a useless way of saying ten thousand years, or some other length of time". It "seems disproportionate" to the mere "ten years before the Flood".

At first sight indeed Marvell's lines seem merely fanciful. He will love the lady for a long time in the past, she shall refuse him till a long time in the future. The two propositions appear to have no more in common than this. Ransom might indeed have noticed an apparent failure in the parallelism: the Ganges is far distant in space, as Noah's Flood is in time; but the Humber is just round the corner — especially if — as is highly likely — the poem was written either in Hull or in Fairfax's house in Yorkshire where Marvell was tutoring Mary Fairfax in the early sixteen-fifties. The parallel would be more exact if we could think of the conversion of the Jews as imminent — as near as Humber, so to speak.

That, I shall suggest, is exactly what many of Marvell's contemporaries did think. I want to look at seventeenth-century ideas about the conversion of the Jews.

II

The conversion of the Jews was seen in the sixteenth and seventeenth centuries as part of a package of events announcing the approach of the end of the world and the millennium. We need not bother with the detailed calculations, based on Daniel and Revelation, which occupied some of the best mathematicians from Napier in the late sixteenth century to Newton at the end of the seventeenth. The ultimately agreed consensus was that 1260 years ("a time, times, and half a time") should be added to the date at which Antichrist set up his power. Protestants took Antichrist to be the Pope, whose rise was estimated to have occurred in 390-6 A.D. Alternatively, 1290 years were to be added to the years 360-6 A.D., taken as the dates of Julian the Apostate and/or the destruction of the Temple at Jerusalem. Both these calculations pointed to the years 1650-56 for the destruction of Antichrist, the gathering of the Gentiles, the conversion of the Jews and their return to Palestine. If — as some did — you placed the usurpation of the Bishop of Rome in A.D. 400-6, then 1260 added to that gave the year 1666 as an alternative.[4]

The conversion of the Jews and the spreading of Christianity to all nations were necessary conditions without which the millennium could not take place. Another was the destruction of the Turkish Empire, which controlled Palestine and under whose rule most Jews lived. Some thought the Great Turk was Antichrist: Christianity could not spread over the whole globe so long as Turkish power survived. (China and India hardly occur in these discussions, so ignorant were most Europeans still of the significance of their vast civilizations).

This time-table is particularly associated with protestantism. Martin Bucer and Peter Martyr of Strasburg preached it in England in the reign of Edward VI. It was taken up by Béza, and the Geneva New Testament of 1557 expressed concern for the conversion of the Jews.[5] Catholics, naturally, did not accept the equation of the Pope with Antichrist. They held that Antichrist had not yet come; when he did appear he would be a Jew. This doctrine was proclaimed in England by the Laudian Robert Shelford.[6] The Laudian campaign to accept Rome as a true church and to reject the identification of the Pope with Antichrist helped to convince many protestants that Laud was preparing for a restoration of popery in England.

There are mediaeval heretical precedents for these protestant attitudes. Wyclif and Hus both interpreted literally the Biblical texts relating to the return of the Jews to Palestine. Fifteenth-century Hussites had been eager for the conversion of the Jews.[7] Lollards had no doubt that the Pope was Antichrist. But interest developed in England especially after the Reformation; it naturally heightened as the sixteen-fifties approached.

There was an additional pointer to the mid-seventeenth century as the time for the series of events leading up to the millennium. Protestant chronologers generally accepted that the date of Noah's Flood was *anno mundi* 1656. Matthew's Gospel said "as the days of Noah were, so shall also the coming of the Son of Man be".[8] Osiander argued from this analogy that the last judgment would come in or soon after 1656 A.D.: his book was translated by George Joye in 1548.[9] A century later this had become a commonplace. In 1639 Thomas Goodwin, writing in exile in the Netherlands, gave the parallel with Noah's Flood as a reason for expecting Antichrist's reign to end in 1655 or 1656.[10] In 1651 Samuel Hartlib published a translation of the anonymous *Clavis Apocalyptica* in which the parallel was drawn, though the years were given as 1655 a.m. and 1655 A.D.[11] On Guy Fawkes Day 1651 Peter Sterry, preaching to Parliament, dated the Flood 1656 a.m., and continued "How near is that year 1656. . . . A flood of fire is coming upon all the world. The windows of heaven are already open". Luther, like Noah, had foretold the day of doom 120 years before it came.[12]

The millenarians John Tillinghast, John Rogers, Henry Jessey and Nathanael Homes, all expected "the flood of God's wrath upon the idolatrous Antichristian world" to be poured out in 1656: the redemption of Israel would follow.[13] "As in Noah's Flood, after the doors were shut up, there was no mercy. . . . Haste — haste — haste" cried Rogers.[14] Robert Gell, in a sermon preached to the Lord Mayor of London and the Drapers' Company, published in 1655, said that the years from Adam to Noah were 1656, and "many believe that the next year [1656 A.D.] will bring with it a notable change in the world; yea, many place the end of the world in that year".[15] William Oughtred, a very serious mathematician, said — also in 1655 — that "he had strong apprehensions of some extraordinary event to happen the following year", because of the correspondence with the year of the Flood. Perhaps the Jews would be converted by "our Saviour's visible appearance".[16] Quakers shared the expectation that the conversion would begin in 1656.[17] Thomas Traherne experienced a spiritual crisis in 1656 which he associated with the Flood, the renewal of God's covenant and the forgiveness and restoration of the Jews.[18]

Andrew Willet in 1590 seems to have been the first English Biblical scholar to devote a whole treatise to the calling of the Jews.[19] But the subject was discussed by William Perkins, Richard Hooker, and many others from the turn of the century onwards.[20] Gradually an agreed time-table emerged. The great mathematician John Napier, inventor of logarithms, committed himself to the view that "the day of God's judgment appears to fall" between 1688 and 1700: 1786 was the latest date to which the world could continue.[21] But this date was soon brought forward.

The crucial figure for England was the learned Puritan Thomas Brightman, who made the most elaborate study of the last days to date. Brightman died in 1607. All his books appeared posthumously, and had to be published abroad. He wrote in Latin, but English translations were printed in the Netherlands from 1612, and no doubt circulated clandestinely in England. Brightman's *Revelation of the Revelation* was not published in England until 1644, after the episcopal censorship has broken down. Already by the early seventeenth century attempts to date the end of the world were regarded as seditious: so early had the Elizabethan consensus collapsed, and so important were eschatological studies in polarizing men's attitudes. Brightman's English translator claimed that Brightman "hath so cleared the point of the Jews' vocation as I have not seen any writer the like". Brightman put the calling of the Jews much nearer in the future than any of his predecessors, dating their full conversion to 1695, though their "first calling shall be about the year 1650". It would be a process occupying several decades. In 1650, Brightman believed, the Euphrates would dry up to facilitate the passage of the first party of Jews from the lost tribes returning to Jerusalem from the East. Their conversion would follow the destruction of Rome and coincide with the overthrow of the Turkish Empire, whose power would begin to reel in 1650 and would be utterly abolished by 1695. The reign of the saints would follow.[22]

Although Brightman's writings were illegal in England before 1640, they were clearly well-known and very influential there.[23] In 1610, for instance, the Hebrew scholar Hugh Broughton believed that the conversion of the Jews was imminent, and with it the culmination of human history.[24] After 1640 translations of Brightman's writings, abridgments and summaries began to appear in large numbers. But two other writers must be mentioned before we pass on to the revolutionary decades.

Sir Henry Finch was a graduate of Christ's College, Cambridge, Milton's College, and a lawyer of some standing. In 1621 he published *The Worlds Great Restauration or The Calling of the Jews*, the first whole book on the subject in English. It appeared under the auspices of the eminent Puritan divine William Gouge. Finch accepted Brightman's time-table: in 1650 the Euphrates would dry up and the gathering of the Jews would begin, together with the decline of Turkish power.[25] Gouge was imprisoned for nine weeks until he produced a recantation of his share in this publication.

The earlier date was reinforced by the cautious and scholarly work of Joseph Mede, Fellow of Christ's College, when Milton was up there.[26] He too had difficulties with the censorship, and refrained from publishing his major works during the sixteen-twenties and thirties. His *Key of the Revelation* (1627) appeared in English translation only posthumously in 1643, published by order of a committee of the House of Commons. A timid man, Mede was clearly, as his correspondence shows, terrified of reprisals from Laud if he spoke out on the subject of his research. In a tract written in 1625 but not published until 1650 Mede suggested a date between 1653 and 1715.[27]

In the sixteen-thirties the Puritans Richard Sibbes and Thomas Adams were convinced that the conversion of the Jews was imminent.[28] George Hakewill in 1627 had thought this conversion so assured that he used it as one of his many arguments that the world was getting better.[29] Even Hakewill's rival, the arch-conservative Bishop Godfrey Goodman, believed in 1653 that Christ would not long be absent.[30]

III

So when the censorship broke down after 1640, when Parliament itself provided for the printing of translations of Brightman and Mede, a great stimulus was given to thinking about the end of the world. It was shrewd policy to authorize publication of scholarly works discussing the coming millennium, since Parliament's case against a Divine Right monarchy could be legitimated only by appealing to the higher authority of God. If the last days were at hand, and with them the overthrow of the papal Antichrist, and if Charles's Laudian advisers — and later his military commanders — were no better than papists, then it was right to call on ordinary people to fight for their overthrow. The subversive possibilities of this approach had already been demonstrated in New England, where in 1637 John Wheelwright preached an inflammatory sermon which got him into trouble. In this he declared "We know not how soon the conversion of the Jews may come". It "must come by the downfall of Antichrist, and if we take him away, we must burn him; therefore never fear combustions and burnings".[31] The spread of popular millenarian doctrines in England was like fire along a well-laid trail of powder.

In 1639 Thomas Goodwin foreshortened the dating still further by placing the downfall of Turks and Pope, and the return of the Jews, in 1650 or 1656, at latest 1666.[32] The Jews themselves, he added, have an eye on 1650 for the appearance of the Messiah. Their conversion, Goodwin thought, may fall out even sooner.[33] Pamphlets such as *Napiers Narration* (1641) and *A Revelation of Mr. Brightmans Revelation* (1641), both in dialogue form, helped to popularize the idea. William Sedgwick in a Fast Sermon of 29 June 1642 referred to the forthcoming conversion of the Jews and their calling "to a happy estate in their own country", though since this latter point "is subject to controversy ... we will waive it".[34] In the same year the author of an anonymous pamphlet — an astrologer — said of the millennium "some do assign one year, some another, yet all agree ... that it is near and even at our doors".[35] Next year a pamphlet entitled *The Rev. Mr. Brightmans Judgement* thought that "Rome must be in the destroying in 1641 in some of his dominions"[36] — a reference presumably to events in England and Scotland, Robert Maton in 1642 advocated the return of the Jews to Israel.[37] So did Ephraim Huit's commentary, *The Whole Prophecie of Daniel Explained* (1644).[38]

So preachers and pamphleteers agreed on the years 1650-6 as the crucial period — John Archer in 1642, Raphael Harford in 1643, and many more, including John Cotton in New England.[39] In July 1644 Stanley Gower assured the House of Commons that the Jews would be converted in 1650. Next month William Reyner confirmed to them that the overthrow of Antichrist either had already begun or was imminent.[40] Thomas Shepard in 1647-8 expected the Jews to return to Zion within the next few years: so did James Toppe.[41] In 1650 Thomas Tany (Theaureaujohn) published a broadsheet *I Proclaime from the Lord of Hosts the Returne of the Jewes*, and did his best to speed the process.[42] Mary Cary, in *The little horns doome and downfall* (1651), looked for the conversion and return of the Jews in 1655-6, leading up to the millennium in 1701. Her book included introductory material by Henry Jessey, who was not absolutely convinced that 1656 was the year. But he knew the conversion would come before 1658.[43] In 1653 John Canne thought that in the year 1655 the Lord will "most eminently appear"; there will be "great revolutions ... everywhere in Europe". The Jews would return to their own country and there wage war against the Turks until 1700. Meanwhile the "Antichristian state shall be wholly destroyed before the year 1660".[44] In 1641 the great Czech reformer Comenius had plans for the conversion of the Jews, since the last days were imminent; but like all the schemes which he devised in England, this one was frustrated by the outbreak of civil war. His disciple Samuel

Hartlib accepted the year 1655, and Hartlib's friend John Dury in 1649 felt that "the conversion of the Jews is at hand".[45]

So the excitement originally built up by the scholarly chronologists and exploited by Parliamentarian publicists continued and expanded as millenarian radicals became more and more involved in politics. A pamphlet of 1648 referred indeed unsympathetically to "all these Cabbalistical Millenarians and Jew-restorers".[46] Among scores of divines and pamphleteers who accepted the mid-fifties (or 1666 at latest) as the time for the conversion of the Jews, many were indeed radicals.[47] But they also included such relatively respectable characters as Archbishop Ussher, John Cotton, the Presbyterians Samuel Rutherford, Edmund Hall and Christopher Love, and the Directory of the Westminster Assembly.[48] Even so hard-headed a figure as Benjamin Worsley, in or after 1647, noted that most divines conceive that the conversion of the Jews is shortly to be expected. He had no doubts himself.[49] In 1650 the diarist Ralph Josselin was much preoccupied with the subject: he thought 1654 might be the year in which the conversion would begin, to be completed by 1699.[50] In 1651 the Ranter Joshua Garment published *The Hebrews Deliverance at Hand*, and Nicholas Culpeper expected their conversion within the next five years.[51] Milton's friend, Moses Wall, also in 1651, looked for the conversion during "this present ... age in which we live", suggesting 1655 as the date.[52] Thomas Tomkinson, later a Muggletonian, had a dream early in 1652 telling him the "joyful news" that "the Jews are now called; ... the day of judgment is at hand".[53]

Among those who totally rejected a special conversion was the Scot Robert Baillie. Richard Baxter observed sceptically that it would take a long time to convert all the Jews.[54] A radical who believed "the day of the Lord" was "near at hand" but nevertheless rejected any "general visible calling of the Jews in all nations" was John Reeve, founder of the sect later to be called Muggletonians. "The Lord Jesus", he declared, "will never spiritually gather the seed of those Jews who rated a bloody Barabbas above the Lord of life". But Reeve also used the word "Jew" to cover those who justify religious persecution.[55]

IV

What we see then is a cumulative process. First the Biblical scholars and the mathematical chronologists evolve techniques for interpreting the prophecies which enable them to arrive at agreed conclusions about dating the events of the last days. These dates are progressively brought back to the first half of the sixteen-fifties. This date is seized upon by the popularizers, the pamphleteers, the Parliamentarian propagandists and preachers in an effort to whip up enthusiasm for the Parliamentary cause and an expectation of the millennium in the foreseeable future. For many radicals the conversion of the Jews was significant primarily as a harbinger of the reign of the saints on earth which was to proceed the Second Coming. Soon achieving this reign became an end in itself, by comparison with which the Jews fell into the background.

Gerrard Winstanley for instance equated the English with the Israelites, the chosen people, and declared that "all the prophecies, visions and revelations of Scriptures, of prophets and apostles, concerning the calling of the Jews, the restoration of Israel and making of that people the inheritors of the whole earth," referred to the coming communist society which the Diggers were starting to build in England.[56] Winstanley and Everard told Fairfax that they were "of the race of the Jews".[57]

Echoes of discussions on the conversion of the Jews can be heard in literature. Giles Fletcher the elder was an early believer in the restoration of the Jews, though his views on the subject were not published until 1677, and I can find no trace of them in the writings of his sons Phineas and Giles the younger.[58] Francis Bacon's Bensalem in *New Atlantis* (1627) was inhabited by converted Jews. Twenty years later, in Samuel Gott's *Nova Solyma* (1648), an ideal society was created after the restoration of the Jews. The Turks had been expelled and the Jews converted fifty years before they left for Palestine — by ship from Dover.[59]

In Sir William Alexander's *Dooms-day* (1637) the "signs foreshown" of that event included "some Jews convert".[60] Henry Vaughan in *Silex Scintillans* wrote of the conversion "sure it is not far".[61] The date of publication (1650) suggests that it must be nearly contemporary with Marvell's 'Coy Mistress'. Abraham Cowley, perhaps in Marvell's more sceptical vein, wrote in the Preface to his *Poems* (1656): "there wants, methinks, but the conversion of [poetry] and the Jews for the accomplishing of the kingdom of Christ".[62]

V

But other factors contributed to an interest in the conversion, factors perhaps less immediately obvious. The conversion of the Jews and "the gathering of the Gentiles" were necessary before the millennium could arrive. This gathering could be furthered by English acquisitions of territory in the New World. (Spanish conquests in America of course only extended the kingdom of Antichrist). Take, for instance, Thomas Cooper's *The Blessing of Japheth, Proving The Gathering in of the Gentiles and Finall Conversion of the Jewes*, dedicated in 1615 to the Lord Mayor, Aldermen and Sheriffs of London and the Commissioners for Plantations in Ireland and Virginia. "As the Lord hath enlarged himself abundantly unto this honourable City", Cooper said, so "your hearts and purses are enlarged plentifully to the furtherance of this great and glorious work of the gathering in of the Gentiles" by the colonization of Ireland and Virginia. Not for the last time in English history, piety and profit went hand in hand. "Can you do God better service than in promoting his kingdom and demolishing daily the power of Satan? Can you do better service unto yourselves than not only to ease the land of that rank blood which threatens some great sickness, but especially to provide some retiring place for yourselves if so be the Lord for our unthankfulness should spew us out".[63] (Here Cooper touches on two anxieties which beset his contemporaries and which historians sometimes forget — fear of the hordes of unemployed vagabonds, and of international Catholicism's threat to England's protestant independence).

His immediate concern is to strengthen the political and economic might of his country. "Hath the Lord begun to enlarge us far and near to Virginia and Ireland, and are not their hopes vain that seek to root God's church out of England? ... Hath not God wonderfully preserved this little island, this angle of the world, that in former ages was not known or accounted to be any part of the world? Have not all the neighbour-nations taken hold of the skirts of an Englishman? Have they not joined themselves to us because the Lord is with us? Are they not happily sheltered under our gracious government?" The reference is to the union of England and Scotland, and perhaps looks forward to the sort of union with the Netherlands which the Commonwealth government was to offer in 1651. Already, presciently, Cooper links Parliamentary government, protestantism, liberty and trade. "So bless thou O Lord the holy meetings of the state that in continuance and increase of the liberty of the gospel we may secure our liberty and advance thy glory, we may provide for the liberty of our posterity, in conveying thy worship unto them, more glorious than we found it".[64]

Those are significant if cautious words: remember that the Parliament of 1614 had just been dissolved without doing anything to secure the liberty of posterity or to advance the glory of protestantism. But Cooper looks forward with confidence to unlimited economic expansion. "Should we not possess all things even when in a sort we have nothing? ... Ought not then the church to strive even for the best with the best? Must she not so run that she may obtain?" (In Cooper's phraseology "the church" means "the commonwealth").[65] Despite Cooper's title, the Jews come in almost as an afterthought to this programme for British expansion: but they do come in. "The Jews shall then have a full and glorious conversion, before the Second Coming of the Lord Jesus. ... Have we not daily experience of the Jews coming in again? ... This great coming in of the Jew cannot be far off, seeing the fullness of the Gentiles is well-near come in". Meanwhile English merchants must soldier on.[66]

The economic basis of religious belief was not often so nakedly exposed. But John Rolfe in 1616 thought the English were "a peculiar people marked and chosen by the finger of God" to possess North America.[67] Conquest of America was linked more closely with the conversion of the Jews by the theory that at least some American Indians were descended from the lost tribes of Israel. This hare seems to have been started in the Netherlands. A Portuguese Jew swore that he had talked Hebrew to some Indians, and the idea spread that the lost tribes were living in America.[68] John Dury among others took the story up.[69] Thomas Thorowgood in *Jewes in America* (1650) (with introduction by Hartlib) linked religion and commercial expansion as crudely as Cooper had done. "Look westward then, ye men of war, thence you may behold a rising sun of glory with riches and much honour, and not only for yourselves but for Christ". The Spaniards are thin on the ground in North America: Indians, Creoles and negroes will turn against them.[70] It reads like a blueprint for Oliver Cromwell's Western Design of 1655. Major-General Harrison was said to have seen similar millenarian possibilities in the Anglo-Dutch war of 1652-4: "The Dutch must be destroyed and we shall have an heaven on earth," thanks to control of the seas.[71]

We are told that those seventeenth-century Puritans in North America who recorded their opinions believed "almost without exception" that the Indians were descended from the ten tribes.[72] This conviction inspired John Eliot, the "Apostle to the Indians", since their conversion would accelerate the Second Coming. Eliot contributed "Conjectures ... Touching the Americans" to the 1660 edition of Thorowgood's pamphlet, seizing the opportunity to distance himself from Thorowgood's commercial approach. "We chose a place where nothing in probability was to be expected but religion, poverty and hard labour, a composition that God doth usually take most pleasure in".[73] Thorowgood, in the less ebullient circumstances of 1660, echoed Cooper's vision of America as a refuge for the godly from "not the violence of enemies so much as our own national and personal sins". The threat now came not from the "encroaching innovations" of (presumably) the Laudians, but from "the falsehood and hypocrisy, the backsliding and apostacy, the avarice and selfishness, the pride and security" which had accompanied the last years of the Commonwealth and which "do portend no less than a deluge of destruction" unless we repent. Thorowgood seems to have been as unenthusiastic about the restoration as was Milton, whom some of these phrases recall.[74]

In 1649 Parliament established a Society for the Propagation of the Gospel in New England, which among other things subsidized John Eliot. Henry Whitfield in 1652 supported this society because he hoped that thereby "the calling of the Jews may be hastened".[75] It survived the restoration, and won the continuing support of Robert Boyle, among others.[76] As late as 1707 William Whiston argued on its behalf that spreading the gospel to all nations would quicken the conversion of the Jews.[77]

VI

"The chiefest place where the Jews live is the Turkish Empire", Menasseh ben Israel told Oliver Cromwell in 1655.[78] In the early seventeenth century English trade with the Levant was prospering, outstripping that of France and Venice, anticipating that of the Netherlands, thanks to expanding production of new draperies, light cloths suitable for a Mediterranean climate. As early as 1591 the condemned heretic John Udall was offered commutation of his death sentence if he would go to Syria as minister for the Turkey Company merchants there; but he died in jail whist negotiating.[79] By 1646 there were at least twenty-two English merchants in Smyrna alone. They normally conducted their trade through Jewish middlemen: there was little intercourse with Turks. The father of the future Messiah Sabbatai Sevi acted as agent for English merchants in Smyrna. The merchants were held responsible for the behaviour of all their countrymen, and made a point of entertaining English travellers. They would be relatively well-informed about Jewish affairs.[80] As English trade opened up, visits to the Levant became feasible. By 1640 there was an extensive literature dealing with the area, from Hakluyt and Purchas to Richard Knollys, William Biddulph, William Lithgow, George Sandys, Fynes Moryson and Sir Henry Blount. This helped to spread knowledge not only of the religion but also of the growing anticipations of the Jews for the coming of the Messiah, especially prevalent in the Near East.[81] The Zohar was said to have predicted a return of the Jews to Israel for 1648.[82]

Among English radical millenarians the idea of leading the Jews back to Jerusalem, or travelling there to assist in the restoration of the Jews, frequently recurs in the two generations before 1640. Ralph Durden in 1586, who thought that the Tudor monarchy was the Beast of Revelation, proposed to lead the Jews and all the saints to rebuild Jerusalem; after which they would defeat all the kings of the earth.[83] Francis Kett, burnt in 1589, grandson of the Norfolk rebel leader of 1549 and friend of Christopher Marlowe, claimed that Jesus was currently in Jerusalem gathering the faithful; all God's people should go and join him there. Whoever will be saved must go to Jerusalem before he died[84] — an interesting survival in a radical heretic of the mediaeval idea of pilgrimage.

Richard Farnham and John Bull, prophets who died in 1642, were believed by their supporters to have sailed away in a boat of bull-rushes to convert the lost tribes.[85] Mrs Attaway was said to have left London with William Jenny some time before 1646 to await the universal salvation in Jerusalem.[86] The Ranter John Robins was inspired by the Holy Ghost to lead 144,000 men to Palestine, and started training some of them for their arduous expedition on a diet of dry bread, raw vegetables and water.[87] His associate Thomas Tany (Theaureaujohn) learnt Hebrew with the object of leading the Jews back. In April 1650 he assumed the title of King of the Jews and issued a proclamation announcing the return of his people. Some time later — perhaps as late as 1668 — he was said to have disappeared in a small boat which he had built for himself in the hope of getting to

Palestine.[88] In the sixteen-fifties Quaker missionaries went to convert the Grand Turk — by whom they were received with more tolerance than in New England.

Intense interest in the return of the Jews led to many stories circulating, most of them without foundation in fact. On All Fools Day 1645 *The London Post* reported that the Jews had sent letters to collect themselves into one body to return to Palestine.[89] Four days later Ralph Josselin in Essex had heard rumours of the Jews' return, no doubt derived from *The London Post*. "Can it be?" he asked doubtfully.[90] In 1647 an anonymous pamphlet, *Doomes-Day: or the great Day of the Lords Judgement proved by Scripture*, announced that the Jews were assembling in Asia Minor, and that the final overthrow of Antichrist was "near, even at the door".[91] There were similar excited expectations in 1648.[92] In 1650 George Foster announced that the Jews were to meet in 1651 in Italy. The Pope would lose his life in 1654, the Head Turk in 1656; after that there would be no Pope, and a classless society would prevail.[93] Samuel Brett's *Narrative of the Proceedings of a great Council of Jews assembled in the Plain of Ageda in Hungary on 12 October 1650* (published in 1655) had a very circumstantial though largely apocryphal account of the meeting. The author regarded it as "a hopeful sign of the Jews' conversion". The Jews, he added, believe that England has a great love to their nation, because they pray for their conversion. The greatest obstacle to the conversion of the Jews is Rome's idolatry.[94] Johnston of Wariston had heard of this Council three years before the publication of *A Narrative*.[95]

VII

Millenarian excitement and commercial interests both contributed to demands for a militant foreign policy which would expedite Antichrist's overthrow, the gathering of the Gentiles and the conversion of the Jews. In 1643 Robert Leslie, commanding the Scottish army in England, was reported as advocating ultimate use of his army to "go to Rome, drive out Antichrist and burn the town".[96] John Eachard in 1645 wrote that "the civil war [now] begun shall last till Rome be burnt and the Jews called". With this magnificent prospect it was absurd for Presbyterians and Independents to squabble among themselves.[97] Peter Bulkeley in *The Gospel Covenant* (1646) similarly anticipated the imminent conversion of the Jews and fall of the Great Turk.[98] The radical Puritan Robert Parker, who died in exile in 1614, left a pamphlet called *The Mystery of the Vialls opened*. Unpublishable before 1640, it appeared opportunely in 1651. Parker argued that England would soon take the lead in sacking Rome and converting the Jews — the former a theme of some of Milton's university writings.[99]

Peter Sterry in 1649 told Parliament that "the outward calling though not the inward conversion of the Jews" was expected near this time, adding that "perhaps the affairs of Constantinople, as they now stand, may make way to this desired conclusion".[100] In 1651 the astrologer William Lilly foretold that "we Christians shall recover the Holy Land ... out of the hands of the Turks; then also shall almighty God by miracle withdraw the people of the Jews from their hard-heartedness, and from the several parts of the world where they now live concealed, and they shall believe in the true Messias".[101] A year later John Owen, preaching before Parliament, rebuked M.P.s for their inactivity: "the Jews not called, Antichrist not destroyed. ... Will the Lord Christ leave the world in this state and set up his kingdom here on a molehill?"[102] A Fifth Monarchist preacher proclaimed whilst Barebone's Parliament was in session that Blake's fleet would carry the gospel "up and down to the Gentiles".[103] Morgan Llwyd and the Fifth Monarchists Christopher Feake, John Rogers and John Tillinghast, all promised that the Army of the saints would overthrow the Turks and the Pope and his helpers.[104] In 1657 George Fox — not yet a pacifist — rebuked Cromwell's Army for its failure to attack Rome.[108]

The Jews' potential usefulness to the development of a forward colonial and commercial foreign policy was an additional reason for English interest in them. As early as 1643 Jews in the Netherlands were said to be financing Parliament. Their command of bullion was enormous; they controlled the Spanish and Portuguese trades; the Levant trade was largely in their hands; they were interested in developing commerce with the East and West Indies. To governments they could be useful as contractors and as spies.[106] If the ambitious scheme for Anglo-Dutch union put forward by the Commonwealth in 1651 had come off, then the Jews in the Netherlands would have been taken over together with the Dutch colonial empire and its trade. When the Dutch refused to be incorporated into the British Empire, Dutch merchants were totally excluded from all British possessions by the Navigation Act of 1651. This development made many Jews in the Netherlands — especially those

trading with the West Indies — anxious to transfer to London; and
it redoubled the interest of the English government in attracting
them there.[107] The policy paid off: Jewish intelligence helped the
preparations for Cromwell's Western Design of 1655.[108]

VIII

So we come to Menasseh ben Israel's attempt to get the Jews
formally readmitted to England, from which Edward I had expelled
them. In 1648 a pogrom had driven Jews from the Ukraine. It was for
them as well as for Jewish refugees from the Iberian peninsula that
Menasseh hoped to find a home in England.[109] There was a contradiction in English attitudes which the Leveller Richard Overton
noted in 1645: "our kings and our rulers, our bishops and our
priests", would not "suffer a Jew by authority to live amongst
them". "What hopes then", he asked, "is there the Jews should be
converted?"[110] "We have prayed these 80 years for the conversion of
the Jews", William Erbery was reported as saying in 1647; "yet we
will not suffer a Jew to live amongst us". Selden's friend Christian
Ravis made a similar observation in 1648.[111]

Robert Maton in 1642 had combined philo-Semitism with
millenarianism, attacking those — too numerous among Christians,
he thought — who condemn or revile the Jews.[112] In 1644 Bishop
Griffith Williams had called for full toleration for the Jews in
England, as a step towards their conversion.[113] In January 1649 a
petition on behalf of the Jews was presented to the Army leadership.[114] The English delegation to the Netherlands in 1651, and
especially its secretary John Thurloe, saw a great deal of Menasseh
ben Israel. Menasseh's *Declaration to Parliament* of 1655 stressed
that both Jews and Christians "believe that the restoration time for
our nation into their native country is very near at hand". To admit
Jews to England might expedite their conversion, he hinted, and so
hurry on the last days.[115]

The cause of the Jews had many advocates. Moses Wall translated
Menasseh ben Israel's *The Hope of Israel* in 1650, and added his
Considerations Upon the Point of the Conversion of the Jews to the
second edition (1651). The influential John Dury was a staunch
supporter. In 1652 Robert Norwood and Thomas Collier called for
permission for the Jews "to live peaceably amongst us, ... whose
conversion is promised and we pretend to expect it".[116] So did Roger
Williams and William Strong.[117] Samuel Hering told Barebone's

Parliament to call the Jews to England "for their time is near at hand".[118] J. W. in 1653 wanted "the Jews to be admitted".[119] In 1655 Ralph Josselin heard "great rumours of the Jews being admitted into England, in hopes thereby to convert them".[120] Henry Jessey argued for admission, speaking of "hopes of their conversion, which time (it's hoped) is now at hand, even at the door".[121] Margaret Fell, who later married George Fox, was the most active Quaker propagandist for the conversion of the Jews. Between 1656 and 1677 she wrote no less than five pamphlets addressed to the Jews, whilst Fox wrote two.[122]

George Wither advocated complete toleration for the Jews in England

> More than most nations we are thought
> Their restoration to have sought;

but when it came to the push "we/ Grow fearful what th'events may be".[123] In 1657 Henry Oldenburg, future Secretary of the Royal Society, was discussing the coming of the Messiah with Menasseh ben Israel.[124] By 1656 the Jews' admission was being officially considered. There was alleged to have been a proposal to this effect in Barebone's Parliament. Pressure for their admission was said to have given a fillip to Fifth Monarchists and other sectaries;[125] but the reasons for considering it were not merely religious or political. It was a development from the economic policy initiated by the Navigation Act of 1651.[126] "Doubtless, to say no more", commented Major-General Whalley, "they will bring very much wealth into this Commonwealth".[127]

Edward Nicholas, in *An Apologie for the Honourable Nation of the Jews* (1648), had deplored "the strict and cruel laws now in force" against the Jews.[128] But in fact the judges advised, no doubt under pressure from Cromwell, that there were no legal obstacles to their admission.[129] Jews had long been in England unofficially. In 1652 Elias Ashmole arranged to take lessons in Hebrew from Rabbi Solomon Frank.[130] No official decision to admit the Jews was taken, but Cromwell extended his personal favour to cover *de facto* admission, despite strong and unpleasantly anti-Semitic opposition from William Prynne and others. Permission was given for building a synagogue in London.[131] The wider implications for religious toleration of admitting the Jews were raised in the Nayler debates of 1656-7. "Will you suffer the Jews to walk upon the Exchange that deny Christ", expostulated Bodurda, "and put this man to death that acknowledgeth Christ?"[132] Harrington in 1656 saw Ireland as a possible refuge for Jews;[133] many in fact settled in British colonies in Surinam and the West Indies.[134]

IX

So I see converging trends. First the chronological experts fixed on the early sixteen-fifties, and the religious and political propagandists used this in support of Parliament's cause, especially radicals hoping for the rule of the saints. Secondly, from the time of Richard Hakluyt men had advocated an expansionist policy in North America which would extend God's kingdom and bring profits to Englishmen. Thomas Cooper in 1615 associated this with the conversion of the Jews, an association later reinforced by the idea that the American Indians were the lost tribes. Others, at least from Robert Parker, who died in 1614, called for an aggressive policy in the Mediterranean against Pope and Great Turk. This would protect exporters of new draperies as well as being a necessary preliminary to the conversion of the Jews. Finally there was the campaign for the admission of the Jews to England, in which commercial motives were once more mixed with those of religious radicalism.

By 1656 the Jews had been admitted *de facto*, Cromwell's Western Design had given England a foothold in the Caribbean, and Blake's fleet dominated the Mediterranean. Millenarian expectations of the conversion of the Jews had stirred up popular excitement and hopes. But as the crucial dates passed in the sixteen-fifties with no sign of the millennium, and as the rulers of the Commonwealth grew increasingly conservative, so active millenarianism rapidly declined. In 1658 the Independents' Savoy Declaration of Faith spoke of "the latter days, Antichrist being destroyed and the Jews called", but it gave no dates. Charles II did not become "the great deliverer of the Jews", as Arise Evans and Walter Gostelow had predicted; the thought was repeated by a royalist pamphleteer in 1660.[135] Charles's restoration put "enthusiasm" of any kind out of favour. The time-table had to be recalculated. Owen, Bunyan and no doubt many others came to think such calculations had perhaps been mistaken in themselves.[136] A certain interest attaches to Edward Lane's *Look unto Jesus*, published in 1663, since he had been a school-fellow of Milton's. His book contained an appendix showing the certainty of the calling of the Jews.

The brief career of Sabbatai Sevi in 1665-6, and the exploits of Valentine Greatrakes in England, caused a flutter of millenarian excitement around the year 1666, but it was short-lived.[137] In 1665 Increase Mather heard "rumours of motions [towards conversion] among the Jews in several parts of the world", which gave him hopes that the millennium might be coming.[138] In December 1665 the Secretary of the Royal Society was asking Spinoza for information about rumours that the Jews were about to return to their country.[139] The Rev. Samuel Lee in 1677 still believed in the restoration of the Jews to Palestine, but by now the date had been moved forward until 1766-1811.[140] It was not until the next great revolutionary age, the seventeen-nineties, that millenarians who favoured the French Revolution hoped that it would give occasion for the conversion and calling of the Jews.[141] Napoleon in Egypt at least got nearer to Palestine than Cromwell did. When in the present century a Jewish national state was established in Israel it did not coincide with "the conversion of the Jews".

X

The conversion of the Jews had been eagerly expected until about 1656 — a date after which it is unlikely that 'To his coy mistress' was written. So we come back to Marvell. He might, I hope you will agree, have heard of the conversion of the Jews. His contemporaries, accustomed to thinking in analogies, would naturally expect Noah's Flood to lead on to the conversion of the Jews. It is not, *pace* Ransom, "the logic of a child", but of a sophisticated seventeenth-century wit; not "disproportionate" but carefully calculated. "Ten years before the Flood" would be *anno mundi* 1646. 'To his Coy Mistress' was hardly written before 1646 A.D. If the end of the world is coming in 1656, Marvell's lady may not have so long as we thought for her refusal, or indeed as she may have thought. "And *the last age* should show your heart" (my italics). I am not suggesting that Marvell himself expected the conversion in 1656. We do not know, but my guess would be that he did not. An interesting paper by Hugh Ornsby-Lennon recently suggested that in 'Upon Appleton House' Marvell plays with modish alchemical ideas in a way that seems serious but is almost certainly ironical.[142] That is exactly what I am suggesting he does with fashionable millenarian ideas in 'To his Coy Mistress'.

The conversion of the Jews would have a clear connotation for

Marvell's contemporaries, and its association with the Flood would
in no way surprise them. Stanzas LIX-LXI of 'Upon Appleton
House' perhaps repeat the connection.[143] So the light elegance of the
opening of 'To his Coy Mistress', with its contemporary relevance,
leads up to the ironically courtly couplet:

> For lady you deserve this state;
> Nor would I love at lower rate.

It hardly prepares us for the clutch at the throat in the terrifying lines
which follow, the axis upon which the poem turns.

> But at my back I always hear
> Time's winged chariot hurrying near.

In the Bible chariots of fire could be images of God's power to rescue
his people (II Kings 6. 17; Psalm 68. 17); but they were also a symbol
of hostile might, Egyptians trying to prevent the Israelites from
leaving for the promised land (Exodus 14.7; I, Samuel 13.5; II, Samuel
10. 18; Psalm 20.7). Marvell's chariot carries not the Messiah but
Death, and a death which appears to offer no immortality:

> Yonder all before us lie
> Deserts of vast eternity.

C. S. Lewis called Milton our first poet of space.[144] Marvell has some
claim to be our first poet of an eternity which is associated neither
with the bliss of heaven nor with the torments of hell. Its blankness
and emptiness correspond to the blank infinity of the Copernican
universe. Marvell's lines recall Pascal's cry as he contemplated the
consequences of the new astronomy: "le silence éternel de ces espaces
infinis m'effraie", "ces effroyables espaces de l'univers qui m'enfer-
ment", "abîmé dans l'infinie immensité des espaces que j'ignore et
qui m'ignorent".[145] Pascal was writing at almost exactly the same
time as Marvell.

We had been prepared for the vastness of space by Marvell's
reference to the Ganges[146] — a river so remote that Marvell has to tell
his readers where it is — and by the lines about the poet's vegetable
love growing "vaster than empires, and more slow". The conversion
of the Jews, contemporaries would need no reminder, will come at
the same time as the overthrow of the papacy, the fourth vast

(Roman) empire, and will usher in the Fifth Monarchy, the kingdom of Christ on earth.

Marvell returns to this theme in 'The First Anniversary of the Government under O.C.' The ponderous movements of "heavy monarchs, ... more slow and brittle than the China clay" impede Oliver's millenarian potentialities, just as the vegetable growth of empires was contrasted with the love that could make the sun run. 'The First Anniversary' begins, unexpectedly, by picturing human life as a weight dropped into a smooth stream. "Like the vain curlings of the watery maze", man

> disappears
> In the weak circles of increasing years;
> And his short tumults of themselves compose,
> While flowing Time above his head does close.

This leads on to a contrast between ordinary men and the heroic Oliver, who

> The force of scattered Time contracts,
> And in one year the work of ages acts.

"Princes and cities" had made the protestant reformation. If princes all over Europe would only co-operate with Oliver's efforts

> Fore-shortened Time its useless course would stay,
> And soon precipitate the latest day.

We can perhaps trace analogies between the "private" love poems and the public poems. The slow movements of Time culminating in death frustrate the eager lover; the possibility of influencing the great world of affairs seems to offer an alternative to a perhaps illusory private happiness. Marvell makes the contrast in 'The Garden', the Mower poems, 'An Horatian Ode' and 'Upon Appleton House'. In 'An Horatian Ode' the poet applauds Cromwell's necessary emergence from

> his private gardens where
> He lived reserved and austere,
> As if his highest plot
> To plant the bergamot.

Cromwell urged his "active star"; his "industrious valour" made

him "the force of angry heaven's flame" which ruined "the great
work of Time".[147] In 'Upon Appleton House', less confidently,
Marvell accepted Fairfax's withdrawal from activity. "The world will
not go the faster for our driving", as he put it philosophically and (as
usual) ambiguously in the much later *The Rehearsal Transpros'd*.[148]

In the contrast between public activity and private happiness
Marvell mostly comes down on the side of public activity, despite his
sympathy for Fairfax. The 'Horatian Ode' seems to give expression
to a turning point in Marvell's own life: the forward youth henceforth sought public employment. Maria Fairfax is a much less
convincing heavenly force than Oliver Cromwell in the 'Horatian
Ode'. She recalls rather the somewhat perfunctory "Pan met me" in
'Clorinda and Damon'; the couple decide to commit suicide in order
to get to heaven quickly.

But in the conflict between *carpe diem* and eternity the outcome is
even less clear-cut. Marvell's attitude in 'To his Coy Mistress' has
been called Puritan rather than libertine. The strategy of the poem is
for lovers to take the counter-offensive against Time and so avoid
languishing in his slow-chapped power.

> Pretty surely 'twere to see
> By young Love old Time beguiled,

as the poet put it in 'Young Love'. But, as Marvell tells us in 'The
Unfortunate Lover', lovers cannot

> to that region climb
> To make impression upon Time.

'To his Coy Mistress' offers no really consoling conclusion. The
lovers in their private world may temporarily triumph over circumstance by making their sun run, but the gates of life remain iron. The
ultimate privacy is the grave; and "none I think do there embrace".[149]

XI

By 1656 the millennium had not come, nor had there been conver-
sions in any significant number of either Jews or American Indians.
But the new English foreign policy had been triumphantly achieved
by the Navigation Act, by Blake's fleet in the Mediterranean, by the
conquest of Jamaica in 1655. The Jews had been unofficially
admitted to England. Their conversion seemed less urgently relevant.

What survived was a secularized millenarianism in which the conversion of the Jews plays little part, and English commercial enterprise is central.

The 'Horatian Ode''s lines,

> As Caesar he ere long to Gaul,
> To Italy an Hannibal,

perhaps catch something of the earlier revolutionary internationalism. But in 'The First Anniversary of the Government under O.C.' Marvell recognized that millenarian hopes were now doubtful.

> If in some happy hour
> High grace should meet in one with highest power ...
> Fore-shortened Time its useless course would stay
> And soon precipitate the latest day.

Cromwell was the obvious focus for such hopes:

> If these the times, then this must be the man.

But too many

> Unhappy princes, ignorantly bred,
> By malice some, by error more misled,
> Indians whom they should convert, subdue;
> Nor teach, but traffic with, or burn, the Jew.
> Hence that blest day still counter-poised wastes,
> The ill delaying what th'elected hastes.

It is the only mention of Jews in the poem: note their association with Indians.

What matters now is England's national power and national trade. In this respect Charles II could easily succeed to Oliver Cromwell. Dryden, like Marvell a former Cromwellian civil servant, resumed the theme of national commercial greatness in 'Annus Mirabilis', whilst ignoring any idea of an anti-Catholic crusade or the conversion of the Jews. After Dryden pseudo-millenarian predictions of a glorious imperial and trading future for London and England became common form.[150] We are back where we started, with Thomas Cooper. Just as the defeat of "the Puritan Revolution" allowed the Church of England to take over Sabbatarianism and "the protestant ethic", so the secular content of the millenarian foreign policy could be taken over once millenarianism was no longer dangerous.[151]

Milton was much less committal on the conversion of the Jews than he was on most theological subjects. In his *De Doctrina Christiana* he merely cited the relevant texts and said "some authors think" that the calling of the Jews will be a further portent of the Second Coming.[152] In *Paradise Regained* the Son of God leaves the question open:

> Yet he himself, time to himself best known
> May bring them back repentant and sincere.[153]

Milton's eager millenarian expectations had been disappointed so many times that his caution is understandable. Yet I should like to end by recalling Northrop Frye's argument that "the prophecy of Michael in *Paradise Lost* presents the whole Bible as a miniature contrast-epic, with one pole at the apocalypse and the other at the Flood".[154] The pattern does not depend on the dating 1656 a.m./1656 A.D.; but it is a suggestive thought for our theme. If the whole Bible proceeds from Flood to conversion of the Jews, Marvell hardly needed his rhyming dictionary: nor was it very difficult to supply a context for the Jews.

NOTES

1. Based on a Clark Lecture, delivered at the Clark Library, Los Angeles, in 1981.
2. J.C. Ransom, *The New Criticism* (1941), pp. 311-13.
3. Taylor, *A Very Merry Wherry-Ferry-Voyage* (1622), pp. 18-19, in *Works of John Taylor* (ed. C. Hindley, 1872).
4. E. Rogers, *Some Account of the Life and Opinions of a Fifth Monarchy Man* (1867), pp. 12-13, 148-51; Capp, *The Fifth Monarchy Men*, p. 192. Since I wrote this piece, David S. Katz's *Philo-Semitism and the Readmission of the Jews to England, 1603-1655*, has added greatly to our knowledge of the subject.
5. B.W. Ball, *A Great Expectation: Eschatological Thought in English Protestantism to 1660* (Leiden, 1975), p. 107n.; A. R. Dallison, "Contemporary Criticism of Millenarianism", in *Puritans, the Millennium and the Future of Israel* (Ed. P. Toon, 1970), pp. 104-14.
6. R. Shelford, *Five Pious Learned Discourses* (1635), p. 314. For Shelford see my *Antichrist in Seventeenth-century England*, pp. 38, 180.

7. Ruth Gladstein, "Eschatological Trends in Bohemian Jewry during the Hussite Period", in *Prophecy and Millenarianism: Essays in Honour of Marjorie Reeves* (ed. A. Williams, 1980), p. 248; cf. M. Vereté, "The Restoration of the Jews in English Protestant Thought, 1790-1840", *Middle Eastern Studies*, January 1972, p. 14.

8. Matthew 24. 37. John Tillinghast made the point that the precise date of Christ's death was uncertain, and so calculations might be a couple of years out at the start; 1654 rather than 1656 might be the operative date (*Knowledge of the Times, Or, The Resolution of the question, how long it shall be unto the end of the wonders*, 1654, pp. 303-8).

9. Joye, *The coniectures of the ende of the worlde* (Antwerp, 1548), Sig. B i-iii.

10. T. Goodwin, *Works* (Edinburgh, 1861-3), III, p. 196.

11. *Op. cit.*, p. 34. John Dury contributed a preface, accepting the date 1656. *Clavis Apocalyptica* was probably written by Abraham von Franckenburg, a great admirer of Jakob Boehme. Cf. Elizabeth Labrousse, *L'Entrée de Saturne en Lion: L'Eclipse de Soleil du 12 Août 1654* (La Haye, 1974), p. 7.

12. P. Sterry, *Englands Deliverance from the Northern Presbytery* (1652), pp. 43-4.

13. Tillinghast, *Knowledge of the Times*, pp. 41-97, 306; *Generation-work: Or, An Exposition of the Prophecies of the Two Witnesses*, Part III (1655), pp. 22, 122; Homes, *The Resurrection Revealed* (1654); R. H. Popkin, "Rabbi Nathan Shapira's Visit to Amsterdam in 1657", in *Dutch Jewish History* (ed. J. Michman, Jerusalem, 1984), p. 187. For further examples of parallels between 1656 a.m. and 1656 A.D., see Labrousse, *op. cit.*, pp. 7-8.

14. Rogers, *Sagrir or Doomes-day drawing nigh*, quoted in E. Rogers, *op. cit.*, p. 83. Lady Eleanor Davies also expected a new Flood in 1656 (Theodore Spencer, "The History of an Unfortunate Lady", *Harvard Studies and Notes in Philology and Literature*, XX, 1938, p. 58).

15. Gell, *Noahs Flood* (1655), p. 17.

16. Ed. E. S. de Beer, *Diary of John Evelyn* (Oxford U.P., 1955), III, p. 138. See now Katz, "English Redemption and Jewish Readiness in 1656", *Journal of Jewish Studies*, XXXIV (1983), pp. 73-6.

17. R. H. Popkin, "Spinoza and the Conversion of the Jews", in *Spinoza's Political and Theological Thought* (ed. C. De Deugd, Amsterdam, 1984), p. 171.

18. Traherne, *Poems, Centuries and Three Thanksgivings* (ed. A. Ridler, Oxford U.P., 1966), pp. 409-13; cf. D. Brady, "1666: the year of the Beast", *Bulletin of the John Rylands University Library*, No. 61 (1978-9), p. 334, quoting Sprat in 1692. Cf. my *Writing and Revolution in Seventeenth-Century England* (1985), p. 231.

19. Willet, *De Judaeorum vocatione* (Cambridge U.P., 1590). Cf. Mayir Vereté's important article, "The Restoration of the Jews in English Protestant Thought", p. 15. See also T. K. Rabb, "The Stirrings of the 1590s and the return of the Jews to England", *Transactions of the Jewish Historical Soc. of England*, XXVI (1974-8).

20. Perkins believed that "it is not possible for any to find out the time of the end of the world" (*Works*, 1609-13, III, p. 467). Cf. T. Draxe, *The Worlds Resurrection or the generall calling of the Jewes* (1608), Elnathan Parr, *A Plaine Exposition upon the 8, 9, 10, 11 chapters of the Epistle of St. Paul to the Romans* (1618), Thomas Sutton, *Lectures upon the eleventh chapter to the Romans* (1632).

21. J. Napeir, *A Plaine Discovery of the whole Revelation of St. John* (1593), esp. pp. 12, 16, 179-80.

22. Brightman, *The Revelation of St. John Illustrated* (4th. edn., 1644), pp. 518-19, 543-5, 555, 781, 808, 836, 894, 967. For Brightman see Vereté, *op. cit.*, pp. 16, 30.

23. In 1612 Nicholas Fuller, Puritan lawyer, also expected the return of the lost tribes from the East. He had no doubt been reading Brightman.

24. Broughton, *A Revelation of the Holy Apocalypse* (1610), pp. 50, 264, 269; M. Reeves, "History and Eschatology: Medieval and Early Protestant Thought in Some English and Scottish Writings", *Medievalia et Humanistica*, N. S., No. 4 (1973), p. 112 and *passim*.

25. Finch, *op. cit.*, esp. pp. 3, 59-60. For Finch see Vereté, *op. cit.*, pp. 16, 30 and W. R. Prest, "The Art of Law and the Law of God", in *Puritans and Revolutionaries* (ed. D. Pennington and K. Thomas, Oxford U.P., 1978), pp. 94-117. The Puritan judge, Sir Henry Yelverton, heard a sermon during James I's reign on the signs of the coming millennium: "remaineth but a full conversion of the Jews" (Cliffe, *The Puritan Gentry*, p. 206).

26. Milton asked in his Seventh Prolusion — why seek fame on earth when "there will be few succeeding generations to remember us?" (*M.C.P.W.*, I, p. 302). Already Christ appears to be "shortly expected King". It is hardly likely that Milton was unaware of Mede's views.

27. J. Mede, *Remains, or Some Passages in the Apocalypse*, in *Works (1672)*, pp. 600, 766-7, and *passim*, Cf. Vereté, *op cit.*, pp. 17-18, 48.

28. Sibbes, *Works*, I, p. 99; Adams, *A Commentary or Exposition upon the Divine Second Epistle General, written by . . . St. Peter* (1633), pp. 1136-8.

29. Hakewill, *An Apologie or Declaration of the Power and Providence of God* (3rd. edn., 1635), p. 549.

30. Goodman, *Trinity and Incarnation* (1653), p. 192.

31. Wheelwright, *A Fast-Day Sermon*, in Hall, *The Antinomian Controversy*, p. 165; cf. P. Greven, *The Protestant Temperament* (New York, 1977), p. 118. See also p. 130 above.

32. T. Goodwin, *Works*, III, pp. 28-9, 72, 157, 201-2. Goodwin quoted Mede for 1656 (*ibid.*, III, p. 196).

33. *Ibid.*, pp. 196, 202-3; *A Glimpse of Syon's Glory* (1641), in Woodhouse *Puritanism and Liberty*, pp. 233-41. Goodwin may have been reading Sir Henry Blount's *A Voyage into the Levant* (1636) — see p. 281 above. Or he may have talked to Dutch traders.

34. W. Sedgwick, *Zions Deliverance and her Friends Duty* (1642), pp. 5, 21-2.

35. [Anon.], *The Worlds Proceeding Woes and Succeeding Joyes* (1642), Sig. B.3.

36. *Op. cit.*, Sig. A 3v-A 4v.
37. Maton, *Israels Redemption* (1642).
38. *Op. cit.*, esp. pp. 58-63.
39. Cotton, quoted in Zakai, *Exile and Kingdom*, p. 383.
40. Gower, *Things Now-a-days, or The Churches Travail Of the Child of Reformation now-a-bearing* (1644), pp. 11-12, 18, 41-2; Reyner, *Babylons Running-Earthquake and the Restauration of Zion* (1644), pp. 28-33.
41. J. F. Maclear, "New England and the Fifth Monarchy: The Quest for the Millennium", in *Early American Puritanism: Essays on Religion, Society and Culture* (ed. A. T. Vaughan and F. J. Bremer, New York, 1977), p. 76. Toppe, *Christs Monarchicall and Personall Reigne upon Earth* (?1648), quoted in *Biographical Dictionary of British Radicals*, III, p. 249.
42. For Tany see *Puritanism and Revolution*, p. 143; *W.T.U.D.*, pp. 225-6.
43. *Op. cit.*, pp. 207-9; B. R. White, "Henry Jessey: A Pastor in Politics", *Baptist Quarterly*, XXV (1973), p. 101.
44. Canne, *A Voice from the Temple to the Higher Powers* (1653), pp. 28-30, 20-1.
45. Ball, *op. cit.*, p. 108; G. H. Turnbull, *Hartlib, Dury and Comenius: Gleanings from Hartlib's Papers* (Liverpool U.P., 1947), pp. 257-8, 261-2, 267.
46. [Anon.], *The Great Day at the Dore* (1648), title-page.
47. For example, William Aspinwall, John Carew, Henry Danvers, John and Thomas Goodwin, Nathanael Homes, Henry Jessey, Morgan Llwyd, Robert Norwood, Robert Purnell, John Rogers, John Sadler, Thomas Shepard, John Spittlehouse, William Strong, John Tillinghast.
48. Ball, *op. cit.*, pp. 147, 150; Dallison, *op. cit.*, pp. 107, 112-14; E. H[all], *A Scriptural Discourse of the Apostasie and the Antichrist* (1653), pp. 72-3; Love, *Heavens Glory* (1653).
49. C. Webster, *The Great Instauration*, pp. 381, 565.
50. Josselin, *Diary*, pp. 227-8; cf. pp. 257, 266, 268; Lamont, *Richard Baxter and the Millennium*, p. 41.
51. Capp, *Astrology and the Popular Press*, p. 172.
52. M. Wall, *Considerations upon the Point of the Conversion of the Jewes*, in Lucien Wolf, *Menasseh ben Israel's Mission to Oliver Cromwell* (Jewish Historical Soc. of England, 1901), p. 53.
53. Quoted by Lamont, "The Muggletonians: A 'Vertical' Approach", *P. and P.*, No. 99 (1983), p. 26.
54. Baillie, *A Disswasive from the Errours of the Time* (1645), *passim*; Lamont, *Richard Baxter and the Millennium*, p. 56; cf. T. Hayne, *Christs Kingdom on Earth* (1645), *passim*.
55. Reeve, *A Divine Looking-Glass* (3rd. edn., 1719), pp. 184-5.
56. Sabine, *op. cit.*, pp. 260-1. Cf. p. 207 above.
57. *Ibid.*, p. 15. Winstanley's *The New Law of Righteousness* (1649) was dedicated to "the twelve tribes of Israel that are circumcised in heart".
58. Vereté, *op. cit.*, pp. 31-2, 49. Fletcher's *The Tartars or Ten Tribes* was

published in Samuel Lee's *Israel Redux; Or the Restoration of Israel* (1677).

59. I owe this point to J. C. Davis, *Utopia and the Ideal Society: A Study of English Utopian Writing, 1516-1700* (Cambridge U.P., 1981), pp. 113-15, 146.

60. Quoted by Ball, *op. cit.*, p. 90. Cf. George Herbert, 'The Jews'.

61. Henry Vaughan, *Works* (ed. L. C. Martin, Oxford U.P., 1914), II, p. 499.

62. A. Cowley, Preface to *Poems* (1656), reprinted in *Poetry and Prose* (ed. L. C. Martin, Oxford U.P., 1949), p. 71.

63. *Op. cit.*, Sig. A 2-3.

64. *Ibid.*, pp. 33-5

65. *Ibid.*, pp. 33-4, 42-3.

66. *Ibid.*, pp. 53-5. Cooper, agreeably enough, defended moderate usury (*The Worldlings Adventure*, 1619, pp. 63-4).

67. Quoted by A. Calder, *Revolutionary Empire: The Rise of the English-Speaking Empires from the Fifteenth Century to the 1790s* (1981), p. 141.

68. Wolf, *Menasseh ben Israel's Mission to Oliver Cromwell*, pp. xxiv, 1-8, and *passim*; Vereté, *op. cit.*, p. 49.

69. See p. 276 above. Dury published *An Information Concerning the Present State of the Jewish Nation* in 1658.

70. *Op. cit.*, Sig. c 3v. Much later the radical Quaker Benjamin Furly and the freethinking deist Anthony Collins each had Thorowgood's book in his library (See p. 198 above).

71. B. Capp, "The Fifth Monarchists and Popular Millenarianism", in McGregor and Reay, *op. cit.*, p. 188.

72. Alden T. Vaughan, *New England Frontier: Puritans and Indians, 1620-1675* (New York, 1979), pp. 19-20. Cf. Thomas Shepard, *The Clear Sun-shine of the Gospel breaking forth upon the Indians in New England* (1648); Gura, *op. cit.*, pp. 133-4.

73. Thorowgood, *Jewes in America* (2nd. edn., 1660), p. 23.

74. *Ibid.*, p. 51. Cf. *The Experience of Defeat*, pp. 281-2.

75. Whitfield, *Strength Out of Weaknesse* (1652), Sig. a, quoted by Ball, *op. cit.*, p. 109.

76. J. R. Jacob, *Robert Boyle and the English Revolution*, *passim*.

77. M. C. Jacob, *The Newtonians and the English Revolution* (1976), p. 167. Sir Hamon L'Estrange wrote a pamphlet entitled *Americans no Jews*, published in 1652.

78. Wolf, *op. cit.*, p. 85.

79. *D.N.B.*, s.v. Udall.

80. A. C. Wood, *A History of the Levant Company* (Oxford U.P., 1935), pp. 43-4, 73, 214, 219-20, 235-6; Gerschom Scholem, *Sabbatai Sevi: the Mystical Messiah, 1626-1676* (1973), p. 107. I am grateful to Richard Popkin for advice about Sabbatai Sevi.

81. Blount, *A Voyage into the Levant* (1636), pp. 102-3. See S. P. Chew, *The Crescent and the Rose: Islam and England during the Renaissance* (New York, 1937), esp. Part I, Chapter 3.

82. [J. Sadler], *Rights of the Kingdom: Or, Customs of our Ancestours*

Touching The Duty, Power, Election or Succession of our Kings and Parliaments (1649), pp. 38-48; cf. *Nova Solyma* (1648) (ed. W. Begley, 1902), I, Excursus F. This was by Samuel Gott, though Begley attributed it to Milton.

83. Capp, *The Fifth Monarchy Men*, p. 29.
84. W. Burton, *Davids evidence, or the Assurance of Gods love* (1592), p. 125, quoted by D. D. Wallace, "From Eschatology to Arian heresy: the Case of Francis Kett (d. 1589)", *Harvard Theological Review*, 67 (1974), pp. 461-2.
85. Ed. J. Lindsay, *Loving Mad Tom: Bedlamite Verses of the XVI and XVII centuries* (1969), p. 104; K. V. Thomas, *op. cit.*, p. 135. Cf. J. Reeve, *A Divine Looking-Glass* (1661), p. 10.
86. T. Edwards, *Gangraena*, III, pp. 26-7. For Mrs Attaway see pp. 102, 199-200 above.
87. G. H., *The Declaration of John Robins the false Prophet* (1651), pp. 4, 6.
88. See my *Puritanism and Revolution*, p. 143, and references there cited.
89. In J. Frank, *The Beginnings of the English Newspaper* (Harvard U.P., 1961), p. 83.
90. Josselin, *Diary*, p. 38.
91. Ball, *op. cit.*, p. 153.
92. See G. Nuttall, *Visible Saints: The Congregational Way, 1640-60* (Oxford, 1957), p. 144. At least one Jew was converted to Christianity, and there was one false conversion.
93. G. Foster, *The Pouring Forth of the Seventh and Last Viall* (1650), pp. 64-6.
94. In *Harleian Miscellany* (1744-6), I, pp. 369-75. There had in fact been a Jewish Council late in 1650 to deal with the consequences of the Ukranian massacres of 1648 (R. H. Popkin, "Jewish Messianism and Christian Millenarianism", in *Culture and Politics: From Puritanism to the Enlightenment*, ed. P. Zagorin, California U.P., 1980, p. 78).
95. Ed. D. H. Fleming, *Diary of Sir Archibald Johnston of Wariston*, II *(1650-1654)* (Scottish History Soc., 1919), p. 178.
96. Ed. J.G. Fotheringham, *The Diplomatic Correspondence of Jean de Montereul* (Scottish History Soc., 1888-9), II, p. 550.
97. Eachard, *Good Newes for all Christian Souldiers* (1646), Sig. A 4v, pp. 1, 3.
98. The passage was dropped from the 1651 edition of this tract.
99. Parker, *op. cit.*, p. 11.
100. Sterry, *The Comings Forth of Christ* (1650), p. 11.
101. W. Lilly, *Monarchy or no Monarchy in England* (1651), p. 55.
102. J. Owen *A Sermon Preached to The Parliament, October 13, 1652* p. 126.
103. My *Puritanism and Revolution*, p. 134; cf. p. 136.
104. Tillinghast, *Knowledge of the Times* (1654); Capp, *The Fifth Monarchy Men*, p. 151.
105. *Puritanism and Revolution*, p. 146.
106. Wolf, *op. cit.*, pp. xviii-xix, xxx.

107. *Ibid.*, pp. xxx-xxxi, xl-xli.
108. *Ibid.*, pp. xxxvi-vii.
109. *Ibid.*, pp. xxxvi-ix.
110. R. Overton, *The Araignement of Mr. Persecution* (1645), in Haller, *Tracts on Liberty*, III, p. 233; cf. p. 225.
111. F. Cheynell, *An Account Given to the Parliament by the Ministers sent by them to Oxford* (1647), p. 35; Christian Ravis, *A Discourse of the Orientall Tongues* (1648), pp. 61, 70; cf. H. Peter, *A Word for the Armie* (1647), pp. 11-12.
112. Maton, *Israels Redemption.*
113. G. Williams, *Jura Majestatis, the rights of kings both in church and state*, quoted by W. K. Jordan, *The Development of Religious Toleration in England (1640-1660)*, II, pp. 433-4.
114. C. V. Wedgwood, *The Trial of Charles I* (1964), p. 89.
115. Wolf, *op. cit.*, p. 79; cf. p. 53.
116. Norwood, *Proposals for the propagation of the Gospel, Offered to the Parliament* (1651[-2]), p. 17; Collier, *The Pulpit Guard Routed* (1652), p. 41.
117. R. W[illiams], *The Fourth Paper, Presented by Maior Butler* (1652), p. 9; Strong, "The Doctrine of the Jews Vocation", in *XXXI Select Sermons* (1656), esp. pp. 287-91. Strong died in 1654.
118. Ed. J. Nicholls, *Original Letters and Papers of State Addressed to Oliver Cromwell* (1743), pp. 99-100.
119. J. W., *A Mite to the Treasury* (1653), p. 17.
120. Josselin, *Diary*, p. 358. In 1656 Josselin dreamt that Thurloe was a Jew (*ibid.*, p. 337).
121. Jessey, *A Narrative of the late proceedings at Whitehall concerning the Jews* (1656), quoted by B. R. White, *The Separatist Tradition*, p. 107. Even a conservative like Thomas Barlow, Bodley's Librarian, urged "the toleration of the Jews" (Nuttall, *Visible Saints: The Congregational Way*, 1640-1660, Oxford, 1957, p. 146).
122. Isabel Ross, *Margaret Fell, Mother of Quakerism* (1949), pp. 89-97.
123. G. Wither, *Vaticinia Poetica, or, rather A Fragment of some Presages long since written* (1666), pp. 13-21, in *Miscellaneous Works* (Spenser Soc.), IV (1875). Joseph Frank records an anonymous work of this title as published in 1656 (*Hobbled Pegasus*, New Mexico U.P., 1968, p. 357). From internal evidence that would seem to be the correct date of first publication of Wither's poem.
124. Ed. A. R. Hall and M. B. Hall, *The Correspondence of Henry Oldenburg*, I, *1641-1662* (Wisconsin U.P., 1965), pp. 123-5.
125. Ed. T. Birch, *Thurloe State Papers* (1742), I, p. 387; Wolf, *op. cit.*, pp. xxxvi-vii.
126. Wolf, *op. cit.*, p. xli.
127. *Thurloe State Papers*, IV, p. 108.
128. Nicholas, *op. cit.*, p. 4. Nicholas expected his book to be attacked by "the Pope and his clergy", especially Jesuits. For Jews, like Puritans, hate idolatry (*ibid.*, p. 14).
129. See *A Collection of Original Letters and Papers* (ed. T. Carte, 1739),

I, p. 233, for a curious suggestion in 1648 that Parliament "had revoked the laws that were made against the Jews".

130. Ed. C. H. Josten, *Elias Ashmole (1617-1692)* (Oxford U.P., 1966), I, p. 92; II, pp. 560, 606, 609; cf. C. Roth, *The Resettlement of the Jews in England in 1656* (Jewish Historical Soc., 1960), pp. 10, 19, 23.

131. W. Prynne, *A short demurrer to the Jews long discontinued remitter into England* (1655), pp. 65-6, 89-90; Wolf, *op. cit.*, pp. lvii-ix, lxvii. John Sadler was said to have helped to win permission for the synagogue (A. Woolrych, *Commonwealth to Protectorate*, Oxford U.P., 1982, p. 207).

132. Burton, *Parliamentary Diary*, I, p. 121.

133. J. Harrington, *Political Works* (ed. J. G. A. Pocock, Cambridge U.P., 1977), p. 159.

134. J. A. Williamson, *English Colonies in Guiana and on the Amazon (1604-1688)* (Oxford U.P., 1923), pp. 164-5; Wolf, *op. cit.*, pp. xxxvi-vii; C. and R. Bridenbaugh, *No Peace Beyond the Line* (New York, 1972), pp. 147, 199, 326-7.

135. Gostelow, *Charles Stuart and Oliver Cromwell United* (1655); my *Change and Continuity in 17th-Century England* (1974), pp. 55, 58, 70-1, 77, 158, 310. See Popkin, "Rabbi Nathan Shapira's Visit", p. 188; cf. p. 204 for continuing hopes in 1662. Menasseh ben Israel quoted a Frenchman who thought that the King of France would be leader of the Jews "when they returned to their country" (Wolf, *op. cit.*, p. 124). Traditional nationalism is taking over from the religious inter-nationalism of the interregnum radicals.

136. See pp. 233-4, 253 above.

137. Capp, *Fifth Monarchy Men*, pp. 213-14; cf. Ida Macalpine, "Valentine Greatrakes", *St. Bartholomew's Hospital Journal*, LX (1956), pp. 361-8. Marvell was a co-signatory with Boyle and others of Greatrakes's *Brief Account* (J. R. Jacob, *Henry Stubbe*, Chapter 3). Cf. R. H. Popkin, "Jewish Messianism and Christian Millenarianism", pp. 67-90, and p. 334 below.

138. D. Levin, *Cotton Mather: The Young Life of the Lord's Remembrancer, 1663-1703* (Harvard U.P., 1978), p. 5. Cf. Vavasor Powell, *The Bird in the Cage, Chirping* (2nd. edn., 1662), Sig. A 6; [Anon.], *The Life and Death of Mr. Vavasor Powell* (1671), pp. 44-5.

139. Oldenburg, *Correspondence*, II, pp. 635-7.

140. Lee, *Israel Redux*, pp. 120-2. Lee's book was reprinted several times. Cf. Vereté, *op. cit.*, pp. 31-2, 49.

141. Vereté, *op. cit.*, pp. 10-13, 26-7, 39-41.

142. Ornsby-Lennon, *Futurist Poets of the English Civil War* (xerox, 1981), I am grateful to Mr Ornsby-Lennon for allowing me to read this article.

143. Cf. A. E. Berthoff, *The Resolved Soul: A Study of Marvell's Major Poems* (Princeton U.P., 1970), p. 187.

144. C. S. Lewis, *Words* (Cambridge U.P., 1960), p. 251.

145. Pascal, *Pensées*, Nos. 194, 205-6 in Brunschwigg's edition.

146. Why does the lady find rubies by the side of the Ganges? No doubt Marvell had read some travel book associating rubies with India. In

seventeenth-century lore rubies divert the mind from evil thoughts (Brewer, *Dictionary of Phrase and Fable*, s.v.); the philosopher's stone sought by alchemists, Sir Epicure Mammon declared in *The Alchemist*, "the perfect ruby which we call elixir,/ ... Can confer honour, love respect, long life" (II, i). And, as the Bible tells us, wisdom and a virtuous woman's price are both above rubies (Job 28. 18; Proverbs 3. 15, 8. 11, 31. 10).

147.. Cf. T. W. Hayes, "The Dialectic of History in Marvell's *Horatian Ode*", *Clio*, I (1971), p. 34.

148. *The Rehearsal Transpros'd* (ed. D. I. B. Smith, Oxford U.P., 1971), p. 135. Marvell is cautiously defending the Good Old Cause. Cf. W. Chernaik, *The Poet's Time: Politics and Religion in the work of Andrew Marvell* (Cambridge U.P., 1983), esp. pp. 39-41.

149. Many poets made time run. Marlowe's Edward II told "bright Phoebus" to gallop apace ... through the sky" to "shorten the time"; his Faustus called on the "ever-moving spheres of heaven" to stand still when his time ran out. Cartwright thought Sir Henry Spelman's researches made the sun "backward run" (*To the Memory of the Most Worthy Sir Henry Spelman*), and Crashawe tells us that love "lends haste to heavenly things"; Christ "spurns the tame laws of time and place" (*Against Irresolution and Delay in Matters of Religion*). Cf. Joseph Hall, *Meditations: the First Century* (1605), in *Works* (Oxford, 1837), VIII, p. 6. In 'Last Instructions to a Painter' Marvell called for the obliteration of the day of England's defeat:

Thee, the year's monster, let thy dam devour.
And constant Time, to keep his course yet right,
Fill up thy space with a redoubled night (lines 737-42).

It all goes back to Joshua 10 and II Kings 20. Cf. Ruth Nevo, *The Dial of Virtue: A Study of Poems on Affairs of State in the Seventeenth Century* (Princeton U.P., 1962), Chapter 4.

150. McKeon, *op. cit.*, pp. 63, 153, 174-5, 249, 268-81.

151. *Society and Puritanism in Pre-Revolutionary England*, pp. 490-4.

152. *M.C.P.W.*, VI, pp. 617-18.

153. Milton, *Paradise Regained*, Book III, lines 433-4.

154. Northrop Frye, *Anatomy of Criticism: Four Essays* (Princeton U.P., 1957), p. 324, quoted by J. A. Wittreich, *Visionary Poetics* (San Marino, 1979), p. 266.

14. *Occasional Conformity and the Grindalian Tradition*[1]

"We ourselves, every Justice of Peace in his station, must make it his business strictly to find them [nonconformists] out; for the country people are generally so rotten, that they will not complain of them, though they see and know of these seditious meetings before their eyes daily."[*]

Occasional conformity, the dissenting habit of going to a service of the Church of England once or so a year, has been much maligned. In the later seventeenth and eighteenth centuries nonconformists qualified themselves for state or local government office this way. Without occasional conformity Tories might well have established permanent control of most boroughs, and so guaranteed themselves a permanent majority in the House of Commons. Hence their repeated attempts to make the practice illegal.[2] Consequently it suited them to denounce occasional conformity as a hypocritical practice, as no doubt it often was. Contemporary dissenters may have thought it essential to the survival of such toleration as the act of 1689 vouchsafed them. But the practice was not new. It had been advocated by the Independent Henry Jacob in 1616, long before there was anything to be gained by it: it has a very respectable intellectual ancestry. I want to try to put it into some sort of historical perspective.

We may find one clue in the fact that the fiercest opponents of occasional conformity came from the extremes of the political spectrum. Quakers denounced it as a cowardly compromise; a high Tory like William Bromley spoke of "that abominable hypocrisy, that inexcusable immorality".[3] Occasional conformists saw themselves as following a *via media*.

---

*Ed. E. M. Halcrow, *Charges to the Grand Jury at Quarter Sessions, 1660-77, by Sir Peter Leicester* (Chetham Soc., third series, V, 1953), p.91: charge at Nether Knotsford, Cheshire, 2 October 1677.

On Guy Fawkes Day, 1709, Henry Sacheverell preached a sermon before the Lord Mayor and the London City Fathers which was to become famous, or notorious. His main target was occasional conformity. He took for granted the wickedness of dissent, of separation from the national church. But he delivered a rather surprising backhand blow at one of Queen Elizabeth's Archbishops of Canterbury, whom Sacheverell even down-graded — "that false son of the church, Bishop Grindal". Against Sacheverell's rejection of Archbishop Grindal we may set John Owen's claim that he and his fellow dissenters "do sacredly adhere unto ... the doctrine of the Church of England ... as it is contained in the Articles of Religion, the Books of Homilies, and declared in the authenticated writings of all the learned prelates and others for sixty years after the Reformation."[4] He was claiming that dissenters were the true Church of England, the successors of Archbishops Grindal and Abbott.

Sacheverell's hero would presumably have been Laud, an Archbishop of Canterbury whose concept of the church was very different from that of Grindal or John Owen. Two years after Laud's death the Presbyterian Francis Cheynell declared that it was the Archbishop who had been "schismatical, imposing such burdens, [rather] than the people in separating from external communion".[5] And — to round off my argument that the idea of continuity from the pre-Laudian church to dissent had a long history — Henry Jessey as early as 1633 was recalling nostalgically Grindal's stand for preaching, Michael Sparke in 1652 looked back to the days of "that learned, pious, painful preaching Bishop Abbott".[6] The perspective in which I want to put the practice of occasional conformity goes back for 150 years before Sacheverell's sermon.

There were problems about a protestant state church. Calvinists had a dual concept of the church — in one sense it was the whole community, in another it was the true believers only. In Geneva, Scotland or Massachusetts the dualism could be resolved to the extent that church and state worked closely together: by excommunication and exclusion from the sacraments, and by stressing the authority of elders, the sovereignty of the godly within the church could be upheld. But in England, where discipline was imposed from above by bishops and their deputies, the situation was less satisfactory: there were Calvinists (as well as Anabaptists) who advocated separation from the national church *in order that* the congregation might be able to excommunicate the ungodly. Bishops were able to score many valid debating points against the Puritan demand for the right of congregations to elect their own ministers — a practice recommended by Luther, Tyndale and Calvin. How absurd to entrust the election of ministers to the ungodly dregs of the population, said Whitgift.[7] The negative point was more effective than the positive argument that in England the patron "represented" the congregation when he presented a minister to a living; no bishop, said one of them in 1570, would think of accepting a minister not presented by a nobleman or a rich gentleman.[8] Presbyterian Puritans were reduced to protesting that by election they did not mean selection by the people proper, but by the well-to-do and godly members of the congregation, with all the difficulties which even they recognized in equating these two categories. They at once laid themselves open to attack from Brownists, though of course the latter no more believed in the democracy of all parishioners than prelatists or Presbyterians: theirs would have been a democracy of the *separated godly*, not of the whole people. This seems the logical conclusion to draw from the two propositions that (i) ministers should be elected and (ii) the mass of the people are unregenerate. But most Calvinists managed to avoid this logic, so strong was the surviving ideal of a national church.

If the visible church must consist of believers only, then the godly should logically contract out of the state church, to reunite as a voluntary congregation. But constructing models like this is a way in which historians deceive themselves. Looking through the wrong end of the telescope the distinction between national church (all inhabitants) and sect (the separated godly) seems clear, simple and absolute. But history was not like that. A missing term is millenarianism, the belief that in the very near future *all* will be believers — either forcibly under the rule of the saints, or convinced by Christ's Second Coming. So separation from the national church is a short-term operation, not an end in itself: withdrawal in order to return, just as many of those who went into exile in the Netherlands or New England hoped to come back to a better England in the very near future. Hankerings after a national church lurked in most of those to whom posterity looks back as the founders of separatist sects, to be shed gradually only as their millenarian hopes faded into the light of common day. Historians have a natural tendency to read back what later became self-evident truths (the millennium is not just round the corner) into the men of the sixteenth and seventeenth centuries, by whom these truths were discovered, if at all, only after long and painful search.

It seems obvious to us that an appeal to Scripture is an appeal to the anarchy of individual consciences: that men have an infinite capacity to read into Scripture what they want to find there. But our recognition of this fact is the result of much disillusioning experience. In the sixteenth century, with the long-secret text of the Bible at last made available, it seemed crystal clear to its readers. Similarly in mid-seventeenth-century England many men believed that once episcopal hindrances had been abolished, it was only a matter of time before all good men agreed on what the Bible said. The spirit of Christ *must* be the same for all men; otherwise why should God allow the Scriptures to be translated, bishops to be overthrown? University-educated divines might try to confuse simple Bible-readers: but in the apocalyptic atmosphere of the sixteen-forties there was widespread confidence in the clarity of the text for honest mechanics, such as the Apostles themselves had been. The early Christian belief that the time was short reappeared: separation or exile would be only of brief duration. Our knowledge of the end of the story is an obstacle to understanding.

Let us remind ourselves of the historical sequence of events. Many of the sincerest English reformers were disappointed with the half-way and erastian nature of the English Reformation, which allowed the survival of bishops and patronage and failed to use church property for education or poor relief. The experience of the years 1547 to 1559 led them to hope for continuing reformation. After surviving the testing period of Mary's reign, convinced protestants, whether they had been exiles or had remained at home, soon felt that Elizabeth's settlement did not go far enough. Once it was clear that she would survive, inevitably schemes for further reformation were put forward.

Grindal's elevation to the see of Canterbury in 1576 and his "opening to the left" seemed to offer prospects of a Scottish type of episcopacy modified by Presbyterian institutions — the social pretensions of the higher clergy reduced, the shire rather than the diocese the unit of church administration, weaker church courts working with the natural rulers of the countryside, the J.Ps., the Geneva Bible replacing the Bishops' Bible. Elizabeth's suspension of Grindal in 1577 was a parting of the ways. His successor, Whitgift, was soon accused of setting "himself against the gentry".[9]

Presbyterianism was predominantly a clerical movement. But its sponsors needed the magistrate's support, since otherwise there would be no coercive power behind the church's discipline once bishops lost their political power. Hence the hope for reform by Parliament. When, as in the classis movement, local groups tried to introduce a form of Presbyterian discipline in advance of Parliamentary legislation, they soon found that their censures could be effective only if backed by the authority of a friendly J.P. or even a bishop.[10] But Elizabethan Presbyterians were never a sect: they hoped for the transformation of the English church into a Presbyterian church. They were perfectly straightforward in their appeals to Queen and Parliament against bishops. They had no more wish to abolish the Church of England than had Henry VIII and Cranmer; like them, the Presbyterians wished to change its government, in a further (and final) instalment of national reformation.

In the nineties the bishops broke up the classis movement, and drove some of its supporters into separatism, or into appealing for popular support. This in its turn lessened Parliamentary enthusiasm for the movement. By the end of the century the hierarchy's counterattack, backed up by Hooker's theoretical statement, had been very successful; and this produced a new situation. The Marprelate Tracts' mocking exposure of the defects of the bishops and their government was intended to bring the whole hierarchy into disrepute. They contributed to drive many to believe that the Church of England was so fundamentally corrupt that reform from within was hopeless: that the only correct solution was withdrawal. Browne was followed into sectarianism by John Penry, probably at least part author of the Marprelate Tracts. On the other hand the scurrility and popular appeal of the tracts shocked and frightened some clerical and gentlemen supporters of the Presbyterian movement (including Thomas Cartwright himself); together with the rise of separatism this helped to complete the rout of its defenders in Parliament. The appeal to the people failed to produce rapid reformation; the Presbyterian policy of reform by political coup had failed. Only two alternatives remained — separatism, which might mean exile and would certainly involve persecution; or conformity and a longer-term, slower policy of permeation from within by preaching, moral reform, self-discipline.

For those who clung on to reformation from within there were many possibilities, varying from inaction to what was later to be called non-separating congregationalism. A congregation could often *in fact* (though not in theory) control its own affairs in many ways. There were some urban livings (fourteen or so in London) where patronage lay in the parishioners or the town corporation. The patronage of a friendly gentleman could on occasion be used: advowsons could indeed be bought.[11] In a poor living (and there were many such) judicious granting and withholding of an augmentation to the minister's stipend made it easier to obtain a man with the right theological outlook. Where it was impossible to influence the incumbent of the living, members of the congregation could subscribe to bring in a lecturer who would meet their doctrinal wishes. As Professor Haller put it, "every Puritan group which at any time joined together to engage a lecturer tended to become a gathered church".[12] This *de facto* Independency was expressed by Henry Jacob and William Bradshaw, insisting on the right of each congregation to control its own affairs under the King, who would be the head of the churches in England rather than of the Church of England.

So far we have been looking at the disintegration of what we may call "official" Puritanism — the nonconformity of clergymen, gentlemen and merchants. But we must not forget — as contemporaries never forgot — the much older stream of lower-class heresy, into contact with which the separating congregations inevitably came after the watershed of the nineties. In England we can trace, from Lollards through Marian martyrs to Elizabethan Familists and the radical sectaries of the sixteen-forties and fifties, a tradition of hostility to the state and its church, to clerical pretensions, to tithes, church courts and oaths, to military service. The state existed to maintain privileges. The radical sects were the organizations of the unprivileged. They were far more difficult to suppress than a national Presbyterian movement. The fact that they lacked the backing of a Walsingham or a Leicester was a help rather than a hindrance: they had to exist underground. As units the congregations might be broken up or driven into exile, but only as units. The movement could not be utterly stamped out, since it met deep spiritual and social needs of the people.[13]

Conformist Puritans differentiated themselves sharply from lower-class sectaries, and indeed claimed that their preaching, their discipline, would help to protect the English church and state from this threat no less than from that of papistry. Even a Commonwealth man like John Hales thought that Anabaptists and libertines, who "would have all things in common", had helped to cause the English risings of 1549.[14] Anabaptism became a shorthand expression for traditional lower-class rejection of the state church, though rejection of tithes was no Anabaptist innovation, going back at least to the Lollards. But anyone who believed in adult baptism would naturally have scruples about paying tithes. This challenged the economic stability of the state church at its most sensitive point. The claim to collect tithes held by many thousand impropriators made their rejection seem a threat to lay as well as to clerical property. All commentators agree that separatists were drawn from and attempted to appeal to the poorer classes. Henry VIII spoke sharply of those who "whilst their hands were busied about their manufactures had their heads also beating about points of divinity".[15] A rare point of agreement between Archbishop Laud and Roger Williams was that "most of the separation" were "of the lower sort of people". John Lilburne described Brownists as "the base and obscure fellows of the world".[16] An early Baptist like Leonard Busher, writing in 1614, was concerned with social reform for the benefit of the poor — the abolition of hanging for theft and of whipping, and putting an end to begging and to the exploitation of the poor by usury and low wages.[17] Walwyn and Winstanley, the most radical reformers, and the men of greatest social compassion who wrote during the interregnum, came from Baptist circles.

For many years the bishops and their supporters had been arguing that "if you had once made an equality . . . among the clergy, it would not be long or you attempted the same among the laity".[18] It was perhaps an unfair argument for Elizabethan bishops to use against those who wanted to establish a Presbyterian discipline; but the events of the sixteen-forties were to show that opponents of religious toleration had a case. Even Lord Brooke in 1641 distinguished between those Anabaptists who "hold free will; community of all things; deny magistracy; and refuse to baptize their children" on the one hand, and the other sort "who only deny baptism to their children till they come to years of discretion, and then they baptize them; but in other things they agree with the Church of England". The former type were "heretics (or atheists)"; the latter were to be pitied. Brooke was quite clear about the "twofold" nature of the sect.[19] Unlike Oliver Cromwell later he felt that no toleration should be vouchsafed to its seditious lower-class wing.

It is worth emphasizing the deep historical roots of the Puritan *via media*, of the call for further reformation *in order* (among other things) to avoid the threat from socially subversive sectaries. Calvin himself began his chapter "Of Civil Government" by observing that he wrote at a time when "on the one hand, frantic and barbarous men are furiously endeavouring to overturn the order established by God", whilst on the other hand "the flatterers of princes, extolling their power without measure, hesitate not to oppose it to the government of God". He thought it his duty to "meet both extremes". But he first demonstrated the necessity for a coercive state machine, against "those who would have men live pell-mell like rats among straw".[20] Calvin's object was to show that true religion is completely consistent with the maintenance of private property, and yet does not necessitate an entirely uncritical acceptance of the existing state.

So when the bishops' campaign of the fifteen-eighties and nineties forced Puritans to choose between submission and separation, most educated, middle-class responsible Puritan laymen chose the former and so avoided being forced into the company of seditious sectaries. It was a preview of the dilemma of 1662, and on both occasions there was much disagreement among those who were faced with it. We must understand the position of "non-separating congregationalists" in this light. They wanted to preserve links with the state church, for social as well as for theological reasons. Even though tarrying for the magistrate had failed, and some with Robert Browne argued for reformation without tarrying for any, the ultimate hope of most of those whom we call Congregationalists was still to take over and modify the state church. Browne himself — Lord Burghley's cousin — returned to the fold. Others went to New England, where they made it clear that they wished to maintain a state church and that they had no use for religious toleration. The settlement of New England was at first envisaged as a sort of revolution by evasion: many New Englanders did in fact return to England in the sixteen-forties and fifties.

Attitudes towards conformity among the respectable separatists varied. Henry Jacob and his church allowed occasional conformity. John Robinson and his followers could hear preaching in the Church of England, but would communicate only privately with godly members of that church. Thomas Hooker also thought it lawful to hear preaching in the state church, but not to communicate either with that church or with Brownists. Henry Ainsworth and Francis Johnson were against any form of occasional conformity.[21] Helwys criticized refusal to break away from the national church.[22]

In 1610 James I appointed an Archbishop of Canterbury in the Grindal tradition, George Abbott; and for nearly two decades life was relatively easy for those who still hoped for further reformation of the national church. But the advent of Laud changed all that. He suppressed the Feoffees for Impropriations who were buying in patronage and augmenting livings; he forced subscriptions of conformity on ministers who were anxious only to have a blind eye turned on them; he suppressed lecturers, driving many of them into exile; his effective control of King and government made it clear that a loose federation of fairly self-governing congregations under the royal supremacy was no longer practical politics. Laud seemed to Puritans the true schismatic, not only because of his attempt to enforce new doctrines and ceremonies, but also because he ended intercommunion with the Dutch and Huguenot churches. This isolated England from the Calvinist international at a time when the threatened advance of Catholicism in the Thirty Years War seemed to make unity among protestants politically as well as theologically essential. Oliver Cromwell thought of emigrating; in fact he stayed on and led the policy of co-operating with lower-class sectaries to rescue England from what was seen as the threatened return of popery.[23]

It is in this perspective that we must see the conflict between those whom we too loosely call Presbyterians and Independents in the sixteen-forties. Both groups wanted to shift the centre of government of the Church of England so as to incorporate Calvinist Puritans. But the experience of the Dedham Classis[24] and New England — and of Scotland — had shown that the full discipline could be established and maintained only with the aid of the civil magistrate. "Presbyterians" were those who feared the social consequences of religious toleration most of all: "Independents" would ideally have favoured a system of congregational Presbyterianism such as existed in New England, but when they were forced into accepting more radical allies they had sufficient social confidence to believe that they could ride the storm. They had no wish to replace the tyranny of old priest by that of new presbyter: there was never much support for Presbyterian discipline from lay members of congregations. Before 1640, by temporarily withdrawing from the state church, and either going into exile or risking persecution at home, the congregations ensured — however unintentionally — that they were composed exclusively of picked and devoted men and women; they acquired confidence, determination, experience in self-government and an ability to manoeuvre and compromise without fear of being swamped. When the Revolution came "Independents" led its radical wing with assurance: "Presbyterians" on the contrary always had one eye looking backwards to the church and state machine within which they had flourished, and which they had only wished to modify to their own advantage. They could, in fact, regain the position they had held from 1644 to 1648 only by restoring monarchy and bishops to check the lower orders.

So both "Presbyterians" and "Independents" proved right, the former in believing that religious toleration would threaten the existence of a state church subordinated to the natural rulers, "Independents" in believing that in the long run they could contain the radicals and win through to a state church which would neither be clerically dominated nor wield a strict coercive discipline. That is why so many "Independent" M.P.s became elders when a Presbyterian state church was set up after 1646. They had wanted a greater share for laymen in running the episcopal Church of England, and certainly did not want to abolish a national church. If a Presbyterian establishment was the best that could be had, it was their duty to help to run it in the hope of continuing reformation.[25]

But these experiments were not carried out in a vaccum, and here "Presbyterian" fears proved more justified than "Independent" confidence. The *de facto* religious toleration of the sixteen-forties allowed the really radical sects to emerge from underground, to meet and discuss in public, to organize themselves under mechanic preachers, free from all control, either of the state church or of their social superiors. Liberty of the press, and the cheapness of publishing, allowed their views to be printed: the New Model Army spread these views across the country as it advanced to victory. Separatism ceased to be what it had been for the respectable godly, a regrettable necessity forced on them by the bishops; it became a principle, as it long had been for the radical sectaries. In the liberty of the forties and fifties the latter were able to work out a much more sophisticated theology and theory of church organization.

So the real dividing question was nakedly revealed: a state church or none? The leading "Presbyterians" and "Independents" came from social groups which could hope to control a state church, either from on top through Parliament, or by infiltration from below, through patronage and local influence. Most of those who whole-heartedly believed in religious toleration came initially from social groups which had no such aspirations — at least not until there had been a radical reform in the state as well as in the church, such as Levellers and others came to advocate.

I express this in what some may consider excessively sociological terms, in deliberate reaction against those denominational historians who are apt to push the origins of their own sect *in an organized form* too far back. The Dissenting Brethren in the Westminster Assembly in 1643, for instance, still envisaged a state church.[26] The New Model Army's Heads of Proposals of 1647 shared the Dissenting Brethren's attitude to the church which they nevertheless wished to retain: there should be no coercive jurisdiction, no penalties for failure to attend parish churches, the Solemn League and Covenant should not be enforced. Liberty not to attend parish churches, legally esta-blished from 1650, was denounced by Presbyterians as schism, just as Whitgift had denounced their practice of electing ministers as schism.

Barebone's Parliament of 1653 contemplated abolishing tithes and patronage. But the moderates, in reaction against what they regarded as the "excesses" of Ranters and Quakers, forced a change of attitude. Masson was quite right to say that "the protectorate came into being in the interests of a conservative interest generally, and especially for the preservation of an established church and the universities".[27] Cromwell's state church reunited moderate Epis-copalians, Presbyterians and many Congregationalists, together with some Baptists, in a loose federation of fairly independent congregations; it preserved tithes (until some better form of main-tenance could be devised) and patronage. It would have perpetuated a more liberal form of the *de facto* Independency which many congre-gations had enjoyed in the pre-Laudian church. There was a great extension of election by parishes. Triers were not empowered to impose any doctrinal test. John Gauden, a Presbyterian who later became a bishop, tells us that in 1656 Episcopalians, Presbyterians and Independents were in a fair way to be reconciled and "upon a very calm temper".[28] It has been estimated that nearly a quarter of the 1760 ministers ejected after 1660 were Congregationalists. Cromwell's church also contained Baptist ministers: six out of thirty-eight of the Triers of 1654 were Baptists.[29] But we should remember that Baptists and Congregationalists were still not precisely differentiated; inter-communion was frequent. In 1672 John Bunyan described himself as a Congregationalist.[30] Many ministers who objected on principle to tithes were prepared to accept state stipends financed from confiscated church lands, as ministers in New England received stipends from towns, not tithes from parishioners.

Cromwell's was a last attempt at a broad-based national church, under lay control. Parliament repeatedly tried under the Protectorate to narrow the standards of orthodoxy to be imposed on ministers before they were eligible for public maintenance; and Quakers and the radicals among the Baptists fiercely attacked the whole conception of a state-endowed church and a professional ministry. So the lines of division hardened. Any Parliament elected on a property franchise insisted on some ecclesiastical jurisdiction, on the maintenance of tithes, patronage and professional clergy against the mechanic preachers of the radical sects. In 1656 the Nayler case was a turning point, convincing conservatives that a definition of orthodoxy enforced by persecution was the only alternative to anarchy and social unrest. It split the radicals, many of whom felt Nayler had gone too far. It finally destroyed the illusion that agreement could be reached among God's people. Presbyterians and Independents clung on to the idea of a state church; receipt of public maintenance was accepted in the Independent Savoy Declaration of 1658.[31]

Even the Levellers (in the 1649 Agreement of the People), Winstanley and Harrington had favoured some sort of national church whose ministers should be elected by parishioners (all of them, not only the godly). Those who rejected a national church were those who rejected a professional clergy, carrying the priesthood of all believers to the logical conclusion that a church can exist without a minister. If there were ministers, they should (in the words of the London Baptists in 1660), "freely minister to others", and the congregation ought in return "freely to communicate necessary things to the ministers (upon the account of their charge)".[32]

In time the sects abandoned hope of recapturing the state church from which they had seceded. The unique freedom of the forties and fifties hastened acceptance of a more permanent sectarian status by enabling far more national organization than had ever before been possible. The Particular Baptists for instance had a confession by 1644. But in the fifties Baptists were still quarrelling among themselves about the lawfulness of taking tithes — which means about the lawfulness of a state church.[33] By the end of the fifties Quakers, General and Particular Baptists were organized as sects. The Westminster Assembly of Divines produced a Presbyterian confession which it had hoped would be accepted as that of the Church of England. The Congregationalists significantly adopted no separate confession till 1658, when they were rightly becoming nervous about the future of the state church to which they had hitherto accommodated themselves.

Who gained from the Restoration? Sociologically it represented a reunion of the natural rulers against the radical lower orders. The royalist/Anglican position had always been clear and consistent. Edward Hyde in the early forties was unable to conceive how religion could be preserved without bishops, who were necessary to control the lower clergy who control the people; nor could the law and government of the state subsist if the government of the church was altered.[34] This social argument for episcopacy was often used. Henry Oxinden in 1643 called on all gentlemen "rather to maintain episcopal government ... than to introduce I know not what Presbyterial government, which will ... equalize men of mean conditions with the gentry".[35]

In 1660 the lay descendants of the conformist Puritans got a national church purged of its dependence on a would-be absolutist monarchy and of divine-right bishops: a church subordinated to Parliament. The political "Presbyterians" were the real beneficiaries of the Restoration, but they owed their victory to their own earlier defeat by "Independents" and sectaries; and they accelerated their triumph by sacrificing those who had made that victory possible, together with the Presbyterian clergy. The latter, however, were relieved at the restoration of their fear of the radicals. Richard Baxter told the House of Commons in April 1660 that now "the question is not whether bishops or no but whether discipline or none".[36] The point was vividly put by Henry Newcome, looking back after his dispossession: "Though soon after the settlement of the nation [note the phrase] we saw ourselves the despised and cheated party, ... yet ... I would not change conditions ... to have it as it was then, as bad as it is". For then "we lay at the mercy and impulse of a giddy, hot-headed, bloody multitude" and faced "a Münsterian anarchy ... far sadder than particular persecution".[37]

The restoration purges, and especially the Corporation Acts, checked the spread of radical sectarianism in towns; reassertion of the rule of parson and squire, plus the Act of Settlement, stopped the sects from spreading to the countryside. As a contemporary put it, "conventicles can be suppressed in the country where the gentry live and the people have a dependence on them, ... but in corporations it will never be carried through by the magistrates or inhabitants, their livelihood consisting altogether in trade, and this depending one upon another, so that when any of these shall appear to act in the least measure, their trade shall decline, and ... their credit with it".[38] Tithes were preserved.

The saints had tried and failed to build God's kingdom on earth. After 1660 Puritanism subsided into nonconformity: the sects were more concerned to disclaim responsibility for the execution of Charles I than with positive political ideals. Pacifism and withdrawal from politics became the order of the day, reinforced by the Clarendon Code's exclusion of dissenters from national and local politics, and from the universities. The Calvinist international no longer existed, and indeed religion had ceased to be a prime mover in international affairs. The French Huguenots were as anxious as English dissenters to proclaim that theirs were peace-loving, nonpolitical bodies. A further factor in the retreat of aggressive Puritanism was the fact that the state church quietly stole many of its clothes. Bishops no longer discouraged preaching and sabbatarianism, and the bourgeois virtues secured the patronage of men like Archbishop Tillotson, who thought that "virtue promotes our outward temporal interests".[39] The thinking of those whom we call Latitudinarians (many of them former Presbyterians) retained much of the social content of Puritanism. Refusing to be excluded from the state church, they continued the Elizabethan struggle on two fronts, against popery and against enthusiasm.[40]

Clearly neither Presbyterians nor Independents could any longer aspire to control the Church of England. Yet neither took kindly to the status of sectary. Twelve days after St Bartholomew's Day, 1662, Henry Newcome and his Presbyterian friends in Cheshire resolved "to stick close to the public ordinances, and not to separate" from the national church.[41] In the same year the Presbyterian Philip Henry was "loath ... to encourage the people to separation", even though he himself felt constrained to resign his living. When Charles II issued his Declaration of Indulgence ten years later, Henry feared that "the danger is lest the allowance of separate places help to overthrow our parish-order ... and beget divisions and animosities amongst us which no honest heart but would rather should be healed". He faced a "trilemma" — "either to turn flat Independents, or to strike in with the conformists, or to sit down in former silence and sufferings till the Lord shall open a more effectual door". The Independents, in Henry's view, "unchurch the nation; ... they pluck up the hedge of parish order". Henry's choice of words is significant. He remained an occasional conformist.[42] Baxter continued in the sixteen-sixties and seventies to discuss with John Owen and other leading Independents the conditions for re-inclusion.[43] Andrew Marvell, friend of both Baxter and Owen, defended against Samuel Parker the doctrines held by "most of our ancient and many of the later bishops nearer our times".[44]

Attitudes towards the restored church among those "who separate, or are rather driven from, the present worship",[45] varied even more dramatically than they had varied after the fifteen-nineties. Some ministers managed to retain their livings without conforming at all — for example Henry Swift at Peniston, Yorkshire, who had the support of the chief families in the parish. Richard Heyricke continued Warden of Manchester collegiate church. The Latitudinarian Bishop Wilkins of Chester, who conformed in 1660, was very helpful to his old Puritan friends in such matters. Ralph Josselin in Essex for two decades avoided wearing the hated surplice.[46] Other clergymen, like John Ray, resigned their benefices and became lay conforming members of the Church of England. Presbyterians favoured occasional conformity more than others: there were no Presbyterian ordinations before 1672. Baxter, William Bates, Thomas Manton, Francis Chandler, Thomas Jolly and the members of his church, were all occasional conformists. Oliver Heywood attended his parish church from time to time.[47] John Humfrey, although pastor to a nonconformist congregation, was "a conformist parishioner", who never received the sacrament elsewhere than at his parish church.[48]

In 1702 Calamy and other dissenters told Bishop Burnet that occasional conformity had been "used by some of the most eminent of our ministers since 1662, with a design to show their charity towards the church".[49] Norman Sykes observes that it is likely that acceptance of occasional conformity as a test for office took this practice into account. "No man," said John Howe sensibly, "can allow himself to think that what he before accounted lawful is by this

supervening condition become unlawful." Occasional conformity no
doubt increased when the laws were more strictly enforced between
the mid-seventies and mid-eighties.[50] Pressure to accept a separatist
position perhaps came from the Presbyterian laity rather than from
the clergy. Congregations, wrote Joseph Williamson in 1671, "are
now come to ride their teachers and make them do what they will . . . .
All the Presbyterians are grown to Independents, and so must the
teachers".[51]

Among the Independents, Thomas Goodwin thought that in most
parishes, "where ignorance and profaneness overwhelm the generality, scandalousness and simony the ministers themselves", occasional
conformity was inadmissible. But in others there were godly members of congregations, under a godly minister whom they had chosen
to cleave to. With such it was lawful to communicate, as with the
reformed churches on the continent. It was indeed a duty to "break
down this partition wall"; "nothing provokes more than . . . to deny
such churches to be true churches of Christ." John Owen, however,
after arguing the case at length, came down against occasional
conformity.[52] William Bridge threatened to excommunicate members of his flock who even went to hear an Anglican service. Philip
Nye thought it was not only lawful but a duty to *hear* ministers of the
state church, though not to join in common prayer or communion.
His son Henry favoured occasional conformity. Some Baptists even
were occasional conformists — John Tombes and Thomas Grantham, for instance.[53]

Patriotism came into it too. The breach with Rome had been a
national act, or at least was so represented. Under Elizabeth and
again in the sixteen-twenties and fifties Puritans had been the
spearhead of English patriotism against Spain and the Pope. Under
Laud, patriotism and prelacy seemed to be diametrically opposed.
But in the sixteen-seventies and eighties the Church of England
revealed itself as firmly anti-Catholic, anti-French and therefore
patriotic. The trial of the Seven Bishops probably did more to make
occasional conformists than the mere desire for office. Presbyterians
were eager to be comprehended in the Church of England after
1688.[54]

After 1660 England again enjoyed a "balanced constitution". The
existence of nonconformity checked effective reform of the Church
of England; but the strength of urban dissent made the state church
necessary to prevent any spread of radicalism to the countryside. The

Tory/Anglican gentry bitterly resented the existence of dissent, which prevented the balance being tipped their way. In 1664 Elias Ashmole had told his Presbyterian brother-in-law Henry Newcome that "nonconformity could be nothing but in expectation of a change". A change may have seemed likely to alarmed Tories in 1679-81, when the number of dissenting M.Ps. increased significantly.[55] They therefore had the less objection to governmental interference with borough charters, until James II actually began to flirt with Quakers and to re-open local government to real radicals.[56] The one constant factor from 1640 to 1689 is that any House of Commons elected on the traditional franchise favoured persecution, at least of radical sectaries.

Surveying the period from 1559 to 1689 we might again conclude that the first century of the Church of England was also its last. After 1660 the state church was no longer inclusive of the whole nation. Some of the most truly religious English men and women had chosen to withdraw from it, or had been driven out of it. The failure of the millennium to arrive and of the revolutionaries to implement their ideals led to the exclusion of their successors from the main stream of national, political and intellectual life. Nonconformity was forced into a position in which it became provincial, "sectarian" and "Puritan" in the pejorative sense of those words.

One of the problems which Puritans failed to solve was the relation of the godly minority to the ungodly masses of the population. Puritans and sectaries had seemed to threaten the traditional rural way of life, its (pagan) festivals, its cakes and ale and cock-fighting. Presbyterians wanted the lower orders to be more severely disciplined; the sects would have offered them preaching, but would not have compelled them to come in. In the late forties and fifties we often find conservative Puritans like Baxter complaining that the ungodly rabble hankered after the old episcopal church.[57] They had their revenge in 1660. The Church of England survived primarily because of its deep roots among the landed ruling class, whose interests it shared in so many ways; but also because "the rabble" preferred its conservative laxity to an enforced Presbyterian discipline, or the voluntary self-discipline of the sects. In the last resort the main numerical support for the episcopal church may have come from those who least believed in his doctrines. The church and king mobs which bawled for Sacheverell in 1709 came from parts of London where there were fewest parish churches. Outside

London, his strongest backing came from the Welsh border region.[58]

The sects, despite many attempts, never succeeded in reuniting: they managed to survive in so far as they got respectable middle- or lower-middle-class support; and nearly died of it in the eighteenth century. Those which lacked such support — Muggletonians and the like — continued to exist only in a vestigial form. Wesley had to start from scratch in appealing to the lowest classes; and there was no room for Methodism in the state church either.

After 1660 the radical sectaries were driven out of politics, into which they had intruded during the revolutionary decades. They abandoned political aspirations, partly because of their own recognition that Christ's kingdom was not going to be realised on earth now, partly because three decades of fierce persecution weeded out all but the most convinced believers, at a time when belief was becoming more other-wordly. The final result was a disastrous split in English social and educational life, the consequences of which are still with us. The Church of England defined the privileged sector. Chamberlayne's *Angliae Notitia* of 1669 complained that "it hath been observed even by strangers, that the iniquity of the present times in England is such that of all the Christian clergy of Europe ... none are so little respected, beloved, obeyed or rewarded as the present ... clergy of England".[59] The practice of occasional conformity was not only a way of qualifying insincere merchants for membership of town corporations; it was also a last symbolic attempt to bridge the gulf between the two cultures and proclaim the unity of the protestant nation.

NOTES

1. First printed in *Reformation, Conformity and Dissent: Essays in honour of Geoffrey Nuttall* (ed. R.B. Knox, 1977).
2. G.F. Nuttall. "Nonconformists in Parliament, 1661-1689", *Baptist Quarterly*, XX (1970); D.R. Lacey, *Dissent and Parliamentary Politics, 1661-1689* (Rutgers U.P., 1969), appendix III.
3. G. Holmes (ed.), *Britain after the Glorious Revolution* (1969), pp. 167-8.
4. H. Sacheverell, *The Perils of False Brethren* (1709), p. 135; J. Owen, *Works*, VII, pp. 74-6, 133, 249; cf. III, pp. 243-5; V, pp. 164, 174; XV, pp. 184-5.
5. F. Cheynell, *The Rise, Growth and Danger of Socinianism* (1648), pp. 62-6.
6. *Collections of the Massachusetts Historical Soc.*, Fourth Series (1863), p. 458; M. Sparke, *Crumms of Comfort*, Part II, 1652, Sig. para., pp. 7-8,

quoted in J.S. McGee, *The Godly Man in Stuart England* (Yale, U.P., 1976), p.76.

7. Whitgift, *Works* (Parker Soc., 1851-3), pp.308, 405-6.
8. Cf. *The Writings of John Greenwood, 1587-90*, ed. L. H. Carlson (1962), pp.247-50.
9. I have drawn heavily in this paragraph on Collinson, *The Elizabethan Puritan Movement*, esp. pp.164-7, 185-9 and 334. Cf. Chapter 6 above.
10. R. G. Usher (ed.), *The Presbyterian Movement in the Reign of Queen Elizabeth* (Camden Soc., third Series, VIII, 1905), pp.53-7, 102, and *passim*.
11. Cf. G. F. Nuttall, *Visible Saints*, pp.23-4; my *Economic Problems of the Church*, Chapter 4.
12. W. Haller, *Liberty and Reformation in the Puritan Revolution* (New York, 1955), p.119.
13. For this and the following paragraph see Chapter 7 above.
14. H.C. White., *Social Criticism in Popular Religious Literature of the Sixteenth Century*, p.121.
15. Quoted in R.M. Jones, *Studies in Mystical Religion* (1909), p.402.
16. Roger Williams, *The Bloody Tenent of Persecution*, 1644 (Hanserd Knollys Soc., 1848), p.425; J. Lilburne, *Come out of her my people*, (1639), p.19.
17. L. Busher, *Religious Peace* (1614), pp.70-1.
18. Whitgift, *op. cit.*, II, p.398. See pp.55, 58 above.
19. Brooke, *A Discourse ... of ... Episcopacie*, p.96, in Haller, *Tracts on Liberty*, II.
20. J. Calvin, *The Institutes of the Christian Religion* (trans. H. Beveridge, 1949), II, pp.651-4.
21. C.E. Burrage, *Early English Dissenters*, I, pp.171, 293, 305; II, pp.163, 301-2.
22. T. Helwys, *The Mistery of Iniquity* (1612), pp.86-94, 101-23. I quote from the Baptist Historical Society's reprint, 1935.
23. Cf. Cliffe, *The Puritan Gentry*, Chapter 10.
24. Usher, *op. cit., passim*.
25. Cf. J. Hexter, "The Problem of the Presbyterian Independents", in *Reappraisals in History* (1961), pp.163-84.
26. J. Waddington, *Congregational History, 1567-1700* (1874), p.426; cf. p.430 and p.6 above.
27. D. Masson, *Life of Milton* (1859-80), IV, pp.566-8.
28. *Thurloe State Papers* (1742), pp.598-601. Gauden was the author of *Eikon Basilike*.
29. Nuttall, op. cit., pp.22-6, 37-8, 135-41; A.C. Underwood, *A History of the English Baptists* (1947), pp.80, 96, 103-5; A.G. Matthews (ed.), *Calamy Revised* (Oxford U.P., 1934), pp.xiii and xli.
30. Cf. B.R. White, "Henry Jessey in the Great Rebellion", in *Reformation, Conformity and Dissent: Essays in Honour of Geoffrey Nuttall* (ed. R.B. Knox, 1977), pp.140, 150.
31. R.W. Dale, *History of English Congregationalism* (1907), pp.387-8; cf. Nuttall, *op. cit.*, pp.64-8, 99-100.

32. Nuttall, *op. cit.*, pp. 85-8; R. Barclay, *The Inner Life of the Religious Societies of the Commonwealth* (1876), p. 338; E.B. Underhill (ed.), *Confessions of Faith … of … the Baptist Churches of England in the Seventeenth Century* (Hanserd Knollys Soc., 1854), p. 115.
33. Nuttall, *op. cit.*, pp. 135-41.
34. Clarendon, *History of the Rebellion* (1888), I, pp. 406-7. See pp. 57-8 above.
35. D. Gardiner (ed.), *The Oxinden and Peyton Letters, 1642-1670* (1937), pp. 36-7.
36. R. Baxter, *A Sermon of Repentance* (1660), p. 43.
37. H. Newcome, *Autobiography* (Chetham Soc., XXVII, 1852), p. 118-19.
38. *C.S.P.D.*, *1675-6*, p. 1. Cf. the epigraph to this Chapter.
39. J. Tillotson, *Sermons on Several Subjects and Occasions* (1748), IX, pp. 134-6.
40. M.C. Jacob, *The Newtonians and the English Revolution*, Chapter I *passim*, pp. 189-96, 266.
41. H. Newcome, *Diary* (ed. T. Heywood, Chetham Soc., XVIII, 1849), pp. 119-20.
42. Ed. M.H. Lee, *Diaries and Letters of Philip Henry* (1882), pp. 99, 250, 277, 328-9.
43. Lamont, *Richard Baxter and the Millennium*, pp. 210-19.
44. Marvell, *The Rehearsal Transpros'd*, p. 33. He was echoing views held by a great many nonconformists (see my *The Experience of Defeat*, pp. 307-9).
45. Owen, *Works*, XV, p. 102.
46. Josselin, *Diary*, pp. 627-8.
47. C.E. Whiting, *Studies in English Puritanism from the Restoration to the Revolution, 1660-1688* (1931), pp. 32-3, 60-1; Joan Thirsk (ed.), *The Restoration* (1976), p. 63.
48. Matthews, *op.cit.*, pp. 284-5; Lacey, *Dissent and Parliamentary Politics in England, p. 23.*
49. E. Calamy, *An Historical Account of My Own Life* (ed. J.T. Rutt, 1829), I, p. 473.
50. N. Sykes, *From Sheldon to Secker* (Cambridge U.P., 1959), pp. 96-7; Lacey, *op. cit.*, p. 26.
51. *C.S.P.D.*, *1671*, p. 496. For the influence of lay members of congregations before 1640 see pp. 69, 78 above.
52. T. Goodwin, *Works*, I, pp. 557-8; Owen, *Works*, XV, pp. 65-8, 345-58, 378-9; XVI, pp. 241-53.
53. Lacey, *op. cit.*, p. 17; See p. 9 above.
54. See p. 9 above.
55. Newcome, *Autobiography*, I, p. 145; Lacey, *op. cit.*, p. 119.
56. For examples see J. Miller, *Popery and Politics in England, 1660-1688* (Cambridge U.P., 1973), pp. 209, 219-22.
57. Cf. J. Morrill, "The Church in England, 1642-1649," *passim*.
58. G. Holmes, *The Trial of Dr Sacheverell* (1973), Chapters 7 and 10.
59. Edward Chamberlayne, *Angliae Notitia* (1669), p. 401; see pp. 58-9 above.

15. *God and the English Revolution*[1]

"When they [the Jews in the Old Testament] *had a mind to change the government, to enter into civil war, to change a royal family, to reform religion, and to dismember their kingdom, ... they presently had a voice from heaven to assure their actions and secure their courses."**

"When the Fifth Monarchy Men ... raised a rebellion against King Charles for the restoring King Jesus, ... everyone was crying out, it was a senseless, mad action, unaccountable and preposterous. 'Ay', says the old woman, 'that's true; but what should we have called it if it had succeeded?'"†

"Take heed of hooking things up to heaven."‡

From way back in the nineteenth century, and still when I was at school, the seventeenth-century English Revolution used to be known as the Puritan Revolution. This name lost favour after Marx, Weber, Tawney and many others taught us that religion was not a self-sufficient motivating factor. Yet even Marxists have been known to speak of Puritanism as the ideology of the English Revolution. God still has a role in seventeenth-century politics. I want to conclude by looking at the effects of God on this Revolution, and its effects on God.

God was not only on the side of the Parliamentarians. Far from it. There seem indeed to have been three gods — a trinity — at work during the Revolution. First there was the God who blessed the established order, any established order, but especially that of England. Kings and bishops ruled by Divine Right, the clergy had a Divine Right to collect ten per cent of their parishioners' income as tithes — so conservatives said. The Elizabethan Homilies extolled

---

*Anthony Ascham, *Of the Confusions and Revolutions of Governments*, p. 109.

†Daniel Defoe, *Review*, I, p. 127, quoted by F. Bastian, *Defoe's Early Life* (1981), p. 19.

‡Marvell to Samuel Parker, *The Rehearsal Transpros'd*, p. 255.

the existing hierarchical social structure, the great chain of being which ran through nature and society, and which Shakespeare stated — probably ironically — in *Troilus and Cressida*. "Take but degree away, untune that string/And hark what discord follows". All change was bad and dangerous, because the mass of mankind had been irredeemably wicked since the Fall of Adam. The state exists to prevent the horrors which sinful humanity — and especially the lower orders — would perpetrate if not held in by law and power.

The second God, the God of the Parliamentarians, was also in favour of order; but he stressed justice rather than mere defence of the *status quo*. The Hebrew prophets in the Bible denounced the injustices of rulers and called for reformation. But only certain kinds of change were permissible: reformation should go back to Biblical models, to the primitive church of the New Testament. The Bible was used as litmus paper to test existing institutions. Were bishops to be found in the New Testament? If not, they should be abolished. This was a dangerously wide-ranging principle.[2] Milton and many others could not find the Trinity in the Bible. Colonel Rainborough in 1647 searched the Scriptures in vain to find a justification for the 40/- freeholder Parliamentary franchise. This did not lead him to reject Parliaments, but to call for manhood suffrage. Others, more conscious of the risks of uncritical application of the Bible to seventeenth-century society, thought that change, however desirable, could be justified only if supported by the authority of the magistrate. Lesser magistrates might take the initiative if the sovereign did not, Dutch and French Calvinists thought. So they authorized revolt if supported by the respectable classes. Calvinists also found the protestant ethic in the Bible — thrift, sobriety, frugality, discipline, hard work, monogamy: a discipline which it was the duty of the magistrate to enforce on the labouring classes lest social chaos should result.[3]

But in the course of the Revolution some people discovered a third God, a God who — like the Holy Ghost — was to be found in every believer. And since it was difficult to ascertain who were true believers, this came to mean that God could be found in every man (some daring spirits said in every woman too). The full horrors of this doctrine were plumbed only in the sixteen-forties, but worshippers of the second, Calvinist, God were early aware of the existence of this third deity, and from the first tried to safeguard against his emergence. The Bible after all said many things, and untutored readers of it might draw very remarkable conclusions. Arise Evans, a Welsh-man, tells us of the impact that coming to London made on his thinking. "Afore I looked upon the Scripture as a history of things that passed in other countries, pertaining to other persons; but now I looked upon it as a mystery to be opened at this time, belonging also to us". In Amos and Revelation he found descriptions of what was happening in revolutionary England. In Amos 9.1 the Lord said "smite the lintel of the door, that the posts may shake"; Evans thought this could only refer to Speaker Lenthall.[4] Others used Biblical texts for more consciously subversive purposes.

The God within sometimes looked like a God of pure anarchy: there might be as many gods as there were men, as Fulke Greville and Gerrard Winstanley both came to the recognize, the former with disapproval, the latter with approval.[5] But this is something which developed fully only after the breakdown of all authority in the sixteen-forties, when lower-class sects of every heretical kind could meet and discuss freely. The three gods favoured different forms of worship. The first liked ritual and ceremonies; the second preaching; the third discussion and participation by the congregation in church government. So the first god attached most importance to the institutional church and its clergy; the second to an educated mini-stry; the third had no real use for ministers at all.

There is of course nothing surprising in this many-facedness of God. Any state religion which survives for any length of time has to perform a multiplicity of tasks: it has to console the down-trodden as well as to maintain the mighty in their seats. It has to persuade the rich to be charitable as well as the poor to be patient. Usually orthodox Christianity had interpreted the consolatory passages in the Scriptures as referring to an after life. But this is sometimes difficult to square with the Biblical text. As the Bible became available in English after the Reformation, and as literacy moved down the social scale, so men and women began to take literally the more subversive texts of the Bible which their betters preferred to read allegorically.

In the century before 1640 many had seen England as a chosen nation, which God continually intervened to protect. In 1588 he blew with his winds and the Spanish Armada was scattered; a century later the protestant wind wafted William of Orange safely over to England to replace the papist James II. Even the revolutionary Great Seal of the English Commonwealth claimed that freedom had been "by God's blessing restored." But great favours entailed great responsibilities.

God punished both individuals and societies for their misdeeds. Sylvester translated Du Bartas's explanation of a plague epidemic:

> For our sins, so many and so great,
> So little moved with promise or with threat,
> Thou now at last (as a just jealous God)
> Strik'st us thyself with thine immediate rod,
> Thy rod of pestilence.[6]

Lancelot Andrewes confirmed that "sin provokes the wrath of God, the wrath of God sends the plague among us".[7] One reason for emigration to New England in the sixteen-twenties and thirties, to which historians perhaps do not attach sufficient importance, was a desire to escape from the wrath to come. Thomas Cooper in 1615 reminded the Lord Mayor, Aldermen and Sheriffs of London of the need "to provide some retiring place for yourselves if so be the Lord for our unthankfulness should spew us out".[8] Fourteen years later John Winthrop, soon to be first Governor of Massachusetts, was "verily persuaded God will bring some heavy afflictions upon this land, and that speedily". "God is packing up his Gospel", said Thomas Hooker in 1631, "because nobody will buy his wares". "God is going from England".[9]

So God regularly showed his approval and disapproval of human actions, particularly those of rulers. One way of propitiating the God who was angry with our sins was to hold a private fast, as Alexander Leighton did in 1624, Hugh Peter in 1626. Such a fast might be semi-public. But "a land or nation ... must be longer in the fire than one particular person".[10] Parliaments of the sixteen-twenties implied criticism of the government by calling for a public fast. Laudians thought fasting "as hateful as conventicles," and sought to suppress fasts in Essex and East Anglia. Their discouragement of fasting deprived the godly of what seemed to them the most hopeful way of averting the calamities which threatened the nation.[11] The Long Parliament made the point neatly when it met in November 1640. It proclaimed a day of national humiliation, to be held on Queen Elizabeth's accession day, 17 November. The sermons preached on that day did not fail to make the contrast between the victorious protestantism of Good Queen Bess and her successors' ineffective

Laodiceanism.[12] Fast sermons preached during the civil war continued to be used to whip up support for the cause. On the eve of Charles I's trial Thomas Brooks reminded the House of Commons that "execution of justice and judgment will free you from the guilt of other men's sins".[13]

One problem was to interpret the signs so as to understand God's wishes. For many, success seemed evidence of God's support, and failure witnessed to divine disapproval; but sometimes, confusingly, it was left to a tiny remnant of the faithful to preserve the truth in secret. Arguments of this type were naturally used when convenient as the fortunes of civil war swayed backwards and forwards between 1642 and 1645. After Brilliana Harley's Brampton Brian had surrendered, triumphant royalists asked the defenders where their God was now?[14] In 1645 preachers before Parliament attributed the defeat of the Earl of Essex in Cornwall to God's objection to toleration of heretics. John Goodwin on the contrary suggested that it was God's judgment against Parliament's intolerance.[15]

In September 1641 Stephen Marshall doubted "whether God ever did such a thing for matter and manner in these two unworthy nations, ... giving us in one year a return of the prayers of forty four years".[16] "A miracle of Providence", Jeremiah Burrough called it; "a mercy that is a foundation of mercy to the generations to come, ... to the Christian world".[17] "It is the Lord's great work that is now a-framing", Brilliana Harley had told her son in May 1642.[18]

In retrospect Parliamentarians came to claim that it was God, not man, who called the Long Parliament in 1640; that God, not man, created the New Model Army and brought about the trial and execution of Charles I in 1649. The Fifth Monarchists Thomas Harrison and John Carew, no less than the Quakers Francis Howgil and Isaac Penington, all saw "the finger of God" in England's deliverances: "the Lord hath appeared in our day to do great things", declared the republican Edmund Ludlow. Even a relative conservative like the Scottish Presbyterian Robert Baillie told the Westminster Assembly that "the Lord ... has led us by the hand and marched before us" against the prelates.[19] "The God of the Parliament ... hath gone with you", the Independent divine John Owen assured Parliament in a sermon preached in June 1649 to celebrate the defeat of the Levellers at Burford. Oliver Cromwell believed that the Army had been "called by God", and fiercely defended "the revolutions of Christ himself", God's "working of things from one period to another". "God hath done great and honourable things" by the agency of the Long Parliament, the Quakers Edward Burrough and Miles Halhead admitted: the Bristol Baptist Robert Purnell, the Fifth Monarchist John Tillinghast, the Independents Thomas Goodwin and John Cook, the antinomian William Dell, the Quaker George Bishop, all agreed.[20]

William Sedgwick, famous Army preacher, in December 1648 denounced the Army's intervention in politics, since it prevented a peaceful settlement with the King which he had hoped would reunite the country. But a few months later he completely reversed his position. The trial and execution of the King, the establishment of the Commonwealth, the abolition of the House of Lords — these events overwhelmed him by their sheer magnitude. *Because* the Army's actions had been so unprecedented they must have been inspired by God. The only problem, as Sedgwick saw it, was to bring this fact home to the generals so as to make them live up to their responsibilities now that God "is upon motion, marching us out of Egyptian darkness and bondage into a Canaan of rest and happiness".[21] "You are the rod of God", Joseph Salmon told "the commanding powers in the Army". "In this day of the Lord's wrath you strike through King, gentry and nobility, they all fall before you".[22] God's people, George Joyce agreed, were going to do "such things as were never yet done by man".[23] We may compare Marvell's sense of Cromwell as "the force of angry heaven's flame", which " 'Tis madness to resist or blame".[24] Even royalists, Baxter assures us, were "astonished at the marvellous providences of God, which had been against that family [the Stuarts] all along".[25]

The ultimate in divine intervention would be the Second Coming. Prophecies in Daniel and Revelation established that a great conflagration will mark the end of the world. Any Christian who takes these prophecies seriously must be anxious to ascertain when the holocaust will take place. I believe many middle-western American Christians are today looking forward with relish to helping to expedite it with nuclear warfare.[26] In the late sixteenth and early seventeenth centuries there seemed to be good reasons for supposing that the end of the world was imminent. When John Milton in 1641 spoke of Christ as "shortly-expected King", he was probably thinking of the sixteen-fifties, though he may have extended the possibilities a decade or two.[27]

For Milton the Second Coming would put "an end to all earthly

tyrannies", including that of Charles I. It involved political revolution. Here we come to a great divide. The orthodox view was that
after the destruction of the world a new heaven and a new earth
would be created, in which the elect would henceforth lead blissful
and quite different lives: it was a totally other-worldly concept. Many
millenarians however interpreted the Biblical prophecies to mean
that after Christ's Second Coming he would rule on earth for a
thousand years (the millennium). Whether Christ would rule in
person or through the saints was a question: radicals tended to
foresee a rule of the saints (i.e. themselves). One can see how such
widely held ideas could turn into theories justifying a dictatorship of
the godly minority. Millenarian ideas could lead to rejection of
régimes which seemed to be excluding Jesus Christ from his proper
authority. For many — like William Sedgwick — the execution of
Charles I only made sense if it cleared the way for King Jesus. When
the Army went to conquer Scotland in 1650 its watchword was "No
King but Jesus". But only three years later the Fifth Monarchist
Vavasor Powell had to tell his congregation to ask God "Wilt thou
have Oliver Cromwell or Jesus Christ to rule over us?"[28]

Millenarian ideas could also beget a sort of revolutionary inter-
nationalism. Hugh Peter told Parliament in December 1648 that
"this Army must root up monarchy, not only here but in France and
other kingdoms round about". Marvell foresaw Cromwell in this
liberating role:

> As Caesar he ere long to Gaul,
> To Italy an Hannibal,
> And to all states not free
> Shall climacteric be.

In 1651 Admiral Blake, commanding the world's strongest fleet, said
on Spanish territory that monarchy was on the way out all over
Europe — in France as well as in England. He gave it ten years in
Spain, a slower-moving country. John Rogers the Fifth Monarchist
declared in 1653 "We are bound by the law of God to help our
neighbours as well as ourselves, and so to aid the subjects of other
princes that are either persecuted for true religion or oppressed under
tyranny". Part of the English Army should be sent to France or
Holland, to conduct a revolutionary war. The Quaker leader George
Fox many times in the late sixteen-fifties rebuked the Army for not
going to Spain, to overthrow the Inquisition. "Never set up your

standard until you come to Rome", he urged, in words which show that he was not yet a pacifist.[29]

But God could also speak directly to private individuals. Lady Eleanor Davies, a slightly eccentric person, in 1633 prophesied that Charles I would come to a violent end. She was sent to Bedlam, but was taken more seriously after the King's execution.[30] In the political freedom of the forties and early fifties quite humble men and women could be entrusted by God with political messages. Gerrard Winstanley heard a voice telling him to set up the communist colony whose necessity to solve England's economic problems he had long been working out.[31] In 1652 John Reeve received a special commission from God, and he went on to found the sect later known as the Muggletonians, which lasted until 1979.[32] God dictated reams of rather mediocre verse to Anna Trapnell. George Fox and John Bunyan received messages, as did innumerable less well-known characters.

It was thus *natural* for perfectly normal people to hear God speaking to them: it was not, as it would be today, *prima facie* evidence of insanity. This followed indeed from what I described as the third manifestation of God, the theological assumption that God dwells in all his saints, perhaps in all men and women. The early Quakers became the best-known exponents of this theology, but it was widespread during the revolutionary decades. Gerrard Winstanley believed that God was the same thing as Reason; the Second Coming was not Jesus Christ descending from the clouds but Reason rising in sons and daughters[33]. So the logic of protestant heresy led to something very like secularism.

Political discussion was invariably carried on in religious language and imagery. Winstanley used the stories of Cain and Abel, Esau and Jacob, to express his class analysis of society: the younger brother would overcome his oppressing elder brother. David and Goliath, Samson and the Philistines, were symbols of revolt against tyranny. Existing corrupt society was designated as Sodom, Egypt, Babylon. The Pope had been Antichrist for Foxe and many protestants, as he had been for Lollard heretics earlier. Winthrop hoped that New England would become a "bulwark against the kingdom of Antichrist".[34] The Parliamentarian revolutionaries saw their royalist adversaries as "the Antichristian faction". Stephen Marshall, in a famous sermon preached to the House of Commons in February 1642, declared that "many of the nobles, magistrates, knights and gentlemen, and persons of great quality, are arrant traitors and rebels against God". What more desperate incitement to class war than that? "The question in England", he said in 1644, "is whether Christ or Antichrist shall be lord or king". In the same year some Parliamentarian soldiers believed that "the people, the multitude" would pull down the Whore of Babylon; "we are the men that must help to pull her down".[35]

But soon Parliament itself was being called Antichristian, and the adjective was applied to Presbyterianism in the sixteen-forties, to Cromwell in the fifties. Any national church was Antichristian, many sectaries asserted. Cromwell himself said that the distinction between clergy and laity was Antichristian. Richard Overton and Henry Denne thought intolerance Antichristian: Baptists said the same of infant baptism. Bunyan put the social point more subtly by describing Antichrist as a gentleman.[36] For Winstanley covetousness, buying and selling, were Antichristian: property was the devil, Christ community.[37] There was a whole code of Biblical shorthand on which (among many others) Winstanley and Milton drew with great effect. Winstanley argued that all the Scripture prophecies "concerning the calling of the Jews," foretold the work which the Diggers were carrying on.[38] Milton could not attack monarchy directly in *Paradise Lost*, since he was a marked man who had been lucky to escape execution in 1660; instead he merely recalled that monarchy had been founded by a rebel "of proud ambitious heart", who

> not content
> With fair equality, fraternal state,
> Will arrogate dominion, undeserved,
> Over his brethren.[39]

Milton did not even need to name Nimrod, of whom Charles I had spoken with approval: he could rely on his readers' Biblical knowledge.

During the Revolution the idea that God might be in every believer, or indeed in every man and woman, worked powerfully against traditional social deference, and for human equality: the eighteenth-century Great Awakening may have had similar effects in preparing for the American Revolution.[40] In England in the sixteen-forties and fifties God said unexpected things to and through his saints. The Ranter Abiezer Coppe, for instance, announced that God, "that mighty Leveller", would "overturn, overturn, overturn".

"The neck of horrid pride" must be chopped off, so that "parity, equality, community" might establish "universal love, universal peace and perfect freedom". "Thou hast many bags of money, and behold I (the Lord) come as a thief in the night, with my sword drawn in my hand, and like a thief as I am — I say deliver your purse, deliver sirrah! Deliver or I'll cut thy throat. . . . Have all things common, or else the plague of God will rot and consume all that you have".[41]

George Foster had a vision of a man on a white horse who cut down those higher than the middle sort and raised up those that were lower, crying "Equality, equality, equality. . . . I, the Lord of Hosts have done this. . . . I will . . . make the low and poor equal with the rich. . . . O rich men, I will utterly destroy you". For Foster too God was "that mighty Leveller".[42] Laurence Clarkson preached a permissive morality. "Till you can lie with all women as one woman, and not judge it sin, you can do nothing but sin". Coppe had a similar libertine theology. "External kisses have been made the fiery chariot to mount me swiftly into the bosom of . . . the King of Glory. . . . I can kiss and hug ladies, and love my neighbour's wife as myself, without sin".[43]

Clement Wrighter and the Quaker Samuel Fisher argued that the Bible was not the infallible Word of God but a historical document to be interpreted. Some radicals rejected the immortality of the soul, heaven and hell. "When men are gazing up to heaven", Winstanley argued, "imagining a happiness or fearing a hell after they are dead, their eyes are put out, that they see not . . . what is to be done by them here on earth while they are living".[44] To Winstanley the personal God above the skies, the God of priests and landlords, looked like the devil.

Conservatives began to feel freedom could go too far, that it was time to stop God communicating through the common people, or at least prevent his words being freely discussed, verbally and in print. Hence the suppression of Levellers, Diggers, Ranters and Fifth Monarchists and the restoration of censorship in the sixteen-fifties. Hence the move to restore authority to the state church. Alderman Violet made the point succinctly in May 1650, reporting upon the economic crisis to the Committee of the Mint: "I propose as remedies, first, to settle able and godly ministers in all churches throughout the nation, that will teach the people to fear God, to obey their superiors and to live peaceably with each other — with a competent maintenance for all such ministers".[45] He had got his priorities right. Ten years later Richard Baxter justified the restoration of episcopacy in the interests of discipline.[46]

One can see too why men desperately searched for certainty. There were so many rival accounts of God's wishes, so many differing interpretations of the Bible, that men sought either an infallible interpreter of God's will, or some other way of replacing the old certainties with a new consensus. The episcopal church had collapsed, and no single church took its place. An infallible prophet like John Robins or John Reeve, or the infallible inner light, were possible saviours. But prophets died, and the inner light said different things to different people. Winstanley rejected human Saviours, but his Reason was as difficult to define as the inner light.[47]

A more promising alternative was to look for secular solutions, for a science of politics which would guide human action. Thomas Hobbes in *Leviathan* (1651) argued that a ruler could claim the allegiance of his subjects only in so far as he could protect them. When Charles I was defeated in the civil war, he could no longer do this, and so subjects had a *duty* to switch their allegiance to the *de facto* power of the commonwealth. Political obligation had nothing to do with claims by Divine Right; it was a question of fact: could the sovereign do his job by protecting his subjects? Hobbes destroyed claims by any group to rule because God favoured them: the restoration of monarchy in 1660 in any case made nonsense of such arguments by Parliamentarians. So Hobbes undermined all traditional theories of obligation based on the will of God. It is the beginning of modern secular political theory. Every individual has a right to his own ideas; no subject and no church can claim a right in God's name to subvert the *de facto* sovereign. But Leviathan the mortal God also supplanted the third God who had rejected deference and promoted revolt.

In 1656 the republican James Harrington advanced his own science of politics — the idea that political structures depend on economic structures, that when the economic base changes the political superstructure (Harrington's word) must change too. During the English Revolution, he argued, there had been a transfer of power to those who had amassed landed property in the century before 1640: no government could be stable which did not recognize their right to rule. The events of 1660-88 appeared to confirm Harrington's analysis, and hammered another nail into the coffin of religious theories of political obligation and resistance. "A commonwealth is not made by man but by God", declared Harrington piously; but God acted through secondary causes, through the balance of property.[48]

The return of Charles II in 1660 ended the Revolution by restoring monarchy to preside over the rule of the propertied. When men took stock, these secular theories seemed to make sense. Charles was proclaimed King by the grace of God, but everyone knew that God had needed earthly agents to get Charles restored. Clarendon said of the restoration "God Almighty would not have been at the expense and charge of such a deliverance but in the behalf of a church very acceptable to him".[49] But that was in November 1660. During the interregnum each party had claimed God on its side in the hour of victory; each side had to rethink its position in the years of defeat, including no doubt Clarendon himself after he had been driven into exile in 1667. Either God was very unstable and erratic, or his ways were incomprehensible to mere human intelligence: better to leave him out of account altogether. This sceptical trend was strengthened by the alarm which the third God had caused, the God within the consciousness of lower-class sectaries. So the keynote of upper-class thinking after 1660 is opposition to "fanaticism", "enthusiasm", to claims to inspiration, whether in literature or in religion or politics. The royalist Sir William Davenant described inspiration as "a dangerous word".[50] Claims to literary inspiration fell out of fashion until they revived with romanticism after the French Revolution. It was Hobbes's undermining of deference that seemed to Clarendon his greatest betrayal of "the nobility, by whose bread he hath bin always sustained".[51] The restoration of the episcopal church confirmed the presence in every parish of an authorized, approved interpreter of the Scriptures, and confirmed the survival of the universities which trained these interpreters. God is one thing, the church is another.

For those Parliamentarians who believed they had been taking part in the revolutions of Christ, the total defeat which the restoration implied was a shattering blow. "The Lord had spit in their faces", Major-General Fleetwood wailed.[52] In December 1659, when Sir Arthur Haslerig seized Portsmouth on behalf of the Rump against the Army, he acknowledged that "the Lord hath wonderfully appeared with us in this business". Just one year later Sir Arthur died in prison; the Rump and the Army were no more.[53] A condemned regicide found it difficult to answer the question "Have you not hard thoughts of God for this his strange providence towards you?"[54] Men had to stress the justice of an avenging God rather than his mercy. "God did seem to be more cruel than men", Muggleton admitted. Milton was thus only one of a large·number who found it necessary to justify the ways of God to men, to account for the apparent triumph of evil over good. God was on trial, for Traherne, Bunyan, Rochester and Dryden as well as in *Paradise Lost* and *Samson Agonistes*.[55]

It is a turning-point in human thought. After 30 January 1649 kings never forgot that they had a joint in their necks. And God was never quite the same again after he had been put on trial in popular discussion. He slowly withdrew into the Newtonian stratosphere.[56] The idea that God watches over each individual's actions is perhaps more plausible within a small community. Once we get trade on a world scale God's immediate interest is more difficult to imagine. Would he organize a storm in the Indian Ocean in order to punish a London merchant with the loss of his ship? God may favour a particular nation, but belief in his direct intervention in the everyday affairs of individuals varies, as Adam Smith nearly said, with the extent of the market.

The belief that God might be in all men, rather than a distinct person above the skies, diminished the likelihood of a personal devil, and so of witchcraft. The former radical John Webster published a definitive *Displaying of Supposed Witchcraft* in 1677. *The Decline of Hell*, which Mr Walker has traced in the seventeenth-century, accompanied the decline of the torture chamber after the abolition of Star Chamber and High Commission. Fasts and fast sermons had faded out in the sixteen-fifties; in 1657 an M.P. was jeered at when he "cited a Scripture to confirm what he said".[57] Judicial oaths and oaths of allegiance could be taken seriously only if the religious sanction behind them was generally accepted. John Locke would refuse toleration to Roman Catholics and atheists because the former owed allegiance to a foreign power; the latters' oaths could not be trusted because they did not believe in the rewards and punishments of an after life. So long as church and state were one, oaths harnessed God to their use. But the existence of permanently organized dissent created new problems: Quakers refused oaths on principle, and ultimately had to be accommodated by a statutory declaration. It was another advance to secularism through religious radicalism.[58].

The God of early eighteenth-century England bore as little resemblance to his predecessor of a century earlier as Archbishop Tillotson did to Archbishop Laud; though Tillotson was rather more approachable than the Supreme Being. After Charles II's reign bishops no longer participated in government, and the state ecclesiastical itself had lost its coercive power. Divine Right, whether of bishops or kings, was forgotten; sovereignty belonged to secular Parliaments, and ecclesiastical law was finally subordinated to the common law.

After 1660 the restored episcopal church was slowly taken over by "Latitudinarians", mostly former Puritans, who abandoned Divine Right claims for bishops and tithes, and based their claims on the law of the land. The Latitudinarians played a prominent part in the newly-founded Royal Society, whose scientists also did much to talk down "fanaticism" and "enthusiasm". Their rejection of "extremes", their stress on moderation, common sense, etc., etc., helped to hold scientific thought within acceptable bounds.[59] Charles II was wise to become patron of the Royal Society as well as head of the Church of England. Here too the intellectual climate favoured a secular science of politics, an empirical probabilism. Common sense of course led to intellectual muddles. Some Fellows of the Royal Society proclaimed a belief in witchcraft, based on the evidence of the senses and the authority of the Bible. "No spirit, no God", declared Henry More, later F.R.S.[60] "No devil, no witches", was in effect Webster's retort. The lives of lonely old women as well as the existence of God were at stake.

The point is made by Eamon Duffy in a discussion of Valentine Greatrakes, whose cures by stroking were admitted by the Royal Society to be "stupendous performances". But his successes made people wonder about the exclusive royal touch for curing the King's evil (which Greatrakes claimed to cure), and even ask how Greatrakes's cures differed from those of Christ in the New Testament. Moreover, Greatrakes had a radical past; and in 1666-7 there was a great deal of renewed millenarian excitement, which Greatrakes shared. It was all very embarrassing for the Latitudinarians. "The development of a particular religious point of view", Duffy concludes, "is never a matter of intellect or spirit alone; the reactions to his cures were dictated as much by fear of democracy or anarchy, of popery or religious enthusiasm, of the upsetting of the Restoration social, political and religious order, as by the intellectual demands of science or reason. Rational theology was the lubricant for a piece of social engineering."[61]

In the early fifties the Ranters had abolished sin. But history abolished the Ranters, and sin came back in strength after 1660. The Quakers, who had denounced the state clergy for preaching up sin, found a place for it in their post-restoration theology. James Nayler had been feeling his way towards such a conclusion after his "fall" in 1656.[62] The sinfulness of the mass of humanity had always been used to oppose change. Even Milton, in *Paradise Lost*, explained the defeat of the Revolution by the sinfulness of the English people, who had failed to live up to the high ideals and aspirations put before them.

Dissenters, excluded from the state church, now formed a separate nation, huddled into their self-supported congregations, desperately concerned with survival in a hostile world. They were cut off from national political life and the national universities. Most of the sects followed Muggletonians and Quakers into pacifism and abstention from politics. Their God now presided over a provincial, stunted culture; he was no longer capable of transforming nations. Accepting that religion should not concern itself with high politics, the sects' emphasis henceforth fell more on questions of conduct and personal morality, such as arose in the confusing growth of capitalist society with its new standards. As they adapted themselves to this new world, the sects became — to adapt Lenin's phrase — schools of capitalism. The nonconformist conscience was to revive as a political force only after internalization of the work ethic had helped many dissenters to prosper: but that was far ahead in 1660.

For those whose lack of property put them below the line which marked off "the political nation", restoration of the familiar, consoling rituals of the traditional church may have been acceptable. Others no doubt just opted out. Church courts no longer enforced church attendance; but perhaps Sir Roger de Coverley's watchful eye over his tenants was more effectual in ensuring their presence. Parson and squire collaborated to keep the rural poor in order. Dissenters could not be suppressed in towns, but church and king mobs could always be used against them.[63] After 1672 the practice of licensing dissenting ministers ensured that nonconformist congregations too were presided over by some sort of recognized interpreter of the Scriptures; they could not now be mere discussion groups chaired by an elected mechanic preacher. The strenuous virtues which Milton had expected of the English people were no longer demanded. They lapsed into the old assumption that politics was for their betters. Church and state, King and country, the royal touch healing scrofula, monarchy as spectacle, after 1688 safely controlled by the King's ministers.

1640 was the last national revolution whose driving ideology was religious. Milton's *De Doctrina Christiana* was so heretical that it could not be published, even in Latin. When his literary executor tried after his death to publish it in the Netherlands, all the power of English diplomacy was exerted to prevent it. The confiscated manuscript lay among the State Papers until 1823. When it was published — on the orders of a King, translated by a bishop — the dynamite of the sixteen-sixties had become a damp squib. Since the American and French Revolutions revolutionary doctrines were no longer expressed in religious idiom. The Revolution had no need of God.

What remained after 1660 was a secularized version of the myth of the chosen people, which Charles II still proclaimed.[64] The millenarian Thomas Goodwin had wanted England to be "top of the nations".[65] The republican James Harrington had advocated "a commonwealth for increase". "The late appearances of God unto you" were not "altogether for yourselves". If "called in by an oppressed people" (Scotland? Ireland? France?) England had a duty to respond. "If you add unto the propagation of civil liberty ... the propagation of liberty of conscience, this empire, this patronage of the world, is the kingdom of Christ".[66] As we saw, Marvell, and Dryden in *Annus Mirabilis*, took up the idea, the latter with minimal religious underpinning.[67]

Ireland — the first English colony — was a case in which the Cause of God got hopelessly mixed up with economic and strategic considerations. Most of the English revolutionaries believed that Charles I and Laud had been part of, or at least had connived at, an international Roman Catholic plot for the conquest of England and the subversion of protestantism. In this plot Ireland's role was crucial. It was an open back-door to foreign Catholic invasion. Spanish troops had landed there in the fifteen-nineties, French troops would land there in the sixteen-nineties in an attempt to restore James II to the English throne. The collapse of English power in Ireland in 1640 unleashed the rebellion of 1641, which was soon headed by a Papal Nuncio. So the Cromwellian re-conquest of

Ireland seemed a necessary defensive blow against Antichrist, to prevent the restoration of monarchy by invasion through Ireland. The radicals, fiercely attacking Cromwell on internal matters, offered no real opposition to the conquest and enslavement of Ireland — with a few notable exceptions, such as the Leveller William Walwyn.[68] The English republic, in Karl Marx's pregnant phrase, "met shipwreck in Ireland". "The English reaction in England had its roots . . . in the subjugation of Ireland".[69] If ever God showed himself a conservative it was in thus allowing religion to mislead the radical revolutionaries.

So God played many parts in the English Revolution. First came the landslide of 1640-1, when suddenly the apparently all-powerful government of Charles and Laud found itself unable any longer to persecute the saints: and when by overwhelming majorities in Parliament the repressive machinery of the prerogative courts was swept away. When the King tried to resist, God raised up an army against him; when stalemate seemed likely to occur, God and Oliver Cromwell created the New Model Army. After bringing about the second great revolution of 1648-9 God continued his favour by permitting the conquest of Ireland and Scotland, the Navigation Act of 1651 and the consequent successfully aggressive colonial foreign policy — Dutch War, Spanish War, Dunkirk seized, piracy brought under control. In turn the events of 1660 came to seem as providential as those of 1640-1 and 1648-9. But with a difference. In 1649 the Army had acted positively as God's instrument, had brutally but effectively shattered the image hitherto worshipped as divine: in 1660 it was the return of the traditional rulers that seemed providential.

> Neither man's power nor policy had place; . . .
> The astonished world saw 'twas the mighty work of heaven,

sang Sir Francis Fane.[70] God had changed sides, and was now overwhelmingly on the side of the traditional establishment, as he had previously been on the side of shocking innovation: the restoration came in spite of rather than because of the royalists. Those who had been the instruments of the omnipotent God in 1648-9 were now revealed as impotent mortals, for whom the God of history had no more use.[71]

The Glorious Revolution of 1688 was an additional providence, another landslide like those of 1640 and 1660, another reassertion of

the predetermined social order. It also confirmed England's new
right to rule the world. Further confirmation came from the
Industrial Revolution, another unplanned gift from heaven. The
secular millenarian interpretation of England's manifest destiny was
validated by these providential social transformations.

In the sixteen-forties the belief that men were fighting for God's
Cause had been a tremendous stimulus to morale. A popular slogan
in the north said that "God is a better lord than the Earl of Derby".[72]
The theoretical duty of a feudal lord was to protect his underlings;
what impressed them was his ever-present power. If you lived in
Lancashire or on the Isle of Man it was difficult to think that there
could be a greater power than the Earl of Derby. Yet in the sixteen-
forties confidence in God's overlordship gave the Puritan citizens of
Lancashire towns courage to resist even the Earl of Derby, who
ultimately in 1651 was executed "for treason and rebellion ... in a
town of his own", Bolton.[73] It seemed a great blow against traditional
deference. Yet in 1660 his son reappeared in Lancashire to wield
much of his father's old authority: in the long run God proved the
weaker lord.

After 1660 a new ruling-class consensus formed, when a more
remote God again presided over the established order, and sanctified
it. To suggest "that religion is a cheat", Chief Justice Hale declared
in 1676, "tends to the dissolution of all government and therefore is
punishable here" — i.e. in the common-law courts.[74] Religion must
not be allowed to decline with church courts. God = history = what
happens. So the Revolution, which at one time looked like a historic
triumph for the third God, ended with his utter defeat. Mammon,
Winstanley's God of this world, who played a very covert role in the
initial stages of the Revolution, fared much better in the end.

One conclusion we may perhaps draw is that any religion can serve
any social purpose, because of the ambiguity of its basic texts.
Enemies of the revolutionary radicals noted the similarity of many of
their theories to those of the Jesuits. We should not think of
protestantism as causing the rise of capitalism, but rather of
protestantism and Puritanism being moulded by capitalist society to
suit its needs. After 1660 God continued to offer consolation in the
after life to those who were unhappy on earth. But between 1640 and
1660 God had also stimulated protest, rejection of an unjust society
and its laws; he had legitimized movements for change. "True
religion and undefiled", Winstanley said, "is to let everyone quietly

have earth to manure, that they may live in peace and freedom in their labour".[75] Land for all might have been the basis for a different consensus. Collective farms making two blades of grass grow where one grew before might have led England out of scarcity into abundance without the expropriation of smallholders in the interests of large-scale capitalist agriculture, without the disappearance of the peasantry. But the victorious God willed otherwise.

How much of the radical tradition survived underground we do not know, for censorship closed down again after 1660, and victors write history. At the end of *Samson Agonistes* Milton envisaged God's Cause as an undying Phoenix; "and though her body die, her fame survives,/ A secular bird, ages of lives".[76] I do not myself think that ideas like those of the radicals get totally forgotten: men were discussing Winstanley's writings in a Welsh valley in the seventeen-nineties — an interesting place and an interesting time.[77] In 1850 God was called the first Chartist, [78] just as Italian socialists in 1893 thought "Jesus was a true socialist".[79] In Blok's *The Twelve* the revolutionary soldiers were led by Jesus Christ. A popular song of the Spanish civil war celebrated Christ as a revolutionary, contrasted with the fascist clergy. God the great Leveller who wants everything overturned is active today in Latin America and parts of Africa. But in England he seems no longer to exercise his power of stirring masses of men and women up to political action.

NOTES

1. This chapter is based on a lecture given at a History Workshop and printed in *History Workshop Journal*, 17 (1984).
2. Cf. pp. 37-8 above.
3. See pp. 123-5 above.
4. Evans, *A Voice from Heaven to the Commonwealth of England* (1652), pp. 26-7, 33, 45, 74-5; *An Eccho to the Voice from Heaven* (1653), p. 17, quoted in my *Change and Continuity in 17th-century England*, pp. 59-60.
5. "No man shall be troubled for his judgment or practice in the things of his God" (Winstanley, *The Law of Freedom and Other Writings*, p. 379; Fulke Greville, "A Treatise of Religion", in *Remains*, ed. G.A. Wilkes, Oxford U.P., 1965, p. 207).
6. *Du Bartas his Divine Weekes and Workes* (translated by Joshua Sylvester), in Sylvester, *Complete Works* (ed. A.B. Grosart, 1880), I, p. 224.

7. Andrewes, *Works* (Oxford U.P., 1854), V, pp. 224, 234. Cf. R. Sibbes, *Works*, VI, pp. 153-4, and E. K. Chambers, *The Elizabethan Stage* (Oxford U.P., 1923), IV, p. 197.

8. See p. 278 above.

9. Collinson, *The Religion of Protestants*, p. 283; E. S. Morgan, *The Puritan Dilemma: the Story of John Winthrop* (Boston, Mass., 1958), p. 40. It was suggested to Sir Simonds D'Ewes in 1638 that he should "make provision of refuge for harsh times, if they should happen in England" by a plantation in Massachusetts (ed. E. Emerson, *Letters from New England: The Massachusetts Bay Colony, 1629-1638*, Massachusetts U.P., 1976, p. 225).

10. S. Foster, *Notes from the Caroline Underground*, pp. 17, 50; S. Rutherford, *The Tryal & Triumph of Faith* (1645), p. 30.

11. Hunt, *The Puritan Moment*, p. 274.

12. They were preached by Cornelius Burges (*The First Sermon*) and Stephen Marshall (*A Sermon*). For fasting see pp. 129-30 above.

13. Brooks, *Gods Delight in the Progresse of the Upright* (1649), pp. 17-18; cf. pp. 46-7.

14. *H.M.C., Bath MSS.*, I, pp. 29-32.

15. J. C. Spalding, "John Goodwin", *Biographical Dictionary of British Radicals*, II, p. 16.

16. Marshall, *A Peace-Offering to God* (a sermon preached before the House of Commons, 7 September 1641) (1641), pp. 3, 40; cf. pp. 45-6.

17. J. Burrough, *Sions Joy* (1641), pp. 43-4, 49-50; cf. p. 38. Preached on the same day as Marshall's sermon.

18. Ed. T. T. Lewis, *Letters of the Lady Brilliana Harley* (Camden Soc., 1854), pp. 157-8.

19. W. Sewel, *The History of the ... Quakers* (1722), p. 87; Baillie, *Letters and Journals* (Edinburgh, 1775), II, p. 86. Cf. Johnston of Wariston, quoted in *The Experience of Defeat*, pp. 79-80.

20. I give evidence in *The Experience of Defeat*, pp. 86, 173, 319-20; ed. Abbott, *Writings and Speeches of Oliver Cromwell*, I, pp. 696-8, III, pp. 590-3; Dell, *Sermons*, esp. pp. 71-6; Sewel, *op. cit.*, pp. 215, 513. Cf. R. Fitz-Brian, *The Good Old Cause, Dressed in its Primitive Lustre* (1659), *passim*.

21. Sedgwick, *Justice upon the Armie Remonstrance* (1649), *passim*; and *A Second View of the Army Remonstrance* (1649), p. 15 and *passim*.

22. Salmon, *A Rout, A Rout* (1649), p. 4.

23. C. H. Carlton, "Joyce", *Biographical Dictionary of British Radicals*, II, p. 148.

24. Marvell, *An Horatian Ode upon Cromwels Return from Ireland*.

25. *Reliquiae Baxterianae*, I, p. 100.

26. See a forthcoming article by Richard H. Popkin, "The Triumphant Apocalypse and the Catastrophic Apocalypse".

27. See pp. 270-4 above.

28. E. Rogers, *Life and Opinions of a Fifth-Monarchy Man*, p. 127; S. R. Gardiner, *The Commonwealth and Protectorate* (1903), III, p. 5.

29. *Puritanism and Revolution*, pp. 133-4, 140; G. Fox and E. Burrough,

Good Counsel and Advice Rejected by Disobedient Men (1659), pp. 26-7, 36-7; G. Fox, *To the Counsell of Officers* (1659), pp. 2, 8; Fox, *Gospel-Truth* (1706), pp. 196-7; M. R. Brailsford, *A Quaker from Cromwell's Army: James Nayler* (1927), pp. 23-5.

30. T. Spencer, "The History of an Unfortunate Lady", pp. 43-59.
31. See pp. 202-7 above.
32. *The World of the Muggletonians*, pp. 23, 64. See Chapter 12 above.
33. Pp. 191, 208-12, 226-7 above, and references there cited.
34. Morgan, *op. cit.*, p. 40.
35. *Antichrist in Seventeenth-Century England*, pp. 79-82, 86. Cf. Feake, quoted on p. 219 above.
36. *Antichrist in Seventeenth-Century England*, pp. 93-6. 108, 110, 121-3; Bunyan, *Works*, II, p. 54.
37. Pp. 214, 216 above.
38. Winstanley, *The Law of Freedom and Other Writings*, p. 88.
39. Milton, *Paradise Lost*, XII. 24-37.
40. Patricia V. Bonomi, "'A Just Opposition': The Great Awakening as a Radical Model", in *The Origins of Anglo-American Radicalism*, pp. 243-56.
41. Coppe, *A Fiery Flying Roll* (1649), in Smith, *A Collection of Ranter Writings*, pp. 86-8, 90, 100-1.
42. G. Foster, *The Sounding of the Last Trumpet* (1650); *The Pouring Forth of the Seventh and Last Viall* (1650), both quoted in *W.T.U.D.*, pp. 210-11.
43. Clarkson, *A Single Eye* (1650), in Smith, *op. cit.*, pp. 169-73, 180-1; Coppe, *op. cit.*, ibid., pp. 107-8. See pp. 170-1 above.
44. *W.T.U.D.*, Chapter II; Winstanley, *The Law of Freedom and Other Writings*, p. 353.
45. *C.S.P.D.*, *1650*, p. 180.
46. See p. 313 above.
47. See pp. 39, 47 above for this and the following paragraphs.
48. Harrington, *Political Works*, p. 704.
49. R. W. Harris, *Clarendon and the English Revolution* (1983), p. 301.
50. Davenant, *Gondibert*, 1651 (ed. D. F. Gladish, Oxford U.P., 1971), p. 22; cf. P. W. Thomas, "Court and Country under Charles I", pp. 192-3.
51. Clarendon, *A Brief View and Survey of the dangerous and pernicious errors ... in Mr. Hobbes's ... Leviathan* (Oxford U.P., 1676), pp. 181-2.
52. *Clarke Papers* (ed. C. H. Firth, Camden Soc.), IV (1901), p. 220; *Clarendon State Papers*, III, p. 633.
53. D. Dymond, *Portsmouth and the Fall of the Puritan Republic* (Portsmouth, 1971), pp. 9-11.
54. H. G. Tibbutt, *Colonel John Okey, 1606-1662* (Bedfordshire Historical Record Soc., XXXV, 1955), p. 154.
55. *The Experience of Defeat*, pp. 307-8; *M.C.P.W.*, VI, pp. 397-8; *M.E.R.*, pp. 351-2, 358-60.
56. Very slowly, we must emphasize. As late as the sixteen-eighties a Whig politician heard God's voice advising him on his speculations, his bets,

his sex-life. He planned to marry the Queen of the fairies. The fact that both God and the fairies repeatedly let him down did nothing to diminish Goodwin Wharton's belief in either (J. Kent Clark, *Goodwin Wharton*, Oxford U.P., 1984, *passim*). Cf. Wildman, quoted on pp. 135-6 above.

57. *The Diary of Archibald Johnston of Wariston*, III, *1655-1660* (Scottish History Soc., 1940), p. 71; cf. p. 120.

58. Cf. pp. 131-4, 233 above.

59. J. R. Jacob, *Robert Boyle and the English Revolution, passim*; M. C. Jacob, *The Newtonians and the English Revolution, passim*.

60. H. More, *An Antidote to Atheism* (1653), p. 164; cf. Joseph Glanvill, F.R.S., *Sadducismus Triumphatus* (1666), *passim*.

61. Duffy, "Valentine Greatrakes, the Irish Stroker: Miracle, Science and Orthodoxy in Restoration England", in *Religion and Humanism* (ed. K. Robbins, Ecclesiastical History Soc., 1981), p. 273 and *passim*. For Greatrakes see J.R. Jacob, *Henry Stubbe*, Chapter 3 and Epilogue.

62. I. Breward, "James Nayler", in *Biographical Dictionary of British Radicals*, II, p. 258.

63. See pp. 132, 313-14 above.

64. *The Experience of Defeat*, pp. 248-9. See p. 30 above.

65. T. Goodwin, *A Sermon of the Fifth Monarchy* (1654), p. 18.

66. Harrington, *Political Works*, pp. 329-33.

67. See chapter 4, p. 314 above.

68. [Anon.], *Walwyns Wiles* (1649), in Haller and Davies, *op. cit.*, pp. 288-9, 310; cf. H.N. Brailsford, *The Levellers and the English Revolution* (1961), pp. 501-5.

69. K. Marx and F. Engels, *Correspondence, 1846-1895: A Selection* (ed. D. Torr, 1934), pp. 279, 281; cf. p. 264. See now my "Seventeenth-century English radicals and Ireland", in *Radicals, Rebels and Establishment* (ed. P. J. Corish, Belfast, 1985).

70. Quoted by James Sutherland, *English Literature of the Late Seventeenth Century* (Oxford U.P., 1969), p. 3.

71. *The Experience of Defeat*, pp. 321, 323-5.

72. See my *Economic Problems of the Church*, p. 23, where I acknowledge discussions with Mervyn James on this point. See also pp. 27-8 above.

73. The shocked words are those of Edward Hyde, Earl of Clarendon, in his *History of the Rebellion*, V, p. 184.

74. Quoted by Susan Staves, *Players Scepters*, p. 290; cf. p. 263.

75. See pp. 207-8 above.

76. Milton, *Samson Agonistes*, lines 1706-7.

77. P. Jenkins, *A Social and Political History of the Glamorganshire Gentry, c. 1650-1720* (Cambridge University Ph.D. Thesis, 1978), p. 298. Cf. pp. 108-9 above.

78. *The Northern Star*, 26 October 1850, quoted by John Saville, *Ernest Jones, Chartist* (1952), p. 112.

79. Eric Hobsbawm, *Primitive Rebels* (Manchester U.P., 1959), p. 183.

Index

343